Imagined Futures

This study provides the first substantial history and analysis of the To-Day and To-Morrow series of 110 books, published by Kegan Paul Trench and Trübner (and E. P. Dutton in the USA) from 1923 to 1931, in which writers chose a topic, described its present, and predicted its future. Contributors included J. B. S. Haldane, Bertrand Russell, Vernon Lee, Robert Graves, Vera Brittain, Sylvia Pankhurst, Hugh McDiarmid, James Jeans, J. D. Bernal, Winifred Holtby, André Maurois, and many others. The study combines a comprehensive account of its interest, history, and range with a discussion of its key concerns, tropes, and influence.

The argument focuses on science and technology, not only as the subject of many of the volumes, but also as method—especially through the paradigm of the human sciences—applied to other disciplines; and as a source of metaphors for representing other domains. It also includes chapters on war, technology, cultural studies, and literature and the arts.

This book aims to reinstate the series as a vital contribution to the writing of modernity, and to reappraise modernism's relation to the future, establishing a body of progressive writing which moves beyond the discourses of post-Darwinian degeneration and post-war disenchantment, projecting human futures rather than mythic or classical pasts. It shows how, as a co-ordinated body of futurological writing, the series is also revealing about the nature and practices of modern futurology itself.

Max Saunders is Interdisciplinary Professor of Modern Literature and Culture at the University of Birmingham. He directed the Arts and Humanities Research Institute at King's College London from 2012–18. He is the author of *Ford Madox Ford: A Dual Life*, 2 vols. (OUP, 1996); *Self Impression: Life-Writing, Autobiografiction, and the Forms of Modern Literature* (OUP, 2010); the editor of five volumes of Ford's writing; and has published widely on Modernism, life writing, and Impressionism. He was awarded a Leverhulme Major Research Fellowship to research *Imagined Futures,* and an Advanced Grant from the European Research Council for the collaborative project *Ego Media.*

Imagined Futures

*Writing, Science, and Modernity
in the To-Day and To-Morrow
Book Series, 1923–31*

MAX SAUNDERS

OXFORD
UNIVERSITY PRESS

Great Clarendon Street, Oxford, OX2 6DP,
United Kingdom

Oxford University Press is a department of the University of Oxford.
It furthers the University's objective of excellence in research, scholarship,
and education by publishing worldwide. Oxford is a registered trade mark of
Oxford University Press in the UK and in certain other countries

First published 2019
First published in paperback 2023

Published in the United States of America by Oxford University Press
198 Madison Avenue, New York, NY 10016, United States of America

British Library Cataloguing in Publication Data
Data available

Library of Congress Cataloging in Publication Data
Data available

ISBN 978–0–19–882945–4 (Hbk.)
ISBN 978–0–19–888644–0 (Pbk.)

DOI: 10.1093/oso/9780198829454.001.0001

For Zachary and Ezra, eventually

Preface and Acknowledgements

The To-Day and To-Morrow series of 110 short books published from 1923 to 1931 constitutes one of the most interesting bodies of literature of the period—the period between the wars; the period of modernism. It is a unique corpus of often superb writing, which develops as a genre what had seemed *sui generis* when produced earlier (by H. G. Wells in particular): the extended expository prose imaginings of possible futures, which, though they have their moments of science-fiction, utopianism, or journalism, are mostly distinct from those genres, and which are perhaps best described with a paradox, as speculative non-fiction. To-Day and To-Morrow speculates about the futures of a vast range of subjects. The series contains discussions of science, technology, what would now be called post-humanism, society, sexuality, the arts, language, and everyday life. Its defining contrast of present and future is often handled differently from utopian or dystopian fiction, fostering the progressive imagination; the imagination of change and innovation as both inevitable and desirable. This enables some strikingly far-sighted projections, elaborating themes usually thought to have flourished later: genetic modification; the cyborg; the two cultures; networked intelligence. In doing so, it offers a revealing case-study of the pervasiveness of ideas of the future in cultural life; and enables insight into the nature of futurology in a scientific age.

At the same time, it is an extraordinarily rich resource for modernist studies, and the literary and cultural history of the period. Many outstanding writers contributed, a number of them well-known. Leading contemporary writers followed the series closely—especially Huxley, Joyce, and Eliot, but also Lewis, Waugh, Graves, the Woolfs, and F. R. Leavis—and responded to it creatively and critically. Yet bizarrely little trace of it is to be found in the received literary or cultural histories—even despite its being reissued nearly complete in 2008 by Routledge. Some of the science volumes have received periodic comment, but mainly in terms of science popularization. The few discussions of the series as a whole are riddled with inaccuracies (even down to getting the number of volumes wildly wrong).

This study provides the first substantial history and analysis of the series, combining a comprehensive account of its interest, history, and range, with a discussion of its key concerns, tropes, and influence. The argument focuses on science and technology, not only as the subject of many of the volumes, but also as a method—especially through the paradigm of the human sciences—applied to other disciplines; and as a source of metaphors for representing other domains. It also includes chapters on war, technology, cultural studies, and literature and the arts.

This book has three main aims. First, to reinstate the series as a vital contribution to the writing of modernity. Second, to reappraise modernism's relation to the future, establishing a body of progressive writing which moves beyond the discourses of post-Darwinian degeneration and post-war disenchantment, projecting human futures rather than mythic or classical pasts. Third, to show how, as a co-ordinated body of futurological writing, the series is also revealing about the nature and practices of modern futurology itself; about what works, and what does not, and why. It enables insightful comparison with today's data-driven and team-authored scenario planning and foresight exercises. The series tell us much about how the future could be imagined in the 1920s and early 1930s. Hindsight enables us to assess its foresight. But, more importantly, analysis can illuminate why its vision succeeded in some areas, and was affected by blind-spots in others.

When I noticed a copy of Vera Brittain's *Halcyon, or The Future of Monogamy* in a second-hand bookshop, I hadn't known of the To-Day and To-Morrow series, or why the volume had its curious title. From the list and descriptions at the end of the other ninety volumes by then in the series it was immediately clear that To-Day and To-Morrow was a publishing exercise unlike any other. What I couldn't foresee was how much this oracular series would engross me for the next ten years.

The resulting project began as a European collaboration, when I proposed research on To-Day and To-Morrow as a topic for part of a European Community (EC) funded European Thematic Network Project called ACUME-2, run from the University of Bologna. I'm grateful to Vita Fortunati and Elena Lamberti for encouraging the idea, and for inviting me to co-ordinate one of the sub-projects, with Brian Hurwitz, on cultural representations of science. Two of its meetings focused on the scientific volumes of To-Day and To-Morrow: an Atelier on 'Narrativity, Temporality and Discourse at the Interface' at the Fondation Maison des Sciences de l'Hommes in Paris on 29 June 2007; and a conference held at King's College London on 29-30 September 2007 on the theme of 'Human and Post-Human: Cultural Origins and Futures'.

Earlier versions of parts of Chapter 1 were presented at those meetings, and I'm grateful to the participants—and particularly Patrick Parrinder and Brian Hurwitz—for their commitment, and for helping me to see just how significant the series is; and to Willard McCarty, for devoting a special issue of *Interdisciplinary Science Reviews* in March 2009 to papers from these meetings. An earlier version of the section in Chapter 1 entitled 'Matter, Consciousness, Time, and Language' appeared as 'Science and Futurology in the To-Day and To-Morrow Series: Matter, Consciousness, Time and Language', *Interdisciplinary Science Reviews*, 34:1 (March 2009), 69–79; in a special issue devoted to To-Day and To-Morrow, ed. Max Saunders and Brian Hurwitz. DOI: 10.1179/174327909X421461 An earlier version of part of Chapter 6 entitled 'Aldous Huxley' was given as an invited lecture, 'Aldous

Huxley: Today and tomorrow', at the conference 'The Condemned Playground: Aldous Huxley and his contemporaries', incorporating the Fifth International Aldous Huxley Symposium, University of Oxford, 3 September 2013. I am grateful to the late David Bradshaw for the invitation.

I am especially grateful to George Myerson, for inspiring discussions about the series and its achievement. I should also like to thank the contributors to two seminars at Modernist Studies Association Conferences, in Long Beach on 2 November 2007, and at the University of Sussex on 1 September 2013. I am very grateful to Melba Cuddy-Keane and Peter Marks for their help in organizing them.

This book could not have been written without the generous support of a Major Research Fellowship from the Leverhulme Foundation from 2008 to 2010; two sabbatical leave semesters from King's College London; and an Advanced Grant from the European Research Council (ERC) for the project 'Ego-Media: the impact of new media on forms and practices of self-presentation' (FP7/2007–2013; grant agreement No. 340331: see http://www.ego-media.org/).

The design of that project includes a series of speculative talks on 'Life Online To-Day and To-Morrow', recognizing the ever-increasing futurological pressure of the web. The connections proved to run much deeper—the just-pre-digital series' projections of increasing communicative interconnection, of the idea of a 'compound mind', and of human-machine interactions, reading as a pre-history of the digital world.

Two friends—David Herman and Patrick Parrinder—very generously read the entire manuscript, and made invaluable and detailed suggestions. Several others read long excerpts and made useful suggestions, notably Clare Brant, Brian Hurwitz, Patrick Wright, Rob Gallagher, Alexandra Georgakopoulou, Becky Roach, and Neil Vickers.

I should also like to record my gratitude to Steve Fuller, Gabriel Gbadamosi, Sara Haslam, Ian Henderson, Nick Hubble, Pat Kane, Christoph Meyer, Leone Ridsdale, Trudi Tate, and Shaf Towheed for discussing the project, and for their sage advice and assistance; to Kaitlin Staudt for helping me establish the story of the series' appearance in the US; and to the mysterious Jesse for generously sharing digitized versions of some of the volumes.

Contents

List of Illustrations   xiii

Introduction   1

PART I. SCIENCE, IMAGINATION, LANGUAGE,
AND COMMUNICATION

1. 'A Scientific Age': Science, Imagination, and Popularization   63

2. Conflict, Connectivity, and the Tropes of Futurology   121

PART II. HUMAN SCIENCES

3. Human Sciences   169

PART III. TECHNOLOGY, MEDIA, CULTURE,
AND THE ARTS

4. 'The machine man of 1925': To-Day and To-Morrow
and the Technological Extension of Man   221

5. To-Day and To-Morrow, Cultural Studies, and Everyday Life   257

6. To-Day and To-Morrow, Literature, and Modernism   287

Conclusion   337

Appendix A: The Book History of the Series   367
Appendix B: Complete Chronological Listing of the To-Day
and To-Morrow Series   393

Bibliography   399
Index   415

Fig. 1. C. K. Ogden at Antibes, 1930. William Ready Division of Archives and Research Collections, McMaster University Library.

List of Illustrations

C. K. Ogden at Antibes, 1930. William Ready Division of Archives and Research
Collections, McMaster University Library.   xii

John Desmond Bernal. Photograph by Ramsey & Muspratt, 1933   60
© National Portrait Gallery, London

Vera Brittain. Photograph by Howard Coster, 1936   165
© National Portrait Gallery, London

Bertrand and Dora Russell, outside the experimental Beacon Hill School,
20th September 1931   166
© Getty Images

Illustration for 'The Machine Man of Ardathia', by 'Francis Flagg'; *Amazing Stories*
(November 1927); public domain; image © Alamy   255

J. B. S. Haldane (left), Aldous Huxley (centre), and Lewis Gielgud at Oxford, 1914 285

This material has been provided by the Wellcome Library and Cold
Spring Harbor Laboratory Archives and Genentech Center for the
History of Molecular Biology and Biotechnology NY, USA, under a
Creative Commons Licence

Verso of early (and possibly the first state) dust-jacket for *Icarus*, early 1924.   370

The 'Classified Index' from *Aphrodite*.   379

The first printing (June 1926) and second printing (July 1929) of one of
Dutton's editions. In this case the one bearing the later label was also printed
in the US—presumably because it was a reprint rather than a new title.   384

The earlier and later style of Dutton's dust-jackets for the series; here for the
first and third impressions of *Lysistrata* (June 1925 and March 1926)   385

WIRELESS POSSIBILITIES

By
PROFESSOR A. M. LOW

Wireless, the author claims, is still in
its infancy. He gives a short sketch
of progress up till the present day,
and then reveals some of the wonders
which he believes Wireless has in
store. The talking cinema, seeing by
Wireless, Wireless and detection of
crime, business and Wireless; and
finally the possibilities of
Wireless
expected
Wireless
the
to-day

SIBYLLA
OR
THE REVIVAL OF PROPHECY

By
C. A. MACE, M.A.

"An entertaining and instructive
pamphlet."—Morning Post.

"The prophet has made a scientific
study of prophecy itself. Mr Mace is
not completely logical, neither is he
completely serious. But his lively mix-
tures stimulating ideas.
—Times Literary Supplement.

"Passages in it are excellent satire,
but on the whole the speculations may
be taken as a trustworthy guide to the
probable
scientific
is very

METANTHROPO
OR
THE BODY OF THE FUTURE

By
RONALD CAMPBELL MACFIE
M.A., LL.D.

The incredulist
author contemplates
who is in
either
another
evolve
both
body
will
subject
human
and

HERACLITUS
OR THE FUTURE OF FILMS

ERNEST BETTS

ICARUS
OR
THE FUTURE OF SCIENCE

By
BERTRAND RUSSELL, F.R.S.

"Startling possibilities of the future."—
Daily Express.

'Utter pessimism."—Observer.

"Mr Russell refuses to believe that the
progress of Science must be a boon to
mankind."—Morning Post.

"The whole essay deserves to be read."—
Daily Chronicle.

"A stimulating book, one that braces one
up, stirs up the controversial faculty, leaves
one not at all discouraged."—Daily Herald.

SECOND IMPRESSION

Introduction

Introductions to To-Day and To-Morrow

On the 4th February 1923 a 30-year-old scientist read a coruscating paper to a student society in Cambridge called 'The Heretics', which had been founded in 1909.[1] The President of the Heretics (a title he must have relished) was C. K. Ogden, freelance thinker, bookseller, and collector, whose influential role in British intellectual life in the first half of the twentieth century deserves to be better known. He had been one of the founders of the society, and its president since 1911. The Heretics society was 'the most prominent forum for public intellectuals to speak at in Cambridge'.[2] Ogden invited scientists, psychoanalysts, anthropologists, philosophers such as Russell and Wittgenstein, and literary writers including Shaw, Chesterton, Forster, Frank Harris, Rupert Brooke, T. S. Eliot, Rebecca West, Walter de la Mare, Edith Sitwell, and Woolf. The speaker that February was J. B. S. Haldane, who had left his post-war fellowship at New College Oxford for a Readership in Biochemistry at Cambridge University. The paper was published, probably in late 1923, as *Daedalus; or, Science and the Future*.[3] It was a small hardback pocket-book of ninety-three pages from the London publishers Kegan Paul, Trench, Trübner & Co.[4] Ogden worked for Kegan Paul, first as the editor of the journal *Psyche*—presumably pronounced 'C. K.'—from 1920, then as a consulting editor

[1] The paper began as one Haldane wrote while an undergraduate in Oxford before the war, called 'The Future of Science'. Back in Oxford at New College, he revised it when asked to speak at short notice, and gave versions of it to various Societies there from 1919 to 1922, adding the details of some of his war experience. It was revised again for the Heretics, and retitled 'Daedalus'. See Damon Franke, *Modernist Heresies: British literary history, 1883–1924* (Ohio State University Press, 2008), 229. However, its first publication was in a magazine under the title 'If You Were Alive in 2123 A. D.', in *Century*, 106 (August 1923), 549–66. This shorter version excludes the war memories, any mention of Daedalus, and also the coda quoting Buchanan and describing the 'ghastly mission' of the 'scientific worker of the future'. Ronald Clark, *JBS: The life and work of J. B. S. Haldane* (London: Hodder and Stoughton, 1968), 70, dates the first version as 1912, but Haldane himself, in the 'Preface to the Fifth Impression' of *Daedalus* (London: Kegan Paul, Trench and Trübner, 1925), viii, says 1914.
[2] John Forrester and Laura Cameron, *Freud in Cambridge* (Cambridge: Cambridge University Press, 2017), 110.
[3] While the later impressions of the book give the date of the first as November 1923, the first impression is actually dated 1924; but it was probably forward-dated for the New Year to let it appear to keep up to date. Fredric Warburg, who published it, confirms the November 1923 dating: *An Occupation for Gentlemen* (London: Hutchinson, 1959), 109.
[4] In 1911 Routledge took over Kegan Paul, Trench, Trübner & Co to form Routledge & Kegan Paul Ltd; but they continued publishing under the separate imprints. See Leslie Howsam, *Kegan Paul—A Victorian Imprint: Publishers, books, and cultural history* (Toronto: University of Toronto Press, 2015), 3. Warburg describes Kegan Paul as 'the twin imprint of Routledge and in effect inseparable from it' (92).

Imagined Futures: Writing, Science and Modernity in the To-Day and To-Morrow. Max Saunders, Oxford University Press (2019). © Max Saunders. DOI: 10.1093/oso/9780198829454.001.0001

for the rest of his life, overseeing five book series, one of which is the subject of this study. Haldane was working on enzymes and genetics, and became a pioneering geneticist as well as a leading commentator on the relations between science, society, and politics. *Daedalus* was to become one of the most influential works of science popularization of the twentieth century. According to its publisher, 'it received glowing reviews and made an impact on the public which was electrifying'; 'In many ways it altered the thinking of at least part of a generation'.[5] It also sparked off the idea of a whole series of such books, mostly bearing classical titles, and predicting the future of a wide range of subjects and topics. Later impressions of *Daedalus* were incorporated into this series, which was called To-Day and To-Morrow, and eventually ran to over a hundred titles appearing until 1931, edited by the maverick polymath Ogden.[6] Haldane's effortless flow of ingenious and provocative suggestions inspired the other gifted contributors. The series includes some of the most interesting writing of the interwar period—about the future, about science and technology, about developments of the human, about war, about gender, about culture and media, and much besides. To-Day and To-Morrow merits our attention as a surprising and revealing chapter of the intellectual and cultural history of the interwar period. It has a more enduring significance too, for what it can tell us about how we imagine the future. Those are the twin emphases of this book.

Daedalus not only inspired the idea of a series, but also invented the style, not just for many of its subsequent contributors, but for post-war popular science. As historians of science John Forrester and Laura Cameron put it, the book was

> The first of the series to be riotously successful, the one that set its tone and established a new style, in tune with the outré 1920s, for writing about popular science—daring and outrageous, rather than worthy and superior […].[7]

It was prefaced by an 'Introduction' of just a single short paragraph that throws down the gauntlet to conservatives or prudes, and gives the flavour of Haldane's display of witty self-assurance. But it also (though he couldn't know it at the time) was to set the agenda for To-Day and To-Morrow as a whole. His book, he says, 'will be criticized for its undue and unpleasant emphasis on certain topics'—in other words, reproduction, and scientific intervention in it: 'This is necessary if people are to be induced to think about them', he continues, 'and it is the whole business of a university teacher to induce people to think' (vii).

Part of Haldane's Daedalean ingenuity was to light on exactly the right mythological figure, whose story would lead into the labyrinthine modern issues being imagined, while offering readers a reassuring thread to link them to familiar

---

[5] Warburg, *An Occupation for Gentlemen*, 109, 112.

[6] The genesis and course of the series are detailed in Appendix A, which draws on the Kegan Paul archive at University College London.

[7] Forrester and Cameron, *Freud in Cambridge*, 180.

knowledge. It is written in part as a parody of a mediocre undergraduate essay of the future describing scientific advances that hadn't yet taken place by 1924 as if they were well-known: especially what Haldane calls 'ectogenesis': not just the fertilizing, but the full gestation of babies outside the womb; and cloning[8] and other forms of genetic engineering. Haldane gives the book what Joyce called 'the name of the fabulous artificer' not for Daedalus' most famous talents as a physicist (achieving flight) or an architect (designing the Labyrinth) but as a proto-geneticist and bio-technician, devising the wooden cow which King Minos' wife, Pasiphaë, used to mate with the white bull sent by Poseidon, producing the Minotaur as a result.[9] (To that extent, Bertrand Russell's attempt in his answering volume *Icarus* to clip the wings of Haldane's optimism falls short. Though Russell's point is that Icarus's fatally rash use of his new technology has a chastening new relevance so soon after the invention of powered aircraft and their first use in war.) The fact that the biological developments Haldane imagines are no longer entirely the science fiction they must have appeared to *Daedalus'* original readers indicates the shrewdness of his predictions. It was announced in May 2016 that human embryos had been successfully grown in an 'artificial womb' for thirteen days—just one day short of the legal limit, prompting the inevitable ethical row; and in April 2017 that an artificial womb designed to nurture premature human babies had been successfully trialled on sheep.[10]

There can be few people as influential in scientific and philosophical publishing in the early twentieth century as Charles Kay Ogden. In 1922, modernism's *annus mirabilis*, he launched the first of his book series for Kegan Paul: The International Library of Psychology, Philosophy and Scientific Method[11]—starting with G. E. Moore's *Philosophical Studies*, and Wittgenstein's *Tractatus* (which Ogden had helped Frank Ramsey translate), and including landmark works by Carnap, Mannheim, Piaget, Malinowski, Jung, Adler, and W. H. R. Rivers. It played an important part in the intellectual life of the period, introducing many major contemporary thinkers. From 1926 he also oversaw a series of Psyche Miniatures, which ran to over one hundred volumes. In between, he edited the more speculative and

[8] It was Haldane who later coined the term 'clone': 'Biological Possibilities for the Human Species in the Next Ten Thousand Years', in *Man and His Future*, ed. Gordon Wolstenholme (London: J. & A. Churchill, 1963), 337–61.

[9] James Joyce, *A Portrait of the Artist as a Young Man*, ed. Jeri Johnson (Oxford: Oxford University Press, 2000), 169. Tom Greer's utopian romance of 1885, *A Modern Daedalus*, often linked to Joyce's use of the name, is thus unlikely to have influenced Haldane's modernizing of the mythological figure. Greer's Irish narrator achieves flight with Daedalean wings, eventually securing an Irish republic with a squadron of airmen.

[10] See Sarah Knapton, ' "Artificial Womb" Breakthrough Sparks Row Over How Long Human Embryos Should Be Kept in Lab', *Telegraph* (4 May 2016): http://www.telegraph.co.uk/science/2016/05/04/artificial-womb-breakthrough-sparks-row-over-how-long-human-embr/ and Hannah Devlin, 'Artificial Womb for Premature Babies Successful in Animal Trials', Guardian (25 April 2017): https://www.theguardian.com/science/2017/apr/25/artificial-womb-for-premature-babies-successful-in-animal-trials-biobag accessed 23 July 2017.

[11] It was later extended into Routledge's International Library of Philosophy.

ingenious To-Day and To-Morrow series, covering topics such as sciences, medicine, the arts, society and politics, psychology, sexuality, education, law, morality, and everyday life. This series too was very much a product of the modernist era. It started to appear just a year after *Ulysses*, *The Waste Land*, and *Jacob's Room*; its last volumes came out in the same year as *The Waves*, and the year before *Brave New World*.

Ogden is probably best known in literary studies for his close association with I. A. Richards, with whom he wrote *The Meaning of Meaning* (1923). Besides editing a journal and his various book series, he had edited the *Cambridge Magazine* from 1912-23, and ran the Cambridge Magazine Bookshop. He was an extraordinarily dynamic intellectual omnivore, but was especially preoccupied with psychology and communication. He was also the driving force behind the 'BASIC English' project for a simplified international auxiliary language, not only establishing the Orthological Institute to promote it, but, somehow, also finding time to write his own books, several on and in BASIC. Ogden was clearly fiercely individual, and his series are an individualist's reinvention of the encyclopedia; sharing its breadth without its formality, finality, and assumed impersonality and impartiality. It was entirely characteristic that when a new three volume supplement to the *Encyclopaedia Britannica* appeared in 1926, Ogden should have reviewed it; not only criticizing its inclusions, but noting its omissions.[12] But his indefatigable series editing (there was also a 'The History of Civilisation') was a commitment to collective intellectual labour.

According to one of the contributors, L. L. Whyte, Ogden 'brought European continental thinking to insular Britain'.[13] Whyte's *Archimedes; or, The Future of Physics*, which draws out some of the philosophical implications of relativistic and quantum physics, and (like Haldane) recognizes the convergence of physics, chemistry, and biology, is representative of the fascinating light To-Day and To-Morrow sheds on the conception of disciplines at the time, and about how disciplinary thinking is shaped by humanistic rhetoric, as well as how literature is shaped by scientific discourses. (As one listens to our contemporary biotech or nanoscience or even molecular biology specialists we can see how visionary these authors proved.) The series is also revealing about the changing status of public intellectuals between the wars. It is an invaluable resource for scholars and students of the period. Indeed, it is exactly the kind of material sought in literary studies in the turns towards New Historicism and interdisciplinarity.

Ogden believed fervently that in an age when science and technology could be seen to have an ever-increasing impact on people's lives, the popularization of

---

[12] These three volumes were intended as a supplement to the famous eleventh edition of 1910, replacing the 1921 'War Volumes'. See *C. K. Ogden: A collective memoir*, ed. P. Sargant Florence and J. R. L. Anderson (London: Elek Pemberton, 1977) . Ogden's review is reprinted on pp. 192–212.

[13] 'L. L. Whyte 1896–1972', obituary, *British Journal for the Philosophy of Science*, 24:1 (1973), 91–2. doi: 10.1093/bjps/24.1.91.

scientific ideas was a vital necessity. In a preface he wrote for a later book of essays by J. B. S. Haldane he explained:

> At a time when public opinion may have increasingly important effects on the future of science, the general reader is a person the experts would do well to take more seriously; and the current view that any newspaper story is good enough for the public may do great damage to the cause of science.[14]

Frankenstein Foods or Designer Babies, anyone?

Futurology

The rationale for the To-Day and To-Morrow series was to combine the popularization of expert knowledge for the general reader with predictions about the future. The essential form of the books is to describe the current state of a particular art, science, discipline, or social phenomenon, and then—the distinctive twist—to project how those fields might develop over the next fifty years or more. The aim for the series was to facilitate intelligent debate by producing a co-ordinated act of comprehensive futurology; a kind of Mass Speculation, or Mass Future Observation (by analogy with Mass Observation), which differentiates it from both the idiosyncrasy of individual futurologists such as H. G. Wells, and the conformity of the professionalized foresight groups which have since come to dominate futurology. As one influential contemporary, Dean Inge, commented: 'They are all (*Daedalus*, *Icarus*, and *Tantalus*) brilliantly clever, and they supplement one another.'[15]

A unique experiment in concerted foresight, then, the series includes both utopian and dystopian imaginings. Sometimes these feature as a debate between authors, as when Haldane's buoyant utopian advocacy in *Daedalus* of the potential of science to enhance human reproduction or devise new fuel economies is countered by Bertrand Russell's cynical caution in *Icarus; or, The Future of Science* (1924) about how power will use and misuse such knowledges. The reviewer for the *Observer* described Russell's argument as 'Utter pessimism'; and just these two words were lifted and—with charming shrewdness—placed on the dust-jacket as unique selling-point. Sometimes the mix of utopia and dystopia occurs in the same book, as when *Aeolus; or, The Future of the Flying Machine* (1927) by Oliver Stewart imagines air travel improved, then anticipates London being bombed from the air.[16] The series can thus be read as expressing opposing attitudes towards the

---

[14] J. B. S. Haldane, *Science and Well-Being* (London: Kegan Paul, 1935), 9.

[15] Dean Inge in the *Morning Post*. Quoted from the end-matter to C. P. Harvey's *Solon; or, The Price of Justice* (1931).

[16] See Clare Brant, '*Aeolus*: Futurism's flights of fancy', *Interdisciplinary Science Reviews*, 34:1 (March 2007), 79–90.

future, as, on the one hand, a source of anxiety due to accelerating technological and cultural change; and on the other, as something increasingly intelligible through that very technological, and scientific matrix, and therefore more predictable and plannable than before.

The scope of the futurology of To-Day and To-Morrow varied: those treating social trends tended to limit themselves to a few decades; those dealing with topics like evolution or cosmology needed to take a longer view. In many cases history has caught up with these imagined futures. In many others—genomics, computer science and electronics, atomic energy, medicine, neuroscience, etc.—scientific and technological knowledge has so overtaken and transformed what was known in the 1920s that the basis for some of its futurology is inevitably outmoded. So such a project may seem to have a purely antiquarian interest now. Yet the current avatar of its publishing house, Routledge, reissued almost the entire series in 2008, rightly suggesting that it has a more enduring interest.[17]

This book offers the first full-length study of the To-Day and To-Morrow series as a whole. Given how many important writers were involved, how good many of the volumes are, their contemporary prestige, and how important they are for modern literature and culture, it is surprising that after almost a century the series remains so under-researched. There are signs it is beginning to be rediscovered. Some adventurous critics have discussed a few of the volumes; there have been two conferences and a journal special issue devoted to it.[18]

---

[17] *To-Day and To-Morrow*, 25 vols (London and New York: Routledge; Tokyo: Edition Synapse, 2008).

[18] The only previous extended treatment of the series is in Paul Marett, 'Making Science Public: The Today and Tomorrow series and the place of science in early 20th century Britain' (Senior Thesis, University of Pennsylvania, 2015). Roy Lewis, 'C. K. Ogden's To-Day & To-Morrow Series', *The Private Library*, 3rd Series, 10:4 (1987), [140]–52, gives a good bibliographic sketch (though his listing omits *Achates* and *Chronos*). Ian F. Clarke, *The Pattern of Expectation: 1644–2001* (London: Cape, 1979), 230–1; 239–40, gives a brief but inaccurate account of the series, as discussed below. Susan M. Squier, *Babies in Bottles: Twentieth-century visions of reproductive technology* (New Brunswick, NJ: Rutgers University Press, 1994), and Angus McLaren, *Reproduction by Design: Sex, robots, trees, and test-tube babies in interwar Britain* (Chicago: University of Chicago Press, 2012), include discussions of *Daedalus* and ectogenesis. McLaren refers to several other volumes, but wrongly says the series ran to 86 titles: p. 169n.37. Peter Bowler's *A History of the Future: Prophets of progress from H. G. Wells to Isaac Asimov* (Cambridge: Cambridge University Press, 2017), discussed below, mentions fewer than a third of the volumes. The following important books also touch on the series: Gary Werskey, *The Visible College: A collective biography of British scientists and socialists of the 1930s* (London: Allen & Unwin, 1978); Patrick Parrinder, *Utopian Literature and Science* (Basingstoke: Palgrave Macmillan, 2015); and Forrester and Cameron, *Freud in Cambridge*; and figure in Chapter 1.

Recent scholars exploring other aspects of the series include Morag Shiach, '"To Purify the Dialect of the Tribe": Modernism and language reform', *Modernism/modernity*, 14:1 (January 2007), 21–34; Tim Armstrong's *Modernism, Technology, and the Body: A cultural study* (Cambridge: Cambridge University Press, 1998), discussed in Chapter 4; and John Attridge, '"A Taboo on the Mention of Taboo": Taciturnity and Englishness in *Parade's End* and André Maurois' *Les Silences du Colonel Bramble*', in Ford Madox Ford's Parade's End: *The First World War, culture and modernity*, ed. Ashley Chantler and Rob Hawkes (Rodopi: Amsterdam and New York, 2014), 23–35. The conferences formed part of the European Thematic Network ACUME-2, run from the University of Bologna; and the March 2009 issue of *Interdisciplinary Science Reviews* (ed. Brian Hurwitz and Max Saunders) focused on its scientific volumes. Brett Holman's Airminded site includes a fairly complete list of the series with useful links to texts and biographies: https://airminded.org/bibliography/to-day-and-to-morrow/

Popular Science

This study will necessarily be selective, focusing on the best volumes which were also the most influential on and relevant to the popular imagination of science and technology, and to literary modernism; but also because they exemplify a binocular vision: in presenting particular imaginings of the future, they also speculate on the practice and process of futurology; and explore ingenious formal ways of conducting and representing it.

Some thirty of the volumes were devoted to scientific or technological subjects, including physics, chemistry, cosmogony, psychology, mechanization, transport, communication, and so on, and these provide the focus for Chapters 1 and 4. Most of the writers on other subjects could see that science and technology would be the most determining, transformative factors to their disciplines as well (a view explored in Chapter 3). Curiously, it is the volumes on the sciences that have remained the most enduring. In part, this is because the pressing scientific debates of the 1920s have returned in new guises. As the Large Hadron Collider at CERN begins to provide new insights into the nature of matter, which might tell us more about the Big Bang and black holes, it is clear that in the contemporary quest for a Theory of Everything we are still teasing out the implications for our understanding of matter, energy, space, and time of the Theories of Relativity and Quantum Mechanics—theories which for the writers of To-Day and To-Morrow were still news that needed to be urgently conveyed to their audience.

The To-Day and To-Morrow volumes convey what a fertile period the 1920s were for formulating themes such as robotics, cyborgs, and cloning which have proved a staple of science fiction and popularization ever since; some of the striking parallels between the series, and the novels, drama, and cinema of the time will be explored here.

The pair of volumes which lifted the series off—*Daedalus* and *Icarus*—invigorated a classic modern debate about the ethics of scientific developments. These, and their authors' other two volumes—Russell's *What I Believe*, and Haldane's *Callinicus; A Defence of Chemical Warfare*—together with J. D. Bernal's *The World, the Flesh, and the Devil*, were not only among the most brilliant and provocative of the series, but also the most influential. This was partly, perhaps, because other volumes in the series kept referring to them, and extending the debate. Indeed, To-Day and To-Morrow was designed to set up oppositions between different viewpoints so as to stimulate intelligent discussion of important issues. It was also largely because of their imaginative power, which appealed to writers; especially writers of science fiction. And this suggests another reason why the series as a whole has remained relevant. In many ways it addresses the problem of what C. P. Snow was to call 'The Two Cultures':[19] the growing separation between the sciences

---

[19] C. P. Snow, 'The Two Cultures and the Scientific Revolution', *Encounter*, 12 (June 1959), 17–24; 13 (July 1959), 22–7.

and the humanities. Yet writers like Haldane and Bernal are seen here to be confronting—and confuting—it three decades before Snow. Most of the To-Day and To-Morrow volumes had a Greek or Latin name in their title and bore a subtitle which connected the name to a modern topic, such as *Delphos; The Future of International Language*, by Sylvia Pankhurst; *Nuntius; Advertising and its Future*, by Gilbert Russell; or one that self-reflexively looks back to look forwards, *Sibylla; or, The Revival of Prophecy*, by Cecil Alec Mace.

As this Janus-facedness suggests, the authors were bringing the European cultural heritage to bear upon pressing questions of international modernity and radical modern thought. Indeed, one of the volumes was called *Janus; The Conquest of War*, using its about turn to turn war against itself (as discussed in Chapter 2). It is also in the texture of the writing that this remarkable synthesis of the classic and the modern is played out. Many of the volumes are dazzlingly written. You might expect that from the literary writers who were drafted in, such as Robert Graves, Vera Brittain, or André Maurois. But the scientists too are remarkably stylish and literate, quoting and alluding to poetry, mythology, and theology. The texts are thus fascinating not only as exercises in the popularization of technical ideas, but for what they can tell us about the relation between insight, concept and language (in which they echo Ogden's and I. A. Richards' earlier foray into this area in *The Meaning of Meaning*).

In 1995 John Brockman identified what he called the 'Third Culture': a new generation of leading scientists who were also adept popularizers of complex and challenging ideas. These were figures such as Richard Dawkins, Stephen Jay Gould, Steve Jones, Marvin Minksy, Steven Pinker, and Martin Rees, who had become masters of communication not just through journalism, but also television. The medium of television was not yet developed enough for To-Day and To-Morrow writers to use in the 1920s, though a few, such as Robert Graves and Hugh MacDiarmid, would eventually appear on it. Some, like Bertrand Russell, took to the air waves for occasional radio broadcasts. At least a couple became radio personalities: Gerald Heard, who was the BBC's first science correspondent from 1930 to 1934—H. G. Wells was reported as saying of him 'Heard is the only man I ever listen to on the wireless. He makes human life come alive';[20] and C. E. M. Joad, who was a regular participant on the panel discussion show *The Brains Trust* through the 1940s. But it was in their writing that many of the contributors to the series proved gifted popularizers; and demonstrated that, just as some among them were anticipating the diagnosis of a schism between 'The Two Cultures', the scientific contributors in particular testified to a 'Third Culture' golden age.

---

[20] See 'The Gerald Heard Official Website', at: http://www.geraldheard.com/ accessed 27 December 2016. The quotation appears in print in the *St. Louis Post-Dispatch* (24 June 1951), 30; and *Faith and Freedom* 8:10 (June 1956), 6; though as the latter draws on interviews with Heard, he may have been the source himself.

According to its publisher, the series 'showed also that the highbrow, when he can be persuaded to write for the multitude, does a much better job than the popularizer and the hack'.[21]

It is an axiom of modernist studies that modernism in literature and the arts is a response to rapid technological and social change; and that that response can take diametrically opposite forms. One of the striking features of the series is how it is poised intriguingly close to the genres of science popularization, expository projections of the future, bursts of science fiction and utopianism, and imagined histories of the future. Yet it is distinct from them. What is distinctive about it is how it shifts its shape, moving between these different genres and registers. Even in volumes on non-scientific subjects, the authors get excited imagining new technologies such as transmitting power by wireless or extra-terrestrial weapons. That is because science fiction is the modern literary form imagining possible future social life which is most familiar today—whether utopian, or, more often, carrying with it hints or elaborations of dystopia. But the prominence and cultural spread of science fiction has tended to obscure this other mode in which modernism and the avant-garde mapped the form of possible futures for humanity: namely, by speculating about such futures in expository prose. There has thus been a dual neglect: both of speculative *non*-fiction; and of modernism's futurology.

The establishment of science fiction as a genre is roughly contemporary with the emergence of modernism. Sometimes it takes the form of a horrified flight from modernity's future, and looks instead to the past; as in the 'mythic method' of high modernists such as Joyce, Eliot, or Pound.[22] The debates between both attitudes in To-Day and To-Morrow, also staged around other modernist trigger themes—sex, machines, radio and other media, war, the classics, the East, language, psychology—makes the series an important resource for virtually every branch of modernist studies.

It is scarcely surprising that science loomed so large in a twentieth-century series about the future. Insofar as the central through-line of the present book concerns science and its cultural impact, it aims to contribute to studies of modernism and science. But the breadth of the series means that it also contributes to the study of modern culture and discourse more widely. Given that we know modernity is so future-obsessed, it is extraordinary that these thought-provoking books have largely gone missing from scholarship about interwar literature. (All the more surprising given the Routledge reissue.) If you want to find cutting-edge thought of the period about the probable futures of almost any topic, To-Day and To-Morrow should be among the first ports of call.

---

[21] Warburg, *An Occupation for Gentlemen*, p. 117.
[22] T. S. Eliot coined the phrase in the essay, 'Ulysses, Order, and Myth' (1923); in *Selected Prose of T. S. Eliot*, ed. Frank Kermode (New York: Harcourt, 1975), 178.

Many of the volumes discuss contemporary writers, artists and thinkers, some of whom are modernist. The authors include several major writers, scientists, and thinkers who were either already well-known or destined to become famous subsequently, such as Bertrand Russell, Vernon Lee, Vera Brittain, James Jeans, C. M. Grieve (who would become known as Hugh MacDiarmid), Sylvia Pankhurst, and Lewis Grassic Gibbon (under his given name of Leslie Mitchell). Important women writers are particularly strongly represented. Ogden was a pioneering feminist.[23] Less than a tenth of the authors were women. But they included leading feminists, and a larger proportion of the titles were on feminist and gender issues, such as the education of women, sexuality, birth control, monogamy, and the family.

Inevitably uneven, the standard of writing is generally scintillating; the volumes lively and stimulating. Though just under a quarter of the titles sold widely, the series was reviewed enthusiastically (as evidenced by the reviews quoted in each chapter). It certainly made its mark in progressive circles, and was being read by modernist writers and critics, as discussed in Chapter 6.

Most of its authors were British (perhaps to distinguish the series from Ogden's International Library), but cover world civilization, culture and history, and world politics. There is a strong European dimension, and a particular concern for the future of Britain and its Empire. There are volumes on India and Canada, as well as on Scotland and Ireland. But the books were also published in the US by E. P. Dutton (who added three extra volumes).[24] This transatlantic dimension is important, especially given the sense that America was leading the way towards the future. There were duly three volumes devoted to the US; and several others written by Americans. The context for the series is the aftermath of the First World War (the first volume opens with memories of its mechanized battles, and several others are devoted to future warfare), the Versailles Treaty, the founding of the League of Nations, British Imperial decline, the Bolshevik Revolution in Russia, and the rise of fascism in Europe. A few volumes were revised and reissued in 1936. The series thus spans most of the interwar period (up to the Moscow Show Trials and the Spanish Civil War, say), and represents a compendium of its hopes and anxieties.

To-Day and To-Morrow was clearly an internationalist project in many ways. But it originated in the UK. For this reason, and also because of its renewed availability, references given here to it are to the first UK editions (generally used for the 2008 Routledge edition), unless otherwise indicated. This makes possible a simplified form for references to the series, necessary because all the volumes are referred to, many of them several times. The full title, and date of first publication,

---

[23] See for example *Militarism versus Feminism* (1915), which he co-wrote with Mary Sargant Florence: *Militarism versus Feminism: Writings on women and* war, ed. Margaret Kamester and Jo Vellacott (London: Virago Press, 1987).
[24] See Appendix A for details of the extent of Dutton's involvement.

is given at the initial citation of each volume. Where page numbers alone are given in brackets after quotations or citations; 'London: Kegan Paul, Trench, Trübner and Co.' is implied in each case.[25] The complete list of volumes, in order of publication, is provided in Appendix B.

The range of topics covered was both encyclopedic and occasionally eccentric, from cosmology to cookery, juvenile delinquency to opera, politics to humour, sexuality to automation, genetics to craftsmanship, half-track vehicles to nonsense. There were titles on technological developments: aviation, wireless, chemical weapons, cinema. The arts are represented both by books on entire disciplines— architecture, music, etc.—but also specific forms such as the novel, poetry, opera. Some volumes are devoted to the media—the press and advertising—and several on language.

As the series grew, it acquired a 'Classified Index', not only listing all the existing volumes (to entice readers of the latest to explore the back-catalogue) but also arranging them (if not always entirely convincingly) into an easily intelligible set of overarching categories:

GENERAL
MARRIAGE AND MORALS
SCIENCE AND MEDICINE
INDUSTRY AND THE MACHINE
WAR
FOOD AND DRINK
MISCELLANEOUS
SOCIETY AND THE STATE
GREAT BRITAIN, THE EMPIRE, AND AMERICA
LANGUAGE AND LITERATURE
ART, ARCHITECTURE, MUSIC, DRAMA, ETC.
SPORT AND EXPLORATION

If such a project were being devised today it would clearly have to be organized differently. Some of these headings reveal the biases of the time and place, and would no longer serve. 'Great Britain, the Empire, and America' is doubly dated, by its Anglophone-centred bias as well as by the fate of the British Empire. (Interestingly, it was retained in the Routledge reissue, along with many of these headings, but presumably to preserve the flavour of the series' mindset.) The separation of 'Science and Medicine' and 'Industry and the Machine' is inimical to technology as the marriage of science and machine. 'Marriage and Morals' now sounds prim (though in the series, 'Marriage' more often than not means 'Divorce'). Routledge's adaptation into 'Women, Marriage and the Family' may have tidied

---

[25] This applies to all the 107 volumes published by Kegan Paul. For the three published only in the US by Dutton, full bibliographic references are footnoted.

away those awkward morals, but they get smuggled back in the suggestion of family values. Anyhow it still shies away from the gender and sexuality that the volumes mostly discuss (in their own terms), and which would be more likely to headline a group now.[26]

Ogden's way of structuring the series is revealing in other ways. It brings out the importance of science to the project. It also brings out not only how some topics figure which seemed pressing at the time, but would be unlikely to be included now; and also how they are categorized. It is telling that the volume on psychical research is placed in 'Science and Medicine', say, rather than 'General' or 'Miscellaneous'. (Admittedly, a contemporary version might well include an account of alternative remedies, and place it under medicine; though such a decision would be controversial.) That war is given its own section is also a sign of the post-war times; especially since it contains only three volumes.[27] Again, the aftermath of the war, and anticipations of wars to come, permeate the series.

There are some surprising omissions in terms of authors—H. G. Wells? Aldous Huxley? Julian Huxley? I. A. Richards? Ezra Pound?[28] The series might have done even better had Ogden managed to persuade his friend John Maynard Keynes to contribute; especially given Keynes's congenial view that '*the importance of money essentially flows from its being a link between the present and the future*'.[29] Perhaps some did not contribute because they were warier of futurology, or felt they were better at criticizing the past or the present. It is difficult to imagine T. S. Eliot, say, or F. R. Leavis going in for it. There are also surprising omissions in terms of topics. Though mentioned in other books, Africa, Economics, automobiles, Painting, Surrealism, Psycho-analysis, don't get separate volumes. (R. E. Money-Kyrle's psycho-analytic study *Aspasia; The Future of Amorality* looks like it was written with the series in mind, but appeared, too large and just too late, in 1932.)[30] Yet the series raises many questions still central to the Humanities and Cultural Studies: in

---

[26] See Appendix A for an illustration of a Classified Index, and further discussion of the headings and Routledge's recasting of them.

[27] The Classified Index in the four last volumes, all from 1931—*Solon*, *Ethnos*, *Chiron*, and *Aphrodite*—only includes *Janus* and *Callinicus* under this heading. The omission of *Paris* (1925) was presumably an oversight; or at least a casualty of trying to fit too many titles onto two pages.

[28] According to Lewis, 'C. K. Ogden's To-Day & To-Morrow Series', pp. [140]–52, Wells, 'though he had the highest regard for Ogden, was apparently too busy with his own prophesies to join the team. So too was John Maynard Keynes who was Ogden's friend and close neighbour' (141). Wells's letters to Ogden published in *The Correspondence of H. G. Wells*, 4 vols (London: Pickering & Chatto, 1998) are certainly friendly, and indicate interest in Ogden's work on meaning and language, but also suggest Wells was trying not to get drawn into his projects. The Huxleys and Richards were also friends of Ogden's, as will become apparent.

[29] J. M. Keynes, *The General Theory of Employment Interest and Money* (London: Macmillan, 1936), 293.

[30] Given the future psycho-analysis has had, the lack of a volume in the series is perplexing. The main reason is probably that psychology was the main focus of Ogden's journal *Psyche*, and of his other series, Psyche Miniatures and the International Library. But it is perhaps also explicable by Ogden's view of Freud as offering just one among many fruitful approaches to the mind—as exemplified by the breadth of consideration in his *ABC of Psychology* as well as his editorial activities.

particular there is a recurrent focus on the body, its techno-cultural transformations, and the ethical issues these pose: there are books dealing with 'the body of the future' (*Metanthropos*, by Ronald Campbell Macfie; 1928); 'the future of the mechanical man' (*Automaton*, by H. Stafford Hatfield; 1928); 'the mechanical extension of mankind' (*Ouroboros*, by Garet Garrett; 1926, which deals with the Economic consequences of the machine age); and 'the soul of the machine' (*Hephaestus*, by E. E. Fournier d'Albe; 1925). The last three are discussed in Chapter 4. Several volumes deal with changes in sexuality and contraception; others with anthropological questions of race and taboo. Some of them make disturbing reading now; not least because we can see their race theory echoed in our debates on immigration and multiculturalism; their obsessions with Taylorism reflected in today's managerialism.

Time, Modernity, and Futurology in To-Day and To-Morrow

Such an unusual project as To-Day and To-Morrow, so complex and rich in interest and ideas, deserves multiple introductions from different angles. So we move from the books, their authors, the series, its editor, and its structure, to some further preliminary considerations of its intellectual and cultural contexts, its themes, its contemporary reception and influence; before asking how history has dealt with its predictions, and how it relates to subsequent developments in imagining the future.

Modernism in literature is notoriously preoccupied with time; an expression of what Wyndham Lewis denounced as the 'time-mind'.[31] The volumes do not approach time in a monolithic manner. The contributors do futurology in different ways. Some talk more than others about the past; about the history of their topic. Some take bigger risks: attempt more distant futures and more ambitious speculativeness. But an aspect shared by several—and which they share with other modern, and modernist, writers—is a sense that the predominant temporal paradigm has shifted from one based on evolutionary epochs to the concept in the new physics of space-time. The popular science books by scientists like Eddington and Jeans, and the articles popularizing science in periodicals, continue to be studied in revealing ways.[32] The extensive thought experiment—which is also an experiment with time[33]—conducted by To-Day and To-Morrow brings something different to

---

[31] Wyndham Lewis, *Time and Western Man* (London: Chatto & Windus, 1927), 3. See Stephen Kern, *The Culture of Time and Space, 1880–1918*, new edition (Cambridge, MA: Harvard University Press, 2003).

[32] See for example Michael Whitworth, *Einstein's Wake* (Oxford: Oxford University Press, 2001).

[33] The time-experiments conducted in the series are different from J. W. Dunne's best-seller about what appeared to be precognitive dreams, *An Experiment with Time* (1927). But Dunne's book is referred to at the start of Vera Brittain's *Halcyon*, which playfully offers her narrative as confirmation of his theory of temporal 'serialism'.

that discussion. Its futurology gives it a different relation to time, which reflects the experience of modernity, defined by Anthony Giddens in these terms:

> a shorthand term for modern society, or industrial civilization. Portrayed in more detail, it is associated with (1) a certain set of attitudes towards the world, the idea of the world as open to transformation, by human intervention; (2) a complex of economic institutions, especially industrial production and a market economy; (3) a certain range of political institutions, including the nation-state and mass democracy. Largely as a result of these characteristics, modernity is vastly more dynamic than any previous type of social order. It is a society—more technically, a complex of institutions—which, unlike any preceding culture, lives in the future, rather than the past.[34]

To-Day and To-Morrow certainly exemplifies these definitions, even if it covers a lot else besides. Many of its authors are preoccupied by that dynamic quality of modernity; arguably their sense of the ever-accelerating pace of technological change was already a cliché before the series began, even as it is one that is still with us. The theme of 'the idea of the world as open to transformation, by human intervention' is one many of the authors take up. Indeed the two ideas are often combined, as when *Quo Vadimus? Glimpses of the future* (1925), by E. E. Fournier d'Albe anticipates 'The unification of the planet' as the infrastructure connects everywhere and everyone increasingly closely (82; this trope is discussed in Chapter 2). Others discuss the built environment, expressing anxieties about the encroachment of the suburbs and the proliferation of ribbon developments along roads—notably *Lares et Penates; or, The Home of the Future* (1928) by H[arry] J. Birnstingl; *Rusticus; or, The Future of the Countryside* (1927) by Martin S. Briggs; and *Diogenes; or, The Future of Leisure* (1928) by C. E. M. Joad. (Such topics provide the focus for Chapter 5.)

The volumes on science have a popularizing aspect. But that mode generally describes only existing developments. These books—certainly the more futuristic of them—have the quality of something like a guide book to *terra incognita*, or a user's manual for a perplexing new technology. Most were written by experts— criminologists, biologists, literary critics, military historians, psychologists— explaining the direction of their disciplines to lay readers. But that popularizing function assumes a degree of instrumentality: that readers need to know what lies ahead. Science fiction sometimes assumes that responsibility: familiarizing readers with technological possibilities such as robots or space travel. But speculations like those in the To-Day and To-Morrow books are generally less invested in the pleasure of imagining other 'possible worlds' (as Haldane, put it in the title of another book). Though some elaborate an imaginative vision of what it might feel

---

[34] Anthony Giddens, *Conversations with Anthony Giddens: Making sense of modernity* (Stanford, CA: Stanford University Press, 1998), 94.

like to live in the future, the emphasis falls more on what sort of futures are possible and—more to the point—which are most likely.

Many of the volumes are instrumental in a further sense, of not only projecting what the future will be, but what it *should* be. The volumes, in short, are not just manuals of how to live in a future that could be glimpsed as arriving imminently; but they are also manuals of how to predict that future, and of how to bring it into being, or to try to avert it.

The series covers material often dealt with in the mass media then and now: speculating on such things as the cars, houses, devices and entertainments of the future. Three features set it apart from the futurology pervading journalism— even the higher forms of journalism. First, precisely the fact that many of its writers were experts. Second, the greater length of the series' pamphlet-style form, which allowed for a fuller development of the ideas. Third, that it is a collective and cumulative and intertextual project. While some of the authors were already established, many were younger figures, making their mark as representatives of the avant-garde across a range of fields. In contributing their futuristic projections the authors might be said to be doubly avant-garde: not just ahead in their present views and beliefs, but ahead in thinking ahead.

To-Day and To-Morrow not only exemplifies Giddens' claim that modernity lives in the future; and that the modern experience of time is therefore fundamentally different—future time. It also signals a major shift in the imagining of futurity, as prophecy gives way to a forecasting based on scientific knowledge and method; in other words, that technology affects not only the content but also the methodology of futurology. Such developments of futurology are discussed from a more general and theoretical standpoint in the second half of these introductions.

Eugenics

One way in which interwar modernity inhabited the future was through what might be termed the eugenic imagination. As Mendelian genetics was becoming understood and refined, and offered an explanation of the mechanism of Darwinian evolution, the question arose of the implications for humans. The discourse of Eugenics, then at the peak of its prestige, threads its way through several of the To-Day and To-Morrow books. See for example Bertrand Russell, *Icarus*;[35] Dora

---

[35] Parrinder, *Utopian Literature and Science*, p. 62, writes that *Icarus* 'explicitly advocated racist eugenics'. He refers to pp. 47–8, in which Russell says: 'If, however, a world-government is established, it may see the desirability of making subject races less prolific [...]'. He is airing the common Eugenicist anxiety that the white educated middle classes who use birth control will find themselves in an out-bred minority, and arguing that 'Governments will oppose the teaching of birth control among Africans for fear of losing recruits', thus running the risk of 'a mutiny of mercenaries'. In my reading, what he is advocating is extending knowledge of birth control to the 'subject races' too, so as to avoid

Russell, *Hypatia; or, Woman and Knowledge* (1925); C. P. Blacker, *Birth Control and the State* (1926); Norman Haire, *Hymen; or, The Future of Marriage* (1927); George Godwin, *Cain; or, The Future of Crime* and *Columbia; or, The Future of Canada* (both 1928), Eden Paul, *Chronos; or, The Future of the Family* (1930); J. F. Roxburgh *Eleutheros; or, The Future of the Public Schools* (1930); and Ralph De Pomerai, *Aphrodite; or, The Future of Sexual Relationships* (1931).[36] It might have appeared that a series including F. G. Crookshank's *The Mongol in Our Midst* (1924) among its earliest volumes was brazenly advocating a racist, ablist, and alarmist Eugenics. But in fact, rather than merely reflecting the contemporary enthusiasm for such ideas, To-Day and To-Morrow makes a more sceptical and critical contribution to the debate. Indeed, some volumes present devastating counter-arguments to the standard Eugenic claims of the time.

Eugenics represents an attempt to apply genetic knowledge to social engineering. Mark S. Morrisson describes it as 'the emblematic expression of programmatic modernism'.[37] Eugenics was founded on the notion of humans taking control of the selection process.[38] It characteristically responded to three kinds of anxiety about the course of evolution. First, that unless humans intervened in the process, evolution might lead us in undesirable directions; especially through degeneration, whether physical or moral;[39] so that we might end up like the sinister, predatory Morlocks of Wells's *The Time Machine*. Second, the spread of sex education and birth control aroused fears among the middle classes of being out-bred, and thus bred-out, by the working class. Third, several of the writers discussing biological issues are concerned that humanity's advances in medicine, science and technology, and its transformation of the environment might have effectively shut off the

---

what he saw as a problem by humane and enlightened means. It was an argument also advanced by Norman Haire in *Hymen; or, The Future of Marriage* (1927), pp. 85–6 (as discussed in Chapter 3).

[36] Eugenics are also referred to in passing in other volumes; such as *Pomona; or, The Future of English* (1926) by Basil de Sélincourt: 'Never did the future beckon more enticingly...' (9) i.e. because of our ability to improve ourselves. Colette Leung, in the 'Encyclopedia' section of the 'Eugenics Archive' website, writes: 'One of the most popular venues for prominent scientists, doctors, philosophers, intellectuals, and literary figures to disseminate eugenic themes to an educated audience was the *To-day and To-morrow* series [....] The goal of the series was to analyze important topics related to cultural, historical, and popular representations of science. The series sought to predict and assess the repercussions of science on society' (Ferreira, 2009; Schraner, 2009). Often, these important concepts were illustrated alongside examination of popular culture including film, literature, fashion, and music (Schraner, 2009). Eugenic topics were often discussed, such as Mendelian genetics, Darwin's theory of evolution, mechanical extensions of mankind, the family, marriage, motherhood and pregnancy, birth control, sexual relationships, race, disease, crime, psychiatry, and even the future of Canada (Holman, 2013)'. See: http://eugenicsarchive.ca/discover/encyclopedia/535eed7a7095aa00000 0024a The 2009 references are to the special issue of *Interdisciplinary Science Reviews*, 34:1 (2009) on the series, edited by Brian Hurwitz and Max Saunders. The final reference appears to be to Brett Holman's 'Airminded' site: http://airminded.org/2010/01/10/to-day-and-to-morrow/

[37] Mark S. Morrisson, *Modernism, Science, and Technology* (London: Bloomsbury, 2017), 139.

[38] For a good account of Eugenics, see Morrisson, *Modernism, Science, and Technology*, pp. 138–43.

[39] See Daniel Pick, *Faces of Degeneration: A European disorder, c.1848–1918* (Cambridge: Cambridge University Press, 1993).

process of natural selection, and thereby halted the clock of human evolution.[40] As E. E. Fournier d'Albe poses the question in *Quo Vadimus? Glimpses of the future*:

> Will a new race have arisen, as much above humanity as man is above the arboreal ape? Or will the further differentiation of man have come to a definite end, and progress be confined to an ever-increasing richness of intellectual, artistic, and emotional life?   (88)

A number of the authors simply accept this claim that humanity is no longer subject to natural selection;[41] and are persuaded of the eugenicist sequel that man should now take control of his own evolutionary destiny through consciously willed selection. This generally involved reducing the numbers of those deemed as 'unfit' in terms of natural selection, or 'degenerate' or otherwise undesirable in Eugenicist terms (because criminal, or physically or mentally disabled or subnormal); the reduction to be effected through sterilization or even extermination. Either way, the Eugenicist programme sought to bring human evolution under human control: to replace Darwinian natural selection with human selection.[42]

We know it today as misguided: as pseudoscientific in the ways it stretches biology to try to connect it with social and moral discourses of race, degeneration, criminality and sexology; and as sinister in its resulting susceptibility to appropriation by murderous totalitarian movements such as Nazism. Yet contemporary developments in genetic modification are giving us precisely the power to control and alter evolution. The transformation which that thought summons up—and which arouses the greatest fascination and anxiety—is the idea that man is poised to start transforming his own nature; his own species. It began to appear increasingly likely that any further changes in the species would be brought about no longer by random mutations affecting populations over immense timescales, but soon, through human design, and implemented by Eugenics.

If they didn't talk then in quite our terms, one of the most intriguing aspects of the series is the way it anticipates debates that we take to be of our time. We can thus see the origins of modern-day discussions about genetic modification, or the transgenic and post-human in their speculations about the future of the human.

---

[40] Aline Ferreira's claim that 'The control of human evolution is the unifying theme of the "To-day and To-morrow Series"' overstates the case. The series has no single unifying theme; though her essay demonstrates effectively how the seven or eight volumes she discusses dealing with evolution and the body shared that interest: 'Mechanized Humanity', in *Discourses and Narrations in the Biosciences*, ed. Brian Hurwitz and Paola Spinozzi (Göttingen: V&R unipress GmbH, 2011), 145–58 (145).

[41] See *Tantalus*, 14, for example, discussed in Chapter 1; also C. P. Blacker, *Birth Control and the State* (1926), 30; George Godwin, *Cain; or, The Future of Crime* (1928), 33; Eden Paul, *Chronos; or, The Future of the Family* (1930), 28; Ludovici's *Lysistrata*, 21; and also Heard's *Narcissus*, which proposes an eccentric version of the argument, claiming that natural selection was now working through clothing rather than bodies: 'evolution is going on no longer in but around the man, and the faster because working in a less resistant medium' (11).

[42] See Daniel Kevles, *In the Name of Eugenics: Genetics and the uses of human heredity* (Cambridge, MA: Harvard University Press, 1985).

Bronwyn Parry says that Bernal was 'along with Haldane, among the first to propose the idea of genetic engineering'.[43] One volume explicitly takes up the very question of the post-human, but using a Greek term for it: *Metanthropos; or, The Body of the Future*, as Ronald Campbell Macfie put it in the title of his 1928 volume, drawing on the word used in 1915 by the Italian physician Enrico Morselli.[44] *Metanthropos*: literally 'beyond the human'. Macfie recapitulates man's evolutionary journey, then asks:

> Such then is the far past of man—a creepy-crawly, slimy, slithery, finny, furry past. Can we perhaps from such a past foretell his far future? Can we map out a curve from the nebula through the amoeba, and worm, and pithecanthropus, and man, to the Metanthropos of the future?   (10).

He is a more cautious predictor than many in the series, since his subject has taught him that it is reckless to prophesy when 'development has been so much an emergence of the novel, and unexpected, and astounding [...]' (11). Anyway, he feels 'there seems little room for further improvement' (38) in the body of today, and that new faculties or senses are unlikely—a striking contrast with the prosthetic advocacy of Haldane and Bernal, and others discussed in Chapters 1 and 4. Nor does he see any future for psychical research, in contrast to several contributors, commenting tartly that 'the alleged new psychic faculty is a sign chiefly of a degeneration of old intellectual faculties in those who claim it' (46). Nevertheless, like many in the series, he is convinced that 'the question of man's control over his own evolution is perhaps the most interesting and most important in all biology' (51).

Today's echoes of 1920s futurology reveal how important it is for us to attend to the earlier arguments; and rather than patronize them where their science is unscientific or their predictions wrong, we should realize that it is exactly by studying where they go awry that we can learn most from them. Utopians of the 1920s should not be uncritically accused of the crimes of Nazism. But there are chilling moments in some of the volumes when the authors imagine future societies sterilizing or even exterminating 'defective' or criminal citizens;[45] though again it's not always clear whether they are endorsing the policy or warning us against it.

---

[43] Bronwyn Parry, 'Technologies of Immortality: The brain on ice', *Studies in History and Philosophy of Science*, 35:2 (June 2004), 391–413 (392). Also see Patrick Parrinder's essay, 'Robots, Clones and Clockwork Men: The post-human perplex in early twentieth-century literature and science', *Interdisciplinary Science Reviews*, 34:1 (2009), 56–67.

[44] Francesco Cassata, *Building the New Man: Eugenics, racial science and genetics in twentieth-century Italy* (Budapest: Central European University Press, 2011), 18–21.

[45] See for example Godwin's *Cain*, 33: 'Ruthless elimination is the remedy. One of the most disturbing facts of the problem of the degenerate is his appalling fertility'.

Some texts air anxieties that even if we don't degenerate, just by staying still in evolutionary terms we might get left behind by others evolving beyond us.[46] H. G. Wells is the elephant in this room too, but this time it's the Martians in his *War of the Worlds* who provide the evolutionary nightmare. What's striking about *them* is that they have evolved in relation to their machines; limbs atrophying when replaced by machines performing the same function more effectively. They represent a paradoxical position where physical degeneration coexists with technological might.

On the other hand, some powerfully dissentient voices also contributed. Arthur Keith, in *Ethnos; or, The Problem of Race Considered from a New Point of View* (1931) considers but rejects the institutionalization of eugenics as murderous as well as impracticable. Bertrand Russell identified another problem, not with the science but with the ways in which it would probably be implemented:

> When men of science envisage a possibility of this kind, they are prone to a type of fallacy which is common also in other directions. They imagine that a reform inaugurated by men of science would be administered as men of science would wish, by men similar in outlook to those who have advocated it.   (*Icarus*, p. 50)

> These are, of course, delusions; a reform, once achieved, is handed over to the average citizen. So, if eugenics reached the point where it could increase desired types, it would not be the types desired by present-day eugenists that would be increased, but rather the type desired by the average official. Prime Ministers, Bishops, and others whom the State considers desirable might become the fathers of half the next generation. Whether this would be an improvement it is not for me to say, as I have no hope of ever becoming either a Bishop or a Prime Minister.   (*Icarus*, p. 51)

This good joke is made funnier by the fact that Russell 'received from private tutors an education fit for the future prime minister his grandmother hoped and expected him to become', his own grandfather having been prime minister twice under Queen Victoria.[47]

The series also features two further impressive dissentient voices among its biological experts. One is in *Metanthropos* itself, in which Ronald Macfie, a Scottish physician, poet, M.P., and science writer, gives a list of experts arguing that the human race has become decadent without natural selection, then counters that the death rate has declined 'chiefly because the death-rate from infantile enteritis has declined', but that there is no reason to believe that that disease discriminated between strong and weak (63-4). He also comments that 'It is commonly believed that malaria pretty well extirpated all the geniuses of Greece' (65); in which case

---

[46] See for example F. C. S. Schiller's *Tantalus; or, The Future of Man* (1924), 36–45. In *Birth Control and the State* (1926), C. P. Blacker considers this claim, though believes that it is an argument for more rather than less extensive birth control.

[47] Ray Monk, entry on Bertrand Russell in the *Oxford Dictionary of National Biography*.

any eugenicist programme using physical weakness as the criterion for elimination would be unlikely to have beneficial psychological or cultural consequences.[48]

H. S. Jennings, Professor of zoology at Johns Hopkins University, in one of the best of the series' books on biology, *Prometheus; or, Biology and the Advancement of Man* (1925), offers a robust criticism of the inadequacy of any theoretical basis in genetics for inhumane policies.[49] He gives an ironic presentation of the eugenicist anxiety:

> This effect of improved conditions has given rise to a pessimism of unrelieved blackness, through-going, irremediable. Every improvement in conditions, it holds, inevitably weakens the stock. By a dreadful paradox, present amelioration means later deterioration. The more rapid the upward movement in conditions, the more headlong the downward plunge into degeneration.   (76)

He then proceeds to demolish the eugenic case on three grounds. First, there is no evidence for the link between improved civilization and genetic deterioration:

> No one knows that the vigour of later generations is not increased by the greater well-being of the bodies in which the genes live and develop. There is no certainty that the invention of fire, clothing, social organization, and vaccination have not augmented the well-being and staying power of the race.   (78)

Hence Prometheus, bringer of fire, as his standard-bearer. Second, Jennings argues that all characteristics are both hereditary and environmental (67), and that it is impossible to know which are the result of genetic improvement with respect to the characteristics alone. In other words, if you wanted to breed longer-living people, and found some families with records of longevity, you'd have to be sure that their longevity wasn't the result of other, environmental factors, such as diet, social support, reduced stress or pollution, or sensible lifestyle choices about tobacco, alcohol, or drugs, and so on. You would need statistically significant control groups for all these factors. Whereas Jennings shows how eugenicist arguments regularly fail to provide the necessary evidence. For example, he points to the way:

> The same fallacy reappears in discussions of racial problems. The recent immigrants into the United States show certain proportions of defective and diseased persons; and we are informed that 'these deficiencies are unchangeable and heredity will pass them on to a future generation'. There is no warrant in the science of genetics for such a statement; under new conditions they may not appear. It is

---

[48] Macfie's comment in *Metanthropos* on race that 'the real boundaries between men are not varieties of language or colour but varieties of mind' (91) might sound comparably humane; but is less so when preceded with the claim that 'It is chiefly in mind that races and individuals differ' (91), which reintroduces the notion of racial superiority exactly while appearing to eschew it.

[49] For a good discussion of *Prometheus* and the other biological or medical volumes in the series, see Alison Wood, 'Darwinism, Biology, and Mythology in the To-Day and To-Morrow Series, 1923–1929', *Interdisciplinary Science Reviews*, 34:1 (2009), 22–31.

particularly in connection with racial questions that there has been a great throwing about of false biology.   (65)

Third, he demonstrates how eugenic selection can be effective with lower organisms such as cultivated fruits, whose individuals can multiply by producing offspring with identical genes (82-3). When a superior variant occurs, it can be propagated selectively and can become widespread:

> This is what the eugenicist desires to do in man. But in man and other higher animals no combination is permanent. None ever lasts beyond the life time of the single individual. No individual can be multiplied in such a way as to retain the same combination of genes. No matter how vigorous, how well adapted to the conditions, how valuable from every point of view, every combination must disintegrate and a differently constituted one must appear for the next generation.   (84)

The element of *un*predictability can never be eliminated. We know now that through cloning it is possible to multiply individuals with the same combination of genes, and are warier of the ethical implications than eugenicists before Nazism tended to be. But *Prometheus* was received in its time as the definitive rebuttal of eugenics. One reviewer noted that 'The importance of this little volume is out of all proportion to its size. In it Professor Jennings shows the inadequacy of the genetic conceptions at the basis of the eugenic programs and other schemes of racial improvement', through shrewdly objecting to only one section in which he 'lays himself open to the accusation of being guilty of the very errors that he warns against'.[50] This where he asserts that 'the freedom and encouragement of reproduction among the feeble-minded, the criminal, the insane' 'should obviously be stopped' (78). The reviewer objected to the assumption that criminality was genetically determined. Our era adds further objections invoking human rights—sometimes disregarding the fact that we practice eugenic selection pre-natally as a matter of course. The other error objected to was the assumption that 'the troubles of humanity' were attributable to the presence of individuals with 'undesirable' combinations of genes. These are fair criticisms, but do not detract much from the significance of the book. *Metanthropos* and *Prometheus* exemplify the strengths of the series, which does not merely reflect contemporary views and debates but intervenes with significant critiques and sceptical alternative positions.

That notion of Eugenics accelerating evolution, as natural selection becomes human selection, is perhaps one reason why the timescale of the prophecies in the series is relatively short—usually a matter of fifty to a hundred years (probably in response to the editorial brief; and possibly because shorter-term predictions are less likely to go awry than longer-term ones). Where they do take a longer view, it

[50] E. B. Reuter, '*Prometheus or Biology and the Advancement of Man.* H. S. Jennings', *American Journal of Sociology*, 31:5 (March 1926), 692. DOI: 10.1086/213969

brings into focus a problem confronting attempts to narrate the future, given that narrative is normally retrospective. Several of the volumes thus proceed by using a trope Chapter 2 terms 'future history'; narrating the late twentieth century from the imagined vantage point of a more distant future, from where it is already all over. In some—Vera Brittain's *Halcyon*, for example—developments in women's rights that in 1929 were still to come, are narrated from the perspective of a female historian writing thousands of years hence, as already having unfolded with the inevitability of the Whig interpretation of history.

Prosthetics

Several of the To-Day and To-Morrow volumes approach the questions of time, evolution, and interconnection differently, though. They see technology as a kind of prosthesis, and celebrate its power to transform human nature in four separate ways. First, there are the books which consider the ways knowledge affects human development. The philosopher F. C. S. Schiller, for example, in *Tantalus; or, The Future of Man* (1924), advances the argument that technologies of writing/printing alter man's place in the world and his ability to transform it (19). But Schiller sees a disparity between this 'social memory', which allows civilization to build on past achievements, and our biological nature, which he sees as still essentially Palaeolithic—stuck in the state of what he calls 'yahoo-manity' (37).

In an odd book called *Narcissus*, Gerald Heard proposes the idea that evolution now moves outside the body, and into technology. He takes a broad view of such technology as including clothes and architecture. If one accepts the premise, then it is through such technological development that we have escaped our prehistoric origins.

Then, third, in *Ouroboros; or, The Mechanical Extension of Mankind*, Garet Garrett argues for the ways in which interaction with machines has changed our ways of being in the world. Writers like Heard and Garrett are thus saying something more than that new technology changes our abilities or our mentalities; but that it changes our *nature* too. Such arguments figure in Chapter 4 on the trope of 'Machine Man'. If you accept that idea of evolution stepping outside the body, working through the environments we create—whether clothes, architecture, the countryside, machine technology, etc.—then you're also accepting the notion that human nature changes as these environments change. According to this view, we are post-human because humanity has evolved through technology.

A sceptic might argue that what distinguishes humans is not just the ability to use tools (which other species seem capable of) but to keep inventing new ones; and that just because we change our technology doesn't mean we change our nature—though epigenetics has recently been providing evidence to the contrary. That kind of argument between culture and genetics might seem stale now. But there is a fourth way, that figures in the two most striking of the To-Day and To-Morrow volumes, Haldane's *Daedalus* and *The World, the Flesh and the Devil* by J. D. Bernal: this is to redesign humanity through engineering rather than genetics, and usher in the future of what we now call the cyborg. The forms their imagined cyborg futures take are not those of our world of pacemakers, hip replacements, heart-lung machines, and retinal implants. But in salient ways their visions are still strikingly ahead of our time. The discussion of them runs through most of the chapters here, though there is a concentrated analysis of both in Chapter 1.

The Value of Past Predictions

A number of the series' imagined futures predict technological developments with impressive accuracy, anticipating today's world of video phones, air travel, space travel, and robotics. Such predictions have been a staple of science fiction too. Not all the authors in the series were as reliable prophets; and other volumes sometimes feel like science fiction precisely when their futures are comically not our world of today. In *Hygieia; or, Disease and Evolution* (1926), Burton Peter Thom makes the arresting case for the importance of disease as a factor in evolution (through its elimination of the less fit).[51] But if his prediction that 'Disease will disappear' because man will reach 'an absolute immunity' (90) still seems an immeasurably distant prospect, his confidence 'That the increase of the population will within a few centuries tax the food resources of the earth is improbable; it may even be said to be impossible' (104–5) seems as inconsistent as it was short-sighted.

The futuristic sublime has a disconcerting habit of turning into the antiquarian ridiculous. That's the fate of all but the best science fiction (think old episodes of *Dr Who*, without the Daleks), as of many of yesterday's prophecies. Nothing dates like the future. *Nineteen Eighty-Four* or *2001? Passé*. Several of the series' tomorrows have proved spectacularly wrong. Oliver Stewart, in a spirited contribution— *Aeolus; or, The Future of the Flying Machine*—foresaw skies full of flying boats and autogiros. He was to know (though he couldn't have known) that, as his pages were flying off the presses, Lindbergh was making history flying across the Atlantic and into the future of aviation. With hindsight it might seem easy to be patronizing. But before the development of the jet engine and the helicopter, Stewart's was a perfectly reasonable (and feasible) speculation. And though his vision now seems the stuff of period science fiction films, as we argue about noise pollution and the social unacceptability of extra runways to our major airports, his projection of small aircraft able to glide noiselessly down to short landings, and large ones

---

[51] (New York: Dutton, copyright 1926); one of the three To-Day and To-Morrow volumes published only in the US.

landing offshore, makes one wonder whether it wouldn't have been better if some of his speculative thinking could have taken more hold. As Peter Bowler has shown, Stewart's vision of the future of air travel was one of several contesting alternatives in the period, competing with airships and larger conventional aircraft; and in such cases it seemed by no means inevitable which technology would prevail.[52] By contrast, Stewart's projection of devastating air-attacks on London is a vividly accurate prophecy of the Blitz (if it draws on the bombing of New York in Wells's *The War in the Air* of 1908, as well as the Zeppelin and Gotha raids on London from 1915-18).

J. Leslie Mitchell, writing his first book, *Hanno; or, The Future of Exploration* (1928), before he started publishing as Lewis Grassic Gibbon, had been in the RAF since 1920. He realized that reliable helicopter flight was imminent (in fact there had been some short helicopter hops already), and insists on its value to the explorer:

> The time is probably very near when the Wright invention, with its pitiful inability to achieve vertical ascents or descents, its clumsy and continuous stalling dangers and general untrustworthiness, may be superseded by craft that will indeed transform normal land exploration; craft capable of hovering (i.e. of being maintained in the air with the propulsion screw shut off) are almost within the inventor's view. The autogiro has pointed the way.   (28)

He also correctly predicted that man would reach the moon within half a century ('even though the main explosive force behind the projectile may be Signor Mussolini in pursuit of an Italian Empire'; 84). But his Jules-Vernean vision of subterranean journeys to the centre of the Earth has proved a fictionist's fantasy.

Ernest Betts, in *Heraclitus; or, The Future of Films*, thought in 1928 that what gave cinema its credibility as a serious art was its bracketing off of sound. 'The film of a hundred years hence', he held, 'if it is true to itself, will still be silent, but it will be saying more than ever'. He couldn't have seen, or rather heard, *The Jazz Singer* in London before September 1928. But he had clearly heard of it by the time *Heraclitus* was published (the film had been out in the US in late 1927), since he had a slip inserted as a footnote, acknowledging the ground was shifting under his feet as he wrote, not so as to retract his position, but to dig himself into an even deeper hole:

> Since the above was written speaking films have been launched as a commercial proposition, as the general pattern of the film of the future. As a matter of fact, their acceptance marks the most spectacular act of self-destruction that has yet come out of Hollywood, and violates the film's proper function at its source. The soul of the film—its eloquent and vital silence—is destroyed. The film now returns to the circus whence it came, among the freaks and fat ladies.

---

[52] Bowler, *A History of the Future*, pp. 122-3, 205.

Maybe in a sense Betts is not so wrong, despite the various offences against today's political correctitude he packs into what looks like an 'Erratum' slip, though he recalcitrantly refuses to acknowledge error. You might think the addition of language would return the cinema to the theatre whence it came; as indeed in many respects it did. But the sound in *The Jazz Singer* was used for the songs more than the talk. Another of the most impressive volumes in the series, *Timotheus*, by the literary critic Bonamy Dobrée, imagines '*The Future of the Theatre*'. In a mixture of Wellsian time-travel and Swiftian satire of monomaniacal projectors, the narrator describes a visit to a theatre in the future. Here, language has all but disappeared—one might say the theatre has tried to imitate the cinema. And what has moved to the foreground instead is the gimmickry of what we'd now call special effects: modulations of light and rhythm that arouse emotions in the viewer. It's almost the 'Feelies' of *Brave New World*; unsurprisingly, since Aldous Huxley, a friend of Haldane's, was doubtless reading the series as it appeared. But it also prefigures our multimedia popvideo world of 3D, CGI, fantasy, and the rest (Dobrée actually imagines a 3D video recorder).

What's interesting in both these cases is the relation between technological understanding and aesthetic judgement. Both men are spurred by their understanding of changing technology to take conservative positions about the respective art-forms. Even if they didn't want art to go there, they could see where it was heading.

One explanation for the neglect of the series may be the speed with which some of its imagined futures have been overtaken by history in this way. The 1920s couldn't, or didn't, anticipate many of our developments in science, technology and society, so that their predictions of our world often appear to come from another world. To take the most obvious example: though the authors of To-Day and To-Morrow could imagine technologies we now take for granted—increased use of machines as prosthetics; auto-pilots to navigate ships; nuclear power; even a networked society—yet there is a computer-shaped hole at the centre of many of their projections. The computer is the most consequential technological development none of the authors were able to predict in the 1920s and early 30s. The first computer, Bletchley Park's Colossus, was working by 1943-4, only twenty years after the series began, and thirteen years after it finished in 1931. But how such a machine might be made, let alone how it might transform our world, was unimaginable to this group of a hundred leading scientists and intellectuals.[53]

So what is the value of returning to study their predictions now, other than to illustrate the history of error? What makes past prophecy alive to posterity is less what it mistakes about ourselves, but what it tells us about our past; and what it

---

[53] See Bowler, *A History of the Future*—discussed further below—on how this blind spot persisted long after the development of initial computers, into the second half of the century: pp. 69–70; 81–2.

tells us about the importance of futurity to modernity; about the ways in which we imagine, or fail to imagine, our futures. The To-Day and To-Morrow books are still intensely but differently fascinating now. They bring together some of the best minds and writers of Modernism's *Wunderjahre*, often fortuitously in the same persons, giving a razor-sharp cross-section of the preoccupations and fads of a period that felt itself unprecedentedly accelerating, fermenting, destabilizing, and globalizing. At their best they don't just give a snapshot of their moment, but frame the issues and debates that have made our moment.

What that reveals is how what is at stake in the series is not just the natures of the futures that the volumes are predicting; it is the nature of prediction itself. This is clearest in the volume *Sibylla; or, The Revival of Prophecy* (1926), by C. A. Mace. Traditionally prophecy derives from the supernatural: from magic, visions, manifestations. But technological modernity projects its future through planning, management, quantification, calculation, and scientific knowledge. *Sibylla*'s dustjacket advertises it by saying:

> Science, seeking new fields for conquest, has directed its gaze to the Future. The man of science will succeed where the older prophets failed. He will foretell the course of the future because its reins are in his hands.

This overstates the case for marketing purposes, with a crassness not found in the book, nor indeed in the series as a whole; though it is touching that it is itself cast in the form of prophecies. Mace argues from the predictive nature of scientific hypotheses to observe a new prophetic confidence among scientists. He names Haldane, in *Daedalus*, as 'The first of the prophets of the twentieth-century school' for his 'frank abandonment of the pose of scientific reserve about the future' (12). Or futurologists, or futurists, as we would call them now. Scientists understand how their discoveries could drive future technological change; and in modernity it is technological change that transforms people's lives.

Not all the authors are so confident that scientists will get the future right. Some think scientists should not be trusted with the future. Some—as we saw in Russell's *Icarus*—think they won't be trusted with it. But even this mirror image to the Haldane-style optimism, derives from a confidence that the future can be predicted more accurately through a scientific, rational, logical study.

By examining what sort of worlds seemed possible to the contributors to To-Day and To-Morrow, we can learn about the limits of prediction; about the ways in which imagined futures are informed by their own cultural moment; about the motives of prediction—whether made from hope and desire, fear and contempt, or creativity and irony; and about the forces that cause some prophecies to be fulfilled and others to be frustrated. Some volumes are poignant for envisaging worlds—of peace, emancipation, art, and leisure—which we know did not come to pass for the projectors (especially because of the Depression, then the Second World War, then the Cold War), and arguably still haven't come to pass for us.

Is it our knowledge of the failed utopias of industrialization, communism, and globalization that, as Perry Anderson has argued, push today's futurology towards the dystopian?[54] Imagined futures nowadays are more likely to be shadowed by risk; by anxieties about catastrophes, whether natural or man-made: asteroid collision, mega-tsunami, climate change and other pollution; crises induced by capitalist misuses of the planet's resources of food, water, and fuel; artificial intelligence (AI) and its robots turning against its human creators; or medical crises such epidemics (including those against which we have squandered antibiotic resistance).

Prestige and Influence

The series had massive impact on the intelligentsia. The vision of ectogenesis in *Daedalus* clearly provided the scientific basis for key ideas about the industrial management of child-rearing in his friend Huxley's *Brave New World* (1932).[55] Haldane's book was read by Churchill, prompting his influential essay 'Shall we Commit Suicide', immediately preceding his re-election to Parliament in 1924.[56] Bernal's bracing visions of huge space-travelling biospheres, interplanetary colonization, brains in vats, prosthetic enhancement, and a universe-wide web of shared consciousness, inspired countless philosophical thought experiments and science fictions, as well as later scientist-futurologists such as Freeman Dyson. Bernal is thought to have been a model both for Orwell's O'Brien in *Nineteen Eighty-Four* and for Lord Feverstone in the final volume of C. S. Lewis' Space Trilogy.[57]

The series won high praise from contemporary reviewers both sides of the Atlantic. These comments are representative of the reception the series received in the UK press:[58]

Spectator: 'Scintillating monographs.'

Observer: 'There seems no reason why the brilliant To-day and To-morrow Series should come to an end for a century of to-morrows. At first it seemed impossible for the publishers to keep up the sport through a dozen volumes, but the series already runs to more than two score. A remarkable series…'

---

[54] Anderson, 'The River of Time', *New Left Review*, 26 (March–April 2004), 67–77. See especially p. 73 on Bernal and Huxley.

[55] Huxley's relation to the series is discussed in Chapter 6.

[56] Graham Farmelo, *Churchill's Bomb* (London: Faber, 2013), 30–2.

[57] See for example Susanna Hornig Priest, ed., *Encyclopedia of Science and Technology Communication* (Los Angeles: Sage, 2010), 914. C. S. Lewis, *That Hideous Strength* (London: The Bodley Head, 1945). Robert Bud, 'Life, DNA and the Model', *British Journal for the History of Science*, 46 (June 2013), 311–34, quotes Feverstone's comment 'If Science is really given a free hand it can now take over the human race and re-condition it: make man a really efficient animal' (the comment is in *That Hideous Strength* (London: The Bodley Head, 1945), 45), describing him as a 'Bernalian figure' (319). Haldane wrote a scathing review of Lewis' trilogy in the Communist Party journal *Modern Quarterly* in 1946: See Parrinder, *Utopian Literature and Science*, p. 61.

[58] The following excerpts are quoted from the end-matter of many of the UK volumes.

Daily Herald: 'This series has given us many monographs of brilliance and discernment.... The stylistic excellences of this provocative series.'

Field: 'We have long desired to express the deep admiration felt by every thinking scholar and worker at the present day for this series. We must pay tribute to the high standard of thought and expression they maintain.'

Reviewers in the US were comparably enthusiastic:[59]

No more interesting and significant books are being published.

(Evanston News Index)

The mildest appearing 16mos that ever scuttled our human complacency with the picture of such vast horizons or such acute despairs.   *(New York Times)*

A series steadily progressing through further volumes as provocative of thought, if not always as intrinsically as important as those to which Messrs. Haldane and Russell lent the authority of their names.

(Ernest Boyd, in *The Sun* (New York))

Each is a compendium of science and excitement. You can read any one of them in an hour and be certain of shocks, surprises and intoxicating ideas. They violate the literary Volstead act, and may well be suppressed or denatured.

(Commercial Tribune (Cincinnati))

The 'outspoken' nature of the series drew predictable attacks from moralistic conservatives such as the *Sunday Express*' notorious James Douglas. Frederic Warburg, the publisher who looked after the series for the twin firms of Routledge and Kegan Paul, described how:

In the beginning, when he thundered his comminations against the sexual explicitness of one or other of the books, alarm and despondency was created in the board-room. But soon we become inoculated against attacks, and smilingly ordered another printing of 2,000 copies on the Monday morning following an outburst.[60]

For Warburg—who would later publish Orwell too: 'It was a unique publishing event. Many now distinguished personages made their debut in this series or contributed an early work.'[61] And so they did. At the time they wrote for the series, writers such as Haldane, Bernal, Liddell Hart, Vera Brittain, Robert Graves, André Maurois, and others were far from being the household names they became later on. Sarvepalli Radhakrishnan, who contributed *Kalki; or, The Future of Civilization* (1929) was already a well-published academic, but would become President of India.

Many of the other contributors were well-known experts and authors at the time—figures such as Russell Brain, F. C. S. Schiller, J. W. N. Sullivan, C. E. M. Joad,

---

[59] The following excerpts are quoted from the jacket flap of several of the Dutton issues.
[60] Warburg, *An Occupation for Gentlemen*, p. 115.   [61] Ibid., p. 114.

Gerald Heard, Dyneley Hussey, or Gerald Gould. Some of the individual volumes are familiar to specialists of their authors, and individual volumes have been discussed for their contributions to specific debates. *Daedalus* and *Icarus* have earned their place in the history of science and science popularization.[62] Yet there has been only glancing work on To-Day and To-Morrow as a whole; and it is the collective project that makes it so unusual and in many ways a representative project of the intelligentsia between the wars, and an excellent indicator of the intellectual life of the era. In short, there are so many good reasons for attending to the series that, rather than asking why we might be interested in it, the more salient question is why one of the most interesting examples of modern thought about the future became so *un*familiar? The series had effectively—and unaccountably—disappeared from cultural memory. Even Ogden's entry in the *Oxford Dictionary of National Biography* omits to mention it, crediting him only with 'the planning and editing of two major series: "The history of civilisation" and "The international library of psychology, philosophy and scientific method" '. Routledge's 2008 reissue as a library edition attracted little attention.[63]

As suggested, the scientists were not only at the frontiers of their disciplines, but could see how those disciplines were becoming increasingly federalized as physics was being 'invaded' by biology and chemistry. The volumes cross disciplinary frontiers in other ways too, making stimulating connections between apparently disparate fields: comparing nonsense to Einsteinian physics; sport to war; arguing that nonsense makes war impossible, and so on.

To-Day and To-Morrow also arguably contributed to the development of cultural studies, through its attention to everyday life, to the media, to press barons and their control, to taste in houses, clothes, books, food, drink; and through its consideration of pursuits such as sport, gambling, and other leisure activities. Chapter 5 explores this claim in detail.

There are other good reasons why it should be better known to literary scholars. It isn't just that many of the books are extremely well-written—intelligent, witty, often accurate in their prophecies, or revealing when wrong—or that those by major writers can reveal a new facet of a familiar talent. Who would have thought Vera Brittain in 1929 would sound so upbeat about the women's movement, while she was also working on the unbearably poignant *Testament of Youth*? Who knew that suffragette Sylvia Pankhurst was also a formidably erudite expert on international language projects? It's also that the debates aired here influence literature in important ways. Conversely, they are fascinating about the literature and culture of their time, and respond to it in ways that are revealing. A rather flat book on Canada by George Godwin suddenly springs to life when it quotes a passage

---

[62] See for example K. R. Dronamraju, ed. (1995) *Haldane's* Daedalus *Revisited* (Oxford: Oxford University Press, 1995).

[63] The only review I saw was my own: 'Future Sublime', 'Commentary', *TLS* (26 June 2009), 14–15.

supposed to exemplify what an American language of the future might look like—the kind of 'interlanguage' Sylvia Pankhurst's volume *Delphos* is about—and we recognize the opening passage of *Finnegans Wake*—though it hadn't even been published as a book under that title at the time. The engagements of major modern writers like Huxley, Joyce, Eliot, Wyndham Lewis, and Evelyn Waugh with To-Day and To-Morrow are explored in Chapter 6.

The series is a modernist project in its commitment (in Ezra Pound's phrase) to 'make it new'; in its approach to modernity via myth;[64] in its formal and stylistic self-reflexivities. Yet in other ways it is very far from the high modernism of Pound's, Eliot's, or Lewis' authoritarian classicizing. It is still anarchist and revolutionary when the modernists aligning themselves with the political right were issuing a *rappel à l'ordre*—a call back to the order of tradition, history, and religion. To-Day and To-Morrow is a salutary reminder that the modern in the aftermath of the First World War could take very different forms.

For all these reasons, the series includes much essential reading for modernist studies, for cultural studies, for science studies and for the history of ideas. It contains some of the most important and interesting writing of the period on dozens of subjects; and some of the best writing on any subjects. For readers who care about the relation between science and the arts, the aftermath of the First World War, politics between the wars, feminism and gender and sexuality, culture, media, technology, or literature, language and the arts in the period, it frequently illuminates these topics in unexpected and intriguing ways. It is a cornucopia, not just for literary scholars but several other disciplines: cultural historians, people studying popularization, science fiction, book history, everyday life, futurology, and many others.

The Unique Character of the Series

There were plenty of other books series, not all of them edited by Ogden, popularizing science, the arts, and the history of civilization, such as the International Scientific Series that ran from 1871-1911 publishing monographs by the likes of T. H. Huxley and Herbert Spencer; or Williams and Norgate's *Home University Library of Modern Knowledge*, published from 1911.[65] But the To-Day and To-Morrow volumes are not designed to impart the core knowledge of part of a

---

[64] Some use myth as a reference point (like Schiller in *Cassandra*, or Dora Russell in *Hypatia* as a kind of frame). Fournier d'Albe in *Hephaestus* and Garret Garett in *Ouroboros* write whole essays in mythological mode, as an allegory of technology and industry.

[65] See Leslie Howsam, 'An Experiment with Science for the Nineteenth-Century Book Trade: The International Scientific series', *British Journal for the History of Science*, 33:2 (June 2000), 187–207. I am grateful to Sara Haslam for telling me about this article, and to the late Robert Gomme for his insights into the Home University Library.

discipline like text-books. Ogden's International Library took up that role for the newer, human sciences. Instead, they are meta-epistemological: not knowledge of chemistry, say, but thinking about that knowledge, and its potential. Many of the contributors, such as Bertrand Russell, James Jeans, F. C. S. Schiller, or C. E. M. Joad, had written the popularizing disciplinary survey-type books too. In To-Day and To-Morrow they were trying to do something different.

In her memoir of Ogden, Dora Russell calls them 'lighthearted […] booklets', by contrast with the 'learned series' of the International Library.[66] True, Robert Graves's mercurial, anecdotal tours around humour or swearing, or Joad's one-liners about morality or suburbia, are light by comparison with the field-changing concepts of Wittgenstein about language and science, or Malinowski about anthropology. But in the best volumes light doesn't mean slight. Rather, the term captures the imaginative panache inventive exuberance of the writing, and the passion about the subjects. As Russell added, the volumes were on 'vital topics'.

There have been comparable series devoted to individual thinkers, such as the influential Fontana Modern Masters series of the 1970s, or the Oxford Past Masters. But even the Modern Masters volumes were essentially backward-looking, assessing the body of work of a usually dead innovator. But for the most part, To-Day and To-Morrow was focused not on thinkers whose thought was already known, but in producing new thought, not about existing individuals, but about the possibilities and probabilities of everyday life no-one had yet lived.

In some ways it is a recognizable forerunner of the 'Short Introductions' and 'Beginner's Guides' prevalent nowadays. But there are two key differences. Rather than mapping a body of knowledge for a predominantly student audience, To-Day and To-Morrow sought to provoke thought in the public sphere, and was aimed at intelligent general readers. Second, it was not only analyzing contemporary developments and trends; but predicting where they might lead. As an encyclopaedic networked performance of futurology there are few parallels, and no serious precursors.

A representative journalistic counterpart would be the 1999 collection, *Predictions*, edited by Sian Griffiths.[67] This assembles '30 great minds on the future', as the dust-jacket has it. The predictive texts were originally solicited to supplement interviews given to the *Times Higher Education Supplement*, and are themselves very short, at between one and five pages. Though in many cases the arguments are familiar from the thinkers' more extended work, the ideas are important and interesting—as is the fact that they mostly adopt a similar, straightforwardly predictive expository prose. Umberto Eco, predictably, comes up with a witty meta-futurological bagatelle called 'Never Fall in Love with Your Own Airship' (104-5)—a warning the author of *Aeolus* would have done well to heed.

[66] Dora Russell, 'My Friend Ogden', in *C. K. Ogden: A Collective Memoir*, pp. 82–95 (93).
[67] Oxford University Press, 1999. Discussed in the Conclusions.

The millennium was a stimulant to such futurological imaginings, both in terms of analytic projections like these, and new age fantasies. The fact that both a century and a millennium were ending and beginning seemed to double the futurological stakes, encouraging people to think about both shorter-term and longer-term futures, as they had also been doing in To-Day and To-Morrow. Perhaps the closest contemporary equivalent to the series would be another millennial product, the short paperback volumes, also called *Predictions*, published by Phoenix in 1997–8, and described on their back covers as: 'a series of 24 short books in which some of the world's most distinguished academics and writers in their particular fields attempt to forecast the future, over the next fifty years, across a range of social, economic, political, geographical and technological subject areas'. Or the similar series *Prospects for Tomorrow*, edited by Yorick Blumenfeld for Thames and Hudson in 2000–1.

Those are all print collections aimed at general readers; attempts to popularize expert thinking about the future. But of course the closest contemporary equivalent of getting numbers of people together to think about the future is the think-tank— the professional consultancy group hired by corporations, governments, or special interest groups, to produce reports on specific topics. Its aim is to influence security, policy or profits; and much more stress is laid on methodologies, data, and accuracy; and the computer has become the essential tool. In some ways it might seem to represent the logical development of the desire a century ago to make futurology more scientific. But the power of think-tanks and foresight groups has drawn criticism of different kinds: not just suspicion of political bias and hidden agendas, but concern that the replacement of the thought experiment by the algorithm reduces the imaginative dimension, and blinds us to the sheer unpredictability of things, which was precisely why we felt the need to try to understand the future in the first place. As J. B. S. Haldane put it: 'In forecasting the future of scientific research there is one quite general law to be noted. The unexpected always happens. So one can be quite sure that the future will make any detailed predictions look rather silly'.[68]

The Sociology of the Series

Like the International Library, To-Day and To-Morrow was in some ways an Oxbridge project. It was closely associated with the Heretics. Besides Ogden and Haldane, several contributors had given papers to the society: Bertrand and Dora Russell, F. C. S. Schiller, E. J. Dent, W. J. Turner, L. L. Whyte, Bonamy Dobrée, and Vernon Lee.[69] The series used a number of other Oxford and Cambridge authors

---

[68] Haldane, 'The Future of Biology', pp. 139–53.
[69] See Franke, *Modernist Heresies*, pp. 219–29.

and recent graduates. Graves, Brittain, C. P. Blacker, and Joad had studied at Oxford, for example (as had Haldane and Schiller). Ogden and Haldane were based in Cambridge, where Russell had been till he was dismissed from Trinity College after being prosecuted under the Defence of the Realm Act in 1916 for his pacifist activities. Ogden and Russell had studied at Cambridge, as had Bernal and Dobrée. The series also keyed into a sense that Cambridge in particular was where so much cutting-edge thinking and research was happening—especially in physics, philosophy, economics, psychology, neurology, and literary criticism. Otherwise, it does not issue from a single group associated with a social or literary movement like the Fabians or the Bloomsbury Group. Nor is it exclusively a product of what Noel Annan defined as the British 'intellectual aristocracy' of the late nineteenth and early twentieth century: the Darwins, Huxleys, Thackerays, Macaulays, Stephens, and Stracheys who had dominated the intellectual and cultural life of the period;[70] though its two most prominent contributors, Haldane and Bertrand Russell, were from such families. Some of the authors (Russell, Bonamy Dobrée, Gerald Gould, and F. G. Crookshank) had written for Ogden's *Cambridge Magazine*. Most were public-school-educated. Some went to elite schools: Haldane to Eton, Schiller to Rugby, Graves to Charterhouse, Bernal to Stonyhurst. Others attended less well-known schools. Joad went to Blundell's School in Devon. Ogden, less privileged and more of an outsider from the metropolitan elite, went to Rossall School, Lancashire, where his father taught. In general the authors came from diverse professional backgrounds: they were doctors, academics, scientists, educators; lawyers, journalists; men and women of letters. The essential qualification for providing a volume was the one so divisive nowadays: expertise.

Ogden's mission with his publishing ventures as with the Heretics was to expose young minds to ideas and positions they hadn't encountered at school—a range of views about the war during wartime; continental philosophy; radical ideas on atheism, birth control, language, etc. Those who encountered him often found the experience mind-stretching.[71] This was the readership To-Day and To-Morrow aimed at: the public school product whose mind had not yet closed.

The pricing of the books (at two shillings and sixpence apiece) and their modest initial print-runs (usually 2,000 each) position them as designed for an influential elite rather than a mass-market. But it would be misleading to claim that the inclusion of volumes discussing public schools, Oxford and Cambridge, clubs, the 'servant problem', or opera, suggest a traditionalist bias. For example, though it's true that the P. Morton Shand who wrote *Bacchus; or, Wine To-Day and To-Morrow* was the grandfather of Camilla, Queen Consort, he was also an advocate of

---

[70] Annan, 'The Intellectual Aristocracy' (1955), in *The Dons: Mentors, eccentrics and geniuses* (Chicago: University of Chicago Press, 1999), 304–41.

[71] See for example Sargant and Dora Russell in *C. K. Ogden: A collective memoir*, pp. 53–4 and 82.

Modernist architecture and design, championing the Bauhaus, and setting up a company to import Alvar Aalto's furniture to the UK.

If the classical titles imply public school- and university-educated readers, they also have a progressive edge; trying to wrench mindsets away from tradition-orientedness and swivel them round towards the future. Janus-faced indeed. Education, certainly, is central to the entire project. It does not just permeate the content (and often provide the answer to the problem under discussion, whether sexuality, crime, or superstition, and so on) but determines the form, and also accounts for some of its formally striking moments, such as Haldane's pastiche of an undergraduate essay, or the occasional mock-Platonic dialogue.

The series covers mass media as well as high culture; the demotic as well as the mandarin; the radical as well as the conservative. Like Modernism it makes sparks fly by rubbing the two together. It is a product of the period when its public-school authors and readers were as likely as not to be socialists. If some of the books are written in the style of student debating societies, the aim was, precisely, to foster intelligent discussion—informed by innovative ideas—on the controversial questions of the day. Overall, though, the project is markedly radical: secular, rationalist, modernist, internationalist, utopian, iconoclastic.

The series investigates and embraces change and modernity as they are being and will be worked out in Society. You would be hard pressed to find a Burkean Tory among the contributors. Even J. F. Roxburgh (Charterhouse, Cambridge, the Sorbonne), the first headmaster of Stowe School and author of *Eleutheros; or, The Future of the Public Schools* (1930), putting the case for the moral qualities inculcated through studying the classics, was a reformer with liberal and aesthetic tendencies.[72] As Eden Paul puts it in his volume, *Chronos; or, The Future of the Family* (1930), the series is 'obviously not addressed to hide-bound conservatives' (5), going on to characterize himself as an irreligious radical (5, 34).[73] There are satirists of radical modernity among them, like Dobrée in *Timotheus*. But the satire is generally markedly benign and good humoured. In fact humour is very prevalent, enhancing the optimistic note of the series.

What the contributors mostly have in common is that the views being advanced are often radical ones, in the sense of being in the avant-garde, anticipating the rapid abandonment of traditional religious, social and sexual conventions; and also in the sense of challenging the root of the subject under discussion, whether the distinction between matter and mind, the basis of race, or the basis of morality.

Several of the authors—Bertrand Russell, Haldane, Holtby, Brittain, Joad, Norman Haire—contributed to the *Realist* magazine which ran from 1929-30, dedicated

[72] Noel Annan's biography of him, *Roxburgh of Stowe* (1965), views him as one of the greatest of public school heads.

[73] Compare Julian Hall's *Alma Mater; or, The Future of Oxford and Cambridge* (1928), pp. 32-3, arguing that a young reformer in the Wellsian mould would gain confidence from the series.

to 'Scientific Humanism'. Some later became involved in the Progressive League, founded in 1932 by Joad, who was President of the Federation and Wells, who was a Vice-president, as were A. S. Neill, Barbara Wootton, Miles Malleson, David Low, Cyril Burt, Aldous Huxley, Kingsley Martin, Harold Nicholson, Beverley Nichols, Olaf Stapledon, Rebecca West, Leonard Woolf, and the psychologist and psychoanalyst J. C. Flügel; and also several other To-Day and To-Morrow contributors: Russell, Brittain, Haire, and Geoffrey West.

To-Day and To-Morrow—the field of interest—is conceived in terms of the present and the future. No past. That was the implicit rebuke in the *Essays of To-day and Yesterday* series which appeared from 1926, and for which writers like Hilaire Belloc, Arnold Bennett, A. C. Benson, G. K. Chesterton, and Edward Thomas contributed volumes of essays. For thinkers like Belloc or Chesterton, a tomorrow that wasn't based on yesterday wouldn't make any sense, or would only make sense understood as a failure: a falling away from the religious and cultural traditions. Traditionalists, conservatives, classicists, nostalgics, all find their visions of excellence and human achievement in the past. The moderns vest their hopes of human potential, improvement, transformation, in the future. Most of the To-Day and To-Morrow authors were Futurist in orientation. If they do not go as far as Marinetti and advocate destroying museums, they simply ignore them, or have virtually nothing to say about them. 'The Museum of the Future' doesn't figure in To-Day and To-Morrow and doesn't seem a possible title in the series. It is a stark contrast with the current fetishisation of the archive and of digital 'curatorship'.

To-Day and To-Morrow, like any cultural work, is a product of its time. The eight-year span during which the volumes were published was framed by Britain's first two Labour governments, led by Ramsay Macdonald: the first in 1924, the second from 1929-31. The rethinking of man's relation to past and future in the series was to some extent a product of the First World War; and inevitably the war haunts many of the volumes (as discussed in Chapter 2)—whether they are projecting images of the past war into future destruction; or expressing a desperate aspiration to avoid a recurrence of such slaughter.

Studying these works today from nearly a century ago might seem an antiquarian endeavour; the archaeology of the lost tribe of modernist future-people. It is done here not just for the fascination of the material; but in the hope that the idealism and creativity of these texts might help us to recover their sense of human potentiality to imagine that the world could be different, and perhaps better.

These Introductions to To-Day and To-Morrow and its writers have attempted a contextualization of the whole series, in terms of its moment and milieu, Ogden as editor, its relation to his other publishing projects, and to other popularizing series, the areas it covered as it developed, and its reception. (A more detailed account of the book history of the series appears as Appendix A.) It is followed by a second introductory section, focusing on futurology, considered both in the context of the early twentieth century, and in terms of theoretical perspectives.

The remaining chapters attempt to offer three main things. First, brief accounts of key volumes, which quote enough to bring out their styles and modes, and analyses which seek to bring out their interest and relevance. Second, a critical study of the series as a whole, looking at a range of themes and ideas, from the perspectives of futurology, popular science, history, literary criticism and literary history, intellectual history, cultural and media studies, and book history. Third, the nature and quality of the writing. One of the most striking features is the different and often creative ways the writers go about their task. Some write dialogues; some jeremiads; some satires. I shall explore these modes, and the rhetorics the volumes experiment with. Another curious feature of the series—in part perhaps to do with the way the authors refer to each other—is how the subject of one book returns in the figurative language of another. And that is true of most of these themes. Networks, conflict, eugenics, robotics, science, all lead this double or multiple life through the series, as discourses from one discipline or science (or pseudo-science) get used to advance views in another field.[74] The energies of interdisciplinary metaphorization—the way sexual attraction gets described in terms of atomic physics, communication networks as a nervous system, machines as ideas, or the body as a machine—are also considered. A particular focus over the entire book is on the communication between literature and science in various forms.

Introductions to the Future: The Future in Theory

Our society is flooded with claims of insight into the future. Some issue from governmental institutions and programmes and their reports, such as the European Union Institute for Security Studies (EUISS)'s report on Citizens in an Interconnected and Polycentric World: Global Trends 2030;[75] the UK government's Foresight Annual Review 2012;[76] or the US National Intelligence Council *Global Trends 2030* website, also from 2012.[77] Much government forecasting operates secretly (when it concerns issues such as security or weapons). Forecasting is vital in the financial markets and the commercial sphere too, and also covert. Access to the best intelligence in anticipating future trends and demands offers the promise of greater profits. Forecasts are also produced by non-profit foundations such as the innovation charity NESTA, which published *Don't Stop Thinking*

---

[74] Morrisson, *Modernism, Science, and Technology*, pp. 85, 63, describes two theoretical models for this migration of concepts and tropes. Anthropologist Marilyn Strathern defines as 'domaining' the way in which habits of thought reproduce themselves in varying contexts each with its own associations and logic. Whereas Michael Whitworth takes a more rhetorical perspective, analysing the way ideas move more easily across boundaries as the different disciplines and practices share metaphors.
[75] http://www.iss.europa.eu/uploads/media/ESPAS_report_01.pdf
[76] https://www.gov.uk/government/publications/foresight-annual-review-2012-2
[77] http://gt2030.com/about/

about Tomorrow: *A modest defence of futurology*, and supports London's annual FutureFest.[78] Journalism, television documentaries, online lectures such as TED and TEDx talks, self-help books, all live looking forward.

Studies of futurology are mainly advocacies or manuals for improved prediction, such as Nate Silver's *The Signal and the Noise* (2013). There is a large theoretical and critical literature on utopias exemplified by scholars such as Lyman Sargent, Fredric Jameson, or Patrick Parrinder. Major sociological accounts include Ulrich Beck, *Risk Society* (1992), and Arjun Appadurai, *The Future as Cultural Fact* (2013). Sceptical futurologists such as Nassim Nicholas Taleb in *The Black Swan* (2007), or dystopians such as Jörg Friedrichs, *The Future Is Not What it Used to Be* (2013), are well represented. The two main lines of, on the one hand, practising or popularizing futurologists, and on the other, academic study of the utopian imaginary, have kept separate. The example of To-Day and To-Morrow shows why this is unfortunate; and demonstrates superbly the ways in which combining them enables writers to analyse, challenge, and enhance both utopian thinking and futurological practice.

The analysis of imagined futures offers clear access to people's values, concerns, hopes and anxieties. Yet, as Appadurai argues, our crucial future orientation has been neglected by the social sciences and especially by the arts and humanities.[79] Though science fiction studies is now well-established, Utopian studies has until recently been more common in the social and political sciences than in literary research. Nevertheless, we are currently witnessing what gets described as a 'future boom'[80] across many disciplines, as politicians, governments, policy makers, scientific and market researchers, journalists, experts in all disciplines, are increasingly being pressured or incentivized to pronounce upon the future: to plan scenarios, engage in strategic foresight exercises or horizon scanning; to spot trends and analyse risks, whether collaboratively or competitively, as in the betting on financial futures; in the kind of 'forecasting tournaments' employed by the US Intelligence Advanced Research Projects Agency (IARPA). We expect the future not only to be predicted, but managed; or at least, we require at least the illusion of its measurability and manageability, as experts conduct future mapping, and devise 'road maps' to get us there; devise 'anticipatory governance',[81] 'responsible innovation', or, in a more pessimistic version, to enhance the 'resilience' of economic and social structures against ungovernable or unpredictable 'black swan' shocks or disasters through the use of 'stress testing'.

---

[78] http://www.nesta.org.uk/publications/dont-stop-thinking-about-tomorrow-modest-defence-futurology and http://www.futurefest.org/

[79] Arjun Appadurai, *The Future as Cultural Fact* (London: Verso, 2013), 285–6.

[80] See Rosalind Shaw, 'Provocation: Futurizing memory': http://www.culanth.org/fieldsights/376-provocation-futurizing-memory

[81] See http://www.forwardengagement.org/ and https://www.wilsoncenter.org/event/anticipatory-governance-upgrading-government-for-the-21st-century

Different schools and practices of futurology abound, and mostly have established methodologies. But there has been little attempt (as Appadurai implies) to gain a theoretical purchase on the system of futurology itself; and how it relates to other disciplines and practices. This study poses futurology as both a vital apprehension of the present, a practice where past and future collide, virtual and real intermingle, fact, speculation, and fiction fuse.

Contemporary futurology is radically different from its origins at the start of the twentieth century. It is dominated by professionalized, group practices led by models, variables and ever bigger data, funded by governments or multinational corporations, and focused on security, power or profit. Its scientific or social science methodologies contrast with the versions of the future in popular science fiction, generally originating in individual imaginations, and presenting dystopian narratives of the failure of atomic or biological or ecological and climate science.

The To-Day and To-Morrow series inhabits the space between these worlds. The project has been described as 'Perhaps the first systematic attempt to create a "Think Tank" to make predictions about the future of society'.[82] Though it was not established as a funded institution, and though the books were produced by individual writers, the contributors were connected both by social and intellectual networks, and through rhetorical engagement. They built on each other's projections, as they debated with each other both inside and outside the series. Its publisher hoped to profit from it, as did the authors. Ogden too took a commission on all the works he had procured for Kegan Paul.[83] But they were contributing to the public sphere, and the pursuit of knowledge and understanding were equally strong motives. The contributors also spanned the divide between professional expertise and imagination, in two ways. The line-up of writers included those best known for their professional contributions to scientific and social science disciplines, alongside popular writers of fiction, poetry, memoir and journalism. It also included a number of contributors with a gift for the popularization of technical subjects—the sciences, law, human and social sciences, and the arts.

According to George Myerson and Yvonne Rydin's spirited account of 'Scenario development as flawed compromise', 'the group means of scenario production, with its dependence on many diverse inputs from multiple experts', too often issues in 'bland statements of future trends'.[84] Yet the dystopian, often apocalyptic, fictional futures offered by science fiction, are liable to the opposite objection. From John Christopher's *The Death of Grass* (1956) and Neville Shute's *On the Beach* (1957), to Cormac McCarthy's *The Road* (2006) or the film *The Day after Tomorrow* (2004), the visions are anything but bland: powerful, shocking, haunting. The problem—and perhaps also the source of their power—is that they do not tell us

---

[82] Roy Lewis, 'C. K. Ogden's To-Day & To-Morrow Series', pp. [140]–52 (141).

[83] Warburg, *An Occupation for Gentlemen*, p. 94.

[84] George Myerson and Yvonne Rydin, 'No Limits to Imagining London's Future', *Imagining the Future City: London 2062*, ed. S. Bell and J. Paskins (London: Ubiquity Press, 2013), 155–8 (156). DOI: http://dx.doi. org/10.5334/bag.w

anything we don't already know. They are warnings about dangers that were already known: biological warfare, atomic weapons, climate change. One point of horizon-scanning is to be the first to see the danger that is on its way but has not yet appeared or arrived. They also elide the mechanisms and processes that have led to apocalypse. The plague or the nuclear fallout has been unleashed; the environmental catastrophe has already occurred. The narratives jump over precisely the evidence the foresight scientists would concentrate on, of how the virus escaped, what risks could trigger nuclear holocaust, what levels of emissions and pollutions will produce irreversible disaster. It is not that these fictions are not based on well-documented scientific fact. Rather, they are not concerned with scientific methodology. After all, they do not need it for narrative purposes. They have no need to provide evidence for their hypothetical futures; they simply choose the future they want to explore.

To-Day and To-Morrow was able to negotiate effectively between these two positions. Contributors drew on their own expert knowledge, or upon the expertise of others. They were not writing fiction or inventing parallel worlds—or not most of the time. Conversely, they could liberate themselves from the bonds of verisimilitude that science fiction tends to depend upon for its credibility (in formal terms it is often a realist method applied to an unreal world). Not answerable to the demands of corporate advantage or government agendas, they were able to root their futurology, as Myerson and Rydin advocate, 'in the unfettered play of ideas, and trust to the coherence of a well-imagined story'.

The historical dimension of this study contributes to the cultural history of the future. But it also aspires to enhance our understanding of how predictions get made; and thus in principle to contribute to better futurological approaches in future. Study of historical futurology risks getting trapped in discussion of the prescience or otherwise of individual predictions. While this remarkable series is certainly illuminating for the successes and failures of some of its individual predictions, it is more revealing for the projections that are still far from realization; and for the topics crucial to lives today but which it didn't anticipate at all. Published on the threshold of the emergence of molecular biology, and envisaging (in *Daedalus*) the genetic modification of plants, it barely contemplates the implications of such modification for humanity. What it can tell us about the limits of futurology, its blind spots, is among its most valuable lessons for future horizon-scanners. Study of such a corpus of imagined futures can thus illuminate the broader processes of imagining forwards, and the history of discourses we might otherwise assume to be contemporary. The writers of To-Day and To-Morrow were confronting for the first time what are now real possibilities—globalization, interconnectivity, robotics, prosthetics, and planned fundamental changes to the nature of humanity—what Steve Fuller calls 'Humanity 2.0'.[85] To consider such past futurology alongside contemporary equivalents has the potential to help us

[85] Steve Fuller, *Preparing for Life in Humanity 2.0* (Basingstoke: Palgrave Macmillan, 2012).

understand not only why we envision the futures that we do, but also why we don't envision those we don't (but which nonetheless sometimes come to pass). Why were the To-Day and To-Morrow authors able to predict biospheres, mobile phones, and virtual reality, but not the digital processor, the crisis in obesity, or the resurgence of religious fundamentalisms? And what will being able to answer such questions tell us about the blind-spots in our own forward vision and horizon scanning?

To-Day and To-Morrow is a key document in the history of modernism and modernity, and deeply characteristic of the early twentieth century's imagination of the future as a site of technological and sociological solutions—the period of H. G. Wells, Futurism, Henry Ford, Le Corbusier, the Bauhaus. The contrast with today's catastrophe-driven futurological discourses in environmentalism, demography, urban planning, nutrition, economics, astronomy, genetics, AI, and other disciplines is evident. Reading the series now enables us to use past futurologies to cast light on present versions; and using the overview of past and present versions to theorize the genre and project forward to possibilities of future futurology.

The series also casts revealing light on the ways in which knowledge is configured. The vertiginous paradigm shifts in the physical and biological sciences in the early twentieth century destabilized the traditional disciplinary separations. To-Day and To-Morrow exemplifies very different visions of what new disciplines might emerge from the epistemological flux. Scientists like Haldane and Bernal, working at the frontiers of the territory that would later be codified as molecular biology, provide a vision of science that is still recognizably mainstream; even if their predictions for what such science would enable are still far from being realized, and may never be realized. Others, as we shall see, thought that the counter-intuitive aspects of relativity and quantum mechanics promised a rapprochement with beliefs in the immaterial world of psychical research. If such strivings after disciplinary synthesis can be seen as pioneering exercises in interdisciplinary thought, they can also chasten contemporary enthusiasms for interdisciplinarity, showing the need for a rigorous questioning of the validity of disciplinary combinations.

The series considered collectively represents the best document we have of how the interwar years thought about the future. Study of it brings out the exhilarating multiplicity of particular imagined futures. But it produces another effect, in some ways more surprising, which is to reflect back on how the notion of the future operates more broadly across culture, and to show how the future is implied everywhere in everyday life; not just in the fiction and journalism we read and the films and television we watch; but in the experience of reading, narrating, remembering, watching. Christine Brooke-Rose, for example, commented on this extraordinary pervasiveness of futurological discourse throughout culture in relation to her novel *Amalgamennon*, written entirely in the future tense—the tense, paradoxically, as she observed, of much news reportage.[86] It also enables a comparative understanding of the relations between futurologies in different fields, and how they might affect each other; as for example when literary then cinematic imaginings of video phones (which make an early appearance in To-Day and To-Morrow) influence subsequent consumer technology design.[87]

The series models the affect evoked by reflecting on the future—not only enthusiastic anticipation but also hope, anxiety, bewilderment, etc.—and how such cares often themselves join past, present and future, not least because they are often the same emotions stirred by thinking backwards: denial, forgetting, trauma, nostalgia, mourning. Study of this unique and diverse corpus of futurological imaginings thus helps us understand futurology in psychological terms: why we do it, what it does for us; what it fails to do; what are its pleasures; what it does to our desire.

The early reviews indicate how the series was greeted in the press with considerable excitement, as something that stood out. Reviewers were familiar with popular science writing; with the kind of science fiction with which Wells had made such an impact; even with the kind of futurological thinking Wells himself had also developed, as we shall see. They were familiar too with the futurological forms of the political manifesto, social critique, journalistic fantasy. One advantage of studying To-Day and To-Morrow is how it reveals the multiplicity of modes of futurology. It draws on all these modes. Yet it seemed also to be offering something new. That sense of novelty may be attributable in part to the novelty of some of its specific predictions. Haldane's ectogenesis in particular became a kind of signature of the series; a concept many of the other contributors invoked as signalling not only a new kind of future, but a new kind of futurology. Bernal's biospheres were to have a comparable effect on subsequent futurologists and science fiction writers. But the novelty of the series is also a function of its form: a particular hybrid, positioned not within the field of popularization (there was, after all, no established science of ectogenesis that Haldane was popularizing, though he could discern the basis of what such a science might turn out to be); nor within science fiction; nor within journalism or political or social advocacy; but placed carefully in the space between such forms. The length of each volume— equivalent to a pamphlet or short story or an extended essay—fell between that of a journalistic essay or political speech on the one hand, and a science fiction novel on the other. This positioning and scale is not unprecedented. But it allowed

---

[86] 'A Conversation with Christine Brooke-Rose By Ellen G. Friedman and Miriam Fuchs', from the *Review of Contemporary Fiction*, 9:3 (Fall 1989), 81–90. See: http://www.dalkeyarchive.com/a-conversation-with-christine-brooke-rose-by-ellen-g-friedman-and-miriam-fuchs/

[87] E. M. Forster's 1909 story 'The Machine Stops' includes an earlier, and pre-war, appearance of a video phone, and indeed of a form of multimedia mechanical web ('cinematophote', p. 15): *The Eternal Moment and Other Stories* (London: Sidgwick and Jackson, 1928), 1–61.

for a free play of imaginative and intellectual energy uncommon elsewhere; a combination of visionary power and plausible elaboration that gave contemporary readers the impression that the future was being made palpable to them.

Future Orientation

In *All That Is Solid Melts into Air*, Marshall Berman considered the new kind of people envisaged in the communist *Manifesto* as required by the permanent revolution of industrial modernity:

> They must learn not to long nostalgically for the 'fixed, fast-frozen relationships' of the real or fantasized past, but to delight in mobility, to thrive on renewal, to look forward to future developments in their conditions of life and their relations with their fellow men.[88]

Berman traces this 'developmental ideal' to the German romantic humanism of Goethe and Schiller and their utopian followers. He teases out the complex relations between past, present, and future in the experience of modernity. But, like Giddens, he clearly—and rightly—sees as foundational this shift of emphasis from traditionalist retrospect to modernity's faith in future possibilities. Such a shift was implicit in the ideals of the French Revolution, and the belief that an aristocratic and theocratic era was giving way to a future of republican rationality. The Industrial Revolution forming the background to Romanticism is generally identified as the pivotal point at which people define themselves less in terms of the past, and were less likely to live and work in the same way as their parents, but feel they are entering a future that would be different.[89]

By the middle of the nineteenth century, orientation towards the future had become a discernible ideology. Berman quotes from the Preface to Baudelaire's 'Salon of 1846', his review of that year's showing of new art. The Preface is addressed 'To the Bourgeois', to whom Baudelaire says: 'you have combined together, you have formed companies, you have raised loans', not just to make money, but for what Berman calls 'a far loftier purpose': 'to realize the idea of the future in all its diverse forms—political, industrial, artistic'.[90] Their speculation, one might say, was not just financial.

Visions of the future are as old as religions and literatures. But with the advent of technological modernity the mythological, apocalyptic or millenarian prophecies are replaced by a new form of imagined future: more sustained attempts to speculate on the ways in which everyday life might be transformed, especially

---

[88] Marshall Berman, *All That Is Solid Melts into Air* (New York and London: Penguin, 1988), 96.

[89] See for example Jeremy Black, 'Why the Industrial Revolution Happened Here', BBC 2, 14 January 2013: http://www.bbc.co.uk/programmes/b01pz9d6 accessed 9 October 2016.

[90] Berman, *All that Solid*, pp. 134–5.

through science and technology. The anthropologist Marc Augé distinguishes between 'the two main modalities of relation to the future observed in the diversity of human societies': one 'makes the future a successor to the past'; the other 'makes it a birth, an inauguration' (3-4). The future that mattered shifted from the theological and eschatological certainties of Heaven and Hell, and the Last Judgement, to the future as created through human agency. If its possibilities were exhilarating, its uncertainties made it a site of anxiety. Little wonder that the science fiction romances pioneered by writers such as Jules Verne and H. G. Wells emerge in the nineteenth century, since they both provide a space in which the future's possibilities can be elaborated imaginatively, and also appear to offer the prospect of delivering what Augé calls the 'ideology of the future *now*'— something he sees as the problematic creation of a contemporary finance capitalism driven by technological innovation; but the origins of which appear to lie in the mid-nineteenth century.[91]

By the time Chekhov wrote *The Three Sisters*, in 1900, the futuristic fantasies of scientific romance and utopian politics were pervasive enough already (in Russia as well as the West) to feel like clichés:

TUZENBAKH.   Very well then. When we're dead people will fly around in balloons, there will be a new style in men's jackets and a sixth sense may be discovered and developed, but life itself won't change, it will still be as difficult and full of mystery and happiness as it is now. Even in a thousand years men will still be moaning away about life being a burden. What's more, they'll still be as scared of death as they are now. And as keen on avoiding it.[92]

Yet the very fact that futurology could be treated comically or parodied, or aestheticized as steampunk,[93] testifies to how it had become second nature. One way futurology changed through the twentieth century was from imagining the future as something distant in time—something that took place 'after our time', and that you needed a time machine to reach—to something that needed to be grasped in the present. The *Daily Mail* devoted a special issue to the Ideal Home exhibition of 1928 bearing the date 'Jan. 1st, 2000' and the title 'News of the Future'.[94] Radio having dragged news reports from being something you would read in the morning paper about the previous day, to something you could hear being reported as it happened, the media wanted to push the news from the present to the future. That paradoxical title combines the retrospect of 'news' with the prospect of futurology.

[91]   Marc Augé, *The Future*, trans. John Howe (London: Verso, 2014), 3.
[92]   Chekhov, *Ivanov, The Seagull and Three Sisters*, trans. Ronald Hingley (London: Oxford University Press, 1968), 148.
[93]   See for example *Futuredays: A nineteenth-century vision of the year 2000* (New York: Henry Holt and Company, 1986), with text by Isaac Asimov to accompany Jean Marc Côté's 1899 cigarette card illustrations depicting everyday life a century on. I'm grateful to Rob Newman for drawing my attention to these wonderful drawings.
[94]   'News of the Future', *Daily Mail* Ideal Home Exhibition Special (28 February 1928).

But there is still a suggestion that the future in question is not where you are. News has to be brought to you from it. Contrast that with the demonstrative rhetoric of post-W.W.II futurology. *The Future is Now* (a short film from 1955 about the products being developed in government research laboratories); *This is Tomorrow* (an exhibition of architects and artists at the Whitechapel Gallery in 1956); or the BBC's science programme 'Tomorrow's World', that began in 1965.

The literature and culture of modernism and modernity is saturated with pre-occupation about the future, whether in political tracts, books on the Condition of England or the Empire, utopian or dystopian novels. Speculative and science fiction, social progressives, Futurists, Vorticists, utopianists, dystopian visions, Jeremiads, city planners, advertisers, were all busy looking forwards. Even the author of *Looking Backward*, Edward Bellamy, had been looking forward; imagining, in his book of 1888, how his time would appear when seen from the vantage point of the future—his future, that is: the year 2000. It was a manoeuvre, as we shall see, which established a paradigm for some of the best writing in To-Day and To-Morrow.

In the case of Bellamy, the prospect of the end of a century provokes imagining the end of the millennium. The plague of futurological speculation unleashed by the end of the millennium itself occurred not only in journalism and fiction but in films, exhibitions, and TV programmes. Often such projections try to present a vision of a whole future world. What's distinctive about To-Day and To-Morrow is how each author focuses on a specific topic. The *fin-de-siècle* was notoriously beset with anxiety about the changes the future might bring, and produced a surge of futurological fiction. After Bellamy's, came William Morris' *News from Nowhere* (1890), Wells's *The Time Machine* (1895) and *The War of the Worlds* (1898), and Ford and Conrad's *The Inheritors* (1901), in which a mysterious stranger is described as an invader from the fourth dimension.[95] If the lines of futurology had thus been drawn in the last Victorian years, the Edwardian period was also to prove intensely futurological.

Futurology before the First World War

Wells was the dominant figure in the early years of the twentieth century too, inventing new modes of futurological speculation in works that were not romances or novels, but expository prose. Such modes are occasionally described in the following book as 'speculative non-fiction', but always with the proviso that futurology can never be distinguished entirely from fiction. First the book from

---

[95] See Max Saunders, 'Empire of the Future: *The Inheritors*, Ford, liberalism and imperialism', *The Edwardian Ford Madox Ford*, ed. Laura Colombino and Max Saunders (Amsterdam and New York: Rodopi, 2013), 125–40.

1901—poised on the threshold of the new century—*Anticipations of the Reactions of Mechanical and Scientific Progress upon Human Life and Thought*. As a result Wells became identified with a futurology based on an imaginative but scientifically-informed speculation about the future, shifting prediction from mystical prophecy to a scientific method. When the book was being serialized in the *North American Review*, it bore the tellingly jarring subtitle 'An Experiment in Prophecy'.

Anticipations covers a number of the main areas that To-Day and To-Morrow would explore: transport, the centripetal creep of cities, changes to the class system, the threat to democracy from technocracy, war, language, and the creation of a world state. Indeed, Haldane quotes Wells's prediction that 'by 1950 there would be heavier-than-air flying machines capable of practical use in war', calling it 'singularly modest', and guaranteeing that he would make '*no prophecies rasher*' in *Daedalus* (9-10). I. F. Clarke describes *Anticipations* as 'the first comprehensive and widely read survey of future developments in the short history of predictive writing'.[96] But the futurology text by Wells even more likely to be known to the To-Day and To-Morrow contributors, and which set out the agenda for what the series would try to do, was 'The Discovery of the Future', read as a paper at the Royal Institution in 1902 and published later the same year.[97]

'The Discovery of the Future' begins by contrasting 'two divergent types of mind': 'types which are to be distinguished chiefly by their attitude towards time' (7). But instead of a broad-brush distinction between past-orientated traditionalists and future-orientated modernisers, he contrasts two attitudes towards the future; and specifically 'the relative importance they attach and the relative amount of thought they give to the future of things' (7):

> The first of these two types of mind—and it is, I think, the predominant type, the type of the majority of living people—is that which seems scarcely to think of the future at all, which regards it as a sort of black non-existence upon which the advancing present will presently write events. The second type, which is, I think, a more modern and much less abundant type of mind, thinks constantly, and by preference, of things to come, and of present things mainly in relation to the results that must arise from them [....]

> While from that former point of view our life is simply to reap the consequences of the past, from this our life is to prepare the future. The former type one might speak of as the legal or submissive type of mind [....] The latter type of mind I might for contrast call the legislative, creative, organising, or masterful type, because it is perpetually attacking and altering the established order of things,

[96] Clarke, *The Pattern of Expectation*, p. 197.
[97] H. G. Wells, *The Discovery of the Future* (London: T. Fisher Unwin, 1902). Subsequent references in the text are to this edition. I am grateful to Patrick Parrinder for drawing my attention to this work. See his *Shadows of the Future: H. G. Wells, science fiction, and prophecy* (Syracuse, NY: Syracuse University Press, 1995).

perpetually falling away from respect for what the past has given us. It sees the world as one great workshop, and the present is no more than material for the future, for the thing that is yet destined to be.   (7-10)

It is clear enough which category Wells places himself in. The rest of the essay is devoted to how the work of such 'modern', 'masterful', and future-orientated thinkers might be enhanced. He approaches the cliché about the future's unknowability sceptically, wondering 'how far some application of intellectual methods may not attenuate, even if it does not absolutely set aside, the veil between ourselves and things to come' (37). A brilliant turn in the argument shows how this can be more than a pious hope. Geological and Darwinian theories have taken a few apparently disparate signs and resemblances and used them to transform our vision of the past, from a created world just a few thousand years old, to an evolved world millions of years old. Why cannot science do the same for the future, he asks, believing that 'an inductive knowledge of a great number of things in the future is becoming a human possibility' (48-51; 52-3). What he is forecasting is forecasting itself: 'a systematic exploration of the future' (52-3); and he warns that his listeners 'must not judge the practicability of this enterprise by the failures of the past', because: 'So far nothing has been attempted, so far no first-class mind has ever focused itself upon these issues' (52-3).

That was the task Wells was to set himself. It was nothing less than to put prophecy on a properly scientific basis. Though note how he believes it can be achieved by a single 'first-class mind'. With a characteristic Wellsian flourish he gives the argument a further twist. Science *is* prophecy: 'the aim, and the test, and the justification of the scientific process is not a marketable conjuring trick, but prophecy. Until a scientific theory yields confident forecasts, you know it is unsound and tentative' (55). It was a move that was certainly prophetic of his own direction as a thinker. Over the next four decades he would produce a whole series of works (including such partly-fictionalized prophetic landmarks as *A Modern Utopia* of 1905 and *The Shape of Things to Come* in 1933) pursuing the line of *Anticipations*, and sketching out his visions of the future for the world, in fiction and expository speculations.[98] Even when writing history Wells could not help writing the history of the future. The final section of his 1920 *Outline of History* considers 'The Next Stage in History'.

Many of the ideas in these books anticipated and shaped the things to come in To-Day and To-Morrow; and to some extent Wells represents an inspiration for the entire series, given that he was effectively a one-man version of the whole project. Certainly, the radical motivation of such prophesying was one which most of them shared. Wells joked to one correspondent that the purpose of

---

[98] See Simon J. James, *Maps of Utopia: H. G. Wells, modernity and the end of culture* (Oxford: Oxford University Press, 2012).

Anticipations was 'to undermine and destroy the monarch, monogamy, faith in God & respectability—& the British Empire, all under the guise of a speculation about motor cars & electric heating'.[99] The futurological imperative of To-Day and To-Morrow put a number of the contributors in mind of *The Time Machine*. But Wells is a presiding figure in other ways too. *The Open Conspiracy* (1928) is his other work most often invoked in the series: an elaboration of the project of future-thinking progressives working towards the world state that he had envisaged at the start of the century.

The Open Conspiracy was one of several works by Wells that appeared during the years the To-Day and To-Morrow volumes were being published. So we need to consider what else the leading futurist of the first half of the twentieth century was producing between 1923 and 1931. *Men Like Gods* (1923) is what Wells called a 'scientific fantasy'[100] about a utopia in a parallel universe. In 1924 he published a collection of recent newspaper articles under the title *A Year of Prophesying*. His novel of the same year, *The Dream*, playfully reverses the direction of the prophetic vision. In it, Sarnac, a biologist already living in a utopian future about two thousand years ahead has a dream of living an entire life from a previous era—the immediate past of the late nineteenth and early twentieth centuries; which lets Wells present his own moment as a transitional one, in which scientific planning will rescue humanity from 'the dark Ages of Confusion'.[101] The scenario of the future scientist looking back to the writer's present parallels that in *Daedalus*. The discussion in the epilogue about the possibilities implied by this re-experienced life of human immortality and of memories surviving death is redolent of the period's hopeful experiments in psychical research. But its implication that future scientific developments will be able to comprehend such recurrences anticipates the vision of one of the most important volumes in the series, J. D. Bernal's *The World, the Flesh and the Devil* (1929).

In 1927 Wells published *Meanwhile*, a novel which mentions the 'Open Conspiracy' he was to treat in full the following year. In 1930 he produced *The Science of Life* (with his son, G. P. Wells, and Julian Huxley); as well as a contribution to a symposium on another topic exercising To-Day and To-Morrow contributors: *Divorce as I See It* (and indeed organized by one of them: Bertrand Russell). The following year saw both *The Work, Wealth and Happiness of Mankind* and his contribution a collection on *The New Russia*. His pamphlet *What Should be Done—Now: A Memorandum on the World Situation* appeared in 1932, the year after the series had terminated; but it shows that Wells was still very much engaged in trying to shape as well as forecast the future into the 1930s; that he was

---

[99] Wells, letter to Elizabeth Healy, quoted by Michael Sherborne, *H. G. Wells: Another kind of life* (London: Peter Owen, 2010), 147.
[100] H. G. Wells, 'Preface' to *Seven Famous Novels* (New York: Alfred A. Knopf, 1934), x.
[101] H. G. Wells, *The Dream* (London: Cape, 1924), 319.

still 'the Futurity Man'.[102] The same year he gave a radio broadcast entitled 'Wanted—Professors of Foresight'.[103]

The question is then why he did not contribute to To-Day and To-Morrow. As Haldane said, 'The very mention of the future suggests him' (*Daedalus*, p. 9). If invited, did he turn Ogden down, preferring to publish his work independently of the projects of others? No evidence survives of an invitation. It isn't plausible that it did not occur to Ogden to include Wells, with whom he was on good terms. Did he decide not to? And if so, why? Could it have been that Wells's futurology was simply already too familiar; over-exposed? Or perhaps too pre-war? Ogden may have shared Wells's sense, as expressed (if prematurely) in 1917, that he was no longer modern enough, when he lamented: 'My boom is over. I've had my boom. I'm yesterday'.[104]

As Wells's example shows, the future boom in fact began well before the First World War. Further evidence is provided by the popularity of the phrase 'Today and Tomorrow' as a title for chapters or books from the beginning of the century. The turn of the century prompted forward as well as backward glances towards the arts as well as technologies of the future. Isadora Duncan, for example, was speaking of 'The Dance of the Future' in a lecture in Berlin in 1903.[105] Dora Marsden's programme in her magazine *The New Freewoman* in 1913 for 'The Art of the Future', which would represent the 'movements of the soul', which 'breaks into evidence as readily as pain breaks into a cry', showed that such prognostications went on right up to the war.[106] Horace B. Samuel's book *Modernities*, published in New York in 1914, even has a chapter whose title anticipates that of John Rodker's To-Day and To-Morrow volume: 'The Future of Futurism'.

If the war put some future-oriented cultural projects on hold, it prompted others. The London magazine the *Future*, to which Ezra Pound contributed several pieces, started in late 1916. As a disruption of the normal rhythms and chronologies of everyday life, the war incited both repression of the future (because you might not be alive to witness it), and an intense looking forward—to a period of rest, home leave, cease-fire... or to a new world after the war. The war, in its demonstration of new technologies of greater powers, was a revelation of the future: a source of anxiety about future insecurity, violence and destruction; but also a source of hope about how society might be transformed in utopian ways. In *All Quiet on the Western Front* (1929), Erich Maria Remarque describes his protagonist being haunted by the thought that since a 'word of command' has transformed the

---

[102] Claire Harman, 'Futurity Man', *TLS* (6 August 2010), 7–8, reviewing Sherborne, *H. G. Wells*.

[103] Reprinted in the *Listener*, 8 (23 November 1932), 729–30. See David Bradshaw, ed., *The Hidden Huxley* (London: Faber, 1995), 132n.

[104] Quoted by Harman, 'Futurity Man'.

[105] Isadora Duncan, *The Dance of the Future* (Leipzig: Eugen Diedrichs, 1903).

[106] Dora Marsden, 'The Art of the Future', *The New Freewoman*, 1:10 (1 November 1913), 181–2 (182).

combatants into enemies, so might words after the war transform them back into friends: 'It is not now the time', he says:

> but I will not lose these thoughts, I will keep them, shut them away until the war is ended. My heart beats fast: this is the aim, the great, the sole aim, that I have thought of in the trenches; that I have looked for as the only possibility of existence after this annihilation of all human feeling; this is a task that will make life afterward worthy of these hideous years.[107]

Such utopian aspirations are at the heart of To-Day and To-Morrow, and are discussed in Chapter 2. They suggest one reason why it was prescient of Haldane to make ectogenesis the centrepiece of *Daedalus*. His narrative of the scientific future of birth is also a prognostication about the birth of a new scientific future. On the home front too, the future was what seemed at stake in the fighting: not just the future of victory or defeat; nor that invoked by the recruiting poster, in which men would have to answer their children's question: 'Daddy, what did YOU do in the war?'; but the future of culture too. To Ford Madox Ford, writing propaganda for the Government before he enlisted, it appeared that: 'the problem that is now before humanity is whether the culture of the future, the very life and heart of the future, shall be materialist or altruist'.[108]

Futurology after the War

In his excellent *A History of Modernist Literature* Andrzej Gasiorek argues that the war not only 'interrupted the modernist effort at cultural renewal and called its vaunting ambitions into question', but also 'led modernism's exponents to wonder if pre-war energy and optimism had been dissipated or could still be recaptured'.[109] While this is persuasive about canonical modernist figures like Lewis and Pound, there was what Brian Stableford has described as a 'boom in futurology' between the wars—though, as we have seen, it was really an on-going boom that had started at the end of the previous century.[110] He is discussing science fiction. But other modernists were turning futurologist too. Ford was thinking about 'the vocabulary for both the prose and the verse of the future' in 1921—though he characteristically advocated *reculer pour mieux sauter*, confident that such vocabulary would ultimately achieved by going back to the previous

[107] Remarque, in *The Penguin Book of First World War Prose*, ed. Jon Glover and Jon Silkin (London: Penguin, 1990), 227–8.
[108] Ford (as Ford Madox Hueffer), *When Blood is Their Argument: An analysis of Prussian culture* (London: Hodder and Stoughton, 1915), xx.
[109] Andrzej Gasiorek, *A History of Modernist Literature* (Chichester: Wiley-Blackwell, 2015), 232.
[110] Brian Stableford, 'Science Fiction Between the Wars', in *Anatomy Of Wonder: A critical guide to science fiction*, ed. Neil Barron, fourth edition (New Providence, NJ: Bowker, 1995), 62–114.

century, and 'the methods of Flaubert and Maupassant'.[111] His future of English was the Impressionism of France. Dorothy Richardson wrote on 'Women and the Future' in 1924.[112] Paul Valéry considered 'The Future of Literature' in an essay of 1928.[113] To-Day and To-Morrow was a site where comparable post-war modernist future hope flourished.

Not all modernists were futurologists. But the series brings out how futurology was one mode through which writers could maintain their modernity. As Augé notes, for modern man: 'it is precisely the faculty to evoke the future, near or remote, that determines how interesting life is'.[114] Indeed, by the twentieth century it had become a distinguishing sign of modernity that the way to demonstrate that you were up-to-date was to be able to think beyond the date you were up to. As Augé continues: 'Being contemporary means concentrating on those things in the present that sketch something of the future'.[115] Which is exactly the structure of the series: to study today for what clues it might give about tomorrow: in Wellsian terminology, to seek anticipations in the world of today of the shape of things to come. As suggested, it also simultaneously asserts a break between that future orientation and the world of the past. That sense of the present as marking the inauguration of the new—of the really modern—is articulated by Alain Badiou in his magisterial analysis of the twentieth century:

> we find ourselves in the real moment of commencement. The nineteenth century announced, dreamed, and promised; the twentieth century declared it would make man, here and now.

> This is what I propose to call the *passion for the real*. I'm convinced it provides the key to understanding the century. There is a conviction, laden with pathos, that we are being summoned to the real of a beginning.

> The real, as all key players of the century recognize, is the source of both horror and enthusiasm, simultaneously lethal and creative.[116]

Badiou sees this conviction of new beginning as one of the two opposed maxims shaping the era. 'The century thought itself simultaneously as end, exhaustion, decadence *and* as absolute commencement', he writes.[117] The former, dominant

---

[111] Ford, *Thus to Revisit* (London: Chapman and Hall, 1921), 161. This follows a passage to which Ogden would have assented: 'communication between man and man is the most important, the most beneficent of human gifts—and just and true communication can only be achieved by an appallingly serious study of Language.... And do not believe that any literary quality, of whatever nature, can be achieved without this seriousness' (161).

[112] First published in *Vanity Fair* in April 1924, Dorothy Richardson's 'Women and the Future' was reprinted the following month in the British edition of *Vogue*. Reprinted in Bonnie Kime Scott, ed., *The Gender of Modernism* (Bloomington: Indiana University Press, 1990), 411–14.

[113] Valéry, 'The Future of Literature', trans. Malcolm Cowley, *New York Herald Tribune, Books* (April 1928): *Collected Works, Volume 11: Occasions*, ed. Roger Shattuck and Frederick Brown (Princeton, NJ: Princeton University Press, 2015), 151–7.

[114] Augé, *The Future*, 24.   [115] Augé, *The Future*, 39.

[116] Alain Badiou, *The Century* (Cambridge: Polity Press 2007), 32.   [117] Ibid., p. 31.

from the collapse of the Soviet empire till now, 'calls for renunciation, resignation, the lesser evil, together with moderation, the end of humanity as a spiritual force, and the critique of "grand narratives"'; the other, 'which dominated the "short century" between 1917 and the 1980s—inherits from Nietzsche the will to "break the history of the world in two", and seeks a radical commencement that would bear within it the foundation of a reconciled humanity'.[118] Many in the 1920s thought of their lives as divided in two, whether by the war or the October Revolution of 1917. To-Day and To-Morrow is an early product of this conviction of 'radical commencement', which also bears the traces of anxieties about decadence, and a sense of ending. As such, it constitutes a magnificent illustration of Badiou's thesis.

One advantage of Badiou's argument, for modernist scholars, is that it accounts for the split in modernism of responses to modern life. As Andrzej Gasiorek summarizes, modernism's 'responses to the modernity with which it critically engaged varied widely, ranging from naive forms of technophilia to reactionary invocations of a hierarchical agricultural way of life that was thought to offer a viable alternative to a predatory capitalism'.[119] So To-Day and To-Morrow contributors varied widely in their responses to modernity. Gasiorek follows Anthony Giddens in arguing that 'modernity is characterized less by a cult of the new than by "the presumption of wholesale reflexivity—which of course includes reflection upon the nature of reflection itself"'.[120] 'This doubled reflexivity lies at the heart of literary modernism', according to Gasiorek. It is also a prominent feature of To-Day and To-Morrow, which rarely embraces the new in an uncritical fashion, but which certainly embraces thinking about it. Furthermore, it does not just think about the new, but thinks about thinking about it: both in terms of frequently considering the nature of prediction, and in terms of the narrative devices and literary tropes through which the future might be imagined (explored here in Chapter 2). To make the point, the US avatar of the series even included a volume called Thinking about Thinking (1926). The volumes of the series are not written in the high modernist registers of The Waste Land or Ulysses. Nevertheless they too constitute an important expression and critique of modernism as well as modernity.

Modernist future hope was frequently Marxist future hope in the period, as Badiou's dating implies. For the Marxist utopian Ernst Bloch, Marxism provided the only sound basis for futurology. As the historian of Marxism, Lesjek Kołakowski explains, paraphrasing Bloch's magnum opus The Principle of Hope:

> Marxism, and it alone, has given humanity a full and consistent perception of the future. What is more, Marxism is wholly future-oriented: it recognizes the past only in so far as it is still alive and is therefore part of the future. Marxism has achieved the 'discovery that concrete theory-practice is strictly bound up

---

[118] Ibid., p. 31.   [119] Gasiorek, A History of Modernist Literature, p. 445.
[120] Ibid.; Anthony Giddens, The Consequences of Modernity (London: Polity, 1990), 39.

with the observed mode of objective-real possibility' (236). Marxism is a science, but one that has overcome the dualism of being and thought, of what is and what ought to be; it is both a theory of the future paradise and a praxis which brings it about.

> Marxism is an all-embracing Utopia, but, unlike the dreams of previous ages, it is a concreted and not an abstract one.[121]

During the Cold War, the future of Marxism came under sceptical denunciation; not least where it had certainly made general predictions about the future of society—about the inevitability of capitalism's self-destruction and supercession by the dictatorship of the proletariat. Karl Popper, for example, in *The Poverty of Historicism* (1957), famously attacked Marxism's claim to have established, in dialectical materialism, a theoretical science of history with the predictive power of the physical sciences. 'The course of human history is strongly influenced by the growth of human knowledge', he argued. 'We cannot predict, by rational or scientific methods, the future growth of our scientific knowledge'; 'We cannot therefore, predict the future course of human history', because 'There can be no scientific theory of historical development serving as a basis for historical prediction.'[122]

After the collapse of communism in Eastern Europe and the Soviet Union from 1989, this became the standard view: that Marxism's futurological credibility had expired; and was anyway ill-founded, given the unpredictability of humans. Thus Stephen Jay Gould, invited to contribute to the millennial series of *Predictions* in 1991, offered instead a meta-futurological scepticism about prediction. Though note how he pushes back a little from the extreme scepticism of Popper's position. After all, though we may not be able to predict the future growth of all scientific knowledge, some discoveries are easier to predict than others; especially when they are implied by previous discoveries. This is especially true of theoretical postulates which are then sought for in experimental conditions, such as the Higgs boson or gravitational waves. According to Gould:

> human futures are unpredictable and it is futile to think that past trends will forecast coming patterns. The trajectory of technology might offer some opportunity for predicting the future—as science moves through networks of implication, and each discovery suggests a suite of subsequent steps. But even the 'pure' history of science features unanticipated findings, and must also contend with nature's stubborn tendency to frustrate our expectations—factors that will cloud anyone's crystal ball.

Moreover, any forecast about the future must consider the incendiary instability generated by interaction between technological change and the weird ways of

---

[121] Lesjek Kołakowski, *Main Currents of Marxism*, revised omnibus edition (New York: W. W. Norton, 2005), 1132.

[122] Karl Popper, *The Poverty of Historicism* (London: Routledge 2002), xi–xii.

human conduct, both individual and social. How can the accidents that shaped our past give any meaningful insight into the next millennium? Pasts can't imply futures because a pattern inherent in the structure of nature's materials and laws too often disrupts an otherwise predictable unfolding of historical sequences.[123]

Popper's argument about the unforeseeability of changes in scientific knowledge could be said to have anticipated another influential work it could not have foreseen, Thomas S. Kuhn's *The Structure of Scientific Revolutions* of 1962. Kuhn introduced the concept (and terminology) of the 'paradigm shift' as the mechanism through which science develops, as new ways of thinking about whole branches of science supersede earlier ones with which they are irreconcilable.

To-Day and To-Morrow, as a network of exercises in prediction, provides a complex test case of such ideas, both bearing them out and complicating them. Three of the advances in the twentieth century that had most impact on the progress of science—atomic power, digital computing, and the discovery of the structure of DNA—developed within just over two decades after the series finished. That the contributors disagreed about the feasibility of controlling nuclear power,[124] and were unable to predict the other two, could be taken as evidence for the way in which prevailing paradigms limit conceptual possibilities. Yet, as we shall see, it was not exactly that the idea of such ideas had not occurred to thinkers of the 1920s and early 30s. They were the answers to problems the solutions to which To-Day and To-Morrow was trying to envisage. AI and modifications to human nature were certainly considered, though the contributors could neither foresee the electronic computer nor knew the precise structure and operations of DNA. The fact that such ideas were already 'in the air'—imagined future possibilities, not yet realized or proven—could be taken as evidence of how paradigms were already beginning to shift. (In 1927, for example, Nikolai Koltsov proposed the idea of a 'giant hereditary molecule' consisting of 'two mirror strands that would replicate in a semi-conservative fashion using each strand as a template', to account for the inheritance of characteristics.[125]) But they do not conform to the Kuhnian model according to which results that are not consonant with existing paradigms are judged as experimental errors. Futurology is, among other things, an attempt to imagine what the next paradigms might be like; a space in which the limits of the existing ones can be explored and tested—another aspect of the reflexivity that marks it as a product of modernity.

It was after the Second World War that future studies became a much larger, more sophisticated, professionalized, and a computerized military-industrial process. One especially influential figure was Herman Kahn, the RAND Corporation

---

[123] Stephen Jay Gould, 'Unpredictable Patterns', in *Predictions*, ed. Sian Griffiths (Oxford: Oxford University Press, 1999), 145–6 (145).

[124] See Chapter 1, n.88.

[125] See Valery N. Soyfer, 'The Consequences of Political Dictatorship for Russian Science', *Nature Reviews Genetics*, 2 (2001), 723–9.

strategic analyst who founded the Hudson Institute think tank in 1961. During the Cold War he cultivated a distinctive style of *Thinking about the Unthinkable* (the title of one his popular books, from 1962), an attitude that Stanley Kubrick satirized in the character of Dr Strangelove, said to be based on Kahn. Besides his significance in envisaging post-nuclear holocaust humanity, Kahn is equally known for having launched one of the most extensive forecasting exercises of the century, and arguably a successor to To-Day and To-Morrow. In 1967, he and Anthony J. Wiener published *The Year 2000: A framework for speculation on the next thirty-three years*, including contributions from other members of the Hudson Institute.[126] It incorporated a list headed 'One Hundred Technical Innovations Very Likely in the Last Third of the Twentieth Century', predicting such developments as the proliferation of nuclear power stations, reliable birth control, automated banking systems, home computers, and pocket phones.

Yet three years earlier, Isaac Asimov had given a bravura demonstration of the ability of the individually-imagined future to see further and with comparable accuracy. Responding to the New York World's Fair of 1964, he imagined the equivalent of 2014.[127] In the way of these things, his fifty-year predictions are hit and miss. The misses testify to the fertile imagination of the science fictionist. If 'underwater housing', 'moon colonies', and 'Algae Bars' serving 'mock-turkey' and 'pseudosteak' have not caught on; and though the world's population passed his estimate of 6.5 billion nearly a decade early; nonetheless, the accuracy of most of his other projections is extraordinary. Asimov too foresaw fission power-plants producing half our power needs. But he also envisioned self-driving cars; ready meals; rudimentary robots; moving sidewalks, video phones that can also transmit media; and the transformation of education and labour through computers.

It is beyond the scope of this study to map out the entire field of future studies and its extensive bibliography, which includes not just landmark books such as Alvin Toffler's *Future Shock* (1970) or Ray Kurzweil's *The Age of Intelligent Machines* (1990), but also dedicated journals such as *Futures, Journal of Futures Studies, Foresight, Technological Forecasting and Social Change, Earth's Future, World Future Review (formerly Futures Research Quarterly)*, and *World Future*. For the reasons given at the start of this section, a survey of such material would be of only limited relevance to the series. Instead, this chapter will conclude with a brief consideration of five critical works which are among the most significant for an approach from the point of view of literary and cultural studies to the kinds of futurology exemplified in To-Day and To-Morrow.

---

[126] I am grateful to Steve Fuller for drawing my attention to Kahn's work.
[127] *New York Times: Books* (16 August 1964):
   https://archive.nytimes.com/www.nytimes.com/books/97/03/23/lifetimes/asi-v-fair.html accessed 21 November 2016. In April 1964 the *New York Times Magazine* had marked the occasion of the Fair with a special issue, containing a section of essays on 'The Future' by Arnold Toynbee, Henry Steele Commager, Margaret Mead, and others. It included one of Haldane's last acts of futurology: 'A Scientific Revolution? Yes. Will We Be Happier? Maybe', *New York Times Magazine* (19 April 1964), 90, 113, 114.

The first is I. F. Clarke's ground-breaking panoramic survey of writings about the future, *The Pattern of Expectation: 1644–2001*. He quotes from *Icarus*, and later includes a brief discussion of the series.[128] It is just a paragraph, and not a particularly accurate one. He says there were eighty-six titles (rather than 107; or 110 if the three published only in the US are added). Oddly omitting *Daedalus* and *The World, the Flesh, and the Devil*, he lists six of 'the more interesting forecasts' in a note: *Socrates, Ouroboros, Prometheus, The Next Chapter, Aeolus*, and *Archimedes* (though for the last he gives not the title but only the subtitle). Nonetheless, it is a significant appraisal of To-Day and To-Morrow, correctly identifying some of the most important volumes, and identifying the series as a turning-point in futurological terms: an early phase of what he calls 'a serious and rational investigation of the future'.[129]

The same year, 1979, also saw the publication of the first version of Lyman Tower Sargent's bibliography, *British and American Utopian Literature*. Its latest, and now online, iteration, *Utopian Literature in English: An annotated bibliography from 1516 to the present* dauntingly lists more than eight thousand primary texts.[130] These include the volumes by Brittain and Bernal, and Fournier d'Albe's *Quo Vadimus*, but surprisingly omits Haldane's *Daedalus*. Sargent's comments are brief and essentially descriptive; and his selection of volumes debatable. But what his decision to select them brings out, is how—by any criterion—To-Day and To-Morrow is only partially or obliquely utopian. It does not systematically map out programmes for future improvement, though some volumes do (such as the three he includes).

The series' complex relation to the utopian needs to be borne in mind when turning to the third exemplary study of writing about the future, Fredric Jameson's *Archaeologies of the Future: The desire called utopia and other science fictions* (2007). As his subtitle indicates, science fiction is Jameson's primary concern here, and utopia is admitted as one of its forms among others. As such, his analysis may seem to have little purchase on To-Day and To-Morrow, which does science fiction as episodically as it does utopianism; and which Jameson does not discuss. And yet several of his observations are germane to the series. For example, his framing discussions of 'the well-known shift in Utopias from space to time, from the accounts of exotic travelers to the experiences of visitors to the future'; and of how 'few other literary forms have so brazenly affirmed themselves as argument and counterargument', are applicable to the series' speculative non-fiction and polemical structure.[131] In Ursula Le Guin, Jameson writes:

> we confront something like a binary alternation between the reality principle of
> SF and the pleasure principle of fantasy. Perhaps in that sense Utopia does

[128]   Clarke, *The Pattern of Expectation*, pp. 230–1; 239–40.   [129]   Ibid., p. 239.
[130]   Sargent, *Utopian Literature in English: An annotated bibliography from 1516 to the present*: http://openpublishing.psu.edu/utopia/ accessed 29 October 2016.
[131]   Frederic Jameson, *Archaeologies of the Future: The desire called utopia and other science fictions* (London: Verso, 2007), 1–2.

constitute a working synthesis of these two incommensurables: the supreme creativity or shaping impulse of fantasy marshalling the most recalcitrant raw material of all, in the state and the social order.   (74)

Change 'SF' to 'science' or 'history', and what he says here of Utopia also catches the tension in the imagined futures of To-Day and To-Morrow. That 'recalcitrant raw material', though, would need to include, as its metaphor suggests, the natural order in addition to the social, to capture the series' imagining of new technologies. It would also need to include the area where the natural and the social combine: in the nature of the human. It is here that Jameson is most suggestive, not just about Utopia in general, but about some of the more utopian strands of To-Day and To-Morrow:

This brings us to what is perhaps the fundamental Utopian dispute about subjectivity, namely whether the Utopia in question proposes the kind of radical transformation of subjectivity proposed by most revolutions, a mutation in human nature and the emergence of whole new beings; or whether the impulse to Utopia is not already grounded in human nature, its persistence readily explained by deeper needs and desires which the present has merely repressed and distorted.   (168)

As with most of the major issues it addresses, To-Day and To-Morrow has things to say on both sides of this dispute. Some contributors—the Eugenicists or transhumanists—imagine subjectivity being transformed in revolutionary ways into something startlingly different. Others—those interested in the psyche or the psychic—imagine the future realizing our full human potential. Jameson argues that this tension cannot be resolved in Utopian writing. Transform the human and you end in science fiction. Whereas 'if Utopia is drawn too close to current everyday realities' then it reduces to political reformism and social democratic politics, losing the possibility of radical transformation of the system (168).

To-Day and To-Morrow cannot be said to have 'resolved' this dispute either, not least because not enough was known then, nor is it now, about how practically to transform human nature, or what it might be transformed into. Yet the series' speculative *non*-fiction, and its dialectical structure, enable it to negotiate the dispute differently from science fiction, especially where (as in the scientific volumes) its imagined futures are based on a scientific understanding of biology and psychology. To put it like that might seem to deliver the series to Bertrand Russell's merciless distinction: 'There are two ways of writing about the future, the scientific and the Utopian. The scientific way tries to discover what is probable; the Utopian way sets out what the writer would like'.[132] This is to characterize the utopian as being as much a purveyor of fantasy as the science fiction writer. Yet to

---

[132] Bertrand Russell, 'Some Prospects: Cheerful and otherwise', in *Sceptical Essays* (London: Routledge, 2004), 202–17; p. 202.

accede to this pitting of 'fantasy', 'the desire called Utopia', or 'what the writer would like', against the probable or the real, is to miss one of the real strengths of To-Day and To-Morrow. It isn't just that the series offers a *range* of ways of imagining the future, from rigidly probabilistic extrapolations of already existent knowledge, to more audacious and challenging visions. It is that these visions—in Haldane's and Bernal's cases especially—are themselves neither simply 'probable' nor expressions of utopian wishful thinking. Rather, they are thought experiments in possibility; experiments the otherness of which summon up doubts and anxieties in their authors; but which seem worth investigating precisely to try to understand what potential there may be in humanity for further self-realizations. The situation is comparable to our own a century later, as we begin to be outsmarted by our own computers at an increasing number of specific tasks, and confront the possibility of AI exceeding human intelligence all round within a few decades. There is perhaps a utopian side to this: a hope that AI might be able to help us solve scientific and philosophical problems, and that it might do a better job than we are doing at running the planet, and not ruining it. Yet we are just as aware of the dystopian possibilities: that our liberty might be compromised; that computers, becoming our masters, might deem us useless, unwelcome competition, or even dangerous, and thus find it necessary to eliminate us. AI may thus be neither probable nor utopian. Yet scientists are nevertheless racing to realize it.

Futurology is sometimes viewed as the preserve of testosterone-crazed techno-enthusiasts, blithely unaware of the human and social costs of their excitements, or the hazards of robot servants and flying cars. But the scientists and engineers among To-Day and To-Morrow contributors, even if they were laying the groundwork for future developments in mobile technology, bioscience, and bionic prosthetics, and even AI, were not actually working on those projects. Their aim was not only to imagine future applications for existing concepts and technologies, but also to imagine the next stages. Imagining more distant, different, futures offers a particular perspective, which can make us think harder, and differently: not only about our aims and hopes and plans for the future, but about the purpose and value of present practices which we might otherwise take for granted.

The fourth critical text bearing importantly on To-Day and To-Morrow is Paul Saint-Amour's *Tense Future: Modernism, total war, encyclopedic form* (2015). This ingenious book finds its imagined futures across a range of genres: fiction, military theory, psychoanalysis, postcolonial theory, archive theory, and poststructuralist critical theory. It argues that the emergence of the idea of 'total war' dominated the interwar imagination, generating intense anxieties of anticipation that were akin to the effects of trauma, but directed at the future rather than the past. In contrast to Jameson's book, *Tense Future* is thus primarily concerned with apocalyptic dystopias. To that extent, his thesis fails to capture some of the series' most interesting qualities, since (as I argue in Chapter 2), though intensely conscious of the experience of the First World War, the contributors are mostly surprisingly hopeful about the future; more interested in a future after war, than a future war. Saint-Amour does discuss one of the volumes, Liddell Hart's *Paris; or, The Future of War* (1925), though he does not mention the series. This is unfortunate, not only because To-Day and To-Morrow represents the best archive of writing about the future in the period, but also because it offers a clearer (and indeed transformational) example of the 'encyclopedic form' that he sees novels like Joyce's *Ulysses* and Ford's *Parade's End* as assuming by way of resisting the logic of total war. I discuss his sophisticated arguments more fully in the conclusion, and how the series resists them in other ways.

Finally, Peter J. Bowler's *A History of the Future: Prophets of progress from H. G. Wells to Isaac Asimov* gives a broad survey of the history of futurological thought during the first two-thirds of the twentieth century. He devotes slightly more space to To-Day and To-Morrow, briefly mentioning thirty of its volumes—mostly those concerned with techno-scientific developments. Yet even he has very little to say about the individual volumes and their qualities, except to pick out some key themes; and some of what he does say is wrong.[133] Nor has he much to say about the scale or scope of the series as a whole, except to describe it as consisting of an unspecified 'huge number of books' (206). The main strength of his study is the contextualization it offers, putting such works alongside the fiction and popularization of the period, and its magazines such as *Armchair Science*, *Popular Mechanics*, or even *Meccano Magazine*; what he describes as 'a vast range of literature produced by scientists, engineers and popular writers who were already taking the business of prediction seriously' (206). His recovery of this pervasive and even feverish enthusiasm for the future in popular culture is a useful counter for the student of future discourses to Saint-Amour's account of modernist future-shock. As Bowler says, 'The literary scholar focusing on high-brow novelists is much more likely to encounter pessimistic views about the future development of science and technology than the historian of popular science' (10). But what he fails to acknowledge are the qualities that stands out when the series is read against this context. For what most of the other material he quotes repeatedly shows is how far ahead of the curve the To-Day and To-Morrow writers often were: in their pioneering speculations; in their wit; and in their intelligence—which frequently escapes Bowler's reductive binary of dystopian pessimism and utopian technophilia. Indeed, one of the surprises of the series, as suggested, is that it is some of its highbrow literary writers most closely associated with the view of the war as traumatic who feature as among its more optimistic and high-spirited futurologists.

In discussing To-Day and To-Morrow in relation to the history and criticism of writing about the future, I am making two claims. First, that the series constitutes a significant chapter of that history, and that its qualities deserve

---

[133] For example, his claim that 'The contribution to the "Today and Tomorrow" series on physics didn't even mention the study of the atom' bizarrely disregards the extensive discussions of atomic theory throughout *Archimedes*.

recognition—not least for its combination of the best features of imaginative autonomy and depth with the rigour of collective speculative thought. Second, that historical and critical accounts of writing about the future would benefit from greater awareness of the series. This is not only a matter of numbers: over a hundred books omitted from the bibliography, a number by well-known writers; over a million words of high-quality futurology; though it is partly that. It is also, and more importantly, that in the sheer inventiveness of many of the volumes, in terms both of content, but also of genre, rhetoric, and style, they expand the repertoire of futurology, in ways that challenge critical accounts of the mode; and which, conversely, impoverish the practice of futurology if they are neglected.

Humanity has many motivations for imagining the future. Accurate predictions are the keys to power and prosperity. Such political and economic concerns run through To-Day and To-Morrow as they do through today's futurology, though some of the emphases are different. In politics, both are concerned with peace and security; though To-Day and To-Morrow's concerns about world war have nowadays been displaced to the background, as jihad and civil war have dominated the foreground. In economic terms, both focus on the disruptive effects of technological development (and why politicians need to anticipate them). But where the main driver for contemporary futurology is corporate profit, for the progressives of To-Day and To-Morrow the concern was, rather, how to ensure that better technology would lead to a more equitable distribution of wealth and to greater personal fulfilment. Our psychological motives for prediction are related to the political and economic ones. Desire for power and satisfaction are matched by anxieties about attack or want. Such anxieties may be entirely rational, but are in turn supercharged by unconscious anxieties about control.

However, the range and complexity of the futurological imagination in To-Day and To-Morrow brings out a further, more philosophical motive; something the contributors, at their most reflective, themselves touch on. This is that thinking about the future forms an essential element of the ways in which we understand and give meanings to our lives. Samuel H. Scheffler, in his book *Death and the Afterlife*, argues for a secular way of apprehending the notion of the afterlife.[134] Invoking thought experiments which curtail the future of humanity (imagine all people rendered infertile; or the Earth facing an impending catastrophic meteor collision) he argues that our lives would be drained of meaning if we could no longer imagine our legacies; no longer assume that our acts would have consequences that continued after us. But the afterlife, shorn of its metaphysical and theological dimensions of immortality, is simply the future. It is indeed our imagination of the future which gives meaning to our projects; and these in turn illuminate the meanings we give to, or find in, our lives. Futurology is the secular mind's alternative to eschatology. Study of a generation's futurology does not just

---

[134] Samuel H. Scheffler, *Death and the Afterlife* (Oxford: Oxford University Press, 2014). See Amia Srinivasan's review, *LRB* (25 September 2014), 13–14. http://www.lrb.co.uk/v36/n18/amia-srinivasan/after-the-meteor-strike

give us a set of outmoded predictions, damned if they did come true (because thereby consigned to the past), and damned if they didn't (because thereby condemned as error). In telling us what that generation thought its life could, or should, be, it tells us what they thought their life was, and what mattered in it, and why it mattered.

If you wanted to get people today thinking about their future, how would you set about it? Found a think-tank? Publish a supplement to a newspaper picking out a handful of early career researchers who look set to have the greatest impact on us? Get a respected scientist to front a BBC4 series about the technologies most likely to change our lives? Run a competition for university students? Set up a brand consultancy? Establish a 'FutureFest'? In the 1920s, and if you were C. K. Ogden, you started a book series, and got some of the most talented writers of the age to contribute to it.

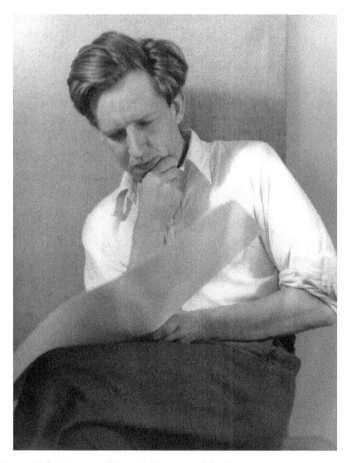

Fig. 2. John Desmond Bernal. Photograph by Ramsey & Muspratt, 1933
© National Portrait Gallery, London

PART I

SCIENCE, IMAGINATION, LANGUAGE, AND COMMUNICATION

DAEDALUS
OR
Science and the Future
By J. B. S. HALDANE M.A.

KEGAN PAUL, TRENCH, TRUBNER & CO., LTD.

ICARUS
OR THE FUTURE OF SCIENCE

BERTRAND RUSSELL

GALLIO
OR
THE TYRANNY OF SCIENCE
By
J. W. N. SULLIVAN

"It is a good book, but so crowded with ideas that it is not possible to do them justice in a short review. We are grateful to Mr. Sullivan..."

EOS
OR THE WIDER
ASPECTS OF COSMOGONY
By
SIR J. H. JEANS, F.R.S.

"He has given us, in simple and attractive language, a fascinating account of..."
—Times Literary Supplement

THIRD IMPRESSION

THE WORLD
THE FLESH AND
THE DEVIL
THREE ENEMIES OF THE RATIONAL SOUL

By
J. D. BERNAL

"His speculations in the sphere of the victory over space and over flesh and blood are absorbingly interesting."
—Times Literary Supplement.

"A brilliant book."—Spectator.

ARCHIMEDES
OR THE FUTURE OF PHYSICS

L. L. WHYTE

1

'A Scientific Age'

Science, Imagination, and Popularization

> Science is no longer our servant. We know it for something greater than
> our little individual selves. It is the awakening mind of the race [....]
>
> (H. G. Wells, The World Set Free, p. 257)[1]

Haldane and Bernal

Science has a very high profile in the To-Day and To-Morrow series; higher, for
example, than in the Home University Library series published by Williams and
Norgate from 1911—a comparable venture in an encyclopedic popularizing book
series, using some of the same contributors.[2] But the period of To-Day and
To-Morrow coincided with the first wave of books popularizing the new physics.
The landmark texts included Bertrand Russell's *ABC of Atoms* (1923), *ABC of
Relativity* (1925), and *The Analysis of Matter* (1927); A. N. Whitehead's *Science
and the Modern World* (1926); and the best-sellers, Arthur Eddington's *Space,
Time and Gravitation* (1920)—which became 'the authoritative popularization of
Einstein's theory',[3] *The Nature of the Physical World* (1928), and James Jeans's *The
Mysterious Universe* (1930).[4] Works such as these continued to create the sense
described by the *Times Literary Supplement*'s reviewer of *Daedalus*:

> The extent and profundity of the modern universe of science as revealed in this
> book, and the vigorous optimism and enthusiasm of the author, typical, we

---

[1] The chapter title is a quote from Winifred Holtby in *Eutychus; or, The Future of the Pulpit* (1928),
20; discussed in Chapter 3. The full reference for the epigraph is H. G. Wells, *The World Set Free*
(London: Macmillan, 1914), 257.
[2] See Peter J. Bowler, who provides a useful anciliary list of publisher's series to accompany his
Science for All: The popularization of science in early twentieth-century Britain (Chicago: University of
Chicago Press, 2009). See http://press.uchicago.edu/books/bowler/Bowler_ancillary_serials_list.pdf
[3] See the *Oxford Dictionary of National Biography* entry on Eddington.
[4] See Michael Whitworth, *Einstein's Wake: Relativity, metaphor, and modernist literature* (Oxford:
Oxford University Press, 2001), 46. Whitworth's argument is that popularization was important in
periodicals too. But the shift of focus to modernist magazine culture has eclipsed the significant
experiment in popularization represented by book series like To-Day and To-Morrow or the Psyche
Miniatures.

Imagined Futures: Writing, Science and Modernity in the To-Day and To-Morrow. Max Saunders, Oxford University
Press (2019). © Max Saunders. DOI: 10.1093/oso/9780198829454.001.0001

believe, of the modern scientific outlook, will help any reader to understand why science is the dominating intellectual activity of our age.[5]

Two of these leading science popularizers—Russell and Jeans—contributed to To-Day and To-Morrow.

In his book *Einstein's Wake*, Michael Whitworth distinguishes between 'vertical' popularization on the one hand, 'with the expert scientist being located above the layman reader', and with 'the hierarchical model of high-priests and laymen still fully operative'; and on the other hand, 'horizontal' popularization, in which readers are treated as equals, and 'may expect to be spoken to as part of an educated elite'.[6] Doubtless the best popular science tends to combine the two modes, and To-Day and To-Morrow generally manages to balance them effectively, as witnessed by the number of reviewers finding the volumes exciting and entertaining. The futurological dimension effectively guarantees that they cannot read like authoritative textbooks (except parodically), since the experts must relinquish the mode of explaining expert knowledge, and acknowledge the uncertainty of predictions. As Russell puts it in *Icarus*: 'I do not wish to be supposed to be making prophecies: I am only suggesting possibilities which it may be instructive to consider' (43).

To-Day and To-Morrow was not restricted to scientific topics. But around one third of the volumes deal with subjects in which science and technologies figure prominently. At least fifteen of them deal with pure sciences and medicine.

The volumes discussed most in this study—*Daedalus*, *Icarus*, and *The World, the Flesh and the Devil*—do not choose a particular science and stay focused on it, as did the volumes on Chemistry, Physics, Biology, or Cosmogony, considering their developments as disciplines. Instead, they are concerned with ways in which all sciences, and also the technologies derived from them, will transform human life, and the understanding of human life.

The present chapter begins with discussions of *Daedalus*, and of J. D. Bernal's searching elaboration of possible practical applications of new scientific knowledge in *The World, the Flesh and the Devil*. It then analyses the volume devoted to Physics, as an example of how the series not only popularized pure science disciplines, but used popularization to extend the discussion of new scientific theories to the understanding of human life, the mind, and language. It closes with a consideration of the role of language and narrative in popular science writing, proposing ten theses about the relation between science and the arts, so important across To-Day and To-Morrow, as it is framed by the series.

---

[5] 'Scientific Prophecies', *Times Literary Supplement* (7 February 1924), 74.
[6] Whitworth, *Einstein's Wake*, pp. 36, 45, and 30.

Haldane's *Daedalus*

Arthur C. Clarke, who said Haldane was 'the finest intellect it has ever been my privilege to know', described him as: 'perhaps the most brilliant scientific popularizer of his generation'.[7] Given the importance of *Daedalus*—as a major work of popular science and literature in its own right; for setting the tone and inspiring other contributors to the series; and for its legacies in science and literature—a granular description of it is warranted.[8] The book opens with two scenes of destruction: one of battles on the Western Front; the other of the explosion of a dying star. These, Haldane says, 'suggest, very briefly, a part of the case against science':

> Has mankind released from the womb of matter a Demogorgon which is already beginning to turn against him, and may at any moment hurl him into the bottomless void? Or is Samuel Butler's even more horrible vision correct, in which man becomes a mere parasite of machinery, an appendage of the reproductive system of huge and complicated engines which will successively usurp his activities, and end by ousting him from the mastery of this planet?[9] Is the machine-minder engaged on repetition-work the goal and ideal to which humanity is tending? Perhaps a survey of the present trend of science may throw some light on these questions.   (4-5)

This establishes at once an intelligence which can not only move effortlessly from Greek myth to modernity (Haldane had a first class degree in classics and mathematics from Oxford), but also use literature to reflect upon science, and science to reflect upon literature.

Arguing that the future of science seems assured, since it will be protected by both capitalism and socialism, Haldane goes on 'to show how far from complete are any branches of science at the present time' (9). Here too his scope is breathtaking. He has the assurance to talk not only about what each science has achieved, but about what still remains to it to do. In some ways his panache recalls that of Wells, whom he invokes to make two points. First, that Wells as a prophet was 'modest' and accurate. So modern prediction based in science can be realistic, not hubristic. Second, that Wells is now 'a generation behind the time' (10). 'When his scientific ideas were formed', says Haldane, 'flying and radio-telegraphy,

---

[7] Arthur C. Clarke, 'Haldane and Space', in *Haldane and Modern Biology*, ed. K. R. Dronamraju (Baltimore: Johns Hopkins Press, 1968), 243–8 (248, 243).

[8] Much has been written about *Daedalus* as a work of popular science. See for example K. R. Dronamraju, ed., *Haldane's* Daedalus *Revisited* (Oxford: Oxford University Press, 1995). But it has received little attention from a literary-critical point of view, though I am indebted to chapter 4 of Patrick Parrinder's excellent *Utopian Literature and Science: From the scientific revolution to brave new world and beyond* (Basingstoke: Palgrave Macmillan, 2015).

[9] Haldane's reference is to 'The Book of the Machines' from Butler's satirical utopia, *Erehwon* (1872).

for example, were scientific problems, and the centre of scientific interest still lay in physics and chemistry' (10). But these are now 'commercial problems', says Haldane. For him, 'the centre of scientific interest lies in biology' (10).

A discussion of Einstein and quantum physics leads to the claim, echoed with variations through the series, that 'Kantian idealism will become the basal working hypothesis of the physicist and finally of all educated men, just as materialism did after Newton's day' (14). Nonetheless, Haldane believes that 'all that applied physics can do for us' is to abolish checks on human activity such as darkness or distance. Such developments in travel and communication, he says, 'are tending to bring mankind more and more together, to render life more and more complex, artificial, and rich in possibilities—to increase indefinitely man's powers for good and evil' (20).

This leads him to consider two forms of power: human and mechanical. Haldane is optimistic that the impact of technology on industry and society will be to maintain the stability of industry and increase social justice, because it magnifies injustices to the point where they can no longer be borne. Surveying the available sources of power, he predicts that wind and solar power will have to replace coal and oil, but is sceptical about the feasibility of 'the commercial possibility of induced radio-activity' (27).

At this point he pauses 'to consider very briefly the influence on art and literature of our gradual conquest of space and time. I think that the blame for the decay of certain arts rests primarily on the defective education of the artists. An artist must understand his subject matter' (27-8). Keats and Shelley 'were the last English poets who were at all up-to-date in their chemical knowledge', he says (28-9). If we want poets able to interpret science as Milton or Shelley did, 'we must see that our possible poets are instructed, as their masters were, in science and economics' (29). After all, if a scientist can be well-educated in Classical and modern literature...This is a diagnosis of a cultural failing. Artists cannot be expected to express the philosophy of an age if they do not understand it. But it also indicates what is at stake in popular science writing for Haldane: not merely bringing people's knowledge of a field up-to-date, but *interpreting* science for them. That interpretation is more than an explanation of scientific thought. It is also an understanding of how such thought and its applications affect people—their society, their religion, their art and culture. Other contributors would expand on this argument too, as we shall see, some urging that literature had a duty to interpret scientific developments; others anxious that the arts followed the sciences at their peril.

Haldane then turns to chemistry, arguing that though it has 'vastly increased the production of various types of substance' such as metals, 'there were explosives, dyes, and drugs before chemistry was a science', and it has 'introduced into human life no radical novelty of the importance of the heat-engine or the telegraph' (31). He imagines future production of a 'vast array of substances like wine, coffee and tobacco, whose intelligent use can add to the amenity of life and promote the expression of man's higher faculties' (37). Meanwhile he expects chemistry will develop synthetic food within 120 years (38).

Then he arrives at his main topic: biology. Whereas 'the average prophet' here restricts himself to medicine, surgery, and improvements through breeding and eugenics (about which he is scathing), Haldane anticipates more radical departures: in reproductive technologies, and genetic modification. He considers six 'biological inventions': 'four were made before the dawn of history. I refer to the domestication of animals, the domestication of plants, the domestication of fungi for the production of alcohol' (42) and the advent of face-to-face copulation. The two modern inventions are 'bactericide and the artificial control of conception' (43). 'The first point that we may notice about these inventions is that they have all had a profound emotional and ethical effect. Of the four earlier there is not one which has not formed the basis of a religion' (43). This question of the transformative effect of science and technology on morality and religion becomes the keynote of the rest of the book. 'There is no great invention, from fire to flying, which has not been hailed as an insult to some god. But if every physical and chemical invention is a blasphemy, every biological invention is a perversion.' (44). As Krishna Dronamraju observes, 'The distinguished physicist Freeman Dyson notes that Einstein and Haldane were almost alone in the early twentieth century to discuss the ethical issues that are brought on by scientific progress.'[10]

Daedalus is then introduced, as 'the first modern man'. Haldane alludes to 'his only recorded success in experimental genetics' (47), the facilitation of the breeding of the Minotaur. 'He was the first to demonstrate that the scientific worker is not concerned with gods' (48). Haldane believes medicine has had almost as deep an effect on European society as the industrial revolution. Besides 'the partial substitution of the doctor for the priest', increased longevity has meant that 'religion has come to lay less and less stress on a good death, and more and more on a good life, and its whole outlook has gradually changed in consequence' (54).

The next section of the book takes the playful form of: 'some extracts from an essay on the influence of biology on history during the 20th century which will (it is hoped) be read by a rather stupid undergraduate member of this university to his supervisor during his first term 150 years hence' (56-7). This enables Haldane to narrate his imagined future as schoolbook history for the student (57-68). (This trope of future history was popular in the series, and will be discussed in future.) The essay comments on the crudeness of eugenics, and notes the practical abolition of infectious diseases. It then recounts genetic experiments

---

[10] Krishna Dronamraju, *Popularizing Science: The life and work of JBS Haldane* (Oxford: Oxford University Press, 2017), 68; referring to Dyson, '*Daedalus* after Seventy Years', in Dronamraju, *Haldane's* Daedalus *Revisited*, pp. 55–63.

with zoology and botany, which include genetic modification. The development of a purple algae as fertilizer multiplies plant yield and causes a food glut. It leaks into sea, which it turns purple, causing environmental problems but also an abundance of fish. A lichen has been devised to bind the sands of deserts.

The student then recounts the history of 'ectogenesis', the growing of embryos outside the mother's body. This was to prove the single prospect that had the most impact of anything in To-Day and To-Morrow, both across the series and beyond it. Haldane didn't invent the term, which was available since at least 1909 to refer generally to 'The production of structures or bodies outside the organism'.[11] But he certainly gave it currency outside the lab. It is not certain that he invented the specific concept of the gestating of human children in artificial wombs either. As Susan Squier has shown in her study *Babies in Bottles*, that image can be traced back to Kingsley's *The Water Babies*, and its twentieth-century scientific reprise to Julian Huxley's reading of that book as a child.[12] As we shall see in Chapter 6, *Daedalus*' imagining of ectogenesis had at least three fathers: not only Haldane and his friend Julian Huxley, but Julian's brother Aldous as well. But what is clear is that *Daedalus* offered the most elaborate and authoritative projection of ectogenesis, and became the standard reference point for subsequent discussions of it.

'As we know ectogenesis is now universal' (65), writes the student, arguing that it saved civilization, which otherwise 'would have collapsed within a measurable time owing to the greater fertility of the less desirable members of the population' (66-7). The double-voiced mode of *Daedalus* ingeniously allows Haldane to propose the idea of ectogenesis as a scientific future possibility, while simultaneously ironising the eugenicist arguments likely to be advanced in its favour. After ten pages of mock-essay he returns to his own voice to consider two kinds of future freedom. First social freedoms: 'If reproduction is once completely separated from sexual love mankind will be free in an altogether new sense' (68); the sense of sexual freedom, and associated freedoms of conduct, of pleasure, and of morality. Second, biological freedoms: 'We can already alter animal species to an enormous extent, and it seems only a question of time before we shall be able to apply the same principles to our own' (69). He even anticipates hormone replacement therapy. Furthermore, he imagines physiological control of our more 'spiritual' faculties; and predicts that when lives are longer and fuller, death will lose its terrors.

Concluding his tour of incomplete sciences, Haldane then turns to psychology, stating that, like biology, it is 'hardly a science yet', its abstract generalizations still a matter of controversy (74-5). 'I have tried', he writes, 'to show why I believe that the biologist is the most romantic figure on earth at the present day' (77). That may sound self-aggrandizing, but he then performs a doubly self-deprecating

---

[11] See the *Oxford English Dictionary* (OED), citing the *The Century Dictionary: Supplement*, first edition (New York: Century, 1909): '*Ectogenesis*, the production of or the giving rise to structures from without'. Though the *OED*'s second historical example is from *Daedalus*.

[12] Susan M. Squier, *Babies in Bottles: Twentieth-century visions of reproductive technology*. New Brunswick, NJ: Rutgers University Press, 1994, pp. 29–30.

manoeuvre. Though to lay eyes the biologist may cut a sad figure 'groping blindly amid the mazes of the ultra-microscopic' (77), Haldane writes, 'he knows he has a responsibility which he dare not disclaim'; he is urged on 'by something or someone which he feels to be higher than himself' (79). This recasts the Olympian omniscient tone and its stylish ironies as in the service of an ideal greater than the individual: something perhaps best called—and something *Daedalus* best exemplifies—the scientific imagination.

In summing up, Haldane then stands back from the achievements and challenges of particular sciences to consider their impact: 'at present reason not only has a freer play in science than elsewhere, but can produce as great effects on the world through science as through politics, philosophy, or literature'; a situation which he sees as making further scientific revolutions more probable. (79) 'It is of course almost hopeless to attempt any very exact prophecies as to how in detail scientific knowledge is going to revolutionize human life, but I believe that it will continue to do so, and even more profoundly than I have suggested' (80). The book ends with a contemplation of the political, moral, and spiritual developments that might follow such scientific revolutions. Haldane discusses the notion of a 'world state', as proposed by H. G. Wells and others (83-4). He argues that as science alters human life, moral boundaries will inevitably keep shifting. Christianity is more flexible than most religions. But, Haldane says, that may be 'an argument for Christianity as against other religions, but not as against none at all, or as against a religion which will frankly admit that its mythology and morals are provisional. That is the only sort of religion that would satisfy the scientific mind, and it is very doubtful whether it could properly be called a religion at all' (91-2). 'The scientific worker of the future will more and more resemble the lonely figure of Daedalus as he becomes conscious of his ghastly mission, and proud of it' (92-3). 'This small book of ninety-one pages might well become the testament in a new faith', wrote the *New York Tribune*' reviewer: 'It is profoundly revolutionary and it envisages startling possibilities. It is a work of imagination and of logical reasoning from exact science.'[13]

Haldane has already noted that were he to learn how to unleash the power of the atom man could destroy his world: a possibility envisaged in the speculation about the birth of a new star. The book closes on an equally Nietzschean-sounding verse-epilogue (though written before *Thus Spake Zarathustra*'s announcement of the Death of God), slightly misquoted from Robert Buchanan's 'Homunculus; or, The Song of Deicides' from his 1870 poem *The Book of Orm*:

> All through his silent veins flow free
> Hunger and thirst and venery,
> But in his eyes a still small flame

---

[13] (11 May 1924), 21.

Like the first cell from which he came
Burns round and luminous, as he rides
Singing my song of deicides.[14]

It is from a section of Buchanan's poem entitled 'The Devil's Mystics'. But one senses here that Haldane is seeking to overturn the tradition of moralized science epitomized by *Frankenstein*, say, in which hubristic scientific curiosity interferes with the mysteries of life and suffers as a result. His 'scientific worker' is a deicide not out of diabolic rebellion for its own sake, but for the sake of knowledge; and because the resulting prospect of the power to create new forms of life renders gods unnecessary, irrelevant. Buchanan's Satan is not only 'the last of the gods', but the first scientist; a biologist, studying humanity through a microscope.[15] The terminology of 'scientific worker' signals Haldane's Marxism too, though he seems no more utopian in his political philosophy than his science: because the scientist's 'ghastly mission' isolates him from his fellow men rather than confirming their solidarity. After all, they are human, whereas what he is ushering in is effectively the post-human.

Bernal's *The World, the Flesh, and the Devil*

The Devil appears in the To-Day and To-Morrow volume by another great British Marxist scientist of the period, J. D. Bernal—*The World, the Flesh and the Devil*, subtitled: *An Enquiry into the future of the three enemies of the* rational *soul* (my emphasis). Bernal's extraordinary book is another of the most visionary, post-human, and also one of the strangest, in the series.[16] It is also one of the few to have a title not from classics but medieval theology.[17] The phrase is in Abelard and Aquinas, and gets into the Litany of the Book of Common Prayer: '[. . . F]rom al the deceytes of the worlde, the fleshe, and the deuill: Good lorde deliuer us'. It is traditionally taken to refer to the three main temptations to a Christian soul—the

---

[14] *Daedalus*, p. 93. See http://www.robertbuchanan.co.uk/
[15] Parrinder, *Utopian Literature and Science*, in an illuminating discussion of Haldane's quotation from Buchanan, pp. 56–61, cites Archibald Stodart-Walker's study *Robert Buchanan: The poet of modern revolt* (London: Grant Richards, 1901), which characterizes his Devil as 'the spirit of science as opposed to the spirit of Theology, the inspirer of research as opposed to the upholder of authority and tradition' (253).
[16] Like *Daedalus* and other volumes, it had begun as a university talk. An earlier version had appeared—also as 'The World, the Flesh and the Devil'—in *Psyche*, 9:4 (April 1929), 3–26, with a note (on p. 3) saying: 'This rough draft of Mr. Bernal's forthcoming volume, here adapted from a paper read in Cambridge in March 1929, is printed in *Psyche* by arrangement with Messrs. Kegan Paul'. See Andrew Brown, *J. D. Bernal: The sage of science* (Oxford: Oxford University Press, 2007), 71–7, on the book.
[17] See Appendix A on the book history of the series on the various forms of title. On Bernal's life in science, see D. M. Hodgkin, 'John Desmond Bernal', 'Biographical memoirs of the Fellows of the Royal Society', *Proceedings of the Royal Society*, 26 (1980), 17–84.

antithesis of the trinity. Bernal wants to update them for a post-Christian world-view, so imagines how science might master each of the three. Each section is vertiginously modern, pushing the logic of contemporary developments in science and technology as far as he can.

His trio are the resistances human reason needs to overcome in order to fulfil its possibilities. The World is the physical universe: matter; the planet Earth, and its place in the cosmos. He speculates how future generations could exploit the physical world, not just of our Earth, but of other worlds, through a willed diaspora of space-travelling artificial ecosystems. In more eco-conscious times, the thought of surviving by merely plundering other planets might not seem very reassuring. But it is survival that's precisely at issue. Because we can't know what risks Earth may face, we'd be rash not to keep our eggs in other planetary baskets too, if we have the capability. Bernal imagines humans colonizing space by constructing what we would now call biospheres, capable of supporting large populations and traveling through the universe to explore other worlds, while remaining in communication with each other:

> Imagine a spherical shell ten miles or so in diameter, made of the lightest materials and mostly hollow [....] The globe would fulfil all the functions by which our earth manages to support life. In default of a gravitational field it has, perforce, to keep its atmosphere and the greater portion of its life inside; but as all its nourishment comes in the form of energy through its outer surface it would be forced to resemble on the whole an enormously complicated single-celled plant.
>
> (*The World, the Flesh, and the Devil*, pp. 24–5)

By the flesh he means the limitations of the human body, both in terms of its vulnerability and short life-span, and the constraints on its range of perceptions. Because what he cares about is rationality, he imagines in a bizarre section a future in which our brains are able to live longer because removed from our bodies and kept alive in machine hosts. It is one of the earliest elaborations of what has become known as the 'brain in a vat' hypothesis—teasing out how much of our personal identity and experience inheres in our brain.[18] In the philosophical

---

[18] The 'brain in a vat' hypothesis—seen as a variant on Descarte's idea of the evil demon deceiving us into thinking our bodily sensations are real—is usually attributed to Gilbert Harman's *Thought* (Princeton, NJ: Princeton University Press, 1973), 5. Also see John Forrester, 'The Psychoanalytic Passion of J. D. Bernal in 1920s Cambridge', *British Journal of Psychotherapy* 26 (2010), 397–404; C. Gere, introducing a special issue on 'The Brain in a Vat', *Studies in History and Philosophy of Science*, 35:2 (June 2004), 219–25; and B. Parry, 'Technologies of Immortality: The brain on ice', *Studies in History and Philosophy of Science*, 35:2 (June 2004), 391–413. Gere (223) says *The World, the Flesh, and the Devil* describes 'the first properly immortal envatted human brain in literature'. Parry (391) says that 'The science fiction scenario of the disembodied brain in a vat had its genesis in a futuristic treatise, published in the 1920s by the visionary Marxist, physicist, and mathematician John Desmond Bernal'. Though, as Gere observes in her introduction (222), John Tresch, in another article in the same special issue, discovered an earlier example, though in a 1914 fictional text, which she calls 'the earliest example of the trope', by Raymond Roussel. John Tresch, 'In a Solitary Place: Raymond

thought experiments, questions are asked such as: if a brain were isolated from a body, but given electrical impulses corresponding to those received when walking, would it think it was walking? But Bernal isn't interested in virtual reality; he doesn't want to fool the brain about the outer world, but give it a new lease of inner life. He's more interested in thinking than walking.

Furthermore, rather than simply proposing to replicate our awareness of the outside world, he wants to enhance it. Our five senses are fine so far as they go, he argues; but wouldn't it be better if we could add others?

> We badly need a small sense organ for detecting wireless frequencies, eyes for infra-red, ultra-violet and X-rays, ears for supersonics, detectors of high and low temperatures, of electrical potential and current, and chemical organs of many kinds.   (*The World, the Flesh, and the Devil*, p. 44)

(Remember Chekhov's Tuzenbach: 'perhaps they'll discover a sixth sense and develop it'.) He doesn't leave it there. If we were able to communicate directly with others via radio waves, what then? If you think of the technological paraphernalia needed to complete a 'phone call in 1929 you can see his frustration: intercontinental cables; local exchanges and operators; stationary handsets in cold hallways. In a way he postulates the mobile phone without having to invent the technology.[19] Partly because the microchip didn't yet exist. But also because he obviates the need for handsets by imagining simply implanting the transmitters and receivers directly into the body, or rather the brainy vat. It is a disturbing idea; a mad one, even, if taken literally as a programme for humanity. But as a thought experiment it enables a fuller sense of what might be at stake with such bio-engineered interventions. As with the brain in a vat, what he has really pioneered is another early version of the crucial trope in the imaginary of the post-human: the idea of what we now call the cyborg, or the bionic human—not the first, certainly, but the first to be thought through so elaborately.[20] He possibly also provided the inspiration for the Daleks in *Dr Who*.

The figure of the cyborg was already available in popular culture, notably in Francis Flagg's pulp fiction 'The Machine Man of Ardathia', published in *Amazing Stories* in 1927.[21] In this story, while the elderly narrator is writing,

---

Roussel's brain and the French cult of unreason', *Studies in History and Philosophy of Science*, 35:2 (June 2004), 307–32: 'Raymond Roussel's novel *Locus solus* depicted a brain-in-a-vat apparatus in which the head of the revolutionary orator Georges Danton was reanimated and made to speak' (307).

[19] A. M. Low in *Wireless Possibilities* had already envisioned portable telephones in 1924: see the discussion in Chapter 4.

[20] Cyborg figures appear in the works of Edward Page Mitchell (1852–1927), such as 'The Ablest Man in the World' (1879). See Alessandra Calanchi, '"I lost my body in an experiment": Reshaping the Human in Edward Page Mitchell's Short Stories'. Conference paper given in London, 29 September 2007.

[21] Francis Flagg, 'The Machine Man of Ardathia', *Amazing Stories* (November 1927), 798–804. See Richard J. Bleiler and Everett F. Bleiler, *Science-Fiction: The Gernsback years* (Kent, OH: Kent State University Press, 1998), 122.

there is a flash, vaporizing his rocking chair, as a strange creature materializes in its place: a three-foot high homunculus-like figure with atrophied limbs and a tadpole-like body, sealed in a crystalline cylinder like a large test-tube. Unlike H. G. Wells's Martians, this visitor is a benign figure, on a mission of scientific exploration. Like Wells's time traveler, but in reverse, he is visiting from the far future. He explains to the narrator that he is an Ardathian; a distant descendant of the human.

The Ardathians do not have males and females. They are not grown from ova, but from synthetically produced cells. After fertilization they are sealed into their unbreakable transparent cases. 'As the embryo develops, the various tubes and mechanical devices are introduced into the body by our mechanics and become an integral part of it' (802). They are nourished by a chemical fluid circulating in place of blood and removing waste products. They use rays to extend their limbs outside the casings. (As the rays play across the narrator's apartment, the capsule suggests a cathode ray from an early television.) The Ardathians can live for 1500 years.

This machine person is from around the year 30,000, and talks of humans as 'pre-historic'; his earliest recorded ancestors are the 'Bi-Chanics', from around 15,000, who 'vaporized their food substances and breathed them through the nostril, excreting the waste products of the body through the pores of the skin. Their children were brought to the point of birth in ectogenic incubators. There is enough authentic evidence existing to prove the Bi-Chanics had perfected the use of mechanical hearts [...]' (801).

Flagg had thus either read *Daedalus* (or perhaps its *Century* magazine avatar with the science-fiction title, 'If You Were Alive in 2123 A. D.'[22]) or Haldane's ideas had reached the more popular culture of pulp science fiction magazines through a more general diffusion. As Susan Squier has shown, this tale is one of a number of texts appearing in the decade after the pioneering popular science writing by Haldane and his friend Julian Huxley.[23] Huxley had experimented on Mexican amphibious axolotls, feeding them minced thyroid, which resulted in an artificial maturation, turning them into salamander-like land animals. The *Daily Mail* picked up the story, and its futurological glimpse of the potential to control ageing, announcing in 1920 that 'Young Huxley has discovered the Elixir of Life'.[24] Huxley responded to the continuing journalistic interest with an article of his own, describing 'Searching for the Elixir of Life', and turning futurologist himself:

The speculative mind looks forward into the future and there sees great institutions for graft operations—human repair-shops. Men will have found methods

---

[22] J. B. S. Haldane, 'If You Were Alive in 2123 A. D.', in *Century*, 106 (August 1923), 549–66.
[23] Squier, *Babies in Bottles*, chapters 1 and 2, pp. 24–99. Also see Angus McLaren, *Reproduction by Design: Sex, robots, trees, and test-tube babies in interwar Britain* (Chicago: University of Chicago Press, 2012).
[24] *Daily Mail* (20 February 1920); cited by Squier, *Babies in Bottles*, p. 36.

for keeping organs alive outside the body, or they will be able to make grafts from tissue cultures. Thyroids, pituitaries, adrenals, pineals, interstitial tissue, and many other regulating organs now unknown, will be in their several places, and aging humanity will come in to have their bodily system reanimated as cars come in to a garage to be overhauled.[25]

This sense of imminent transformation of humanity through science was part of the background to Haldane's case for the biologist as the 'most romantic figure' of the age. (Indeed, Huxley's essay had appeared in the same magazine which would publish Haldane's 'If You Were Alive in 2123 A. D.') Julian Huxley later turned science fictionist too, producing an influential story based on these ideas, called 'The Tissue-Culture King.'[26]

In Flagg's story, the mechanical is not just a metaphor for spare-part surgery. Man and machine have been fundamentally combined. The Bi-Chanics 'were the first among men to realize that man's bodily advancement lay in and through the machine. They perceived that man only became human when he fashioned tools; that the tools increased the length of his arms, the grip of his hands, the strength of his muscles. They observed that with the aid of the machine, man could circle the earth, speak to the planets, gaze intimately at the stars.' (802) However, 'they had only partly subordinated machinery to their use' (801). The Ardathian, by contrast, exemplifies the complete fusion of the biological and the mechanical.

The narrator proudly tells the Ardathian that the Bi-Chanics weren't the first to attempt such experiments: 'a year or two ago I read an article in one of our current magazines telling how a Vienna surgeon was hatching out rabbits and guinea pigs in ecto-genic incubators' (801). His desire to speak up for our 'prehistoric' species is touching, even if 'hatching out rabbits' sounds a little like conjuring rabbits out of hats. The Ardathian contrives to vanish as suddenly as he appeared, leaving the narrator with only the disappearance of his rocking-chair to convince him the encounter was more than a dream. The Author's Note at the end explains that the narrator has since gone mad; leaving it open whether the madness produced the vision, or was produced by it. But the figure of the machine man will be back, in a future chapter.

The story exemplifies how tropes such as the artificial human or the cyborg circulate between popular science, popular culture and literature. The parallels with *The World, the Flesh, and the Devil* are striking: the evolutionary trajectory towards the cyborgian; the prosthetic exoskeleton extending longevity to what seems from our point of view to be virtually immortality. Bernal describes his

---

[25] Julian Huxley, 'Searching for the Elixir of Life', *Century* (February 1922), 621–9 (626).
[26] Julian Huxley, 'The Tissue-Culture King', *Yale Review*, 15 (April 1926), 479–504. The story was reprinted in *Amazing Stories*, 2:5 (August 1927), 451–9; the volume also containing a story called 'The Ultra-Elixir of Youth', by A. Hyatt Verrill, 476–85.

brains in cylinders as 'the first stage of mechanized humanity' (47). Yet it is where his elaboration develops the trope beyond its popular fiction avatars that it gets more interesting, stranger and still more disturbing. He is not interested in the Wellsian machinery of time-travel. He compresses the evolutionary process into a single life, making 'ontogeny' (the development of the individual) recapitulate 'phylogeny' (the evolution of the species). It is where he focuses on communication technologies that his projection resonates with our information age.

With a radio-sense we should not only be able to communicate directly with our chosen interlocutor, but could do it without speaking; simply by transmitting our thoughts directly. In short, telepathy: what might seem a quaint fictional hope; though it is rapidly being realized in today's research using brain activity to activate machines. What Bernal is effectively doing here is offering a possible scientific grounding for the phenomena previously considered the preserve of psychical research. This part of his argument can thus be read as countering a volume which testifies to the series' ability to act as a barometer to the intellectual pressures of the age, E. N. Bennett's *Apollonius; or, The Present and Future of Psychical Research* (1927).

It gets stranger still. Bernal doesn't stop with abolishing god and the devil, and many of the constraints of embodiment and aging. He was thoroughly conversant with psycho-analytic theories of not only of reason, anxiety, and the unconscious, but of their relation to embodied experience. And he knows that most people will find his vision of the future appalling. Indeed, he admits to being disturbed by his own speculations, acknowledging that we cannot really imagine what it would be like to abandon our bodies. But he also knows that the greatest human fear is of death; and he thinks science can challenge mortality itself.

In the boldest move in the book—and arguably in the entire series—Bernal imagines developments which might allow transcendence of individuality in a non-spiritual manner, by not only abandoning our bodies but our individual minds too. The thought signals would not be confined to telephone wires but would radiate out everywhere. Pushing even further this vision of enhanced humans communicating with each other directly, no matter how far away they are, he sees that the logic of this possibility is that each human will be connected, or could be, to all others. Bernal wonders about the possibility that his longer-living but still mortal brains, encased in their life-support machines, would be able to communicate their ideas so fully to each other that they would combine to form a single super-brain or 'compound mind' (54)—what science fiction writers (since at least Olaf Stapledon) have called a 'group mind' or 'hive-mind'. Here too he knows such experience cannot be imagined fully within the limits of the human.

Yet, even more strikingly, he wonders whether, as our thoughts are all transferred electronically to the network (or as we would now say, 'uploaded'), that would not give us an immortality more real than any dreamed up by theologians: the eternal existence of the most intimate and creative and valuable part of the human animal—not the soul, but the rational mind. That is, the ability to connect up individual intelligences would mean the end to mortality, since your consciousness, as it would be shared by others, would be able to outlast your individual brain. The cynical abuse of today's communication technologies might make us cynically think of the risk of 'brain-hacking' in such a future. But Bernal—a committed Marxist—is thinking collectivity rather than predatory competition. For him the idea that an individual's thoughts could be propagated into others' brains would effectively not only unite workers of the worlds but also offer the hope of a form of immortality after the vat can no longer keep the brain alive, and gives up the ghost in the machine. 'The new life would be more plastic', he says, 'more directly controllable and at the same time more variable and more permanent than that produced by the triumphant opportunism of nature' (57).

There is a sort of logic to the idea: if you reduce significant human life to brain activity; to having thoughts; then as long as those thoughts keep being thought, and helping to produce other thoughts, then that life could be said to continue. After contemplating the freeing of the brain from the limitations of the body, he is then drawn to imagining freeing the mind from the limitations of the physical brain. It is not unlike the way writers have traditionally hoped their written words would guarantee their immortality by being read after their deaths; though again, in Bernal's scenario the mediation of speech or reading is bypassed.

The 'compound mind' may be different in scale and duration from the individual human brain, but it is not clear that it is different in kind. The limit Bernal's project appears to come up against is imagining an intelligence as artificial as its cyborg container. That is an easy criticism to make with our hindsight after some seventy-five years of electronic computing, and as machine learning begins to open up radically new possibilities of AI. Nevertheless, Bernal takes the trope running through the series of a prediction of greater interconnection (explored in Chapter 2) further than anyone. His notion of a human race dispersed through the galaxy, each communicating directly with all, has major problems. It is not clear why a multitude will guarantee the immortality of your thoughts any more than a single recipient (except that any individual will die, whereas the multitude will keep reproducing itself). Nor is it clear how an individual brain would be able to prevent the multiplicity of messages coming to it from everyone else from drowning each other out in cacophony. Welcome to the twittersphere, we might say. Because that is what seems one of the most surprising things about this extraordinary book. It appears also to have foreseen something uncannily like the wireless internet, though again without having had to invent the computer first. That vision of the unimpeded flow of messages connecting the human race is both deeply rooted in the popular science discourse of the period, and also stunningly far-sighted.

Arthur C. Clarke called *The World, the Flesh and the Devil* 'the most brilliant attempt at scientific prediction ever made'.[27]

The transformations of modern life come with disorientating rapidity in Haldane's and Bernal's books, so as to render modernity utterly bizarre and perplexing. Having networked humanity, Bernal is off imagining artificial life; then turning, in his third section, to psycho-analysis as the science attempting to master the devils within man's mind. The enemies are not temptations but limitations, which he sees it as his job to outwit. For a scientifically rational soul, the devil isn't Satan, but an utterly secular one: the unconscious and its irrationality, standing for everything that jeopardizes our rationality—our destructive desires, aggressions, self-deceptions and our religions. Bernal, who was an early convert to Freud, sees psychoanalysis as the science that can liberate us from its tyrannies.[28] Which is what must have really disturbed C. S. Lewis; the anti-theological stance Bernal as a Marxist shared with Haldane. Reading Haldane and Bernal reminds us that what has become known as 'the new Atheism' of Richard Dawkins or Christopher Hitchens is nothing new; but rather, a legacy of this science-inspired intellectual avant-garde. One can only imagine the dismay of such writers at the current return to the dark ages of religious fundamentalisms and New Age calls for 're-enchantment'. An anonymous review in Ogden's journal *Psyche* of Louis Berman's book *The Glands Regulating Personality* characterizes research on hormones as promising to understand 'the Chemistry of the Soul'.[29]

Bernal was doing what Haldane projected medical science as doing in *Daedalus*: effecting the 'substitution of the doctor for the priest' (54). Which is hardly surprising, given that in *Daedalus* Haldane had effectively mapped out Bernal's triad (and the scope of much of the rest of the series too):

> We must regard science then from three points of view. First it is the free activity of man's divine faculties of reason and imagination. Secondly it is the answer of the few to the demands of the many for wealth, comfort and victory [....] Finally it is man's gradual conquest, first of space and time, then of matter as such, then of his own body and those of other living beings, and finally the subjugation of the dark and evil elements in his own soul.   (*Daedalus*, pp. 81-2)

In that phrase 'the free activity of man's divine faculties of reason and imagination' Haldane lulls the theologically-inclined into a false sense of security. He could

---

[27] Arthur C. Clarke, *Greetings, Carbon-Based Bipeds* (New York: St Martin's Griffin, 2000); cited in Brown, *J. D. Bernal*, p. 70. See also Maurice Goldsmith, 'The World, the Flesh, and the Devil', *Futures*, 10:2 (1978), 148–53; in 'From Prophecy to Prediction: A serialised survey of the movement of ideas, developments in predictive fiction, and first attempts to forecast the future scientifically'.

[28] For a fascinating account of Bernal's youthful development and engagement with Marx and Freud, and of *The World, the Flesh and the Devil*, see John Forrester and Laura Cameron, *Freud in Cambridge* (Cambridge: Cambridge University Press, 2017), 157–86.

[29] Anon., 'Survey of Current Literature' section, *Psyche*, 3:4 (April 1923), 375–8 (376).

almost be accepting the Christian view that reason is divine because given by God to man so as to exercise free will. But what he means is the opposite: it is only by ceasing to take gods seriously that man can be free. The divinity is in the human, not outside it. So with Bernal's Devil. For these scientists, it is man who is the measure of all things; not in his current physical or social state, but in his imagination of other possibilities.

BBC4's 2007 series 'Visions of the Future' was described on the BBC website as follows:

> In this new three-part series, leading theoretical physicist and futurist Dr Michio Kaku explores the cutting edge science of today, tomorrow, and beyond. He argues that humankind is at a turning point in history. In this century, we are going to make the historic transition from the 'Age of Discovery' to the 'Age of Mastery', a period in which we will move from being passive observers of nature to its active choreographers. This will give us not only unparalleled possibilities but also great responsibilities.[30]

Bernal's vision of 'possibilities' is very much one of 'Mastery'. This is unsurprising in 1929, perhaps. But it *is* surprising, and bears out the argument about the 'Two Cultures', that Michio Kaku seemed blithely unaware of the post-modern critique of instrumental reason, and today's humanists' anxiety about the imperialisms of the enlightenment. That notion of possibilities and responsibilities echoes the perennial cliché about knowledge offering powers that can be used for good or for ill. And that's one of several such ideas that science writers today tend to articulate as if they hadn't already been clichés by the early twentieth century—rather as the phrase 'today and tomorrow' itself. Kaku spoke of the ever increasing speed of change, as if he'd made a new discovery.

What marks Kaku's argument as of its time are the technologies he is discussing. He sees the science of the future as a fusion of biotechnology, nanotechnology, and information technology. That just as we have discovered that what assembles and controls our physical existence is a vastly complex genetic code (that it has taken computers to crack), we are beginning to discover ways not only to rewrite that code, but to write other codes that will allow matter to assemble and repro-duce itself, to produce substances—organisms, even—that will interact with our bodies (to cure diseases through nanotechnological interventions, say). That's what he means by the mastery of matter: we'll no longer be at the mercy of what's already there, we'll be able to make new structures—much more complex ones than synthetic chemistry can manage alone.

Seen in this context Bernal appears an unreliable prophet. We are much more likely to find ways of extending longevity by manipulating the bodies and brains we have than abandoning them for machines and become Dalek-like cyborgs.

---

[30] See http://docunow.blogspot.co.uk/2013/05/dr-michio-kaku-revolution-series.html

But in 1929 Bernal didn't know about the structure of DNA—it wasn't till 1953 that Crick and Watson, drawing on Rosalind Franklin's X-ray diffraction images, worked it out. Though he would have known about senile dementia (until 1977 the diagnosis of Alzheimer's Disease was reserved for pre-senile dementia), he was not to know the extent to which it would increase with extended life-expectancy. Nor did he know about digital computers, as we have seen. He was in no doubt of the significance of such discoveries and inventions once he was aware of them. In a Foreword added for a reissue of *The World, the Flesh, and the Devil* in 1970 he wrote that his 'essay in prediction was written on the eve of the greatest discoveries and inventions in science'; in short, 'before the atomic age' (9):

> Increases in the supply of energy have certainly far exceeded my predictions, hopeful though they were.
>
> Then the next possibility, referred to in the book and now a reality, is the practical achievement of space navigation by rockets—the space age.
>
> There have been two more triumphs in the field of physics, the laser and the electronic computer, the latter now being used in all guidance and communications systems.
>
> Yet, in my opinion, the greatest discovery in all modern science has been one in molecular biology—*the double helix*—which explains in physical, quantum terms the basis of life and gives some idea of its origin. It is the greatest and most comprehensive idea in all science [...]'.[31]

Yet his 1929 vision of networked intelligences does anticipate recent research on AI, and our experience of information networking. So it turns out to be in the areas he couldn't know about that he now seems the most prophetic.

Why this is, has to do with the book's most dazzling properties, which though they have much to do with rationality, have much to do with imagination too. It demonstrates imagination as a part of reason; even a form of reason, given full play and with everyday constraints removed. What comes across is Bernal's extraordinary intelligence, which makes one wish it could have been preserved in other forms than books. In envisioning the future of science Bernal—like Haldane, and many other of the To-Day and Tomorrow writers—is writing something which requires the inspiration of a visionary or a science fiction writer, but framing it in non-fictional, and expository rather than narrative form.

There are two points that follow from this; one about futurology, and one about fiction. First, the series brings out the way our writing and thinking about science is inescapably futurological. Whether it's 'Visions of the Future', or even the old BBC series 'Tomorrow's World', part of the interest of today's scientific advances lies in what they tell us about future possibilities. This is inherent to the structure

---

[31] Bernal, 'Foreword to the Second Edition' of *The World, the Flesh, and the Devil* (London: Jonathan Cape, 1970), 9–10 (9).

of scientific development, whereby one discovery becomes the foundation for the next. And it is inherent to our harnessing of scientific knowledge in technological forms, whereby they become part of forward-looking projects (to cure disease, increase longevity, improve communication, discover new worlds etc.). But it also produces Augé's 'ideology of the future *now*'.[32] Chapters to come will demonstrate the converse effect too: how the imagination of the future is permeated by science, even for those writing the volumes about other topics.

The other point is that such projects necessarily involve imagination and fiction; the imagination of possible, but presently non-existent worlds, towards which we may want to strive; or, of course, as Bernal also imagined—since he also postulates a branch of humanity that wants nothing to do with his cyborg future—future possibilities that we may want to avoid.

Its early assessments of relatively new technologies and theories (flying, wireless, behaviourism, films, or caterpillar-tracked vehicles) constitute one fascination of the series. It is also revealing about the changing boundaries of more traditional disciplines. An influential biographer of Bernal was to employ the term 'boundary rider' to characterize his fostering of novel and productive connections not only between the sciences but between politics and world views.[33] In the sciences the authors were sharply aware of the convergence of the traditional subjects towards new fields such as biochemistry and 'mathematico-physico-chemical morphology', a matrix of physical techniques and theories applied to the study of biological organisation which attracted the support of three of the To-Day and To-Morrow contributors, and is now seen as a precursor of what became labelled molecular biology.[34] The discovery of radioactivity and X-rays at the turn of the century had undermined the Daltonian view of the stable separation of elements, and begun to disintegrate the boundaries between chemistry and physics.[35] This sense of disciplinary convergence can be seen in Lancelot L. Whyte's book *Archimedes; or, The Future of Physics* (1927) discussed in the next section. The concept of the unity of science, or—in more dialectical terms—of its 'synthesis' was to become an important focus for debate through the 1930s and beyond.[36] Both Ogden and Russell were on the International Committee organizing the Second International Congress for the Unity of Science in Copenhagen in 1936, which Haldane attended.[37]

---

[32] Marc Augé, *The Future*, trans. John Howe (London: Verso, 2014), 3; discussed in the second part of the Introduction.

[33] Gary Werskey, 'The Visible College Revisited: Second opinions on the red scientists of the 1930s', *Minerva*, 45 (2007), 305–19.

[34] Pnina Abir-Am, 'The Biotheoretical Gathering, Transdisciplinary Authority, and the Incipient Legitimation of Molecular Biology in the 1930s: New historical perspectives on the historical sociology of science', *History of Science*, 25 (1987), 1–71.

[35] See Mark S. Morrisson, *Modernism, Science, and Technology* (London: Bloomsbury, 2017), 57–61.

[36] See Jay Clayton, 'The Modern Synthesis: Genetics and dystopia in the Huxley circle', *Modernism/modernity*, 23:4 (November 2016), 875–96 (879); and Julian Huxley's *Evolution: The modern synthesis* (London: George Allen and Unwin, 1942).

[37] 'The Second International Congress for the Unity of Science', *Science*, 83 (17 April 1936), 363; for Haldane's attendance, see Clayton, 'The Modern Synthesis', p. 879.

Haldane's vision of 'ectogenesis' not only proved the most provocative idea of the series, but, as we have seen, also interacted most productively with science fiction. Such further interactions are analysed admirably in an essay by Aline Ferreira.[38] Leading scientists, too, like Freeman Dyson, have acknowledged a debt to Bernal's book (Dyson even gave a J. D. Bernal Lecture of the same title in 1972); and another generation of undergraduate students were introduced to Bernal's text after it was excerpted as part of an Open University collection, *Health and Disease* (U205) in 1984.[39] In 1995 Oxford University Press published *Haldane's 'Daedalus' Revisited*, edited by Krishna R. Dronamraju, which reprinted Haldane's text, and included discussions of it by Dyson, and Nobel Laureates Max Perutz and Joshua Lederberg. Bernal and Haldane were to become prominent figures, not only for their own research—Bernal on x-ray crystallography and molecular biology; Haldane on enzymes, evolutionary biology, genetics and population genetics—but also for their engagement with Marxist political thinking which they developed through a sustained focus on the social function of science and involvements with interventions in the politics and sociology of scientific work.[40] Bernal had first joined the Communist Party of Great Britain as a Cambridge undergraduate in 1923 (his membership had lapsed when he returned to Cambridge in 1927, but was renewed in 1933).[41] Haldane had become a socialist during the war. He supported the Communist Party at the time of the Spanish Civil War, and joined it in 1942. Bertrand Russell too had been prominent as a philosopher and radical intellectual since the war. As Gary Werskey has shown, Marxism's claims to provide a scientific philosophy of history gave it a powerful appeal to scientists, especially during the 1930s.[42] Its framing of the theory of class conflict in terms of scientific laws that would inevitably determine the future lent confidence to these writers' predictions of scientific futures. Thus the debates about the future of science begun in the To-Day and To-Morrow books have remained vital not only to scientists, but to historians of science and scientific practices, cultural historians, sociologists, and literary critics. That they have done so is in part due to the way they ride the boundaries between science and other fields—philosophy, politics, society, culture, and the arts. The books by Haldane

[38] Aline Ferreira, 'The Sexual Politics of Ectogenesis in the "Today and Tomorrow" Series', *Interdisciplinary Science Reviews*, 34:1 (March 2009), 32–55. See *Ectogenesis: Artificial womb technology and the future of human reproduction*, ed. Scott Gelfand and John, R. Shook (Amsterdam: Rodopi, 2006) on the legacy of *Daedalus*.

[39] Black, Nick, David Boswell, Alastair Gray, Sean Murphy, and Jennie Popay, *Health and Disease: A Reader* (Milton Keynes: Open University, 1993), 305–9 includes all of chapter 3 of *The World, the Flesh and the Devil* ('The Flesh'; 37–57). The first edition was in 1984. The module was taught from 1985-2007.

[40] Bernal's reputation was later damaged by his support in 1949 for the pseudo-scientific Lamarckianism of Lysenko's agricultural theory after it became official Communist Party policy.

[41] Brown, *J. D. Bernal*, p. 108.

[42] Gary Werskey, *The Visible College: A collective biography of British scientists and socialists of the 1930s* (London: Allen & Unwin, 1978).

and Bernal stand out even in this generally well-written series, for the intensities of their speculative imaginations.

Besides their radicalism and interdisciplinarity, they are representative of To-Day and To-Morrow, and of Ogden's designs for it, in a number of other ways. They are markedly polemical. The university debating society from which they both sprang was a model Ogden drew upon as the architecture of the series developed. As Russell debated with Haldane about science, so the series would pair up volumes taking opposing or at least contrasting positions on some topics—feminism, the United States, Canada, Scotland, eugenics, architecture, music, humour, religion, education, Oxbridge, and so on. Or volumes would stage debates internally. Some do this by juxtaposing different positions, as do both Hamilton Fyfe, in *Archon; or, The Future of Government* (1927), and Edgar Ansel Mowrer in *Sinon; or, The Future of Politics* (1930). Others stage the debates literally, in dialogue form, as does Winnifred Holtby in *Eutychus; or, The Future of the Pulpit* (1928). Douglas Woodruff's entertaining *Plato's American Republic* (1929) understandably adopted the Platonic dialogue mode; as did *Eleutheros; or, The Future of the Public Schools* (1928), by J. F. Roxburgh, defending classical education. Some volumes incorporated sections of dialogue within them, such as Whyte's *Archimedes*; or André Maurois' *The Next Chapter; The War against the Moon* (1927) and C. E. M. Joad's *Diogenes; or, The Future of Leisure* (1928). *Timotheus; The Future of the Theatre* (1925), moves in and out of theatrical dialogue form.

This debate model of rational enquiry testifies to the series' commitment to, and belief in, education. Several volumes explicitly address education—not just *Eleutheros*, but also *Hypatia; or, Woman and Knowledge*, by Dora Russell (1925), *Procrustes; or, The Future of English Education*, by M. Alderton Pink (1926), or *Chiron; or, The Education of a Citizen of the World*, by M. Channing Pearce (1931). Other volumes address education in passing, concerned with how their subjects are taught—as in Haldane's parody of a student of the future.[43]

Furthermore, *Daedalus* and *The World, the Flesh, and the Devil* are representative of a pair of concerns that run through the series, and which were especially close to C. K. Ogden's heart: language and communication on the one hand, and psychology on the other. Ogden is perhaps best-known nowadays internationally for his invention of and campaign for 'BASIC English'—the name a punning acronym for 'British, American, Scientific, International, Commercial'—a regularized form of English for use as an auxiliary language, reduced to 850 core words—an idea said to have suggested Orwell's Newspeak.[44] Ogden devoted

---

[43] The volumes on education, politics, and other human sciences are discussed in Chapter 3.

[44] Orwell quoted Lancelot Hogben on BASIC in 'Politics and the English Language'. He also produced a BBC programme about it, and wrote to Hogben on the topic. See Mark Thompson, *Enough Said: What's gone wrong with the language of politics?* (London: Bodley Head, 2016), 144–6. Also see Howard Fink, 'Newspeak: The epitome of parody techniques in *Nineteen Eighty-Four*', *Critical Survey*,

much of his considerable energy to this utopian project, himself writing some twenty books on the subject, and commissioning others to write about it, and to translate classic and contemporary works into it.[45] He was developing BASIC from the late 1920s, in collaboration with I. A. Richards.[46] By the beginning of 1928 he had articulated the idea of simplified English as the future.[47] But he only began publishing intensively on it from 1929, towards the end of the run of To-Day and To-Morrow; so it is not surprising the series does not discuss it directly.[48] One volume, though—*Automaton; or, The Future of the Mechanical Man*, by H. Stafford Hatfield—refers in 1928 to 'the plan for the simplification of English proposed by Mr C. K. Ogden', and to the Orthological Institute Ogden set up to propagate BASIC.[49] Interestingly, this section of the book is about the possibility of machines being able to type from dictation; and Hatfield sent this passage to the Institute, printing its 'translation' into what is effectively BASIC as an appendix (93-100).

But the To-Day and To-Morrow volumes certainly discuss language. Basil de Sélincourt's blithely imperialist *Pomona; or, The Future of English* (1926) was countered by J. Y. T. Greig in *Breaking Priscian's Head; or, English as She Will be Spoke and Wrote* (1928), which argues against the ossification of a 'Public School Standard'.[50] Robert Graves contributed the surprising *Lars Porsena; or, The Future of Swearing and Improper Language* (1927). Archibald Lyall's *It isn't Done; or, The Future of Taboo Among the British Islanders* (1930) is similarly exercised over what cannot be said in Britain, at least by the middle classes. But it is *Delphos; The Future of International Language* (1927) by Suffragette and communist Sylvia Pankhurst that is closest to Ogden's own interests: a lucid and scholarly account of the rival systems on offer before BASIC, such as Esperanto, Interlingua, and Volapük.[51] Volumes focusing on other subjects introduce the topic of language, sometimes in surprising ways. Bonamy Dobrée's *Timotheus* worries that the theatre (like the silent cinema), was in danger of abjuring the potentialities of verbal communication in favour of immersive rhythm and sensation. George Godwin's *Columbia; or, The Future of Canada* (1928) is mostly a lacklustre argument that

5:2 (Summer 1971), 155–63; and Kristin Bluemel, *George Orwell and the Radical Eccentrics: Intermodernism in literary London* (New York: Palgrave Macmillan, 2004), 112–15.

---

[45] See Gordon, W. Terrence, *C. K. Ogden: A bio-bibliographic study* (Metuchen, NJ, and London: The Scarecrow Press, 1990).

[46] Gordon, *C. K. Ogden*, p. 22.

[47] Ogden, 'Editorial' in *Psyche*, 8:3 (January 1928), 1–2. Gordon, *C. K. Ogden*, p. 84.

[48] In his 'Editorial' for *Psyche*, 9:3 (January 1929), 1–9, Ogden 'Introduces the first publication of the 850-word list under the name of "The Universal Language"'. Gordon, *C. K. Ogden*, p. 85. BASIC was named in print for the first time in *Psyche*, 9:5 [10, 1] (July 1929), 1–30. Gordon, *C. K. Ogden*, p. 86.

[49] Hatfield, *Automaton*, pp. 45, 93n. In his 'Editorial', *Psyche*, 8:1 (July 1927), 1–7, Ogden announced 'An Orthological Institute', and discussed 'The Future of English'. Gordon, *C. K. Ogden*, p. 84.

[50] J. Y. T. Greig in *Breaking Priscian's head; or, English as She Will be Spoke and Wrote* (1928), 9.

[51] *Delphos* is discussed in Chapter 2.

Canada will inevitably be incorporated into the USA; that is, until its startling closing section, 'Phantasmagoria', which begins: 'Let us borrow Mr H. G. Wells' time machine...'. Like a number of the To-Day and To-Morrow volumes (from *Daedalus* on), this casts its prediction in the form of history written from the distant future about the period still ahead of us. Godwin imagines looking over the shoulder of a future historian, writing in Saskatchewan, correcting the proofs of a book *United America: A retrospect*; this footnoted as Kegan Paul, 'To-Day and Yesterday Series'[52]. He quotes a passage ostensibly as example of 'the American language', which is a sort of interlanguage: 'Drawing upon English, German, French, Swedish, Norwegian, Spanish and Italian, it fused those languages into something unlike any of them, but flexible, vigorous and rich'.[53] One short quotation must suffice, he teases: 'riverrun brings us to Howth Castle and Environs, Sir Tristram, violer d'amores, fr' over the short sea has passencore rearrived from North Amorica on this side the scraggy isthmus of Europe Minor to wielderfight his penisolate war'. How many of his readers would have recognized this as the most avant-garde form of contemporary English, from the 'Opening Pages of a Work in Progress' that had begun to appear in the Paris magazine *transition* from April 1927, and would later be heavily revised, and retitled as *Finnegans Wake*?[54] For some of its early readers (as for many of its later), Joyce's portmanteau style seemed less a crafted interlanguage than 'the universal language of nonsense', to quote from another To-Day and To-Morrow volume concerned indirectly with words, meanings, and universal communication (and perhaps making a dig at Ogden-type utopian schemes for universal languages: *Pons Asinorum; or, The Future of Nonsense* (1929) by barristers and biographers George Edinger and E. J. C. Neep; 24). But Ogden was fascinated by Joyce, and got him to record a reading of the 'Anna Livia Plurabelle' section of *Finnegans Wake* in 1929.[55] Nonetheless he also felt the need to counter Joyce's Babelized experiment in maximizing linguistic complexity, ambiguity, and difficulty with his customary attempt to demystify and simplify: he translated part of 'Anna Livia Plurabelle' into BASIC.[56]

It was, then, while Ogden was reading and editing the To-Day and To-Morrow books that he was increasingly focusing in his own work on the future of language. He got the inventor and thinker Richard Paget to contribute the volume *Babel; or, The Past, Present and Future of Human Speech* (1930).[57] Ogden's own

---

[52] George Godwin's *Columbia; or, The Future of Canada* (1928), 80–95 (80).   [53] Ibid., p. 87.
[54] James Joyce, 'Opening Pages of a Work in Progress', *transition*, 1 (April 1927), 9–30 (9).
[55] See—or, rather, hear: https://archive.org/details/JamesJoyceReadsannaLiviaPlurabelleFrom FinnegansWake1929
The recording was made under the auspices of Ogden's Orthological Institute.
[56] C. K. Ogden, 'The Orthological Institute', *Psyche*, 12:2 (October 1931), 92–6; reprinted in *transition*, 21 (March 1932). Gordon, *C. K. Ogden*, pp. 90–1.
[57] Ogden had published Richard Paget's 'The Origin of Language' in *Psyche*, 8 (July 1927), 35–9; his book, *Human Speech*, also first appeared in 1930. 'His famous theory of pantomimic action of the

book of 1931 is his response: *Debabelization: With a survey of contemporary opinion on the problem of a universal language.* The Benthamite title announces the utopian and post-war programme: a panoptic language that will offer the hope of eliminating confusion, ambiguity, and misunderstanding.

Thus, although I have argued that Haldane's belief in scientific knowledge is not unambiguously utopian, the To-Day and To-Morrow series overall, and Ogden's work as a whole, does evince utopian attitudes to education and communication. True, the experience of the war lent a panicky edge to the insistence that greater interconnection and communication are humanity's best hope of avoiding similar and worse conflicts. But the hopes of faster travel and better communication technologies; of the development of an international language; and of an improved understanding of psychology are all predominantly optimistic. Such views may seem antithetical to modernism's foregrounding of fragmentation, disconnection, incommunicability, and language as in crisis; as well as its proffering of tradition, myth, and difficulty as salves for such predicaments. Yet from another point of view, it is precisely the radical focus on language, psychology, and change that makes the series avant-garde.

Debabelization appeared in another of Ogden's series, Psyche Miniatures. Over a third of the main ('General') series of just under a hundred volumes of these (there was also a 'Medical Series' of at least a further fifteen) was devoted to BASIC, in the form of monographs by Ogden and others, and also translations of classics of World Literature into BASIC. Many of the Psyche Miniatures were written by contributors to the journal *Psyche*, which Ogden had also edited, from 1923 for three decades, the magazine ending in 1952. Indeed, some of the Miniatures contained versions of material previously published in *Psyche*.

This brings us to the final strand of Ogden's many interests: Psychology. *Psyche* was originally entitled the *Psychic Research Quarterly*, but changed its name after only a year to *Psyche: A quarterly review of psychology, in relation to education, psychoanalysis, industry, religion... & c.* This '& c.' in the journal increasingly included language among its broad range of topics (alongside subjects such as entomology, astronomy, anthropology, class, and statistics) from the later 1920s: the same shift we have seen in its Miniatures. Nevertheless, the centre of Ogden's entire project was the psyche, its thought, and the symbolic systems in which that thought was expressed. He took the term 'orthology' from Karl Pearson's *The Grammar of Science* (1892), to designate 'the science of correct symbolism'.[58] Symbolism was how the mind created meaning, and the orthological project of

tongue and lips explained lucidly how language arises at all and related it directly to the senses and affections.' And is said to have influenced Kenneth Burke's gestural theory of expression. See also Jean-Michel Rabaté, 'Joyce and Jolas: Late modernism and early Babelism', *Journal of Modern Literature*, 22:2, Joyce and the Joyceans (Winter, 1998–9), 245–52.

[58] Gordon, *C. K. Ogden*, p. 146, n. 170a.

BASIC was the net with which he hoped to catch 'the meaning of meaning'. Ogden's view of language, in short, was always a psychological one. As he put it in his excellent *ABC of Psychology*, characteristically riffing effortlessly on his literary knowledge: 'the proper study of mankind is "mind"'.[59] In particular it was the psychological effects of language that concerned him—what he sometimes described as 'word magic',[60] and the reason he was so influential on literary thinkers such as I. A. Richards and William Empson. Empson 'put into BASIC' (translation didn't seem the right term for moving a text from one form to another of the same language) two science volumes by Haldane in 1935 for the Psyche Miniatures: *Science and Well-Being*; and *The Outlook of Science*; the latter being selections from *The Inequality of Man* and *Possible Worlds*.

Ogden's work on psychology is too vast a topic to treat further here—not least because, in addition to books like the *ABC*, and the thousands of pages of the journal *Psyche* and its Miniatures, it includes his most enormous venture: The International Library of Psychology, Philosophy, and Scientific Method. This is described further in Chapter 3, in a discussion of psychology's place in To-Day and To-Morrow, among the other human sciences. Meanwhile, the rest of this chapter continues the discussion of science in the series, and its exploration of how to think about science is necessarily to think scientifically about both mind and language.

*   *   *

To-Day and To-Morrow was effectively book-ended by the two major volumes of speculative science popularization explored in this chapter: Haldane's *Daedalus* (1923), which generated the idea for the series, and is a key reason why science is so central to it; and Bernal's *The World, the Flesh and the Devil* (1929)—not exactly the last volume, but near the end: probably ninety-second out of 110; and a comparably mind-bending work, which has resonated with other writers and scientists.

What is impressive about these volumes is their speculative energy and adventurousness; their thinking of 'Possible Worlds'; not just sketches of possible futures, but a sense that the scientist's and intellectual's duty is to speculate on future possibilities; to ensure that human potential isn't wasted just because no one thought of a key invention or discovery or solution; or because they kept pusillanimously to traditional beliefs rather than trusting the insights of the new sciences. Haldane and Bernal thus sketch out the high stakes that the series was playing for. If the other volumes couldn't all live up to their high-octane high standards, many certainly realized the nature of the debate they were taking part

[59] C. K. Ogden, *ABC of Psychology* (London: Kegan Paul, 1929; third edition 1934), 33. The *ABC* was a revised version of his *The Meaning of Psychology* (New York: Harper & Brothers, 1926), but this passage was an addition.
[60] See Gordon, *C. K. Ogden*, pp. 45, 79.

in, and often referred to Haldane's inaugurative volume. My aim in the coda to this section is to draw from them the paradigm for the series; which is what makes it especially significant, and especially relevant to modernism and modernist studies. At its most general level this is a belief that science and technology will transform our world(s) utterly in the future in multifarious ways. As such it was a widespread view; a truism, even—especially after the experience of the First World War (the intellectual aftermath of which is the subject of Chapter 2). But it is the complex ways in which the writers develop that idea, which make the series cumulatively so distinctive. We can pick out seven aspects of the impact of science outlined in *Daedalus* which mark out the terrain of many of the subsequent volumes, and which are then re-articulated in *The World, the Flesh and the Devil*. Haldane's and Bernal's point of view is one that is foundational for twentieth-century thought across many disciplines.

First, and most tangibly, science is seen by most of the To-Day and To-Morrow writers as providing the main engine of change; and this change ramifies out across our entire experience. A particular scientific idea or discovery might enable new forms of relationship to our world; new experiences. (Our awareness of the Anthropocene makes it hard—perhaps foolhardy—to entertain such thoughts as inspirational in the way they were for these 1920s visionaries). New technologies in turn enable new forms of industry, economics, politics, creativity, destructiveness.

Second, as many of the writers of To-Day and To-Morrow point out, the pace of change, and especially technological change, is accelerating. That was not quite the cliché in the 1920s that it is in the twenty-first century; we are used to more up to the minute formulations like Moore's Law about the exponential increase of computer processing power. But, as in Anthony Giddens' analysis (discussed in the Introductions), one of the main shifts in modernity is from a view of history as essentially static to one that is dynamic. It was assumed that the natural state of affairs was for things to remain the same, barring occasional cataclysmic events— acts of God, or wars. Modernity assumes they will change, rapidly. Postmodernity and neoliberalism assume they will change increasingly rapidly; that 'innovation' is the new stasis. Or rather, the new 'disruption'. As that term has gained traction for paradigm-shifting entrepreneurship, it becomes apparent that the commercial disruptors achieve their mastery of the universe by disrupting everybody else's lives. That is, people experience change as passive victims (as they lose their jobs, their local businesses and services) rather than as agents.

Whereas (third), though To-Day and To-Morrow's authors understood the disruptive potential of mechanization, they could still see it as freeing up time for the pursuit of alternative agencies. By the same token, the progress of science enabled them to see humans as having more agency in their history than before; as having more effect on their destiny than religions, diseases, natural disasters and so on. According to this view, the future is more under our control than before. In Christianized parts of Africa today it's considered impious to use the future tense without adding 'God willing'; as if it would be presumptuous of man to trespass on the divine omniscience; or to dare to make plans that might not comply with God's plans. The Arabic tag '*insha'Allah*' works in the same way. Critics of instrumental reason might say yes, it is man's attempt to control the world that has got us into this mess of global warming, pollution, overpopulation and food crisis. But they should recognize that only better science and technology are going to enable more responsible custodianship of the planet now, rather than any amount of prostration in prayer or trusting in the will of God.

This is not to claim that awareness of how science and technology have enhanced human agency dates from the 1920s. I. F. Clarke notes of nineteenth-century futuristic utopias that 'From the evidence supplied by contemporary technology the writers look forward to a future completely changed by the powers of applied science'.[61] He sees this conviction as completed by Darwinism. However, in the Einsteinian realm of the twentieth century, the scientific picture of the universe had shifted dramatically; an effect which in turn altered perceptions of the power of science, not only to understand the world, but to change it. Science and technology seemed humanity's best hope.

Fourth, a new belief in human agency implies transformations not only in religion but in politics too. What most of the writers are anticipating in the series is not the will of god; natural disaster; apocalypse; pandemics; but the scientific and technological developments that will help humanity negotiate such things. A scientifically-orientated politics such as Haldane's is representative of the period and the series in steadfastly opposing religion. Some of the To-Day and To-Morrow contributors were or became Marxist, like Haldane and Bernal, and many were left-inclined. Yet whereas Marxism sees the future as the inevitably unfolding process of class struggle, they often seem to be looking beyond class-war.[62] Some, like Vera Brittain and Dora Russell, are very much concerned with the struggle for women's rights or pacifism. But the general assumption is that what will make the future seem most different is technology rather than politics—if only because (as in Brittain's *Halcyon*, discussed in Chapter 2) technology effects changes in labour and society which make political changes feasible. We may respond (as indeed Bertrand Russell did respond in *Icarus*) that technology is always politicized. But the sense of science as the most pervasive agent of change pervades the series, especially in these volumes, which suggest that the politics of the future will be barely recognizable to a twentieth- or even twenty-first century mindset.

---

[61] I. F. Clarke, *The Tale of the Future: From the beginning to the present day* (London: Library Association, 1961), 13.

[62] For instance, Cecil Chisholm argues in *Vulcan* that increased production of goods, higher wages, and shorter working hours limit the appeal of Marxism (94).

One reason it is so hard to imagine the future is because science and technology do not just change science, or history, or our mode of living. They also change our modes of thinking and feeling about how we live (this is the fifth aspect). It is hard enough to imagine new machines or new bionic implants. The difficulty of imagining how such developments would alter our thinking, or our imaginations, is of another order of magnitude. As Bernal puts it: 'to predict even the shapes that men would adopt if they would make of *themselves* a harmony of form and sensation must be beyond imagination' (47). New technoscience will not just change our way of thinking about science, but about *every* aspect of life—as the internet keeps showing us. The approach to topics which contemporary disciplinary categorizations would place under the arts and humanities, social science, or cultural studies, is the subject of Chapter 3's demonstration of how the series presents this continually broadening application of scientific approaches to the field of the human—what if we were to apply technological invention to the body? To consider clothes in terms of evolution? To think systematically about sleep? Significant claims were increasingly being made by the emergent human sciences of sociology, anthropology, psychology, psycho-analysis, and economics to be able to identify laws and quantifiable patterns in natural and social phenomena. The impact of science on the series is thus not confined to the volumes on scientific subjects. Other volumes, covering topics such as society, education, history, warfare, reproduction and eugenics, longevity, prosthesis, travel, communication and so on, tend to register the impact of scientific and technological developments upon those aspects of human life. (Conversely, the volumes on science and technology do not restrict themselves to advances in scientific knowledge, but consider its applications and their effects on life and society.)

But the concept of the human sciences comes under pressure once the concept of the human comes under pressure. We saw in the Introductions how the series engages with the view that genetics, specifically through Eugenic intervention, would be able to take over from the evolutionary process, and modify human nature. Haldane and Bernal envision more immediate genetic or surgical modifications. The argument is extended in Chapter 4's analysis of how the machine changes the human—not just our bodies but our minds.

One mode of thinking subject to transformation by science is futurology. Many of To-Day and To-Morrow's writers on scientific topics don't just prophesy about science; they also have something to say about science transforming prophecy. The futurology of science in this series is thus bound up with the science of futurology. The historian of futurology is likely to see things differently. In retrospect, futurology is likely to seem the accomplice of pseudo-science. There are two routes by which hypotheses (including those about the future) can end up labelled as pseudo-scientific: one where ideas run so counter to scientific orthodoxy that they are denounced at the time (as with many 'alternative' remedies such as homoeopathy nowadays); the other where ideas that are widely accepted by the scientific community at one time are later discredited as paradigms shift (as with phrenology or eugenics). Whether eccentric compared to the paradigm of the day, or adhering slavishly to an idea later discarded, past futurology all too often appears as pseudo-scientific wishful thinking.

But the writers in the series felt it was now possible to speculate about the future based on something other than history or religion or metaphysics. Scientific prediction enables a new way of imagining the future; and introduces a new reliability into the proceedings; as we saw in C. A. Mace's *Sibylla; or, The Revival of Prophecy* (1926). Mace's point is not that classical Greek sibylline divination is making a comeback—prophecy's days in that form are past—but that science enables prophecy to make a comeback in an entirely new form: as what we would nowadays call forecasting or foresight or horizon scanning.[63] Making prophecy more scientific will not make it infallible; but at least it can be based on something demonstrable and testable and improveable. Science transforms prophecy from vatic vision, based on belief in gods, fate, or a stable tradition, to the formulation, testing, and improving of hypotheses. Modern foresight thus needs to sound scientific, rationalist, and evidence-based in order to be more credible than the products of visionary inspiration and oracular pronouncements. This is bound up with the belief that it is scientific rationality that is going to be the chief agent of change in the future; and that since science itself proceeds in rational steps, working out the direction it is likely to take, at least in the short to medium term, is not difficult; or at least is less difficult than with unpredictable humans or natural phenomena. We saw Karl Popper roundly reject this view of predictability, which he associated with Marxism's false belief in historical inevitability.[64] But it was widely held between the wars; often resulting from a sense that the new science was opening up new vistas of possibility. Once Einstein had theorized that matter could be converted into vast quantities of energy, one didn't have to be Einstein to realize that that energy could be used as a power source or in weapons. But the transformative effect of science on foresight goes further than using science to predict the development of more science; or of equipping future-thinking with a scientific method. The challenge was (and is) to imagine a futurology of the future.

That was point six. The seventh and final aspect concerns the rhetorics of speculation: how the future is represented. What were the essential modes of thinking about the future in the past? In addition to the static conception of history, there was a variation on it, the cyclic. The cycles might be seasons, generations, reigns, dynasties, eras; but the principle is that what goes around comes round, again; any variation is recuperated as just confirming the

---

[63] See the discussion of *Sibylla* in the first half of the Introductions, and of today's professionalized futurology in the second.

[64] See the Introductions, 51–52.

established pattern. You could make predictions based on precedent; or on nature, such as someone's character as understood through the lens of the theory of humours. But that too assumes human nature is essentially static.

Otherwise, there was prophecy. You could work yourself up into a trance or a frenzy, and convince others, and possible yourself too, that you were having a vision; that the god or goddess was speaking through you. Best to speak in riddles, so you can't be proven wrong. You don't have to be Nietzsche to feel that vatic prophecy is at best delusional and at worst a con-trick; and most major religions have given it up; or at least confined their prophecies to the afterlife, where they can't be tested. Of course other than these modes of foresight there has always been at least an element of pragmatic calculation, or strategy; working out how to outwit your opponent in battle, or in chess, or in business. But again the techniques are based on an assumed essential human nature, and only give short-term foresight. They might help you win the war but don't tell you what the peace was going to be like.

Berman's account of modernity's future-orientation is good on its origins in liberal capitalism and socialism's critique of it, but has little to say about its rhetorical strategies. What To-Day and To-Morrow's cumulative futurology make clear is how clean the break was not just from pre-modern ways of thinking about the future, but ways of speaking and writing about it. The conclusion to this chapter extrapolates from the series a set of general theses about the relations between science and imagination in the twentieth century. Chapter 2 develops this argument, exploring the poetics of post-war futurology in the series. First, though, we continue our investigation into the volumes on science, looking at how, in the one devoted to physics, the science of matter becomes inextricable from questions of mind and language.

Matter, Consciousness, Time, and Language

We're so used to scientific advances being the result of double-blind trials and reiterative assays, 'evidence-based' medicine, or statistical modelling, that we might risk forgetting how, at the beginning of the twentieth century, scientific genius, especially as personified by Einstein, seemed to work by a kind of poetic or metaphoric imagination. Imagining riding on a beam of light, say, rather than designing experiments to measure the speed of light in differing situations. Scientists today certainly still speculate about future developments in their fields. Indeed, discussions of innovative science are inescapably future-orientated. But— unless they work in the already abstract and poetic world of theoretical physics— the researchers are perhaps less likely to think of such speculation as science.

Mace's *Sibylla* begins with just the question touched on at the end of the last section: 'Can Prophecy be a science?', which it sees as cognate with the idea that

'Science, at any rate, appears to aim at prophecy'. For Mace, as for H. G. Wells, the verifiability of a hypothesis depends on its predictive accuracy. *Sibylla* has some interest for literary historians too; it cites science-fiction texts by Capek, and Wells, and perhaps Odle, as discussed by Patrick Parrinder.[65] But it is a rather one-dimensional volume. Its main idea is that what it calls 'scientific management', essentially Taylorism, and 'Industrial Psychology', will be able to plan social developments that are based on science rather than political or theological drives.

Such ideas of prophecy and temporality are given a different twist in one of the most interesting volumes, L. L. Whyte's *Archimedes; or, The Future of Physics* (1927), which is the main focus of this section. Lancelot Law Whyte (1896-1972) had a curious career, split between being a theoretical physicist, financier, industrial engineer, and author. He later supported Frank Whittle in his development of the jet engine. He had deferred his university education to enlist in the Army in 1915, and had served as an artillery officer during the Battle of the Somme. But he was a young Cambridge physicist of 30 or 31, who had been working under Rutherford, when C. K. Ogden recruited him to write for the series. In the later 1920s he spent time in Germany, where he met Einstein and discussed his work.[66]

In *Archimedes*, it becomes clear that it isn't just that his vision of the future is based on advances in the physical sciences; but also that our sense of time, and our place in it, have been altered by these ideas:

> We stand at the eve of a new epoch. Physics, biology, and psychology are converging towards a scientific synthesis of unprecedented importance, whose influence on thought and social custom will be so profound that it will mark a stage in human evolution.   (9)

Besides the accuracy with which he predicts the scientific situation of our brave 'neuro-' world, there are two striking features here. First, the excitement at the sense of old disciplinary boundaries being swept away. It is comparable to the argument put forward by Haldane in *Daedalus*, that mathematical Physics is about to be invaded by Physiology (15-16). This idea is borne out in other volumes in the series devoted to science. *Prometheus; or, Biology and the Advancement of Man* (1925), by H. S. Jennings, starts with an interesting idea of how science develops; how a theory is constructed to account for observed facts; but how then more and more facts accrue which don't fit the theory, but are ignored for as long

---

[65] The reference to 'clockwork' in *Sibylla* (16) in this context of science fiction is the possible allusion to E. V. Odle's *The Clockwork Man* (1923). See Patrick Parrinder, 'Robots, Clones and Clockwork Men: The post-human perplex in early twentieth-century literature and science', *Interdisciplinary Science Reviews*, 34:1 (March 2009), 56-67.
[66] Lancelot Law Whyte, *Focus and Diversions* (London: The Cresset Press, 1963). On pp. 95-6 he gives a succinct review of *Archimedes*. His conversations with Einstein are discussed on p. 102. I am grateful for research assistance from Elise Schraner in tracing this information, and for providing annotations on the text of *Archimedes*. See his obituary by O. J. Whitrow, 'L. L. Whyte 1896-1972', *British Journal for the Philosophy of Science*, 24 (1973), 91-2.

as possible, until the theory collapses, and a new one has to be substituted (6-7). It is effectively Thomas Kuhn's notion of paradigm shifts a third of a century before Kuhn formulated it in *The Structure of Scientific Revolutions* (1962). Jennings doesn't explicitly make the point about the new paradigm involving a fusion of the traditionally separated realms of physics, chemistry, and biology. On the other hand, *Hermes; or, The Future of Chemistry*, by T. W. Jones, simply moves between the three, looking at the organic chemistry of fossil fuels and fibre production; considering transport in relation to energy; and then moving on to the biochemistry of nutrition and the endocrine system.

In many ways Whyte and Haldane were proved right. Disciplines such as Genetics, Molecular Biology, or Neurology have been precisely fusions of the three disciplines; though one might equally see the transformation as a translation of biological science into physical and chemical properties and processes; and note (with Kuhn) that these disciplines have fused with a fourth, the codes and networks of computer science, which contributors to the series could not foresee. This is where Whyte is also heading in *Archimedes*—though his argument leads him to the limits of rational foresight as well:

> We really have to deal in human beings with a whole series of forms of behaviour of increasing complexity and integration: reflex and instinctive actions, deliberate activity, and finally the intuitive whole-natured creative functioning which leads to ends which could not have been intellectually foreseen. To each of these must correspond a certain type of awareness, and in my view, a brain process of a definite degree of complexity. [....]   (68-9)

This is a voice in a dialogue: 'the physicist', who is debating with 'a psychologist'. It is a little disconcerting here, since the separation of voices as speaking for their disciplines seems at odds with the argument that the disciplines are converging.

But Whyte's argument, or at least his physicist's, is that the consciousness the psychologist studies corresponds exactly to the brain-processes that a physical scientist would study. Indeed, he goes on to suggest that 'we may be able to infer from the structure of the central nervous system of an organism what sort of awareness it can experience' (69).[67] And that is exactly what he means by convergence: the electrical and chemical processes in the brain account for, and predict, the mental experiences of that brain.

It is, as his voices agree, a determinist and physicalist form of the behaviourist position (though it reinserts consciousness back into the picture from which the behaviourists sought to airbrush it, as correlated with the neural structures it expresses). As such it is diametrically opposed to the argument of another volume in the series, *Gallio; or, The Tyranny of Science* (1927), by the journalist

---

[67] A position famously countered by Thomas Nagel, in 'What Is It Like to Be a Bat?', *Philosophical Review*, 83:4 (October 1974), 435–50.

and popular science writer J. W. N. Sullivan.[68] Arguing against I. A. Richards' concern in *Science and Poetry* that 'poetry may be destroyed by science' (25), Sullivan mounts an essentially Idealist argument against scientific materialism as incapable of addressing anything beyond matter, such as metaphysics: 'All that depends on the *structure* of reality belongs to physics, including other universes than ours. All that depends upon the *substance* of reality for ever lies outside physics'.[69] Whereas for Whyte, that 'substance of reality' is a product of the structure of reality, and the assertion that it is different is an unfounded piece of mysticism.

So far, so predictable, as a determinist literary critic might put it. A clear case of Idealism vs. Materialism; Cartesian dualism vs. reductive determinism. If the debate sounds theological, that is how Winifred Holtby presents it in her witty volume, *Eutychus; or, The Future of the Pulpit* (1928). Though, from another point of view, she extends the idea of preaching to include all forms of belief and advocacy. As the young Bloomsburyite, Anthony, explains to a churchman:

> we have the two extremes, those who deny the reality of matter and those who deny the reality of anything save matter; and in between them lie an infinite gradation of sects demonstrating the imperfect separation of natural and ethical philosophies. Each sect has its appropriate pulpit, adorned by scientists and pseudo-scientists, pseudo-theologians, and theologians. From these pulpits are preached the Health Cults, originating mostly in this country and in Germany, the Hypnotic Cults, originating chiefly in India and the Far East, the Vegetarian Cults and Simple Life Cults originating in Welwyn Garden City. Sometimes all these are mingled; sometimes they are treated in turn.   (78)

There are two ways in which Whyte's argument in *Archimedes* becomes more interesting than a rehearsal of a debate about dualism, as he engages with the nature of matter and the nature of time. First, his argument about convergence has the opposite effect from the normal mechanistic one. Instead of saying that matter and mind are the same thing—because mind is only brain-structure—he feels that the new physics reveals that neither was the thing we thought it was.

---

[68] On Sullivan, see David Bradshaw, 'The Best of Companions', *Review of English Studies*, 47 (1996), 188–206, 352–68. Sullivan's own *Aspects of Science* (London: R. Cobden-Sanderson, 1923) puts a case closer to the synthesis between science and metaphysics which appealed to many contributors to the series.

[69] J. W. N. Sullivan, *Gallio; or, The Tyranny of Science* (1927), p. 37. Though, like other contributors, he sees the New Physics as approaching metaphysics, arguing that, if Richards is right: 'I suggest that the poets who are so depressed by law and order should study besides the theory of relativity, Quantum Theory. They will find there much that is, at present, agreeably miraculous. But one need not fly to miracles to get rid of the bug-bear of "unalterable law". It is only necessary to understand the true status of the unalterable laws, and this is just what relativity theory enables us to do' (30). Gallio was the Roman proconsul mentioned in *Acts* xviii 12–17. When the Jews bring Paul to him to be judged, he refuses on the grounds that his jurisdiction was only over immoral or criminal deeds, rather than questions of 'words and names, and of your law'. See Ali Wood's discussion of *Gallio* in 'Darwinism, Biology, and Mythology in the "Today and Tomorrow" series, 1923–1929', *Interdisciplinary Science Reviews*, 34:1 (March 2009), 22–31.

Cartesian dualism relies on a commonsensical notion of matter as inert, solid, inanimate stuff. But this is exactly the view undermined by atomic theory, quantum mechanics, the theory of gravitation and relativity. Matter is mostly insubstantial, dynamic, neither just one thing nor exactly in one place. Even the subatomic particles behave in such strangely dual ways as to seem no longer like anything solid or material, but instead something that can act as much like waves as particles. With the famous equation $E = mc^2$, Einstein had shown how mass could be thought of as equivalent to energy. Whyte pushes this even further, arguing that features of matter that are traditionally thought of as purely aspects of its structure—attraction, say, or the number of electrons an atom can have in each 'shell', could equally be described as forms of intention or 'conscious purpose'. This might seem like its own form of mysticism. But what he means is that the new physics reveals matter as really 'process'; as is consciousness. What he wants to do is break down the old dualism between 'mind and matter' by presenting matter as already characterized by the kinds of processes that characterize consciousness too. For him there is no essential difference between the energy level of an atom changing, and what happens when a synapse fires. Conversely, because of this equivalence, consciousness, purposiveness, and behaviour aren't quite what we thought either. Because, as he says, they take many different forms, some of them so basic and instinctive as scarcely to be conscious at all. If this is the psychologist speaking, it isn't quite the Freudian model of the unconscious on offer. In a way it's closer to how his contemporary, D. H. Lawrence, understood the mind.

Lawrence's objection to Freudian psychoanalysis makes this clear: namely, that the desires it finds in the unconscious aren't different from conscious desires. Indeed, they were conscious desires that were then banished from consciousness. They are thus too tarnished by the intellect for Lawrence, who writes:

> Trigant Burrow says that Freud's *unconscious* does but represent our conception of our conscious sexual life as this latter exists in a state of repression. Thus Freud's unconscious amounts practically to no more than our repressed incest impulses.[70]

Whereas Lawrence is the advocate of the pre-conscious rather than what he sees as this post-conscious view of mind:

> We have actually to go back to our own unconscious. But not to the unconscious which is the inverted reflection of our ideal consciousness. We must discover, if we can, the true unconscious, where our life bubbles up in us, prior to any mentality [....][71]

---

[70] D. H. Lawrence, *Psychoanalysis and the Unconscious*, in *Fantasia of the Unconscious* and *Psychoanalysis and the Unconscious* (Harmondsworth: Penguin, 1983), 206.
[71] Lawrence, *Psychoanalysis and the Unconscious*, p. 212.

That paradox, of trying to 'discover', and thus to be conscious of, a nature that precedes consciousness, was the challenge Lawrence's art repeatedly set itself. From one point of view it might seem antithetical to Whyte's account of the world, in which even the inanimate can be thought of as conscious. Yet Whyte's view of consciousness as something that is only different in degree rather than kind from unconscious physical processes shares Lawrence's sense of the inhuman but vital processes that underlie human experience.[72] And, when he discusses 'Creative aspiration', his language and position are surprisingly close to Lawrence's: 'It seems that in some matters our organic body is wiser than ourselves, or rather wiser than our very immature consciousness' (77-8).

To cite Lawrence is not to imply that Whyte was aligning himself with anti-rationalistic art as opposed to mainstream science, but to indicate that the views of the era's scientific pioneers were transforming the mechanistic, Newtonian understanding of science into something that sounded much more like a paradoxical and metaphorical idealism or mysticism; and also that literary and expository writers were quick to recognize this.[73] As another To-Day and To-Morrow author was to put it, wondering about the mystifying nature of sub-atomic matter:

> Our greatest scientists like Einstein, Jeans, Schrödinger, Planck, Eddington, and innumerable others believe that its dominant characteristic is consciousness. 'Consciousness is fundamental', declares Professor Max Planck. 'I regard matter as derivative from consciousness'. This is a vastly different conception from that of the old mechanistic type of science which sought to derive consciousness from inert matter. And here we come to the heart of our investigation. The whole cosmos is derivative from, and related to, a universal and absolute consciousness, and man, as a conscious being, is capable of appreciating this fundamental unity, and can fully realize his own nature only when his relationship to the Absolute is conscious and harmonious.[74]

This might be assumed to be from a book about physics, but in fact it is from Ralph de Pomerai's *Aphrodite; or, The Future of Sexual Relationships* (1931). But that is the point: just as it seemed reasonable for a humanist to move from sexuality to quantum physics, it seemed reasonable to a physicist like Whyte to move from matter to consciousness. Tempting though it is to joke about 'atttraction' or 'getting physical', the To-Day and To-Morrow series helps us see how such views and rhetorical tropes were by no means as eccentric as they might appear to

---

[72] For a further discussion of this contrast between Freud and Lawerence, see Max Saunders, 'Lawrence, Freud and Civilisation's Discontents', *D. H. Lawrence Review*, 27:2–3 (1997–8), 269–88.

[73] See for example Michael Whitworth, *Einstein's Wake*.

[74] Ralph de Pomerai, *Aphrodite; or, The Future of Sexual Relationships* (1931), 87. Of the scientists he cites here, James Jeans was also a contributor to the series: see his *Eos; or, The Wider Aspects of Cosmogony* (1928), discussed below.

us at first glance. They are instances of the mobility of ideas and sharing of metaphors across fields described by Michael Whitworth; and signs of the consequent 'domaining' analysed by Marilyn Strathern as concepts signify differently as they shift contexts.[75] Gillian Beer writes of the 'transformations undergone when ideas enter other genres or different reading groups, the destabilizing of knowledge once it escapes from the initial group of co-workers, its tendency to mean more and other than could have been foreseen'.[76] Such conceptual agility helps us understand the unfamiliar, the mobile metaphors enabling the translation of the unknown into the known. (What is an atom? A plum pudding? A mini-solar system? Waves? A jumping between 'shells'? Clouds of probability? String?) One thing To-Day and To-Morrow helps us see more clearly, in its multiple interconnections between different fields, together with its futurology, is how such improvisatory metaphorical thinking is itself a process of thought experiment; one which is integral to our thinking about the future, and conducive to invention and discovery.

The reason the relation between matter and consciousness mattered so deeply to the intelligentsia in this period was that it was not an abstract philosophical or theoretical question, but a political one too. The idea, fundamental to Marx, that matter determines consciousness, was elaborated into the concept of 'dialectical materialism' first by Lenin, and then by Lukács at about the same time To-Day and To-Morrow was launched, and was energetically debated throughout the Third International.[77] Seen from this point of view, it is the opposite of a mystical view of the physical world, but rather, a rationalist, secular, and indeed anti-religious view.

It is also a medical and therapeutic view in the series. In *Pygmalion; or, The Doctor of the Future* (1925), R. McNair Wilson proposes what he calls, unconvincingly, 'a new law of medicine' (31), that instead of seeing a symptom as 'a sign of disease' (6), we should think in terms of stimulus and response, and realize that 'symptoms are signs not of reaction to *disease, but of altered reaction to life, occasioned by the presence of disease*' (13). The thesis becomes a little more persuasive when he moves from physical examples such as wounds to various kinds of stimuli which aren't diseases but produce disease-like symptoms: unaccustomed heat, noise, light. Where it becomes decidedly more interesting, and characteristic of its time, is when he then considers psychological techniques by which we are able to reduce anxieties related to unbearable stimulation: *esprit de corps*; psycho-analysis; faith healing. He notes that it is not just the sense organs, but the nervous system, which can become hyper-sensitized, and imagines that the

---

[75] See the Introductions, n. 74.
[76] Gillian Beer, *Open Fields: Science in cultural encounter* (Oxford: Oxford University Press, 1996), 115.
[77] I'm very grateful to Neil Vickers for suggesting this parallel. See Lukács, *History and Class Consciousness: Studies in Marxist dialectics* [1923], trans. by Rodney Livingstone (London: Merlin Press, 1971).

doctor of the future 'will possess, in all human probability, the secret of the desensitization of nerves'; and so will be able to cure 'a vast host of men and women...labelled at present as sufferers from "heart disease", "nervous disease", "neurasthenia", "hysteria", and so forth—the population of sufferers which throngs the spas and the health resorts' (55-6). Readers of Ford Madox Ford's *The Good Soldier* take notes. The import of this shift in perspective is to align medicine with the new physical sciences and its scepticism about dualism. '[T]he age of materialism is past' (63), says McNair Wilson, and medicine needs to move from materialist specializations to a more humanistic approach, and no longer separate body and mind. Here, as in other volumes, there is an optimism about the liberating and transformational powers of the human mind. Since it can generate its own stimuli without reference to the material world, man can learn to use his mind to develop his nature.

Though *Pygmalion* is not without interest (dare one say, primarily of a symptomatic kind), like the other medical volumes in the series it is disappointing compared to the science volumes. *The Conquest of Cancer* (1925) by H. W. S. Wright, has little to offer apart from education, early diagnosis, and hope. It was based on a lecture, and even with the addition of an introduction by F. G. Crookshank, comes in at just over fifty pages—one of the shortest volumes. The other contributions by medics get led astray by the period hobbyhorses of race and evolution. Crookshank wrote several books for Ogden. His *The Mongol in Our Midst* (1924) is not about medicine, except insofar as it takes the medical condition of Down's Syndrome to be a form of evolutionary 'throwback'—an idea which is then used as the basis for theory or racial evolution so preposterous as to make it difficult to work out whether it is more insulting to the disabled, to Africans, Asians, or Caucasians, or to the Gorillas, Orang Utangs, and Chimpanzees from which he argues those races respectively derive.[78] A second volume by Crookshank was advertised in 1925—*Æsculapius; or, Disease and the Man*—but appears not to have been published.[79]

The only other medical volume is, if possible, even stranger. *Hygieia; or, Disease and Evolution* (1926), by visiting prison syphilologist Burton Peter Thom, was published only in the US series. It has an unexceptionable argument about disease being an essential factor in the evolutionary process. 'The struggle of mankind with the myriad legions of disease is a biologic epic that has never been told', he writes.[80] But this leads him into prophecies as baseless as they are counter-intuitive and contradictory. 'Disease will disappear' because man will reach 'an absolute immunity' (90), he says. But also that 'disease will be conquered

---

[78] The expanded edition (London: Kegan Paul, Trench and Trübner, 1931) was given short shrift in review by leading zoologist Solly Zuckerman, 'Apes, Idiots, and Men', *Spectator* (13 June 1931), 939–40.

[79] See Appendix B.

[80] Burton Peter Thom, *Hygieia; or, Disease and Evolution* (New York: Dutton, 1926), 6.

by the mind of man long before his body is rendered immune to it' (90-1). Despite this, he thinks 'That the increase of the population will within a few centuries tax the food resources of the earth is improbable; it may even be said to be impossible' (104-5). After such defective visions, it comes as something of a relief to fall back on the conclusion's queasy mixture of mystical hope and familiar eugenicist assumptions about degeneracy: 'the passing of disease will bring about the passing of crime and vice' (106). Given the significant medical advances of the period, such as those largely resulting from the war, in surgery and neurology, it is unfortunate that Ogden was not able to commission volumes that did justice to the field and future of medicine.

The view of matter and mind as interrelated rather than antithetical is expressed by a number of other contributors. To some extent it derives from the Bergsonian notions of the *élan vital* or creative evolution—the hope that spirit can will itself into new forms and potentialities. In discussions of the biological sciences, this Bergsonianism is combined with a neo-Lamarckian disbelief that random mutations alone can account for the directions evolution takes. In *Galatea: or, The Future of Darwinism* (1927), W. Russell Brain asks:

> Is it not possible that the ancestors of man began to stand upright on their legs, not because their legs suddenly altered, nor because there was a shortage of trees, but because they were pioneers? To suppose that all evolutionary change is the effect either of germinal mutation or of environmental influence is a pure assumption. Only this assumption prevents us from believing that there occurs in nature a novelty of another kind, which is of the spirit that bloweth where it listeth and the manner of whose coming is known to no man—not even the biologist.
>
> The idea that initiative is a factor of importance in evolution will certainly be contested.   (46-7)

He concedes that contemporary biology had no clue how changes to an individual's body could be 'mirrored in the germinal material' (59)—that is, how characteristics such as might be acquired by an individual could then get into the genes to be passed on. Brain thinks it possible that the problem is a product of our mode of thinking (60). The series testifies to a resurgence of interest in Lamarckianism at this time; but also to the emergence of the work which would eventually discredit it. Haldane was one of the mathematically minded young Cambridge biologists associated with embryologist Joseph Needham who, in Steven Rose's words: 'strove to unite three biological sciences that had become divorced earlier in the century: evolution, genetics and embryology (soon renamed "development")'.[81] Together they worked in the 1930s to bring

---

[81] Steven Rose, 'How to Get Another Thorax', *London Review of Books*, 38:17 (8 September 2016), 15–17 (15). It was Julian Huxley who provided the classic account of the scientific history of this development in *Evolution* (1942).

'Mendelian genetics and natural selection together in what became known as the Modern or neo-Darwinian Synthesis, a comprehensive theory of evolution which persisted throughout much of the rest of the twentieth century.'[82]

Though Brain's biological ideas read as pseudo-science from our perspective, they lead him into a discussion about modes of conceptualization that is instructive in relation both to popular science writing like Whyte's, and to modernist ideas of art, architecture, design, time, and the abstract. 'Two such abstractions of the greatest biological importance are form and function', he says; 'Form, especially such form as is visible to the naked eye, is much more easily dealt with than func-tion' (61-2). The differences is that 'Function involves duration; duration has been abstracted from form' (66); 'Form possesses extension in space, but it has been divorced by thought from the flow of time. Function is, therefore, as a conception immensely fuller than form' (67).

> Our minds feel at home in dealing with form. Our habits of thought have been built upon our experience of inanimate objects, the form of which can often for practical purposes be regarded as unchanging. We therefore tend to look upon form as reality and function as an elusive activity generated in some way by form. We hold fast to the apparently stable in the changing world of life. We do not recognize that the apparent stability is a construction of our own minds and that in the living organism form is more remote from reality than function.   (68)

Like other volumes on science, or interested in scientific developments, *Galatea* comments on how the paradigm shift occurring in physics ripples outwards to affect other bodies of thought:

> The Mechanistic philosophy has to its credit the remarkable achievement of having for a century convinced a large proportion of the most thoughtful people that the more you take away from reality, the truer the account you give of it. Everything, if we only knew enough, could be explained in terms of electrons and their movements. Life, mind, art, beauty and religion are thus phantasmagoria, fleeting eddies set up by the electronic dance.   (88)

The argument is disconcerting here. What starts out sounding like a rejection of materialism, then dematerializes matter into impressionistic fluctuations in something electronic. 'Electronic' presumably means 'of electrons' here; but even so, the phantasmagoric eddies sound relatively immaterial and no longer mechanistic. Brain's argument, close to that of Sullivan's *Gallio*, is that what is false is to reduce all biological functions to those of physics; to treat the animal as all matter and no mind. He says: 'evidence is accumulating that the tyranny of the Mechanistic philosophy is coming to an end' (90). But (as in the writing about

---

[82] Rose, 'How to Get Another Thorax', 15.

physics in the series) the strange new world of particle physics has already disturbed the material world, showing it already to reveal mind and matter as inseparable: 'Mechanism has been shaken to its foundations by the discovery that time and matter are not the all-sufficient raw material of the universe, but merely products of the mind's attitude towards the four-dimensional world of point-events' (90). That is why Brain is so critical of the attitude that space is more important than time, or form than function; and why, for so many intellectuals in the period, Einsteinian physics completely changes the way we think of traditional dichotomies such as mind/matter, mind/body, space/time, or form/function. In working these ideas through, *Galatea* is a good example of the attempt to synthesize the different disciplines that E. O. Wilson would later designate as 'consilience'[83]—an ideal also implied in Brain's aphorism: 'Darwin is the Newton of biology: she still awaits her Einstein' (91).

Returning to Whyte: the second aspect of his rhetorical strategy is a compelling argument about time. This takes us back to that first quotation from *Archimedes*:

> We stand at the eve of a new epoch. Physics, biology, and psychology are converging towards a scientific synthesis of unprecedented importance, whose influence on thought and social custom will be so profound that it will mark a stage in human evolution.   (9-10)

The other striking feature (besides Whyte's excitement about the convergence of disciplines) is what this sentence does with time. One way of describing it would be to say that it seems at odds with the idea of a projection into the future based on current scientific knowledge; since he's arguing that scientific knowledge is about to change so radically that the future it produces will be discontinuous from the past: a new epoch or stage in evolution. Then there's a strange loop in the argument whereby science, which has only recently become able to theorize evolution, itself becomes part of that evolution. Note how he puts in 'social custom' too. That shows how the linkage between thought and evolution might work. For he is not just using 'evolution' in a metaphorical way, applied to the history of ideas (as Dawkins does with his notion of 'memes', say). What he means is that a new way of thinking makes us behave differently, and that could actually impact upon our biological evolution—as when our ancestors decided to leave the forests and become hunter-gatherers and farmers; a period which coincides with the development of larger brains. 'Behaviour', you recall, was the term Whyte used in talking of the congruence between mind and matter. This is another example of that congruence. The evolution of human consciousness is congruent with the evolution of human bodies. Though, in imagining this new epoch, or stage in evolution, isn't he beginning to imagine what would need to be called the 'post-human'?

---

[83] Edward O. Wilson, *Consilience: The unity of knowledge* (New York: Knopf, 1998). See the Conclusion for further discussion of 'confluence' in the series.

Archimedes is permeated by ideas on time in another way. The emphasis on 'process', as a concept that can redescribe the relation between mind and matter, derives from a concern about a problem in post-Einsteinian Physics. Whyte argues that laws of physics still assume a pre-Einsteinian concept of time that has been undermined by Relativity, so their basis needs restating. This is presumably where the title-character comes in (though, unusually for the series, he is not mentioned in the course of the text). Archimedes boasted that, given a long enough lever and a secure fulcrum, he could make the earth move. Whyte's point is that Relativistic physics has done just that: moved the ground it was standing on—and that this might be tantamount to pulling the rug out from under your own feet.

In fact Whyte poses two related arguments about why time needs to be rethought. One is that Relativity has revealed that time is no longer the fixed, regular measure of events and processes that it was taken to be in Newtonian mechanics. The other is that classic scientific laws required that processes be reversible. If a force makes a mass accelerate, an opposite force will make it decelerate, and so on. Such a principle is adequate for traditional mechanics. But Whyte thinks it's wrong that the idea of reversibility has been taken to be a more general requirement for a scientific law, because it doesn't always apply to a science like biology. If light makes a plant grow, for example, putting that plant in the dark won't make it return to its seed. He makes much of this notion of irreversibility, claiming that whereas Newtonian physics assumes processes must be reversible, even the more interesting physical ones often are not—processes involving heat, light, electricity, explosions, collisions, etc.—and that we need new laws to explain these, of which the Newtonian ones will be shown to be an approximate sub-set. These new laws, based on ideas of process, would dissolve the old Cartesian dualism between mind and matter. That is partly what he means when he says he agrees with Haldane that physiology will invade mathematical physics, or at least synthesize with it to produce new science. If it was not yet possible to foresee the detail of such science—which would require computers to elaborate—Whyte nevertheless identifies the area that later twentieth-century theories of Chaos and Complexity would develop.

These ideas of consciousness, time, space and process were fundamental to developments in the arts during the period of modernism. I hope the attempt to tease some of Whyte's ideas out of his use of language gives some sense of why the work in the To-Day and To-Morrow series is of interest to those who study literature as well as the history and philosophy of science. But I also want to demonstrate why literary criticism is indispensable to an approach to such texts.

First, there is one argument, which is either fundamental or trivial depending on your point of view, which is that all science is 'textual', and so amenable to, or requiring, literary analysis. Disturbing though it can still prove to many scientists, such a view is widely accepted in the humanities. But it doesn't get us very far distinguishing between a scientific paper and a book like Whyte's, which is popularizing science, and consciously contributing to a debate about science and its future directions. On three counts a work like *Archimedes* is very different from a Nobel prize-winning piece of research, say. In terms of theme, form, and audience, it is different. The theme of prophecy is ironically un-scientific. The form is consciously literary—especially in the play with Socratic dialogue; or the allusion to Nietzsche's transvaluation of values (77). And the work is addressed to the non-specialist, in clear layman's terms with virtually no technical jargon.

However, these distinctions aren't very precise either, and counter-examples are easily found—such as major scientific works—Darwin's, say—that are intensely literary and addressed to general as well as specialist readers.[84] There are more productive ways in which literary scholars might approach a work such as *Archimedes*. One way, which I have tried to bring out in analysing the passage about a new epoch, is to trace how the language, the shape of the sentence, seems to work through the ideas being explored. That this might sound like the old formalist manoeuvre of saying that the form 'enacts', 'mimes', or even 'embodies' the meaning is perhaps unsurprising. It was Ogden's collaborator, the Cambridge critic I. A. Richards, who founded and named the method of 'Practical Criticism'. Whyte may well have known Richards and his circle too, though he had left Cambridge before Richards' methodology of experiments in 'close-reading' became widely established. Richards' work sought to establish literary criticism as securely as scientific theory, by applying recent developments in psychology, neurology, social science, and linguistic philosophy, to literary questions.[85] Kegan Paul was Richards' publisher; his *Principles of Literary Criticism*—with its grounding of the theory of literary responses in neurology—appeared in Ogden's International Library in 1924, and three of his other books—*Science and Poetry*; *Basic Rules of Reason*; and *Basic in Teaching, East and West*—appeared as Psyche Miniatures in 1926, 1933, and 1935, respectively.

What is at stake in *Archimedes*, however, is something more specific than a superficial echoing of ideas in forms that became a mantra for Practical Criticism, and its transatlantic offspring, the 'New Criticism'. What is arresting about such a passage is that it appears to be working out in terms of the history of human intellectual development the same kind of problem he identifies with regard to time in astronomy and physics: that is, just as he says Physics still bases its laws on a concept of time that it has itself undermined, so the sentence about evolution uses the very concepts of the human and of evolution of its day, to try to imagine the epoch beyond: its tomorrow. Imagining the 'post-human' is not an easy thing for the human to do; though several others writing for the series attempt it, as we have seen: not just Haldane and Bernal, but Fournier d'Albe in *Hephaestus; or, The*

---

[84] See for example Gillian Beer's landmark study of Darwin's literariness, *Darwin's Plots: Evolutionary narrative in Darwin, George Eliot, and nineteenth-century fiction* (London: Routledge & Kegan Paul, 1983).

[85] See for example I. A. Richards, *Principles of Literary Criticism* (London: Kegan Paul, 1924); *Science and Poetry* (London: Kegan Paul, 1926); and *Practical Criticism* (London: Kegan Paul, 1929).

Soul of the Machine, and Macfie in *Metanthropos*. On the other hand, as discussed in the Introductions, others began to worry that we might have inadvertently produced a situation where the species would no longer be able to evolve; would be unable to get beyond the human. F. C. S. Schiller, for example, in *Tantalus; or, The Future of Man* (1924), is the most eloquent exponent of this view. He worries that as we have learned to control our environment and generally outwit our predators, the 'unfit' now survive alongside the 'fit'; and that therefore we shall remain human, all too human, unless we invoke eugenics to replace natural selection with human selection.

But then, in a sense, the problem of thinking beyond human thought is the mirror-image of the problem of language. Language is a human product. But the printed word is not a voice; even if it's presented in inverted commas as speaking in a Platonic dialogue. The human produces non-human words which gesture back towards the human or the post-human. Another way of putting this would be to say that the meaning that Whyte's syntax is trying to mime or enact is that of language's perpetual eluding of the meaning it seeks: as such, it is what literary theorists after Derrida would call a 'deconstructive' move as much as a formalist one. Indeed, his argument about time in post-Einsteinian physics is something of a deconstructive one too, showing how the discipline has undermined its own fundamental concept. That is, perhaps, an anachronistic way of putting it. A more useful account for the history of literature and criticism might be to say that in this kind of discursive response to the new science, one isn't just seeing writing that is energized by the new criticism; but one is also seeing the origins of the post-humanist; since the kind of scepticism and relativism we find in post-structuralism, though they can be traced back to Nietzsche and Marx philosophically, were paralleled by the deconstructing of time, space, and matter in the new physics of the early twentieth century. Which is one reason why popular science writing like this from the period of Modernism in the arts reads so interestingly in our Postmodern times.

This approach might appear to place too much weight on one or two sentences. But it is worth taking seriously for another reason, since it takes us back to Whyte's argument that a particular state of consciousness corresponds to a particular brain process which corresponds to a particular structure of nervous system. Even listening to today's neuroscientists, it remains hard to understand exactly how that leap can be made from anatomical structures and functions to experience and consciousness. As the philosopher Jerry Fodor put it in 2004, with characteristic force and humour, in a review of a novel by Dan Lloyd called— rather ominously—'Radiant Cool: A novel theory of consciousness':

> Nobody has the slightest idea what consciousness is, or what it's for, or how it does what it's for (to say nothing of 'what it's made of') [....] There are several reasons why consciousness is so baffling. For one thing, it seems to be among the chronically unemployed. It's been increasingly clear, since Freud, that

psychological processes of great complexity can be unconscious. The question then arises: what does consciousness add to what unconsciousness can achieve? To put it another way, what mental processes are there that can be performed only because the mind is conscious, and what does consciousness contribute to their performance? Nobody has an answer to this question for any mental process whatever [....] There is, to repeat, no science of consciousness. Nor is there any understanding of what a science of consciousness would be like. Nor is there any understanding of what an account of what a science of consciousness would be like would be like.[86]

Neuroscience has made spectacular advances since then on aspects of consciousness, such as on the electro-chemical processes of memory, and the visualizing of neural networks. Scientists working on the European Union's Human Brain Project may not yet have a science of consciousness, but they certainly have a theory of what such a science would be like. It would be like the digital reconstruction of part of a rat's brain (which is also being attempted), only cleverer. Fodor would doubtless disagree that even a digital reconstruction of a complete human brain would not provide a theory of consciousness, just a model that may or may not demonstrate properties we might want to label consciousness. But he is reviewing a novel in the passage above. There may be no science of consciousness yet, but there is certainly an art of consciousness, or a literature of consciousness; and never was literature more a literature of consciousness than in the 1920s, when the novel was preoccupied with the 'stream'—or process—'of consciousness', and interior monologue. With the new physics of the early twentieth century fusing the matter and consciousness that Cartesian dualism had separated, it is unsurprising that a writer like Joyce was interested in a series like To-Day and To-Morrow (as we shall see in Chapter 6). Whyte's argument about how matter and consciousness are inextricable may be hard to grasp in neuroscience; but where we can grasp it is in writing. For writing is a perfect example of something neither exactly material nor exactly mental, but a fusion of the two. It is by reading someone's writing that we can infer their state of consciousness, without having to have recourse to their brain scans. *Archimedes* is very conscious of words, of language, of literariness. A work that is conscious of its allusions to classical scientists and classical and later philosophers, is surely, or at least is arguably, conscious of its own status as a work of language. In a crucial passage from the chapter about 'Physics and Mind', Whyte explicitly considers words. Here, again, he's arguing against the reductive form of behaviourism that refuses to read behaviour as evidence of consciousness:

Eventually we must expect to be able to give a complete scheme of all organic behaviour in terms of the organic processes and their laws, but none the less it

---

[86] Jerry Fodor, 'You Can't Argue with a Novel', *London Review of Books* (4 March 2004), 30–1 (31).

will remain a great deal more convenient in some cases to refer to what happens to human beings by using words that suggest their conscious experience.   (69)

Whyte was to continue his anti-dualistic futurological thinking in books such as *The Next Development in Man* (London: The Cresset Press, 1944) and *Everyman Looks Forward* (The Cresset Press, 1946); and his thought about psychology in *The Unconscious Before Freud* (New York: Basic Books, 1960).

Narrativity, Temporality, and Discourse:
Ten Theses on Science and the Arts

Whyte's *Archimedes* exemplifies how the series was committed to verbalizing not just difficult abstract concepts like Relativity or quantum mechanics, but also a spectrum of human characteristics, and practices that generally go without saying, or without saying much: consciousness, sleep, the home, leisure, language, sex, humour, nonsense. Or rather, even where much has been said and written about these everyday life topics, they are not often analysed, nor their futures predicted. (The series' pioneering role in thinking theoretically about everyday life is explored in Chapter 5.)

Whyte's utopian hope that the medium of language will be able to mediate the debates between the arts and sciences reminds us that such discussions can prove as sectarian as any theological dispute. Practitioners in the humanities and the sciences both tend to see their own disciplines as taking priority. For most scientists, it seems axiomatic that their scientific work *precedes* the communication of it as papers or lectures. And for post-Derridean theorists of the humanities it seems axiomatic that there is no intellectual work conceivable outside language. Of course 'language' here is a somewhat flexible concept. It seems more helpful to think of systems of signification. Clearly much thinking can happen in non-verbal systems, such as pictures, patterns, numbers, equations, software code, or music.

The concluding section of this chapter will focus on areas where the contestation of the interface between science and communication might prove most productive, and most relevant to To-Day and To-Morrow. Areas of narrativity and temporality; of the ways in which science could be seen as the product of social and discursive construction; and the idea of discourse itself, and the tropes it uses, as sites where sciences and humanities can be seen to shape each other.

The books already introduced by Haldane, Russell, Bernal, and Whyte are all good examples of how To-Day and To-Morrow inaugurated new forms of art-science interfaces or hybridity. Haldane poses science as enabling; as augmenting human powers of human reason and imagination. Russell offers a characteristically pithy and cynical antithesis. This leads me to the first of ten theses on the relations between science and the arts, which are intended to crystallize the preceding arguments and highlight the enduring relevance of the series:

(i)   *Science is not self-sufficient, neutral knowledge. It is up for debate. It can't just be the 'free activity of man's [...] reason and imagination', because of these very demands that society makes of it; and because what it produces can, and probably will, be used and abused. It is moral, social, and political; therefore it is also rhetorical.*

To take the example Haldane made famous in *Daedalus*: to speculate about the technical possibility of 'ectogenesis' isn't just neutral speculation: it is advocacy, believing that such developments could be beneficial, convenient, and socially desirable; and it knows the kinds of rhetorical opposition it will meet from traditionalist and religious groups. Haldane's response? 'We must learn not to take traditional morals too seriously' (90).

Russell, who had been so appalled by the war, felt that there was too little evidence for any confidence in Haldane's hope that science could achieve for man the 'subjugation of the dark and evil elements in his own soul'. He wrote in his autobiography that it was only his curiosity about mathematics that had kept him from committing suicide on several occasions when young, so perhaps he should have had more faith in science. But instead such experiences made him all too aware that, as he puts it in *Icarus*: 'Our unconscious is more malevolent than it pays us to be' (60). His position is that whatever utopian potential any advances in scientific knowledge might have, they are more likely to be put to dystopian use in the quest for power. 'Possibly some day politics may become more rational', he says, 'but so far there is not the faintest indication of a change in this direction' (28). By the time science gets round to 'finally' subjugating the dark and evil elements, the same science will probably have already ensured it is too late.

Russell responds to Haldane's idea that science can only answer to the 'demands of the many for wealth, comfort and victory' in times of 'peace, security and stagnation' (*Daedalus*, p. 81), by making the political basis more explicit. It is a matter of organization, says Russell. The war may not have delivered wealth and comfort, but it certainly accelerated technology. As Haldane almost says, bringing that sequence of peace and security to a pause on the word 'stagnation', perhaps science wouldn't do so well without conflict. And anyway, Russell suspects that the human rivalries that lead to war and competition are a defining and ineradicable part of our humanity; so much so that if we could organize them out of human life we'd get bored (and presumably kill ourselves or start a war to liven things up).

Such attention to the social and political dimension of science is of course characteristic of much between-the-wars writing. Haldane's and Bernal's Marxism gave them an understanding of the interface between science and society as dialectically porous from both directions. Society needed to think about the uses of science; about its future, because its future was also society's future. But in turn, science had begun to offer new tools to extend that thinking. Not only a political science, Marxism, that explicitly modelled itself on the natural sciences— the laws of mechanics, thermodynamics, and evolution. But also psychology, and in particular the new science of psycho-analysis, enjoying a new prestige as a result of the scale of war-trauma and psycho-somatic reactions to it.

The sciences of psychology and of psycho-analysis had begun to change what people meant by human 'reason and imagination'. And this leads to my second proposition. For all these men:

> (ii)   *Science has a psychological dimension too. As the product of human 'reason and imagination', it is also their expression; an expression of part of what it means to be human; and to that extent comparable to art. Post-war developments in neurology as well as psychoanalysis held out the possibility that such sciences would also be able to help us understand the mind they expressed.*

After Bernal's setting out of his vision of our space-travelling, bionic, networked future, the last thing we might expect from him is that he would add a philosophy of art—that he was as interested in aesthetics as prosthetics. Yet that is exactly where his argument does lead, in quasi-Hegelian fashion:

> It is here that prediction is most difficult and most fascinating. Under the influence of psychology it may well be that, just as all the branches of science itself are coalescing into a unified world picture, so the human activities of art and attitudes of religion may be fused into one whole action-reaction pattern of man to reality. The recognition of the art that informs all pure science need not mean the abandonment for it of all present art, rather it will mean the completion of the transformation of art that has already begun. Art expressing itself on one side in a kind of generalized architecture, massive or molecular, gives form to the infinite possibilities of the application of science; on the other a generalized poetry expresses the ever-widening complexities of the understanding of the universe, while religion clarified by psychology remains as the expression of the desire that drives man through the universe in understanding and hope.
>
> (*The World, the Flesh, and the Devil*, p. 69)

> The art of the future will, because of the very opportunities and materials it will have at its command, need an infinitely stronger formative impulse than it does now. The cardinal tendency of progress is the replacement of an indifferent chance environment by a deliberately created one. As time goes on, the acceptance, the appreciation, even the understanding of nature, will be less and less needed. In its place will come the need to determine the desirable form of the humanly-controlled universe which is nothing more nor less than art.   (78-9)

That comparability between arts and sciences is expressed in To-Day and To-Morrow not only by the fact that so many separate sciences and arts had individual volumes devoted to them, but above all in the tendency of its writers to ride the boundaries between arts and sciences.

When Haldane gave his paper to the 'Heretics' society in Cambridge he was arguing that modern poets needed to know contemporary science; but also that scientists needed to know literature:

> I am absolutely convinced that science is vastly more stimulating to the imagination than are the classics, but the products of this stimulus do not normally see the light because scientific men as a class are devoid of any perception of literary form. (*Daedalus*, pp. 28-9)

There was already a debate in progress over the relevance of a classical education in the twentieth century. A. C. Benson, who had been a schoolmaster at Eton before moving to Magdalene College Cambridge, was writing books suggesting wistfully that perhaps teaching Latin verse wasn't the most appropriate training for the modern world.[87] In Haldane's comments there is doubtless an element of alpha-male (and especially Oxbridge high table) one-upmanship, as he both devalues the classics, and shows that he knows as much about literature as the arts specialists in his audience, peppering his text with quotations in Latin from Boethius and Prudentius, as well as from English poems by Chesterton and Buchanan. It's possible to make too much of such proficiency. After all, snatches of Latin verse would have been the property of every public-school-educated boy of the age; and Chesterton was at the peak of his considerable fame during Haldane's youth. But there is perhaps a more significant comparison at stake in Haldane's title. For the year before he gave his talk, Joyce's *Ulysses* had been published. It would have been hard for Haldane to have read a copy then, while it was banned in England. But he is unlikely not to have known about it, or even not to have read about it. Even if he hadn't known that it continued the story of Stephen Dedalus, he would probably have known of that character in *Portrait of the Artist as a Young Man*. And Joyce's story of how the artist must use his ingenuity to escape the limitations of family, religion, and nation, offers a paradigm for the plot of Haldane's and Bernal's books, of how science can help humanity metamorphose itself.

This was the Cambridge of Ogden and Richards and (a little later) the young William Empson too, where thinking about poetry was being vastly stimulated by the sciences—not just physics, psychology, and neurology, but also astronomy, anthropology, and psychoanalysis[88] I don't know if Empson had formulated his eventual reading of *Ulysses* by the 1920s. But he arrived in Cambridge in 1925 and was soon closely involved in Ogden's circle, through Richards, his tutor at Magdalene. Empson later wrote that he thought the implicit plot of Joyce's novel

---

[87] See for example A. C. Benson, *The Upton Letters* (London: Smith, Elder, 1905), 158–61.
[88] As described by Forrester and Cameron in *Freud in Cambridge*.

was that Bloom was trying to engineer a sexual encounter between his wife and Stephen, which he could get aroused by watching, in order to rekindle his and Molly's sex life. It is either an interpretation of perversity, or a perverse interpretation, depending on your point of view or point of voyeurism. This is not to argue that Haldane was implying this reading of the novel, or even wanted us particularly to think of Joyce. Simply that Joyce's novel may have been why he had Daedalus in mind. But Haldane's monograph, celebrating the figure of Daedalus less as engineer and more as biologist facilitating bestiality, may have set Empson thinking about adultery and perversity in *Ulysses*, and that such a possibility is indicative of Haldane's cachet in the literary world at the time.

Literary scholars are familiar with Eliot's image (in 'Tradition and the Individual Talent') of the poet as like a platinum catalyst in a chemical reaction, whose presence produces a poem-event which is somehow strangely impersonal. And we're familiar with the New Criticism's fascination with the Metaphysical Poets, drawing on the new learning of their day in their poetry. Eliot's own poetry rarely becomes the twentieth-century equivalent—metaphysical, yes; knowledgeable about science, not visibly. (He gets the chemistry wrong: sulphur dioxide reacts with oxygen to produce sulphuric, not sulphurous, acid.[89]) But the To-Day and To-Morrow books help us see the basis for a third thesis:

(iii)   *Science offers* matter *for literature too. Not just the poetry Haldane is talking about, but the emerging genre of science fiction too, that his and Bernal's books both draw upon and stimulate.*

Jules Verne had imagined an expedition to the moon in 1865, and submarines in 1870. But it wasn't until H. G. Wells's scientific romances of the 1890s that the genre could be said to have become established in English. His Martians in *The War of the Worlds* of 1898 in many ways could be said to anticipate the future for humans imagined by Bernal: not only extending their bodies prosthetically (in ways which seem to cause their own structures to atrophy), but achieving space travel, and attempting to colonize other worlds.

The To-Day and To-Morrow books, science fiction and what we might call science poetry, are all works existing on the interface. (One of Empson's finest poems, 'Arachne', makes a love poem out of entomology and the physics of surface tension: 'King spider, walks the roof of velvet streams'.) But such attempts at mediation are indicative of a tension between the arts and sciences; between Snow's 'Two Cultures'.[90] Snow in the 1950s was labelling a process he thought had

---

[89]   See *T. S. Eliot and the Concept of Tradition*, ed. Giovanni Cianci and Jason Harding (Cambridge: Cambridge University Press, 2007), 9, n.12.

[90]   Snow first used the famous phrase in 1956 as the title for an article in *The New Statesman*. The article provided the germ for his 1959 Rede Lecture at Cambridge University, 'The Two Cultures and the Scientific Revolution', which was subsequently printed in *Encounter*, 12 (June 1959), 17–24; 13 (July 1959), 22–7. Whitworth, *Einstein's Wake*, p. 47, notes that 'Though the phrase "the two cultures"

already happened; and the label seemed more pressing in the atomic and genetic age. But one of the many striking features of Haldane's and Bernal's books is that they show that the debate about the two cultures had in fact already started a quarter of a century beforehand. This is my fourth thesis:

(iv)   *The To-Day and To-Morrow series is the first sustained attempt in the twentieth century to address the sense of a split between the 'two cultures' of science and the humanities.*[91] *It does so by putting volumes on science alongside volumes on the arts and society; in the project of trying to popularize technical ideas for generally-educated readers; in the use of classical titles for modern topics such as post-Einsteinian physics, post-Freudian psychology, or cinema; and in the juxtaposition of cultural history with technological futurity.*

This gives the series an extraordinary cultural significance. But what makes it even more significant to literary scholars is the way it anticipated, in some cases directly influenced, major cultural developments. Later chapters will trace the lines from Haldane, Russell, and Bernal to the key speculative fictions of the twentieth century, *Brave New World* and Orwell's *Nineteen Eighty-Four*. Just as *Daedalus'* vision of possible developments seems to have incited his friend Huxley to imagine as fully as possible the world which Haldane had showed was scientifically possible, so Bernal's volume (which was itself originally advertised earlier in the year of its publication as 'Possibilities',[92] indicating the speculative energy of the best of these books, and which ends with a section on 'Possibility') imagines a breath-taking range of tropes of subsequent science fiction, as we have seen: space travel, space stations, artificial planets, cyborgs—both as prosthetic enhancements of human senses and functions, and as keeping brains animated when bodies fail—artificial human intelligence, the networking of artificial human intelligences to form a complex or compound mind, in a forerunner of contemporary speculations about 'artificial life'... That the responses of progressive writers like Huxley and Orwell—and indeed Russell before them—took such dystopian forms sounds an alarm about how these scientists came across as not so much morally naïve but morally reckless about the Pandora's box they were opening. (Is it surprising that no-one wrote a *Pandora* volume? It probably would

---

had not been applied to the arts/science divide' before Snow, many of the popular science works of the 1920s and 1930s 'begin by alluding to the schisms created by intellectual specialization'.

[91] The terms of the debate opposing the arts and sciences has often been traced back to the lectures given in the 1880s by Thomas Henry Huxley and Matthew Arnold. See for example Paul White, 'Ministers of Culture: Arnold, Huxley and liberal Anglican reform of learning', *History of Science*, 43 (2005), 115–38.
[92] Bernal's volume was advertised as *Possibilities* in the end-matter of Vera Brittain's *Halcyon* (1929), 4. Ogden's International Library had published the American philosopher Scott Buchanan's first book, *Possibility*, in 1927.

have been too anti-science for Ogden.) But that alarm signals the extremity of their radicalism, and the depths of the reactions it consciously provoked.

Two further theses follow from this. First, we're now so used to speculative fiction, whether in literature or cinema, turning dystopian, that when we read these essays by Haldane and Bernal, their exhilaration at the imagination of possible futures might seem naïve. We are so used to being disillusioned about science, so aware of the dangerous consequences of what are advertised as scientific advances, that such speculations about radical change are likely to made us think their speculators are worse than naïve: mad scientists. $E = mc^2$? Atom bomb; Chernobyl; anxieties about terrorists acquiring atomic weapons or targeting nuclear facilities...Human genome? Fascist eugenics; human cloning; Frankenstein...and so on. But the objections to a technocratic futurity, already voiced within Haldane's and Bernal's visions, and elaborated in Russell's *Icarus*, show that:

(v)   *What we like to think of as Postmodern scepticism about the claims of science and its Grand Narrative of progress is in fact a modern or modernist scepticism; a product of the First World War as much as of the Second.*

Such scepticism can be traced even further back. Victorian thinkers felt their idea of the human and of religion subverted by Geology and by Darwinism; just as earlier readers had felt their ideas of the human and religion subverted by a text like *Frankenstein*, and experiments like Galvani's which lie behind it. Perhaps an idea of the human or of religion that isn't subverted by science isn't worth much; and perhaps art that doesn't challenge us on these points isn't worth much either. But my argument is historically more specific than this. The scientific ideas that our authors are responding to are new: atomic theory, behaviourism, relativity; genetics and eugenics; psycho-analysis; biochemistry; the electromagnetic spectrum; quantum mechanics. And it is precisely their novelty that incites the imagination of novelists like Aldous Huxley—as it excited the writers of To-Day and To-Morrow. The sudden arrival of so many new ideas and new technologies— cars, aeroplanes, radio, talkies, television, U-boats, tanks, chemical weapons, and so on—itself felt like something new: part of the condition of modernity. In *Eos; or, The Wider Aspects of Cosmogony* (1928), James Jeans gives a beautiful sense of the awe scientists were feeling at the extraordinary, counter-intuitive, and above all previously unimagined world the new sciences were opening up:

The need for caution in our interpretation of the universe is borne in upon us with overwhelming force when we reflect that the new world in which astronomy moves to-day is all a discovery of the present century. It is not merely that our present concepts of the extent of the universe in space and of its duration in time are new revelations to us; our understanding of its fundamental mechanism is equally new. The conversion of matter into radiation, which appears to be the primary physical process of the universe, did not come within our terrestrial purview at all until 1904. The primary matter of the universe appears to consist of elements whose existence we are only just beginning to suspect, and to exist in the state of almost completely broken-up atoms, a state of matter which, again, was not contemplated before 1917. The primary radiation of the universe is not visible light, but short-wave radiation of a hardness which would have seemed incredible at the beginning of the present century. Indeed, our whole knowledge of the really fundamental physical conditions of the universe in which we live is a growth of the last quarter of a century.   (71-2)

Whyte's sense that 'We stand at the eve of a new epoch', similar to Jeans's comment here about the newness of the new science, sheds light on why it was that the period kept the 'future boom' booming. As we shall see, that sense of the transformative power of new scientific ideas ripples out through other disciplines and practices too. Recalling his education in the materialist science of the nineteenth century, the musicologist and poet W. J. R. Turner in his volume *Orpheus; or, The Music of the Future* (1926) commented: 'The great creative scientists of this age have disintegrated those old hard ideas, and it now *appears* that the Universe is a miracle of rhythm [...]' (17). He wonders whether 'the world of music may be like the universe of Einstein, "finite but unbounded"' (10).

Jeans's repeated image for the experience of contemporary cosmology as like that of an infant in his cradle suddenly becoming aware of the immensity of the universe doesn't just evoke feelings of childlike wonder and excitement. It also evokes the sense of being at the beginning of something. Fate, he says, 'has selected for us what is, perhaps , in some ways the most sensational moment of all in the life of our race' (17)—because we have only just become aware of the immensity of the universe, and begun wondering where beyond earth it might all lead. New ideas or techniques, whether in science, industry, politics, sexuality, psychology or wherever, imply the future; or a series of possible futures. Being at the beginning of something is to wonder what the middle or the end will be like. Being at the beginning of so many new things at the same time made the future— the question of the future, of what it would be, could be, should be—suddenly immensely pressing and rich in potentiality.

That exhilarating awareness of genuine innovation (before it acquired the vacuity of a neoliberal corporate mantra)[93] was heightened by the way that one insight led rapidly to another. At least since Newton wrote: 'If I have seen further it is by standing on the shoulders of giants', scientists understood how indebted their discoveries were to those of their precursors.[94] Not since the Early Modern period had so many heaven-shattering discoveries come so quickly in succession.

---

[93] See Augé, *The Future*, chapter 6.
[94] Letter from Sir Isaac Newton to Robert Hooke, 5 February 1675: see http://digitallibrary.hsp.org/index.php/Detail/Object/Show/object_id/9285.

Copernicus, Kepler, Galileo, Hooke, and Newton transformed how people saw the world, and its place in the solar system. They also transformed the act of seeing: the telescope and microscope offering prosthetic extensions of the eye, to enable new orders and scales of things to become visible, some of which provided evidence for the planetary theories. Newton transformed the understanding of light, of motion, and of gravity.

Jeans combines his image of infant awareness with another of the birth of a new civilization: 'Utterly inexperienced beings, we are standing at the first flush of the dawn of civilization. Each instant the vision before us changes as the rosy-fingered goddess paints a new and ever more wonderful picture in the sky' (83). The night sky is a light show; an entertaining spectacle. This too is a vision about changing visions. That image of the vision changing each instant turns it into an image of the movies, but one in which the stars are the stars, illuminating a goddess in no need of a screen. Ernest Betts's volume on the future of film was entitled *Heraclitus*, alluding to the philosopher of universal change. But Jeans means something more than that when we look through a telescope we see heavenly bodies in motion; or that we can see the sun rise. (In fact what we mainly see in the night sky, barring the occasional shooting star or satellite, or at sunrise, gives the impression to human vision and temporality of being static.) His rosy dawn is a metaphor for a sequence of ideas of the universe, from Homer, who uses the epithet 'rosy-fingered' to describe the dawn goddess Eos, to the modern cosmologist studying the creations and destructions of heavenly bodies.

Subsequent cosmological theory has done nothing to diminish that sense of the unimaginable sublimity of the extra-terrestrial: the big bang;[95] black holes; event horizons; wormholes; dark matter, God particles, the multi-verse...Popularizers of cosmology in the later twentieth century and beyond have continued Jeans's line of awe-inspiration, from Patrick Moore and Carl Sagan to Stephen Hawking and Brian Cox. 'No book in the series surpasses *Eos* in brilliance and profundity', said the *Spectator* reviewer, 'for one of the best brains engaged in research gives us here the fruits of long labour in terms that all may understand'.[96] Jeans is also struck by the way the scales and forces and energies of the cosmos are incommensurate with humanity. Some of the best passages in the book invent images to convey this disparity. He takes Hubble's estimates of the number of nebulae visible to the biggest telescope of the day (two million), and that the whole universe is itself about a thousand million times bigger than the part of space the telescope can see:

---

[95] Hubble's Law, postulating an expanding universe and implying an originary event wasn't formulated till 1929, the year after *Eos* was published. But the idea had been proposed in 1927 by the French astronomer Georges Lemaître.

[96] Quoted from the end-matter of C. P. Harvey's *Solon; or, The Price of Justice* (1931).

Let us now multiply 1000 million by 2 million, and the product by 1000 million. The answer (2×10^{24}) gives some indication of the probable number of stars in the universe; the same number of grains of sand spread over England would make a layer hundreds of yards in depth. Let us reflect that our earth is one millionth part of one such grain of sand, and our mundane affairs, our trouble and our achievements, begin to appear in their correct proportion to the universe as a whole.

It is not just a matter of scale. If it were, all those other grains of sand might have their Earths, their Englands, their inhabitants; and we might still be able to think of the universe anthropomorphically, or at least biomorphically. But Jeans argues that 'the physical conditions under which life is possible form only a tiny fraction of the range of physical conditions which prevail in the universe as a whole' (73). So that: 'it does not at present look as though Nature had designed the universe primarily for life; the normal star and the normal nebula have nothing to do with life except making it impossible' (86). Arghol in Wyndham Lewis' pre-war Vorticist play had better reason to be *Enemy of the Stars* than he may have realized.

Clearly it wasn't only novelists, like Lewis or Huxley, who could imagine such anti-humanist implications of the new sciences. They are already prefigured in Haldane's ambivalent response to the war. Indeed, it is the point he starts from. It is worth quoting at length to let Haldane's modernity and his imaginative and stylistic energies manifest themselves:

> As I sit down to write these pages I can see before me two scenes from my experience of the late war. The first is a glimpse of a forgotten battle of 1915. It has a curious suggestion of a rather bad cinema film. Through a blur of dust and fumes there appear, quite suddenly, great black and yellow masses of smoke which seem to be tearing up the surface of the earth and disintegrating the works of man with an almost visible hatred. These form the chief part of the picture, but some where [*sic*] in the middle distance one can see a few irrelevant looking human figures, and soon there are fewer. It is hard to believe that these are the protagonists in the battle. One would rather choose those huge substantive oily black masses which are so much more conspicuous, and suppose that the men are in reality their servants, and playing an inglorious, subordinate, and fatal part in the combat. It is possible, after all, that this view is correct.   (1-2)

Then what at first appeared to be the second scene, rather disconcertingly seems to be one he did not witness.

> Had I been privileged to watch a battle three years later, the general aspect would have been very similar, but there would have been fewer men and more shellbursts. There would probably, however, have been one very significant addition. Then men would have been running, with mad terror in their eyes, from

gigantic steel slugs, which were deliberately, relentlessly and successfully pursuing them.   (2–3)

There's a curious detachment about all this. Was he there or wasn't he? Are the humans in control of the technologies or is it the other way around? (A line that leads out of Butler's *Erewhon* and into speculative fictions like those that make up *The Matrix*, say.) The gigantic steel slugs sound at once like something from *Star Wars*, as well as the tanks on the Western Front. These images invite us to think of cinema. You might say that's the genius of the science popularizer: make the general reader think they're watching a war film and they'll put up with the technical information. But it also raises a more interesting point. Thesis six:

(vi)   *To relate science to the human we need to turn it into narrative and metaphor; to engage with cultural forms such as literature or film. As in Eos, another energizing feature of the To-Day and To-Morrow books is the clarity with which they exemplify this. Haldane's ectogenesis, or Bernal's geriatrics choosing to lose their bodies rather than their reason, are developed with such imaginative flair that we witness science speculation metamorphosing into a curious hybrid between speculative fiction and non-fiction.*

Here there are two levels of narrative. Micro-narratives: in one scene this is happening; in the next, this. Macro-narratives: between this scene and the next, technology has invented a new expression of human power and destructiveness. Arguably, the History of Science is the chief way we humanize science in this way. But Haldane's opening isn't a history of science exactly. It's more an example of the literary form he said 'scientific men as a class are devoid of any perception of'. At a time when Modernist poetics advocated juxtaposing images without much by way of connective, Haldane starts his essay with two images, disjoined in time. Towards the end of his essay he engages with literary form in more playful ways, prophesying through parody and poetic quotation. One of the superb features of the series is the way it fosters this kind of playfulness about literary form.

But this is a double-edged pen. Part of the point of Haldane's detachment describing the Western Front becomes clear as he develops another scene—in the course of which it becomes clear that the two images of the war were in fact two aspects of his first 'scene'—as it were, two clips from a film of the Western Front. (And that hesitation over temporality, as I shall go on to suggest, may be very much to the point.) In what he then calls the second scene, 'three Europeans in India' are 'looking at a great new star in the milky way'. Haldane had been sent to India to recuperate after he was wounded in the war.[97] He explains the current cosmological explanation of the event as a 'collision between two stars, or a star and a nebula'. But then he ponders:

---

[97] See Dronamraju, *Popularizing Science*, p. 359.

There seem, however, to be at least two possible alternatives to this hypothesis. Perhaps it was the last judgement of some inhabited world, perhaps a too successful experiment in induced radio-activity on the part of some of the dwellers there. And perhaps also these two hypotheses are identical, and what we were watching that evening was the detonation of a world on which too many men came out to look at the stars when they should have been dancing.   (3-4)

There is Haldane's ability to encapsulate the dystopian within his utopian imagination, to suggest that the sense of a new beginning might also be a sense of the beginning of an ending.

My last three propositions are all closely interrelated, and all crucial to the cultural understanding of modern science.

(vii)   *Science enables humankind to make its own future for the first time. (This is a major theme of Bernal's book too, which ends by implying that science has humanized and aestheticized the future: it can liberate man from the enemies of reason.) With this responsibility comes the freedom to mess things up, and destroy ourselves.*

But note how Haldane is ambivalently (or relativistically) placed: he is on a world like the one being destroyed, so could be as easily destroyed, or could as easily destroy himself; but he is also watching from a safe distance; learning about human folly with the advantage of cosmological knowledge. If the event was a cosmic collision, it's unlikely any human-type agency could have stopped it. Worlds have been ending since soon after the beginning of the universe. And from biblical stories of Flood or Apocalypse, to scientific stories of the inevitable heat death of the universe, people were accustomed to narratives of ineluctable destruction.[98] In the twentieth century a new story became possible: that instead of being destroyed by inevitable natural processes, man might do the job himself. Wells had imagined this narrative before the First World War, in *The World Set Free* (1914), which prophesies radioactivity being harnessed by 1933 and weaponized by 1956 (only eleven years later than the dropping of the first atom bombs in the Second World War). In the interwar years, the conjunction of Einsteinian physics and the devastation of world war made such a narrative more compelling. As Haldane would write the following year in *Callinicus* (1925), his second volume for the series: 'Of course, if we could utilize the forces which we now know to exist inside the atom, we should have such capacities for destruction that I do not know of any agency other than divine intervention which would save

---

[98] One such example is Harold Jeffreys' *The Future of the Earth* (London: Kegan Paul, Trench, Trübner and Co., 1929). Why this was published in Ogden's Psyche Miniatures series is unclear. It is a work of astronomy and physics, narrating the future diminution of the sun, the cooling of the Earth, and the crashing of the Moon into it. Psychology does not come into it. The title suggests it may have been intended for To-Day and To-Morrow.

humanity from complete and peremptory annihilation' (15) But he then thought it a very remote possibility, because 'we cannot make apparatus small enough to disintegrate or fuse atomic nuclei', so 'can only bombard them with particles of which perhaps one in a million hit', which is 'very uneconomical' (17). By then the first atomic bomb was only twenty years away. It was not that Haldane's science was wrong so far as it went; simply that he didn't yet know about and couldn't foresee chain reactions. These were not theorized until 1933, by Leó Szilárd, the year after the atom was split at Cambridge's Cavendish Laboratory under Rutherford. Nevertheless, Haldane certainly did not think the problem was 'ultimately insoluble' (19).[99]

> (viii)   *This new possible ending, in which the destruction of one world or the creation of another is determined not by divine intervention, or the inevitable working out of universal laws such an inevitable thermo-dynamic 'heat death', but by human agency, is the most egregious example of how twentieth-century science and technology had changed the possibilities of story and plot.*

This is different from the Garden of Eden story, because then humanity just got expelled from the Garden, and became mortal; but not extinct. Now, if we misuse our new knowledge, we not only kill ourselves but destroy the whole race, and even our world. The crucial point is that it is a story not about our past, but about our possible future; and that this imagined end of the human is achieved by human agency, not divine intervention or judgement.

> (ix)   *Modern Temporality is thus different from earlier temporalities. In one sense this follows from Einsteinian Relativity, which makes time more permeable; a category or function of human perception and thought rather than an absolute scale. The big bang that ends one person's world is the creation of a new world for another observer. (Note how Haldane takes an exploding world as the starting point of his book.) In another sense, historical time now appears potentially finite; a fact we learned to live with in the Cold War, and associate with the post 1945 atomic age. But it is already in Haldane's work, and in To-Day and To-Morrow, in the 1920s.*

Of course finite time is something readers have to live with, so I'll end this chapter's story with one final proposition. But first let us return to Haldane's hesitation over time. When we thought we were getting two scenes from the world war, he then gives us two worlds: one ending; one observing (like a scientist or an artist). Imagining the exploding world as having destroyed itself with its own knowledge,

---

[99] T. W. Jones, in *Hermes; or, The Future of Chemistry* (1928), was also sceptical about the feasibility of nuclear power (27–8). Whereas Cecil Chisholm's *Vulcan; or, The Future of Labour* (1927) assumes its development would be only a matter of time (70–1).

he imagines its ending as the ending of our world too. Its today is our tomorrow. The temporality of cosmic observations is even more surreal, since the images coming from so many light years away are already ancient history as we see them: the big bangs ending and creating worlds not only show us how ours might have begun and might end, but might have happened at roughly the same time that ours began. So:

(x)   *To think about Science is inevitably to think about temporality and futurity. This isn't just because technological developments had been accelerating rapidly since the late nineteenth century. New knowledge poses questions about its future uses, as well as about further knowledge it might lead to. Science, that is, always involves a consideration of To-Day and To-Morrow.*

It will have become apparent from this chapter that science in the series is not confined to the volumes devoted to scientific or technological subjects. A distinctive feature of the books is how such concerns are often integrated with a broad range of other social, cultural and everyday-life subjects. Two-thirds of the volumes focus on subjects other than techno-scientific ones; and the discussion of them in the rest of this book perforce ranges widely, touching on many other disciplines and vocations. But we shall see how scientific paradigms, and ideas of science and technology, are rarely far from the writers' minds.

CALLINICUS
A DEFENCE OF CHEMICAL WARFARE

by

J. B. S. HALDANE
Sir William Dunn Reader in Biochemistry, University of Cambridge
Author of "Daedalus"

"Mr Haldane's brilliant study. There can
be very few men who will not learn something from his book."
— *Times*, Leading Article.

"When a man knows his subject thoroughly, he is sure to write something worth
reading. When he possesses his thorough
with a light and humorous touch, reading
becomes a pleasure. Mr Haldane's book
has all these qualities. Though small in
bulk, it is weighty in matter, yet the reader
relieves it of all heaviness."
— *Times Literary Supplement.*

"A book to be read by every intelligent
adult."
— *Spectator.*

"This brilliant little monograph, cynically
realistic and audaciously fantastic by turns."
— *Daily News.*

"Has followed ... ... should
an activities ... ...
that clear ... ...

CASSANDRA
OR
THE FUTURE OF THE
BRITISH EMPIRE

By

F. C. S. SCHILLER
M.A., D.Sc., Fellow and Tutor of
Corpus Christi College, Oxford

"An independent examination of the basic
depressing problems that the British Empire ...
We commend it to the consideration of all
parties." — *Saturday Review.*

"Highly suggestive discussion."
— *Daily Herald.*

"Deserves a great audience. The book is
small but, very, very vitality ; brilliantly
written, it ought to be read by all shades
of politicians and students of politics."
— *Yorkshire Post.*

"A first-rate analysis philosophy has made
yet another addition to that bright contribution of ..."
— *Spectator.*

" ... ...
... ... from
... ...
... ... appeared
... ... *Chronicle.*

DELPHOS
THE FUTURE OF
INTERNATIONAL LANGUAGE

E. SYLVIA PANKHURST

JANUS
THE CONQUEST OF WAR

By

WILLIAM McDOUGALL, F.R.S.

QUO VADIMUS?
SOME GLIMPSES OF THE FUTURE

By

E. E. FOURNIER D'ALBE, D.Sc.

"Progress is moving towards greater
happiness and a fuller life, says the
author ... ... a graphic peep into the
scientific future."
— *Westminster Gazette.*

"Interesting and singularly plausible."
— *Daily Telegraph.*

"What will the world be like a thousand
years hence? A much pleasanter place
than at present according to the visions
of this famous scientist."
— *Evening Standard.*

"A wonderful vision of the future."
— *Daily Sketch.*

"A remarkable contribution to a remarkable series." — *Manchester Dispatch.*

SECOND EDITION

THE NEXT CHAPTER
THE WAR AGAINST THE MOON

By

ANDRÉ MAUROIS

This imaginary chapter of world-history
from 1951 to 1964 from the pen of one of
the most brilliant living French authors
mixes satire and fantasy in just proportions.
He tells how the newspapers of the world
are controlled by five men, how interest is
focussed on an attack on the moon made
possible by a scientific invention, and how
the threat of a world-war is averted by
this sensational 'stunt.' How the moon re-
taliates and subsequent events brings to an
end a book which will leave the reader
begging for more. A penetrating bitter
criticism of human character is concealed
beneath the light fancies of this imaginary
history.

2
Conflict, Connectivity, and the Tropes of Futurology

War

This chapter places To-Day and To-Morrow in its interwar context, and examines how it engages with politics, especially through its discussions of war, race, and the state. It examines the language and rhetoric of futurology in the series; and explores how its narrative and discursive forms relate to its politics. It also considers how such debates relate to Ogden's own work on language, communication and meaning.

To-Day and To-Morrow exemplifies the claim—elaborated by Marshall Berman out of Marx—that modernity is essentially future-oriented.[1] The series assumes life in the future will be different; that it has the potentiality to be better; and that no aspect of life—however intimate or apparently essential it may seem—should be excluded from its speculative transformations. After the Second World War, the Holocaust, and the prospect of thermo-nuclear annihilation, such confidence appeared misplaced, especially to the Frankfurt School's critique of the Enlightenment and of instrumental reason.[2] Many major literary texts of the 1920s— whether modernist or testimonies of the war—express an earlier version of this loss of faith in, or even a horror at, modernity.[3] Yet To-Day and To-Morrow remains more balanced about the future, and especially about science and technology. The series shows a generation, many of whom had experienced the war on the Western Front and elsewhere, not disillusioned, but all the more determined to assert utopian future lives as possible and worth imagining. Rather than causing them to reject technological modernity, their experience of how the advance of scientific knowledge can cast a nightmarish shadow appears to have left many of these writers determined to exercise human ingenuity to avert future catastrophes. To hazard a generalization possibly modernist in its diagrammatic reduction: where postmodernism views utopia in the knowledge of the disastrous totalitarianisms of Nazism and Stalinism, as something that can only slide into

---

[1] See Marshall Berman, *All That Is Solid Melts into Air* (New York and London: Penguin, 1988), 96.
[2] See Max Horkheimer and Theodor Adorno, *Dialectic of Enlightenment* (*Dialektik der Aufklärung*) (Amsterdam: Querido Verlag, 1947); and *Eclipse of* Reason (New York: Oxford University Press, 1947).
[3] See Andrew Frayn, *Writing Disenchantment* (Manchester: Manchester University Press, 2014).

Imagined Futures: Writing, Science and Modernity in the To-Day and To-Morrow. Max Saunders, Oxford University Press (2019). © Max Saunders. DOI: 10.1093/oso/9780198829454.001.0001

dystopia (and sees Zamyatin and Huxley as its prophets), the futurological modernism of To-Day and To-Morrow aspires to move in the other direction: to turn the dystopia of world war into a utopian future. As for so many of the war's survivors, the problem was not the new—the technology that mechanized slaughter—but the old—the political, imperial, social, and religious *status quo* that seemed to have brought the war about. The determination to prevent future mass slaughter led many to socialism or communism after the war.[4]

According to Georg Lukács, modern mass warfare produced a new experience of history as dynamic and unfolding. 'It was the French Revolution, the revolutionary wars and the rise and fall of Napoleon', he argued, 'which for the first time made history a *mass experience*, and moreover on a European scale'.[5] The propaganda needed to create a mass army had 'to reveal the social content, the historical presuppositions and circumstances of the struggle, to connect up the war with the entire life and possibilities of the nation's development'.[6] That is to say that a nation's justification for war goes beyond the defence against a present existential threat, to contemplate a postwar national and geopolitical future. After the greater mass conscription and propaganda saturation of the First World War, the futurological tendency was...only to be expected.

As Marc Augé argues:

> In the immediate post-war period, people thought they could change society and establish the foundations of a new solidarity: they believed in the future [....] above all it was unthinkable, after such a punishing, mutilating ordeal, not to look towards a different horizon.[7]

Except that he is describing not the post First World War period, but Sartrean existentialism and the legacy of the Second World War. If this analysis introduces a necessary qualification to any claim that the cataclysm of the Second World War necessarily destroyed utopian rationalism, it also could be applied to the period immediately after the First World War—certainly as exemplified by many of the To-Day and To-Morrow texts. In a brief essay called 'The Future of Poetry' published in August 1919, Richard Aldington explained how the motives for that turn to a different horizon included not only psychic and social sanity, but the desire that the war generation's legacy should be something other, something better, than war:

> Now that the war is over, the world's youth is approaching freedom again, still weary perhaps with the struggle, but with an intense eagerness for life. And out

---

[4] See for example the excerpts from Herbert Read's *The Contrary Experience* and Henri Barbusse's *War Diary* in the *Penguin Book of First World War Prose*, ed. Jon Glover and Jon Silkin (London: Penguin, 1990), 289, 291, 190, 196; and Ernst Toller, *I Was a German: The autobiography of a revolutionary*, trans. Edward Crankshaw (London: John Lane, The Bodley Head, 1934).

[5] Lukács, *The Historical Novel*, trans. Hannah and Stanley Mitchell (Harmondsworth: Penguin, 1976), 20.

[6] Ibid., p. 21.   [7] Marc Augé, *The Future*, trans. John Howe (London: Verso, 2014), 91–2.

of this intensity should grow poetry, not, perhaps, large in bulk but yet enough for us to be able to say to future generations: 'We hooligans who fought for those long years in the mud and in spiritual darkness could yet make a few songs to test your emulation'.[8]

The Versailles Treaty had been signed at the end of June.

A comparable note was sounded by Haldane, whose imagining of possible futures for science appears to have led Ogden gradually towards the idea for another series.[9] Dora Russell, who had been an old friend of Ogden's, recalled him persuading her husband 'Bertie' 'to do one, following one by Haldane called *Daedalus; or, Science and the Future*, on *Icarus; or, The Future of Science*', and then inviting her to produce a feminist reply to Anthony Ludovici's anti-feminist *Lysistrata: Woman's Future and Future Woman*, which built up to a vision of women taking power, and slaughtering most men, apart from the few spared for breeding.[10] This is suggestive of Ogden's way of working informally through his extensive contacts. But it is ambiguous about how clearly Ogden had worked out the idea of the series at this stage. Had he already decided he wanted a volume on the future of science, and wanted it called *Icarus*?[11] Or did he just think Haldane's book merited a response, or presented a superb publishing opportunity? The latter appears more likely, since the next two volumes did not adopt classical titles: F. G. Crookshank's *The Mongol in our Midst*; and *Wireless Possibilities* by A. M. Low.[12] The design of the books had been changed for these, to the deep maroon boards and elegant cream labels, giving the rest of the series (in the UK version) its distinctive visual identity (the US versions published by Dutton were duller, clothbound books in various colours; but their eventual jackets were more striking, with elegant Art Deco designs. Kegan Paul used plain cream jackets with descriptions or reviews but no illustrations). None of these first four volumes bore any internal indication yet that they were part of a series; nor were their lengths

---

[8] Richard Aldington, 'The Poetry of the Future', *Poetry*, 14:5 (August 1919), 266–9 (266).

[9] The development of the series is discussed in greater detail in Appendix A.

[10] Dora Russell, 'My Friend Ogden', in *C. K. Ogden: A collective memoir*, pp. 82–95 (93).

[11] In fact Russell had already given a lecture in October 1923, before the publication of *Daedalus*, on 'The Effect of Science on Social Institutions'. This was given to the Fabian Society in a series 'Is Civilization Decaying?', which also included Shaw, Harold Laski and R. H. Tawney. A version of Russell's lecture was published in four parts in George Lansbury's *Daily Herald* under the title 'Science and Civilization' (16, 19, 20, and 21 November 1923, p. 4 each issue). Ray Monk says these 'later formed the basis for his little book *Icarus or the Future of Science*'—*Bertrand Russell: The ghost of madness: 1921–1970* (London: Vintage, 2001), 28. But *A Bibliography of Bertrand Russell* by Kenneth Blackwell, Harry Ruja, and Sheila Turcon, 3 vols (London: Routledge, 1994), vol. 2, pp. 66–7, suggests the *Herald* version's informality may indicate that it was reported rather than published from Russell's text. The formal version was published as 'The Effect of Science on Social Institutions', *The Survey: Graphic number*, New York, 52:1 (1 April 1924), 5–11; and it was this version which was revised into chapters 1, 2, and the conclusion of *Icarus*.

[12] It is also perfectly possible that *Daedalus* did inspire Ogden to solicit a companion volume called *Icarus* (in which case the book Russell delivered was an argumentative companion); and saw the pair as heading as series on the future, but was not at this stage thinking of using the classical titles throughout the series.

or the form of their titles standardized; but the fifth—Gerald Heard's *Narcissus: An anatomy of clothes*—included a list under the series title of 'To-Day and To-Morrow'.[13]

What is clear from Dora Russell's reminiscence is that Ogden wanted the series to stage rational argument between its contributors; and to stimulate discussion among its readers. I. A. Richards recalled him characteristically asking: 'Will you change your mind, if I convince you?'[14] The pairing of *Daedalus* and *Icarus* set up a debate between the benefits and risks of science—one of several debates which run through the series, and are very typical of the adversarial polarizations of the period; others including those on the political conflict between left and right, eugenics, sexuality, and education. To-Day and To-Morrow was thus a forum for the post-war world to debate the kinds of future it wanted to create.

The first third of this chapter traces the presence of the war in the series, and considers the impact of the war on its futurology. The following two sections analyse key rhetorical devices it uses to imagine the future, each examining one of its most distinctive and recurrent tropes, both of which are antithetical to the anxiety or disillusion of war (and thus arguably minister to such feelings). First, the device of imagining the very distant future, from which the writers can look back to their present and immediate future: a trope which implies that, for all its follies and self-destructiveness, humanity nonetheless *has* a future. Second, a rhetoric of unification: familiar enough in the political internationalism and communication technophilia of the period, but striking in the series for the way it plays across so many diverse fields—often with surprising effects. Both tropes have their ambivalences, certainly. But what they keep in play in the aftermath of war is, precisely, play: the spirited sense of the exhilaration of thought and the imagination of possibility which the science volumes were seen to embody.

Janus; The Conquest of War (1927), by William McDougall, exemplifies the relation between war anxiety and utopian thought with particular clarity. McDougall was an influential popularizer of psychology, writing about instinct and what he termed the 'group mind' (a concept which has been reprised in recent research in the form of the 'social brain' hypothesis).[15] Like other contributors, he approached parapsychology with scientific seriousness. In its analysis of the problems faced by humanity between the wars *Janus* is a powerful work. A very vivid foreword starts with several traumatic scenes from the war, to convey the widespread horror of conflict, and to explain the widespread peace movement. 'Yet the next great war draws nearer' (12); 'a war which, if it shall break out, will

[13] The evolution of the series is elaborated in Appendix A, which argues from the use of the series title on an early dust-jacket of *Icarus*, that it was probably conceived between the printing and publication of that book.

[14] I. A. Richards: 'Some Recollections of C. K. Ogden', in *Encounter*, 9:3 (September 1957), 10–12; also 'Co-Author of the Meaning of Meaning', in *C. K. Ogden*, pp. 96–109 (96).

[15] See for example Robin Dunbar, 'The Social Brain Hypothesis', *Evolutionary Anthropology: Issues, news, and reviews*, 6:5 (1998) 178–90.

far surpass in horror and suffering and destructiveness even the Great War of 1914-1918' (19). McDougall is particularly striking on how technological developments have made war so destructive and total that now man faces the possibility of destroying himself:

> These developments, and especially the development of aircraft, of the explosive bomb and of the poison gases, have made it only too clear that in the next Great War the civilian populations, and especially the populations of the great cities, will be the first and greatest sufferers, that wounds, mutilation and death, terror and famine, will be broadcast among them with awful impartiality; that no woman, no family, no little child, no church, no treasury of art, no museum of priceless antiquities, no shrine of learning and science will be immune; but that in a few days or hours great cities may be levelled with the dust, while their surviving inhabitants scrape for crusts amid mangled bodies of fair women and the ruins of the monuments of art and science.   (17-18)

(The verb 'broadcast' there is an interesting touch: deriving from sowing, the metaphor can refer to any form of distribution; but as it was becoming increasingly associated with radio, it acquires here the sense of the reach, penetration, and invisibility of radio waves, but given an ominously lethal twist.) McDougall sees more advanced technology as increasing everyone's fear of aggression, and thus racking up armament.

This increased anxiety is entirely rational, on two counts. First, says McDougall, people felt stunned after the war, but 'the causes of war have been in no way removed' (26-7). Second, mankind finds itself in a situation both without precedent, and, possibly, facing a future of having no future. He quotes a counterfactual passage from Winston Churchill's essay 'Shall We All Commit Suicide?' asking 'What War in 1919 Would Have Meant':

> It is probable—nay, certain that among the means which will next time be at their disposal will be agencies and processes of destruction wholesale, unlimited, and, perhaps, once launched, uncontrollable.
>
>   Mankind has never been in this position before. Without having improved appreciably in virtue or enjoying wiser guidance, it has got into its hands for the first time the tools by which it can unfailingly accomplish its own extermination. That is the point in human destinies to which all the glories and toils of men have at last led them.   (25-6)[16]

Nearly a decade on from the war, McDougall too knows that war technology has already become more destructive; and that air-power is the main agent of transformation. Indeed, his description of it anticipates the *Blitzkrieg* of Guernica and the invasion of Poland: 'And the coming of aerial warfare has immensely

---

[16] Churchill's essay first appeared in *Nash's Pall Mall Magazine* (September 1924), 12–13, 80–1, and was subsequently re-issued in pamphlet form in Britain and the US.

accentuated both this rapidity and this advantage, and has thus intensified this universal fear of sudden overwhelming aggression' (51).

But the logic of this grim vision of military futurity is that future warfare will only become more appallingly and ingeniously brutal; as Churchill had projected, in the exercise in futurological sensationalism McDougall continues to quote:

> Might not a bomb no bigger than an orange be found to possess a secret power to destroy a whole block of buildings nay, to concentrate the force of a thousand tons of cordite and blast a township at a stroke? Could not explosives even of the existing type be guided automatically in flying machines by wireless or other rays, without a human pilot, in ceaseless procession upon a hostile city, arsenal, camp, or dockyard?
>
> As for Poison Gas and Chemical Warfare in all its forms, only the first chapter has been written of a terrible book. Certainly every one of these new avenues to destruction is being studied on both sides of the Rhine, with all the science and patience of which man is capable. And why should it be supposed that these resources will be limited to Inorganic Chemistry? A study of Disease—of Pestilences methodically prepared and deliberately launched upon man and beast—is certainly being pursued in the laboratories of more than one great country. Blight to destroy crops, Anthrax to slay horses and cattle, Plague to poison not armies only but whole districts such are the lines along which military science is remorselessly advancing.   (27-8)

The conclusion Churchill draws from these new technological possibilities is perversely ahistorical: 'The liberties of men are no longer to be guarded by their natural qualities, but by their dodges; and superior virtue and valour may fall an easy prey to the latest diabolical tricks' (29)—as if arrows, gunpowder and rifles were 'natural qualities', or had no effect on courage and resilience. After the Gotha and Zeppelin raids during the war, many in the period were contemplating the devastation of future aerial bombardment (though some, like Wells, had been imagining it even before the war).[17] But it is characteristic of To-Day and To-Morrow not just to recirculate the received debates but to inspire further possibilities. Churchill had been Secretary of State for Air from January 1919 to February 1921, and was clearly well-informed about the weapons futurology of the day. Nonetheless, the far-sightedness of the predictions is striking, as he anticipates several technologies that were not to be realized for decades: not only atomic, but biological warfare; not only missiles, but drones. His grim vision of technological devastations offers the vision of future warfare that *Janus'* proposal is intended to prevent. McDougall takes issue with those ex-soldier contributors—J. F. C. Fuller and Basil Liddell Hart; he could also have included Haldane—who argued that

---

[17] Paul Saint-Amour's *Tense Future: Modernism, total war, encyclopedic form* (Oxford: Oxford University Press, 2015) gives an excellent account of the discourse of air power and total war in the 20s and 30s.

more technologically advanced wars will be surgically swift and clean.[18] To make matters even worse, the war had also shown up the inadequacy of the system that was supposed to be able to regulate international disputes:

> The Great War showed us also the futility of another form of international agreement. The leading nations of the world had maintained by mutual consent the agreeable fiction that there existed a body of international law governing their relations and their conduct towards one another[.]   (21; cf. also 88)

He is also clear-sighted about how the League of Nations had demonstrated itself incapable of maintaining peace (97). Such an analysis might be expected to lead to a cynical denunciation of man's inevitable barbarity, perhaps framed in terms of psychological instincts. But instead—and this is where the utopian dimension comes in—McDougall has a solution to propose. In fact it is something of a hobbyhorse, since he had already put it forward twice, as an Appendix to his book *Ethics and Some Modern World Problems* (New York: Putnam's Sons, 1924), and also in an article, 'Psychology, Disarmament, and Peace' in the *North American Review* for November 1924. It would be easy to caricature him for his conviction that he has the answer to world peace, and frustration that people keep ignoring it. Also for what might appear to us now the quaintness and unfeasibility of the proposal. Yet the idea is by no means absurd. McDougall's suggestion is that, just as 'Without police force our civilized life could not continue a day' ([*sic*]; 112), so in the international arena what is required is an international police force.[19] One might say that the idea has been realized, at least to some extent, in the deployment of multi-national UN peace-keeping forces. But the difference, and what makes McDougall's proposal very much of its time, is that what he advocates is an international air force to keep the peace. Unlike Wells, McDougall does not advocate a world state. Instead, he sees a stronger international organization, along the lines of the League of Nations, but backed up by international military force, as guaranteeing rather than threatening individual nations; though these need to accept that the concept of International law sets limits to their sovereignty (92-3).[20]

---

[18] Fuller is referred to as 'J. T. C. Fuller', the error not corrected despite his having written two volumes for the series; *Pegasus; or, Problems of Transport* and *Atlantis; or, America and the Future* (both 1925). In fact there is common ground between *Janus* and Liddell Hart's volume *Paris; or, The Future of War* (1925), which also correctly identifies air power as becoming the foremost branch of the fighting forces, and argues for the need for a shift from the Napoleonic strategy of inflicting the maximum possible damage on an enemy, to a more moral approach (91), as discussed below, p. 129.

[19] Chapter VI, pp. 122–40, is the proposal: 'INTERNATIONAL AIR-FORCE AS A PREVENTIVE OF WAR'.

[20] Sarvepalli Radhakrishnan's *Kalki; or, The Future of Civilization* (1929)—discussed in Chapter 3— makes a comparable point: 'So long as the Great Powers are not prepared to relinquish a jot or tittle of their sovereignty which they are ready to uphold by force, whenever necessary, the League and the pact are all a mockery' (96).

McDougall argues that such policing would need to be combined with a ban on states having their own military aircraft, to ensure that any aggressors could be dealt with swiftly:

> If nations could be induced to forego the possession of national air-forces, a comparatively small international air-force, stationed at a few well-chosen centres, could serve effectively as the International Police which is required to render International Law effective and to assure International Justice. (126-7)

That is one of the weak points in the proposal, as German rearmament would soon demonstrate. Another difficulty he is aware of is that commercial aircraft could easily be converted to military use. In his initial formulation McDougall had proposed that 'it would be necessary to suppress entirely the use of aircraft for commercial purposes' (128). Now he argues that it would be enough to enforce a maximum speed of 100 miles per hour for commercial purposes (128-9). The Ford Tri-Motor, one of the most influential airliners of the period, was capable of 150 miles per hour before the end of the decade, so it was never likely that countries would voluntarily reduce speed in an emerging business for which speed was of the essence.

It is a safe prophecy that the expression 'it seems safe to prophesy' is likely to preface something risibly improbable. So it is with McDougall's optimism that: 'it seems safe to prophesy that the sure protection afforded by the International Air-Force would soon make large armies and fleets old-fashioned and foolish luxuries' (138). Seeming safe is an aspiration he takes seriously, though, and he is by no means the naïve eccentric that a paraphrase of his fascinating book—one of the longer volumes in the series—might make him appear. For example, he envisages combining the international police force with the idea of sanctions, in a way that presages the operations of the United Nations: 'It is therefore proposed that the whole world, acting through the League of Nations, shall use the economic boycott and the threat of it to repress the warlike tendencies of nations' (84).

Ultimately what drives his vision is the determination that a possible solution has to be found, since the alternative is unthinkable; coupled with an optimism—shared by writers like Haldane and Bernal—that the technology that has unleashed the spectres of modern warfare can also offer our best hope against them:

> Must each nation continue as hitherto, arming itself to the teeth, playing for a place in some strong combination of nations, and hoping for luck on the outbreak of the next world war?
>
> Fortunately, the march of science, which has rendered modern war so intensely hideous and destructive, has put into our hands just such an instrument as International Justice needs for its police work [....] (125)

It is a grim thought that the UN may have deterred more conflicts than it has failed to avert. But McDougall's prophecies about specific potential future conflicts have proved all too accurate. His is one of several volumes realizing that Japan was likely to make war again (43). He also anticipates future Muslim 'barbaric force' against the Christian world (58-9). Dean Inge said of *Janus*: 'Among all the booklets of this brilliant series, none, I think, is so weighty and impressive as this'.[21]

The volume by Liddell Hart that McDougall is countering is *Paris; or, The Future of War* (1925). Where McDougall wants the Great War to have been the war to end war, Liddell Hart is more of a realist. He wants to learn from the experience of the war how to fight better. *Paris* aims to rethink military strategy and tactics. 'The goal in war is the prosperous continuance of national policy in the years after the war', he says: 'the only true objective is the moral one of subduing the enemy's will to resist with the least possible economic, human, and ethical loss—which implies a far-sighted choice, and blend, of the weapons most suitable for our purpose' (91). As nations become increasingly interconnected through trade, large scale destruction of an enemy damages the victor too. Both the objective and the morality were lost sight of as the Western Front got bogged down in trench warfare:

> The last war was the culmination of brute force; the next will be the vindication of moral force, even in the realm of the armies. From the delusion that the armed forces themselves were the real objective in war, it was the natural sequence of ideas that the combatant troops who composed the armies should be regarded as the object to strike at.
>
> Thus progressive butchery, politely called 'attrition', becomes the essence of war. To kill, if possible, more of the enemy troops than your own side loses, is the sum total of this military creed, which attained its tragi-comic climax on the Western front in the Great War.
>
> The absurdity and wrong-headedness of this doctrine should surely have been apparent to any mind which attempted to think logically instead of blindly accepting inherited traditions. (80–81)

He argues that the real objective should have been the enemy's Achilles heel (hence his invocation of Paris); its command and communication centres behind the front lines. In fact J. F. C. Fuller, who had been a staff officer with the Tank Corps, had devised 'Plan 1919', for a tank strike at these 'nerve centres of the German army' rather than the 'flesh and blood' of its troops. Fuller had learnt from the chaos caused in the British Army by the German offensive in the Spring of 1918 that 'its extent was due far more to the breakdown of command and staff control than to the collapse of the infantry resistance'.[22] Plan 1919 did not need to be implemented, because the German army collapsed in August 1918, for similar reasons. Fuller was the more innovative of the two. He had written *Tanks in the Great War* (1920) and then *Tanks in Future Warfare* (1921), and contributed a

---

[21] Review in the *Evening Standard*, quoted from the end-matter of C. P. Harvey's *Solon; or, The Price of Justice* (1931).
[22] See Patrick Wright, *Tank* (London: Faber, 2000) for an in-depth account of Fuller and Liddell Hart.

volume to To-Day and To-Morrow on advocating the use of half-track vehicles: *Pegasus; or, Problems of Transport* (1925). Liddell Hart quotes Ludendorff saying 'Divisional staffs were surprised in their headquarters by enemy tanks'. He compares this defeat to that of the Roman Empire at Adrianople by the Goth cavalry, arguing that:

> The lesson to be drawn from this historical analogy is that the tank attack is the modern substitute for the cavalry charge, the supreme value of which lay in its speed and impetus of assault, and the demoralizing effect of its furious onset. The deadliness of modern fire-weapons brought about the extinction of the cavalry charge, and with its disappearance warfare became lopsided and stagnant. The stalemates of recent campaigns are to be traced to the lack of any means of delivering and exploiting a decisive blow. If, instead of regarding cavalry as men on horseback, soldiers thought of it as the mobile arm, the main cause of the interminable siege warfare of the Russo-Japanese and Great Wars would be apparent. The practical view of history lies in projecting the film of the past on the blank screen of the future.   (78-9)

The military theory is cogent enough, and indeed is said to have influenced German Panzer *Durchbruch* (breakthrough) tactics in the Second World War.[23] The requisite weapons existed to win the war more humanely, but the right way to use them had not yet been invented. Because men on horseback were outmoded against machine guns in trenches, tacticians did not think hard or early enough about how to regain the *mobility* of cavalry. (He too is of course aware of the difference made to war by the even greater mobility of air and submarine power, adding a vertical dimension to tactics: 'just as the value of armies has been radically affected by the conquest of the air, so has that of surface fleets by the coming of that other new and three-dimensional weapon, the submarine' (63). Though the logic of the parallel between cavalry and tanks is clear, as metaphor it is problematic—tending to mythologize machine war with the enchantment of a heroic past. In Liddell Hart's use it is more double-edged than that; the metaphoricity (dare one say it) more mobile. He is not telling us to think of tanks as being as glamorous as cavalry, so much as saying that modern war should make us think of what is cavalry-like about tanks; so that we abstract the essential tactical value of mobility. Metaphor is important here because what is at issue is how to think war, and how to see it; how to represent it. If 'any mind which attempted to think logically' had seen cavalry projected onto tanks as 'the mobile arm', the solution to trench stalemate might have been clearer. Nevertheless, the most interesting metaphor here is that of the film, which is both of its modernist time, and characteristic of the connectivity of the series, moving between technologies and media and times. For there are several times in play in this clip: the fall of ancient Rome;

---

[23] I. F. Clarke, *The Pattern of Expectation: 1644–2001* (London: Cape, 1979), 239–40.

the Russo-Japanese War of 1904-5; spring 1918; August 1918; 1919; the now of the practical historian; the future. The screen of the future is blank because its history has not yet taken shape. But what does Liddell Hart imagine us seeing when we project the film of the past onto it? It cannot mean seeing the future as repeating the past. That would be the blind acceptance of inherited traditions that he thought had blinded the commanders. It is a vision of the future; a metaphor for futurology itself, and one which casts it as like cinema: a *pro-jection*—a throwing forwards, in order to see where you have come from, and where you are going. Wars had been filmed from the last three years of the nineteenth century (during the Graeco-Turkish, Spanish-American, and Boer Wars). But film was used much more intensively during the First World War for newsreel and propaganda purposes; and the mid-1920s was when the major films about the war began to appear. King Vidor's *The Big Parade* was released in 1925, the year *Paris* was published. Liddell Hart thus invokes the technology of his today to visualize war tomorrow.

In Chapter 1 we saw how the scenes of war and destruction with which Haldane begins *Daedalus* turn on similar questions of cinematic representation and point of view. Haldane presents his arresting contrast between two opening scenes as 'a part of the case against science'. First, troop movements on the Western Front, seen without tanks, then with them. Second, the more Apocalyptic contrast, describing three Europeans in India looking at birth of 'a great new star in the milky way'. Those with any astronomical knowledge debate the cause: 'the most popular theory attributed it to a collision between two stars, or a star and a nebula', he says, then adds: 'There seem, however, to be at least two possible alternatives to this hypothesis'. One is that it might be 'the last judgement of some inhabited world'; but then he speculates that it might be the result of science on the part of another form of intelligent life, which had managed to produce a nuclear reaction and destroyed itself. The war-time context cannot but suggest the thought that it might have been a war-related explosion. But Haldane sets against that hypothetical disaster, the three Earthlings speculating about it. I suggested that such imaginative speculation offered a hope of the kind of knowledge and intelligence needed to avert such disasters; to set against not only the 'cosmoclastic' disaster, but against the war on Earth. After all, the birth of a new star is both a destruction and a creation—not just of the star itself, but of its potential to evolve another solar system, that might in turn lead to the birth of new life-forms and intelligences.

Haldane gave another of his books—a collection of essays—the title *Possible Worlds* (1927); and his language here of 'possible alternatives' plays across the differences between hypothetical worlds. Speculative imagination is both what makes science progress, and what gives hope that it may progress in ways that offer humanity other possibilities than abjection or suicide. The contrast between the two scenes on the Western Front is comparably neutral. The image of men terror-stricken by the unforeseen manifestation of tanks is appalling in its vision of man helpless in the face of his own machine creations. But where you might expect that to introduce a warning about man's technological inhumanity to man, and the risks of science, on the contrary he sees science as the only hope in averting such catastrophe. It figures an advance, offering the hope of breaking out from the more appalling deadlock of trench attrition, in which men are at the mercy of the more appalling high explosive bombardments. He might stand accused of lacking empathy for the infantrymen had he not been one of them.

Similarly, if his later volume for To-Day and To-Morrow, *Callinicus; A Defence of Chemical Warfare* (1925), with its argument that weapons like poison gas might actually prove more humane (that the better the science the fewer the victims), is unfashionable now, it is not because Haldane was insensitive to the sufferings involved. Not only had he witnessed the brutal injuries caused by conventional weapons, but he had actually been subjected to gas asphyxiation in experiments performed with his father, the scientist John Scott Haldane (with his sister, Naomi, later Naomi Mitchison, and Aldous Huxley, as helpers ensuring the gas chamber was effectively sealed) during the war, in an attempt to analyse and devise defences against the chlorine gas being used by the Germans in 1915.[24] As he explains in *Callinicus*:

> I regard the type of wound produced by the average shells as, on the whole, more distressing than the pneumonia caused by chlorine or phosgene. Besides being wounded, I have been buried alive, and on several occasions in peacetime I have been asphyxiated to the point of unconsciousness. The pain and discomfort arising from the other experiences were utterly negligible compared with those produced by a good septic shell-wound.   (21-2)

Haldane is most vigorous in his defence of the poison gas that has acquired the most opprobrium:

> The most interesting thing, however, about mustard gas is that, though it caused 150,000 casualties in the British Army alone, less than 4,000 of these (or 1 in 40) died, while only about 700 (or 1 in every 200) became permanently unfit. Yet the Washington Conference has solemnly agreed that the signatory powers are not to use this substance against one another, though, of course, they will use such humane weapons as bayonets, shells, and incendiary bombs.   (27)

Such writing is characteristic of the way To-Day and To-Morrow can challenge the received view of the war, and of its literature. Reading Haldane need not diminish our sense of the humane outrage at horrific suffering in a poem like Wilfred Owen's 'Dulce et Decorum Est' in which the narrator watches the agonizing death of a gas victim; but it will certainly make us think again about how

---

[24] See Stephen Jay Gould, *The Lying Stones of Marrakech* (Cambridge, MA: Harvard University Press, 2011), 305–14 on Haldane, *Callinicus*, and the problems of futurology. Haldane tells of his auto-experiments in *Callinicus*, 67–9.

representative of the war such a scenario might be; and about whether other responses might not also be possible. Haldane is scathing about the childish mentality of a General who only wants gas that can kill (48-9). Like Liddell Hart in *Paris*, Haldane is advocating tactics to avoid mass slaughter:

> It seems, then, that mustard gas would enable an army to gain ground with far less killed on either side than the methods used in the late war, and would tend to establish a war of movement leading to a fairly rapid decision, as in the campaigns of the past.[25]   (50)

Like several other volumes—*Aeolus, Janus, Paris*—*Callinicus* imagines the catastrophe of an intense aerial bombardment of a city (56-7). The difference here though is that Haldane's point is that aerial bombing would be much worse than a gas attack, by subjecting unprotected civilians to severer injuries, and making the Home Front more like the Western Front. The *Spectator*, which gave the series more encomia than might be expected, judged that 'Mr. Haldane has followed up his success in *Daedalus* with a still more brilliant book *Callinicus*'. But its reviewer grasped the author's motivation: 'Everyone who has any interest in the prevention of war for the future should read Mr. Haldane's volume'.[26]

These writers, and many others in the series, show how war creates a new relation to time. They put the war behind them, say *Goodbye to All That*, in the phrase Robert Graves used to title his 1929 war memoir. *But It Still Goes On*, for some, as he wrote in the follow-up book the next year. One way it still goes on is in foreshadowing the future, both as the reason for imagining peaceful utopias, and as future wars that have to be averted in order to achieve peace. Aldington wrote that:

> Adult lives were cut sharply into three sections—pre-war, war, and post-war. It is curious—perhaps not so curious—but many people will tell you that whole areas of their pre-war lives have become obliterated from their memories.[27]

---

[25] An earlier version of *Callinicus* was published as 'Chemistry and Peace' in the *Atlantic Monthly*, 135:1 (January 1925), 1–18, which was paraphrased in *Current Opinion*, 78 (March 1925), 333–4, as 'Chemical Warfare Is Called Humane: Poison gas not so barbaric as firearms, says noted chemist'. Andrew Ede 'The Natural Defense of a Scientific People: The public debate over chemical warfare in post-WWI America', *Bulletin of the History of Chemistry*, 27:2 (2002) 128–35 (132), is misleading here, suggesting the *Current Opinion* article was a reprinting of 'Chemistry and Peace', and the essay was 'subsequently expanded into a book', *Callinicus*. The preface to the book version says it was based on lecture given August 1924, and published nearly as given. Apart from minor variants in paragraphing and punctuation there is little difference, and no expansion between the *Atlantic* and book texts, which anyway were published in the same month. (The *Spectator* reviewed *Callinicus* on 31 January 1925.) One of the changes Haldane made for the second, revised, book edition of 1925 was to add an explanatory sentence to the end of the Preface, glossing the title: '"Callinicus" means "He who conquers in noble or beautiful manner"' (viii). Kallinikos was a Byzantine architect said to have invented Greek Fire. When the *Times Literary Supplement* reviewed the book favourably (19 March 1925), 206, the *Times* ran an editorial the same day also commending it.

[26] 'Books', *Spectator*, 134:160 (31 January 1925), 160.

[27] Richard Aldington, *Death of a Hero* (London: Chatto & Windus, 1929), 224.

That obliteration resulted partly from a feeling of the incommensurability of wartime trench life and pre-war existence. In Aldington's own case, a feeling of disgust was added, not only for the war, but for the pre-war society that let it happen (or, he suggests, desired it). But the war did not only alter people's relation to their pasts. It created a new relation to the future. The war could not but summon up a time 'When This Bloody War is Over', as the popular song had it. When it was, the future seemed different from pre-war futures. In the third volume of his *Parade's End* tetralogy, *A Man Could Stand Up—*, Ford Madox Ford presents the Suffragette Valentine Wannop thinking of the Armistice at the end of the war as a 'parting of the ways'; a 'crack across the table of History[.]'[28] It is an ambiguous image. The 'crack' could be a fault-line between the war and the post-war world, as anatomized by Aldington. But Valentine is also thinking of the girls in the school she is teaching in: will they respect authority, or get out of control in the victory carnival? So the 'parting of the ways' is also the divergence of different kinds of possible post-war future worlds. The war seemed an ending, but the ending of the war seemed a beginning. No wonder the war begat discourses of both apocalypse and utopia; or begat, as in To-Day and To-Morrow, reflexivity about such tendencies. As we saw in *Daedalus*, when Haldane considers 'the last judgement', it is as 'hypothesis'. He was an atheist,[29] and offers his visions frankly admitting that their 'mythology and morals are provisional' (91-2) in a way he argued religions could not.

Future History

Part of the challenge of imagining the future is the question of how to narrate it. Even if To-Day and To-Morrow attempted to reground futurology on the basis of scientific knowledge, as we have seen, nonetheless it remains an act of imagination and product of human creativity. The future does not yet exist, so it has to be created each time it is invoked. In Kenneth Burke's description:

> Anticipation is by very nature an abstractive process, a simplification; as such, it has an interpretative or 'philosophic' consistency which events in actuality do not have. The future itself is a 'work of art' until it is actually upon us.[30]

As Arjun Appadurai has observed, academic disciplines have only recently started attending to what he calls, in the title of an important essay, 'The Future as

---

[28] Ford, *A Man Could Stand Up—*, ed. Sara Haslam (Manchester: Carcanet, 2011), 17.
[29] See his essays 'The Duty of Doubt' and 'Science and Theology as Art Forms', in *Possible Worlds* (1927), 211–24, 225–40; and see the discussion of the essay 'The Last Judgement' in the Conclusions. Krishna Dronamraju, *Popularizing Science: The life and work of JBS Haldane* (New York: Oxford University Press, 2017), 3, 66.
[30] Kenneth Burke, *The Philosophy of Literary Form* (Louisiana: Louisiana State University Press, 1941), 237.

Cultural Fact'.[31] Our social institutions, whether for government, education, health, or rehabilitation; our financial institutions and instruments, whether investment, saving, insurance, or trading, are not just future-directed but involve specific relations to concepts of futurity that vary from culture to culture.[32] Yet that very relativism signals that, while it is a fact that the future is culturally central to most aspects of everyday life, it is also true that our different versions of the future are fictions. We frame them in hope or anxiety and they may turn out to be true; but we cannot know that for sure in advance. The future is a story that faces forwards rather than back. But it is nonetheless a story. As such is subject to the same types of analysis and criticism as other stories or literary inventions.

This section considers the rhetoric of imagined futures in the series. It asks a set of questions related to the general question of how we imagine the future, but focusing specifically on how modernity narrates the future. The ancient vatic modes of prophecy and divination began to appear ridiculous after the Enlightenment; vestiges of superstition rather than portals to knowledge. For a modern mystic such as T. S. Eliot, such modes are signs of a legitimate attraction to the supernatural; it is just that, from his Anglo-Catholic perspective, they are the supernatural of the wrong sort. In the *Four Quartets* he says of pursuits such as spiritualism, astrology, divination, or dream interpretation:

> all these are usual
> Pastimes and drugs, and features of the press:
> And always will be, some of them especially
> When there is distress of nations and perplexity [...][33]

Other than such supernatural versions of prediction, the prevalent forms were mainly proverbial, moral, religious, strategic, or promissory. Proverbs compact the wisdom of past experience with practical advice for the future. They might be cast in the present tense—'The early bird catches the worm'—but the inference from the distilled insight is clear: be quick and you *will be* rewarded. In the mor-alized fable, the narrative is cast in the past, but the moral applies the situation to the future, whether implicitly or explicitly. Beware flatterers, or like the crow you will be tricked by the fox; if you're an idle artist grasshopper, you'll be at the mercy of the prudent ants. In a sermon, sinners will be punished physically in a meta-physical future. Promissory language acts can be private or public, to do with friendship or finance.

The future is thus present even in traditional, past-oriented societies. In the modern age and the developed world, futurity is omnipresent. Its grammar has changed. In the public sphere its most common articulations include the

---

[31] Arjun Appadurai, in *The Future as Cultural Fact* (London: Verso, 2013).
[32] See Augé, *The Future*, p. 96.
[33] T. S. Eliot, *The Dry Salvages*, V. *The Poems of T. S. Eliot*, vol. 1, ed. Christopher Ricks and Jim McCue (London: Faber, 2015), 199.

promissory statements made by politicians. As these are intended to certify individual agency, they sound more plausible (at least in theory) than predictions about impersonal processes. A candidate saying 'the economy will get better' is unlikely to garner many votes; whereas 'I will create new jobs' or 'I will cut taxes' sound like achievable aims. The other most common forms are probably those in the media, as Eliot says. His phrase 'features of the press' puns between the characteristics of mass-circulation newspapers, and the 'feature' articles they include. A proportion of these have always been predictive (of the kind Tuzenbach in *The Three Sisters* may have been reading, about balloons, or the discovery of a sixth sense). Remember the experimental novelist Christine Brooke-Rose's observation that news broadcasting, which you might think was reporting what had happened, in fact often says what will happen. 'In a speech tomorrow the Chancellor will say...'. The speech has been circulated in advance, or the main points, often precisely to trail them in advance to ensure they don't cause outrage (or in the hope the shock will have dissipated before the speaker confronts a live audience). So the utterance has effectively already been made; just not formally delivered at a public occasion. But the effect is to make the bulletin seem impeccably up to date. In a culture of rolling twenty-four-hour news, reporting what happened an hour ago already sounds passé.

What forms did the (mostly) rationalist To-Day and To-Morrow writers find to articulate their curiosity about the time-dimension? How did writers articulate their conceptions of the future? What are the styles and forms of thought used?

It is surprising given Wells's popularity at the time, that hardly anyone attempted sustained science fiction. André Maurois almost does, as we shall see, but his fiction of a war against the Moon does not detain him for long; it is a mere pretext for thinking about the future of media and politics in everyday Earthly life. Bonamy Dobrée's *Timotheus*, discussed in Chapter 6, is the only sustained science fiction (and which borrows the Wellsian time machinery), but he uses the mode satirically. It is possible there was something in Ogden's brief to contributors, especially if he recommended *Daedalus* as a model, which discouraged them from using science fiction more than episodically.

It is less surprising that few adopt prophetic registers. Many are quick, like Russell, to disavow any pretension to foresight, lest they be thought mystics or delusional. But some do wax prophetic. Hugh MacDiarmid, say, in *Albyn; or, Scotland and the Future* (1927) projects an alliance between socialism and Catholicism which offers a fusion of two millennial rhetorics. Fournier d'Albe contrasts prophecies about the immediate future, which we often make confidently, with a necessary diffidence about what he calls 'The Farther Outlook':

So far, we have looked but little ahead, a century at most. The prophet's task becomes more arduous as the time is extended. Historical guidance fails us. Familiar landmarks get blurred and disappear. We are in danger of getting lost in a bog of unreal speculation. Yet the task has often been essayed, and it is necessary and desirable that it be essayed now and again. Let me make my own humble attempt, in the light of what knowledge I have acquired and what great thoughts I have encountered in many lands and languages, and in discussions with many thinkers.   (*Quo Vadimus*, pp. 75-6)

Some—like Bernal—are able simply to be prophetic without making these pompous noises of sounding like a prophet, which hamper some of the weaker volumes (*Pomona*, say, or *Thamyris*). The danger in a post-prophetic age is that any prediction might sound like cod-prophecy. One strategy a few contributors find is to write mock-prophecy, the irony acting like a dose of cod liver oil. They rarely keep it up for longer than is needed to signal their awareness of prophecy's rhetorical dilemma. The best sustained example is Garet Garrett's *Ouroboros* (discussed in Chapter 4).

As H. G. Wells put it in the first chapter of *Anticipations of the Reactions of Mechanical and Scientific Progress upon Human Life and Thought* (1901), 'Locomotion in the Twentieth Century', the chief mode available, and in which he had himself been the prime British innovator, was science fiction. But that did not always seem the most suitable mode for serious public consideration about the future that would actually unfold:

It is proposed in this book to present in as orderly an arrangement as the necessarily diffused nature of the subject admits, certain speculations about the trend of present forces, speculations which, taken all together, will build up an imperfect and very hypothetical, but sincerely intended forecast of the way things will probably go in this new century. Necessarily diffidence will be one of the graces of the performance. Hitherto such forecasts have been presented almost invariably in the form of fiction, and commonly the provocation of the satirical opportunity has been too much for the writer; the narrative form becomes more and more of a nuisance as the speculative inductions become sincerer, and here it will be abandoned altogether in favour of a texture of frank inquiries and arranged considerations.[34]

In speculative fiction the narrative is in the past tense, but the time-setting in the future. One form Wells's speculative fiction takes is the utopian. In an example such as *A Modern Utopia* (1905), the modernity is by contrast with Thomas More's early-modern version. Wells's time-setting is in the present. The idea is that the modern Utopia is a parallel world which could have been ours, and still could be. It is a world that exists now, at least potentially; that is, it doesn't require new science and technology to realize it; merely changes of ethos, of social and political structures and beliefs.

[34] H. G. Wells, *Anticipations of the Reactions of Mechanical and Scientific Progress upon Human Life and Thought*, fourth edition (London: Chapman and Hall, 1902), 1–2.

As his 'Anticipations' are grounded on mechanical and scientific progress much of which has already occurred, and consider the effects of such developments, a proportion of his narrative is written in the past tense, outlining the history of technological development. But this gives him permission to switch into a straightforwardly declarative future tense: 'In the next place, and parallel with the motor truck, there will develop the hired or privately owned motor carriage' (15). Many of the To-Day and To-Morrow volumes fit Wells's description of his method in *Anticipations*. They too are relatively orderly arrangements of 'certain speculations about the trend of present forces, speculations which, taken all together, will build up an imperfect and very hypothetical, but sincerely intended forecast of the way things will probably go'. Much of their vision is articulated in the future tense. Writing about hormones, T. W. Jones, in *Hermes; or, The Future of Chemistry* (1928), ends with the vision, common to most of the scientific and technological volumes in the series, that new knowledge will enable mankind to change its own nature:

> Through completer knowledge of the chemical control of the body it will become possible to evolve a physical and mental type finer than any previous generation has ever dreamed. Thus it appears that we may anticipate a great evolution not only in material things and methods but also in man himself.   (88)

Though he uses the language of 'evolution', the fact that he applies it to material things (he has been discussing fossil fuels and industrial processes too) makes it unlikely he means it here in a strictly Darwinian sense. That he is using the term metaphorically suggests a swerve from conviction prediction. (The difficulty with futurology is not to sound mad.) Similarly, we can see a swerve away from the simple future: not 'a finer type will evolve', but 'it will become possible to evolve' it. In the following sentence, rather than predicting that 'there will be a great evolution', he says 'we may anticipate' it; not even 'we can anticipate' it; nor is it definite that we may anticipate it; 'It *appears* that we may[.]' This is all part of the diffidence Wells says is necessary 'to grace the performance'. But it shows Jones encountering difficulties with the future-expounded form just where he needs, in his closing flourish, to sound most rousing. (Though from another point of view the salient fact is the transitive verb. Man evolved, but now evolves other things through his own agency—which he might also turn to evolving himself along eugenic lines.)

Wells had not only identified the difficulties of writing predictions, but also, in finding a solution, had caused a problem for his successors. They had to wrestle with non-fictional futurological form, and they also had to avoid sounding like H. G. Wells. One solution several of the To-Day and To-Morrow writers found was an ingenious trope I term 'future history', in which the narrative is projected forwards to a distant future, from which it looks back and writes as history what was still to come for them.[35] Future history is not the history of the future, but the

---

[35] I had given several papers using this term before noticing that Adam Stock has also coined it in 'The Future-as-past in Dystopian Fiction', *Poetics Today*, 37:3 (2016), 416–42.

distant future's history of the present and its more immediate future. Predictably, it was Haldane who found it first for the series, and it was possibly because he showed the way that others adapted the device. His parody of a 'rather stupid' future Cambridge student essay describes the advances Haldane is predicting as if they've already happened; describing these unfamiliar and even disturbing possibilities in the blasé way we recapitulate the too-familiar.

It produces a curious effect, in which we apprehend an event as both in the future and the past at the same time. The device generally makes for humour, allowing the authors to avail themselves of what Wells calls 'the satirical opportunity'. But the humour or satire is directed not at the imagined future, but at the imaginary historian trying to narrate and understand it. Sometimes the present is also satirized. So Haldane satirizes the student—and doubtless the progressive Heretics of the paper's original audience in 1923 relished seeing in him a caricature of their less gifted contemporaries. But his obtuseness serves to make the most audacious future projects, such as ectogenesis, appear mundane. So the device enables the double achievement of imagining extraordinary transformational discoveries, and also imagining what a world would be like in which they are taken for granted.

It is a common tendency for people to consider how posterity might record their actions. (Think of politicians trying to manage their 'legacy' from even before the time they leave office.) In Evelyn Waugh's, *Decline and Fall*, the prison governor Sir Wilfred Lucas-Dockery keeps imagining 'sentences from the social histories of the future' praising him.[36] This comic version allows us to imagine the fatuousness of the (self-)praise, without Waugh needing to supply it. The social histories are 'of the future' in the sense of being written in the future; rather than about the future. He is imagining how his present will look to posterity. In the future histories of To-Day and To-Morrow, what is being imagined is the future, and also how it will look to its historians. The other two main differences are that the future history in To-Day and To-Morrow has happened to other people—our descendants, not ourselves; and that it has to be elaborated.

The trope might have recommended itself because the writers felt the form of history to be more plausible than that of prophecy—a mode that felt less speculative; more like scientific fact and less like divination. Or at least, a strategy to make foresight like realism. Put like that it might sound like at best, what Wells calls 'diffidence'; at worst, a failure of nerve. But in fact, it is the opposite of playing safe. Instead, it frees the imagination of these writers to even more audacious speculations. It increases the writers' confidence in prediction. Though the effect on the view of the future retrospectively predicted is more ambivalent. For some (Haldane, Vera Brittain) it also enhances confidence in the future itself, and its utopian possibilities; it expresses the feeling that their projects (science, feminism) are heading in the right direction. For others (Maurois, Godwin in *Columbia*, or

---

[36] Evelyn Waugh, *Decline and Fall* (Harmondsworth: Penguin, 1980), 171.

Hartley and Leyel in *Lucullus*) it can serve as a warning about where current developments will lead—all the more effectively for making them seem as if they have already led there. I predict that we shall see how these more dystopian future historians can use the trope with different degrees of satire.

Projected or future history may thus provide another reflection of an unease with prophecy in a rationalistic age; a feeling that prophecy harked back rather than launching forward. On the other hand, the telling of the future through the mode of history might equally suggest an unease with historiography:

> It was of course as a result of its invasion by *Porphyrococcus* that the sea assumed the intense purple colour which seems so natural to us, but which so distressed the more aesthetically minded of our great grand-parents who witnessed the change. It is certainly curious to us to read of the sea as having been green or blue. I need not detail the work of Ferguson and Rahmatullah who in 1957 produced the lichen which has bound the drifting sand of the world's deserts (for it was merely a continuation of that of Selkovski), nor yet the story of how the agricultural countries dealt with their unemployment by huge socialistic windpower schemes.
>
> It was in 1951 that Dupont and Schwarz produced the first ectogenetic child. As early as 1901 Heape had transferred embryo rabbits from one female to another, in 1925 Haldane had grown embryonic rats in serum for ten days, but had failed to carry the process to its conclusion, and it was not till 1946 that Clark succeeded with the pig, using Kehlmann's solution as medium.   (62-3)

As the mind reels from these extraordinary developments, it is mainly the laziness of the essayist that is in the satirical cross-hairs ('I need not detail...'). But as Haldane slips in his own tongue-in-cheek scientific epitaph, isn't he also satirizing the historiography of science which can reduce a life's work to being 'merely a continuation' of someone else's? The result, the ecological catastrophe notwithstanding, is a comic optimism—though with the darker undertone that this cheery future contrasts so starkly with the darker recent past of the war. The sea-change has been brought about by an accidental leak of a man-made algae used for fertilizer (and thus itself prophetic of today's pollution of rivers by agricultural nitrates). But it also provides a further joke at the undergraduate's expense, who appears not to recognize, as Haldane would have, that the sea has turned the colour of Homer's 'wine-dark' epithet. Despite 150 years of all the biochemical advances of the kind Jones was to anticipate in *Hermes*, Cambridge has signally not been able cultivate a better class of undergraduate.

There are other modes of future imagining in To-Day and To-Morrow. William Seagle's *Cato; or, The Future of Censorship* (1930) fantasizes about a future in which censorship has the effect on ideas that Prohibition had on alcohol. A legal 'Inhibition Amendment' spawns 'read-easies', 'play-easies', and 'talk-easies' (43). Imagining a time in which 'the League of Nations will have established its authority' (46), it turns its attention from disarmament to disinfection. Seagle gives his predictions in a simple future tense, or a conditional. The tone is light, and the jokey play on Prohibition and its speak-easies is clear. As with his vision of a psycho-analytically based censorship—'A great crusade in the holy name of the neurosis would be declared' (46)—what's less clear is whether Seagle actually believes in his predictions, or is offering them as amusing possible extreme scenarios:

> With television accomplished, nobody but the intelligentsia would read either [sic] a book or attend a play, look at a picture in an art gallery, or enter a concert hall. There would exist a group of aristocratic arts that would not need to be controlled.   (82)

This has a darker edge, especially in the light (or darkness) of historical retrospect. Seagle's closing prophecy is darker still, and offers another moment which makes one wonder whether Orwell was reading these books: 'The last censorship will be a psychological censorship which will last for countless thousands of years', he writes, adding that 'police officials will be known as "Psychological Comptrollers"' (94).[37]

Future history is not history, of course. It expresses hopes and fears for the future, as well as anxieties about the present. Haldane did not invent the trope. It was already available in late nineteenth century futurology, as we saw with Edward Bellamy's *Looking Backward* (1888). Inevitably, H. G. Wells had himself already used it, in *When the Sleeper Wakes* (1899) revised as *The Sleeper Awakes* (1910).[38] The prospect of the end of the century, together with the Boer War in the case of the Wells, may have been especially conducive to thinking in terms of a cataclysm and time-shifts (in Wells's 1895 *Time Machine* the imminence of the new century was perhaps enough; though that work does not use the future history trope). But cataclysms were all around in the period. A post-war book like Stapledon's *Last and First Men* (1930) deploys future history. So does the first section of Wells's *The Shape of Things to Come* (1933)—a product of the Depression, and published at a time when the thing to come feared by most was a second world war. Wells's title for this section? 'To-day and To-morrow—The Age of Frustration Dawns'.[39]

The sense of war as breaking up time ministers to the imagination of leaping across time. The future history trope suggests that if combatants wanted to jump forward out of war to be able to escape it, they also wanted to imagine what it would be like to be out of it but looking back at it; and looking even further back

---

[37] For further discussion of *Cato*, see Chapter 6.

[38] Wells also used the trope in the prologue and epilogue to *In the Days of the Comet* (1907). I'm grateful to Patrick Parrinder for this observation.

[39] John Gloag, the author of *Artifex; or, The Future of Craftsmanship* (1926) was a friend of both Wells and Olaf Stapledon. In 1932 he published his first science fiction novel, *Tomorrow's Yesterday*—a future history satire apparently playing on the title of To-Day and To-Morrow, in which a race of cat people from the future observe human behaviour.

to before it, and wondering how it all happened. The war, that is, among its many disturbing effects, provoked new ways of writing about the discontinuities as well as continuities between yesterday, today, and tomorrow.[40]

André Maurois' *The Next Chapter; The War against the Moon* (1927) also uses this intriguing trope for trying to narrate the future. In Maurois' version of future history, the mediacrats have a video conference (—yes, in 1927!) and decide that if world peace is to be sustained, the fiction of a common enemy is needed. Fredric Jameson notes how many utopian projections of the period involve a 'conception of a world state or of some higher-level United Nations or *ekumen* which would somehow unify mankind'; and how, as shown by both Sartre and Ursula Le Guin, they therefore 'require an eternal enemy against whom to perform this fusion of humanity as a whole.'[41] That 'eternal' appear to be an error, but even if not, the argument holds for an 'external' enemy. The use of propaganda against an external enemy to unite people was familiar from the First World War, as it would be for Orwell, writing *Nineteen Eighty-Four* soon after the Second. Orwell's vision is not of a world state, but the Cold War, in which three superpowers each use war and propaganda against each other to control their internal populations. He had himself broadcast propaganda during the Second World War for the BBC, so did not need lessons from Maurois as to its political uses. Yet Maurois' vision of a World Newspaper Association, and its cynical control of public opinion, may have contributed to the ideology of Big Brother.

So Maurois' press warlords create propaganda about a hostile Moon-civilization, and persuade governments to start attacking it with a destructive ray (54-8).[42] But they get more than they bargained for, when the Moon starts firing back, and destroys Darmstadt. Of course Maurois did not actually believe the Moon was inhabited and by people as technologically advanced as humans. What he is concerned about is the power of the press, including the propagandistic power to create realities that don't exist; and he is interested in the power of imaginative

---

[40] For a discussion of post-war novels looking back across the war to the pre-war world, see Max Saunders, 'Ford and European Modernism: War, time, and *Parade's End*', *Ford Madox Ford and 'The Republic of Letters'*, ed. Vita Fortunati and Elena Lamberti (Bologna: CLUEB (Cooperativa Libraria Universitaria Editrice Bologna), 2002), 3–21. For a comic example (dating from the year the series began) of future history written from a conservative rather than progressive point of view, see the satirical *Memories of the Future: Being memoirs of the years 1915–1972. Written in the year of Grace 1988* (London: Methuen & Co. Ltd, 1923), was published as by 'Lady Opal Porstock' and merely 'Edited by Ronald A. Knox'—who was actually its true author, the Roman Catholic priest and friend of Evelyn Waugh.

[41] Fredric Jameson, *Archaeologies of the Future: The desire called utopia and other science fictions* (London: Verso, 2007), 219. It is 'external' when, on p. 223, he mentions 'Sartre's dilemma as to whether the truly collective does not require an external enemy to come into existence'.

[42] Maurois may have encountered the idea in Ford Madox Ford's novel of the previous year, *A Man Could Stand Up—* (1926), in which the protagonist Christopher Tietjens hears a cannon firing at long range, and muses: 'It would be a tremendous piece of frightfulness to hit the moon. Great gain in prestige. And useless. There was no knowing what they would not be up to, as long as it was stupid and useless': ed. Sara Haslam (Manchester: Carcanet, 2011), 61.

literature to create worlds that do not exist.[43] (Maurois was a novelist too, though is now best known as a literary biographer.) A working title for *The Next Chapter* had been *Clio; or, The Future of History*, indicating Maurois' reflexivity about historiography.[44] The book is presented as a 'Fragment of a Universal History' published in 1992. What we have is purportedly the next chapter of that book.[45] But it is also what might be the next chapter of world history for the time of writing. 1992 is sixty-five years from publication: around two-thirds of a century. It is a possible indication of the futurological range Ogden was asking his contributors to aim at. The majority of the volumes work within limits of around fifty to a hundred years. That may be because, as several besides Fournier d'Albe argue, one can make informed guesses about where current trends might lead in that time; but imagination of more distant futures have to rely on fantasy rather than evidence. It may also be that sixty-five years was one lifetime ahead—at least by 1920s assumptions about life expectancy.

It is often the mostly playfully fictionalizing volumes in the series that provide the most accurate predictions: evidence of an advantage the imaginative writer may have over the digitally-armed and statistically-loaded foresight team of today. Maurois predicted a world war of 1947—close, but too late and too short. Yet he also predicts the resulting development of knowledge of 'energy within the atom' between then and 1951—thus being only two years out about the start of the atomic age, in contrast to the scientists, who were too aware of the technical challenges to see it coming so soon.

The Next Chapter stimulated another contributor, C. E. M. Joad, to reply, in *Diogenes; or, The Future of Leisure* (1928). In the core of the book, headed 'The Misuses of Leisure', Joad gives a characteristically amusing, cynical dissection of the tawdriness and vacuity of most existing recreations, before shifting into a satirical dystopian prophecy, including the idea that 'A deluge of carefully selected news will descend upon the heads of the community aided by every resource of television and telephotony[46] that science may have succeeded in perfecting' (69).

---

[43] See Charles Marsh, 'The War against the Moon: Andre Maurois' 1927 "Fantasy on the Coming Power of the Press"', *Journalism & Mass Communication Quarterly*, 86:2 (June 2009), 419–38. Maurois' fantasy may have been suggested by Robert Goddard's 1919 work of pioneering rocket science, *A Method of Reaching Extreme Altitudes*, which had received wide coverage, and included the suggestion of firing a rocket at the moon designed to ignite enough flash powder on the moon's surface to be visible through a telescope from Earth.

[44] Discussed in Appendix A.

[45] It is also possible that Maurois was alluding to Churchill's comment, quoted in *Janus* and discussed above (p. 126), that 'As for Poison Gas and Chemical Warfare in all its forms, only the first chapter has been written of a terrible book'.

[46] The *Oxford English Dictionary* does not record 'telephotony', which may be Joad's own coinage by analogy with 'telephony'. But it does include 'telephote', in use from the 1880s, as a device for transmitting either signals by means of light, or (more probably in this case) images by means of electricity—in other words what we would probably now call a videophone. Joad echoed this passage in one headed 'A Vision of the Future' in a later book: *The Untutored Townsman's Invasion of the Country* (London: Faber, 1946), 140–1.

This implicitly alludes to Maurois' book. But in turning to consider 'The Future of Leisure', Joad explicitly invokes him, saying he aims 'to indicate an alternative conception of leisure by the adoption of which mankind may yet escape the fate that he foresees' (70). First, though, he switches into a burst of future history, presenting a two-page fantasy 'with an extract from the work of a Martian historian writing in the year 10,000 P.M.I. (Post Martem Incarnatum)' (70). It is offered as the next chapter of *The Next Chapter*, to 'carry M. Maurois' prophecy a stage further' (70). The Martian has a dim view of man's 'low grade cunning', which would have destroyed all other species if they hadn't started destroying each other. 'The domination of the homunculi was eventually terminated by their discovery of how to release the forces locked up in the atom, a discovery of which they speedily made use to exterminate themselves altogether' (71). This taken as evidence by theologians of 'the providential government of the universe' (71).

Such intertextual high spirits demonstrate how the series was stimulating people to think and write about the future. But part of that stimulation was to get them thinking about *how* to go about it. If human endeavour can be conceived as written, in a book of history or fiction, how shall we write its next chapter? Future history is an ingeniously double-articulated mode, bringing a self-reflectiveness to bear on the writing of both science fiction and of history. Was this something encouraged by Ogden? Linda Hutcheon coined the influential term 'historiographic metafiction' for postmodern novels which are not merely historical novels, but which explore the condition of their own fictionality through meditating on the processes by which history is written (and thereby fictionalized).[47] Future history as practiced in To-Day and To-Morrow is not that. In Hutcheonese it would be something like meta-historiographic speculative non-fiction: a description unlikely to catch on, but which captures both the specificity of the experiment, and also how, when the writers experiment with it, what they are doing is passing from non-fictional to fictional narrative in their speculations.

This trope of future history is typical of what's so engaging about the series, and especially its writing about science. Vera Brittain uses it for the most part unsatirically in her volume, *Halcyon*, subtitled *or, The Future of Monogamy*, but really dealing with feminism and the relations between the sexes. It begins with a dream-vision introducing four chapters from a history book written in the future, and titled *History of English Moral Institutions in the Nineteenth, Twentieth, and Twenty-first Centuries*, written by the equally fictional Professor Minerva Huxterwin. The idea that the University of Oxford might appoint a woman to a full professorship injects a gently satiric note. (It would be the 1940s before that prophecy was fulfilled.) That such a woman appears to (or might need to) be a combination of Huxley and Darwin sharpens the satire. Using the future history

---

[47] See Linda Hutcheon, *A Poetics of Postmodernism* (New York and London: Routledge, 1988), 5, 57.

trope, Brittain is able to imagine a world in which the reforms she advocated have already come about. The second chapter from Huxterwin's book, 'The Period of Sexual Reform', narrates the passing of the Sexual Instruction (Schools and Welfare Centres) Act of 1948, and the Matrimonial Causes Act of 1959, which broadened the possible grounds for divorce, and made consensual divorce legal. The third chapter, 'Scientific Progress, 1950–2000 and its Relation to the Moral Revolution' envisages some of the same technological changes as other contributors, but is more interested in their domestic effects. Wireless and television would stop couples getting bored, as would air travel, which would also facilitate the form of long-distance 'semi-detached marriage' Brittain herself favoured (85). Ectogenesis has become commonplace. But she has Huxterwin disagree with Haldane about the use of it, arguing that couples would still want to conceive and gestate children naturally, helped by scientific advances in reducing the pain of childbirth; though she does envisage *in vitro* gestation for mothers unable to carry a pregnancy to term (77)—an interesting reversal of today's fertility treatment of *in vitro* fertilization.

The shrewdness of many of *Halcyon*'s predictions across a range of technological as well as social and political subjects testify to an outstandingly intelligent and curious mind. Brittain also predicts 'home talkies' via television (54–5); the introduction of maternity leave, known as a 'child-birth year' (51); and that airspeed would have reached 500 miles per hour by 1965 (though the thought that it would cost 'a few shillings' to fly to America or Australia was unduly optimistic; 60–1). *Halcyon* was published only the year after women under thirty were given the vote in the UK, which perhaps accounts for its optimistic tone.

Like Haldane, Brittain plays with the idea of history, which in *Halcyon* appears to have been transformed by psychical research: 'Only one or two examples are needed to illustrate this period', writes Huxterwin, 'now so well known owing to the recent research work of the Historio-Telepathic Institute' (18). The joke is nicely turned. It isn't that Brittain is confusing an academic discipline with a pseudo-science (though she may be warning us that the future might). Rather, she acknowledges that telepathy (the transmission of feelings, thoughts, experiences at a distance) is what both history and futurology have to be, but in the dimension of time rather than space. In doing so, she also acknowledges the limits of futurology, which, despite attempts to ground it in science, can only ever be speculative. Yet the comedy of the idea of a 'Historio-Telepathic Institute' suggests that generalized narratives about past feelings, thoughts, and experiences, despite attempts to ground them in the rigorous accumulation of evidence, can never shed their speculative aspect either.

To advocate sex education and women's independence when they go against the social grain is one thing. To write in 1929 of the 'Married Women's Independence Act' of 1949 (allowing women with children to continue their careers) is quite another. Treat it as a historical fact; an achieved landmark of emancipation, and it suddenly begins to seem more feasible; something everybody could live with. In short, future history is a narrative form that makes prediction feel as robust as its scientific basis is argued to make it. In doing so, it also makes the things predicted seem not only realistic, but familiar, acceptable, desirable.

The surprising observation is that this version of futurology—what one might call the 'Whig interpretation of Futurity' seems to run counter to the standard sociological account of modernity. To-Day and To-Morrow as a project certainly bears out Anthony Giddens' postulate that modern society is one 'which, unlike any preceding culture, lives in the future, rather than the past'. But he develops that idea by seeing the futurological turn as producing what he calls a risk society: 'a society increasingly preoccupied with the future (and also with safety), which generates the notion of risk'.[48] This might describe some of the volumes, like Russell's, or those worrying about future wars (as suggested at the start of this chapter) such as Liddell Hart's *Paris* or Oliver Stewart's *Aeolus*. But in general, what's striking about the series is the relative freedom from anxiety accompanying its predictions. Coming out in the same period as most of the great First World War memoirs and novels, celebrated for their cynicism and disillusion, you might expect To-Day and To-Morrow to be more preoccupied by a repeat of the war. What the series shows, though, is that concepts such as 'risk society' are too general to be especially helpful for analysing interwar modernity. Attitudes to risk are as affected by specific events like a war or financial crisis as much, or arguably more, than by long-term social shifts. Perhaps you had to be optimistic if you had survived the Western Front. Contemplating a reprise of that would have been as intolerable as looking back at it. When Vera Brittain looked back at the war in *Testament of Youth*, about her experiences as a nurse, the devastation inflicted on her patients and on her closest friends produced one of the most poignant and harrowing memoirs of the conflict. *Testament* was published in 1933. It had been massively rewritten, and was possibly being reworked when, in 1929, she looked forwards, and produced a surprisingly upbeat book in *Halcyon*. The *Yorkshire Post*'s reviewer said: 'Of all the brilliant books in the series, I know of few more "squib-like"'.[49] Or perhaps it's not so surprising. As any reader of *Testament* will understand, her pacifism made her want to see a world in which war had been abolished. For those who'd witnessed the war, the future had to be better. Which is to say that To-Day and To-Morrow is a key manifestation of interwar modernism's utopian tendency: its manifestos for a better life.

Which is not to say that all the volumes are optimistic or utopian—as we saw with Joad's. If future history can make utopian hopes seem reassuringly attainable, it can equally make dystopian projects look depressingly inevitable. In *Caledonia; or, The Future of the Scots* (1927), the journalist, historian, and biographer

---

[48] Anthony Giddens, 'Risk and Responsibility', *Modern Law Review*, 62:1 (1999), 1–10 (3).
[49] Quoted from the end-matter to Harvey, *Solon*.

G[eorge] M[alcolm] Thomson gives an unremittingly negative picture of Scotland. The Scots are presented as a 'dying people' (10), due to emigration, plus immigration of Irish Catholics. Thomson finds an 'abject acceptance of the progressive impoverishment of their country' (29). Capital, industry, intelligent youth, are all being drained South. He is dismissive of Scottish achievements, education, culture, and newspapers. To show that the future could nevertheless be even worse, Thomson ends with future history. He imagines an intelligent young New Zealander named 'Macaulay' (after the great nineteenth-century historian and politician Thomas Babington Macaulay)[50] who 'drops out of the London-Reikjavik-Tokio express somewhere over Edinburgh' in 2027 (70). He learns that the Irish have predominated; a 1985 act banning further immigration sparks race riots. The Scots have mostly gone. The Highlands and Islands have been bought up by rich Americans who fight each other like old clan chiefs. Burns's cottage has been transported to Toronto (82). Scottish emigrants worldwide are portrayed as like the Jews: without a homeland, assimilating, but forming a movement 'to create in Scotland a National home for the exiled Scottish people' (92). The picture is all the more dismal in future history mode.

Robert Graves's *Lars Porsena; or, The Future of Swearing and Improper Language* (1927) offers the most bravura example of future history. It is a brilliant comic turn all round, touching on so many of the contemporary concerns of the other contributors—the League of Nations, chemical warfare, Freud, etc.—as sometimes to seem like both a digest and parody of the series in which it took its place. But it deals particularly with language. Part of Graves's joke is that he has an impossible subject, since censorship prevents him using the words he is discussing.[51]

Graves introduces a Sternean digression which is also a Huxleyan *mise-en-abyme*: a paraphrase of an imaginary book of the same title that cannot be written:

> Might not a useful addition be made to this *To-day and To-morrow* series, by some worthier, more energetic, and more scholarly hand than mine? To be called *Lars Porsena; or The Future of Swearing*. Lars Porsena, if we may trust Lord Macaulay, was more fortunate than ourselves: he had no less than nine gods to swear by, and every one of them in Tarquin's time was taken absolutely seriously. (48)

He then gives a synopsis of what its argument might be:

> The imaginative decline of popular swearing under industrial standardization and since the popular Education Acts of fifty years ago; the possibility that

---

[50] Macaulay had famously imagined a future New Zealander contemplating the ruins of London. See his review of Leopold von Ranke's *The Ecclesiastical and Political History of the Popes During the Sixteenth and Seventeenth Centuries* [*Die römische Papste*], trans. S. Austin (London, 1840); *Edinburgh Review* 72 (October 1840), 227–58. I'm grateful to Patrick Parrinder for drawing my attention to this allusion.

[51] Censorship was also addressed in *Cato*, as discussed above, and in Chapter 6.

swearing under an anti-democratic régime will recover its lost prestige as a fine art; following the failure of the Saints and Prophets, and the breakdown of orthodox Heaven and Hell as supreme swearing-stocks, the rich compensation offered by newer semi-religious institutions, such as the 'League of Nations' and 'International Socialism', and by superstitious objects such as pipes, primroses, black-shirts, and blood-stained banners; the chances of the eventual disappearance of the sex-taboo and of the slur on bastardy, but in the near future the intentional use of Freudian symbols as objurgatory material; the effect on swearing of the gradual spread of spiritistic belief, of new popular diseases such as botulism and sleepy-sickness; of new forms of chemical warfare, of the sanction which the Anglican Church is openly giving to contraception, thereby legitimizing the dissociation of the erotic and progenitive principles and of feminism challenging the view that hard swearing is a proof of virility.   (48-9)

He then imagines a puzzled reader asking whether *Lars Porsena* weren't the book he was reading. Graves explains that 'this volume goes as far as it decently can', since 'this is nearest to a *Lars Porsena* that will ever be published':

For as soon as there is sufficient weakening of the taboos to permit an accurate and detailed account of swearing and obscenity, then, by that very token, swearing and obscenity can have no future worth prophesying about, but only a past more or less conjectural because undocumented.   (52)

This is followed by an extended passage—around a third of the book—in the form of an account by an imagined historian from the thirtieth century looking back at the twentieth and its future—and struggling with the historiography of the undocumented:

When a future historian comes to treat of the social-taboos of the nineteenth and twentieth centuries in a fourteen-volume life-work, his theories of the existence of an enormous secret-language of bawdry and an immense oral literature of obscene stories and rhymes known, in various degrees of initiation, to every man and woman in the country, yet never consigned to writing or openly admitted as existing, will be treated as a chimerical notion by the enlightened age in which he writes.   (55)

Graves explains how just as James Frazer took the Golden Bough legend as an exemplary text, so his historian might analyse what Graves calls 'The Bottom Legend', allegedly taken from 'a contemporary historian Roberts' (and in fact about the notorious Horace De Vere Cole):

Shortly before the 'Great War for Civilization' (the indecisive conflict, 1914–1918, between rival European confederations to decide which was to have the right of defining Civilization) there was a student at Oxford University famous for his 'practical joking.' He is said to have been one of the rare persons of the day to whom a peculiar licence was given for such 'practical joking' and for deriding the most sacred taboos of the time. [....]

As Graves tells it, the student's 'most interesting breach of taboo' was a dinner-party he gave in a provincial town, bringing together all the people he had found there 'whose surname contained the syllable "bottom"':

> Ramsbottom, Longbottom, Sidebottom, Winterbottom, Higginbottom, Whetham-bottom, Bottomwhetham, Bottomwallop, Bottomley, and plain Bottom; he insinuated himself into the friendship of every one of these families, but separately, without allowing them to meet in his presence, until finally he was able to invite them all together to a huge dinner-party at his hotel. When each name in turn had been announced by a particularly loud-voiced hotel-servant, he withdrew, promising to return in a few minutes, and begging them to begin dinner without him. The meal consisted merely of rump-steak, and the host was already in a railway train, riding swiftly towards London, and leaving no address.   (56-8)

The reviewer for the *TLS* found Graves's 'outline of a future historian's labours [...] exhilarating'.[52] Certainly his parody of earnest academic dispute with learned sources on and around such a speculative topic are entertaining; not least because the parody is in part about the impossibility of explaining any humour without killing it, let alone trying to make a different time and culture understand what why such an escapade might have been thought funny.

Yet the most striking effect here is rather the allusion to the war: not just the relabelling of it (and in terms which parody the contemporary propaganda about saving civilization from the barbarous Huns), but the labelling it as 'indecisive'. That summons up the prospect of future conflict, which Graves could imagine as the League of Nations proved so indecisive and Italian fascism augured ill for Europe:

> Joyce appears to have defied all taboos in his writing, and it is a pity that the Universal-Fascismo combination of 1929 succeeded in destroying every copy of his most famous work *Ulysses*, which would have been a mine of information for our present inquiry.   (72)

This was written in 1927; and is chilling in its anticipation of Nazi book-burning of 1933. *Lars Porsena* ends by denying that Joyce is an obscene writer. But Graves argues, again with witty paradox, that it is nonetheless appropriate he be censored, since all that most of his readers are interested in are the parts judged obscene; and that by the same token Shakespeare's work should be banned as well.

Where *Daedalus* deploys future history with humour to sweeten several profoundly serious predictions, *Lars Porsena* is more troublingly ambivalent. Though its *jeu d'esprit* is decidedly and explicitly back-shadowed by the war, it doesn't fall into the category of the utopian. Part of the joke at the expense of the future historian is that a time when taboo-based humour is no longer possible or comprehensible may not be a better world (though this too is ambivalent, since it

---

[52] Quoted on the dust jacket of the fourth impression.

simultaneously parodies contemporary antiquarians obtuse to the liveliness of the pasts they dissect).

The volume that uses future history to turn its comedy and satire most squarely against the present is *Lucullus; or, The Food of the Future* (1926) by food writers Hilda (Mrs C. F.) Leyel and Olga Hartley (who also wrote novels and detective fiction). Lucullus was a Roman consul, notorious as a gastronome. Hartley and Leyel wonder what the Lucullus of the future would expect to eat. In the second part of this short volume, taking up nearly half of it (43-77), they imagine that a future 'Professor Lucullus, F.R.S., may broadcast something remotely resembling the following lecture' (43). This begins, rather startlingly: 'In the middle of the twentieth century the world became vegetarian. It has been commonly assumed that the reasons were economic' (43). This transformation allows for a series of comic contrasts in which contemporary innovations in radio, or technologies retain their currency; whereas traditional forms of life, especially those connected with food, become as incomprehensible to the future as was humour to Graves's future historian. The professor is baffled why people still kept dogs, wondering if it was for food. 'It is of course possible that they venerated them for superstitious reasons', he adds: 'and kept them as mascots to bark, either to scare away the spooks the spiritualists were apparently raising in considerable number about this time, or with the idea of averting the calamity of strikes' (50). The book appeared the same year as the General Strike.

Lucullus demonstrates his modernist credentials in his view of farm animals: 'Of course cows and sheep are machines for turning grass not only into meat, milk, butter and cheese, but also into wool, horn and leather' (49). Future history here enables fine satire of contemporary fashions. 'There were also private suburban gardens, but the only plants the inhabitants seem to have had any idea of growing were laurel bushes, privet hedges, and geraniums. It is rational to assume that they *did* eat them: why else should they have taken the trouble to grow them?' (69-70). But the humour at the expense of baffled future historians faced with obscure past practices is equally fine. 'Of course London had Covent Garden but how much fruit was actually grown there is a matter of speculation' (68-9). Lucullus refers to a debate over whether 'tinned foods' refers to food made from tin (55). There are also some sharp comic vignettes aimed at scientists: 'and of course in those superstitious days the credulous people believed everything the scientists told them, in spite of the fact that each generation of scientists told them something quite different from what their predecessors had preached' (51). Mad science is not confined to nutrition. Surprisingly, Hartley and Leyel join the ranks of contributors speculating about atomic science and cosmology—perhaps to sound suitably futuristic:

> in about 1942, in experiments on the atom, scientists blew up the whole of North-west London; it simply disappeared in a cloud of dust and fire. There was

a question asked in Parliament about it, by the Member for North St. Pancras or Hampstead, who was left without a constituency, but beyond that nobody complained, nobody seems to have objected.   (53)

Then a Scottish scientist uses magnets to try to bring Mars near enough for radio contact, but it goes wrong and 'it was Glasgow that was torn up by its roots and whisked up to Mars' (60-1). Such recklessness sparks a 'great reform movement' (62) to hold scientists in check.

All of these writers use the trope of future history for serious purposes, whether to examine scientific interventions in biological processes, the feasibility of extending women's rights, to attack censorship, or to reimagine diet—even as they also find surprising comic potential in the form. There is a long tradition of the rediscovered manuscript from the past. The history of the novel is strewn with them; and there was an Edwardian vogue for them, with writers like A. C. Benson specializing in the wistful, and Maurice Baring in the humorous imagining of the *Lost Diaries* and *Lost Letters* of famous figures from history and literature. In some ways future history turns that genre around in time.

However, the aim of the reading in this section between and across these intelligent texts is to bring out what Raymond Williams used to call a 'structure of feeling', or what in this case might better be called a style of thinking: a rhetoric of knowledge organized around ideas of historical progress and retrospect.

Future history is from one point of view the narrative counterpart to the future anterior tense, used in order to articulate what humanity *will have done* by a point in time in the future. The future anterior imagines a future time by which an action will have been completed.[53] Yet *its* point of view is the present. It is conceiving of that future moment from now. Once that moment has been reached, the tense would be the past (whether simple past or past perfect), describing a completed action—it *happened*; it *has been done*—a tense of retrospect; of historiography. Future history does not just anticipate an event in the future. That would be prophecy or prediction. It anticipates a point of view in the far future from which you can look back. As it is used in To-Day and To-Morrow it has affinities with the 'time-shift' in fiction, as devised by Ford Madox Ford and his collaborator Joseph Conrad in the years between the Boer War and the First World War.

Future history produces an effect of displacement, teletransporting the reader out of the present, to a vantage point from which she can look back at that present, and also at its future. To some extent it is perhaps elicited by the series brief of projecting the self forward, to a future point well outside the writer's own time. It is about seeing your time from outside; and is thus a form of what Viktor

[53] See for example Ben Highmore's discussion of 'future-perfect, or future-anterior' writing 'as correspondents consider their (and others') past and futures in the context of the ever-changing present', in *Ordinary Lives: Studies in the everyday* (London: Routledge, 2010), 92. I'm very grateful to Nick Hubble for drawing my attention to this study.

Shklovskij in 1917 had called 'defamiliarisation'.[54] Shklovskij was a leading member of the Russian formalists, critics approaching literature in scientific and technological terms, as a medium using a set of devices or techniques to produce its effects. To-Day and To-Morrow volumes use a variety of forms of displacement. *Ethnos* uses the anthropologist's (or League of Nations diplomat's) conceit of standing outside race and nation. *Daedalus*, as we have seen, zooms back in cinematic fashion from the trenches to see a tank battle from above. All futurology arguably effects a comparable displacement, in the temporal dimension. Because futurology defamiliarizes chronology, disturbing our familiar sense of situatedness in time, it conduces to a relativistic attitude to time and history. Prediction incited the contributors to future history, that is, because thinking about their future made them think about how their present would look to that future.

But future history offers a more complex form of disorientation—in effect a triple displacement, moving from the present, to the far future, to look back at the present, and its near future. This network of temporal positions may have made the trope particularly appealing at times when, in Eliot's words, 'there is distress of nations and perplexity'; when people were looking back to the last war (the boom of war novels and memoirs crescendoing during the late 1920s); anxiously beginning to anticipate the next; and wondering how posterity would look back, not only on a century which could countenance such avoidable horror, but on the generation living between the wars, whose decisions and actions would determine the next chapter of future history.

Friedrich von Schlegel famously wrote that 'A historian is a prophet in reverse'.[55] The future history trope allows prophets to write history in reverse; looking forwards.

Joined Up Thinking/Thinking Networks: Rhetorics of Unification

Though the series' writers couldn't foresee what Manuel Castells calls 'The Network Society' in the digital/internet/multimedia sense in which we understand it, we have seen how Bernal predicted a form of mental interconnection.[56] Interconnection was a familiar trope through the nineteenth century. Dickensian plots insist on the interconnectedness of urban life. The development of the technologies and institutions of the railways, the postal service, the telegraph and then the telephone

[54] Viktor Shklovskij, 'Art as Technique', *Literary Theory: An anthology*, ed. Julie Rivkin and Michael Ryan (Malden: Blackwell Publishing Ltd, 1998), 15–21.
[55] Schlegel, 'Fragmente', *Athenaeum* Berlin 1798, I:ii.20: 'Der Historiker ist ein rückwärts gekehrter Prophet'; sometimes translated as 'The historian is a prophet looking backwards'.
[56] Manuel Castells, *The Information Age: Economy, society and culture. Volumes I, II & III: The rise of the network society/The power of identity/End of the millennium* (Oxford: Blackwell, 1999).

intensified the sense of manifold networks. But wireless-based technologies take the possibilities of connection to a new level. This heightened sense of interconnection forms another recurrent trope in To-Day and To-Morrow; one which is applied to a wide range of subjects, as this section will demonstrate.

It certainly characterizes the discussions of new communication technologies—something the writers were especially exercised by. For example, television. Though in Britain the first demonstration of television transmission had taken place in January 1926, and the BBC didn't start a regular broadcast service till 1932, in the intervening years, when three quarters of the To-Day and To-Morrow books were written, many of the authors consider the possible impact of the medium, such as Vera Brittain, André Maurois, Cecil Chisholm in *Vulcan*, as well as A. M. Low in *Wireless Possibilities*.

Even the year before Baird's demonstration, E. E. Fournier d'Albe, in *Quo Vadimus? Glimpses of the Future* (1925) gets positively and rather poetically exhilarated by thinking of the possibilities of increased human connectedness:

> The mass of interconnections between human nations and individuals will be like a closely-woven fabric. Even now, the digging up of a city road reveals a tangled network of water pipes, electric mains, gas pipes, and drain pipes suggestive of the dissection of an animal body. It is but a faint foreshadowing of what is to come [....]

> Nobody is conscious of the appalling complexity of his anatomical organization when using his body as a well-poised instrument of thought and intercourse. 'The simple life' is not the old-fashioned country life of England or the primitive life of savage humanity. Real simplicity is constituted by the life in which most things are done by pressing a button, and a man can travel across a continent in such comfort that on arrival at his destination all memories of his journey are dimmed or lost, and he can hardly recall having travelled at all.

> We may, therefore, expect that, as facilities for intercourse become more detailed and widespread, the effect will be, not to increase the tax on our nerve force until it becomes unbearable, but to increase our area of selection. There will thus be more consistency in our actual interests and activities and more real harmony and leisure.

> The unification of the planet which is being accomplished before our eyes will have some astounding consequences. Mankind will assume a definite mastery of his home in the solar system. Attila could boast that when he plunged his spear into the ground, the whole earth trembled. The earth trembles even now to the electric signals of our powerful wireless stations. What will it be in a hundred or a thousand years? In a hundred years the unification of the human race will be complete. The earth and the fulness thereof will be under the full mastery of man. All animal, vegetable and bacterial life will be kept within strict bounds in the interests of humanity. The earth will be under one government, and one language will be written and understood, or even spoken, all over the globe.

There will still be different races and perhaps allied nations, but travel and commerce will be free and unfettered, and calamities will be alleviated and dangers met by the united forces of all mankind.   (81-3)

Fournier d'Albe's argument here effectively counters those who—like Georg Simmel in his essay 'The Metropolis and Mental Life' (1903)—saw urban modernity as an accelerating assault on the nerves.[57] Fournier d'Albe's vision of unification is of world co-operation and League-of-Nations-style alliances, but not racial or political unification. Another contributor, C. P. Blacker, writing on *Birth Control and the State* (1926), also entertains that idea (in the same words) of 'the unification of the human race' (82). 'Unification' there seems to mean peace and harmony— he has been considering whether the war he foresees between Japan and either the US or the UK might be averted. Later he talks of how 'mankind is now economically unified throughout the world by the astounding feats of inter- communication and transport. But as yet the human race has achieved little ethical unification' (85). His book goes through the routine eugenicist arguments (the middle classes will diminish through contraception; 'degenerates' multiply without restraint); and shares the concerns of other To-Day and To-Morrow volumes with the crisis in the League of Nations (74), 'world peace' (95) and the prospect of a future war. But it is unusual in bringing the two topics together. He sees the control of populations as the key to geopolitical crises. Which makes one suspect that, given his overarching subject, the 'unification of the human race' might also be conceived as a racial unification, based on a 'biological criterion of racial fitness' (85).

Quo Vadimus? anticipates globalization and ways of describing it, though in a utopian vein, rather than our more critical analysis of the ways the main drivers and beneficiaries of such discourse have been multi-national corporations rather than a liberated mankind. Fournier d'Albe's utopianism is not unlike the project of To-Day and To-Morrow itself, connecting different fields so as to build up a connected picture of connectivity. It becomes even more utopian in the following pages, as he imagines medicine curing disease and preventing ageing. But I want to pause on that image of unification. One striking feature is that it is unification conceived in many different fields at once: unification of the planet, of humanity, of communication, of language, of government, of travel and trade. From one point of view that was the author's aim: to sketch the future in general, without confining himself to one branch of knowledge. But many of our authors share his perception of increasing intercommunication and interconnection. Indeed, his

---

[57] Georg Simmel, 'Die Grosstadt und das Geistesleben', in *Die Grosstadt. Jahrbuch der Gehe-Stiftung* 9 (1903). Available in English translation in Kurt H. Wolff, *The Sociology of Georg Simmel* (Glencoe, IL: The Free Press, 1950). Also, if Bernal had read this volume, its rhetoric of increasingly widespread connection might lie behind his vision of wireless-connected humanity. If a problem with that vision is that direct exposure to the thoughts of everyone else would just sound like radio interference, Fournier d'Albe here suggests a solution: we would be able to select our Spacebook 'friends' and groups.

sketch here encapsulates the arguments of several of the other volumes, such as Sylvia Pankhurst's *Delphos* (1927), advocating an international language, or 'Inter-language'; or Ernest Betts' championship of the silent film as a universal art medium; in addition to those predictions of advanced communication technologies in Bernal and Low already discussed. Fournier d'Albe takes the idea to the point where it sounds like mysticism, or the science fiction of *Solaris* or *The Matrix*, say:

> *The Earth will have become a sentient being.*—It will be as closely unified and organized as the human individual himself. Mankind will be the 'grey matter' of its brain. (86)

But insofar as such an image is read as metaphor, it is accurate enough: it's hard now for anything to happen in the world without it being sensed somewhere else; by CCTV, satellite, spy-planes, or the monitoring of the various communication technologies, social media, or the internet of things. And the rhetoric of connecting human intelligences together to produce a collective brain is remarkably similar to Bernal's idea (and may even have influenced it). Fournier d'Albe's vision is more modest. He concedes that his sentient Earth 'may not resemble a sentient being high up in the scale of life'. It is, perhaps, more physiological; neurological.

A good historicist might object that such observations are nothing special. They were not only common in the 1920s, but even clichés before then.[58] The artist William Henry Hyde, for example, could title his image of telegraph poles and wires, with a faint outline of St Paul's Cathedral behind them, 'The Nerves of London' in 1907.[59] Hyde's image and title suggest that the 'nerves' are more than technological extensions of our nervous systems. They are both the wires themselves and the effect they have on us: 'nerves' you suffer from as much as a technology of feeling. (To that extent his image bears out Simmel's theory.) The illustration juxtaposes modern neurasthenia with the backdrop of a spirituality increasingly troubled by the incursion of technological modernity. Whereas Fournier d'Albe's point is that increasing connectivity will not 'increase the tax on our nerve force' (82). He sees interconnection as enhancing life; an object of awe and desire. In this respect our predictors of the 1920s were very much of their time. And if that sometimes makes them seem prophetic of our time too, that is because the age they lived in saw the birth, the ectogenesis even, of many aspects of our modernity; aspects they were among the first to grapple with, to seek ways of comprehending and representing.

---

[58] See for example Elleke Boehmer, 'Global and Textual Webs in an Age of Transnational Capitalism; or, What Isn't New about Empire', *Postcolonial Studies*, 7:1 (2004), 11–26.

[59] Hyde, illustration in Ford Madox Hueffer, *England and the English* (New York: McClure, 1907), facing p. 280. C. R. W. Nevinson had much the same idea in 1930 for his modernist view down Fleet Street to St Paul's, through geometrically criss-crossing telephone wires, entitled *Amongst the Nerves of the World* (oil on canvas, H 977 mm; W 725 mm; Museum of London).

But it was also the time of the aftermath of the Great War, as it was then known, or Armageddon, as it was also sometimes known. That period, when humanity had come together primarily to blow itself to pieces, couldn't but cast its shadow over even the most utopian writing of the 1920s. Thus authors in a variety of disciplines are not just writing about their disciplines; but, as here, are writing about how developments in those disciplines will make for, or threaten, the world's peace. Take Sir Arthur Keith, writing *Ethnos; or, The Problem of Race* in 1930. At a time when the popular image of anthropologists was as explorers studying distant, non-European cultures—Africans, Pacific Islanders, Aborigines—Keith applies race theory to the inhabitants of the British Isles. (Another, wittier volume in the series, Lyall's *It Isn't Done* (1930) takes this conceit of 'reverse anthropology' further, looking not at race but the customs of the British, and especially of our class system, as if it were from a strange isolated culture; as his subtitle has it, 'the future of taboo among the British islanders'.) Keith starts from 'the unrest which now disturbs the world', arguing that it 'arises from qualities inherent in human races'. What he has to say about 'patriotism' and 'nation' are thus clearly shaped not only by the war, but by attempts, through the Versailles Peace Treaty and the fledgling League of Nations, to negotiate these issues for the postwar world. He concludes his book arguing that his evolutionary theory of race 'must be constantly applied in the affairs of every-day life; without it we have no clue to the perplexities of racial animosity which ever disturbs the peace of the world' ([92]). It's clear from *Ethnos* that one reason Keith thinks 'racial animosity' is so threatening to world peace is provided by the post-war notion of 'self-determination', applied in Woodrow Wilson's 'Fourteen Points' of January 1918 and subsequently embodied in the Versailles Treaty. As F. C. S. Schiller argues in *Cassandra; or, The Future of the British Empire* (1926), the fragmentation of the pre-war empires into the proliferation of post-Versailles nations created a volatile and unstable geopolitics that even as early as 1926 looked likely to produce another catastrophe. Even if you thought that small nation-states tended to correspond to single races this would be cause for concern about racially-motivated conflict. But Keith's main argument is that 'race' is no more fixed a category than 'species', and that it should be viewed in comparably Darwinian terms, as constantly evolving. Correspondingly, he argues that nations can occupy any position on a scale of racial differentiation, from those in which everyone conforms to a single type, to those in which different types co-exist. His model for this is T. H. Huxley's analysis of the British, according to which the four national identities—English, Scottish, Welsh, Irish—don't correspond to distinct races, but to different combinations of two distinct races, Nordic and Mediterranean. Keith considers how this argument, and indeed Huxley's change of mind (he'd originally thought it needed three racial components), as well as the wildly differing numbers of basic races different anthropologists had come up with, all tended to problematize the notion of race, and its relation to nationality.[60] Huxley, he says, denied that there was any correspondence between nation and race.

Keith has a different view; that a nation is an expression of what he calls 'race-building', or a race-in-progress. He is clearly disturbed by the idea that the war had uncovered primitive traits and impulses which are deeply buried in human nature. He suggests two possible courses for trying to avert such conflicts in the future. One is what he terms 'deracialization'—getting a 'Eugenist' to breed out any nationalistic/tribal tendencies. But this sounds murderous and impracticable. Instead Keith opts for bringing 'all their inborn tribal instincts and racial prejudices under the rule of reason':

> It is only thus that the diverse races of mankind can live in the same world and yet preserve their respective heritages. I am convinced that the problems of race can be understood and solved only by men who approach them with a knowledge of the past.   (91-2)

Haldane expressed a similar view that nationalism's propensity to violence needs to be resisted from an anthropological and evolutionary perspective: 'It took man 250,000 years to transcend the hunting pack. It will not take him so long to transcend the nation' (*Daedalus*, p. 85).

Bolton C. Waller, in *Hibernia; or, The Future of Ireland* (1928) is comparably sceptical about the virtues of nation states, and about the viability of defining them along anthropological or sociological lines of race, religion, or culture (8-9). The Irish Free State had come into force in 1922 (though it would not get its new constitution, without the oath of allegiance to the British crown, till 1937; nor become a separate republic till 1949). So 'It is time that a cheerful book on Ireland were written', says Waller, 'and now it can be done honestly' (5). In order to do this, he has to gloss over the conflict between those (like Michael Collins) who supported the Free State and the Republicans (like Éamon De Valera) who thought it a sell-out. Waller's main terms are Freedom and Unity: 'What use will we make of Freedom?' he asks: 'How are we to achieve Unity?' (6). Ireland's cultural achievements are a source of pride, he argues: 'These things are in fact definitely unifying the Free State, causing us to get beyond the tribal or sectional point of view and to regard the interests of the whole' (66). He is an advocate of the League of Nations, and appears to hope that the League's or Commonwealth's model of linking nations to try to secure peace would also allow sectarian groups within nations to co-exist peacefully. (The Free State was still a dominion within the British Commonwealth.) *Hibernia* ends by arguing that no significant developments

---

[60] For an extended discussion of race theories about Europe in the period, see Max Saunders, 'All These Fellows Are Ourselves': Ford Madox Ford, race, and Europe', in *Modernism and Race*, ed. Len Platt (Cambridge: Cambridge University Press, 2011), 39–57.

are hampered by its remaining in the Commonwealth; and that there would be no gains from becoming a republic (69-72). Those who fought for a Republic couldn't recognize the freedom offered by the Free State, he says: its supporters were wrong to apologize for its falling short of a Republic (74). Waller gives two reasons for preferring the Free State over a Republic: i) 'The day of the wholly independent, sovereign, self-regarding state is even now passing away [...]'; ii) 'Ireland can be united on the basis of the Free State. Ireland cannot be united on the basis of the Republic' (78-9).

In geopolitical terms, as this suggests, particular nation-states appeared as fissile as the pre-war empires. It wasn't just that the colonies and dominions would want to detach themselves from the British Empire; or that Ireland wanted Independence, as would Scotland and Wales. But if these nations, like England, or virtually any modern nation without a history of isolation, were themselves multi-racial and multi-faith, they might as easily tend towards division as towards racial unification. Which perhaps accounts for that strange wobble over the notion of race in the long passage I quoted from *Quo Vadimus*? First Fournier d'Albe writes that 'In a hundred years the unification of the human race will be complete'; but then he says: 'There will still be different races and perhaps allied nations'. If in the first sentence he had said 'races', it would have been clear that he was imagining a bringing together of different races: the united races of man, by analogy with the United States of America, say, or the League of Nations. But as it stands, does he take humanity to be one race, or many races? What has happened, perhaps, is that increasing interconnection has begun to problematize notions of difference and similarity. The very technologies and institutions that purport to unify, might serve to heighten awareness of difference and division. Today we worry about globalization as obliterating local differences through the multi-nationalization or Americanization of the planet; but also that the resulting multi-culturalism might prove fissile in response to Islamic fundamentalist or neo-Nazi terrorism. To-Day and To-Morrow included three volumes on America. But other authors had of course foreseen American Domination. C. E. M. Joad in *Diogenes; or, The Future of Leisure* (1928) quoted Anatole France observing that 'the future is an American future' (14). But in Europe, in the aftermath of the First World War, it was the local differences that had proved more of a problem.

Just as European conflict produced the utopian hope that a repetition of war could be staved off through greater interconnection and unification through the League of Nations, it may also have shaped the hope that greater technological interconnection and unification would make for peace; and, equally, the hope that the safeguarding of national identities (as promised by the Versailles Treaty) would in turn hold the competing racial groups within particular nations in peaceful co-existence.

Our experience of nearly a century later shows that these issues are as pressing as ever. The disastrous wars in Iraq and Syria, and the emergence of Islamic State, are frequently understood as consequences of how national boundaries were drawn after the First World War. Similarly, the post Second World War European settlement is under increasing pressure from the rise of nationalism and anti-immigration sentiment, as the EU begins to unravel, and the Trump administration's commitment to the future of NATO remains uncertain. Britain is split down the middle over 'Brexit', and its own union is no less fissile, with the Scottish Nationalist Party winning fifty-six out of fifty-nine Scottish seats in the 2015 General Election, and the narrow defeat of an Independence referendum having by no means settled the matter.

The notion of 'self-determination', it should be added, is also a post-*imperial*, or anti-imperial, or at least potentially anti-imperial, notion. This comes out clearly in Schiller's *Cassandra*. He sees the Versailles 'settlement' as promoting, rather, 'a general unsettlement' of European affairs, 'of which the consequences, economic and political, will endure until the next convulsion, which they are admirably calculated to precipitate and aggravate' (50). He introduces his volume with the conceit that it is only those prophecies of doom which go unbelieved (like Cassandra's) that prove true, because if people believe a warning they'll try to evade its danger. (Or, as Gerald Gould was to put it in another good volume in the series, *Democritus; or, The Future of Laughter* (1929): 'We are back, indeed, at the old central paradox in which all discussion of the future find, and loses, itself. Aspiration is its own negation'; 43). Unfortunately, as the evidence of these volumes confirms, that fatalistic sense of another inevitable European war was widely believed in the period. The promoting of nationalisms is the main risk according to Schiller. This is because separate nations establish barriers to the traffic and trade that would enable greater interconnection; because they are then put under internal strain insofar as their populations are mixed; but also because some of the nations were in competition as imperial powers too, 'without perceiving the contradiction between the imperial and the national ideal' (54). This somewhat throwaway clause indicates one of the main causes of imperial disintegration. He has other arguments, especially about the geographical dispersal of the British Empire, and the impossibility of a small nation like Britain being able to stop its colonies growing closer to larger and nearer powers like the US. But what drives such a process of a colony growing away from its imperial ruler is precisely the principle of self-determination as it acquires a national identity (as colonies so remote from their rulers are especially likely to do).

Cassandra ends with 'A Note on Locarno', saying that 'Since pp. 55-56 were written the much-belauded Locarno Pact has been compiled [...]' (89). The Locarno treaties, with which Germany, France, Britain, Belgium, and Italy sought to guarantee European peace, were initialed in October 1925 and signed on the 1st December 1925. The book was thus presumably completed in late 1925 or possibly early 1926, and its publication in 1926 probably preceded the 'Imperial Conference'—the third since the war—that took place in London that October and November. (The *Yorkshire Post*, calling *Cassandra* 'small, but very, very weighty; brilliantly written', said: 'it ought to be read by all shades of politicians'.[61]) It was at that conference that the 'Balfour Declaration' of 1926 was signed—not to be confused with the 1917 Balfour Declaration which included support for a Jewish national home in Palestine. The 1926 Declaration accepted the increasing diplomatic and political independence of the Dominions, and granted them equal status with the United Kingdom within the 'British Commonwealth of Nations'. With the 1931 Statute of Westminster they achieved full legislative sovereignty. If Schiller couldn't have known this outcome, he would have been aware of growing demands from the Dominions for autonomy, and the imminent Imperial Conference was part of the context for his book, which may well have been intended to influence the Conference's discussions. The 1926 Conference is also discussed by George Godwin in *Columbia; or, The Future of Canada* ((1928), 8, 66, 77). Godwin's prophecies proved much less accurate than Schiller's. He thought the loosening of Canada's ties to the British Empire made its annexation to the US inevitable.[62] Schiller, by contrast, and with greater prophetic accuracy, argues that it is Britain which needs to ally itself ever closer to America. What unites the two authors, though, is the sense of the Empire's inevitable disunification. Hugh MacDiarmid wrote in *Albyn, or Scotland and the Future* in 1927 that the word 'Empire' was now a misnomer: instead, it should be renamed the 'British Association of Free Peoples' (59). The two books on India which appeared in 1929 both argued along these lines. In *Kalki; or, The Future of Civilization*, Sarvepalli Radhakrishnan wrote that: 'India's independence is only a matter of time' (94). Whereas R. J. Minney in *Shiva; or, The Future of India* not only predicted that within a hundred years India could be 'the greatest and most prosperous country' (5) but that it would no longer be part of an Empire, but something sounding very like the modern Commonwealth (that did not acquire its current republican form until after India gained independence in 1947): a 'confederation or league of independent nations, living, trading and advancing in political and commercial harmony' (94). Minney also thought it was likely that India would itself disunify, as it did with the Partition that separated off Pakistan, also in 1947.

Schiller, like these other contributors, prophesies fission at several levels: individual nation; geographical region (Europe); and empire. He differs from Keith in seeing the fissile forces as not reducible to race (which he scarcely touches upon, though he talks of 'alien populations' within states (54) and a 'great mixture of peoples' within Europe (52)), but also involving economics, politics, and language. But in both, the rhetorics of difference within sameness, and sameness

---

[61] Quoted from the end-matter to Harvey, *Solon*.
[62] W. Eric Harris's *Achates; or, The Future of Canada* (1929) provided a counterblast to *Columbia*, arguing that not only would a self-governing Canada continue to play a role within the British Empire, but that it would have a world-leading role as a model for the resolution of other conflicts which neither the US nor Britain alone could achieve.

within difference, are strikingly comparable. They run through the volumes on techno-science too; though there, the writers are more often 'joiners', emphasizing convergence, greater connection between people, places, or man and machine. Whereas those writing on politics, or issues of evolution, race and eugenics, tend to be 'splitters', focusing on divergences—between nations, races, stages, and qualities of life.

The solution Schiller doesn't exactly propose—he sees the chance as having been missed—but which he would have favoured, was a federal Europe, based on the Swiss model of distinct 'cantons', each with a strong identity but a close political integration. Now there's an idea...Americans probably find it amusing how difficult an idea Europeans find this to swallow nowadays, even despite increasingly close political and legal and economic interconnection—or possibly, as the potentially disastrous outcome of the 'Brexit' referendum showed, because of it. In 1926 it must have seemed downright eccentric to all but Marxist internationalists, which Schiller was certainly not. Yet he also imagines a fourth level of connectedness, or a more extreme kind: what he calls a 'World-State' (78). This may seem even more eccentric to us now, but was an idea that gained currency through the 1920s and 1930s (remember Fournier d'Albe predicting that 'The earth will be under one government'). Aldous Huxley projected it in *Brave New World* (1932). But, as we have seen, it was H. G. Wells who had especially and repeatedly propounded it, and done much to popularize not just the concept but this name for it, from *Anticipations* (1901), through *A Modern Utopia* (1905), and his *Experiment in Autobiography* (1934), to the Second World War and beyond.[63] George Orwell, responding to Wells's *Guide to the New World* (1941), could complain:

> What is the use of pointing out that a World State is desirable? What matters is that not one of the five great military powers would think of submitting to such a thing. All sensible men for decades past have been substantially in agreement with what Mr. Wells says.[64]

Wells wasn't a Marxist either, but could see the attraction of the Internationalist project. It was especially with the publication of his best-selling *The Outline of History* in 1920 that the 'World-State' idea was very much associated with him. In it:

> he argued that the study was the first conscious attempt to tell the story of humankind from a non-nationalist perspective. He used the project to propagate his own sincere beliefs in the globalizing nature of human progress. He argued that, from the start of human evolution, humankind was constantly merging into larger and larger social units.[65]

[63] See John S. Partington, 'H. G. Wells and the World State: A Liberal Cosmopolitan in a Totalitarian Age', *International Relations*, 17:2 (2003), 233–46.

[64] George Orwell, 'Wells, Hitler and the World State', *Horizon* (August 1941), 133–8.

[65] Partington, 'H. G. Wells and the World State', p. 234. Though Wells had proposed the world state as early as *Anticipations* (1901), p. 81. See also *The Open Conspiracy* (London: Waterlow and Sons [printers], 1933), 18, on how the 'main theme' of *The Outline of History* is 'the growth of human

Schiller had thus clearly not invented the idea of the 'world-state' in 1926. His anxiety about how smaller units could be peacefully contained within larger ones was a general anxiety of the interwar period. The map of the West and the imperial powers was being reinvented; a massive disruption which fostered the reimagination of the map of Western thought. As I hope this chapter has demonstrated, it was a concern which a diverse range of issues both summoned up and offered the prospect of resolving: technology, race, nationality, internationalism.

Language should also be added to that list; not only because both Schiller and Keith mention it, but for the way the impressively erudite volume in the series, *Delphos*, by Sylvia Pankhurst, brings out the extraordinary diversity of comparable internationalist linguistic projects still current at the time.[66] The *Spectator* called *Delphos* 'Equal to anything yet produced in this brilliant series'.[67] Pankhurst discusses numerous examples of 'Inter-language', that is, synthetic international languages constructed either a priori on logical grounds, or a posteriori on the basis of shared lexis. Esperanto is still a familiar name, but others are not, and readers today will be surprised what a large following there was for now forgotten tongues such as Interlingua and Volapük. Pankhurst was writing before Ogden had launched his equally active campaign for 'BASIC' English. But she is unlikely to have supported it, believing that such a language, to be successful, needed to be based not on any single national language, but on common Latin roots. She is clear that Interlanguage is intended as everybody's second language, rather than as a threat to anybody's first language (and to that extent precisely mirrors the idea of a League of Nations that aimed to guarantee individual nations rather than trying to swallow them into a larger federation or empire). But BASIC, too, like the other Interlanguage projects, sought to foster intercommunication and interconnection, for peaceful aims.

The volumes of To-Day and To-Morrow are highly varied, and their authors were often chosen for their contrarian attitudes. They are certainly not all uniformly internationalist, even though the series as a whole has a radical cast. Many of the volumes are, or have their moments which are sexist, nationalist, imperialist, traditionalist, racist, classist (and specifically under-classist). Nor are such views necessarily antithetical to their modernism. It is often precisely in their most modern positions that latent prejudices based in gender, race, class, or empire become visible; as where an intoxication with technological futurity and instrumental reason engenders visions of reproduction without women, the elimination of those deemed 'degenerate', and the breeding or engineering of a superior race.

intercommunication and human communities'; how 'myriads of little tribal systems' have 'fought and coalesced' into the sixty to seventy nations of the present, and are now straining 'towards their unison'.

---

[66] See Morag Shiach, '"To Purify the Dialect of the Tribe": Modernism and Language Reform', *Modernism/modernity*, 14:1 (2007), 21–34.
[67] Quoted from the end-matter to Harvey, *Solon*.

If we pose the same question of the texts discussing interconnection as we asked of those writing 'future history', and ask what 'structure of feeling' or thought-style they manifest, what we see here is a rhetoric of knowledge organized around ideas of conflict and unification. Anxieties about disintegration were not only a legacy of world war and the beginning of the end of empire. Social structures were under threat from revolutionaries (as in Russia and Germany), labour activists (as in the General Strike), and women (as with the Suffragettes and campaigners for birth control and divorce reform). To-Day and To-Morrow, representing all these positions, was acutely sensitive to forces making for both connection and disconnection. Given such convulsions that is to be expected; though it may also reflect the interest of many of the contributors in Marx's theory of history, with its repurposing of Hegelian dialectics, and its spiralling reiteration of thesis, antithesis and synthesis.

The two tropes examined here—future history, and the discourse of conflict and unification—may seem incommensurable. Yet as soon as they are juxtaposed, their interdependence becomes palpable. The disintegrations and integrations of peoples and states are the stuff of traditional historiography: the narratives of wars, treaties, alliances, empires and independences. Yet in To-Day and To-Morrow the tropes speak to each other in a more distinctive way as well. The discussion above of the modernist valences of future history (as temporal fragmentation and disorientation) emphasized its disjoining potentiality, evocative of the temporalities of postwar memory. Yet in narratological terms, it can also be seen as a trope of unification: a device that reconnects past, present, and future; and a device which offers hope that future conflicts need not obliterate humanity, but can themselves become matter for future historians.

To conclude, let us consider another globalizing project not directly connected with To-Day and To-Morrow and coming several years later. This was another brain-child of H. G. Wells—so often the *éminence grise* of the series—this time thinking about how to organize not the world's peoples and nations, but the world's knowledge. He called it the 'World Brain: The Idea of a Permanent World Encyclopaedia' in a contribution he wrote in 1937 for the new *Encyclopédie Française,* and reprinted it in his book *World Brain.*[68] He was stirred by the development of the then new information technology of microfilm to imagine new possibilities for the unification of knowledge, writing:

> There is no practical obstacle whatever now to the creation of an efficient index to *all* human knowledge, ideas and achievements, to the creation, that is, of a complete planetary memory for all mankind. [...] It foreshadows a real intellectual unification of our race. The whole human memory can be, and probably in a short time will be, made accessible to every individual.

[68] H. G. Wells, *World Brain* (London: Methuen, 1938). I am grateful to Dr Gert Morreel for drawing my attention to this essay.

Wells was in his 70s when he wrote this. Before criticizing his vision as exemplary of the totalizing grandeur that postmodernism has taught us to be so skeptical of (what of unwritten human memories; the memories of the victimized, amnesia, and so on), we should perhaps recognize an autobiographical investment. If his concern here may reflect a personal anxiety about the ability to recover his 'whole human memory', it also echoes the terms in which he analyses himself in his *Experiment in Autobiography*, the subtitle of which is: *Discoveries and Conclusions of a Very Ordinary Brain (since 1866)*. In it, Wells describes how he has come to see his life-story as a gradual recognition of the necessity and, as he saw it, inevitability, of a world-state. In other words, his own brain was a 'world brain' in another sense.

The notion of a 'world brain', whatever else it does, might also remind us that contemporary notions of the human brain had at the time recently undergone their own unsettlement. Behaviourism and psycho-analysis are among the new branches of knowledge regularly discussed in the series; unsurprisingly given that among Ogden's other vast editorial projects were the production not only of the journal *Psyche* but the series of 'Psyche Miniatures'. As Bernal makes clear in *The World, the Flesh and the Devil*, the post-Freudian psyche was itself a fissile federation, only too liable to conflict—'Our capacities, our desires, our inner confusions', which he said were 'almost impossible to understand or cope with in the present' (58); yet one the understanding of which offered the hope of—precisely, unification; though here the model is a scientific one, reflecting the attempt to develop a unified field theory, or the increasing understanding that the physical and biological sciences were 'coalescing' (69). In *Socrates; or, The Emancipation of Mankind* (1927), H. F. Carlill (who was Inspector-General in Bankruptcy, and later Assistant Secretary to the Board of Trade, as well as a translator of Plato) puts forward just such a holistic concept of mental life: 'what lives and moves at the back of our minds is not the mere *débris*, the rejected by-products of our experience; on the contrary, it is an integral part of our lives, a complex being with a character of its own, rich in memories, impulses, and powers; almost another self' (26). (Though to integrate the content of peripheral consciousness seems here to split the self.) Interestingly, he connects the drive for unification with the experience of war. Many ex-soldiers were struck by the antinomy of scale between the vastness of the military operations and the forces they unleashed, and the smallness of the human figures in the open landscape, dwarfed into insignificance by the juxtaposition. Carlill describes his sense during War of 'being an integral part of a vast organism [...]' (39-40).

But Wells's 'World Brain' project also suggests how the To-Day and To-Morrow series can itself be seen, collectively, as another expression of this tension, anxiety, working through, of the relation of parts to wholes. It is both an attempt to unify the state of contemporary knowledge, collecting it into one series; but also to parcel it out into disciplines, categories, geographic areas, and so on. And within the project, individual writers repeatedly connect their work to that of other contributors and to each other's fields. In terms of the sociology of knowledge, then, the series partakes of the utopian, globalizing aspirations and anxieties of many of its authors. One wonders what they might have made of the internet, which, for all its faults, has effected many of their ambitions. And if microfilm libraries never quite achieved Wells's project of the 'world brain', the world wide web comes closer to mobilizing the 'whole human memory', even if it doesn't help the individual brain to know what to remember or how to think about the 'information' it retrieves. Wells, who for all his progressivist ideals also had a strongly elitist side, may have been disturbed by the ability of readers to edit today's equivalent of the world brain. Which someone perhaps ought to add to the entry on 'World Brain' on Wikipedia...

Fig. 3. Vera Brittain. Photograph by Howard Coster, 1936
© National Portrait Gallery, London

Fig. 4. Bertrand and Dora Russell, outside the experimental Beacon Hill School, 20th September 1931

© Getty Images

PART II
HUMAN SCIENCES

VULCAN
OR
THE FUTURE OF LABOUR
By
CECIL CHISHOLM

"No one, perhaps, has ever held the balance so nicely between technicalities and flights of fancy as the author of this excellent book in a brilliant series. *Vulcan* is a little book, but between its covers knowledge and vision are pressed down and brimming over."—*Spectator.*

"Ingenious and stimulating speculations on the future of industry, of absorbing interest."—*Daily Herald.*

"Both refreshing and stimulating."
—*Economic Review.*

"A pleasant departure from recent publications dealing with labour problems. A penetrating . . . who courses of our present . . . diverting and . . . dustrial . . . thoughtful . . . the subject . . ."

EUTYCHUS
OR
THE FUTURE OF
THE PULPIT
By
WINIFRED HOLTBY

Written in the form of a dialogue between Archbishop Fénelon, who stands for the great ecclesiastical tradition of preaching, a clever young gentleman called Anthony, who stands for the more superficial itself . . . . . . ents in . . . . . . thus, re . . . . . . dinary . . . . . . e study . . . . . . point . . . . . . with . . . . . . ster . . .

WHAT
I BELIEVE
By
BERTRAND RUSSELL, F.R.S.

"In walking sometimes he pinctures the bubble of cruelty, envy, narrowness, and it will which there is authority call these morals."—*New Leader.*

"Simple and brilliantly written."

"One of the most brilliant and thought stimulating little books than I have read . . . better even than Icarus. Mr. Russell's brilliancy is amazing."—*Nation*

THIRD IMPRESSION

PONS ASINORUM
OR
THE FUTURE OF NONSENSE
By
GEORGE EDINGER
and E. J. C. NEEP

What is Nonsense ? The answer of this book is both provocative and stimulating. Where is Nonsense ? Everywhere—in Art, Music, Chatter, Architecture, Plays, Speech, and Literature. Where did it come ? All through History. The book traces its growth from Primitive Ritual through the Medieval Church, the Tudor Masque, Stuart Roads, and Georgian . . . . . . to American knickabout Hells. What is the future ? A new vocational stimulus ? A lecture in International etiquette ? A common language ? A world information ? Or just Nonsense ? The whole thing is amusingly fanciful.

HYPATIA
OR WOMAN AND KNOWLEDGE

Mrs BERTRAND RUSSELL

3

Human Sciences

Introduction

As we have seen, some of the most influential To-Day and To-Morrow volumes were devoted to science. Though the majority—around two-thirds—of the volumes were on other topics, this chapter will argue for a scientific paradigm as a primary motivation of the series; and for an appreciation of the significance of the series as a contribution to thought about modernity and the future. In particular, it will consider the extension of science to study the human. To-Day and To-Morrow does not include extended discussion of the concept of the 'human sciences'. But late-nineteenth- and early-twentieth-century advances in disciplines such as medicine, neurology, anthropology, psychology, sexology, sociology, and economics clearly underpin the arguments of many of the volumes, whose authors shared Haldane's view that: 'It is foolish to think that the outlook which has already revolutionised industry, agriculture, war, and medicine, will prove useless when applied to the family, the nation, or the human race'.[1]

In his *Introduction to the Human Sciences* (1883) Wilhelm Dilthey had defined the 'human sciences' (*Geisteswissenschaften*) as encompassing both the humanities and the social sciences.[2] His aim was to distinguish their methodology from that of the natural sciences (*Naturwissenschaften*). Yet the social sciences such as sociology and psychology are Trojan horses, in that they already combine the methodologies of the traditional humanities with the more empirical and quantitative methods of the natural sciences. To that extent, approaching the facts of human culture and experience from a scientific perspective was not new in the twentieth century. Yet from another (and more Anglophone) point of view, the increasing prestige of social science disciplines like psychology, sociology, and also anthropology, led to a conceptualization of the human sciences as a third, hybrid, category, not subsumed by the humanities, but precisely attempting to combine the humanistic and the scientific, in a way that did appear novel. From

---

[1] J. B. S. Haldane, 'The Scientific Point of View', *Realist*, 1:4 (July 1929), 10–17 (10).
[2] See the *Stanford Encyclopedia of Philosophy* at https://plato.stanford.edu/entries/dilthey/#N188BroaCritFram accessed 8 January 2017. Also see *W. Dilthey: Selected writings*, ed. H. P. Rickman (Cambridge: Cambridge University Press, 1979). Rickman explains that Dilthey used the term ambiguously, to denote both 'moral sciences' ('i.e. the human disciplines like history, sociology, jurisprudence, linguistics and literary criticism') and also 'the disciplines which deal with mind and its products' and which 'are only accessible to understanding and require interpretation'; this second sense in contrast to *Naturwissenschaften* as dealing with matter (12).

Imagined Futures: Writing, Science and Modernity in the To-Day and To-Morrow. Max Saunders, Oxford University Press (2019). © Max Saunders. DOI: 10.1093/oso/9780198829454.001.0001

the vantage point of this century, the Introduction to the first issue of the journal *History of Humanities* describes the genealogy thus: 'Over the twentieth century, other categories were introduced in addition to the humanities and the sciences, in particular the social sciences (or human sciences), which study human behavior in its social context.'[3] This is the predominant attitude of the To-Day and To-Morrow contributors. When not writing about natural sciences, they write about disciplines traditionally grouped under the arts and humanities—literature, language, religion, music, etc.—but they approach them in a scientific spirit: sceptical, experimental, unafraid of challenging dogma. Religion, for example, is considered not in theological terms, but in terms of sociology, politics, and rhetoric. This approach too has its precedents, going back in some cases to the Enlightenment, and certainly to nineteenth-century figures such as Bentham (Ogden's idol) and Mill, Jacob Grimm, or Herbert Spencer. But the series contributors also write about cultural phenomena not yet co-opted into the traditional epistemological categories: the aspects of everyday life and culture which are now the mainstay of cultural studies but which were only beginning to be studied in the early twentieth century; partly because they depend on the technologies of the period such as audio recording, cinema, telephony, wireless, and so on. This pioneering work in the series is discussed in Chapter 5. The focus in the present chapter is on more traditional disciplines, but approached with this newer conception of the human sciences, and with a sense of how that category was coming under pressure from new technologies and ideologies.

In Chapter 2 we saw how the trope of ever-increasing connection played across the series, as writers saw people, places, ideas, connecting or merging (even if they also threatened to disconnect or disintegrate). The subject of this chapter is how the disciplines through which they understood that connectedness were themselves becoming increasingly integrated—precisely through the sharing of scientific method. That integration was the project of what was probably Ogden's major editorial achievement; his International Library of Psychology, Philosophy and Scientific Method; which ran to over 150 hefty and often landmark volumes during his lifetime; and which sought, through a fully interdisciplinary approach (but one which put the philosophical study of the human mind first) to bring together all the human sciences. So 'Philosophy' in that series title covers not just the traditional branches of analytical philosophy such as logic, ethics, and the study of language and meaning; but also more recent and mainly continental developments such as sociology, anthropology, psychology, psycho-analysis, and literary criticism. The aim is to present a coherent picture of a coherent body of thought. The 'Scientific Method' is not there as an additional subject; it provides the basis

---

[3] Rens Bod, Julia Kursell, Jaap Maat, and Thijs Weststeijn, 'A New Field: *History of Humanities*', *History of Humanities*, 1:1 (2016), 1–8 (3).

for the psychology and philosophy. The extent of the picture of international contemporary thought builds up by accretion as volumes are added.

To-Day and To-Morrow works the same idea but differently. There is an idea of totality and self-consistency articulated through the series title from early on, and after the first fifteen volumes or so, in the series page which described the books as providing 'a stimulating survey of the most modern thought in many departments of life. Several volumes are devoted to the future trend of Civilization, conceived as a whole'.[4] The totality the series offers is 'To-morrow', and 'To-day' insofar as it is the basis for thinking about 'To-morrow'. It is an encyclopedia of futurity. It proceeds on the basis that you cannot map the future without charting each discipline, practice, configuration of the social or political order, individually. But as it does that, they begin to accumulate—despite the local disputes along the way—into a coherent picture of human possibility examined from a point of view which is predominantly scientific, or at least which is organized in relation to ideas of the scientific, even in the volumes more sceptical of the paradigm.

The scientific attitude was also being systematized in the philosophy of the Vienna Circle, whose empiricism and logical positivism were founded on their responses to Wittgenstein's *Tractatus*. Ogden had published the translation of the *Tractatus* at the start of the International Library. As its title indicates, that series was another exercise in thought translation, introducing to British and American readers pioneering European works by Alfred Adler, Jung, Malinowski, Karl Mannheim, Piaget, Otto Rank, and others, alongside equally visionary British writers such as T. E. Hulme, G. E. Moore, I. A. Richards, W. H. R. Rivers, and Solly Zuckerman. Lord Zuckerman (who later became Chief Scientific Advisor to the British government) described how from an early stage the books in the series were 'required reading'.[5] *The Logical Syntax of Language* by the Vienna Circle's Rudolf Carnap appeared in the International Library in 1937, translated by Amethe Smeaton, Countess von Zeppelin. Ogden was to incorporate works by members of the Vienna Circle into his other series. He also published two essays by Carnap, *The Unity of Science* (1934) and *Philosophy and Logical Syntax* (1935) in his series of Psyche Miniatures, together with an influential book by another member of the Circle, Otto Neurath, *International Picture Language: The first rules of Isotype* (1936)—Neurath's manifesto for a standardized and logically-based pictogram system standing as a visual equivalent of Ogden's crusade for BASIC English as an International language. Pysche Miniatures was a series on the same scale as To-Day and To-Morrow, but focused on psychology, communication, and BASIC English.

---

[4] See Appendix A on the book history of the series for further details of the promotional paratexts.

[5] Solly Zuckerman, 'Talent Scout and Editor', in *C. K. Ogden: A collective memoir*, ed. P. Sargent Florence and J. R. L. Anderson (London: Elek Pemberton, 1977), 122–32.

The Vienna Circle was certainly attempting to establish a scientific foundation for philosophy:

> The publication of 'The Scientific World Conception: The Vienna Circle', signed by Carnap, [Hans] Hahn and Neurath and dedicated to [Moritz Schlick, the group's notional leader] (who was not wholly pleased by it), coincided with the 'First Conference for the Epistemology of the Exact Sciences' in mid-September 1929 [....] A distinct philosophical school appeared to be emerging, one that was dedicated to ending the previous disputes of philosophical schools by dismissing them, controversially, as strictly speaking meaningless.[6]

Such views were in turn popularized in Britain in the 26-year-old A. J. Ayer's bombshell book of 1939, *Language, Truth, and Logic*, with its provocative first chapter on 'The Elimination of Metaphysics', eliminable because unverifiable and unfalsifiable, unlike scientific hypotheses. What To-Day and To-Morrow shows, in the conception of the overall project if not in every single volume, is the adoption of a comparable version of this logical empiricism as the paradigm applied to every topic under consideration. Contributors could argue for or against traditional gender roles, beliefs about religion, morality, crime, the British Empire or modern poetry. But the point was that they could be argued about; nothing would escape questioning and being challenged simply because it was established, traditional, sacred, or seemed to work. Most of the contributors appear to have been chosen because of their enthusiasm for at least some aspects of the modern; and those putting the reactionary counter-case are doing so precisely in response to the evident modernizing bias of the series. Furthermore, some of those expressing scepticism about the more radical projects were themselves known as radicals in other respects—as with Bertrand Russell, whose mathematical approach to logic paralleled the work of the Vienna Circle, and who had been Wittgenstein's PhD supervisor. His critique of Haldane's optimistic projection of developments in biochemistry and genetics wasn't based on a belief that Haldane's vision of ectogenesis was too radical a transformation of family life. After all, he describes Haldane's utopia as 'attractive' (*Icarus*, p. 5). His objection is that he thought Haldane wasn't being radical enough about politics, and needed a more cynical critique of how such developments were all too liable to be misused.

Russell followed *Icarus* with a second volume for the series, called simply *What I Believe*. It was published in the Spring of 1925, and was probably the tenth in the series (and the first to appear that year). It is quite a contrast. As he explains in the Preface: 'In this little book, I have tried to say what I think of man's place in the universe, and of his possibilities in the way of achieving the good life. In *Icarus* I expressed my fears; in the following pages I have expressed my hopes' (5). There is some irony there, which seemed constitutional to him, and his expression of

---

[6] *Stanford Encyclopaedia of Philosophy*: http://plato.stanford.edu/entries/vienna-circle/ accessed 14 August 2014.

hopes is not much less satirical of the *status quo*. Indeed, what he hopes is that it will be possible to dismantle most of the elements of that *status quo*. The avoidance of a classical title is presumably part of that aspiration. He must at least have considered calling the book *Credo* to conform to the classical template; but that would have connoted an avowal of religious faith, whereas the author two years later of *Why I am not a Christian* (1927) wants to set what he believes squarely against any religious or traditional beliefs.[7] Indeed, his anti-credo is worth quoting, not only for the intellectual flavour it gives of the series' bracing confidence and energy, or out of nostalgia for a time when religion's absurdity seemed self-evident, and when it might actually go away and stop making our lives a misery, as for the way it clearly anticipates the logical positivist elimination of metaphysics:

> God and immortality, the central dogmas of the Christian religion, find no support in science [….] No doubt people will continue to entertain these beliefs, because they are pleasant, just as it is pleasant to think ourselves virtuous and our enemies wicked. But for my part I cannot see any ground for either. I do not pretend to be able to prove that there is no God. I equally cannot prove that Satan is a fiction. The Christian God may exist; so may the Gods of Olympus, or of ancient Egypt, or of Babylon. But no one of these hypotheses is more probable than any other: they lie outside the region of even probable knowledge, and therefore there is no reason to consider any of them.   (13-14)

What I Believe accordingly sets out the programme for Russell's utopia. In many ways it is also the programme for To-Day and To-Morrow, or at least for its progressive contributors. Its cornerstone is scientific method (as witnessed by his concern with the non-verifiability of theology). 'Man is a part of Nature, not something contrasted with Nature. His thoughts and his bodily movements follow the same laws that describe the motions of stars and atoms', he says (9). The new physics and astronomy have transformed our understanding of stars and atoms. Therefore they have changed our understanding of our relation to the universe. 'There are some who maintain that physiology can never be reduced to physics, but their arguments are not very convincing and it seems prudent to suppose that they are mistaken' (11-12). Because 'God and immortality [...] find no support in science' (13) the world-view based upon them has to be replaced by one based on what, in the title of a later book he called *The Scientific Outlook* (1931). He also disposes of a number of modern alternatives—vitalism, evolutionism (erroneously geo-centric: life has no significance in the wider cosmos); optimism or pessimism (mere 'naive humanism': 'the great world [...] is neither

---

[7] Russell published two more, shorter, essays with the same title, 'What I Believe'. The first, in the *Forum*, 82 (September 1929), 129–34, was written for the magazine's 'Credo' series. The essay also appeared as 'How I Came by My Creed', *Realist*, 1:6 (September 1929), 14–21. The second was published in the New York *Nation*, 132 (29 April 1931), 469–71.

good nor bad, and is not concerned to make us either happy or unhappy'). 'All such philosophies spring from self-importance', he says: 'and are best corrected by a little astronomy' (23-4).

What I Believe then moves through most of the subjects of radical debate since the *fin-de-siècle*, outlining how a scientific approach would reinvent them. In addition to theology and philosophy, he considers morality, criminology, sexuality, education, empire, psychology, law, war and politics. 'It is we who create value' (25), he says, articulating what would become a central tenet of Existentialism. He does not believe in ethics: 'Outside human desires there is no moral standard' (40). It then behoves us to understand what those desires are. In the field of sexuality Russell believes the traditional religious positions on consent, illegitimacy, divorce, infidelity, birth control, extra-marital relations, celibacy, sin, and sex education are all illogical and inhumane. So it goes with the other subjects, his discussions of them generally anticipating the more radical volumes in the series devoted to criminology (cure rather than punish!); sexuality, sex-education, and birth control (yes yes yes! The argument mutual with that of his wife Dora Russell's *Hypatia*); or education ('In all stages of education the influence of superstition is disastrous. A certain percentage of children have the habit of thinking; one of the aims of education is to cure them of this habit'; 53). Like many of the contributors, he sees the idea of 'human nature', on which religious and conservative thought is grounded, as something itself undergoing change, or liable to be changed: 'Nature, even human nature, will cease more and more to be an absolute datum' (95), he says—a statement which captures both the ways in which progressive thought was redescribing what human nature was, and also how that human nature might itself be subject to change, whether through eugenics, prosthetics such as ectogenesis, or physiology (*Icarus* had ended with an anxiety about leaders making populations more docile through the control of their hormones.) He does not cite authorities, but seems to be deducing everything from first principles, or inducing it from observation. There's no mention of Einstein or Nietzsche or Freud; but the arguments are in their spirit of leaving no assumption unquestioned. He does not advocate a particular psychological theory, for example (psycho-analysis or behaviourism), but writes well about human aggression and anxiety. 'In the ordinary man and woman there is a certain amount of active malevolence', he argues: 'both special ill-will directed to particular enemies and general impersonal pleasure in the misfortunes of others. It is customary to cover this over with fine phrases; about half of conventional morality is a cloak for it' (75).

Occasionally the insights are startlingly far-sighted. Richard Dawkins may have hit on the concept of the 'selfish gene' before reading *What I Believe*, and coming across this: 'it would seem likely that all altruistic emotion is a sort of overflow of parental feeling, or sometimes a sublimation of it' (31-2).[8] That might

---

[8] Haldane had made more specific proposals about 'the existence of genes for altruism in human populations' in work of 1932 and 1955: Krishna Dronamraju, *Popularizing Science: The life and work of*

seem to cast a cynical light on the basis of Russell's hope for social improvement, since he argues that '*The good life is one inspired by love and guided by knowledge*' (28). But perhaps it should be seen as an example of his subjecting even his own feelings to the same kind of remorseless demystification and scourging of the hypocrisy that he finds in others. In one scathing example, he touches on an area unaccountably missing from the rest of the series, for all its discussions of the British Empire, politics, justice and race: the imperial mindset in Africa:

> At the present moment, polished English gentlemen flog Africans so severely that they die after hours of unspeakable anguish. Even if these gentlemen are well-educated, artistic, and admirable conversationalists, I cannot admit that they are living the good life.   (69)[9]

Not all the contributors were progressives in the mould of Haldane and Russell. Anthony Ludovici, for example, appears to have been chosen to put as diametrically opposed a view as possible. His contribution to To-Day and To-Morrow was *Lysistrata; Or, Woman's Future and Future Woman* (1924): a forcefully anti-feminist tract, which would be countered by other volumes including Dora Russell's *Hypatia* (1925). Ludovici had written *A Defence of Aristocracy: A textbook for Tories* (1915), and *The False Assumptions of 'Democracy'* (1921—note the scare-quotes). He was also an art critic for *The New Age*, in which he attacked Impressionism and Futurism.[10] A sharp and lucid controversialist, he repeatedly positioned himself as a staunch opponent of the modern in questions of gender, politics, or art:

> I am particularly opposed to 'Abstract Art', which I trace to Whistler's heretical doctrines of art and chiefly to his denial that the subject matters, his assimilation of the graphic arts and music, and his insistence on the superior importance of the composition and colour-harmony of a picture, over its representational content.[11]

Yet—despite the suggestion, however playful, of a religious orthodoxy in that critique of 'heretical doctrines', Ludovici was scarcely a conventional traditionalist. He had been Auguste Rodin's secretary, and admired Van Gogh, whose letters he translated. His inspiration was Nietzsche (whom he also translated), and he shared

---

JBS Haldane (Oxford: Oxford University Press, 2017), 161. Dawkins quotes from *What I Believe* in his later book *The God Delusion* (London: Bantam Press, 2006), 397.

[9] Such incidents had been in the news from 1923, after the notorious case in which Jasper Abraham, the son of the Bishop of Norwich, flogged and kicked an African servant so violently that he died that night; his offence having been daring to ride his master's horse home after having to run along beside it for 17 miles on an errand. See Martin J. Wiener, *An Empire on Trial: Race, murder, and justice under British rule, 1870–1935* (Cambridge: Cambridge University Press, 2008), 193–4. A fictionalized version appears in Karen Blixen's *Out of Africa* (1937).

[10] Anthony Ludovici, 'Art: A question of finish', *New Age*, 12:21 (1913), 508; 'Art: An open letter to my friends', *New Age*, 14: 9 (1914), 278–81.

[11] Wikipedia; unattributed.

Nietzsche's antagonism to Christianity as well as democracy. His anti-modernism is thus radical in its own way (and parallels modernism's own opposition to nineteenth-century liberalism): so extreme it goes beyond any conventional Tory notion of tradition, and appears modern itself. His defence of aristocracy is grounded in eugenicist arguments rather than the divine right of rulers. His represents a reactionary modernism, akin to fascism; indeed, he would go on to write approvingly of Hitler in the mid-1930s. Even, then, in contributions as far to the political right, received ideas, beliefs, and practices, conventional pieties, were all under attack, eliminable in imaginable futures. A comparable Nietzschean strain, though without Ludovici's political baggage, runs through other volumes in the series dealing with social topics.

Social Sciences

Here the scientific paradigm is provided by the social sciences, such as the still relatively young discipline of sociology. Sociological studies were to play an important part in Ogden's International Library through the 1930s, notably with Karl Mannheim's *Ideology and Utopia: An introduction to the sociology of knowledge* (1936), a work that has evident bearing on the futurological imagination. Mannheim poses ideologies as 'those complexes of ideas which direct activity toward the maintenance of the existing order', and utopias as 'those complexes of ideas which tend to generate activities toward changes of the prevailing, order', and then shows how their interaction raises consciousness about aspects of social life that might otherwise go unnoticed.[12] Louis Wirth's preface to the book indicates the continuity between To-Day and To-Morrow's scientific utopianism and the International Library's project of mapping and advocating a modern rationality:

> It seems to be characteristic of our period that norms and truths which were once believed to be absolute, universal, and eternal, or which were accepted with blissful unawareness of their implications, are being questioned. In the light of modern thought and investigation much of what was once taken for granted is declared to be in need of demonstration and proof.[13]

Similarly, other sociological contributions to the International Library can be seen as being anticipated by the To-Day and To-Morrow authors.[14] The two volumes on crime bear titles harking back to the Bible and Shakespeare, but take the line characteristic of the series that such categories as law and transgression should not be seen as god-given or as functions of a universal and eternal human

---

[12] Preface (by Louis Wirth), p. xxiii.   [13] Ibid., p. xiii.
[14] The International Library also included: Jerome Michael and Mortimer Adler, *Crime, Law and Social Science* (1933); and Huntington Cairns, *Law and the Social Sciences* (1935).

nature, but need to be understood historically and through the human sciences.[15] In *Cain; or, The Future of Crime* (1928) the lawyer George Godwin predicts that crime will be regarded as disease. From one point of view this is a liberal position, in that he advocates psychoanalytic treatment for criminals as opposed to revenge-driven punishment, which he views as archaic. He claims that by 'common consent' the causes of crime are bad heredity and bad environment (101). This move neatly evades the Nature/Nurture argument—crimes can arise from either cause. But 'bad heredity' signals that we are crossing the border into Eugenica. 'Crime is the disease of the social body; degeneracy is the disease of the race', he says, labelling examples of the latter as 'The Irreclaimables' (31). The future he sees for criminology is thus a combination of sociology and eugenics, with the result that sociologically-defined crime will be treated more humanely, whereas— disturbingly—it would be the end of the line for eugenically-defined criminals: He goes even further, speculating that: 'it may come about that we shall not hang the murderer, but shall take to the lethal chamber some who have no murders to answer for' (56). Perhaps he thinks he has scored a clever debating point, but the proposition is chillingly typical of eugenicist discourse; though his view that 'crimes of tomorrow' might include financial speculation would doubtless be met with more enthusiasm nowadays after the banking scandals of 2008 (75 ff.).

Autolycus; or, The Future for Miscreant Youth, also from 1928, by R. G. Gordon, takes a similarly sociological line, like Godwin following the argument of Samuel Butler's *Erewhon* in viewing crime as a social disease rather than an issue of timeless morality. Ronald Gordon was a psychologist, who had written for the International Library, with books on *Personality* (1925) and *The Neurotic Personality* (1927). The archaic term 'miscreant' in his subtitle is revealing. It had originally meant 'Misbelieving, heretical; pagan, infidel' (*OED*, sense 1), but this underwent a shift to a moral or criminal rather than religious sense: 'Depraved, villainous' (*OED* sense 2); this in turn shifted to a weaker sense of merely 'badly behaved, reprobate' (*OED* sense 2). A 'miscreant youth' is also described throughout the text as a 'delinquent'. Gordon opposes Lombroso's (and also Godwin's) biological and characterological determinism, arguing that there is no such thing as a 'criminal type' (33-4); and he is similarly sceptical of the designation 'moral imbecile' (60). Yet arguably the term 'delinquent' is at least susceptible of such a typological reading: not in its etymology—it simply derives from the Latin *delinquere*, to fail, be lacking or at fault—but in its usage to classify a social type, usually with associations to an under-class. Nowadays such problems would be more likely to be understood as episodic: 'anti-social behaviour', or in the social work jargon, even more episodically, 'behaviours'; to be managed with temporary court orders

---

[15] A similar point is made in one of the two books on the legal system, E. S. P. Haynes's *Lycurgus; or, The Future of Law* (1925), 34, which argues that sanctions in criminal law are still theological, and that whole edifice is 'a peculiar blend of barbaric violence, medieval prejudices, and modern fallacies'.

and professional intervention. Nevertheless, Gordon's approach is fundamentally psychological. Where Godwin anticipated addressing crime through eugenics, Gordon, though sceptical of a psycho-analytic invocation of the Oedipus complex to account for violence against authority, instead anticipates treatment through therapy or analysis.[16]

Religion

The volumes devoted to religion perform a comparable confrontation of tradition with scientific modernity. *Apella; or, The Future of the Jews* (1925) was published anonymously, as by 'A Quarterly Reviewer'. It author, Laurie Magnus, had written an article on 'Zionism and Anti-Semitism' for the *Quarterly Review* in 1902, and is reviewing the topic nearly a quarter of a century on. His argument in both is anti-Zionist, believing that the liberty won in Britain in the nineteenth century (such as the right to enter parliament, under the Jews Relief Act 1858) needed to be preserved, and campaigned for in other countries; but that Zionism represented a dangerous retreat from this 'religious trust' (5). Magnus contrasts Judaism with Zionism: Judaism as a religious identity, without the international organization comparable to a Pope or a Synod (14-15); Zionism as reversing the nineteenth century's processes of assimilation. 'Where Jews had been united by religion, and separate in their national identities, they now formed an international organiza-tion, with a political transcending any religious bond' (24); its mission 'to restore a Nation to a Home' (25). He worries that plays into the hands of anti-Semites, who fear an international Jewish conspiracy and cast doubt on the allegiance of Jews living outside Palestine to their home state (25).

However, Magnus acknowledges that the War transformed the situation. Jewish communities of South-Eastern Europe were vulnerable, and victimized, in the political turmoils during the conflict. This latest experience of the precarious-ness of their existence, together with the Palestine Mandate's creation in 1922 of a 'national home for the Jewish people', gave new impetus to Zionism (23).[17] 'The trouble of the Jews before Zionism was that no one troubled about them *en masse*', argues Magnus: 'Hence they hailed the mass-solution, which treated them as one people, one "nation"' (37). He sees the effect as having caused a splitting of identities and loyalties, along different lines from the Victorian settlement. Now the question was whether Jews would identify as 'members of a religious or of a national community' (45).

---

[16] A comparable science-based approach to crime underpins the volumes on law, especially Haynes's *Lycurgus*; discussed in Chapter 5.

[17] Magnus' original *Quarterly Review* essay was also issued as a separate work. During the war he published *Zionism and the Neo-Zionists* (London: St. Clements Press, 1917), 'Reprinted in revised form from *Aspects of the Jewish Question*, Murray, 1902.'

Oddly, given what he has said about the war boosting Zionism, and given the pervasive anxiety about another world war, he remains convinced that the pendulum will swing back to nineteenth-century assimilation (53). 'Zionism will not swallow Judaism' (58). It is not that he cannot envisage future wars. He does fleetingly concede that 'a war of the twentieth or twenty-first century may wrest Palestine from the League of Nations' (92) (few of the other contributors had such faith in the League's longevity). But his view of the Jews as the paradoxical survivors, repeatedly confuting the prophets of their destruction, seems only to have been confirmed by the war. The Jews 'have been persecuted bitterly in every country, and the remnants of them have been driven across the frontiers, yet they have not anywhere been extinguished' (10). To say this seems naïve, even allowing for the superiority of hindsight, is not to berate a prophet of 1925 for not foreseeing the Nazi future, even two years after the Munich *Putsch*. Rather, it is to wonder at how his wishful religious thinking could blind him to the logic of his own argument; and foreclose any consideration of the possibility of an independent Jewish state; let alone the possibility that the tension between religious and what Magnus calls 'Cultural Judaism' (59) would become a fault-line of that state.

In *The Future of Israel* (1926), a book published only in the American version of the series,[18] James Wise Waterman takes a stance on different ground, neither religious nor Zionist. He prophesies that 'The religion of the future will in truth be the science of life'.[19] (He had perhaps not been keeping up with D. H. Lawrence.) He does not think Jewishness is a matter of religion, or at least of religion alone; but then he sees it as something distinct from culture, race or nation, too, but which transcends all these categories. To that extent the analysis has a social sciences dimension; but in the end Waterman retreats to a characterological assertion more redolent of pseudo-science, positing a Jewish 'bond' which is 'fundamentally *emotional* in character' (84-5).[20] Waterman's talk of 'the religion of the future' indicates how his subject is not religion as such—certainly not conceived humanistically from a theological perspective—but its role in history and society.

Winifred Holtby's *Eutychus; or, The Future of the Pulpit* (1928) is, despite the irony and modesty of its title, another of the outstandingly rich and intelligent volumes in the series. Eutychus was the man in *Acts of the Apostles* who fell asleep and fell out of a window while St Paul was giving a sermon (25-6). Holtby places him, as 'A Common Man', in dialogue with figures from two later epochs: François Fénelon (1651–1715), the Roman Catholic archbishop, theologian, royal tutor and writer; and a fictitious '*Mr Anthony*: A Young Man about Bloomsbury'.

[18] See the complete listing of all the volumes in the series in Appendix B, giving details of the three volumes only published in the US.
[19] James Wise Waterman, *The Future of Israel* (New York: Dutton, 1926), 37.
[20] Nevertheless, the book was reviewed enthusiastically by W. T. Bush in the *Journal of Philosophy*, 26:21 (10 October 1929), 575–81.

Eutychus is one of the relatively few volumes cast entirely in dialogue form, which is odd given the series' commitment to putting opposing views into relation.[21]

Holtby's internalization of the dialogue form makes it harder to locate her opinions than it is in most of the other To-Day and To-Morrow volumes. It is genuinely dialogical, owing something to Fénelon's own writing (dialogue could be a useful insurance policy against accusations of heresy); and in particular his technique in *Dialogue des Morts* (1718) of bringing into contact the dead from different times and places, such as Confucius and Socrates, or Plato and Aristides (as well as pairs who did know each other, like Louis XI and his cardinal La Ballue). But the main reason why Holtby presents *Eutychus* as dialogue is because its form follows its function. Her imagining of 'The Future of the Pulpit' is not concerned with religion alone, but with all forms of authority, including the more secular versions that have supplanted it. She is thus also interested in rhetoric. The speakers go out as anthropologists to observe what the state of public speaking is in the country, and come back and report their findings. Holtby is interested in forms of what might be termed the secular sermon, examining the claims for authority based on science, philosophy, financial success, health, sex, etc.[22] She sees it as a paradox that one form of spiritual authority has been replaced by others; and though the rejection of the religious is often cast as an argument that the common people don't understand the arcane knowledge of the clerics, nor do they understand the scientific basis on which such things are said to be disproved. As Louis Wirth's preface to Mannheim's *Ideology and Utopia* continues: 'The criteria of proof themselves have become subjects of dispute. We are witnessing not only a general distrust of the validity of ideas but of the motives of those who assert them' (xiii). Or, as Anthony puts it: 'To-day the illusion of Authority is shattered. We are no longer prepared to listen submissively without answering back' (19). Post-modernist, or post-truth?

Thus Holtby puts the dialogue form into debate with the more monologic and tendentious volumes advocating single positions; setting the form of her volume sceptically against the radical project of the series; not to oppose it, but to make it more reflexive about its own certainties, and sense of superiority to the forms of authority it prides itself on eliminating. Anthony continues: 'In a scientific age there is no room for appeals beyond logic and experiment to a vaguely defined and apocryphal Authority' (19). Though from another point of view—Anthony's, in fact—the form of the series as a whole is greater than the sum, or summa, of its parts: 'No one but a madman would to-day attempt a *Summa Theologica*' (65), he opines, a little too dogmatically. The belief that knowledge is now too diversified and/or divided for a mediaeval Thomas Aquinas or a renaissance man to master, is the rationale for the collective summations of contemporary thought

---

[21]   See Chapter 1 for further discussion of dialogue in the series.
[22]   See the quotation in Chapter 1, p. 94.

and its aspirations represented by both To-Day and To-Morrow and the International Library.

Anthony is the kind of young modern intellectual who would have been among the most enthusiastic readers of To-Day and To-Morrow. Indeed, he has been reading it. He quotes Russell's comment from *What I Believe*: that 'the central dogmas of the Christian religion, find no support in science' (20; quoting Russell, p. 13), adding: 'And we live to-day, as I have already mentioned, in a scientific age' (20). Other contributors are named in the discussion: Dora Russell, Norman Haire, and Anthony Ludovici (73), for their discussions of women's education and sexuality; also Charlotte Haldane, who had married J. B. S. Haldane and published her dystopian feminist novel *Man's World* in 1926. Anthony may well be supposed to have read his Freud as well, since his view of religion as an 'illusion of human infancy' which 'has no future' (11) echoes Freud's, in *The Future of an Illusion* (*Die Zukunft einer Illusion*; 1927; translated into English in 1928), describing his interpretation of religion's origins, its development, and its (non-)future.

Anthony agrees with Fénelon on one rare occasion, that modern radicals have generated a new dogma and hagiology: 'the religious impulse now sustains men who have rejected the childish anthropomorphism of Christianity' (58-9). But, Holtby subtly suggests, perhaps he doesn't realize the extent to which he is himself enslaved by such dogma and hagiology. He quotes Russell's *What I Believe* again, arguing that we should not ground our values in the natural world: 'It is for us to determine the good life, not for nature—not even for nature personified in God' (68; quoting Russell, p. 25). But if he's letting Russell determine his values for him, has he simply displaced Authority from religious to secular forms? Fénelon unintentionally represents the comic view of this paradox when, having returning from his scouting out of the rhetorical territory, he describes various voluntary social groups forming the 'Service Movement'—such as the Boy Scouts, the Rotary Club, the Automobile Association—as quasi-religious (50). More cunningly, he argues that 'curiosity', which for Anthony would be the engine of science, 'arises from the Grace of God, which has implanted in man a deep intuition, driving him to seek explanations of the universe [...]' (52).

The other volume addressing religion is *Vicisti, Galilaee? or, Religion in England: A survey and a forecast* (1929), by Edward B. Powley, a naval historian, poet, and poetry anthologist. It is one of the longer volumes—119 pages of close type, and a classic document of its period. An introductory page explains the title, which refers to the legend of Julian the Apostate dying with the confession that Christianity had triumphed. Powley asks whether it has, not in the world, but specifically in England. (Contemporary readers would probably have been most familiar with the story via Swinburne's 'Hymn to Proserpine': 'Thou hast conquered, O pale Galilean; / the world has grown grey from thy breath'; lines 25-6). He adopts the scientific attitude in a less ironic way than Holtby, though the book has fine ironies of its own. Turning Julian's concession into a question, Powley aims to put religion into question, examine the evidence impartially, and base his judgement only on fact rather than belief or superstition.

It is divided into three chapters: 'The Past'; 'The Present'; 'The Future'. The first and longest takes up half the book, giving a historical survey of Christianity from the life of Christ to 1830. Written from a sceptical point of view, seeing the Resurrection as based on 'Mary's illusion, or hallucination, the illusion or hallucination of others', and seeing the early church as a form of communism (12). This section ends by observing that up to the seventeenth century Christianity and Christian doctrine concerned the whole populace; and that by 1830 fewer than 10 per cent did not attend church. The second chapter asks whether the State Church's faith is the same as was proclaimed in 1830, and answers that yes, essentially the doctrine is close to the Elizabethan settlement. But it discusses the divisions between Anglo-Catholics and non-Anglo-Catholics, noting further divisions within each grouping. Roman Catholicism has remained closest to the Constantinopolitan orthodoxy. Whereas members of the 'State Church' prefer to treat the creed as a historic document, and to interpret dogma liberally. Now the Church means nothing to three-quarters of the population. 'The War, it must again be insisted, brought the new freedom of thought to full birth. For four ghastly years, men put, not questions about the *Old Testament* or the *New*, but such final enquiries as—is there a beneficent God at all?' (82). The *Guardian*'s reviewer thought *Vicisti, Galilaee?* 'One of the best in the series; a book to be read, thought over, and discussed by all Christians who are not afraid to take the shutters down'.[23] Powley argues that the Church 'fails because orthodox Christianity cannot be made to fit with most of the rest of organized experience' (80). He subjects the creed to a sceptical close reading from this modern and quasi-Tayloristic viewpoint. This section concludes that though Christ's mission has failed, he remains an important leader figure.

The final section asks whether Christianity has a future. Powley sees Christ's 'words of communism and anarchy' as inspiring an inevitable communism (91). He turns to consider mysticism, arguing that the mystic's vision of the Ultimate cannot be reached by reason; but by feeling. Poets and novelists, he says, show how the language of religious ecstasy has been recast in terms of nature rather than religion. Then he argues that the only future for Christianity is to abandon its dogma as 'childish', and follow this path of nature-mysticism. He closes quoting Tennyson's vision of a 'Faith beyond the forms of faith'. This Arnoldian turn from religion to literature is completed as Powley argues that it is the sayings and the story of Christ make up his worth 'to the writer'; and that 'the life of Jesus will be valued by the educated democracy of the years to be' for the same reasons (91). This is not quite what Anthony means in *Eutychus* when he states that 'The salvation which men today are seeking is a salvation of human personality' (66).

---

[23] Quoted from the end-matter of C. P. Harvey's *Solon; or, The Price of Justice* (1931).

Its preachers are many, he says, listing biologists, scientists, pseudo-scientists, moralists, political philosophers, economists, politicians, pacifists, and artists. Salvation has become a matter for everyone but churchmen; and the ground of value in religion has shifted from the theological to the psychological: the 'personality'. Though Powley means his analysis perfectly seriously, his account of Christ as a protocommunist lends a humorous edge to the tone.

Science Sceptics

Humour proves one of the few areas in the series resistant to the scientific approach, both in the volumes devoted to it; and as a tactic used by other contributors to resist what they see as a scientistic reduction of their topic.

Democritus; or, The Future of Laughter (1929), by Gerald Gould, a former academic turned Suffragist and man of letters, provides an illuminating historical survey of different types of humour from Shakespeare, and parodies of him, to Chaplin. He has a good turn of phrase: 'save for the hyena, man is the only laughing animal' (18). 'Man is a risible, not a reasonable, being' (14-15). Yet to say 'Laughing is no laughing matter' (5) is problematic if you have little to offer apart from laughter about laughter. Gould was not the first to feel that attempts to explain humour sink under their own gravity. 'There are big books about it, by psychologists', he says, 'and I have tried to read them; but I still laugh without, at the moment, knowing why' (5). He is especially critical of psycho-analytic-sounding explanations, pronouncing that 'the neo-psychological attempt to associate all fun with suppressed sex is both ignorant and vicious' (88). For all that, all he comes up with by way of explanation is precisely a form of psychological (and sociological) account: 'laughter is the escape from the ego into the common lot' (5-6). When he turns to the future, the same idea returns: 'One may sum up the progress of laughter, and therefore prognosticate its future, by remarking that mankind becomes ever more conscious of the *necessity* of escape' (61)—the difference being that people seem to be availing themselves of the kind of psychological explanation Gould also wants to reject. He does, though, raise a challenging futurological question about Utopias: 'In a perfect world, a world without pain, humiliation and disappointment, there would be no laughter', he predicts: 'For the future of laughter, this is a grave disability. It means that our Utopias threaten as much as they promise' (19). In other words, there would be nothing left to laugh about in Utopia; and Thomas More wasn't as humourless as we thought. Gould spares a humorous thought for technotopia too: 'Wireless, now—it should surely be possible to make a humane joke about wireless?' (45). But that he does not produce the wireless joke interferes with his optimism.

Robert Graves's gossamer volumes approach the subject of humour in very different ways, managing to parody the series in the process. In *Mrs Fisher; or, The*

Future of Humour (1928), he uses the same witty tactic we saw him deploy in *Lars Porsena*, arguing that the nature of his topic makes the book impossible to write. If the humour of tomorrow it prognosticates is to be different enough from today's to be convincingly futuristic, it would be too unintelligible to strike today's readers as humorous. Instead he finds humour in projecting future attempts to understand humour—parodying, in the process, the ambition of the series to shine the light of science on the more obscure aspects of everyday life. He anticipates the creation of a Board of Humour charged with trying to classify jokes into degrees of humour, and to copyright them. His point is that jokes depend too much on specific contexts to be susceptible of such generalizations. Some humour does not survive transportation beyond the intimacies of family or friendship; or its particular location in time and space (hence, he argues, jokes from the war no longer seem funny).

Gould's *Democritus* thought humour had been shifting from the aphoristic to the absurd—a shift we might now associate with the war's undermining of traditional stabilities, as elegant Wildean paradox gives way to trench farce: 'We have been extremely rich in a kind of didactic and paradoxical epigram that cannot now be much more exploited: we are beginning to delve rather in the rich fields of imbecility' (70). That is the type of humour celebrated in *Pons Asinorum; or, The Future of Nonsense* (1929), by George Edinger and E. J. C. Neep. The Latin phrase means 'the bridge of asses': the name given to the fifth proposition in Euclid's *Elements*, Book 1, stating that the two angles at the base of an isosceles triangle are equal. The name may come from Euclid's bridge-like diagram; though another explanation is that this theorem is the first real test of the reader's intelligence, sorting out the asses from the geometricians capable of crossing over to the more complex propositions.

Edinger and Neep's book lives up to its topic. Idiosyncratic and mercurial, it does not have a linear argument; because 'true nonsense must be *aimless* humour—the humour that makes fun as opposed to the humour that makes fun of something' (7). But it appears to attempt two things simultaneously: to characterize the kind of humour most resistant to analytic commentary ('sheer nonsense requires originality'; 11); and then to find it everywhere, using the term 'nonsense' to satirise modern projects to order and understand the world (including science). Here too, the war is seen as ushering in the new humour. After it, 'men found their senses—and, at the same time, found their nonsenses. For when Einstein discovered the kink in space, man discovered the kink in mind' (63). This disposes not only with the madness of war, as a time when men had lost their senses, but also with psycho-analysis as well as relativity. It is a paradoxical example, since even humour's claimed incommensurability with the scientific finds its justification by a parallel with science. It serves as a further example of how the scientific functions as metaphor across the series, as do metaphors based on specific new scientific or technological ideas.

Pons Asinorum similarly brays at the topics explored by many of the other con-tributors—industrialism, mass production, socialism, cinema, language, the American future, etc.—and finds them at once antithetical to nonsense, but also producing it themselves. Nonsense is thus both an inspired refusal of the rational and the systematic—a Blakean 'deliberate non-sense of the intellect' (49); and a critique of any attempts to be rational and systematic about a Protean humanity. Edinger and Neep comment (perhaps with the series in their foresight) that 'all foretell an ultra-Collectivist To-morrow. But nonsense at its best has always been the product of individualism, nay of that ultra-individualism that is eccentricity' (78). 'The twin forces of the immediate future are Utilitarianism and Collectivism', they say: 'both are even now shaping the nonsense of to-morrow' (70). It is a double-jointed performance, in which the word 'nonsense' repeatedly flips from naming a precious quality of mind, to decrying its absence in others; and slips between describing jokes, ideas, and discourses about ideas. The 'nonsense of tomorrow' beautifully captures impracticable political arrangements; the kinds of pointless talk that will circulate around them; and the kinds of jokes that future nonsensologists will be able to make about them. It also manages to have fun at the expense of the language of futurologists. Similarly, when the authors speak of 'the universal language of nonsense' (24), they are saying nonsense is all around us—both in the endless provocations of a mad world, and in the inspired mad-ness with which we make nonsense of them. They are possibly having a dig at the kinds of universal language projects Sylvia Pankhurst and C. K. Ogden were so interested in. (It may also be that Ogden was interested in nonsense as the degree zero of his Orthology: for the meaning of meaninglessness.) But they are also suggesting that nonsense is no respecter of languages or nations. It is the argu-ment made for silent cinema (as by Ernest Betts in *Heraclitus*): that it was a uni-versal language operating free of the restrictions of natural languages. Which is perhaps why Edinger and Neep are so enthusiastic about, but also so critical of, film, saying: 'the greatest medium of entertainment that the world has ever known will perforce be kept at the level of the custard pie until a new age succeeds the age of Utilitarianism' (77–8). Such slapstick cinema is an example of what they diagnose as the 'Mass nonsense' reverberating across the globe (83); which is leading to an 'Internationalization of Nonsense' (84)—the results of mass produc-tion and international trade.

For the interwar generation taking their bearings from Marx and Freud, reli-gion was a form of nonsense too, as it was for Bertrand Russell. But presumably it wasn't for Edinger and Neep, who had co-written *A Handbook of Church Law for the Clergy*.

A number of other individual contributors resisted the scientific paradigm, resisted its incursion on their subject, or resisted its claim to be the sole basis of understanding that subject. We saw (in Chapter 1) how *Gallio; or, The Tyranny of Science* was not opposed to science as such, or its descriptions of the physical world. Sullivan just thought science should not get metaphysical—an increasingly hard position to maintain in the face of the new physics. In *Apollonius; or, The Present and Future of Psychical Research* (1927) E. N. Bennett takes the opposite position to Sullivan, thinking that scientific method *must* be extended to investigate metaphysical claims. He projects the future of something most scientists now would consider not to have one: a field generally considered as pseudo-science.[24] Yet Bennett is keen that his subject be seen as rigorously scientific. The hypotheses investigated by psychical research—the existence of ghosts, evidence of the after-life, telepathy and so on—may run counter to mainstream scientific thinking, yet the methodology nonetheless aspires to the scientific; verifying or falsifying by repeated experiment, leading to new hypotheses. He sees the metaphysical-sounding doctrines of the new physics as making an accommodation possible. As we saw in Whyte's *Archimedes*, one effect of the revolutions of the increasingly abstract and counter-intuitive theories of relativity and quantum mechanics was sometimes (in contrast with the logical empiricism of the Viennese School) to reopen science to more metaphysical speculations such as the effects of mind on matter. In Maurizio Ascari's analysis:

> in the 1920s Einstein's theories seemed to erode the divide between the material and the spiritual domains, legitimising the status of psychical research. According to Bennett, due to these changes in the *metaphysics of science*, psychical research could aspire to the status of science provided it also embraced the *epistemology of science*, that is to say 'the exercise of rigid control and accuracy in our experiments' (43). Yet the author was aware that 'no satisfactory experimental control of these wayward phenomena seems at present feasible' (44).[25]

Thus while from the perspective of a mechanistic and determinist science, *Apollonius* and *Archimedes* are posed antithetically, constituting a debate between orthodox science and pseudo-science, from another point of view one can see both texts as exploring similar problems along parallel, if not quite meeting, lines.

Other volumes mount similar arguments that mechanistic science needs to open its mind to the spiritual. An intriguing case is *The Dance of Çiva: Life's unity and rhythm* (1927) by 'Collum'—Vera Christina Chute Collum (1883-1957), military radiographer, archaeologist, polyglot author and theorist of the Celtic mother-goddess. *The Dance of Çiva* exemplifies the attention in the series to the language and figures used to represent futurity. It combines a highly poetic, meta-phoric language with accounts of scientific developments, especially those in plant biophysics in the work of Sir Jagadish Chandra Bose, an extraordinary Bengali polymath working across several sciences and human sciences (biology,

---

[24] See Maurizio Ascari, 'From Spiritualism to Syncretism: Twentieth-century pseudo-science and the quest for wholeness', *Interdisciplinary Science Reviews*, 34:1 (March 2009), 9–21.
[25] Ibid., p. 10.

physics, botany, archaeology) and who also wrote science fiction. He moved from working on remote wireless signaling to plant physiology. His research on the responses of plants to stimuli demonstrated similarities between botanical and animal tissue structures, and postulated the power of feeling in plants. Collum argues from this that we need to overcome the compartmentalizing mentality of post-Platonic Western thought, embracing an Eastern idea of unity instead. Çiva (the transliteration in French of what in English is generally 'Shiva'), one of the three major Hindu deities, is described as transcendent, without form or limit. Collum offers the image of life as a dance, combining creation and destruction, as providing a matrix to think about issues such as race and nation. Nonetheless, through the figure of Chandra Bose *The Dance of Çiva* frames its plea for a philosophy broader than Western scientific rationalism in terms of an enhanced paradigm of science. Eastern mysticism had been in vogue since Rabindranath Tagore won the Nobel Prize in 1913. He had been a regular visitor to Britain, and was to return in 1930 to give the Hibbert Lectures in Oxford. The resulting book, *The Religion of Man*, included as an appendix a dialogue between Tagore and Einstein, 'Note on the Nature of Reality'.[26] Collum expresses the hope that through the intellectual contact with the East she describes, 'a new civilization and a new social order may arise on the ruins of what we call "Western civilization"' (50).

An ironic perspective on that civilization, and the primacy it accords to science, is provided by *Plato's American Republic* (1929) by Douglas Woodruff. In this entertaining bagatelle, our scientific age is seen from the perspective of classical antiquity, as Socrates is imagined reporting a visit to the USA. To fifth-century Athenian eyes, 'Modern Science' appears as 'A divine priestess' who 'is invoked in all difficulties, whose words are received with great reverence, and that though her oracles are more than usually incomprehensible and fickle and her words long and horrible'; 'she is dear to the Americans', he says, 'because she speaks principally about machines, and tells them there shall be more and more of them, and an increasing number of parts in each' (90).[27]

The strongest case made in the series *against* the scientist view of the human and political realm is *Kalki; or, The Future of Civilization* (1929), by Sarvepalli Radhakrishnan, at the time an academic philosopher—in 1929 he too was giving the Hibbert Lectures in Oxford, where he taught for the next two years—but who was, whether he could foresee it or not, later to serve as the first Vice-President of India for ten years, and its second President from 1962-7. Like Collum and many of the other contributors, Radhakrishnan starts from the premise that 'Civilization to-day seems to be passing through one of its periodic crises' (7). He connects

[26] Rabindranath Tagore, *The Religion of Man* (New York: Macmillan, 1931), 221–5.
[27] *Plato's American Republic* is, accordingly, discussed in greater detail in Chapter 4, on 'Machine Man'.

this sense of crisis with an orientation towards the future; and, like Collum, sees (Western) science as part of the problem:

> Standards, aims, and institutions which were generally accepted even a generation ago are now challenged and changing. Old motives are weakening and new forces are springing up. Anyone who has an insight into the mind of the age is vividly conscious of its restlessness and uncertainty, its dissatisfaction with the existing economic and social conditions and its yearning for the new order which is not yet realized.
>
> All this confusion of thought and unstable enthusiasms for ill-defined ideals show that humanity is about to take a new step forward. One of the chief factors in this unsettlement is modern science. Though science is not peculiar to our civilization, its pace of progress has become latterly too fast and its range too wide and deep for our quick adaptation.[28]   (7-8)

But unlike Collum—and possibly in response to *The Dance of Çiva*—Radhakrishnan is sceptical about viewing 'the history of humanity as a single continuous movement which later divided itself into separate streams on account of differences in milieu and native endowment' (10). He too comments on the increasing and quasi-organic interconnexion of the planet:

> The East and the West are not so sharply divided as the alarmists would make us believe. The products of spirit and intelligence, the positive sciences, the engineering techniques, the governmental forms, the legal regulations, the administrative arrangements, and the economic institutions are binding together peoples of varied cultures and bringing them into closer reciprocal contact. The world to-day is tending to function as one organism.
>
> The outer uniformity has not, however, resulted in an inner unity of mind and spirit.   (9)

Opposing those advocating (both in the series and outside it) the unification of the human race, he argues that: 'The unity of civilization is not to be sought in uniformity but in harmony. Every great culture is due to the blending of peoples of different ideals and temperaments' (13). As in the famous quip attributed to Gandhi at this time, who, when he was asked what he thought of Western civilization, replied 'It would be a good idea', Radhakrishnan clearly does not believe that the West has attained 'great culture' status, and provides a witty analysis of its values. It confuses comfort with civilization, he says (42). 'Sexual promiscuity is getting to be regarded in some circles as a social duty' (19). He is unimpressed by contemporary culture:

---

[28] Compare H. J. Birnstingl, *Lares et Penates; or, The Home of the Future*, 18–19: 'There is a sense of instability and uncertainty about modern life' due to 'the immense speed with which inventions and discoveries are made, the effects of which it is quite impossible for foresee'.

The sort of mental life which prevails is at a low level. Emotional thrills and intellectual sensations, aesthetic occupations and mental excitements attract us and not deep appreciation of great literature and noble art. Mechanical plots, detective stories, crossword-puzzles allure and amuse us.   (40)

While this would be taken today as an elitist snub of popular culture, it is as likely to have been a comment on Oxford high-table-talk. His point is that society has confused matter and spirit: 'We are practically certain that it is only by getting rich that we can pass through the eye of a needle' (26), he says; and that this confusion is true nationally as well as individually:

Economic success is our highest ideal, and almost all our wars are due to economic causes. Economics is our religion. Empire is big business. We wage wars to increase our trade, extend our territories and acquire colonies.   (48)

Radhakrishnan notes that 'The sciences of psychology and sociology, biology and anthropology are undermining the foundations of orthodox theology in every historical religion' (14); and he catalogues the resulting arguments with which the modern mind dismisses the spiritual (similar to those given in Holtby's *Eutychus*), such as that 'Religion is a pursuit of infantile minds, with which the bold thinkers have nothing to do' (16). By contrast, he believes that 'We can never get rid of religion' (55), because: 'Body, mind, and spirit form distinguishable aspects of an inseparable unity' (42). However, as in his model of culture as a harmonious blend of different ideals, he embraces religious multiplicity rather than unifying proselytism:

Every religion represents the soul of the people, the inner law of its being and aspiration [....] When it comes into contact with others, it transforms their ideas and influences into something new. It is better to transform what we take from others than repeat what has been gained elsewhere. A single religion for all mankind will take away from the spiritual richness of the world.   (59)

While this is to be expected from an expert in comparative religion, it leads to an analysis of morality that comes close to relativism:

For morality is nothing else but the current brand of social custom, and any one who insists on doing differently is immoral, though his immorality acquires ethical value in the next generation and becomes a part of the tradition in another. At any one period, we always have a few who are in advance of the highest life-conception of the time and some behind it, while a large number are about it. The first are the rebels, the second the criminals, and the last the normal individuals. All progress is due to the rebels.   (75)

It is perhaps the suggestion that all three categories are moving in the same direction that restrains this view from a completely relativist position. Yet curiously the equation of morality with the social custom of the age speaks the language of the social scientist rather than the theologian. The implied definition of crime as a mis-alignment with social custom is close to that of *Cain* and *Autolycus*, and sounds the Nietzschean note of several other To-Day and To-Morrow volumes.

When it comes to progress in the political sphere, Radhakrishnan warily contrasts it with technological progress:

> Pacifism or internationalism is not a scientific device like the wireless or the telephone which the world can, all on a sudden, take to. It is a delicate plant which it takes long to rear. Patience and forbearance, mutual understanding and respect are necessary for its growth.   (90)

His views on democracy are comparable. 'Paradoxical as it may seem, democracy in its actual workings is anti-democratic' (31); this because it is based on the liberty of the individual. Which is perhaps also why he argues that 'Democracy has succeeded in several countries because it is not true democracy. It is yet an ideal' (86); this because he sees the theory of the sovereignty of the 'general will' as unachievable. Doubtless he didn't cite these insights when campaigning for office. Nonetheless, he believes democracy is better than any of its precursors, and that 'equality of opportunity is a sound social ideal' (87).

Politics

Such volumes are signs of the intense political consciousness, and intense political polarization of the interwar years. 'Not a modern country but is infected with some degree of class war', as one of the contributors has it.[29] Hence my claim for the importance of a scientific paradigm for the series needs to be joined by an argument that a political paradigm is comparably determining. It was there from the start of the series with Russell's warning to heed the politics of science. For the socialist or Marxist contributors, the political and scientific approaches were part of the same paradigm, as we saw in Chapter 1. Marxism had promised a new rationale for political science's claim to be a science, especially as dialectical materialism was reformulated in the 1920s and 30s. In *History and Class Consciousness* (1923), for example, Lukács argued that Marxism was 'the scientific conviction that dialectical materialism is the road to truth'.[30] Inevitably, To-Day and To-Morrow touched on politics and on socialism in volumes on a variety of topics. Inevitably, it included volumes devoted to politics. Curiously though, it is these volumes, which might have been expected to be among the more enthusiastic subscribers to the scientific paradigm, which, like *Kalki*, are among the more

---

[29] Edgar Ansel Mowrer, *Sinon; or, The Future of Politics* (1930), 41.
[30] Lukács, *History and Class Consciousness* (1923), trans. Rodney Livingstone (Merlin Press, 1967), p. 1.

sceptical. (Of course such resistances to the scientific paradigm demonstrate the pressures these writers felt to adopt it.)

Arthur Shadwell, in *Typhoeus; or, The Future of Socialism* (1929) is categorical. Because Marx assumed capitalism would produce increasing misery, but in fact the effect is the opposite, then 'Scientific Socialism is, in truth, quite obsolete' (12). Shadwell's book is a crisp digest of debates about leftist politics in the period, contrasting socialism with communism, distinguishing five models for a socialist organization of society, analysing contemporary experiments in Soviet Russia and Germany; and predicting that in Britain it would begin with the nationalization of the coal mines. But his title says it all: Typhoeus was the deadliest monster of Greek mythology. For Hamilton Fyfe, in *Archon; or, The Future of Government* (1927), 'To suppose that there is, or can be, a science of government, is a perilous delusion'; because 'No science is possible without fixed properties, ascertained laws, the assurance that given causes will produce foreseen effects' (8). This is scarcely promising from someone introducing a book purporting to foresee the effects of the future on government. He would have been unimpressed by the response that the kind of science in question is a *human* science, which may be better at analysing the logic of history than predicting future outcomes, because the notion of a human science is exactly what he thinks needs contesting. 'If there should ever be a science of human nature', he says, 'there may then be a science of government. None is possible until then' (8). One knows what he means. Politics isn't an *exact* science. People are unpredictable, etc. But he had clearly not been keeping up with the progress of the 'hard' sciences over the preceding quarter of a century,[31] in which Newtonian 'ascertained laws' had been redrafted by Einstein, 'fixed properties' had been smashed with the atom, and fixity and determinacy had been thrown out of the window (and presumably through the door at the same time) by the quantum theory arising from the work of Max Planck, Werner Heisenberg and others (though Heisenberg's formulation of the uncertainty principle appeared in 1927, the same year as *Archon*, so Fyfe may (and, like Schrödinger's cat, may not) have been aware of it. He seems not to have been aware of scientific method at all, given that his reason for thinking there can be no science of government is that 'Government must be experimental' [...] (p. 8); whereas science...? Because politics works by 'appealing to the emotions', he says, 'we discover that government is an art' (10).).

Fyfe, who was a journalist, newspaper editor and playwright, is a better guide to politics than he is to science. He sets up an opposition between Italian fascism as subordination of individual to state, and Nietzsche seeing only evil in the state (24-5). Then he discusses the spread of international finance: 'Money Power' has now become supreme (30). This, combined with the Party 'machine' has reduced

---

[31] Fyfe would not have been able to read Whyte's *Archimedes*, which came out at the same time or later.

MPs to robots, who daren't disagree with the party managers (69-70). Fyfe analyses the problems he identifies in the system: education doesn't awaken thought; corruption; the failure of bureaucracies to look to the future. 'Even those who do now know exactly how the system works feel that something is wrong. Hence the vague fancy that "strong man rule" might serve us better. Hence the spreading conviction that Democracy has failed' (72-3). But then he returns upon himself, to argue that when you look at the improvements it has brought about, Democracy hasn't failed, and is still better than the alternatives of dictatorship or oligarchy.

Edgar Ansel Mowrer, in *Sinon; or, The Future of Politics* (1930), is more balanced in the way he sets up the comparison between arts and sciences. His first chapter on 'The Nature of Politics' is divided into 'The Science of Politics' and 'The Art of Politics'. 'All men are born politicians' (11), he argues, but this Aristotelian premise leads into a more modern view, drawing on comparisons with animal behaviour (bears, white ants, dogs) to posit a 'political instinct' (12) which demonstrates the kinds of 'conditioned reflex' responses demonstrated by Pavlov (to whom he refers). His discussion of the will to power is duly Nietzschean, as are the views that 'From the clash of individual wills, some sort of conflict ensues inevitably, and you have politics' (13); and that 'Equality is a conception brought over from ethics or mathematics, where it means something, into politics, where it lacks genuine content' (19). In geopolitical terms this entails that 'War is national Will to Power in international anarchy' (21); and that therefore: ' "Sovereign" nations cannot disarm without risking destruction, and *war is the normal condition between them*, [...]' (21). There is also an echo of the Freudian death drive in what Mowrer calls the 'urge to die' (13). 'The doctrines of the psychoanalysts are particularly stimulating to political conjecture' (34), he says, but thinks that they are untested, so Political Science needs to stick to 'bare but essential [and presumably more scientific] principles'.

In an interesting move in which biological and psychological science is used to critique political science, Mowrer argues that 'Humanity is, however, so complicated, the single mind so stocked with (often contradictory) tendencies, that almost no one has had the wish or the capacity to sever the subjective links that bind politics to ethics and the need for spiritual reassurance' (21); and that accordingly, 'Political Science has been and still is largely distorted or fanciful' (22).

Mowrer criticizes political movements on similar grounds; specifically that they have turned programmes into religions. Communists 'have done nothing less than transform a political belief into a full-blown mystico-materialist religion' (38), he says, then makes the same critique of their opponents: 'Nationalism is a religion' (43). He also objects, in Arnoldian terms, to nationalism's cultural effects: 'Nationalism destroys culture of any known type by subordinating the free play of individuality—the only source of culture—to the supposed national purpose' (44)—which is a good definition of fascism and its aesthetics. He thought that 'so long as international anarchy persists, modern states must remain more or less nationalistic' (44). Yet 1930 seems hardly the time to be predicting that 'It would seem that in the West the apogee of Nationalism has been passed' (44). Mowrer's is not quite the standard self-serving critique from a liberal democracy of the extremes of left and right, since he sees industrial capitalism as effecting its own form of subordination of individuality:

> The present world suffers from the regimentation of minds. Radio, movies, newspaper syndicates, standardized advertising, stimulate this process, which pleases the manufacturers. But it does not make for culture. Hitherto at least, culture and large countries, or even culture and peace, have been found incompatible, since the individuation that made for culture has led to war.   (80)

But he is ambivalent here. If 'regimentation', which sounds warlike, is good for industry and peace, morally and culturally it is disastrous, since 'standardized minds are a relapse of the human race into the tribe' (81).

In this second chapter, analysing 'Contemporary Political Movements', Mowrer has been picking out five ideas of psychological import—human equality; nationalism; individualism; efficiency; and internationalism—'whose influence is predominant' (35), and which he sees as vying for the future. In the third chapter, on 'The Crisis of the Modern State', he contrasts the totalitarianisms of left and right in the USSR and Italy. While the communists' commitment to equality proves them 'the only true democrats' (39), the USSR 'conceals under its name a communist despotism whose rulers govern in the name of the enlightened workers of the world and a materialistic interpretation of history of which each of its important leaders is a living refutation' (52). His strictures on Mussolini's fascism are comparably uncompromising: 'The present Government of Italy is therefore a personal despotism nesting within the framework of a constitutional monarchy'; 'The means used are those traditional to tyranny—censorship, legal and extra-legal police espionage, and violence. There is no equality, small political liberty and only one individual, the *Duce*' (64).

So far *Sinon* might appear an example of what the series did exceptionally well: provide a crisp, incisive sketch of the salient issues of the day—issues already familiar to us from the literature and history of the period. Mowrer was certainly a sharp observer. He was Rome and then Berlin correspondent for the *Chicago Daily News* during the 1920s and 30s, so had first-hand experience of fascist Italy by the time of writing. But he was also able to generalize impressively from his observations; and this enables him to offer a further level of analysis which is original, and characteristic of what the series does best, and why it is often worth attending to even on such familiar territory.

He notes the paradox that whereas traditionally despotic government (implicitly in the East) is 'moving steadily towards representative government of a western type', in Europe by contrast, the despotisms he discussed in Russia and Italy have arisen out of a move in the other direction, and 'as a reaction to parliamentary or constitutional government' (57). In particular, they have arisen because 'large-scale democracy is breaking down' (54). He attributes this breakdown to a structural contradiction in liberal industrial society. This is where 'Efficiency' comes in. Though no supporter, he thinks that: 'The Fascists are right in assuming that the efficiency and power of large centralized States require an equivalent sacrifice of individuality and democracy'; and that as a result 'Everywhere real government is slipping into the hands of a small group of orators, financiers and technicians' (56):

> Government of whatever existing type has, in large countries, become unstable. The political organization is no longer adequate to its technical development and human demands. [...Cyclic] democracy is giving place to oligarchy. But the pre-requisite of modern efficiency and power is large-scale intelligent co-operation. This brings about an increasing claim for participation in power and material benefits, and so tends to lead back to some democratic form.   (69)

So although he thinks 'stable government of any form is in large States impossible under present conditions' (69), he hopes more inclusive, co-operative forms will emerge. The short term outlook is not good. On the one hand, the communist project of producing 'a superior, non-individual Mass Man, whose inner being is entirely social' (60) is flawed, because founded on a dubious form of Lamarckian belief that social characteristics can be passed on genetically (61). On the other hand, he also had the foresight to grasp, as the era of Appeasement loomed, that 'the ultimate meaning of Nationalism is war' (67). What is more, there is little hope that liberal democracy can navigate a course between these extremes. This because the precision of 'machine technique' 'encourages a demand for ever more competent administration', which should 'require ever better popular discern-ment in the choice of legislators'. But instead 'there is a growing preference for "wind bags" and "glad handers"' (54).

In his fourth chapter. Mowrer considers 'The Alternative to Downfall'—that is, to the threats posed to existing nations and civilizations of 'futile and violent ruin' (72) at the hands of revolutionaries of the left or the right. Like Wells, he sees a world government as offering the best hope; though he traces the conception to earlier thinkers, from Dante, through Kant, Mazzini, and Woodrow Wilson (95):

> short of the dominance of one State over all the others—the *Pax Romana*—war can really be abolished only through the formation of an International Government which on the basis of International Authority, formulates inter-national laws [...]   (77).

Given what has come before, his conclusion, on 'The Future of Politics', could not be other than gloomy. 'What is history but one long series of reforms that have failed?' (87), he asks, and quotes George Santayana's *Soliloquies in England* disabusing anyone whose utopianism was founded on a belief in a human decency which had been suspended during the war:

You suppose that this war has been a criminal blunder and an exceptional horror; you imagine that before long reason will prevail and all these inferior people that govern the world will be swept away and your own party will reform everything and remain always in office. You are mistaken. This war has given you your first glimpse of the ancient normal state of the world, your first taste of reality.   (87-8)[32]

As Mowrer puts it superbly: 'The future of politics is simply more politics' (86). All he can offer itself sounds a utopian hope almost impossible of fulfilment: 'to preserve our nations and with them Occidental civilization we must achieve a political organization that will (*a*) forestall successful insurrection within the several States; (*b*) eliminate international war; and (*c*) permit broad decentralization of government' (73). The last because, 'Secure in internationalism, people could transfer their real emotion to the small group [...]' (82), and become more attached to localities. That was all more than the League of Nations was capable of, acting as 'a kind of international Fire Brigade to put out war' (48-9). Yet that doesn't prevent him from making perceptive predictions. He anticipates China and India turning into modern states (68-9). And if his suggestion that three continental groupings would emerge—Asia with Australia, Europe with Africa, and the Two Americas—has transpired only in terms of informal trade relations rather than political integration, his anxiety that large entities will become increasingly hostile—'Capitalism *versus* Communism, Europe against America, Asia opposing its white conquerors [...]' (84)—not only proved more prophetic during the Cold War, but also perhaps suggested Orwell's vision of the hostile three continental superpowers in *Nineteen Eighty-Four*.

Education

The idea in *Kalki* of the need to cultivate civilized mentalities is indicative of another of the series' main concerns: education. As with all such major issues, this both threads its way through volumes on a variety of other topics, as we have seen;[33] and is also allocated specific volumes addressing the subject directly. In fact there are six To-Day and To-Morrow titles on education, covering the field from nursery school to postgraduate research. Though surprisingly, there is no discussion of primary education. The books are mostly concerned with the British public school system and Oxford and Cambridge. The debate focuses particularly on the role of new science as opposed to a classically-based training: in a way, the

[32] Quoting George Santayana, *Soliloquies in England and Later Soliloquies* (New York: C. Scribner's Sons, 1922), 103.
[33] Mace's *Sibylla* also advocates taking a scientific approach to education and government.

contrast focused by the standard form of title in this book series, contrasting the classical past with the modern conception of the future.

Robert T. Lewis' *Romulus; or, The Future of the Child* (1929) considers the pre-school child, and advocates extending nursery education, on the grounds that parents are not prepared for educating children beyond infancy (44). It includes discussions of Winnicott (38), Montessori theory (57-9, 69-70), Adler (72-3), and the nursery pioneer Margaret McMillan (85-6).

In *Procrustes; or, The Future of English Education* (1927), M. Alderton Pink argues that British education is based on the model of training people for university (25-6); but that as only 3 per cent ever reached the universities of the day, it is not well-designed for the others (27). His first chapter argues against the romantic idea of perfectibility (i.e. educability) of humankind. Education should not be seen as a miracle panacea for social ills. We should recognize that conventional education does not suit all. Pink cites Cyril Burt's use of intelligence tests (later notoriously discredited) dividing up the population into five grades of aptitude, and linking these to different grades of labour (33-4). Readers of *Brave New World*, with its cloning of the 'Epsilon'-grade labour force, will not be surprised to learn that Huxley knew of Pink's work—he wrote a preface for Pink's *A Realist Looks at Democracy* (1930).

Yet Pink's position of advocating vocational training for the unacademic does not stem from a desire to preserve academia for the privileged few. On the contrary, it is because he mistrusts academia that he does not think the education system should be designed around it. He quotes the President of Columbia University, Nicholas Murray Butler, saying that 75-90 per cent of research is 'not properly research at all, but simply the rearrangement or re-classification of existing data or well-known phenomena' (87-8). Pink continues:

> Literature at the universities is in even a worse plight. The scientific historical method applied in this field is steadily devitalising literary study. Criticism and enjoyment of the great masters have to give place to the study of tendencies and influences of historical minutiae and bibliographical irrelevancies.   (89)

It was a situation the social-scientific and psychological method of Cambridge criticism was about to revitalize.

The case for the public schools is made by J. F. Roxburgh, the Headmaster of Stowe School from 1923-49, in *Eleutheros; or, The Future of the Public Schools* (1930).[34] This is presented in dialogue form (thus providing an example of the classical training and education it advocates) between four men: Dr Archdale, the Roxburgh figure; Mr Burgess, the businessman; Col. Callaghan, the traditionalist military man; and M. D'Orsay, adding the foreign perspective. Burgess takes a

---

[34] Evelyn Waugh wrote about Roxburgh, who had taught him at Lancing, as one of his 'Two Mentors' in chapter 7 of *A Little Learning* (Harmondsworth: Penguin, 1983), 156–62.

position similar to Pink's, that the classically-based curriculum is outdated, and demotivates students. He sees the public schools as useless and predicts their extinction. Archdale replies:

> We did make a tremendous mistake in giving both Latin and Greek to every boy. They are, as Burgess says, extremely difficult languages, and one is quite enough for the normal boy if he is to get any distance in it and do anything else as well. I firmly believe that every boy ought to have a literary education of some sort, whatever he gets in addition; for everyone, even a scientist, has got to read and write and think and speak.   (22)

He thinks for boys staying at school till 18 or 19 that education should be in Latin. That a literary education might include anything contemporary disturbs Colonel Callaghan, who disapproves of the 'young highbrows' 'who are all for Lenin, Epstein, and that fellow D. H. Lawrence, and so on—a rotten type, I think, though pretty rare still, thank Heaven!' (26). That Roxburgh admits such controversial moderns into his book betokens a more open mind. Archdale is committed to education as intellectual rather than what we would now call 'vocational' training: 'It is an unpractical policy to teach a boy useful accomplishments and leave him with a half-developed brain' (64). 'I call a subject "educational" if it provokes more mental activity than is required for mastering it' (66), he says.

Archdale tries to counter the objection to the social inequality of the division between the public schools and education for the masses, saying: 'There is nothing worse than equality which is achieved by levelling down' (81). But that complacent assurance masks the fact that his vision of the future has no intention of trying to level up. He speaks the language of aristocracy, if his vision is of a meritocracy: 'if the best of the English Public Schools [...] can select and secure the very best young Englishmen of each generation, this country will begin to build up a new aristocracy of character and capacity such as the world has not hitherto seen' (83). This is subtly radical in its way, suggesting that the old class system had failed the country, and the new elite should be based on education and intelligence rather than inherited titles, land or wealth. There is perhaps also a sense that a new elite is needed to replace the war generation's officer-class casualties. Archdale is also modern in saying that the selection process should 'learn from the psychologists and eugenists' (83). But that conjunction rings alarm bells now about IQ tests and spurious racial theory. Which in turn indicates how in other ways it is a deeply conservative vision. That pitting of the best young Englishmen against the world connotes the burdens of empire that they were still being trained to shoulder. Women do not figure in his projection, even though just two years earlier the franchise had been extended to women over 21.

The group concludes that the most serious problem threatening the future of public schools is the Labour government. Unlike most of the series, *Eleutheros* leaves us with a dismaying sense that many of its arguments—about the British being anti-intellectual, the public school system being on the way out, the need to do more vocational training, literary education equipping people for general communication skills—are still with us.

However, a more radical view is offered in *Chiron; or, The Education of a Citizen of the World* (1931), by M. Chaning Pearce—then the headmaster of Alpine College in Switzerland, and a writer on Kierkegaard, theology, and federalism. *Chiron* is written explicitly as a reply to Roxburgh, whom Chaning Pearce does not believe has shown how the future of public schools might be anything other than their past. He lists his qualifications for criticizing the governing class mentality, having served as a soldier, magistrate and secretary to a High Commissioner in the East. His first chapter then anatomizes 'The Public School Type', showing that what the system generally produces is far from Roxburgh's ideal of the well-developed brain. 'Like the good soldier of the pre-War régime, he is most valuable when he does not think fundamentally for himself' (17)—rather like Ford's *Good Soldier*, Edward Ashburnham, perhaps. 'An open-minded, unconventional, cosmopolitan public-school man is a contradiction in terms' (21). Rather than producing well-rounded individuals, the public school system is a 'triumph of British mechanization' in the uniform excellence of its product (23). And what it produces is the 'governing classes'—'a type of man adapted for leadership, administration and command' (24-5). Whatever other motives people might have for sending their children there, that is the 'racial purpose' (28-9) of the schools; not what Chaning Pearce understands by education.

He defines 'The Purpose of Education' in his second chapter, asking whether it is 'the development of individuality or the training of a good citizen?' (32). He appears to reject the former as an ideological mystification, having argued that the public schools claim to develop individuality but in fact produce bureaucrats. He also takes issue with a book by Dorothy Revel, called *Cheiron's Cave*,[35] and which gives him his title-figure (Chiron or Cheiron was the wise centaur who tutored innumerable mythological heroes, including Theseus, Achilles, Ajax, Aeneas, Jason, and Perseus), and which advocated a very progressive, Jungian, antidote to 'slave-education' (33). Where Revel wants to promote creativity and the 'natural life', Chaning Pearce objects that 'the creative type' is 'a deviation from the norm' (37), and that an entire society of them would be inconceivable. Any comprehensive scheme must focus on 'the average man' (38), he says. This might sound like a capitulation to an education he had criticized as mechanical. But when he argues: 'The business of education [...] is not the training of "creative types" but the training of good citizens' (38), it is that notion of the citizen which marks the difference.

---

[35] Dorothy Revel, *Cheiron's Cave, the School of the Future: An educational synthesis based on the new psychology* (London: Heinemann, 1928).

The third chapter, 'Citizenship in the Modern State', elaborates the key argument. 'The two most salient features of post-War society and politics' are the forming of new, and distinguishing of old, national, cultural and social groups; and 'ideas of co-operation, internationalism and federalism which seek to combine those groups' (48-9). His utopian claim is that a federal model can work both nationally and internationally. Within the state, it leads to government by co-operation between classes rather than by a governing class; and internationally, to co-operation between states rather than imperialism (49). This because 'The conceptions of a "governing class" and of a "ruling power" are equally objectionable to the modern mind' (49). 'The key-word of the modern age is co-operation rather than domination' (49). Chaning Pearce is also optimistic that 'The clean division of mankind into ruling and subject races, masters and men […] is passing' (49-50).

Chiron's critique of the public schools is that under their hegemony, 'We are not educated either for class-cooperation or for State-cooperation' (55). Chaning Pearce sees the duty of schools as mediating a number of divisions. He anticipates C. P. Snow's 'Two Cultures' argument even more explicitly than Haldane and other contributors, contrasting the 'old culture', fostered by public schools, with 'a culture proceeding from science' (50-1). But then, by adding to the mix 'a culture which can best be described as proletarian, based largely upon sociology', and, finally, with the conquest of distance, an infiltration of 'the cultures of other races' (50-1), the book becomes an advocacy of what would now be called a multiculturalist perspective which is strikingly avant-garde in its openness to 'many different types of culture' (56-7). Indeed, the labelling of these various mentalities of class, discipline, and ethnicity as 'culture', seems avant-garde in another way, anticipating the perspective of a cultural studies normally thought of as starting thirty years later. That this approach is stirring across the series is the argument of Chapters 4 and 5.

For Chaning Pearce, attempts to secure peace through the League of Nations, and agreements like the Locarno or Kellogg pacts will be stillborn without this corresponding attitude of co-operation (56). His last two chapters outline a proposed revision to the educational system to embody the principle of co-operation within and between nations. '[T]he average public-school product is indisputably insular' (66), he argues. So he proposes a cosmopolitan revision of the syllabus, in which 'a far greater place should be given in the educational curriculum to the history of world civilization, to science and to sociology and civics' (78-9); and an even more radical proposition of educating the British in schools outside Britain, organized on a federal as well as an international basis (78). The point is for the school to act as a microcosm of the state: to be federalist internally, but also in relation to an imagined federation of other schools (80); for 'the scholastic organization' to 'include some scheme of graduated self-government' (79). That is why he can pronounce that 'the key of the future lies not at Geneva but in the schools of the future' (82). Because the League of Nations will only work if people have learned how federalism works in the detail of their everyday lives.

Chaning Pearce finds a surprising ally for his federalist and internationalist project in the Archbishop of Canterbury, who is quoted as making the unexpectedly psycho-analytic observation that 'in English education we have been mainly training the sub-conscious self. . . . English education has been quite unconsciously directed toward the unconscious' (70). It goes back to *Chiron's* point about the public schools producing colonial administrators, who are trained to act decisively in difficult situations without thinking critically about their actions. The implication is that an education premised on co-operation between classes, nations, and races, will help people to see and know themselves better.

This debate about the politics of education is continued in the pair of volumes covering Oxbridge, both of which—appropriately given their futurological intent—focus on the students rather than the institutions and syllabuses of the two universities. Julian Hall's *Alma Mater; or, The Future of Oxford and Cambridge* (1928) is one of several volumes drawing on H. G. Wells's idea of *The Open Conspiracy*, and is dedicated 'To H. G.' Hall distinguishes between two broad types of 'post-War mentality' (18). The first, inspired by Wells and the scientific outlook, is committed to 'the formation of a new world-commonwealth' founded on 'the basis of an economic unity' (18). Hall sees this outlook as 'constructively religious, in that it preaches new ideals for mankind' (18); and (a recent graduate from Balliol himself) says it is 'reputed to be strong in Cambridge' (19). By contrast to these 'conspirators', Hall poses the 'sceptics', who are more prevalent. 'The conspirator's mind is turned towards the future' (21). The sceptical mindset he finds harder to define. It is negative, anarchic, cynical even. It is a product of the war. 'Ruin was in the air which my generation breathed at school', he says: 'The old order had been broken, and its fragments have not been pieced into a new organism' (30). The sceptic 'thinks nothing is worth doing for its own sake' (66). 'In a life which he has emptied of values he can respect nothing, and can take nothing seriously' (41). Evelyn Waugh is the sceptic's best portrayer. Hall does not mention him. Waugh's first published novel, *Decline and Fall*, appeared the same year. But Waugh's Oxford is scepticism's *alma mater*.

Sketching 'the thought of a young conspirator', Hall gives us an insight into the readership of the series (confirming that it was read avidly by university students), and also into what its contemporary readers gained from it:

> He will have gained confidence from the speculations of *To-day and To-morrow*. This series has offered us many visions of the future. It has dealt sometimes with the future of our race as a whole, sometimes with the future of institutions and enterprises which we know to-day. It has made us think of our institutions merely as expedients for the achievement of social ends. It has made us consider what, if any, are the social ends which we should set before us. Many of its writers have

shown how by means of scientific discoveries man may regulate the working of his mind and of his passions. The doyen of *To-day and To-morrow* is Mr. J. B. S. Haldane.   (32–3)

Hall sees the conspirators' views as prevailing in the longer term. When he turns to the future of the universities, he predicts that they will cease to exist in their present form. School will impart the conspirator vision of world unity, and pupils will leave at 16 or 17 having chosen the way they want to serve that end. 'Thus will proceed that subordination of the personal life which the conspiracy demands, and which the modern university combats' (91). So the universities will abandon teaching, and become 'research stations' for 'professional students'. 'Some of them will be concerned with Daedalist problems' (91).

Hall's volume was countered by W. J. K. Diplock in *Isis; or, The Future of Oxford* (1929). Diplock was another recent Oxford graduate, who had read chemistry, but who, according to the summary given on the dust-jacket, had evidently seen the error of his ways.

> From a survey of its social and intellectual life, the author concludes that the University is split into two rival camps: the adherents of the newer culture, typified by Science, and those of the older culture, typified by Classics and Philosophy. These latter, he asserts are the *only* participants in the real intellectual life of Oxford.
>
> In his prophecy of the future, the whole system of Science-teaching, state-scholarship system, women students, and recent benefactors to the University, alike receive the lash of his reactionary scorn; and he looks forward to a time when these influences will have been all banished to a vast technical-school-cum-laboratory that will be Cambridge, leaving Oxford as the last citadel of the older culture.

Here again, this time towards the end of the series, we have an explicit statement of the divide being already apparent between the two 'cultures' of arts and sciences thirty years before C. P. Snow's diagnosis.

The dig at 'the other place' was doubtless intended as a typical Oxbridge jibe, but that 'reactionary scorn' for science, widening participation, and women, is troubling in someone who would eventually become a law lord, and responsible for the juryless 'Diplock Courts' used to try terrorists in Northern Ireland.

The University of London had been the first to admit women to degrees in the UK in 1878. Though women had been able to attend lectures and take examinations at Oxford from the 1870s, it had only been from 1920 that they were allowed to graduate there. In Cambridge they had to wait until 1948. Women's education is the subject of Dora Russell's superb volume *Hypatia; or, Woman and Knowledge* (1925). Hypatia of Alexandria was a Neo-Platonist philosopher murdered by a Christian mob in 415 AD. She taught mathematics and astronomy, and was also credited with inventing the astrolabe and hydrometer with her father, Theon. Or, as Russell puts it in a prefatory note: 'Hypatia was a University lecturer denounced by Church dignitaries and torn to pieces by Christians. Such will probably be the fate of this book: therefore it bears her name'. Kingsley's *Hypatia* would presumably have been the best known Victorian version of her story.

Sexuality and Morality

Russell's book is a rebuff to the views expressed in *Lysistrata*, in which Ludovici argues that women's demands for rights and power result from an unfulfilled maternal instinct. As with *Daedalus* and *Icarus*, Ogden's setting up of debates between opposing views paid off, with both *Lysistrata* and *Hypatia* selling out and going to third impressions. Russell contests the notion of maternal instinct itself, arguing that it 'consists of habit almost imperceptibly learnt' (53). It is an example of what she sees as wrong in traditional education. 'Dualism, as ever, is the culprit' (77), she says. Like many of the contributors, she argues that mind and matter 'are not different forces' (77). The matter that matters most to her argument is the body. The knowledge which needs to be de-repressed is carnal. The book is a rejection of 'the time-honoured theory that renunciation of the world, the flesh, and the devil is the path to duty and salvation' (31). After the opening chapters 'Jason and Medea—Is there a Sex War?', outlining the difficulties still facing feminists despite their partial success with the vote; and 'Artemis—The Early Struggles of Feminism', covering the suppression of women through religion and a lack of sex education, she turns to the future: 'To me the important task of modern feminism is to accept and proclaim sex', she says, rather than 'the lie that the body is a hindrance to the mind' (24-5). Women need to be taught anatomy and physiology (23); to realize that the body is 'a temple of delight and ecstasy: a temple to hold the future if we will' (24).[36] 'To understand sex' (25) will bridge the gap between Jason and Medea. The chapter 'Aspasia—The Younger Feminists' discusses how modern women can advance feminism by breaking with this taboo, which is for Russell both a necessity and 'a revolution' (32). In another instance of the contributors gauging how everyday life had been transformed as a result of wartime, she writes:

> during the years of war, young women took the last step towards feminine emancipation by admitting to themselves and their lovers the mutual nature of sex-love between man and woman [....] with nothing but instability and death around them, our modern Aspasias took the love of man and gave the love of woman, and found this union, free and full on either side, the most priceless gift the immortal gods can bestow.   (32)

---

[36] See Stephen Brooke, 'The Body and Socialism: Dora Russell in the 1920s', *Past & Present*, 189:1 (2005), 147–77. doi: 10.1093/pastj/gti024

Countering the moralists' accusation that this was nothing new, but 'just wickedness' (33), Russell argues that what was new was the throwing off of a sense of sin and guilt about sex. Nor does she accept that sexual experience is only bodily: 'lovers know that it is through sexual understanding they best apprehend the quality of each other's minds' (35). Once *Hypatia* was out 'I began to receive telegrams asking for comment and interviews', said Russell: 'The *Sunday Express* review had described this as a "book that should be banned"; consequently, to the joy of the publishers, it sold 600 copies in a week.'[37]

In the longest chapter, 'Hecuba—Feminist Mothers', Russell discusses the lack of education on birth control, arguing that 'We want better reasons for having children than not knowing how to prevent them' (46). Analysing the problems faced by working mothers, she makes radical social and economic proposals too, arguing for increased social mobility, and that feminist mothers should demand 'the recognition of their work', asking 'for endowment from the community' (67). The final chapter, 'Jason and Admetus—Men', considers male opposition to feminism: 'If we are to make peace between man and woman' and by their unity and partnership change the ideas that govern our politics [...] it is essential that men should make a more determined attempt to understand what feminists are seeking' (78-9). Many of the arguments in Russell's pioneering volume are thus truly futuristic—both in the sense that they remain still to be realized, but also in the sense that they anticipate the second wave feminism of the 1960s and 1970s— as does her remark that 'Philosophy and sex are more important in politics than General Elections' (77), which can be seen as a forerunner of the 1970s slogan that the personal (or the private) is political.

Russell counted Ogden as among her 'best friends', and after a BBC radio broadcast about him in 1963 wrote in to complain that the programme 'involved itself so pompously and patronizingly in assessing what might be his achievements in specialist fields that it entirely missed the real meaning of C. K. to many of his generation' at Cambridge.[38] During the first World War 'many were grateful to Ogden for keeping alive some sort of rational international outlook by his publishing extracts from the foreign press in the *Cambridge Magazine*, for which some jingoists threatened him with violence.'[39] She praised him for encouraging writers (like her) not yet known, 'which made him a first rate editor'. But she also makes it clear why he was important as a scourge of pomposity, referring

[37] Dora Russell, *The Tamarisk Tree: My quest for liberty and love* (London: Virago, 1977), 180.
[38] Dora Russell, 'Portrait of C. K. Ogden', letter to the editor, *Listener* (21 March 1963), 505.
[39] Dorothy Buxton's regular digest of 'Foreign Opinion' in the *Cambridge Magazine* has been recognized as a major achievement of the anti-war movement. See Patrick Wright, *Iron Curtain: From stage to Cold War* (Oxford: Oxford University Press, 2007), 176ff and 430; also Grace Brockington, 'Translating Peace: Pacifist publishing and the transmission of foreign texts', in *Publishing in the First World War: Essays in book history*, ed. Mary Hammond and Shafquat Towheed (Basingstoke: Palgrave, 2007), 46–58 (49–51).

revealingly to 'the saucy To-Day and To-Morrow series', and highlighting his satiric energies:

> The Sunday night meetings of the Heretics in Top Hole were a serious challenge to the fetters of authority in matters of belief. And, though we eschewed solemnity, our discussion, like Ogden's pranks and witticisms, was a challenge to the Establishment itself.

> In fact, C. K. was the forerunner of present-day satire: he would have revelled in TWTWTW,[40] *Private Eye*, and the rest.

The satirical bite of the series is nowhere more evident than in C. E. M. Joad's two contributions. *Thrasymachus; The Future of Morals* (1925) is certainly an uproarious challenge to established views on its subject: crisp, clever, Nietzschean, and fizzing with extreme and perverse Shavian epigrams. The first chapter takes Thrasymachus' position in Plato's *Republic*, Book 1—'Morality as the Interest of the Stronger'—and says that though it is given short shrift there, it is worth exploring. Joad finds 'a double significance' (15) in the idea. First, the morality of the many promotes interests of the few. This is his analysis of Christian morality: 'Of all religions known to man it [Christianity] lays the greatest stress upon those virtues whose practice is advantageous to the stronger' (12). Its 'virtues make good workmen and prosperous employers [...]' (13)—an idea which perhaps helped shape R. H. Tawney's analysis of *Religion and the Rise of Capitalism* published the following year (though equally, both men would have known Weber's *The Protestant Ethic and the Spirit of Capitalism*; 1905). Second, it is the successful few, who benefit financially from the moral system, who are duly awarded honour and a reputation as moral because of that success.

The second chapter, 'Herd Morality and the New Tyranny of Thought', takes up Nietzsche's idea from *The Genealogy of Morals* of a 'herd morality' as having taken over in modern societies from a feudal 'slave morality'. (Joad was perhaps also drawing on the influential book by Wilfred Trotter, *Instincts of the Herd in Peace and War*; 1916.) In democratic societies, he says, the common man, or rather woman, is now 'the arbiter of morality' (17). But 'Those who belong to a herd are in general unable to understand the wish of others to escape from it' (37). The herd mind resents non-conformity; is offended by 'the insulting superiority of the few' (23); by the artist, writer, or genius (the Nietzschean Superman is implied here); by the recluse. Like many contributors, he believes a post-war world requires a reinvented politics. But his panacea is different. He argues that a utopian future requires a government by the young. Because the old are embittered, government should be handed over to men under 35 (21; interestingly, Joad turned 34 the year *Thrasymachus* came out).

---

[40] *That was the Week that was* (also known as TW3): a landmark satirical BBC television satire of 1962–3 devised by Ned Sherrin, and presented by David Frost.

His third chapter, 'The New Liberty of Action', takes up some of Dora Russell's themes of sexual morality and sex education, though handled with cynical paradox rather than earnest advocacy. Joad sees the two main factors in moral change as being the 'growth of economic independence among women, and the practice of birth control' (41). He judges the basis of marriage as purely economic, ridiculing the Church's positions:

> The early Christian fathers, expecting the immediate end of the world, saw no reason to take steps to ensure the continuance of the race. The Christian hostility to the pleasures of the sense was, therefore, allowed to rage unchecked, and sexual intercourse was denounced as both wicked and unnecessary. As time passed, however, it was found that the world showed no signs of coming to an end, an inconsiderateness which led to the necessity for a change of attitude. The Church met the situation with a complete volte face. (41-2)

As he puts it wryly later: 'As regards the Almighty, whether he would agree with the views put forward by those who speak in his name is not known' (52). Joad's account of marriage and prostitution are comparably Shavian:

> Throughout the recorded history of civilization the only recognised way for a woman to make her living has been through her body. Her body being her one saleable asset, she could employ it in either of two ways. She could sell the use of it to one man for an indefinite period, or she could lease it to a number of men for short and strictly regulated periods. (42-3)

He then imagines this view as having led to 'the formation of two unofficial women's Trade Unions, the Trade Union of wives and the Trade Union of prostitutes' (43), both bitterly opposed to women 'prepared to give for love or for nothing what other women were only prepared to give for maintenance' (43). 'The force of female opinion so directed is known as morality' (43). For all this playfulness, he appears to regard as probable 'the endowmen[t] of motherhood' (49) which Russell had advocated.

Joad's prediction that 'we may expect that the practice of birth control will profoundly modify our sexual habits' (58) has proved more accurate. It had already led to 'The New Liberty of Action'. But this in turn has provoked a new Puritanism among those 'outraged in their deepest feelings by the prospect of shameless, harmless and unlimited pleasure which birth control offers to the young' (59). Where Russell saw the fault-line as between men and women, for Joad it is between youth and age. The closing chapter, 'The Coming Clash', considers the outcome. 'Certainly not a relapse into complete promiscuity' (68), he says. 'The belief that people are fundamentally licentious' 'springs from the doctrine of original sin which has always been popular among quiet and well-behaved people' (68); 'pleasantly shocking though it is to the minds of respectable people', the idea that society will collapse into 'a welter of unbridled licence' has 'no foundation in fact' (68). In the short term (the by now familiar fifty-year span) Joad sees 'the beginning of a period of reaction from the license of the war' (87). But he views morality as a swinging pendulum, and doesn't expect 'bourgeois Puritanism' (87) to last.

In a wonderful and surprising coda, Joad stands back from the preceding argument, acknowledging that it 'will seem to many to be cynical and disruptive. I shall be charged with taking a low view of human nature, and speaking slightingly of morality' (89). His defence? That he is not denigrating human nature, but only that part of it 'which expresses itself in what is called morality' (89); and that 'what is called morality is not in any true sense of the word morality at all' (89). He understands by morality something positive; the pursuit of the good. Whereas the new Puritanism appeals to people's fear rather than their hopes. So his morality of the future turns out—unexpectedly—to require religion in order to regenerate it. Doubtless his view of religion is as different from what is called religion. It generates 'emotional enthusiasm', comes from 'the life force' (91), and is the only 'driving force which impels men to change things'. 'Meanwhile the less we write and think about morality the better' (91).

Given what Joad says about the motives of Puritanism, it is perhaps unsurprising that it is sexual morality which is the most hotly contested during this period. Given the recent experiences of the war, it is perhaps surprising the morality of warfare evinces less passion—though we have seen how it is certainly discussed in the series, both by pacifists like Bertrand Russell, and ex-soldiers like Haldane and Liddell Hart. But it is the arguments for sex education, and in favour of acknowledging the reality of female sexual pleasure, for birth control, and for changes to the ethos of marriage and the family that seem especially to define the modernity of the series, and to run through many volumes other than the substantial group devoted to 'MARRIAGE AND MORALS' (which included ten volumes in the Classified Index by the end of the series).

Hymen; or, The Future of Marriage (1927) by Norman Haire, for example, was popular enough to be reprinted twice. The *Sphere* thought it 'An electrifying addition to the series'.[41] Haire's main focus is on sexology: a subject which had been developing in medicine since the 1880s, joined by psycho-analysis from the turn of the century. But the attempt to bring human sexuality into the domain of science still felt new to many readers of popularizing works like these. Haire also takes a much broader view of sexual morality. Like Joad (to whose *Thrasymachus* he refers), he is a relativist, assuming that the one thing you can foretell about morality is that it will change; that it is not transcendental but responds to social change, including technological or scientific change. Contrasting ancient Jewish and Greek views on marriage, he argues apropos of the Greeks (and rather like

---

[41] Quoted from the end-matter to Harvey, *Solon*.

Blacker in *Birth Control*—discussed in Chapter 2) that their attitudes to procreation and sex were determined by their need to ensure the population did not outgrow its limited food-supply. Thus the Greeks condoned homosexuality and prostitution; whereas the Jews needed to multiply because their numbers were so small (18-19). Like Blacker and other contributors, he thinks eugenics a sounder basis for sexual regulation than religion or convention; that sterilization should be used to eliminate defects; so that for him, incest is preferable to letting impaired couples procreate. Indeed:

> There is scarcely a single subject relating to sex on which we seem capable of thinking and acting rationally, and our prejudices give rise to incalculable harm to Society. A flagrant example is the matter of prostitution. Instead of realizing that in the present state of Society, prostitution is inevitable, and doing our best to improve its conditions, we pretend that it is unnecessary and we make the worst of it.   (33)

Haire's argument is the majority of marriages are not happy, largely because of 'sexual unhappiness' (8-9); and that this reflects a mis-match between current 'sex codes' and social needs. 'As social conditions change, the sex-code must undergo corresponding alterations' (38). Like Russell, he not only advocates 'rational sex-education' (51), but tolerance towards 'onanism'; auto-erotic curiosity in children (as something normal and not to be punished, though they should be distracted from excessive forms); polygamous desire (59-60); and divorce reform. He is utopian enough to believe that the sense of property will diminish, as husbands become less proprietorial towards their wives; and he does not see this as contradicted by his advocacy of the legalization of polygamous marriages alongside monogamous ones (64-5—a reference for readers of *Halcyon*, and another for readers of *The Good Soldier*).

Of the series of predictions with which he ends, several have been borne out. Contraception 'will be universally practised by all normal people' (80). If this is rude about Catholics, it is less snobbish than many eugenicists about the lower classes. Haire demolishes the anxiety, often voiced by the middle classes, that contraception will produce dysgenic results, with the working class reproducing faster because not using it. His solution? Teach all classes birth control (85-6). Now why hadn't anyone thought of that? He thinks abortion will be legally recognized in some cases (90); that suicide will be more common; and that it, and euthanasia, will be legalized (92). He is a bit too enthusiastic about the last, leading him to some predictions that to post-Nazi ears only signal the moral dangers of eugenics. 'Later still, Society will probably exercise the right of painlessly destroying persons who are a menace to it, either physically or otherwise' (92). Wait a minute! Does that mean Society will destroy them physically or otherwise? Or that it will destroy them if they are a menace physically or otherwise? It is a lethal confusion, conflating the use of the death penalty (still operative in Britain then) with the eugenic ambition to 'eliminate' the 'degenerate'. He also suggests that some 'sexually abnormal persons' might be killed if they can't be treated or educated (94-5). This because 'The sexual rights of other citizens, and especially of children, must be protected' (94); so he is talking about rapists and paedophiles. Like the series' criminologists, he is confident such people 'will be regarded as the victims of an inborn or acquired defect, for which they will not be held responsible' (94). And like Bertrand Russell in *What I Believe*, he thinks that, otherwise, 'the sexual relations of two mutually consenting adults will probably be considered the private concern of the two individuals involved. We shall cease to persecute the unfortunate abnormals' (95).[42] But we shall still apparently call them 'abnormals', and 'we shall endeavour to cure them' (95). Though insistent that even if cure is impossible, 'we shall not interfere with their rights as long as they do not interfere with the rights of others' (95), it is a precarious guarantee in a future in which society gives itself the right to destroy 'persons who are a menace to it'. The line between 'abnormal' and 'degenerate' is too fine to be relied on.

Haire correctly forecasts the demographic shift as the population becomes older (93). But the topic leads him into the bizarre territory in which factual pseudo-scientific research sounds like science fiction. He had also written a book called *Rejuvenation: The work of Steinach, Voronoff, and Others* (London: George Allen & Unwin, 1924). Voronoff had transplanted monkey ovaries into women, and Haire reports that he had also just performed the reverse operation, transplanting a human ovary into a female monkey, and then trying to inseminate it with human sperm (88). Haire introduces such ideas with a discussion of *Daedalus*, suggesting that the principle could be taken further: by removing 'young embryos—of good heredity on both sides' (87) from the original mother to be 'grown in the uterus of other women who volunteer for the service'— which sounds reassuringly like surrogate motherhood, which we are used to now, until he adds 'or perhaps even in the uterus of other animals' (87); such as in cases where a woman 'particularly suitable for parenthood' had an accidental death (87-8).

'Rejuvenation' was a hot topic in the period. Holtby's *Eutychus* also mentions Voronoff. As John Gray has shown, in *The Immortalization Commission*,[43] his study of science's attempts to solve the problems of aging and mortality, the belief that, with 'the gradual decline in the belief in the supernatural' (*Hymen*, p. 92), science was where humanity should now put its faith in addressing these topics was widely held. Steinach had developed an operation in which a semi-vasectomy was supposed to stimulate hormone production to increase energy and sexual vigour. Though the theory now sounds deranged, the concept is a precursor of

---

[42] See the discussion of homosexuality in the Conclusions.
[43] John Gray, *The Immortalization Commission: The strange quest to cheat death* (London: Allen Lane, 2011).

today's Hormone Replacement Therapy. Haire himself became a 'Steinach surgeon', and famously 'Steinached' W. B. Yeats in 1934.

Aphrodite; or, The Future of Sexual Relationships (1931) by Ralph de Pomerai largely covers the same ground as *Hypatia*, *Thrasymachus*, and *Hymen*, charting the history of sexual taboo, and in as spirited a style, maintaining the series' characteristic progressive and provocative approach to the end:

> The fact that Adam and Eve succumbed to temptation is not surprising; the only surprising thing being that innumerable men and women still continue to revere the perpetrator of this despicable trick. And despicable it surely was, for in this matter the action of the deity resembled nothing so much as that of a class-prejudiced mistress who deliberately leaves money about, hoping that her servant may discover it and yield to temptation, and so offer a sop to her own moral superiority and afford her an opportunity for the exercise of tyrannical vindictiveness. Strangely enough, most sane people are capable of realizing that the action of the mistress is far more reprehensible than that of her maid, though they seem quite unable to appreciate that the reputed action of the deity is even more repugnant than that of the mistress.   (15)

Analysing the factors making repression appear outdated, de Pomerai cites both intellectual and social causes. Among the intellectual he points to 'Scepticism in religion and declining clerical authority', which he attributes in part to the kind of consciousness-raising about science that To-Day and To-Morrow was itself committed to: 'the gradual popularization of the great scientific discoveries of the past seventy years, the effects of which are often underestimated' (61); and the impact of psycho-analytic theories of sexuality and repression:

> Even more emphatic was the verdict of Professor S. Freud, who, as a result of his unequalled researches in the field of morbid and pathological psychology, laid it down that sexual repression or sex-conflict is always the cause of neuroses, hysteria, and most forms of abnormal mentality. Freudian psychology, as is well known, has been subjected to a very considerable amount of adverse criticism, but the general truth of this statement has never been disproved by any competent authority. Thus Dr. G. C. [sic] Jung, who refuses to admit the validity of the Freudian theory of libido, when asked why it was that the erotic conflict, rather than any other, caused neuroses, replied: 'There is but one answer to this. No one asserts that this ought necessarily to be the case, but as a simple matter of fact, it is always found to be so.'   (48-9)

'It inevitably follows', argues de Pomerai, 'that a healthy sex life is essential to human beings, and that copula is valuable in itself [...]' (51).

The social factors he considers include the increasing independence of women (economically, in politics, and from their parents and men); and knowledge of contraception, removing much of the fear accompanying extramarital sex.

Also, like Dora Russell, De Pomerai makes a strong case for how the war had transformed sexual relations:

> For several years men and women lived a life of unnatural strain; privation and death haunted them, and from sheer reaction they attempted to find relief from uncertainty and gloom in the most ephemeral and superficial of pleasures. Men on leave from the front, anticipating an immediate return to the Hell of Flanders and the possibility of a premature and horrible death, sought to crowd as much pleasure and excitement as possible into the few days of life that might remain. The quest for amusement and pleasurable diversion became urgent and all-absorbing; compensations were demanded for untold misery, suffering and privation; time was short, and inevitably the moral standards and conventions of normal life were swept irrevocably to one side. The fate of civilization seemed to hang in the balance; permanence of values was scarcely considered in a world where permanence seemed but a wild dream: each and all lived but for the moment, and the habit once acquired survived the cataclysm responsible for its formation.   (65-6)

'What is required by the world today', he says, 'is not the reinstatement of the old and cramping sexual code, but emergence of a new morality adequate to secure the maximum benefits to the individual and to humanity as a whole' (74). It is that morality which his volume seeks to imagine. Its bases are his convictions that, on the one hand:

> the truth about sexual love is that it is wholly good and one of the most potent and beneficial factors in human life. Sexual love, qua sexual love, can never be immoral in itself, although like every other good thing, it can be, and very frequently is, both degraded and abused.   (60)

And on the other, that: 'It is apparent, therefore, that sexual activity is the parent of creativeness, art, and of the mastery of life'—though (as the gendering of 'mastery' there suggests), he rather spoils the argument with a sexist flourish—'and especially is this true in the case of man' (55). The moral principles that these views lead him to have in common with the free love movement of the nineteenth century are the desire to throw off repression and the facilitation of divorce. But de Pomerai thinks 'free love' is a 'misnomer': 'Free passion may exist', he says, 'but free love never, for the moment love intervenes in a relationship it forges its own emotional, psychical and spiritual chains' (68-9). And where the advocates of free love wanted to remove barriers to passion, de Pomerai goes further, suggesting a duty to maximize it—'One ought no more to be satisfied with but a minimum experience of love than one should with a minimum experience of knowledge or of beauty' (73)—to the extent of being obliged to seek it with multiple partners:

> if we are prepared to admit that the love of a person for another leads to an enrichment of experience and a wider range of sympathy, we are inevitably

forced to the further conclusion that the love of an individual for more than one, supposing this to be possible, must yield even greater benefits. And here we must categorically deny the popular fiction that the majority of human beings are incapable of loving more than one.   (59-60)

Thus many of the volumes anticipate, and hope to bring about by advocating it, what Vera Brittain refers to in her second chapter as having already finished: 'The Period of Sexual Reform'.

Roger Money-Kyrle's *Aspasia; The Future of Amorality* was published in 1932, just after the last of the volumes in the series. It was not published as a To-Day and To-Morrow book, but was probably conceived as a contribution to the series. *Aspasia* is a comparably eccentric text in some ways, but is also comparably revealing about its recently-established discipline, psychoanalysis. Its argument that psychoanalysis transforms our understanding of ethics and morality is indicative of the radical stance of many of the To-Day and To-Morrow books, and of their utopian hope that contemporary advances in knowledge and technology could improve the quality of individual and social lives. In Neil Vickers's account, *Aspasia* attempts 'a psycho-analytic synthesis of anthropology, economics and eugenics', in order to offer something absent from the series: a 'sustained consideration of what difference psycho-analysis might make to the future of human society'; and in particular, how future wars, which might now endanger the race, could possibly be averted.[44] It argues that 'the frustration of the sexual instincts in childhood often results in lifelong hatred of parents and of authority'.[45] 'Money-Kyrle believed that the superego was the main source of individuals' morality and consequently that most moral ideas were fantasies', explains Vickers.[46] It was a conclusion with which Joad would have agreed. *Aspasia*'s 'provocative proposal' is to cultivate amorality, by which he means relaxing parental attitudes to toilet training and sexual curiosity. The book 'addresses a question that lies behind all of Money-Kyrle's early writings'—and which is entirely in the spirit of To-Day and To-Morrow—'namely, *how can people be induced to change their social and political outlook?*'[47]

Another facet of the project of subjecting human society and morality to a science-based and psychological critique is represented in writing about animal behaviour, and its relation, implicit or explicit, to human behaviour. Charles Joseph Patten, in *The Passing of the Phantoms; A Study of Evolutionary Psychology and Morals* (1924) argues from anecdotal observations of animals (some of them his pets) that we can deduce 'the evolution of the mental and moral faculties in lower animals' (5), enabling a new understanding of 'the Evolution of Human

---

[44] Neil Vickers, 'Roger Money-Kyrle's *Aspasia; The Future of Amorality* (1932)', *Interdisciplinary Science Reviews*, 34:1 (March 2009), 91–106 (92).
[45] Ibid., p. 97.   [46] Ibid., pp. 97–8.   [47] Ibid., p. 98.

Morality' (5). Because animals sometimes react to inanimate things as if they were animate, Patten takes this as evidence of imagination, which he sees as the 'tap-root' of superstition. The moral and social senses are evolved by natural selection in animals too, for the benefit of the community. On this basis, Patten argues for an agnosticism which clears away prejudice and superstition, only basing its moral sense on scientific evidence. He claims this does not mean abandoning religion, only dogma; for him it is 'an expansion of religious thought' (69). He sees the great distinction in civilized societies as between the superstitious and non-superstitious, arguing that the latter is still currently in the minority but increasing with the advance of science. In this volume too, then, the interlocking traditional concepts of religion, law and morality are replaced with a modern set of interlinked disciplines: philosophy, sociology, and especially psychology.

Conclusion

This chapter's survey of how the human sciences figure in To-Day and To-Morrow may have created the impression that the series was organized to correspond to academic disciplines. In some cases individual volumes do take a single discipline as their remit: notably in the sciences (physics, chemistry, biology, astronomy); but also in social science areas such as law, politics, education, or psychology; and in the arts (with volumes on the English language, theatre, music, criticism, and so on). However, when the classified index is considered from the point of view of disciplines, two striking features become apparent. First, that a number of disciplines—among them subjects perceived in the period as particularly urgent—have no volumes assigned: for example, economics, sociology, or art history. Given Odgen's association with Wittgenstein, the high profile of philosophy in his editorial activities, and especially Bertrand Russell's involvement in the series, it is even stranger that it does not include any volumes specifically devoted to 'the future of philosophy'. Future volumes were often advertised in the end-matter, but as there are no announcements for these disciplines, they not appear to have been planned. Perhaps Ogden was trying to keep his various series relatively distinct. The International Library featured philosophy prominently, and included sociology. These are foregrounded in the Psyche Miniatures too, as well as in their parent journal.

The second feature which stands out from the To-Day and To-Morrow Index, especially when it is compared with the run of the International Library volumes, is that for the most part it is not really organized by discipline at all. Indeed, one of the main distinguishing features of To-Day and To-Morrow is that most of the volumes do not offer the International Library's textbook style coverage of an academic subject. Conventional—and novel—disciplines run through the series, certainly; but the writers often take an oblique way towards them—as Bernal's predictions lead him to a vision of a psycho-analytic future, say. In the next chapters we shall see how *Ouroboros* has much to say about economics, but in relation to the invention and spread of machines; how sociology comes into books on labour or leisure. But quintessentially, the volumes are organized through *practices* (laughter, sleep, eating, labour, war, exploration, sport); *institutions* (marriage, the home, family, public schools, Oxbridge, the Church of England rather than religion, countries, and empire); *movements* (socialism, futurism); *technology and media* (discussed in Chapter 4); or the *cultural forms of everyday life* (swearing, nonsense humour, the press, the best-seller, films, clothing, taboo, etc., discussed in Chapter 5). Some volumes focus on an individual topic within a discipline. No volume on philosophy as a whole, but ones on morals and logic. No volume on the future of theology, not just because most of the writers did not believe it had one, but because they were writing on superstition; the pulpit; or the Church of England. Anthropology is represented by books on race and taboo; Geography by books on exploration, the countryside, and the geopolitics of empire; the future of history is imagined via future history.

It was inevitable the way human knowledge and activity had been divided up into disciplines would be reflected in the series. The important point is that the writers were not expected to cover them in any traditional or systematic way. What the format encouraged was the choice of a *topic* that they were engaged by, and which seemed likely to be important or interesting in the future; and the projecting of its development as far ahead as the writer could imagine.

The future of philosophy and of psychology are nevertheless central to the conception of To-Day and To-Morrow, and the conclusion of this chapter will briefly demonstrate this by discussing the volumes that have most to say about these subjects. One has only to look at the full title of The International Library of Psychology, Philosophy and Scientific Method to see that for Ogden it was psychology that took pride of place as the pre-eminent scientific paradigm for understanding other branches of knowledge. His *ABC of Psychology* (1929) draws on many of the texts he had published in the International Library, giving a good sense of how he saw the different disciplines as interlocking. He presumably agreed with Schiller, who, in *Tantalus; or, The Future of Man* (1924) took issue with *Daedalus* and *Icarus*, arguing that a truly scientific psychology would be more effective than pharmacology in improving humanity, and was the best prospect we had to 'transform the Yahoo into a man' (67-70). Ogden clearly felt psychology was the discipline that had the potential to transform the human sciences and the humanities as the theories of Darwin, Mendel, Einstein, and Planck had transformed the biological and physical sciences.

The sole volume devoted to philosophy in To-Day and To-Morrow was one published only in the US: *Thinking about Thinking* (1926), by Cassius Keyser. It is a refreshingly crisp volume devoted to what Keyser terms 'Autonomous' or 'Postulational' thinking (thinking taking the form 'If…then…'; in which propositions are deduced from postulates (or axioms), enabling us to say with certainty that the propositions are true if the postulates are). Though the volume does not engage in predictions as such, it makes what might be characterized as a prediction about predictions, touching on futurity in the opening claim that this unique form of thought is not only essential to the greatest scientific achievement, but 'is destined, I believe, to attain pre-eminence among the intellectual and scientific agencies which, it is hoped, will become more and more effective in determining the future course and character of human history'.[48] Not all postulational thinking predicts the future; but all futurology is inherently postulational: if the current trends are X and Y, then we can expect Z to happen.

Keyser shares the sense of many contributors of a paradigm shift; but in his case it is one in mathematics: the invention of non-Euclidian geometry, first by Saccheri in 1733, though he remained unknown (30); then, by both Bolyai and Lobachevski independently of each other, in the nineteenth century (31). These 'strange new doctrines' caused a revolution in epistemology and methodology, and 'the philosophy of science was greatly advanced' (31). In Keyser's own generation, 'scientific doctrines of the autonomous type have risen by the score', 'the most imposing and most beautiful edifices in the modern City of Science' (33). He cites the elliptic geometries of Riemann and Klein (33); Plücker's line geometry and the sphere geometry of Lie (34). That aesthetic appreciation is crucial. Mathematicians talk of the beauty of equations or their solutions; and Keyser recognizes that his City of Science is built in accord with, not in opposition to, art: 'An autonomous doctrine is indeed a work of art of the highest order' (54).

There are three volumes in the series devoted primarily to psychology.[49] The only one of these to name the discipline in the subtitle was *Sisyphus; or, The Limits of Psychology* by Muriel Jaeger; a relatively late addition to the series in 1929. Jaeger, whose closest friend was her Somerville contemporary Dorothy L. Sayers, was the author of a utopian novel, *The Question Mark*, published in 1926 by the Hogarth Press, and a book *Experimental Lives, from Cato to George Sand* (1932). *Sisyphus* is essentially a sceptical contrast between Freud's psycho-analysis and the behaviourism of J. B. Watson.[50] Indeed, it is striking that behaviourism features as prominently as Psycho-Analysis in the series. This contrasts with the privileging of the psycho-analytic in literary studies. That emphasis reflects the fact that

---

[48] Cassius Keyser, *Thinking about Thinking* (New York: Dutton, 1926), 2–3.

[49] Excluding those touching on the topic more obliquely, and discussed above: Patten's *The Passing of the Phantoms*; Bennett's *Apollonius; or, The Present and Future of Psychical Research* (1927); and McDougall's *Janus; The Conquest of War: A Psychological Inquiry* (1927).

[50] Such contrasts were familiar at the time. In a Psyche Miniature volume of the previous year, *The Battle of Behaviourism* (London: Kegan Paul, 1928), Ogden had pitted arch-behaviourist John B. Watson against William McDougall (the author of *Janus*) making the case for a psychology drawing upon the data of consciousness as well as those of behaviour.

many creative writers found psycho-analysis more congenial than behaviourism, and were reacting against behaviourism's negation of consciousness. Whereas behaviourism's experimental methods appealed more to the scientifically-minded, including Ogden. However, the evidence of To-Day and To-Morrow could also be taken to indicate that the modernist stress on consciousness was lagging behind contemporary scientific developments, and was still preoccupied with phenomenology while the scientific agenda had shifted to more experimentally verifiable methods. Ogden was not opposed to Freudian ideas, and devoted a section of his *ABC of Psychology* to a sympathetic explanation of them, arguing that though 'The whole theory is in many quarters rejected', 'its opponents sometimes show either ignorance and misconceptions of it or an emotional attitude towards it which suggest that their theoretical objections are in part rationalizations' (228; by which he meant irrationalizations: 'some more or less plausible and elaborate answer, bearing no relation to the real reason'; 242).

In *Sisyphus* Jaeger sees the scientific claims of psychology as vitiated by the individuality of the observer. She quotes Haldane, in *Possible Worlds* saying that psychology is not yet ready to be a science (89). The book ends with a turn to art, as exemplified by Dostoevsky and Pirandello (the modern masters in fiction and theatre of the irrational); by the sculptor Epstein; and also by Freud, but in his capacity as an artist rather than a scientist. The artist has the advantage because he 'makes a strength of what is the scientist's weakness—his own individuality' (87), says Jaeger.

Vernon Lee's *Proteus; or, The Future of Intelligence* (1925) is poised between philosophy, psychology, and aesthetics. Lee was a pioneer of what she called 'psychological aesthetics'.[51] She chooses Proteus as the mythological embodiment of her topic because she wants to apprehend 'Reality' in its complexity and changeability, and argues that what she means by 'intelligence' is different from received standards of thought; and that it is constantly changing. Like many of the writers in the series, she is responding to a sense of intellectual paradigm shift, and recognizes that it is at least partly attributable to science. She too sees traditional philosophical, moral and religious ideas shifting their shape, arguing that 'until the eighteenth century the only Future which people thought about was the Future in Heaven or Hell', leaving over no interest 'for any other after-life, to wit, that of unborn generations' (16-17). But that science opened up ways of '*thinking in terms of change*', which is an intrinsic part of the thought she privileges: '*thinking in terms of otherness*' (16). As is evident, unlike many of the other contributors, she takes the argument a stage further, suggesting that these changes are changing not just the material our minds operate upon, but the nature of the intelligence we bring to bear on them. In other words, Lee too is thinking about

---

[51] See, for example, her *The Beautiful: An introduction to psychological aesthetics* (1913).

thinking—Keyser's phrase capturing the essence of the reflexivity seen by Anthony Giddens as characterizing modernity.[52]

Lee sees morality as 'already taking a new status, independent alike of an absentee (or absent) Deity, and of an indifferent Cosmos', its 'sanctions and imperatives only the stronger for being man-made and man-regarding' (28). Modern intelligence liberates thought from 'chewing and rechewing the cud of Scripture and the Classics' (17). Lee is contemptuous of the fascist 'rods and axes of antique hangmen figuring (not merely in figurative manner!) as emblems of post-war Italy' (18). She takes the mobile intelligence she is concerned with to be a relatively 'recent human accomplishment'(50), and follows the Arnoldian line that the loss religious consolation can be compensated by art. 'Intelligence is the living, changing mass of unprofessional thought, the averaged, habitual thought of the majority of us' (55), she writes; the statement typifying her agile and, her, itself rather Protean, shifting between the apparently contradictory positions of the democratic and the elitisist, the mystical and the rationalist, or the advocacy of and wariness about science.

Lee closes with a warning about warnings. She notes that what she calls with irony 'men of genius or thereabouts ("Creative Intellects" is the official expression)' have recently 'taken over one of the most remunerative and mischievous employments of all obsolete priesthoods, to wit: of frightening believers with bogies of their manufacture' (57): 'nowadays encyclopedic science and journalistic emphasis are being applied to making our flesh creep with prophecies of Perils' (57-8)—threats from different races, political movements, the eugenically undesirable, 'from unsexed women and over-sexed women' (58) and so on. In many ways what she calls this 'multifold reincarnation of the spirit of prophecy in our Men of Science and of Letters' (59) is what To-Day and To-Morrow was intended to stand as antithetical to, and Lee clearly intended the description as a critique of the scaremongering of the tabloid press. (It is a 'reincarnation' because a throwback to the days of 'obsolete priesthoods'.) The series largely eschews those rabble-rousing tones. *Proteus* was an early volume—the fourteenth or fifteenth in the series. It demonstrates familiarity with earlier volumes; but arguably too few would have been available at the time of writing for her to have countenanced an overall assessment. Yet some of the scare-subjects—eugenics, race, inhumane politics, female sexuality—had already been touched on in the volumes she mentions by Haldane, Russell, and Schiller; and also in *Lysistrata* (probably the eighth volume, out in 1924). So it is possible that the 'multifold reincarnation of the spirit of prophecy in our Men of Science and of Letters' is itself subtly multiform, exhorting To-Day and To-Morrow's multiplicity of experts to strive for an intelligence up to the demands of the challenge.

---

[52] Anthony Giddens, *The Consequences of Modernity* (London: Polity, 1990), 39; discussed in the Introductions.

H. F. Carlill's *Socrates; or, The Emancipation of Mankind* (1927) might sound from its title as if it were going to be about philosophy, but in fact it argues that 'our conception of human nature' has been fundamentally 'altered by recent investigations' (13) in psychology: particularly in the work of Freud, the behaviourists, and Taylorism. Just as Socrates challenged the Athenian world by questioning everything that was taken for granted, he says, the new sciences of the mind and behaviour will transform the human of the future.

> Human behaviour is still governed mainly by impersonal forces, by instinct, habit, and tradition; but the growing realization of this fact, with all the possibilities of deliberate self-development which it implies, will lead in the end to a real freedom based on a real understanding.   (96)

Just as Socrates argued that to know the right is to do it, Carlill envisions a future where politics and morality are no longer necessary. In some ways he too is a proto-existentialist, arguing that: 'Man creates himself by becoming self-conscious' (51); even a proto-performativity theorist, as when he says:

> the self, the free agent is not something given beforehand, something to which you ascribe consciousness and to which you apply motives. It is something that comes into being only in the act of self-consciousness and the adoption or rejection of motives. There is no self until it asserts itself.   (52).

Following William James and others, he considers that abnormal mental states and individuals showing exceptional powers (such as savants) reveal potentialities of the mind that could be unlocked (70-3): 'Half the virtue of the technique of the future by which, I am persuaded, vastly greater powers than we at present use will be commonly developed will consist in knowing how and when to let the machine run free' (74-5). That is the 'Emancipation of Mankind' of his subtitle, and which he sees science as making possible.

In *Pygmalion; or, The Doctor of the Future* (1925), R. McNair Wilson had arrived at a comparable vision of how a new science of the relation between body and mind will liberate human potential. He asks of the doctor: 'Shall he continue to speak of the body as though it may be spoken of apart from the mind?'(69-70). If not, then:

> Realizing that man owes all that he is to his power of self-stimulation by thought, he will perceive that no limit can be set to the extension of this process, and that, under guidance, men and women may, indeed, be evolved mentally and spiritually in a manner not yet generally dreamed of.   (67)

These volumes indicate how the conception of the series is itself psychological, and in two ways—both arguably characteristic of Ogden's thought-style. They are thinking about the power of human thought; what it is already capable of, and what it might yet be capable of. And in doing the latter, they are themselves exercising human thought in one of its most characteristic modes, though one curiously neglected by thinkers: speculation about the future (the neglect is understandable: futurology's associations with prophecy and fantasy and error make academic thinkers nervous). The sense of exhilaration in the writing of much of the series comes from this new sense of the extension of human possibility in thinking about possible worlds, and in thinking about thinking. The idea that the future of thought will be *different* is at least implicit in most of the To-Day and To-Morrow books; even the majority on topics other than science, yet which employ a scientific paradigm. Their future of philosophy is a philosophy of the future.

PART III

TECHNOLOGY, MEDIA, CULTURE, AND THE ARTS

AUTOMATON
OR THE FUTURE
OF THE MECHANICAL MAN

H. STAFFORD HATFIELD

EUTERPE
OR
THE FUTURE OF ART

By
LIONEL R. McCOLVIN

The nature and amount of popular
interest in art is governed largely by
economic and purely commercial influences, and these are not leading to the
development of the best artistic life.
This essay shows why this is so, analyses
the various factors responsible for the
present low standard of popular taste,
and suggests remedies. Some points
are raised concerning the basic
[illegible] ...

NARCISSUS
AN ANATOMY OF CLOTHES

By
GERALD HEARD

With 19 Illustrations

CONTENTS

A METAPHYSIC OF MAN—THE STORY OF
NAILS—THE EXPRESSION OF FASHION—
CLASSICAL DRESS—ORIENTAL RATIONAL-
ISM AND OCCIDENTAL SEXUALITY—EVOLUTION
BEGINS: EGOATISTIC CONSTANCY—THE
INDUSTRIAL DEFECTION—THE CHANGING
IDEA OF THE GENTLEMAN—THE GRANDFATHERS
OF UNIFORMS—THE FUTURE'S FASHION

OUROBOROS
OR THE MECHANICAL
EXTENSION OF MANKIND

GARET GARRETT

PLATO'S AMERICAN
REPUBLIC

By
DOUGLAS WOODRUFF

This is the story of what happened to
the famous Greek philosopher Socrates
when he went on a lecture tour in the
United States. His misfortunes lead him
to a philosophical consideration of the
modern Americans and his ideals, and of
the conditions that are making to-day for
the mass-manufacture of standardised
souls. In the course of a wide survey,
which takes in Great Britain, Socrates
and his friends decide that the Americans
are heading for disaster and unhappiness
and very kindly develop a drastic plan of
national education to change them. The
work is a judicious blend of light
burlesque and subtle criticism.

4

'The machine man of 1925'

To-Day and To-Morrow and the Technological Extension of Man

Chapter 1 argued that To-Day and To-Morrow is informed by a paradigm of scientific thinking, which then informs its presentation of topics beyond the natural sciences; as in the human sciences, surveyed in Chapter 3. But what happens to the idea of the human when science and technology transform human life through the proliferation of the machine? That is the central question of this chapter. It develops the theme of the impact of the war, analysed in Chapter 2, when the new military technologies had introduced new forms of inhumanity, and had questioned the place of the human in war and history and even the cosmos. It also develops Chapter 1's discussion of imagined changes to human nature through genetic modification or biotechnological intervention, asking what happens when science and technology start redesigning the human, to the point where it begins to look like something other than the human? How do culture, media, the arts and everyday life change when the idea of the human comes under such pressure? How does our thinking about these things change? These are the questions pursued here, and in the remaining chapters.

As has become clear from their earlier appearances through this book Haldane and Bernal are posthumanist and indeed transhumanist before either of those terms had been coined. Indeed, *Daedalus* and *The World, the Flesh and the Devil* have both been seen as foundational texts of transhumanism.[1] The transcendence of the human they envisage results from a combination of eugenics, biochemistry and bionic engineering to alter the body's reproductive processes, its genetic makeup, and its physical and mental nature. Such changes could scarcely be more drastic. They involve forms of prosthetic invention that act as life support machines (Haldane's artificial wombs; Bernal's brain vats); in the case of Bernal's book, involving major surgical interventions (primarily the transferring of the brain, and also the attachment to it of enhanced mechanical limbs and senses). To-Day and To-Morrow speculates on a wide range of prosthetic technologies.

---

[1] See for example Nick Bostrom, 'A History of Transhumanist Thought', an early version of which appeared in *Journal of Evolution and Technology*, 14:1 (April 2005), 1–25; revised for *Academic Writing Across the Disciplines*, ed. Michael Rectenwald and Lisa Carl (New York: Pearson Longman, 2011), 1–30. Also see the Wikipedia entry for transhumanism: https://en.wikipedia.org/wiki/Transhumanism accessed 9 January 2017.

Imagined Futures: Writing, Science and Modernity in the To-Day and To-Morrow. Max Saunders, Oxford University Press (2019). © Max Saunders. DOI: 10.1093/oso/9780198829454.001.0001

But most of them are of less invasive kinds—less invasive to the body, at least: prosthetics, tools, technologies which are merely added on to, or used alongside, the existing body. These are the main subject of this chapter.

As the series neared its end in 1931, the Classified Index listed eight volumes on 'Industry and the Machine', and twelve on 'Science and Medicine'—including *Automaton*, which could equally have been placed in the former category. Much of what the series separates into 'Science' and 'the Machine' would now be more likely to be brought together under the heading of 'Technology' or 'Techno-science'.[2]

Many of the To-Day and To-Morrow authors see technology, and especially the machine, as the key to the future. If occasionally they are continuing a romantic or Victorian jeremiad against the dehumanizing effects of industrialization, they are charting a new phase of that industrialization and its effects. For they have a new mode of production to consider—the technique of mass production, pioneered by Henry Ford, and which was coming to symbolize the condition of technological and industrial modernity. They also had new technologies, new machines, and new media, to weigh up: the automobile; the aeroplane; the tank; radio; the phonograph; cinema; television; and so on. It was, commentators agreed, the Machine Age. Three years into the series, a 'Machine-Age Exposition' was staged in New York in 1927, organized by Jane Heap, the editor of the literary magazine *The Little Review*.[3]

These ideas inevitably thread their way through To-Day and To-Morrow, as inevitably constitutive of the future.[4] Ford himself, who knew a mass-produced title when he saw one, called his best-selling autobiography *Today and Tomorrow* (1926). Yet he has little to say about tomorrow, evidently thinking prophecy was bunk. In a passage quoted by F. R. Leavis in his classic essay worrying about what mass production was doing to culture, Ford writes:

> But what of the future? Shall we not have over-production? Shall we not some day reach a point where the machine becomes all powerful, and the man of no consequence?
>
> No man can say anything of the future. We need not bother about it. The future has always cared for itself in spite of our well-meant efforts to hamper it. If to-day we do the task we can best do, then we are doing all that we can do.

---

[2]   See Mark S. Morrisson, *Modernism, Science, and Technology* (London: Bloomsbury, 2017), 22–3, 39.

[3]   The exhibition catalogue, which included an intriguing essay on 'The Aesthetic of the Machine and Mechanical Introspection in Art' by Enrico Prampolini, was reviewed in T. S. Eliot's *Criterion*, 6:3 (September 1927), 284.

[4]   Two volumes specifically set mass production against the idea of craftsmanship. Oliver Stewart's *Aeolus* contrasts 'artist-scientist' craftsman with mass production in the US (18–19). In *Artifex; or, The Future of Craftsmanship* (1926), John Gloag moves from a Ruskinian medievalist celebration of the creative freedom of true craftsmanship to arguing that mechanization should be seen not as the death-knell of the craftsman, but a new opportunity; and that 'The education of craftsmen must be directed to make hand-craft and machine-craft compatible' (73).

Perhaps we may over-produce, but that is impossible until the whole world has all its desires. And if that should happen, then surely we ought to be content.[5]

Others, like Leavis, were less sanguine, and felt that the implications and effects of the new technologies required analysis. Mass production and the idea of 'machine man' became essential components of the lexicon of cultural discourse. *Culture and Environment*, for example, which Leavis wrote with Denys Thompson in 1934, includes a chapter on mass production, and cites Ford again, and also Stuart Chase's *Men and Machines* (1929) as well as a book about the American short story by E. J. O'Brien called *The Dance of the Machines* (1929).

When the To-Day and To-Morrow writers consider the machine, the figure they are particularly drawn to is that of the prosthesis: the machine or tool understood as an artificial addition to the body. In computerized times we tend to visualize mass production as a fully automated process, perhaps overseen by white-coated boffins. It is doubtless an ideological distortion produced by advertising, designed to make the products look futuristic even in their production, and thereby to efface the traces of human labour. But in the interwar imagination of mechanization, machine and man are conjoined—as they had been in the pre-war imagination of Vorticism in works like Jacob Epstein's *Rock Drill*.

In October 1930 the *Magazine of Today*, which had only launched that May, realized it was already out of date, but did not help by changing its name to *Today and Tomorrow* (unless it hoped to poach readers from the series).[6] Its Spring 1933 number included a fine essay by the veteran sexologist Havelock Ellis on 'The Machine and the Future'. It was a meditation on a book by a French architect and engineer, Jacques Lafitte, which had appeared the previous year, called *Reflexions sur la Science des Machines*. It prompts Ellis to ask 'What is a machine?', and to develop the answer thus:

> The hand which wielded that first flint-knife was itself really a machine formed on mechanical principles. Our bodies, in fact, are, all through, a natural machine, with levers and pulleys and pumps and bellows, and all sorts of other mechanical devices. Even when we turn to the receiving and transmitting and reproducing processes of the apparatus of our highest sensory centres of hearing and sight we find already in operation the same sort of application of natural forces which we are now ourselves beginning to devise. In making machinery Man is only doing in his way what Nature has been doing in her own way since life began. Machines are an organised prolongation of ourselves. The house, our

---

[5] Henry Ford, *To-day and To-morrow*, pp. 272–3. Quoted by F. R. Leavis, *For Continuity* (Cambridge: Minority Press, 1933), 46n.

[6] The *Spectator* announced on 2 May 1930 that the *Magazine of Today* would launch that week. Harold Herd (the editor), letter to W. H. Dawson, 12 August 1930, announcing the change of name: Birmingham University Library, Special Collections. The magazine ran under its new title till 'New Year 1934'.

dwelling place, which is the nearest and the most primitive of our machines, not only goes back to early Man, but even to some forms of animal life. We have acquired the delicate and sensitive skin of the creatures that live in shells, and, unlike them, we are able to construct our own shells.[7]

As in the series, Lafitte moves between disciplines, not only considering the body as a machine, but then in turn considering machines from biological and evolutionary perspectives. As Ellis explains:

it is possible (and here to some extent M. Lafitte follows Butler) to regard them as having an evolution in many respects resembling and parallel to our own. We have in the evolution of machines a series closely comparable to a living series, with generation, heredity, development and degradation. It is born and develops and dies out by changes analogous to those in an animal or a vegetable species. A main difference is that the life of machines passes through our moulding hands. But the laws are the same natural laws and cannot possibly be any other. They thus present problems which are very like the problems of biology. And since, save in the most rudimentary shapes, it involves human social activity, the machine becomes 'another flesh of our flesh'. The science of the organised bodies constructed by Man is thus a branch of sociology.[8]

The phrase 'flesh of our flesh' recalls *Genesis* 2:23 in which Adam comments on the creation of woman: 'This is now bone of my bones, and flesh of my flesh'; and alerts us to the gender work done by Ellis' pronouns in the previous quotation: 'Man is only doing in *his* way what Nature has been doing in *her* own way since life began' (my emphasis). The gendering of the machine as masculine, that is, rivals both the creation of woman by god, and the production of children by woman. The language of the description of 'organised bodies constructed by man' contrasts such machine progeny with the bodies gestated by women. We shall see how, as with 'The Machine Man of Ardathia', or Bernal's cyborg, the linguistically unmarked term 'man', while claiming the alibi of standing inclusively for the human, allies the masculine with the machine and the future, against the feminine and the biological and the past.

As Ellis' essay develops, he shows how the science of machines—what we would now call technology—is affecting most branches of human knowledge.[9]

---

[7] Havelock Ellis, 'The Machine and the Future', *Today and Tomorrow*, 3:3 (Spring 1933), 261–6 (262). Lafitte was the brother of Ellis' companion Françoise Lafitte. I'm grateful to Patrick Parrinder for noting this connection.

[8] Ibid., p. 263.

[9] In fact this sense of 'technology' was available from the early nineteenth century. The *Oxford English Dictionary* gives an example of sense 4a: 'The branch of knowledge dealing with the mechanical arts and applied sciences; the study of this' from 1787; and an example of sense 4b: 'The application of such knowledge for practical purposes, esp. in industry, manufacturing, etc.; the sphere of activity concerned with this; the mechanical arts and applied sciences collectively' from 1829.

He is clearly familiar with Le Corbusier's famous claim in *Vers une Architecture* (1923) that 'The house is a machine for living in':[10]

> Today it is becoming a highly complex branch. The organisation of machinery is being ever more thoroughly and elaborately conceived, with a simultaneous development in external form and internal anatomy, well illustrated by the tendencies in architecture, for the house is the most essential of human machines. And in this respect mechanism follows life. The mechanological series, as it is put, runs parallel with the biological series. The increasing place of machines in modern literature, the general intellectual repercussion of this activity in our philosophy, taken in conjunction with the vivid interest of the younger generation today in all kinds of engines as compared with the older generation, show how greatly our conception of the machine is being transformed, and that a general science of machinery is becoming a necessity for mankind.[11]

Our conception of the machine was thus being transformed in multiple ways. To call a house a machine partly reflects how modern technologies were beginning to constitute domestic space. But it also extends the concept of the machine from manufacturing mechanisms to any element of the made environment—tools, devices, means of communications, etc.

Not all the volumes proposing a prosthetic view of human development are machine-focused. Gerald Heard, for example, produced an eccentric volume called *Narcissus: An anatomy of clothes* (1924). In it he picks up a version of the idea in Ellis' essay that we have evolved out of an animal's protective hide, and now need 'to construct our own shells'. He means that 'anatomy' in his subtitle seriously; since his argument is that human civilization has brought evolution to a halt—the view several of the more eugenically-minded contributors shared (and which is discussed in the Introductions), on the grounds that medicine, law and morality had countered all the forces that prevented the survival of the less fit. Therefore, argues Heard, evolution has itself had to evolve, moving into our clothes. It sounds a fairly mad idea, and certainly the exposition of it doesn't do much to dispel that impression. But there is something to be said for its notion of clothing as prosthesis. Some examples are specifically designed to enable us to survive in hostile environments: armour, diving suits, space suits, etc. But his view is perhaps most plausible apropos of clothing that has evolved to enable people to live in more extreme climates, whether desert or Tundra. Or sportswear that lets us jog further or swim faster.

---

[10] Le Corbusier, *Towards a New Architecture*, trans. Frederick Etchells (London: The Architectural Press, 1927), 10.

[11] Ellis, 'The Machine and the Future', p. 263.

When Ellis writes that 'Machines are an organized prolongation of ourselves' it is ambiguous whether he means they prolong our reach (with swords, say, or telephones) or our lives. The sheer size of so much Victorian machinery tends to encourage a view of it as stand-alone installations which humans can engage with or not, turning a handle or pressing a button, and letting the machine do the work. But the prosthetic view sees the machine as not working alongside or instead of us, but as an extension of the human body and human will. That is why it was becoming possible to think of machines in terms previously reserved for biology and humanity: 'generation, heredity, development and degradation'. Conversely, more sophisticated machine technology extended the range of metaphors for describing the human as mechanical. In Ellis' marvellous observation, we find in our bodies whatever we invent in our technology. It was after we had started networking our computers that we began to think seriously about neural networks.

Seeing the hand as a machine, or that our organs work like machines, were not unprecedented ideas. (Witness Ellis' reference to Samuel Butler.) But they also typify a modernist mode of vision, attending to form and function, and the relations between them, rather than to content. It is the basis of the Futurist or Vorticist vision of man behaving as if mechanical. Which illustrates the double-edged nature of machine man discourse. Machines can be assimilated to people; given a taxonomy and the parallel equivalent of a natural history. The fantasy vision towards which that version of the analogy leads is the automaton or robot or android; increasingly mimicking the human to the point where one can no longer tell the difference. Conversely, people can be assimilated to machines. Body parts are like machine parts. The entire body is like a machine. The fantasy vision this version leads to is that of *society* as the machine, with the individual as just a constituent component.[12] Which conjures visions of people mass produced as uniformly as possible to ensure the smooth running of the machinery. As Edgar Ansel Mowrer puts it in *Sinon; or, The Future of Politics* (1930) of the conception of 'applying engineering methods to society': 'with the machine for a model, people expect an ever more frictionless functioning' (47).

It is a vision which corresponds to the rhetoric of interconnection and unification charted in Chapter 2, as the individual is linked ever more intricately into the social network. As we saw in Fournier d'Albe's image of underground pipes and wires as evoking an animal dissection, or his vision of the future in which 'The Earth will have become a sentient being', the machine becomes so complex it acquires the characteristics of the animate; becomes what we shall see Haldane call a 'super-organism'.[13] That was effectively Le Corbusier's view of the machine

---

[12] See the discussion of the Psyche Miniature volume, *The Conquest of Thought by Invention in the Mechanical State of the Future* (London: Kegan Paul, Trench, Trübner & Co., 1929), by To-Day and To-Morrow contributor H. Stafford Hatfield in note 59 below.

[13] See the discussion of J. B. S. Haldane's *Possible Worlds* (London: Chatto and Windus, 1927) in the Conclusions (354–56).

for living in which is a city. His description in *The City of Tomorrow* captures the paradox whereby man's creation is both unnatural and yet organic: 'A city! It is the grip of man upon nature. It is a human operation directed against nature, a human organism both for protection and for work'.[14]

The vision of the state as machine threatens liberalism's valuing of the autonomous individual. It is generally figured in interwar writing as either fascism or communism; the subsumption of individual wills under the will of the dictator or the party. The other machine-figure expressing a major threat to the individual in the period is that of the 'war machine', in which the individual soldier is either a part of the military machine, or the raw material it mass produces into uniform soldiers and then destroys. As the subject has been dealt with superbly by Daniel Pick in his book *War Machine*, there is no need to dwell on it here, except to note its presence in To-Day and To-Morrow both explicitly and implicitly. We saw it in Haldane's vision of the troops appearing subservient to huge explosions or relentless tanks; and saw that its rhetoric of conflict and disintegration is the obverse of that of interconnection and unification. We saw it, too, in Liddell Hart's account in *Paris* of how the slaughter of the Western Front began to blind the strategists to reason.

What all these versions of the group machine share is an anxiety (ideologically liberal, no doubt, but humanly intelligible given the experiences of war, the Depression and mass unemployment) about man losing control. As Ellis notes at the conclusion of his essay: 'It is one of the main objects of M. Lafitte's book to emphasize that now fateful question: Is Man to control the machine or to be controlled by it?'[15] If that question too goes back to Samuel Butler's *Erewhon* too, it was also one exercising the To-Day and To-Morrow contributors, as we shall see; and it is one that has come back in a new form to haunt the era of artificial intelligence, as we contemplate the possibility of what Ray Kurzweil calls 'The Singularity': the point at which machine intelligence overtakes that of its creators; and which Stephen Hawking has warned us could terminate humanity.[16]

Unsurprisingly, it is America which they saw as indicating the future. In *Thrasymachus; The Future of Morals* (1925), C. E. M. Joad wrote that: 'if we want to know what England will be like to-morrow, we cannot do better than look at America today' (32).[17] He clearly didn't like what he saw: 'The objects of American civilisation are to substitute cleanliness for beauty, mechanism for men, and hypocrisy for morals' (33). It is the two intriguing volumes on

---

[14] Le Corbusier, *The City of Tomorrow* [*Urbanisme*] trans. Frederick Etchells (London: John Rodker, 1929), xxi. I am grateful to Simon Vickery for drawing my attention to this quotation.

[15] Ibid., p. 266.

[16] Ray Kurzweil, *The Singularity Is Near: When humans transcend biology* (New York: Viking, 2005). 'Stephen Hawking warns artificial intelligence could end mankind': http://www.bbc.co.uk/news/technology-30290540 accessed 9 January 2017.

[17] In his other volume for the series, *Diogenes; or, The Future of Leisure* (1928), C. E. M. Joad described America as 'the most typical country of the modern world', and cites Anatole France as saying that 'the future is an American future' (14).

America in the series that are among those which address the concept of the machine age most directly.[18]

In *Midas; or, The United States and the Future* (1926), C. H. Bretherton[19] states that 'America is to-day the land of many and efficient machines, the one place where machines are suffered gladly and even welcomed enthusiastically by all sections of the community' (60). He puts what he calls the 'machine man' in an evolutionary perspective, wondering whether his future will be as transformative as that of his 'ape man' past:

> It may be that they will not develop any new attribute of civilization, any new art or new field of intellectual activity. We cannot rule out that possibility because Science forbids us to assume that any further expansion of man's intellectual activity must be one of degree and not of kind, or that the machine man of 1925 has before him an evolutionary horizon less extensive than that which lay before the ape man of 20,000 B.C.   (21)

He is doubtful, on the grounds that the results of invention have degraded man's inventiveness: 'Centuries, however, if not thousands of years, have elapsed since a new art was discovered' (21). This appears wilfully blind to a range of emerging artistries—of photography and cinema in particular.[20] But as his argument develops, it becomes clear that he sees the industrial process as inimical to art: 'We have only to consider the motor car. Here was a new medium for artistic expression if ever there was one, but the automobile remains a machine [...]' (22). Fetishists of classic cars may disagree with this exclusion of the Bugatti Type 35 or the Hispano Suiza H6 from the category of the aesthetic. But Bretherton's point is a version of the nineteenth-century anxiety that machines dehumanize man:

> we may not refuse to entertain the possibility of a wholesale and drastic revolt by the human race against the civilization of to-day which threatens to enthrone the power plant and the machine and make of man an ant toiling in a hill, a robot functioning according to plans over which he has long lost all control.   (60)

---

[18] The third volume about the US, Col. J. F. C. Fuller's *Atlantis: America and the future* (1925) is less admirable. It is mostly supercilious about everything American, dismissing 'Jews, Modernists, Fundamentalists and Whatnots' (71). However, he does predict that 'the "almightiness" of the dollar' will 'crack' (69), as it did in the Wall St Crash of four years later; and also that a Russian Alexander will lead an invading army into Europe, as Stalin was to do after the Second World War.

[19] Bretherton was a US citizen who married an Englishwoman, joined the British Army in the First World War, and became Irish correspondent for the *Morning Post* after the war.

[20] Bretherton was certainly aware of the West Coast's emerging culture industry, and of the cultural divide between the two coasts and middle America, arguing that 'The West being younger will move faster. California will become the centre of whatever essentially American intellectual civilization is developed [...]' (90), whereas it was the people from the central plains who will be the problem—in his terms, the kind of cranks advocating Creationism and Prohibition (92). But his prediction that the US was now emotionally too detached from Europe ever to take part in another European war was not borne out (41).

Yet, as the presence of that ultra-contemporary 'robot' suggests, there is also something new here. For the nineteenth century the scandal was that industrial-ism treated workers without humanity, as if they were inhuman. In Dickens' *Hard Times*, for example, the factory hands are treated as if they were precisely and only that: 'hands', body parts, of interest only for what work they could do, what they could make with those hands—*manu-facture*. Industrialism dehumanizes; and Gradgrind education too risks making people like machines. But robotics makes machines like people. The category distinction between man and machine is thus under pressure from both directions; and the discourse of the conjoined 'machine man' becomes increasingly pervasive.

To-Day and To-Morrow tends to frame prostheses as extending not just the body but the mind as well. In some volumes the effects are seen as negative. For Bretherton in *Midas*, it is what the machine age does to our minds rather than our bodies or our souls that challenges their creativity. Americans, he says, 'have already acquired or are about to acquire the outlook and temper and habit of mind of the machine age' (22). This is partly because—as other volumes observe too—the very mechanization that promised the saving of labour actually results in a consumerist frenzy of production and advertising and consumption, which demands ever harder work:

> In the old world some bitterness and hostility is still expressed. The machine, we point out, was introduced and encouraged in the belief that as it could do the work of anything from three to a hundred men a life of opulent ease lay before us all. To-day with the machine working its hardest we find ourselves also work-ing harder than ever before in our lives, hampered with an incredible number of material possessions, gadgets, utilities and other highly specialized objects that bring no happiness into our lives and still actuated by a far greater number of unsatisfied desires than ever before.   (60-1)

At this point it becomes clear that what worries Bretherton is a particular form of degradation; one which not only treats the body as exploitable mechanism, but which, through doing so, ends up turning the mind into mechanism too. That thought is perhaps implicit in the figure of the robot. But whereas that image tended to connote slave-like drudgery, as it does with the servants of the machines in Fritz Lang's film *Metropolis*, say (in the Czech of Karel Čapek's play *R.U.R*, which introduced the term, *robota* denotes serf-labour), Bretherton is tracking a more subtle, unconscious process, more subtly:

> So it comes about that the American mind is also becoming a machine, one in which the undisciplined processes of reflection and ratiocination and imagination are falling into disuse and thought is becoming an apparatus for registering the ready-made idea or translating it into action.   (61)

That is the effect that for him militates against artistic invention: a passive intellectual consumerism.[21] In that context we can see that his objection to contemporary artistic developments was precisely that they seemed to him to exemplify this mechanization of the mind and imagination. In literature he judges that 'the American passion for *vers libre* is simply a reflection of American superficiality' (76). In music, he asks: 'Is the United States of the future to have no other [atmosphere] than that of the cash register opening and shutting to the neurotic crash and whoop of the jazz band?' (79). His lack of appreciation of jazz seems obtuse too now—Duke Ellington had been recording since 1924, though his recording career only took off in 1926, and his tenure at the Cotton Club at the end of the following year—and that 'whoop' may suggest a racist inflection of taste. The pulsing rhythms of jazz dance music frequently seemed crude or 'primitive' to classically-trained ears.[22] To Bretherton they sound as mechanical as a till; or possibly as a recording ('an apparatus for registering the ready-made idea'; 61). Indeed, the idea that people were buying records rather than making their own music may have offered further evidence of his thesis.

The effect of recording technology on the mind, on sensibility, and on art is a concern for another outstanding volume, *Euterpe; or, The Future of Art* (1926), by Lionel McColvin. Little known nowadays beyond the history of public libraries, where he was influential, McColvin was the Chief Librarian in Ipswich in 1926 (he later became chief librarian at Hampstead and curator of the Keats House Museum in 1931, and city librarian at Westminster from 1938). It would be an exaggeration to claim him as the British Walter Benjamin. But one of McColvin's subjects is certainly the work of art in the age of mechanical reproduction, articulated ten years before Benjamin's famous essay. If this goes to show what cultural studies and New Historicism have taught us—that ideas are produced socially, and have their time, it also demonstrates the acute antennae of To-Day and To-Morrow's editor and authors. The series is continually entertaining ideas that we tend to associate with later periods and thinkers.

In *Euterpe* McColvin asserts that 'the most powerful force in the art-life of to-day is the purely mechanical factor'; that 'this factor is to a great extent determining the nature and amount of art-production and reproduction'; that 'it is causing a decrease in the average quality of the total artistic life of the community'; and that 'this degeneration must naturally continue unless it is counteracted by other influences' (21). The influences he has in mind include education, and the making of good art more accessible by putting 'art-provision as far as possible upon a non-commercial basis' (48). Public libraries had existed in Britain since

[21] David Ockham, in *Stentor; or, The Press of To-Day and To-Morrow* (1927), discussed in Chapter 5, expresses a similar concern about what he terms 'the "Fordisation" of the intellect' (40–1).
[22] W. J. Turner, for example, in *Orpheus; or, The Music of the Future* (1926), describes jazz and popular songs as '[i]nfantile' (13).

the mid-nineteenth century. So McColvin is thinking here less about literature and more about music—Euterpe was the muse of music or lyric—wondering whether libraries should house recordings as well as books. He could thus also be seen as a forerunner of contemporary thought about the nature of media and the archive.

McColvin starts from an explicitly sociological viewpoint (6), seeing aesthetics as produced not only culturally but technologically: 'the quality of public taste has been influenced by mechanical methods of reproduction' (13).[23] He argues that the main factor in the change in cultural pursuits from previous civilizations to ours is 'the development of means of reproduction' (11). He is good on the distinctions between a range of technologies, and what different effects they have on audiences. Here too he can be seen to anticipate the work of thinkers such as Pierre Bourdieu on the sociology of taste, and Friedrich Kittler on new media theory.[24] Scientists, he says:

> have given us within recent years inventions which have revolutionized artistic conditions—the mechanical processes and innumerable secondary inventions such as stereotyping, and mechanical composition and binding, which have facilitated the production of printed matter, the three-colour and other photo-mechanical methods of reproducing pictorial matter, the gramophone, the piano-player, and wireless to aid the distribution of music, and so on, through-out the range of pure and applied art.   (9)

The crucial point is that here is an argument that what will make most difference to the future of aesthetics is not new movements or new geniuses but new technologies.

McColvin's ideas about free dissemination of what is now called quality 'content' parallels, if it didn't influence, the debate in the 1920s about the ethos of public service broadcasting. After all, the BBC had been founded—as the British Broadcasting Company—in 1922. The date, just the year before the first volume of To-Day and To-Morrow appeared, indicates how the series is contemporary with the birth of the BBC, and of the era of public service radio then television. The Company received its Royal Charter, and became the British Broadcasting Corporation, in 1927, just the year after McColvin's Euterpe. He also contemplates extending the provision of art by the state (54)—i.e. beyond art-galleries, museums, and libraries (and the subsidizing of theatres, operas and conservatoires in other countries). In other words, he advocates what would become the Arts Council [established in the 1940s].

---

[23] A less incisive version of the same idea can be found in E. J. Dent's *Terpander; or, Music and the Future* (1926), discussing the impact of mechanical inventions—presumably phonograph or radio—which make us more passive (92).

[24] As in Friedrich Kittler's 1986 book, translated as *Gramophone, Film, Typewriter* (Stanford, CA: Stanford University Press, 1999).

Much of what McColvin says also anticipates the development of media and cultural studies in the second half of the twentieth century—a characteristic of a number of the volumes, which will be discussed later in this chapter and in Chapter 5. Indeed, he makes a plea for just such an approach, writing: 'we must regard art as an inseparable organic element in life, not as a super-imposed culture which may or may not exist in any individual or take any form' (75). The corollary is a massive expansion of the scope of the aesthetic: 'since artistic poten-tialities exist in all men [...] the realm of art will present as large a variety of val-ues, types, and manifestations as does our life itself' (75). That expansion of the aesthetic is the work done by the term 'culture' nowadays (rather than that 'super-imposed culture', which we would term 'elite' or 'high culture'). One can see him feeling the pressure this argument puts on the term 'art', when he coins a variant to capture a sense of the art which is in everyone's everyday, rather than confined to museums and universities: 'art life': 'we must be prepared to view the art life of the community as a whole'; not just the elite connoisseurs, but 'the remainder, which indulges in jazz, "the pictures", light fiction, Bovril pictures, and tin-chapel architecture' (13). 'The quality of their artistic experiences and the standard of their taste and artistic education may be very different, yet they seek the same kind of experience as the others. It is entirely a matter of degree' (13). He thus takes the opposite line to that of the Leavises and their followers, opposing elite and popular culture. He is not arguing, as they did, that 'this world with its many who appreciate the less valuable is worse than the world of the pre-mechanical era' (27). It is better, because 'The actual quantity of good artistic endeavour is much greater, and every increase in the numbers of those who appreciate the least worthwhile is a distinct gain to the community [...]' (27).

This utilitarian justification is unlikely to have appealed to Leavisites. But McColvin's extremely radical educational proposals might have garnered more sympathy—though perhaps not his advocacy of 'the total abolition of the Examination system' (32).[25] There is, he argues, 'a great need for systematic edu-cation in the appreciation of art' (31). But without a plan the teachers take refuge in 'aspects of art-instruction which are not those best calculated to stimulate genuine enjoyment'. Like Pink in *Procrustes*, he opposes 'our addiction to historical and theoretical studies' (31).[26] Instead, he advocates a formalist approach to art, echoing the Bloomsbury aesthetics of Clive Bell and Roger Fry, at exactly the moment that practical criticism was being formulated in Cambridge:

I would suggest as a starting-point the study of *form*, of the anatomy or architecture of art. Apart from the moral value of cultivating a sense of proportion, of

---

[25] *Caledonia* is comparably scathing about how the 'idolatry of examinations' (50) means that they 'take the place of education' (53).

[26] Cf. p. 40. In Chapter 6 we shall see Hubert Griffith take a similar line in *Iconoclastes; or, The Future of Shakespeare* (1927).

perspective, of the inter-relation of part—a sense of which is as essential to a sane life as to the appreciation of a picture or a musical composition—nothing could lead more readily to an understanding of the artist's aims and plan of campaign.   (33)

While the invocation of proportion and perspective resonate reassuringly with the traditional aesthetics of academic pictorial composition, the language of 'the inter-relation of parts', while it might do that too, also connotes the moving parts of a machine.

The argument about the impact of technologies is one which features in one of the other volumes taking the United States as its subject. *Plato's American Republic*, 'Done out of the original' by Douglas Woodruff (1929). This volume too shows To-Day and To-Morrow at its versatile best. It is high-spirited, witty, and intelligent, wearing its learning lightly but using it tellingly. For the *Observer* it was: 'Quite the liveliest even of this spirited series'. According to the *Journal of Education*: 'Possibly no wittier satire has ever been penned in our generation'.[27] It takes the series' classical titles more seriously than most, purporting to be a translation from Plato of a text (dated 1925!) in which Socrates recounts doing what British and European writers often did in the 1920s—going on a lecture tour of the USA. So Woodruff presents aspects of America as if seen under ancient Greek eyes. The irony of the trope works by first making it look like a misunderstanding to try to translate modern phenomena into classical terms (the card index which appears to be treated as a sacred object, say) but then showing that this defamiliarizing turn reveals a modern blindness to contemporary habits. Predictably, mass production, and especially automobiles, provoke some of the most humorous passages:

> they pay a most special and devout worship to a strange god whom they call Progress, and whose will they declare it to be that there shall be made as great a number as possible of all objects that men make, but principally of the machines that are called 'autos' or 'cars', which move men quickly from place to place.   (15-16)

Some of the humour comes from cod futurology, but turned with a fine satiric edge. '[T]he control of these machines gives great joy to the Americans', says Socrates: 'So that it may well happen that they will live altogether in their cars' (16), leading to the 'abolition of offices and the transaction of all business in cars' (17). This because it is getting hard to find parking places:

> at present they must endeavour to find some place in the city where they can leave their car while they go to an office, and he who is successful in doing this is said to have parked his car, and is held in honour. And as among many peoples a

---

[27] Quotations from the end-matter to the seventh impression of J. B. S. Haldane's *Daedalus; or, Science and the Future* (1926).

youth is not granted the dignity of manhood until he has slain an enemy, so among the Americans must he first prove himself by parking a car.   (16)

He predicts that man's love-affair with the automobile will issue in a new race: 'For as the centaurs were half men and half horses, so will these be half men and half motor-cars' (17). It's one of the series' many visions of machine man, if an unusually comic one. The vision turns darker, however, when Socrates moves on to consider the problems of industrialization: 'it will be realized that these iron machines of theirs are a more deadly threat to the life of a city than was the Wooden Horse himself' (111-12). This is about more threats than dangerous driving. It is also about how machines change life, change man; about how mass production produces mass machine man, homogenizing humanity not just within a single country but globally: 'a machine will make Sheffield in the furthest Indies' (111), says Woodruff's Socrates, identifying a problem exercising other writers in the series: that by exporting machinery the developed countries turn their markets into their rivals.[28] When one of his interlocutors, Lysis, wonders if football will make the Americans warlike and destroy other 'barbarians', Socrates answers:

> they are more likely to combine forces in order to industrialize the rest of the world. And though they are very different people yet bonds of similarity are growing up, for machinery sets its stamp upon souls, and the same machines will in the end produce the same souls.   (116-17)

The metaphor of setting a stamp upon something has itself been mechanized here. The human authority that authenticates or authorizes becomes something machines do to humans. Stamping presses were being increasingly used in mass-production processes to shape metal sheets. Imagining such mechanical force impacting on immaterial souls is paradoxical. But Woodruff gives two ingenious examples of what he understands machines to be doing to the mind. Immediately following the passage about machinery setting its stamp on souls he says: 'To take but one instance, among both peoples there has grown up the love of the Dark Cave' (116). Lysis and Phaelon (the other interlocutor) ask what this Dark Cave is. Socrates answers by recalling the allegory of the cave in the *Republic* (514a–520a): 'I there pictured the unhappy lot of men sitting huddled together in a dark place, condemned all to look in the same direction and to watch phantoms and shadows of men as though they saw something real' (117). He pitied them, and sought 'how they might be rescued and brought out into the sunlight and might learn to see men as they were' (117). But the Americans and the English 'are not reasonable and will pay money to be imprisoned in these caves, and to contemplate lies and live altogether in a false world. This is making them one, for the greatest bond of

---

[28]   113. Cf. Garet Garrett, *Ouroboros; or, The Mechanical Extension of Mankind* (1926), 56–7.

union is to share a common experience' (117-18). He recounts how at the end of his visit he visits one of the caves, and tries to reason with the crowd to try to save them from being misled; with the result that he is 'considered disgraced for attacking "our American Movies"' (118).

Woodruff's other example of how machinery affects mind comes earlier, during the chapter about 'Women, Cars, and Men'. 'For do you notice how we have wandered out of our course', Socrates asks, 'as generally happens with these machines, and have quite forgotten the original thread of our discourse' (18). Again, this is more than just a joke about cars coming off the road, or about how easy it is to take a wrong turning. It's more than a joke about how distracting cars can be—their noise, their size, their speed, their fumes; about how they attract attention and demand concentration, whether you are a driver, passenger or pedestrian. For it is also making a serious point about how interaction with machines cannot but affect our ways of thinking. That 'great joy' in controlling these machines leads to the practice of driving for the sake of it, 'going for a spin' for pleasure, without being directed towards a particular goal, or at least the arrival mattering less than the journey. Such habits, he suggests, erode our sense of direction and objectives in argument. The implication is that true Platonic dialogue will no longer be imaginable in a fully Americanized world.

Buried in Woodruff's conceit seeing cinema as the modern form of the cave of illusion, is the familiar argument in the period about mass culture destroying individuality; the anxiety that (as in *Midas*) the machine dehumanizes not just the body but the mind: the kind of concern the Leavises and T. S. Eliot would soon be writing about.[29] Such concern had been growing with the spread of 'mass production'. Indeed, 1926 was the year the *Encyclopaedia Britannica* published an article it had asked Henry Ford to write, which did much to popularize that expression.[30] The anxiety runs through the modernisms of writers as different as, say, Wyndham Lewis and D. H. Lawrence. As Andrzej Gasiorek writes of Lewis:

> Around the time of the First World War, when he was engaged in the Vorticist project, Lewis was both critical of the machine age and cautiously optimistic about its potential to transform social life. Depending on how it was developed, technology might either serve human interests or dominate them so completely that society would effectively become its servant. The danger, he had warned in

---

[29] See for example T. S. Eliot's 'The Man of Letters and the Future of Europe', *Sewanee Review*, 53:3 (Summer, 1945), 333–42: 'Not least of the effects of industrialism is that we become mechanized in mind, and consequently attempt to provide solutions in terms of engineering, for problems which are essentially problems of life' (338). Machine man was also thematized within film, and even earlier than *Metropolis*. See Jesse Matz's fine discussion of Abel Gance's 1922 film *La Roue* in *Lasting Impressions* (New York: Columbia University Press, 2016), 115–16.

[30] The article was actually composed by Ford's spokesman William Cameron, and an earlier version of it appeared in the *New York Times* (19 September 1926). See David A. Hounshell, *From the American System to Mass Production* (Baltimore: Johns Hopkins University Press, 1984), 1, 306. Ogden refers to it in passing in his review of the *Encyclopaedia*; *Collective Memoir*, p. 194.

The Caliph's Design (1919) was that 'we should become overpowered by our creation, and become as mechanical as a tremendous insect world, all our awakened reason entirely disappeared' (*TCD* 76). The opposition here between a fully automated (and hive-like) society and one guided by purposive human agents lies at the heart of everything Lewis wrote about technology in the inter-war period, and as his thinking about it developed he became increasingly concerned that, as Giedion put it, mechanization was inexorably taking command of human life and turning the individual into an adjunct of its all-embracing systems and structures.[31]

In Lawrence too such concern is foundational. It is manifested with particular force in the presentation of Clifford in *Lady Chatterley's Lover* (1928).

A third volume in the series on the US, Colonel J. F. C. Fuller's *Atlantis: America and the future* (1925), describes the country as a 'mechanical monster', poised to 'grow into something terrible or sublime' (96). However, the view we have glimpsed in *Midas* and *Plato's American Republic* of the ways in which mechanization and mass production can alter human mentality, imagination, and creativity are indicative of a different, and more subtle, realization of the how technology was transforming the understanding not only of psychology and society, but of the meaning of what might have been called 'human nature', though the term is no longer adequate to cover the non-natural determinants of machine man.

The long philosophical tradition of thinking about man in relation to machine goes back at least to the eighteenth-century doctor Julien Offray de La Mettrie's 1747 work *L'homme Machine*—though he was responding to Descartes, and denying the existence of the soul as separable from matter.[32] *L'homme Machine* is usually translated as *Man a Machine*, though *Machine Man* would do as well. There was a reprise of the debate in Ogden's vicinity in the 1920s. In 1925 he published Friedrich Lange's *History of Materialism and Criticism of its Present Importance* in the International Library (with an introduction by Bertrand Russell) and described it as 'monumental' in his own *ABC of Psychology* (1929; p. 134). This may have triggered, or at least paralleled, a similar debate the following two years in another of Ogden's series, Psyche Miniatures. *Man Not a Machine* (1926) by Eugenio Rignano was answered by Joseph Needham in *Man a Machine* (1927). One reason why the debate seemed newly pressing was the rise of behaviourism in psychology over the previous decade, ever since J. B. Watson's lecture

---

[31] Andrzej Gasiorek, *A History of Modernist Literature* (Chichester: Wiley-Blackwell, 2015), 464–5. Siegfried Giedion's *Mechanization Takes Command: A contribution to anonymous history* (New York: Oxford University Press, 1948) did not appear until after the Second World War; but it offered a cogent account of 'the period between the two World Wars as the time of full mechanization', when 'mechanization penetrates the intimate spheres of life' and 'impinged upon the very center of the human psyche, through all the senses' (41–2).

[32] See Michel Foucault, *Discipline and Punish: The birth of the prison* (New York: Random House 1975), for a discussion of what he terms 'the great book of Man-the-Machine' in the materialism of Descartes and La Mettrie (136).

of 1913 often described as the behaviourist manifesto.[33] Ogden included a volume of the Psyche Miniatures on *The Battle of Behaviourism* in 1928, staging a debate between Watson himself, who wrote the first half, and William McDougall, who contributed the second (and who also wrote *Janus* for To-Day and To-Morrow). Behaviourism is arguably Machine Man's analysis of himself.[34]

The fact that such a debate exists testifies to a reaction against the machine from some quarters. For some of the writers in the series, doubtless aware of the vitalism of Bergson and Lawrence, modern life and its possible futures had to be understood precisely in terms of that reaction. So Ralph de Pomerai argues in *Aphrodite; or, The Future of Sexual Relationships* (1931), suggesting that industrialism's mechanization of the everyday incites a desire for impulsive, scandalous behaviour, and predicting a consequent increase in freedom from parental control over the sexuality of young adults (66-8). Vera Brittain, by contrast, as we saw, thought broadcast and travel technologies would stabilize monogamy. In *Cato; or, the Future of Censorship* (1930), William Seagle argued that mechanization has inhibited press freedom. Technologies of book publication, radio and cinema involve large numbers of people, and hence potential censors, in the production process. With such forms of mediated communication, the more popular the medium, the greater the degree of censorship likely in future.[35]

Such discussions abound through the series, as writers contemplate the effects of mechanization across the spectrum of everyday experience. In *Vulcan; or, The Future of Labour* (1927), it forms Cecil Chisholm's primary topic, as he considers the increasing role played by mechanized mass production and the consequent changes to our way of life. Chisholm ran a specialist publisher, Business Publications Ltd, and wrote books on management. Though his methods of 'Simplified Practice' make him sound like a forerunner of today's management consultants, he is critical of Taylorism's psychological naivety (27). Chisholm's optimism about machines and management rests on a utopian vision in which productivity increases, working hours shorten, wages rise, and workers are given share incentives. 'The worker has been too modest in his demands on the future', he writes: 'Science and the machine will do for him far more than he dreams' (63-4). However, he had visited enough factories to be able to identify an inherent obstacle (14n): 'Ease is the certain blessing brought to mankind by the machine',

---

[33] The lecture had been published as 'Psychology as the behaviorist views it'. *Psychological Review*, 20 (1913), 158-77. Later incorporated into the first chapter of J. B. Watson, *Behavior: A textbook of comparative psychology* (New York: Henry Holt & Co., 1914).

[34] See for example E. B. Strauss, 'L'Homme Machine: A brief account of Pavlov's conditioned reflexes', *Realist*, 1:4 (July 1929), 89-98. The *Realist: A Journal of Scientific Humanism* (April 1929-January 1930), published a number of To-Day and To-Morrow contributors, including Haldane, Bertrand Russell, Vera Brittain, Winifred Holtby, Norman Haire. Gerald Heard was the literary editor. It also published writers like Aldous Huxley, Rebecca West, Herbert Read, and H. G. Wells, together with writers for Ogden's other series such as Malinowski, Richard Paget, and Solly Zuckerman.

[35] Seagle's arguments are discussed in greater detail in Chapter 6.

he says; but 'monotony is the no less certain curse' (21). Which is his explanation of why despite improved conditions and living standards, social unrest was increasing (41). This might itself sound naïve, but is best understood as a response to the 1926 General Strike, and his attempt to convince himself that class war was not the inevitable future predicted by Marxists, but could be transcended by better management. But in describing the present, Chisholm voices the classic dehumanization argument: ' "You are but a human Robot and our slave", drone the great machines' (43).

In *Pomona; or, the Future of English* (1926), Basil de Sélincourt expresses anxiety about mechanization infiltrating the mind and language of modern man:

> The salient feature of our age is the increasing participation of the masses in the guidance of life and in its interests. Machinery has made this possible, and more and ever more machinery will be required, if we are to attain the broader humanity we desire. Yet machinery symbolizes the ossifying routine, the obstructive red tape, which chokes progress; and machinery always has undue importance for undeveloped minds.   (45)

He sees what he calls 'simple people' as more in touch with natural processes and their emotions, and argues superciliously that: 'As the complexities of civilization pass over them, they become complex, they "grow up", and because they are grown up we think them more mature. They are not really more mature: they are more mechanical' (91). Ogden shared the view that the mechanization of man was audible in language. 'The Machine is now the Manager of the Man', he wrote: 'Its Mark is even on language'.[36]

Other volumes worry that mechanization degrades the products of human labour. Hartley and Leyel, in *Lucullus; or, The Food of the Future*, discuss the problem of the inferior quality of mass-produced food. P. Morton Shand has the same concern about drink in *Bacchus; or, The Future of Wine* (1927).

The argument of this chapter so far has concerned views of the machine as reproducing man in its own image: the machine considered as something external to man, which nonetheless produces effects on his practices and habits, and perhaps even his internal nature. Where To-Day and To-Morrow becomes even more interesting and suggestive is when the writers contemplate much closer synergies of man and machine. They do this especially when thinking of technology as not a separate sphere, but as a prosthetic development of the human: a technology of creativity.

McColvin's *Euterpe* suggested as much in relation to cultural technology such as audio recording. A number of other volumes take that line of argument further, exploring the ways in which technology can be seen not as threatening human thought, individuality, and creativity, but as amplifying, enhancing, and

---

[36]   C. K. Ogden, *Brighter Basic*, second printing (London: Kegan Paul, Trench and Trübner, 1935), 37.

liberating it. They are interested not just in how we think about the future but how the future will change how we think.

The Technological Extension of Man

This section concentrates on To-Day and To-Morrow's discussions of techno-logical enhancement, arguing that these present an alternative view to Hal Foster's account of the proto-fascist 'Prosthetic Modernism' (of figures such as Marinetti and Wyndham Lewis); and that instead they anticipates McLuhan's theorization of media.

But first, some dissentient views. One classic statement of the prosthetic exten-sion of humanity comes in a work contemporary with some of the early volumes of To-Day and To-Morrow, Alfred North Whitehead's massively influential *Science and the Modern World* (1925)

> The reason why we are on a higher imaginative level is not because we have finer imagination, but because we have better instruments [....] These instruments have put thought on to a new level. A fresh instrument serves the same purpose as foreign travel; it shows things in unusual combinations. The gain is more than a mere addition; it is a transformation.[37]

The transformation in this account is of thought, not of the thinker. Whitehead suggests an essentialism here comparable to F. C. S. Schiller's view in *Tantalus* (considered in the Introductions) that our development of technologies of social memory—through language and writing—has enabled greater achievement; but that not only has it not redeemed what he calls our 'yahoo-manity' (37); it has perversely led to institutions becoming increasingly technical and clogged, blocking further development.

But a powerful strand of To-Day and To-Morrow takes the opposite, progressive, line. A number of volumes besides those by Haldane and Bernal discuss and imagine the technological enhancement of humanity. Automata of course have a long cultural history. But, as Patrick Parrinder has shown, the start of the series is contemporary with Čapek's *R.U.R.*[38] And this period is the first when robotics began to emerge as a real technological possibility. Robots are referred to in a number of the volumes, including *Archon, Automaton, Cato, Delphos,* and *Vulcan; Socrates* mentions automata; in *Albyn* Hugh MacDiarmid writes of the 'robotization of Europe' (46). Such a comment generally objects to men being turned into machines. But the To-Day and To-Morrow writers are also interested in

---

[37] Alfred North Whitehead, *Science and the Modern World* (New York: Macmillan, 1925), 166–7.
[38] Patrick Parrinder, 'Robots, Clones and Clockwork Men: The post-human perplex in early twentieth-century literature and science', *Interdisciplinary Science Reviews*, 34:1 (March 2009), 56–67.

something subtler: how such technological prostheses and enhancements alter humanity. So the series can be seen as in many ways a key moment in the emergence not just of an imagination and discourse of the cyborg post-human (as in Haldane and Bernal) but of the phenomenology of technology. The other volumes in this group include:

Low, A. M., *Wireless Possibilities*, 1924
Heard, Gerald, *Narcissus: An anatomy of clothes*, 1924
Fournier d'Albe, E. E., *Hephaestus; or, The Soul of the Machine*, 1925
Garrett, Garet, *Ouroboros; or, The Mechanical Extension of Mankind*, 1926
McColvin, Lionel R., *Euterpe; or, The Future of Art*, 1926
Hatfield, H. Stafford, *Automaton; or, The Future of the Mechanical Man*, 1928
Macfie, R. Campbell, *Metanthropos; or, The Body of the Future*, 1928

As *Narcissus* and *Euterpe* are discussed above, and *Metanthropos* in the Introductions, the remainder of this chapter will concentrate on the others. Low's *Wireless Possibilities*, one of the very earliest volumes, is an impressive example of Ogden's aspirations for the series. Low, a Professor of Physics at the Royal Artillery College, was a dry, laconic writer. *Wireless Possibilities* is one of the few volumes coming in under the norm of ninety-four pages (it only runs to seventy-seven—though this may have been because the norms for the series were then still evolving).[39] Much of it is devoted to technical considerations of how broadcasting technology might be improved. 'The whole point of wireless is that it brings a man into your room', Low says strikingly, 'but it must sound like the man himself if it is to be really effective ; it is this pitiful quality of reproduced sound that has wrecked the talking cinema' (28)—this, three years before *The Jazz Singer*. The blurb on the dust-jacket advertises Low as revealing:

> Some of the wonders which he believes Wireless has in store. The talking cinema, seeing by Wireless, Wireless and detection of crime, business and Wireless; and finally the terrible possibilities of Wireless in warfare. In an unexpectedly short time, he believes, Wireless will have entirely changed the surface of life as we know it to-day.

'Seeing by wireless' is what we now call television, though Low calls it 'radio television', not only arguing that transmitting moving images would be necessary and possible (indeed, John Logie Baird would demonstrate silhouette images in Selfridges the following year), but also anticipating television in colour. He makes further accurate predictions, such as that there would be 'special wave-lengths for [...] Parliamentary debates'. But perhaps the one that seems most clairvoyant now is his anticipation of the mobile telephone:

[39] See Appendix A on the Book History of the series.

In a few years time we shall be able to chat to our friends in an aeroplane and in the streets with the help of a pocket wireless set, and be able to do practically everything by the aid of radio that we now do with our voice. The only thing that will seem intensely strange will be that these comforts never existed before!   (35)

The *New Statesman* was impressed, commenting: 'The mantle of Blake has fallen upon the physicists. To them we look for visions, and we find them in this book.'[40]

Low's title signals right from the start of the series that the idea of media and communication will be crucial; and that they are likely to transform everyday life. It may have inspired some of Bernal's thoughts, as well as his working title of *Possibilities*: some of his most striking thinking involves seeing how far one can imagine our internalization of such technologies.

There are four main arguments to be drawn from the volumes pursuing this line of thinking about technology as a form of prosthesis. First, modernist studies has become very interested in prosthesis; as were a number of To-Day and To-Morrow authors. Tim Armstrong's *Modernism, Technology and the Body*, for example has a chapter on 'Prosthetic Modernism' which identifies the importance of the concept to the series. He defines modernity's relation to the body thus: 'it offers the body as lack, at the same time as it offers a technological compensation.'[41] But this group of books offers an alternative version of the relation of man to machine in modernism: one closer to a celebrated passage of Freud's (part of which Armstrong quotes):

> Man has, as it were, become a kind of prosthetic God. When he puts on all his auxiliary organs he is truly magnificent; but those organs have not grown on to him and they still give him much trouble at times.... Future ages will bring with them new and possibly unimaginably great advances in this field of civilization and will increase man's likeness to God still more. But in the interests of our present investigation, we will not forget that present-day man does not feel happy in his God-like character.[42]

When critics have focused on writers and artists like Marinetti and Wyndham Lewis, the tendency has been to see the convergence of men and machines as protofascist. In Hal Foster's account of the 'Prosthetic Modernism' of these two, for example, Marinetti's desire for the metallization of man is seen, persuasively, as an anti-humanism seeking power over others, and particularly the power to kill.[43] In the fascist imaginary, machine man is a war machine. That desire to absorb the human entirely into the machine is indeed disturbing.

---

[40] Quoted from the end-matter in C. P. Harvey's *Solon; or, The Price of Justice* (1931).

[41] Tim Armstrong, *Modernism, Technology, and the Body: A cultural study* (Cambridge: Cambridge University Press, 1998), 3.

[42] Sigmund Freud, *Civilization and its Discontents*, in the Standard Edition of the Complete Psychological Works of Sigmund Freud, Volume XXI (1927–31) (London: Hogarth Press, 1930), 59–145. Armstrong, *Modernism, Technology, and the Body*, p. 77.

[43] Hal Foster, 'Prosthetic Gods', *Modernism/modernity*, 4:2 (April 1997), 5–38.

Foster understands the aggression in this relation between technology and subjectivity as defensive: the psyche inventing defences against war-damage to both body and mind, which amount to a negation of subjectivity:

> In order to prepare for the new ego, the old bourgeois subject must first be destroyed: thus his persistent attacks, both polemical and poetic, on subjectivity understood as interiority (this is even more pronounced in Lewis). 'Destroy the *I* in literature', Marinetti exclaims in 'Technical Manifesto of Futurist Literature', 'that is, all psychology' (*M*, 87). Again and again he calls on Futurist art and writing to make over bodies and psyches as the new technologies seem to have done.[44]

Though this is a psychological reading (even a psychoanalytic one—as the allusion to Freud in Foster's title implies), it is concerned not with mental prostheses but physical ones, which seek to turn man into machine to avoid the injuries done to man by machine. This is perhaps because the artists in question are less interested in mental prostheses, because they are scathing about interiority. They are more concerned with hard exteriors; turning the body into its own armour. They were not aiming to make over the mind in the way Wells hoped to do with his 'World Brain' project (discussed at the end of Chapter 2); or the way his successor, Vannevar Bush hoped to do with the 'Memex'—his concept of a personal mechanized repository of microfilm pages that would let individuals store their memories and knowledge, and which is seen as an inspiration for the concept of hypertext.[45]

In another essay, tracking 'this logic in critical discourse on technology in the 1930s, 1960s, and 1990s', Foster discusses Ernst Jünger—another war-engrossed modernist—arguing in 1931 that 'technology was "intertwined with our nerves" in a way that subsumed criticality and distraction within "a second, colder consciousness"'.[46] The connection of technology to 'nerves' is comparable to Hyde's pre-war image of telephone wires as 'The Nerves of London' (discussed in Chapter 2). Jünger's 'nerves' are the circuits of feeling. But rather than Hyde's sense of urban modernity overloading the feelings to the point of neurasthenia, Jünger's 'intertwining' of human and technological makes man indistinguishable from machine, and human feeling mechanical rather than pathological. The association of nerves and wires was already familiar (as Hyde's illustration indicates); but it had new currency in the 20s and 30s. The British electro-physiologist Edgar Adrian had discovered the presence of electricity in nerve cells in 1928, and went on to describe his research into the electrical discharges of single nerve fibres in

---

[44] Ibid., pp. 13–14.   [45] Vannevar Bush, 'As We May Think, *Atlantic*, 176 (July 1945), 101–8.
[46] Foster, 'Prosthetic Gods', p. 30, n.1.; 'Postmodernism in Parallax', *October* 63 (winter 1993), 3–20. Ernst Jünger, 'Photography and the "Second Consciousness"', in *Photography in the Modern Era*, ed. Christopher Phillips (New York: Metropolitan Museum, 1989), 207–10 (207).

his book *The Basis of Sensation* (1928).[47] He was awarded the Nobel Prize with Sir Charles Sherrington in 1932. In the digital era we associate such ideas with the electrochemistry of neurons, which enable us to think of the brain and computer as analogous. For Jünger in 1931, though it would have been historically possible to associate an electro-physiological nervous system with the nascent electronics of valves and cathode ray tubes, the more likely association would have been with electrical devices such as the telegraph, telephone, or chart recorder. As the coldness of his 'second' consciousness suggests, the drift of his machine man image is to take the feeling out of feeling; and thereby attain to the anti-Romantic 'impersonality' of classic modernism.

Haldane's and Bernal's visions of the future are very different from this essentially fascist version of prosthesis. True, there are plenty of political objections one might make: feminist objections to ectogenesis as a male fantasy arrogating control over women's fertility, or even envisaging the displacement of women from the reproductive process entirely, in favour of a technological production of machine males;[48] or ecological and postcolonial objections that interplanetary mining is a projection of an imperialist and instrumentalist mindset; and that we contemplate abandoning embodiment or our planet at our peril. But nonetheless they are not fascist or even protofascist ideas; not examples of the paradoxical combination of an embrace of modern technology with a rejection of the Enlightenment and liberal democracy that the historian Jeffrey Herf termed 'reactionary modernism'.[49] Their aim is to preserve life, to liberate humanity from some of its constraints, to enhance human communication and connectedness. Haldane's popular writing is always highly literary. He moves easily between quoting poetry and discussing hormones.

Bernal's spectacularly prophetic vision of thoughts transferred universally by wireless network is also antithetical to the fascist imaginary—exemplified, say, in Xanti Schawinski's 1934 propaganda poster using photomontage to plant Mussolini's head on a body made up of hundreds of people, the leader identifying himself with the mass or the nation. Bernal's interconnectivity is, rather (as suggested), a Marxian collectivism, everyone contributing the ideas they can to the communal knowledge pool. Wikipedia is perhaps the utopian online equivalent; though Twitter shows the potential of such open systems for abuse.

---

[47] See also his 'Animal Electricity', *Realist*, 2:1 (October 1929), 1–12.

[48] Though it should be noted that in offering women freedom from pregnancy and childbirth ectogenesis has been seen as a pro-feminist conception too: John Forrester and Laura Cameron comment that the last pages of Shulamith Firestone's 1970 *The Dialectic of Sex: The case for feminist revolution* are 'infused by Haldane's imagined ectogenesis': John Forrester and Laura Cameron, *Freud in Cambridge* (Cambridge: Cambridge University Press, 2017), 180, n.231. See Donna Haraway's 'A Cyborg Manifesto: Science, technology, and socialist-feminism in the late twentieth century', in *Simians, Cyborgs and Women: The reinvention of nature* (New York: Routledge, 1991), 149–81, for a classic critique of the machine bias of male futurology.

[49] Jeffrey Herf, *Reactionary Modernism: Technology, culture and politics in Weimar and the Third Reich* (Cambridge: Cambridge University Press, 1984).

The second point is about the sheer difficulty of prediction. H. Stafford Hatfield, in *Automaton; or, The Future of the Mechanical Man* (1928), makes a similar point to Whitehead's about the development of 'better instruments'. But where Whitehead argued that such prostheses took humanity to a 'higher imaginative level', Hatfield, who wrote a number of popularizing books about science and particularly invention,[50] identifies an impasse in innovation:

> In our machines we have already developed *limbs* of a power and precision exceeding our own many many thousand-fold. In our instruments, we have developed *senses* exceeding our own, in many cases, a million-fold in sensitivity. Indeed, they are capable of receiving impressions, such as magnetism, which are qualitatively imperceptible to our natural senses. What we have still to develop is the mechanical *brain*, the link between instrument and tool.   (14-15)

Though the emphasis here is on our *not* having been able to develop anything you could call a mechanical brain, the Kegan Paul dust-jacket cranked up the claim for attention:

> Hitherto Man's chief inventions have been extensions of his sense or of his limbs. The author of this work prophecies the dawn of an era in which substitutes will gradually be found even for the human Brain.
>
> Dr Hatfield is the inventor of the 'Chemical Robot' which performed such marvels at recent demonstrations in London.[51] An account is here given of the principles on which a mechanical brain is constructed [...]

This is not exactly the chutzpah of Kurzweil's *How to Create a Mind* (2012); Hatfield isn't talking about the electronic mind that digital computer scientist are aspiring to imitate. Nonetheless, that mechanical brain is what we'd now call a computer. But the fact that he calls it a *mechanical* brain shows he is still locked into the machine man paradigm.

It is an example of the blind spot mentioned in the Introductions, that the most striking case of a major fact of our modernity which these hundred-plus prophets of the 1920s failed to see was the invention of the computer. In the volumes dealing with technological invention, such as *Wireless Possibilities* (1924) or *Automaton* (1928) the basic model of technology is mechanical rather than

---

[50] H. Stafford Hatfield's *The Inventor and his World* (London: Kegan Paul, Trench, Trübner & Co., 1933) was reissued as a Pelican book in 1948. Joseph Agassi, *Science in Flux* (Dordrecht: D. Reidel, 1975), 282, refers to Hatfield as: 'the most important writer on technology, perhaps'.

[51] No trace of Hatfield's 'chemical robot' has been found in the popular press. It is thus probable that the phrase refers not to an android robot but a mechanical control system for a chemical process. Hatfield had filed a US patent in 20 September 1927 for an 'Apparatus for Effecting Chemical Tests and Controlling Chemical Reactions' (Patent no. 1,643,243). And he was reported in the *Journal and Proceedings of the Institute of Chemistry of Great Britain and Ireland*, 54 (1930), 307–56 (327), as describing then demonstrating 'an instrument of his own invention for measuring the hardness of water'. However, the jacket blurb may invoke the interest in 1928 in the UK's first Android robot, 'Eric', who was recreated by the Science Museum for its 2017 *Robots* exhibition. See: http://www.sciencemuseum.org.uk/visitmuseum/plan_your_visit/exhibitions/eric

electronic. Though the Enigma encryption apparatus was a mechanical device to switch electrical circuits in complex patterns, the computer developed to crack it had to be electronic. Even a writer such as A. M. Low, discussing crystals and valves and the development of television, sees the importance of amplification as an essentially mechanical problem; how to turn minute sonic or radio signals into clear, audible sounds. Hatfield is more concerned with the automation of labour than about robots (though he does contemplate these): 'The ruling passion of our maturity is the conquest of power over the material world'. He defines automata as having three parts, corresponding to the senses, brain and limbs of humans. But he has little to say about machines that could begin to do human brain-work. He is mainly concerned with automated control systems. When he contemplates something involving as many variables as air navigation, he assumes the problem is just too complicated for mechanical solution. But rather than laughing complacently as we programme our SatNavs (which are perfectly capable of proving him right by telling us to drive into a river) we should realize how difficult it must have been, some fifteen or twenty years before the wartime experiments such as those with Colossus at Bletchley Park in 1943-4 (which were in turn kept top secret for decades after the war) to predict not only the existence but the rapid evolution of the computer. Even those like Hatfield who were clear about what invention was needed and why could not imagine how the paradigm had to be shifted. It was not only the To-Day and To-Morrow authors who had hit the prophetic wall. However, Bernal nonetheless does predict that human intelligence might somehow be able to be transferred to machines; and that such machines could then be connected so as to 'network' (as we would now call it) individual thinking.

What I called in the Introductions the computer-shaped hole in the series is characteristic of other volumes too; not least since it is computer modelling that has made the greatest difference to our ability to predict situations of complexity. Even Bernal does not imagine that something other than the human brain might ever be able to produce thoughts. Controversial though the concept of 'artificial intelligence' remains, we do at least have the idea; and it appears that computers gave it to us. That is to say that the invention of digital computing then enabled new acts of imagination. Without that technology being quite within reach, Bernal's solution was to keep the human brain, and just plug it straight into mechanical prosthetic senses and limbs, and an electronic communication network.

Nonetheless, part of the interest of the series is in how its futurological visions inspired later ones, both in subsequent popular science writing and in science fiction. Bernal's book (along with *Daedalus*) is credited with influencing Olaf Stapledon, as well as later writers such as Bruce Sterling.[52] Robert Scholes calls

[52] See Brian Stableford, 'Science Fiction Between the Wars', in *Anatomy Of Wonder: A critical guide to science fiction*, ed. Neil Barron, fourth edition (New Providence, NJ: Bowker, 1995), 62–114 (70). On Stapledon's debt to Haldane, see also J. J. Hughes, 'Back to the Future: Contemporary biopolitics in 1920s' British futurism', EMBO Reports. 2008 Jul; 9 (Suppl 1): S59–S63. doi: 10.1038/embor.2008.68 On Bernal and Haldane, see Patrick Parrinder, *Shadows of the Future: H.G. Wells, science fiction, and*

The World, the Flesh and the Devil a 'book of breathtaking scientific speculation' that 'is probably the single most influential source of science fiction ideas.'[53] And Arthur C. Clarke, who invented the geo-stationary satellite (which makes SatNavs possible) and in his futurological *2001: A space odyssey* created in HAL the most memorable of computers with a mind of its own, owned a copy of *Automaton*.

Good though Hatfield's *Automaton* is, and given that he was credited with that spellbinding demonstration of something known as a 'chemical robot',[54] it is surprising that in engineering terms it is very slightly out of date. It has now become a truism of writing about the information age that Norbert Wiener, celebrated as the founding father of cybernetics, based this theory on research done on the automated aiming of anti-aircraft guns during World War Two. It would be an untruism to see that work as without pre-war precedent.[55] David Trotter writes about the Vickers Predictor, 'an analogue computer connected to an anti-aircraft gun. Fed information about the height, speed, and bearing of an approaching aircraft, it calculated trigonometric firing solutions and fed them automatically to the weapon'.[56] He describes a photo in the *Illustrated London News* of the gun being used in a defence exercise while being televised in 1936. But this 'extraordinary real machine' was in fact in service from 1928—the same year *Automaton* appeared—and had been developed 1924.[57] The analogue computer was a mechanical device, still requiring two operators to input the horizontal and vertical movements of the aircraft. Such a device was still a long way from an electronic digital programmable computer, and does not supersede Hatfield's or Bernal's visions of machines as merely prostheses for the human brain. Yet the fact that such a prominent machine was being developed and used throughout the publication span of To-Day and To-Morrow, and was given a name connecting mechanical computation with prediction is striking; as is the fact that no-one in the series comments on it (even though it is exactly the kind of cybernetic mechanism Hatfield discusses), or is drawn to speculate on the future of computation, especially in the service of prediction. If they had, would they have remained inhibited by the mechanical paradigm? (Predictably, it was

---

prophecy (New York: Syracuse University Press, 1995), 140. Bruce Sterling acknowledges the influence of *The World, the Flesh, and the Devil* in the 'Introduction', *Schismatrix Plus* (New York: Ace Books, 1996), calling it 'a stellar masterpiece of cosmic speculation' (2).

[53] Robert Scholes and Eric S. Rabkin, 'Bibliography III: Science backgrounds', *Science Fiction: History, science, vision* (London: Oxford University Press, 1977), 240.

[54] Jacket of H. Stafford Hatfield's *Automaton; or, The Future of the Mechanical Man* (1928).

[55] See Robert Brain, 'Representation on the Line: The graphic method and the instruments of scientific modernism', in *From Energy to Information: Representation in science, art, and literature*, ed. B. Clark and L. D. Henderson (Stanford: Stanford University Press, 2002), 155–78, on how 'the technological crossover from energy to information was accomplished in an analog format' (177).

[56] David Trotter, 'In the Soup', *LRB*, 36:19 (9 October 2014), 27–8.

[57] See A. G. Bromley, 'Analogue Computing Devices', in *Computing Before Computers*, ed. William Aspray (Ames, IA: Iowa State University Press, 1990), 156–99 (188).

Haldane who was to take up the issue later in an essay entitled 'Machines that Think', discussing predictors and also electrical calculating machines.)[58]

It was because the analogue machines were so impressive that the mechanical paradigm was so compelling. When in *Vulcan* Chisolm describes an 'automatic calculator' (18)—that is, a punched card reader—he says:

> Surely its inventor came very near to giving mankind a machine which can think! Already the Robot is nearer than we imagine. It is no far step from the automatic tabulators—those giants which now help many of the chief Governments through the labour of the census.   (19)

Indeed. These data storage machines used in the 1890 US Census were made by Herman Hollerith's company, which became the core of IBM.

It might be countered that the fact Hatfield comments on the failure to engineer a mechanical brain shows he was effectively predicting one; that other technologies had advanced to the point where a sophisticated control system was palpably the next necessary thing.[59] This in contrast to Wells's notion of a 'World Brain', conceived essentially as knowledge-content—a conveniently scaled archive of existing information—rather than as artificial intelligence—the mechanization of the process of thinking. Similarly, the dust-jacket blurb assumes he was not only predicting but describing the principles of a 'chemical brain'. That argument has considerable force. The writers knew something was *required* to perform the brain-function if machines were to evolve to the next stage. But it was impossible to see what it would be. Mechanical? Chemical? Cyborg? It is all the more surprising, given that domestic electricity still felt modern, and electronic devices such as radio and especially television were at the cutting edge of modern technology, that it was not as obvious to them as it is with hindsight that what they were looking for would be an *electronic* brain.[60]

But another volume takes a different tack: not prosthesis as physical defence, nor as an attempt to replicate our mental processes. Instead, E. E. Fournier d'Albe's *Hephaestus; or, The Soul of the Machine* (1925)—his second volume for the

[58] J. B. S. Haldane, 'Machines that Think', *Daily Worker* (29 August 1940) 4–5. Collected in *A Banned Broadcast and Other Essays* (London: Chatto and Windus, 1946), 85–7.
[59] The book Hatfield published the following year in Ogden's Psyche Miniatures series might sound from its title as if it takes up the quest for artificial intelligence: *The Conquest of Thought by Invention in the Mechanical State of the Future*. But in fact it advances the contrary proposition that the increasing mechanization of the state, acting to protect humanity from risk, effectively stifles the generation of new ideas. It thus contributes to the discussion of machine man, from a cynical perspective which sees the mechanized state as much more of a threat than Belloc's 'servile state'. Given Hatfield's concern with the future in this volume, it is another mystery why Ogden did not include it in To-Day and To-Morrow, unless he was attempting to interest readers of the series in his other, more psychologically-focused projects.
[60] One only has to look at a book published just twenty years later to gauge the rapidity of development. In 1944 the US Army published *Electronics Today and Tomorrow*, by John Mills, in an 'Armed Services Edition', aimed at instructing readers in recent developments such as electron tubes, television, ultra-high-frequency generation, and cyclotrons.

series—sees the importance of technology as arising from the relationship between body and mind (67). His argument is that all technology is prosthetic; an extension of the individual body, yes. But that it is correspondingly an expression and an expansion of mind. The idea of the soul of the machine is intriguing; as is the use of the Classical title. Fournier d'Albe posits Hephaestus as the god of machinery; the only Olympian god to have survived into the modern age. 'The God of Fire is the supreme master of the earth' (14). But he is also the god of the industrial revolution: 'His furnaces are roaring [....] He has girdled the world with hoops of steel' (14). Fournier d'Albe is thus able to write *Hephaestus* as a modern myth; a myth of 'the age of machinery' (25) with Hepahestus as its prosthetic god.

Like other contributors, he notes 'an increasing tendency in modern thought to abolish the distinction between soul and body and to regard them as one and indivisible' (33). The direction this leads him in is the opposite one to the nineteenth-century anxiety about dehumanization. On the contrary, thought humanizes the machine. 'The soul of the weapon is the soul of the man who uses it' (33). '[I]f a "soul" animates that man's body and drives it to perform deeds of valour, the same soul will animate his weapon' (33), he argues. Note that 'if'. This is not an argument about spirituality, nor indeed about the 'soul' theologically considered, though Fournier d'Albe—a physicist—had been a believer in spiritualism.[61] What he is writing about is mind and intention: 'Every weapon, every tool, every machine is the embodiment of a human thought and purpose. The user adopts that thought and purpose, and behold—the machine has found its soul!' (34).

This might appear the zenith of the dream of instrumental reason: technology as a realization of human 'purpose'. But it's the opposite. Instead of reason becoming the instrument for imposing the human will on the natural world or social order, the instrument becomes reason; the technology is not only for use but an object of understanding and even aesthetic contemplation. Hence Fournier d'Albe's conclusion, which takes prosthesis a stage further than Freud. Rather than becoming 'a kind of prosthetic God', troubled by his prosthesis, machine man here transcends human nature, to become 'super-"natural"' (90):

> The earth is being organized and unified under the ægis of the human race, the protoplasm of this planet, the race which, transcending the mechanism and long-established traditions of its own germ-plasm, enlarged and multiplied its functions until it acquired the use of fire. Upon that achievement it built an

[61] See Fournier d'Albe's preface to his translation of A. von Schrenck-Notzing, *Phenomena of Materialisation: A contribution to the investigation of mediumistic teleplastics* (London: Kegan Paul, Trench and Trubner, 1920). Also see Leigh Wilson, *Modernism and Magic: Experiments with spiritualism, theosophy and the occult* (Edinburgh: Edinburgh University Press, 2012), 98, 145. Fournier d'Albe was also interested in the philosophical implications of the new physics, and translated Charles Nordmann's *The Tyranny of Time: Einstein or Bergson?* (London: T. Fisher Unwin, 1925).

unprecedented form of life a super-'natural' edifice of infinite power, as yet but dimly realized, but which in its full beauty and perfection will be nothing less than Divine.   (90)

It is a trope that is back with us; for example in Yuval Noah Harari's *Homo Deus: A brief history of tomorrow* (2016), or in Michio Kaku's prediction that 'if you want to see the future, you have to understand physics, and you have to realize that by the year 2100, we will have the power of the gods';[62] but with little sense of the history of the trope, nor indeed of the history of writing the history of the future. Perhaps it is not just that each age is awed by its own technology, but that this represents a moment of strain in the concept of prosthesis itself, as the complexity of technological developments begins to alienate the user. In his book *Feed Forward*, Mark Hansen argues that:

> if twenty-first century media open up an expanded domain of sensibility that can enhance human experience, they also impose a new form of *resolutely non-prosthetic* technical mediation: simply put, to access this domain of sensibility, humans must rely on technologies to perform operations to which they have absolutely no direct access whatsoever [....][63]

This is a different situation from what Günther Anders calls the 'Promethean gap'; a gap 'between what we are able to produce and what we are able to imagine'.[64] Anders' *Die Antiquiertheit des Menschen*, 2 vols (1956, 1980) is not yet translated into English, but the title is usually rendered as 'The Outdatedness of Human Beings' or 'The Obsolescence of Man'. It is a response to the existential and epistemological challenges of the atomic bomb and the Shoah; technologies of human annihilation. The traumatic experience of destructiveness on the Western Front arguably produced a First World War equivalent sense of a gap between the machinery of war and the incomprehensibility of its results. But To-Day and To-Morrow is Promethean in the opposite sense. Rather than reflecting Anders' gap between human production and imagination, it shows imagination running ahead of production; not only in the trivial sense of running ahead in time, by doing futurology; but in the sense of first imagining new technologies then imagining their implications. Alberto Toscano argues in a discussion of Anders, modernism, and machines, that the desire in Futurism to create machine man can be seen as an anxious attempt to close the Promethean gap. Perhaps. But where Futurism merely imagines the idea of the metallized body, To-Day and

---

[62] Michio Kaku, 'The Universe in a Nutshell': http://www.floatinguniversity.com/kaku-transcript accessed 26 July 2017.
[63] Mark Hansen, *Feed Forward: On the future of twenty-first-century media* (Chicago: University of Chicago Press, 2015), 4.
[64] The definition is given by Alberto Toscano, in 'The Promethean Gap: Modernism, machines, and the obsolescence of man', *Modernism/modernity*, 23:3 (September 2016), 593–609 (604).

To-Morrow's prosthetic imagination both imagines the biotechnologies to transform the human, then the effects on mentality of such interventions.

Hansen, by contrast, is concerned with the phenomenology of use, and how while we may be using the internet as an instrument (of information, social life, shopping, etc.) we are simultaneously the objects of other people's (or corporations') purposes, as they aggregate and monetize our data. And that this level of the operation is performed algorithmically and hidden from our view, so we cannot be directly conscious of it. Fournier d'Albe's idea that our technological power is 'as yet but dimly realized' might sound like a Promethean gap. Though his futurology, and that of the series as a whole, exemplifies the opposite: an ability to imagine what has not (yet) been produced. It may, rather, be a glimpse of how future technological interconnection (his future, our reality) might take technology, and modernism, beyond prosthesis.

When Fournier d'Albe ends the book saying that it is fire-related technologies that make divinity, we grasp that the equation is reversible. The soul of the man is, or becomes, the soul of the weapon, the technology. That move from the mechanical to 'Science and invention' is crucial. Machines are the realization of creative minds. Fire enables us to be like gods, if prosthetic ones. According to this view, our souls, our minds, do not just turn the material world into ideas; they are also altered by our prostheses. Ideas change the mind.

> The 'mechanical age', which to some appears as the very negation of the soul, is, on the contrary, the age of supreme psychical achievement.
>
> Science and invention are for ever annexing fresh regions of the universe and subjecting them to the free play of our mental faculties. The process of bringing material things into subjection to our will is a process of sublimation, which does not drag us down to the dust, but raises up dust into the realms of immortal spirit.   (50-1)

At this point *Hephaestus* moves closer to Bretherton's argument in *Midas*, though it had appeared to be arguing in the other direction, that 'it is things and not ideas that mould the destinies of men and races though man, who is much more concerned with what he thinks than with what he makes, refuses to recognize it' (*Midas*, p. 18). It combines with Fournier d'Albe's other main argument (also made in *Quo Vadimus?*): that technology unites humanity into one body. Again, this isn't meant in the totalitarian sense—as when Caligula said he wished all Rome only had one neck so he could cut its throat. It's an example of the trope running continually through this series, that technology is connecting us ever more closely together.[65] As in Bernal's vision of networked thoughts; which also forges humankind into something superhuman; what Haldane was to call a 'super-organism'.[66]

---

[65] See the third section in Chapter 2.
[66] Haldane, 'The Last Judgement', in *Possible Worlds*, p. 304; and see the Conclusions.

Let us develop that idea by taking a spin with one more book from the series, called *Ouroboros*—after the mythical serpent swallowing its own tail. This was published in 1926 by a man with a name that makes you see why he was interested in circularity: Garet Garrett. Like *Hephaestus*, it is concerned with the effect of the machine on man; and it is brilliantly written. He too starts from the thought that evolution may have finished, at least internally; but may now have gone external:

> Suddenly man begins to augment himself by an external process. His natural powers become extensible to a degree that makes them original in kind. To his given structure—the weakest among animal structures in proportion to its bulk—he adds an automatic, artificial member, responsive only to his contact, answerable only to his will, uncontrolled by nature, fabulous in its possibilities of strength, variation, and cunning. His use of it in three generations has changed the design of civilization out of recognition.   (12)

Garrett is also very good on how machines have rapidly both made themselves indispensable to us, and also seem to be gaining the upper hand over us. You wonder if the makers of *The Matrix* had read *Ouroboros*; or Fritz Lang, whose *Metropolis* would appear the following year:

> The riddle is that industrial civilization, having created to its unknown ends a race of mechanical drudges, requires nevertheless a contribution of human toil more intense, more exacting, more irksome than ever.   (21)

He wonders what 'a planetary tourist', coming to visit Earth, would make of our relation to machines; and asks (in Butlerian vein):

> What may you deduce from these facts? First, you will be amused that people are so naive as to think they make machines. Then you may say there are two kinds of people here, agricultural and industrial. The earth makes one kind; machines make the other.   (28)

And he makes it clear that this vision of the machines calling the tune was either a product of the First World War or certainly heightened by it. The conflict was:

> a machine-war. What made that war so terrifying, so destructive, so extensive, was the power of the machine—an inconceivable power except as it disclosed itself from day to day. No one beholding the event from a firmamental point of view could have supposed it was a war between races of men. Man in contrast with the machines he served was pitifully insignificant.   (45)

But again, unlike the fascist attitude (but like Haldane, whom we saw start from a similar vision of the war as fought by weapons, with scurrying human assistance) Garrett concludes not with man's insignificance, but the immense significance of the fact that he created the machines in the first place. And it becomes clear why he has chosen this curious style; it too is the recounting of a modern creation myth—the creation of the machine:

> How strange at least that with an incentive so trivial and naive in itself he should have been able to perform an absolute feat of creation! The machine was not. He reached his mind into emptiness and seized it. Even yet he cannot realize what he has done. Out of the free elemental stuff of the universe, visible and invisible, some of it imponderable, such as lightning, he has invented a class of typhonic, mindless organisms, exempt from the will of nature. We have no understanding of creation, its process or meaning. The machine is the externalized image of man's thoughts. It is furthermore an extension of his life, for we perceive as an economic fact that human existence in its present phase, on its present scale, could not continue in its absence. And what are we ourselves, life to begin with, if not an image of thought? Perhaps it is true as a principle of creation that the image and its creator must co-exist, inseparably.   (92)

Like Freud, Garrett sees the machine as a prosthesis for our fantasy: a technology of wish-fulfilment. But where for Freud modern man is a prosthetic god only in his own fantasy, for Garrett, the godlikeness isn't in what we do *with* our prostheses, but that we have *created* them in the first place. If the sentence 'Even yet he cannot realize what he has done' has you reaching for your Promethean gap, *Ouroboros* closes it, realizing for us and representing our creativity and its effects.

This is the third argument. For Garrett the machine is 'the externalized image of man's thoughts', not just his wishes. It is 'an extension of his life' not just in the sense of stretching it out—making the same nature reach further—but because in doing so it also it makes our life something different. The transformation is qualitative as well as quantitative. The fascist co-option of technology to incorporate the human into the machine state makes one suspect a compensatory fantasy to assuage castration anxiety, the prosthesis providing a reassuring sense of phallic power. Rather than technology compensating for something the body is felt to lack, *Ouroboros* celebrates technology as the gaining of something new, offering new possibilities. This argument shares the view in *Midas*, say, that machines change how we think. But it inverts it, seeing technology not as something that robotizes us, but rather, as something that liberates creativity and innovation.

If we were asked to identify today where we had extended our lives with the externalized images of our thoughts, we should probably say media. *Ouroboros* is clear about the link between technology and media: machines solve the problem of production, but that produces another problem: that of selling what you've produced, and this generates advertising. The series has strong representation of media, as we have seen, with books on wireless, cinema, advertising, and the press. Some of the To-Day and To-Morrow writers do use the word 'media';[67]

---

[67] C. A. Mace, *Sibylla; or, The Revival of Prophecy* (1926), 43; E. N. Bennett, *Apollonius; or, The Present and Future of Psychical Research* (1927), 53; others use it in the sense of a biological medium

but not many, and mostly not in the sense of forms of cultural communication. Yet not only are they often writing about it, but they do so in a way that anticipates the foundational formulation of the concept by Marshall McLuhan, in his *Understanding Media*: (1964).[68] This is the fourth argument.

There is no hard evidence that McLuhan read any of the To-Day and To-Morrow volumes. Ogden is not mentioned in his books, nor is the series credited in his bibliographies. But when McLuhan arrived in Cambridge in 1934, just three years after the last volumes had appeared, they would have still had currency. He was taught by Ogden's friend I. A. Richards, and had certainly read the book they wrote collaboratively, *The Meaning of Meaning*; and he read William Empson, another Ogden had writing for him. Ogden was still in Cambridge, as were many of the contributors to To-Day and To-Morrow and his other book series, others of which were still running: Psyche Miniatures; and especially The International Library of Psychology, Philosophy, and Scientific Method. Lord Zuckerman later described Ogden as 'a man of giant intellect, and a person whose general influence on the intellectual world of his time was almost without parallel'.[69] 'General influence' is a rather woolly concept, certainly hard to demonstrate. But the whole conception of McLuhan's *Understanding Media* is very akin to Ogden's of the series. It is not just the grounding of cultural theory on analysis of language and communication. Where Ogden had become increasingly involved in the campaign for BASIC English as an international auxiliary language, McLuhan saw himself as a Renaissance grammarian analysing modern communicative acts. But more interestingly, it's the table of contents of *Understanding Media* that seems to issue from a similar mind-set, in the way it yokes together mechanical forms of technology with forms of communication. McLuhan's whole project is based on the idea that new technologies like printing or electricity change how we think and communicate; that was what the To-Day and To-Morrow authors were grasping and projecting too. If you return to McLuhan now from a media studies perspective it is surprising to find chapters on: roads; clothes; housing; transport; sport; money; the press; cinema; advertising; the phonograph; weapons; automation; and so on. But this collection of subjects has striking similarities to the list of subjects covered by To-Day and To-Morrow. Admittedly, towards the end of the book, he delivers a series of chapters on the communication technologies we now associate primarily with media studies: the press, the telegraph, the typewriter, the phonograph, radio, film, television. And he focuses less on the way these subjects had featured in To-Day and To-Morrow, especially in McColvin's book, for the way they would impact on the future of art.

---

for cultivating cells (Haldane, *Daedalus*, p. 60) or a physical one for transmitting waves (Hatfield, *Automaton*, p. 43).

---

[68] See Marshall McLuhan, *Understanding Media: The extensions of man* (New York: McGraw-Hill, 1964).

[69] Solly Zuckerman, 'Talent Scout and Editor', in *C. K. Ogden: A collective memoir*, pp. 122–32.

But the main reason for suspecting a line of influence from To-Day and To-Morrow, whether direct or indirect, is in the way McLuhan is thinking of all these subjects as different forms of prosthesis: what, in his subtitle, he calls 'The extensions of man'.[70] He told his son Eric that he took the phrase from Emerson. It is true that, in *The Conduct of Life*, Emerson writes:

> The motive of science was the extension of man, on all sides, into Nature, till his hands should touch the stars, his eyes see through the earth, his ears understand the language of beast and bird, and the sense of the wind; and, through his sympathy, heaven and earth should talk with him. But that is not our science. These geologies, chemistries, astronomies, seem to make wise, but they leave us where they found us. The invention is of use to the inventor, of questionable help to any other.[71]

But his emphasis falls on science rather than technology or media (though they might be indicated by the term 'invention'); and his argument is that science does *not* extend humanity in general. Whereas *Ouroboros*, like other volumes of To-Day and To-Morrow, argues that it does. Bernal still thought so when preparing his undergraduate lectures on the history of science under the title *The Extension of Man*.[72] Garrett was possibly thinking of Emerson too; and the full title of his book—*Ouroboros; or, The Mechanical Extension of Mankind*—may have been intended as a counter to Emerson's scepticism about prosthetic inventions; and could conceivable have reminded McLuhan of the Emerson passage, or prompted him to notice it subsequently. The question of influence aside, the attraction for all these writers of the phrase 'the extension [or extensions] of man' has much to do with its suggestive ambiguity, already there in the Emerson, and which we have seen exercising To-Day and To-Morrow's writers about technology. Do prostheses merely extend the reach of an essential and fixed humanity, allowing us to do more of the same old things? Or do they extend human nature itself in the process; extend us beyond the human?

---

[70] Marshall McLuhan: 'Any invention or technology is an extension or self-amputation of our physical bodies': see Elena Lamberti, *Marshall McLuhan's Mosaic: Probing the literary origins of media studies* (Toronto: University of Toronto Press, 2012), 185, citing *Understanding Media*, 54–6.

[71] Eric McLuhan, email to Max Saunders, 5 August 2016. Unfortunately for my argument, Marshall McLuhan did not have a copy of Garrett's book in his library; though Eric McLuhan thinks it possible he may have read at least Russell's *Icarus* (Eric McLuhan, email to Max Saunders, 4 August 2016). Emerson, 'Beauty', chapter 7 of *The Conduct of Life* (Cambridge, MA: Houghton Mifflin, 1860), 219–40 (223). Other ideas in the series parallel McLuhan's thought. The trope of electrical interconnection discussed in Chapter 2, for example, is a precursor of McLuhan's 'global village'. But such ideas were widespread in the period, and the parallels may be confluences rather than influences. It is not impossible that the title of McLuhan's article 'Tomorrow and Tomorrow' (published in *The Manitoban*, 16 May 1934) played on the title of the series as well as echoing *Macbeth*. But it does not mention the series, and its denunciation of industrialization and of Marxism indicates why he may have found the overall project uncongenial.

[72] J. D. Bernal, *The Extension of Man: A history of physics before 1900* (London: Weidenfeld & Nicolson, 1972).

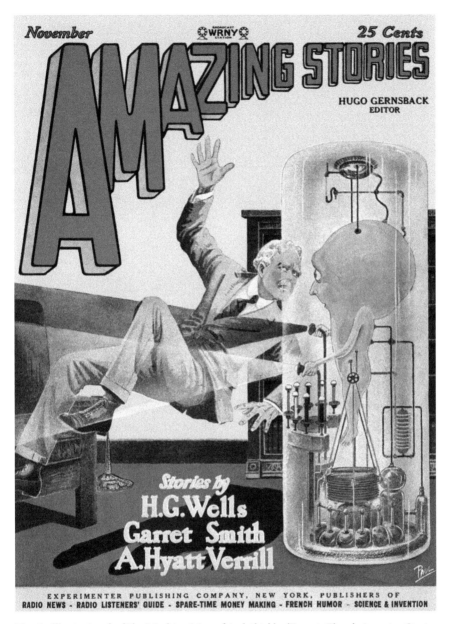

Fig. 5. Illustration for 'The Machine Man of Ardathia', by 'Francis Flagg'; *Amazing Stories* (November 1927); public domain; image © Alamy

5

To-Day and To-Morrow, Cultural Studies, and Everyday Life

Introduction: Cultural Studies

At this point, media shades off into the everyday life it was increasingly becoming a part of and characterizing, as the prosthetic technologies of telephones, gramophones, wireless, then television entered the home of the future, accompanied by labour-saving devices such as vacuum cleaners, washing machines, and even teasmades. Around seventy of the titles in To-Day and To-Morrow—many of which have been discussed or mentioned already—could be described as covering 'everyday life' topics. Insofar as the ambition of the series is to sketch out possibilities for life in the future, all the volumes have something to say about how everyday life might change. In Barthes's paradoxical flourish: 'la marque de l'Utopie, c'est le quotidien'.[1]

The purpose of this chapter is thus in part to thicken the description of this aspect of the series; and to show, as study of the everyday becomes an increasingly important emphasis in modernist scholarship, what a wealth of pioneering material the series offers in this area too. But it also aims to demonstrate that something else significant was stirring in To-Day and To-Morrow that is scarcely found elsewhere, though it relates to representations of the everyday in literature, film, and journalism. This is the emergence of what were later to be called cultural studies and media studies. Chapter 4 touched on the topic of media, concluding with the suggestion that To-Day and To-Morrow's configuring of prostheses and communication technologies anticipated McLuhanite developments in media theory. David Trotter, in his book *Literature in the First Media Age*, makes the case for considering transport as a form of media.[2] That conjunction too is anticipated in the way the series predicts futures of increasingly interconnecting links of transport, communication, and representation. In this chapter the aim is to assess the broader ways in which the series explored and projected the role of culture and media in everyday life.

---

[1] 'The sign of Utopia is the everyday': Roland Barthes, *Sade, Fourier, Loyola* (Paris: Editions de Seuil, 1971), 23.
[2] David Trotter, *Literature in the First Media Age: Britain between the wars* (Cambridge, MA: Harvard University Press, 2013), 218.

Imagined Futures: Writing, Science and Modernity in the To-Day and To-Morrow. Max Saunders, Oxford University Press (2019). © Max Saunders. DOI: 10.1093/oso/9780198829454.001.0001

In the received accounts of the study of culture and media, we are told such things as this:

> In the history of cultural studies, the earliest encounters were with literary criticism. Raymond Williams and Richard Hoggart, in their different ways, developed the Leavisite stress on literary-social evaluation, but turned the assessments from literature to everyday life.[3]

Hoggart and Williams were certainly influential figures. But the historical claim here is apparently blind to the way the Leavises had already made that turn, and indeed that the whole point of their 'literary-social evaluation' was to judge literature against other cultural forms. They may not have liked what they saw in mass culture, but they were paying critical attention. Or we are told that a similar move among historians led to 'the development of the post-war traditions of social history with their focus on popular culture, or the culture of "the people" especially in its political forms', as exemplified by the Communist Party Historians' Group.[4] Post-war here again signifies post Second World War. Whereas in fact the origins of both cultural and media studies lie further back, in the work of the sociologists and urban ethnographers of the Chicago School in the 1920s and 30s; and in the founding of the New School in New York in 1919, which has studied the impact of media from that date, and taught the first College course in film in 1926.[5] Sometimes the cultural histories (such as the one quoted above) focus on the institutionalization of cultural studies in universities, tacitly assuming (counter to the spirit of the discipline) that work only qualifies as cultural studies if it happens inside an academic institution. Even by that definition, the work had already begun between the wars. But To-Day and To-Morrow shows why it is the wrong definition. Jed Esty has posited an 'anthropological turn' in late modernism from 1930 to 1960, as writers responded to imperial decline with a renewed concentration on English life and culture in both literary and theoretical works.[6] To-Day and To-Morrow, in imagining how that life and culture might change, demonstrates that process as already having begun in the 1920s, and contemporaneously with high modernism.

The series is contemporary with some of this foundational work; and it contains some of the earliest, in some cases the earliest, sustained critical accounts of a range of everyday life phenomena, from advertising and domestic architecture to sport, sleep, wireless, and clothing. A further aim here is thus to bring out the

---

[3] Richard Johnson, 'What Is Cultural Studies Anyway?', *Social Text*, 16 (Winter, 1986–1987), 38–80 (38); previously published by the University of Birmingham's Centre for Contemporary Cultural Studies, 1983.

[4] Ibid.

[5] See http://www.newschool.edu/public-engagement/school-of-media-studies-about/; accessed 28 August 2016.

[6] Jed Esty, *A Shrinking Island: Modernism and national culture in England* (Princeton University Press, 2004), 'Introduction', especially p. 2.

contribution of the series to these emerging disciplines; and even to suggest possible lines of influence from the series and its contributors both to contemporary writers, and their interest in the everyday; and also to the first generation of critics and thinkers turning their attention to media and culture between the wars. They also provide some of the sharpest and most entertaining among the volumes. To-Day and To-Morrow does not articulate any over-arching theory of cultural or media studies. Nor did it offer the kinds of systematic theorization of everyday life in the manner of pioneering studies such as Freud's *Psychopathology of Everyday Life* (1901/4); Henri Lefebvre's *Critique of Everyday Life* (1947); Erving Goffman's *The Presentation of Self in Everyday Life* (1956); the Situationist Raoul Vaneigem's *The Revolution of Everyday Life* (1967); or Michel De Certeau's *The Practice of Everyday Life* (1980). But the series is indicative of, and played its substantial part in, the establishment of a new kind of critical attention to everyday life and practices, on which those subsequent theorizations depend.[7] Its implicit theoretical assumptions are the axioms of subsequent cultural studies: that media and cultural practices are crucial constituents of everyday life; that they deserve and require systematic attention; and that they are constantly evolving.[8]

Even if McLuhan was not influenced directly by the series, he certainly was by the emergence of Cambridge criticism while he was there.[9] And its key figures— Richards, Leavis, Empson—were well aware of Ogden and the series. The book Leavis co-authored with Denys Thompson, *Culture and Environment: The training of critical awareness* (1933) which performed Cambridge close reading on newspapers, magazines, and advertisements was an inspiration for McLuhan's *The Mechanical Bride*, and, according to his son, of his subsequent work on media.[10] Leavis had completed his PhD in 1924 and became a lecturer in 1927, by which time To-Day and To-Morrow was well-established. Leavis knew I. A. Richards, and certainly knew about Ogden's work. In his essay *Mass Civilization and Minority Culture*, first published in 1930, he mentions 'a little book called *Babel*, published in the To-day and To-morrow series', by Richard Paget.[11] (Paget's 1930

---

[7] The title of J. B. S. Haldane's *Science and Everyday Life* (London: Lawrence and Wishart, 1939) is indicative of how his thought remained focused on the effects of applied science on the everyday; as it had been in his *Daedalus; or, Science and the Future* (1923).

[8] For recent critical discussions of modernism and everyday life, see:
Michael Gardiner, *Critiques of Everyday Life* (London and New York: Routledge, 2000); Rita Felski, 'Introduction' to Special Issue: Everyday life, *New Literary History*, 33:4 (Autumn 2002), 607–22; Ben Highmore, *Everyday Life and Cultural Theory* (London and New York: Routledge, 2002); John Roberts, *Philosophizing the Everyday* (London and New York: Pluto Press, 2006) Michael Sheringham, *Everyday Life: Theories and practices from surrealism to the present* (Oxford and New York: Oxford University Press, 2006); Bryony Randall, *Modernism, Daily Time, and Everyday Life* (Cambridge: Cambridge University Press, 2007).

[9] See Elena Lamberti, *Marshall McLuhan's Mosaic: Probing the literary origins of media studies* (Toronto: University of Toronto Press, 2012).

[10] Eric McLuhan, email to Max Saunders, 5 August 2016.

[11] F. R. Leavis, *Mass Civilization and Minority Culture*, was first published as Minority Pamphlet No. 1 (Gordon Fraser, The Minority Press: Cambridge, 1930). It was collected in his *For Continuity* (Cambridge: The Minority Press, 1933), 13–46 (42). Paget's gesture-theory influenced the work of

volume not only discussed *Icarus* and *Tantalus*, but carried the usual end-matter advertising the other volumes, by then numbering over one hundred.) In *For Continuity* (1933) Leavis cites Ogden's BASIC English initiative, and shows he also knew of his Psyche Miniatures and his interest in Joyce.[12] He was evidently watching the work of Ogden and his networks closely and critically;[13] also citing other works by To-Day and To-Morrow authors. He knew Paget's major book, *Human Speech* (1930), published the same year as *Babel*. *Culture and Environment* cites other books by two To-Day and To-Morrow writers: C. E. M. Joad's engagingly-titled *The Horrors of the Countryside* (London: The Hogarth Press, 1931); and E. A. Mowrer's *This American World* (London: Faber, 1928), which had a preface by T. S. Eliot. Gilbert Russell followed his To-Day and To-Morrow volume *Nuntius* with *Advertisement Writing* (London: Ernest Benn, 1927). Both appear in the bibliography of Q. D. Leavis' influential *Fiction and the Reading Public* (1932); and *Culture and Environment* quotes from and discusses the latter. To-Day and To-Morrow was by no means the sole source of such ideas (as these works by the Leavises show); ideas which were diffused through journalism, cinema, pulp fiction, comics, and the like. Contributors were often drafted into the series because—like Paget or Russell—they had already written, or were writing, a larger book on the topic.

Media and Everyday Life: The Press, Advertising, and Propaganda

Gilbert Russell's *Nuntius; Advertising and its Future* (1926) is essentially a defence of the profession by an insider. Russell argues for the essential honesty of advertising, which should not be mistrusted because it has occasionally been used unscrupulously. He thinks advertised brands must be superior to unadvertised commodities or people wouldn't buy them. He argues that advertising provides a social service. 'Advertising was the implement that made people want vacuum cleaners' (27).[14] Thus he also sees advertising as a democratizing force; it allows modern inventions to be 'the satisfaction of the many, instead of the luxury of the few' (27-8). 'Advertising is an educative force, a civilizing influence' (21). Yet he is

---

Kenneth Burke. See Debra Hawhee, 'Language as Sensuous Action: Sir Richard Paget, Kenneth Burke, and gesture-speech theory', *Quarterly Journal of Speech*, 92:4 (November 2006), 331–54.

[12] Leavis, *For Continuity*, pp. 43, 215.
[13] In the volume he edited of essays from *Scrutiny*, *Determinations: Critical essays* (London: Chatto & Windus, 1934), Leavis reprinted Michael Oakeshott's critique of Ogden's case for Bentham: 'The New Bentham', pp. 244–80.
[14] Trotter, *Literature in the First Media Age*, chapter 1, 'Telephony', demonstrates the effectiveness of a comparable government campaign to encourage people to invest in telephones.

untroubled by the contradiction: a rhetoric that can create new desires is doing something other than transparently disseminating factual information.

When in the last 60 per cent of the book he turns to the future, he is even more utopian. Modern advertising begins with the reintroduction of argument and description; and thus with the rise of the agency. This role will become increasingly important and professionalized. Like Garrett in *Ouroboros*, he thinks that 'We have solved the problem of production. The problem of the future will be marketing' (56-7). Market research will become more important. Advertising could help solve unemployment. As education improves, advertising can become more informative, more rational (81). In a passage that must have caused apoplexy in the Leavis household, he is even confident that '[t]he literary quality of advertisements in the future will of course be much higher than it is now' (63). Of course. It is at least arguable that in the shorter term he was not so wrong. When he discusses political advertising, he thinks that it will make people better informed. Perhaps it did in the public information films and broadcasts of the New Deal or the Reithian BBC. And yet the longer term story—with its episodes of fascist propaganda and Soviet socialist realism—tells another picture; and Russell appears to be in denial of it.

This blind spot is connected to (and perhaps a product of) the most extraordinary silence in his discussion of 'Advertising To-Morrow'. If it has occurred to him that it might colonize the emerging media of film, broadcasting, and eventually television, he does not mention the possibility. Although he does consider the subconscious effects of advertising, and quotes A. H. Deute in *Printer's Ink* (the first US national trade magazine for advertisers) on how the minority can use its power to sway the majority, he seems either not to grasp the extent to which that fact threatens to negate all his previous arguments, or to be wilfully suppressing the implications. It is all the more surprising since the question of the manipulation of 'public opinion' was extremely topical at the time. Walter Lippmann's books on *Public Opinion* (1922) and *The Phantom Public* (1925), and Edward Bernays' *Crystallizing Public Opinion* (1923) are among the classic examples. Russell's hope that 'perhaps for the first time the great mass of voters will be fully informed and will properly understand not only the issues before the country but the methods which each party would apply to deal with them' (85) cannot but seem catastrophically naïve to an era of infantile vacuity and mendacious negativity in political discourse, let alone a 'post-truth' era of 'fake news' and 'alternative facts'.

We can only hope Russell was a better judge of products than predictions. His rightness that architecture would incorporate posters is undermined by the wrongness of his conviction that electric signs would not last. That is because of his naïve belief that 'Pictures will cease to be used to procure attention and will be used only when they are more efficient than words in the explanation of a point in the text' (72). At least he is addressing the crucial question in advertising about the relation between word and image; even though it must have been evident by the 1920s (and certainly was to Bernays, the nephew of Sigmund Freud) that the prime use of the advertising image was to be fantasmatic: to mobilize desires that slipped around and through language. Russell's claim that advertising could have kept the US out of the war is disturbing, especially coupled with his proposal that an organized international campaign could preserve peace. In other words, in his view if the Mad Men do not already rule the world they should, and a league of advertising agencies would be more effective than the League of Nations.

By contrast, David Ockham in *Stentor; or, The Press of To-Day and To-Morrow* (1927) provides a bracing critique of what he calls 'The Dictators of Public Opinion' (36)—the press barons. 'In the stead of the Delanes[15] and the Northcliffes', he says, 'we have control by self-seeking millionaires with a megalomaniac itch for interference' (49):

> The world has never known anything comparable. A handful of men, sitting over a luncheon table, can decree what the community is to think, what it is to be told, what it is not to be told. So we have reached the 'Fordisation' of the intellect, which works through mass suggestion reinforced by damnable iteration. And this is mainly the work, not of men with missions, not of enthusiasts, or patriots, or men of culture, not even of journalists, but of men who have 'gone into' the newspaper industry as they might have 'gone into' the establishment of bacon-curing factories.   (40-1)

It is like Maurois' vision of the power of the press cabal; though for Maurois' dictators in the future it is a virtual luncheon table. Ockham's are dictators *of* the future: 'Does it require a prophet to forecast the colossal influence of the Dictators on the opinions, the conduct, and the ideals of the next generation?' (41). *The Next Chapter* writes that forecast; and gives it a title making it sound like an instalment of a newspaper serialization of a fiction.

Ockham is satirical about the contents of the papers of the day. 'The Press is still old-fashioned enough to regard Woman (with a very large "W") as a remarkable creature that has only just been discovered' (54), he says. But when he gets on to 'The Newspaper of To-morrow' in a penultimate chapter (65-81), his cynical futurology is an amplified version of a shrewd eye for contemporary trends: the exploitation of niche pursuits rather than the provision of news and analysis. He also predicts more clearly than Gilbert Russell the increasing power of the image:

> One foresees also an immense increase in the number of photographs and other pictures, aided by the development of telephotography,[16] television, and air trans-port. The motorist, the golfer, the collector of antique furniture, the amateur

---

[15] John Delane was editor of the *Times* from 1841 to 1877.

[16] This is probably the transmission of images over long distances, such as by cable or radio, rather than the photographing of distant subjects with telephoto lenses.

gardener, the investor, will find more space devoted to their special interests. There may even be room for an increase in the amount of space (if not of the quality) devoted to book reviews, although this forecast is admittedly optimistic. (What the public is supposed to want is not literary criticism, but 'gossip' about the personal habits, the clothes, the recreations, the holidays, and the monetary earnings of authors.)   (66-7)

The Sabbath will be kept holy by an increase in the space devoted to autobiographies of contemporary criminals and the retelling of old crimes. In short, the Newspaper will have travelled a stage further on the road to supplant the book, to supplement the playhouse.   (69)

Ockham is also refreshingly scathing about the disingenuity of the Dictators' claims to be protecting a free press:

Newspaper proprietors assert that in fact, their editors have a free hand, and attempt to prove this contention by pointing to differences in policy or treatment manifested by newspapers under the same control. One is at some difficulty in deciding whether this argument is the fruit of ingenious or of merely ingenuous minds. The *Evening Standard*, for instance, may not see eye to eye with the *Daily Express* in such matters as the morality of modern dancing or the retention of old churches in the City of London, but a strike, a political crisis, a general election, the issue of war or peace, will witness a unanimity of editorial comment which goes beyond the limits of sheer coincidence. The *mot d'ordre* has been given.   (74)

Memories of the General Strike the previous year were still bitter. Discussing broadcasting, Ockham is equally wary of governmental control, and—again in telling contrast to Russell's blithe confidence in advertising's political benignity— wary of its use for propaganda over transparency:

as a matter of fact, the new British Broadcasting Corporation, which is a Government Department, possesses powers to do almost anything that can be done by a newspaper. Some of those powers it will certainly use, and there is nothing to prevent the Corporation from adding to its functions that of purveyor of propaganda for the Government of the day. The transmission of official news, and the development of an Inter-Empire news service it will certainly undertake.   (76-7)

The BBC's Empire Service was launched in 1932; a forerunner of the World Service, funded through the Foreign Office.

Again unlike Russell, Ockham is sharply aware of the pressures newer media are already exerting on newspapers, and how the technologies and challenges will only intensify. Pathé newsreels and documentaries had been appearing in British cinemas since 1910; though they would only acquire sound in 1928. 'The popular newspapers have lately begun to break out in a pictorial eczema throughout their pages', he writes: 'But the kinema'—like Ezra Pound he prefers the spelling that freeze-frames the classical etymology of the 'cinematograph'—'with its extremely well-organized service for recording and exhibiting events of the hour, leaves the newspaper miles in the rear' (80):

> Television, already a scientific achievement, and tomorrow a possible 'commercial proposition', will also come to the aid both of the Kinema and the Wireless. How does the Press propose to meet the actualities of the picture theatre and the possibilities of new inventions for the photographic recording and reproduction of events?   (80-1)

Communications and Travel

The satirical note had also been sounded—if in more of a Wyndham Lewis vein— in an earlier volume, E. E. Fournier d'Albe's *Quo Vadimus? Glimpses of the Future* (1925). Fournier d'Albe attacks human stupidity, questions enlightenment (claiming implausibly that most humans still think the earth flat, etc.) and democracy. He then projects the future across a range of topics—transport and communications, privacy, clothing, housing, children, education, labour, government—in some ways offering a condensation of the scope of the whole series. It is when he addresses the acceleration and ramification of technological change that he becomes most compelling, not just for his attention to the invention of gadgets, but for his appreciation of their transformation of audiences, forms of publicity, and speech acts; even of the senses and of memory:

> The consequence of that constant acceleration is that new developments and achievements succeed each other with bewildering rapidity. Hardly have we got accustomed to the idea of telegraphy without wires when radiotelephony becomes an accomplished fact, and within a few years there is a rich crop of listeners with their wireless receiving sets counting by the million. An entirely new form of publicity comes into being, and a speaker on Savoy Hill is able to speak to an audience of millions and sway them by his voice more effectively than he can do by cold print in the newspapers.   (76-7)

> And this is only a beginning. Communication will become closer and more general. Already the earth is a network of lines and cables, linking continent to continent. Soon a speaker will have the earth for his sounding board and his hall of audience, and the privilege of addressing the human race will be prized above a coronation. Human sight and hearing will extend its range enormously, not only in space, but in time also. For the cinema film and improvements in the recording of sound will make it possible to make minute and comprehensive records of past sights and sounds for future reproduction, so that nothing of any value may be lost.   (77-8)

The turn at the end of that last thought is still unspooling the future of film; and takes in the development of home movies. But it has taken still newer technologies fully to capture its totalizing imagination ('*nothing* of *any* value')—video cameras first, then their digital heirs, and the associated Web 2.0 capabilities of uploading of such video material onto platforms like YouTube; or the use of wearable tech for 'life-logging'.

Fournier d'Albe also understands well how the development of such technologies of '"signalling" communication' (78) will be imbricated with those of transport, travel, and even mass tourism to achieve a global interconnectedness:

> Our descendants will pay an afternoon's visit to Timbuctoo or Mount Ararat, much as we should visit the British Museum or the Lake District. Everybody will be a globe-trotter, but the 'globe' will not be confined to the ordinary tourist resorts. It will include every part of the world, even the Poles. And wherever they go they will find friendly voices, long familiar in the home through the service of radio-telephony.   (79)

Home and Family

The imagination of how such technological change will reconfigure the spaces of the home and the world plays across many of the volumes; but is the particular focus of *Lares et Penates; or, The Home of the Future* (1928), by the architect H[arry] J. Birnstingl.[17] Birnstingl gives an illuminating account not only of how everyday home life was changing, but of how its changes related to the past as well as the future. 'There are no longer local building materials, for the annihilation of distance makes the whole world local' (41), he writes, developing the idea to show how the globalization of resources and products goes hand in hand with the globalization of information.

> One of the effects of our astoundingly rapid development of the world's resources has been the comparative elimination of time and space. The whole history of the world's past achievement lies on our bookshelves, and actions taking place at all the ends of the earth are made known to us almost at once. Our store of available facts has thus increased quite prodigiously within a comparatively short time; facts relating not only to scientific inventions, and to the various branches

---

[17] Birnstingl had fought at the Somme. After the war he married Phyllis Reid, a friend of Ezra Pound and Stella Bowen (who became Ford Madox Ford's partner). Birnstingl's promising career was cut short by inherited tuberculosis. He died in 1927, the year before *Lares et Penates* was published. His story is told in his daughter Mirabel Osler's charming memoir, *The Rain Tree* (London: Bloomsbury, 2011). The Lares and Penates were the Roman gods said to protect a household and its possessions.

of natural science, but also to the past history of the world itself and to mankind's activity thereon. (70-1)

It is another of many moments in the series when descriptions firmly rooted in the communications and transportation technologies of the period, and the system of imperial trade, also appear to speak for other and future developments—in this case of encyclopedic modernism, as well as the information revolution of the late twentieth century. He is also acute on the drawback of the information revolution:

> unfortunately man's intelligence has not increased at the same rate as his knowledge, and so busily is he engaged in acquiring facts that he has no time for thought, and no time to consider how best to utilize the vast resources of the earth which are piling up about him. (71)

His diagnosis of the effects of this accumulation is also incisive:

> One of the results of the availability of all this knowledge is the growth of the historical sense which has now become so acutely developed as to have a very definite effect upon craftsmanship and upon the furnishing of the home, for it is this over-developed historical sense that is the cause of the desire for period houses and period furniture. (71-2)

T. S. Eliot had famously argued for the importance of the 'historical sense' to poets in his key essay 'Tradition and the Individual Talent', countering forms of modernism such as Futurism gleefully bent on trashing the past.[18] Birnstingl however sees the opposite problem as the more pressing. In his view, the intensification of the historic sense has led to 'a set of values which cuts across the aesthetic, the moral and the efficiency values' (72), and thus led to the production of fakes and reproduction furniture. Another volume in the series, *Artifex; or, The Future of Craftsmanship* (1926), by John Gloag, is also concerned about the threat to traditional hand-craft posed by the machine; though he expresses qualified optimism that 'an enlightened alliance of hand-craft and machine-craft can achieve great progress; but that progress must have the encouragement and support of a public that will demand good workmanship in the commonplace things of everyday life' (95). For Birnstingl the issue is the effect of information rather than mechanization. Before such knowledge of the historic, 'design had hitherto progressed with the very minimum of eclecticism and self-consciousness' (74). That self-consciousness about design history is what has characterized postmodern architecture theory, as articulated by Charles Jencks and Robert Venturi.[19] A future one glimpses in this moment of *Lares et Penates* contains both the rise and the critique of postmodernism at the other end of the century.

---

[18] T. S. Eliot, 'Tradition and the Individual Talent', *Selected Essays*, third enlarged edition (London: Faber and Faber Limited, 1951), 13–22 (14).

[19] See for example Charles Jencks's *The Language of Post-Modern Architecture* (1977).

Birnstingl is soberly diffident about prediction. Yet the way he sees home life developing is comparably perceptive about the role of mechanization in everyday domestic life. He says that coal will be replaced by 'low-carbonized coke' (84); and then:

> eventually all the heating, the cooking, and the hot-water supply will be provided by means of electricity. Electricity, too, will be used to clean the house, to wash up the plates, to do the laundrying. Also, by means of the judicious use of time-switches it will, to some extent, supersede human labour. Anyone, for instance, will be able to arrange to have themselves called in the morning at a certain hour with a cup of hot tea ready by the bedside, and a hot bath prepared a few minutes afterwards.   (84)

He was not inventing any of this technology. The electric vacuum cleaner was invented in 1899 and available from 1908. Washing machines, invented around 1900, were available from 1904. Dishwashers were a much more recent invention (from 1924), but lacked drying elements till 1940. Only the teasmade was still unmade; though that too had already been brewing since the 1890s. Yet his vision of all these machines becoming standard, and controlled automatically, is striking (and again uncannily anticipatory, here of the 'internet of things').

Birnstingl is not an infallible prophet of course. He thinks high-rise will fall. Though he discusses 'the most immense buildings' (90) in the US, he thinks they are planned to be obsolescent. Nonetheless, he predicts that concrete and steel will become the main materials, and anticipates standardized concrete houses, where pre-fab shuttering is supplied (90-1). He has the snobbery characteristic of the architectural critic of the period: 'the professional-class house will retain a modicum of dignity and orderliness of form; not so the lower-middle-class homes, which will be awful in their unmitigated vulgarity' (88). Yet he draws out the implication for the suburbs and rural areas that goes beyond snobbery, and expresses an anxiety about the countryside shared by other contributors (as we shall see): 'These houses will spread out from the towns in all directions in endless ribbon developments […]', he says, and gloomily anticipates a future in which all towns will interconnect:

> then haphazard incisions will be made into the *hinterland*, and as the undesecrated spots become rarer, so the scramble for them will become greater, but no material will be considered too mean, and no design too ugly, for a house to be set in surroundings of whatsoever loveliness, for by that time the senses will be deadened to impressions of ugliness and the mind too shallow to protest at the process of devastation.   (89)

Lares et Penates ends with a curiously literary flourish: a collage of putative journals from 1987, called *Urbanities* (a tasteless *Tatler*, sycophantically celebrating socialites paying vast sums for mid-Victorian vulgarities); the *Labour Savour* (discussing 'the all-galvanized tin housette'); and the *Morning Efficiency* promoting 'The Cotswold Exploitation Company' (92-5). It is not future history, but its parodies from and of the future have a similar effect, as prophecy is replaced by imaginary textual evidence of things to come.

Family and Law

A volume that imagines a very different future for the domestic environment is *Chronos; or, The Future of the Family* (1930), by Eden Paul, the Socialist doctor and writer who had helped Beatrice Webb and Charles Booth, and was the translator of (among other things) Marx's *Das Kapital*, as well as the son of the publisher Charles Kegan Paul. It is a short book even by the series' standard, and essentially advances one argument: that the family is not the same as a home; nor is it a natural but a historical and social category (39-40); that since the family is 'disintegrating' (51) largely due to sexual reform, those best suited to bringing up children are not always those most suited to having them. It is partly a eugenic argument about poor stock ('suspect heredity'; 28); and the belief that children should be regarded as offspring of the 'germ-plasm', rather than of the parents (29). But it also includes a radical proposal following from the latter for reorganizing education through new kinds of institutions which provide caring homes where adults can rear children who might include but are not restricted to their own. It therefore has much in common with the kinds of progressive reinvention of humanist thought along scientific lines discussed in Chapter 3; yet its focus on the institution of the bourgeois family rather than on the discipline of sociology demonstrates its relevance to a discussion of everyday familial and social life as well.

The two volumes on law in the series could also have been considered in Chapter 3, as attempts to rationalize outmoded disciplines. They both criticize the wilful obscurantism and elitism of the legal profession, and share the reformist agenda of many of the other volumes, arguing that the law needs to be made more intelligible, accessible, and affordable, to the masses. Yet that argument is an acknowledgement that law forms a part of everyday life for most people, at least potentially. To that extent, lawyers are the *Lares et Penates* of modernity.

Lycurgus; or, The Future of Law (1925), by E. S. P. Haynes, shares the eugenics-based views of the criminologists and others writing in the series that crime should be reconceived as disease rather than sin. He notes a 'growing tendency to determinism and to regard crimes and punishments purely in relation to social welfare' (34-5). Haynes was a man of letters who specialized in family law. He would act as Evelyn Waugh's divorce lawyer. Family law is a major concern in *Lycurgus*, which covers facilitation of divorce, ease of adoption, legitimization of a child by subsequent marriage, and guardianship in the case of divorce. Haynes predicts that a system of domestic courts will most likely be set up, as it had been in the United States.

C. P. Harvey's *Solon; or, The Price of Justice* (1931), as its title suggests, is more concerned with the economics of law. 'Litigation is a luxury within the reach only of millionaires and paupers' (15), he complains, and advocates an insurance scheme, by analogy with medical insurance. Like Haynes he considers the argument for the 'fusion' of barristers with solicitors, but does not believe it will improve matters. He gives witty and brisk accounts of key elements of the legal system: juries; evidence; pleadings (including an amusing version of the story of Jack and Jill written in this 'repellent' style); and appeals. He then concludes with the argument that to limit the number of appeals, and introduce insurance, would facilitate a 'substantial reduction in the price of justice' (103).

The Environment

The other architectural volume in the series, Christian Barman's *Balbus; or, The Future of Architecture* (1926), takes its engagement with everyday life out of the home and into the built environment. Barman had studied architecture at Liverpool University, and set up his own practice. In the 1930s he edited both the *Architect's Journal* and the *Architectural Review*. He was invited by Frank Pick to take up the post of Publicity Officer at London Transport in 1935, and after the Second World War worked for and wrote on railways. But he is best known as a designer of household appliances such as heaters, irons and hairdryers. His approach to the city is very much in terms of the relation between architecture and everyday life practices: walking, driving, shopping. It is a fascinating text in some ways, troubling in others.

Barman considers a definition of a building—'A building worth of the name of great architecture'—as being 'composed of a succession of spaces or cells'. This enables him to draw the analogy between the building and the body, and to argue that for both, 'the first essentials of beauty are to be found in the shape, disposition, and junction of this sequence of cells' (17). 'These are the important facts about a building', he says; and they 'are more fully revealed in a plan than in any other kind of drawing' (17). Or any other kind of representation, since this leads him into a distinction between plan and photograph:

> It is a significant fact that the chief vehicle of architectural information to-day, the most popular means of recording architectural excellence, is the photograph, not the plan, of which it is the direct opposite. The photograph expresses all that the plan leaves unsaid; it ignores all save a small remnant of the major qualities registered in the plan, and this remnant it twists and falsifies to a degree which renders its testimony worse than valueless. We still have to be shown the photograph that, representing the interior of a room, will convey a modicum of reliable information concerning the shape of that room. For in looking at a room through a photograph we are, be it remembered, looking at it through a small hole in a box. (24-5)

It is a revealing contrast, and one of the things it reveals is Barman's paradoxical position. As that note of vituperation in his dismissal of architectural photography suggests, he is not a monomaniac of the modern. He had written books on Vanbrugh, and St Paul's Cathedral. He is not wild about 'Marinetti's advice to use the altar of art as a spittoon', adding drily that it 'has not been altogether neglected by architects [...]' (24). Yet he was an industrial designer, and his championship of plan over photograph, for its revealing of form over surface, objectivity over point-of-view, is a classic modernist move.

Urban architecture, especially in the era of Trump towers and altitude rivalry, is often seen as the preserve of male egos and corporate phallic fantasies. Barman is more concerned with the ways in which the 'freedom of modern woman' is transforming architecture (21). If this is another note of his modernity, it too is ambivalent. What he means is that, 'as a consumer of wealth' she is the force determining why 'the large new drapery store assumes the characteristic form that will gradually impose itself upon many of our other buildings', because in its design 'no external wall must cut off the ground floor of the building from the pavement of the street, for the business can only succeed if the undreamt-of collection of goods is amply and seductively displayed to the feminine passer-by' (27). The words 'amply' and 'seductively' suggest that it is not only the merchandise causing arousal. This follows immediately from a passage about the Suffragettes, whose 'stones went crashing through the windows of the Government offices in Whitehall', whereas 'the newly erected windows of Mr Gordon Selfridge became the cynosure of the more pacific among feminine eyes' (26-7). Selfridge was a prominent supporter of the Suffragettes, and when one of the windows of his store was smashed he refused to press charges. Women's increased post-war economic independence, and the fact that some now had the vote, had increased their power, yes. But there is something odd about attributing to their agency changes in architecture which the shop owners implemented to profit from women's new disposable income. Barman sees the architect as powerless in the face of such cultural shifts: 'The architect is a servant only, and these things are the business of his master' (21). But when 'the master fails to attend to them [...] we get a building without a content [...] there is nothing to give its cells any particular shape, or to suggest or enforce any particular disposition of these cells'; 'This is the typical building of to-day and to-morrow':

> Inside the buildings [...] no walls are wanted at any point, on any of the floors, and there we find large open spaces offering no obstruction to the view, and allowing counters and show-cases to be moved backwards and forwards with the capricious tides of fashion. No longer is the building composed of an expressive sequence of definitely formed cavities; there is only layer upon layer of formless space, tier upon tier of vacant sites, along which the hundred specialized departments may pitch their glittering booths. It no more resembles a piece of major architecture than does a market-place with awnings and sunshades. (27-8)

He calls it the '[t]he new eviscerated architecture', and says it 'did not take long to gain a very considerable following' (29). He bemoans the transformation by such buildings of London's high-end shopping streets in Kensington, Bayswater, and Regent Street and Oxford Street; and is concerned how the concept is spreading beyond the department store:

> The possibilities of open-floor design for all kinds of building were, then, abundantly exhibited and widely perceived. From shop and factory the new device spread to the office block, whose claim to be in the modern movement is not usually admitted unless it consists of the same succession of shelf-like floors suspended round a central road. Schools and universities have already subscribed to the principle of unformed and undivided space.   (33)

'And what of the house and home?' he asks: 'Are we to meet there, too, with the same undefined vacuity, the same absence of internal form' (33-4). Again, the insistence on form and definition that might sound modernist, but which is pitted against the modernist dogma (which the open-plan store exemplifies impeccably) of form following function. Again, the ambivalent attribution of agency to the modern woman. Barman thinks the post-war house an improvement on the late-Victorian impracticably cavernous houses that seemed 'to derive from the cathedrals and dungeons of the Middle Ages' (61); and he is prepared to give the modern woman credit for the change: 'Instead of losing purpose and definition, like the typical city building, it has gained vastly in both these qualities, and it has gained because, from being the scene of the housewife's activities, it has become her instrument and ally, and sometimes (it must be admitted) her accomplice even' (62). The 'housewife' is of course not necessarily the same as the economically independent consumer, let alone the Suffragette. And there is a hint in that curious comment about the house becoming her 'accomplice' that she has again, architecturally speaking, done something she should not have done. What this seems to mean is that, if she was responsible for restoring a logical, cellular plan to the design of houses, she was now beginning to preside over another architectural revolution, this time throwing the concept of plan, and even the house itself, out of its own window:

> The next step, indeed, has already been taken. It is possible even now to watch the modern residence gradually assuming the properties of a machine. At the beginning of the last century nine-tenths of the cost of a house went into the structure, while the remaining tenth paid for its fixtures and equipment. Nowadays we spend almost as much on drains and plumbing, on baths and closets, on bedroom lavatory basins supplied with hot water, on central heating, electric light, telephones and suchlike, as we spend on the building of the house. So remarkable has been this development that an American writer has prophesied a period when houses will be given away free with the plumbing. It is doubtful whether such munificence will ever become a commercial possibility, but the prophecy contains more than a modicum of truth.

It sounds like Barman too was familiar with Le Corbusier's epigram that 'A house is a machine for living in'; and he presumably saw Corbusier's Pavilion de l'Esprit Nouveau at the International Exhibition of Decorative Arts in Paris that he mentions having visited the previous year (72). Here too, Barman's anxiety is that domestic architecture, which he thought had just regained its sense of the formal logic of space, was now about to lose it again. And once again: if in panic, *cherchez la femme*. Who else would insist on those 'bedroom lavatory basins' (nowadays just called basins or hand-basins), and then even more unreasonably insist they were plumbed in with hot water?

> We may reasonably expect to see all but the most indispensable furniture done away with in the small house of to-morrow, while its walls, ceilings, and doors will assume a blankness and roundedness that has hitherto been thought need-ful only in the operating chambers of our hospitals. In order still to reduce the housewife's labours, the apartments will be brought together in those vast blocks that are meeting with such strenuous opposition from private householders in the United States, an opposition to which the zoning authorities have almost invariably given every support.   (62-3)

Barman is more appreciative of women's new consumer influence on decoration, which he demonstrates curiously via a comparison of two nineteenth-century French novels a generation or two apart. In Gautier's *Mademoiselle de Maupin* (1835), he complains, the romantic nature cult means that landscapes are described in loving detail, but interiors and exteriors of buildings not at all (66-7). Whereas in Zola's *Nana*, he is excited by the heroine's (and Zola's) passion for ever more elegant décor. Few readers of these risqué novels of transvestism, love tri-angles, and prostitution can have been so interested in their implicit history of interior design. Barman's point is that the change in attitude through the century 'has infused new life into modern decoration' (69). But in *Balbus* the 'housewife' is also held responsible for tower blocks. It is not immediately clear why relocating up many flights of stairs or a lift-shaft saves labour. But Barman presumably means that she would be able to live nearer to shops, schools, and the like, so would be saved the labour of driving or travelling. That is why he brings in the idea of 'zoning' here—the restriction of the kinds of use that plots of land can be put to, such as residential, commercial, industrial, and so on. Zoning, he explains, differs from London-style height restrictions (intended for stability, regulation of light, and fire-safety). It is concerned 'to regulate capacity alone' (46), and can be achieved if facades are broken up into 'receding vertical planes, each separated from the next by a narrow terrace' (47).

Zoning matters to Barman because it is a means of regulating traffic congestion, by controlling the relation between population density and road capacity. Though To-Day and To-Morrow shows less interest than we might expect in the city as the site of the everyday life of the future, *Balbus* offers its most serious account of the need for urban planning; and one articulated not through the totalitarian modernist schemes for urban utopias, but through thinking about the everyday business of moving ourselves and our necessities about. He notes that '[w]hile the growth of building merely tended to become proportionate to the growth of the population, it was necessary that the means of communication should increase at a much faster rate' (39). Communication here includes people being compelled to move around more rapidly, but also the need for 'their various belongings, their food and drink, the materials and products of their labour [including the things they send in the post], the waste left over from their individual and corporate metabolism', also to be transported with every greater speed (40). No wonder, he says, that 'the London traffic authorities complain that the more facilities they are able to provide, the greater becomes the demand made upon those facilities' (40-1). He turns poet of the road as he marvels at:

> The long, heroic struggle of nineteenth-century scientists and legislators to perfect this great and complicated thing, the modern road, or marvel to see them extend it hither and thither, and guard it from encroachments, and level and straighten out its trajectory, and search out a firm foundation for it, and render its surface hard and impervious, and dry it, clean it, illuminate it, and at last equip it for the automatic distribution of water and fuel, and for a continuous scavenging of all our towns.

> It is this remarkable achievement of civilized man that to-day threatens to become ineffective.   (41)

A different feeling of threat to civilization disturbs his account of contemporary Paris. He has been discussing the increasing imbalance in numbers of men and women in Western Europe, which he unchivalrously describes as 'the excess of women' (71). But then something other suddenly irrupts:

> One of the most distressing sights to be met with in Paris to-day is the large number of coloured and mostly negroid males that is gradually being assimilated by the white population. There are some even who predict that France will soon have become a bi-coloured republic. Should this unpleasant prophecy be realized, the present excess of white females will no doubt go a long way to account for the change.   (71-2)

'Whether or not this excess has done anything to stimulate the new movement in decoration it is, of course, impossible to say [...]' (72). He thinks it has, because the only modern country where the new decoration has not caught on is the US, where men outnumber women. But it is his racist comment which comes across as 'excess'. It clearly has nothing to do with decoration; only with his 'distress'; which is presumably at least in part a fear that those naughty women, not content with spoiling the architecture of the high street and the home, will mess up the eugenics of the British race as they are doing to the French. Here it is the power of female sexuality, rather than of economic empowerment, that distresses him; and which perhaps explains his recourse to French novels, and especially to those French novels.

That Barman was thinking of eugenics is also suggested by his comment that 'the tenants of the buildings we put up will before long have ceased to multiply' (77). This leads him to prophesy wrongly that the population will fall, building capacity will finally be adequate to demand, and 'the great age of city-building' will be over (78). But when he asks what will follow, his question—'Are we to meet, after failing to grasp the illusive opportunities of town-planning, with new, and real, and unexhausted opportunities of country-planning?' (78)—he touches on a subject exercising a number of contributors; and also sounds an environmentalist note that his discussion of cities does not sustain.

'On every side a wail is rising over the irreparable damage that is being done to the rural England that we all claim to love', begins *Rusticus; or, The Future of the Countryside* (1927), by the architectural historian of the Baroque, Martin S. Briggs. He imagines a traveller (like Doughty or Kinglake) returning after twenty years, and noticing the changes (11). Chalk downs, trees, old walls, have been cut through 'to allow the cars and charabancs to roar through the countryside. But is it countryside any longer?' (10). The 'New Architecture' 'appears to consist mainly of Bungalows' (10). He sketches 'the charm of the unspoiled English village and landscape before coal and petrol began to dominate our whole life' (12), noting that 'Admiration for the beauty of the countryside seems to be a very modern cult' (24)—a function, that is, of its perceived loss. 'For a century coal was the dominant factor in English life', he says: 'but since 1910 petrol has played the main part in altering the aspect of the countryside' (26-7). He then devotes a chapter each to 'King Coal' and 'The Age of Petrol'. His view of the road, by contrast with Barman, is a dystopian one:

> Few of us foresaw that the clumsy and not very speedy vehicles which made their first appearance on our highways some thirty years ago, preceded by a man bearing a red flag, would eventually cause so radical a change in our ideas of the nature of a road. (46-7)

The development of the road system has led to the 'mad race from towns to the fringe of the country [which] is destroying the country for miles round' (45): a race to escape from the towns not just to use the countryside as a playground for day-trips, but also as a place to live and commute from. Hence those objectionable bungalows. In an extraordinary moment Briggs even suggests that what he sees as the destruction of the rural is the product of a war mentality, which has turned the countryside into a war-zone (as it did in Flanders):

> There was a great and genuine demand for houses after the War, which had to be satisfied. Nine people out of ten took what they could get, and they got bungalows. For the most part their *ménage* consisted of a husband, wife, and a two-seater.

Neither servants nor children entered into the picture. There was a prejudice against everything connected with the pre-War period, especially with its social distinctions, and perhaps the ex-service man sought for the antithesis of the suburban villa. Accustomed for four years to scenes of ruin and to leaky Army huts, his mind readily accepted the slap-dash bungalow with its familiar barbed-wire fence and no-man's-land of a garden.   (57)

As the presence (and indeed absence) of those servants indicates, this is an analysis riven by class. Despite Briggs's ostensible sympathy with the needs of the demobilized soldiers, and their financial constraints, his contempt for what they were prepared to accept matches their 'prejudice' *against* class with an aesthetic prejudice which is transparently ideological. The *Daily Telegraph*'s praise of *Rusticus* is thus unsurprising; though it conveys the book's appeal: 'Few of the fifty volumes, provocative and brilliant as most of them have been, capture our imagination as does this one'.[20]

As the towns make in-roads into the countryside, the future for Briggs, as for Barman, is one in which the regime of 'planning' accepted for towns needs to be extended to the country. 'At the present time, when authorities on town-planning have long made it clear that orderly development is both desirable and practicable', he writes, 'the haphazard growth of suburbs into the country is a deplorable and even a painful sight to every intelligent person' (43); and he advocates a new crusade 'for the preservation of rural England' (91). He is more positive about the everyday life of British cities, praising the 'great development of municipal housing after the War' (75), and noting that 'The Underground Railways in and round London are employing clever artists to design their stations and notices and posters' (79). What he most fears is modernity entailing further Americanization:

Untidiness, ugliness, lack of respect for history and beauty, an insane craze for speed in getting from one futile pursuit to another, blatant advertisement, sordid commercialism—these are some of the things we have borrowed from American life to vulgarise our own.   (93)

But when Americans come to the UK, he notes, what they most value is what has been preserved.

Leisure

C. E. M. Joad's *Diogenes; or, The Future of Leisure* (1928) has characteristically trenchant and cynical things to say about many of the topics covered in *Rusticus*. 'Yes, we all love the country, and in confessing it we pay an indirect compliment to ourselves', he says: 'But most of us love it best in books'; adding that: 'In real life

---

[20] Review quoted from the end-matter of C. P. Harvey's *Solon; or, The Price of Justice* (1931).

it is damp, muddy, and liable to give us rheumatism, intolerably dull in winter and most disliked by those whose love is the most vocal' (25). His generation, he says, 'found England a land of beauty and left it a land of "beauty spots"' (35). Like Briggs, though verbally more clinical, he despises 'bungaloid growths' (37), and the 'red rash' of suburbia's 'advancing armies' (28). 'Thus the country changes at our approach and transforms itself into suburb' (28).

Everyday suburban life of cars and commuting cannot expect to escape his scorn, all the funnier for being self-inflected. 'We all of us own cars, and our garages, symbols of the coming domination of machines, impend largely over the pigmy residences of their owners' (37). The paradox of commuter life is that: 'Except for Saturday afternoon, when we go out in the car, we are never in the country at all' (37). Needless to say, we are no more there when we are in the car:

> It has been truly said of our generation that it has discovered the country. We spawn over it in our hideous dwellings, we drive pitilessly over it for our pleasure, we rile it and tame it, and make it tidy and uniform and regular and genteel, and every now and then we dress it up in beauty spots, that we may render it a land fit for stockbrokers and actresses to joy-ride in. We do these things to the country because we do not know how to enjoy it, because it intimidates us when we enter it, making us feel little and strange and vulgar. And to punish it and put ourselves at ease with it we make it vulgar like ourselves, stamping the marks of our civilization indelibly upon it.   (39)

The stockbroker and actress, and their joy-riding, would not be out of place in Auden, though the sadism of their violent subjugation of the natural reaches back to Lawrence and Freud. The humour is Joad's own, though, as when he directs it at 'Motors', and mercilessly dismantles the possible reasons why people spend so much time driving (40-5). You don't see the country. It's not restful. It's not exhilarating. It's not for speed. Indeed,

> [t]he faster we try to go the slower do we succeed in going, so that in London at the hub of civilization, where progress is exhibited at the height of its development clear for all to see, we have almost stopped moving altogether.   (43)

He says he hopes motoring will be prohibited as 'a criminal occupation' (45).

Joad's thoughts about the country and the suburbs are part of his broader thesis about leisure and its future; which is that we do not know how to enjoy not only the countryside, but anything. This because, as he says at the outset,

> Civilised man spends rather more than two-thirds of his waking life in obtaining the means to make life possible; he has only one third left for living. As a consequence, he is a shocking bungler in the art of life through sheer lack of practice.   (7)

People assume 'the knowledge of how to live rightly is instinctive'; but civilized life is artificial, and 'All good tastes are acquired' (7). He diagnoses two errors: the direct pursuit of pleasure; and the 'false notion of entertainment as something for which one pays' (11); false because 'satisfaction can only be momentary' (12). 'This at least is the gospel according to Schopenhauer' (13), he says. By contrast, 'work is the only occupation yet invented which mankind has been able to endure in any but the smallest possible doses' (19), because it offers escape from 'the selfish little pit of vanity and desire which is the self' (20).

But then there is income to be disposed of. The papers are full of experts advising how to make money, but none on how to spend it (53). So 'Having lost the capacity to amuse ourselves we pay other people to do our amusing for us' (53). In a marvellous moment discussing the photographs in the papers of Bank Holiday amusements, he comments: 'The object of these pictures is to show people how they enjoyed themselves' (64), managing to imply that what passes for enjoyment appears so unpleasurable that people are not even aware they are enjoying themselves unless it is explained to them retrospectively. In the example he discusses,

> One picture is of a jam of immobile cars, another of adults struggling for the privilege of riding upon the Zoo elephants, another of a crowd at Brighton looking for Mr. Lobby Lud, another of people queuing up for a performance on the pier. (64)

Brighton Rock, anyone? He is struck by the recurrence of queues, and recounts a story about an interview with a woman who had queued for twenty-four hours for a ticket for a show, who said 'Oh, I just love waiting in a queue. There's always plenty of company and I like someone to talk to', adding that she would 'rather be queuing up for a good show than sitting with the old man at home' (64). 'This is, perhaps, the strangest use of leisure which I have to record' (64), says Joad, strangely, since he has also recorded that 'A frequent use of leisure is for the purpose of hunting and terrifying animals. There are many people who consider that the good life consists in depriving other creatures of life' (49).

The only way of spending one's leisure he does not satirize is reading (60-1). It needs no special apparatus. No other people, special mood, or special weather conditions are required. It is not dependent on time or place. It awakens curiosity and stimulates; diverts attention from matter to thought. Books are 'the great commentators and interpreters of life' (63). What is more, 'a book is an enhancement of rather than a distraction from life' (63); it helps us to see more. The thinking man's prosthesis.

For the last third of his own interpretation of everyday life, Joad turns to the future. Casting aside the virtually obligatory diffidence in tele-prophecy, which restricts most of the contributors to looking no more than fifty years or a generation or so ahead, Joad's shorter-term future dial is set to 300 years, based on (though not entirely subscribing to) a Marxist confidence in a plan with historical inevitability. He postulates 'that people are reasonable and that the transition to Socialism is accomplished gradually without a catastrophic upheaval'. Then 'we may envisage in, say, three hundred years time, a world in which poverty and overwork are abolished' (68). How then, he asks, would people spend their leisure? 'How, assuming the persistence of present conceptions, would they utilize the vast tracts of leisure at their disposal?' (68). The satirical dystopian prophecy he conjures up is, he concedes, 'a depressing picture' (68-71). The countryside will vanish, either from development, or from being transported to America. The sea coast will become like the Riviera. 'Pseudo-religions will spring up like mush-rooms' (69).

Cynics, one might deduce, clearly make the best prophets—even if the version of socialism that is now beginning to look increasingly likely, of governments guaranteeing a basic wage independently of work done, will be driven by hyper-capitalism plus artificial intelligence, rather than acceptance of Marxist doctrine. But when Joad ups the warp factor of his tele-prophecy to 'the beings who will be inhabiting this planet in, say, fifty or a hundred thousand years' (72), his projec-tion of the future of leisure turns decidedly stranger and darker. First, he sum-mons up the imagined world of the last play of George Bernard Shaw's 'Metabiological Pentateuch' *Back to Methuselah* (1921), in which Shaw, whose Nobel Prize was not for diffidence, prophesies a mere 30,000 years ahead in *As Far as Thought Can Reach: A.D. 31,920.* In Joad's summary of the progress of Shaw's 'Ancients' in this play: 'having exhausted the emotions to be derived from sex at the age of two, they proceed to art, which occupies them until they are four' (72). They then turn from 'images only of reality' to reality itself, which for Shaw is a matter of mind: 'the vast tracts of their prodigious lives are indeed devoted entirely to that study of reality, which in its initial stages in logic, mathematics, and science we to-day call thought' (73). 'The body is the last toy to be given up, and, when that final emancipation has been achieved, there will be no people but only thought, so that life becomes a whirlpool of pure intelligence, which began as a whirlpool of pure force' (73).

Given Joad's philosophical bent, love of books, and Schopenhauerian scepti-cism about the pleasures of the body, we might expect him to embrace this Shavian vision. Certainly, thinking is an essential part of his vision of the good everyday life. Yet he calls it an unattractive prospect, saying its

> ultimate destiny of the species is unlikely to be acclaimed with enthusiasm. A life devoid of love, or art, or of amusement, devoted to the contemplation of immutable entities [...] is not likely to appeal to the ordinary sensual, twentieth century man.   (74)

Yet he puts his finger on the ethical paradox of prophecy, observing: 'we have no right to judge the pursuits of the future by the tastes of the present; the amoeba would probably fail to enjoy a modern football match' (74). His concluding sec-tion suggests that:

> there are already to-day certain signs and portents pointing Ancient-ward, and that it is only by giving heed to them and moulding our lives in accordance with

the indications which to the discerning eye they present, that we can escape the hell of boredom and restlessness to which our present misuse of leisure is likely to bring us.   (75)

In other words, just when he seemed to have shifted from the dissection of everyday life into science fiction, Joad then draws out the tendencies of present everyday life that seem to him to indicate a metaphysical future. Considering both the recent stages in human evolution (as the biological volumes like *Galatea* and *Metanthropos* had), and the kinds of biochemical interventions already beginning, and being discussed by Haldane, Joad says: 'Everything points to the view that our present power over the body will be still further increased in the future' (90). That was the direction in which Bernal would be prophesying the following year. Mechanization too Joad sees as a metaphysical affair: 'We have in fact delegated our intercourse with material objects to machines'; the raison d'être of machines being 'to release us from the need to concern ourselves with matter' (91). At this point his thought takes a Bergsonian or Lamarckian turn. Evolution, Joad argues, is 'purposive'; that purpose being to turn to new kinds of experience—he cites the Hegelian triad of goals for the phenomenology of mind: the religious, the ethical, and the aesthetic—and to emancipate itself from 'the necessity to concern itself with matter' (93). But what concerns Joad is that most current leisure puts us back in touch with matter: 'The most frequent use of leisure is to play games, most of which consist in hitting small round bits of matter with long thin ones' (94). This is a cause of anxiety, for the Schopenhauerian reason he has already given: 'Life will resolve itself into a succession of pleasures which increasingly fail to please' (96). Which, besides being depressing in itself, summons up the shadow looming over so much of the series: 'the increase of leisure will produce a restlessness and a craving for excitement which will render war an ever present possibility' (96-7). 'It is often said that the only way by which men may avoid war is by sublimating the energies that make for conflict [...]' (97), he too says. But he thinks we shall need a new method: 'a sublimation which will divert our energies not from killing men to breaking records, but away from the world of matter altogether' (97). Before we dismiss such a notion of pure intellectuality being the answer to human problems as the fantasy of intellectuals, we should consider the ubiquity of computing now, and the incremental emergence of AI.

It is in this last section that the force of Joad's title becomes felt. Diogenes of Sinope was notorious for his indifference to civilized comforts, as well as his mockery of social institutions and establishment figures, including both Alexander and Plato. Joad ends on a surprisingly upbeat note given the tenor of the rest of the book, asserting that 'effort in the world of thought' is 'as real and as exciting as effort in the world of matter'; that 'life has now reached a stage at which such effort alone is permanently satisfying' (99); and that it is 'to thinking, to reading, to writing, and to creating, that our leisure, if it is to be a pleasure and not a boredom, will in the future be devoted' (100). As he acknowledges, such advice is not in itself new. Indeed, his belief that 'the only thing which can give permanent satisfaction is the employment of our best faculties at their highest pitch, alternating with the recreation of the mind in music and art and literature and the conversation of our friends' (100) is reminiscent of the *Principia Ethica* of the Cambridge philosopher and inspiration for the Bloomsbury Group, G. E. Moore a quarter of a century before.[21]

That such views were 'in the air' is also indicated by a volume with an antithetical focus, Cecil Chisholm's *Vulcan; or, The Future of Labour* (1927). As we saw in Chapter 4, Chisholm argued that scientific management would make workers feel increasingly dehumanized. The resulting monotony will strengthen the unions, leading to demands for shorter hours. He sees this as culminating in a one-day week—a prediction that seems extraordinary to our ever longer-working workforce, but which demonstrates why the future of leisure seemed such a pressing concern a century ago. Chisholm's naïvety about the ownership of the means of mass production means that he thinks everyone will be wealthy (again an understandable delusion given that Ford was credited with making the workforce more affluent). This leads him to a conclusion similar to Joad's, that education will help people to cultivate 'the art of living', so that 'the age of extravagance must give way to the age of culture' (95).

As I hope the preceding discussion has brought out, the attention to everyday life produced some of To-Day and To-Morrow's most interesting and also entertaining volumes. One of the best is *Atalanta; or, The Future of Sport* (1928), by the art critic (and later, unsuccessful Labour candidate for Chelsea in 1935), G[eorge]. S. Sandilands. Sandilands shares Joad's gift for observing the absurdities surrounding leisure pursuits. In a chapter on blood sports, he mocks those—like foxhunting—which pit man against animal without giving the animal any chance of victory. Of sports pitting man against man, he says of duelling: 'For some obscure reasons a man's "honour" was supposed to depend upon his willingness to fight for his life when called upon to do so by any unscrupulous scoundrel' (20). Turning to animal v. animal sports produces a marvellous satire of horse-racing:

> To such a frenzy of altruistic enthusiasm does the sight of the exquisite creatures work upon the spectators that all of them almost without exception, are consumed with a passionate desire to give away all their wealth to one another. Here is true sportsmanship at last.   (29)

Unfortunately this aesthetic susceptibility does not issue in aesthetic effects: 'Notwithstanding the fact that the trained race-horse in action is one of the most beautiful sights imaginable, the regular race-going public is one of the most inartistic sections of the whole community' (30). Again like Joad, he turns his irony on ball games; though differently; by treating them (with mock piety) as part of the story of human creativity and genius: 'Among the unhonoured benefactors of

---

[21] See G. E. Moore, *Principia Ethica* (Cambridge: Cambridge University Press, 1903), 188.

humanity surely the one who stands serenely supreme is the man or woman who invented a ball' (34). Conversely, he asks why human ingenuity might not do for sport what it has done for war: 'Considering the destructive and entirely negative use to which great scientific inventions have been put, is it too much to ask that a way of rapidly drying a cricket pitch may be found?' (56).

Women had been participating in some of the Olympic Games since 1900, but were excluded from track and field events. Women's Olympiads were staged from 1921 to campaign for representation in all sports. Sandilands' comments on women in sport sound amusing in a dated, chauvinist way now; as when he writes: 'Like most fast women, Atalanta loved to be pursued' (57). (Though he also turns the myth to prefigure the strange modern phenomenon of people playing sport for a living: 'It had been a very bad year for apples, and Atalanta could not resist the strong temptation to turn professional'; 58.) His remarks on the 1922 Women's Olympiad are nonetheless classically revealing of the changing ethos of the period—and of the immense differences made to everyday life by such details liable to be passed over even by social historians. It was, he says, 'almost a revolution—and extremely immodest. Girls appeared in running shorts, and revealed great lengths of unclad legs. Even naked thighs were displayed—and displayed *as if they didn't matter*' (73); adding that: 'prurient people (i.e. all of us) discovered yet again that a woman's legs are far less indecent than her underclothing' (73). His difficulty in keeping a straight face was not helped by the Secretary of the Women's Amateur Athletic Association explaining that: 'girls were going to be taught how to use their legs' (73). Readers of Ford Madox Ford's *Parade's End* can learn much from *Atalanta* about the context of Ford's presentation of the athletic character Valentine Wannop.

Some of Sandilands' predictions are in a more serious vein. 'The twentieth century will be remembered as the "International Century"' (104). He anticipates cheap air travel and winter holidays in the sun, though was misled by this correct prophecy into a false one that 'the football grounds of the future will be deserted' (107-8). His thought that sport would be used as an antidote to industrial degeneration has been fulfilled in the form of the omnipresent fitness club (112). If we still await the realization of his hope (again close to Joad's) that international sport will reduce the warring spirit (115), it is probably because he is not entirely serious; as in his conclusion, arguing that since hitherto, war has been the main international activity. 'Could we not for a change have the delightful uncertainty of sport?' (116).

Conclusion: War and the Life of Everyday Life

That both Joad and Sandilands end wondering about the future relations of leisure to war provides further evidence of war's shadow; of how it had become impossible to imagine the future without imagining future warfare. As Paul

Saint-Amour argues in *Tense Future*, the traumatic experience of the First World War had produced a future-orientated trauma of the anticipation of war's repetition.[22]

Yet To-Day and To-Morrow tells another story too (as touched on in Chapter 2); one that was also being told in the fiction, poetry, and drama of the period: a story in which one of the after-effects of war is a renewed attention to life. Richard Aldington, for example, attacked what seemed to him the morbidity of T. S. Eliot's poetry, via a parody of 'The Hollow Men':

> A greatly admired poem by the most admired poet of the day may be sum-
> marized in the following excerpted words:
>   Hollow-dried-meaningless-dry-broken-dry-paralysed-death's-hollow-I-dare-
> not-death's-broken-fading-death's-final-twilight-dead-cactus-stone-dead-
> fading-death's-broken-dying-broken-last-sightless-death.
>   The poet's genius is not in question, but I hate this exhibitionism of a perpet-
> ual suicide mania which never, never, comes to the point....It is the War despair
> which involved so many of us and from which the healthy-minded have been
> struggling to escape, not yearning to wallow in.[23]

Yet in *The Waste Land* April is 'the cruellest month' because it is trying to bring 'the dead land' back to life: 'breeding / Lilacs', and 'stirring / Dull roots with spring rain'. Aldington was reinventing his pre-war Imagist poet self as a post-war novelist, and switching allegiances from Eliot to D. H. Lawrence in the process. Lawrence's *Lady Chatterley's Lover* is the classic example of the interwar novel in which war-damaged veterans try to get back in touch with a sense of life and its processes. The best-known passage in Virginia Woolf's best known, and immediately post-war, essay, 'Modern Fiction', starts by asking of the Edwardian fiction of Bennett, Wells, and Galsworthy: 'Is life like this? Must novels be like this?', and answering:

> Look within and life, it seems, is very far from being 'like this'. [....] Life is not a
> series of gig lamps symmetrically arranged; life is a luminous halo, a
> semi-transparent envelope surrounding us from the beginning of conscious-
> ness to the end.[24]

If the attempt to invent new definitions and representations of the nature of everyday life is less present in British drama of the period (then under the sway of the bedroom farce and Hollywood romantic comedy), it is nonetheless audible

---

[22] His book is discussed further in the Conclusions.

[23] Richard Aldington, *Sunday Referee* (15 December 1929): quoted Charles Doyle, *Richard Aldington: A biography* (Carbondale and Edwardsville, IL: Southern Illinois University Press, 1989), 148–9. See my *Self Impression* (Oxford: Oxford University Press, 2010), 426–37, for further discussion of these relationships.

[24] Virginia Woolf, 'Modern Fiction', in *The Essays of Virginia Woolf. Volume 4: 1925 to 1928*, ed. Andrew McNeillie (London: The Hogarth Press, 1984), 157–65 (160).

in work by the two dominating figures in British dramaturgy: Shaw's *Back to Methuselah*, as we have seen; and arguably, though in clipped-down form, in Noel Coward's *Private Lives* (1930) and *Design for Living* (1932).

The redesign of everyday life in To-Day and To-Morrow represents another version of this new attention given to what it means (and what it will mean) to be alive. W. J. Turner, in *Orpheus; or, The Music of the Future* (1926), also turns to Eliot, quoting 'Gerontion', and commenting: 'The bravest, the most intelligent, the most sensitive are oppressed with that profoundest sense of the futility of life which Mr. Eliot expresses so admirably [...]' (83-4). And yet: 'in the midst of futility and inanity, in the midst of desperation and despair, there sounds the music of Beethoven' (85). To Turner, Beethoven's 'agony' makes Eliot's disillusion-ment seem 'feeble and superficial' (85). Turner's use of the Orpheus myth—itself an example of the 'mythic method' Eliot identified in Joyce—is chosen not just for Orpheus' association with the lyre, but for his attempt to win Eurydice back from what Eliot (in 'The Hollow Men') calls 'death's dream kingdom'. Turner is also clearly influenced by Eliot's theory of tradition. But his book is based on the more Lawrentian idea that the new in music is a dialectical experience of life and death together:

> There is a universal tendency to this intellectual formalizing, stereotyping pro-cess which I have called knowledge or death; and contrasted with it everywhere is a complementary process, the process of creation or life. But the one is neces-sary to the other and all experience is the one becoming the other.   (30)

'Music, therefore', claims Turner, 'is experience becoming knowledge and knowledge breaking up and becoming experience [....] Music is the experience of life and death in *sound*' (30).

That sense of everyday leisure pursuits being matters of life and death is in tune with the arguments of Joad, Sandilands and others. But Joad's discussion of *Back to Methuselah* signposts a fork in the paths leading to the future. Shaw's 'Ancients' have evolved via a kind of Lamarckian process to become bodiless vortices of energy travelling wherever they wish. In Shaw's or Joad's view, such development is a natural one, but one which expresses human will and intelligence—merely an extrapolation of the evolution of human intelligence which has already occurred. But even allowing for a Lamarckian means of accelerating evolution by passing on characteristics developed during an individual life, Shaw's 30,000 year span seems too short to accomplish such quantum changes, given the fifteen million years evolution has taken to get from the hominid great apes to *homo sapiens sapiens*. Shaw's metabiology was palpably an influence on and a challenge to J. D. Bernal too, whose *The World, the Flesh and the Devil* has similar ambitions: the liberation of humanity from the constraints of physical location, aging and even mortality; and the emancipation from the body into a world of thought—and of thought that will represent a step-change from existing notions of rationality.[25] Yet for Bernal 30,000 years is too long to wait. Humanity is likely to have destroyed itself long before then if it is not able to transcend its current nature and limitations first. That is why Shaw's self-congratulatory title, *As Far as Thought Can Reach*, was a provocation. Bernal's implication is that Shaw's thought has not reached very far, certainly no further than the kind of Lamarckianism that had made a comeback in the early 1920s in the work of Paul Kammerer on amphibians, but which had been roundly discredited by 1926.[26] For Bernal, what determines the reach of thought is not time but technology. So he (like Haldane) proposes technological and biomedical intervention in the evolutionary process, to transform ourselves by space travel, prosthetics and electro-magnetic interconnexion. He thus provides a methodology he thinks can actually get us to Shavian immortality, extra-terrestriality and pure intellectuality, and get us there much sooner; but a methodology in which these things actually would go beyond what Shaw had imagined, since his immortals seem a throwback to classical or religious metaphysical conceptions of the spirit. Whereas what Bernal envisages is something radically new: a scientifically-achieved collective and interplanetary mentality that would take thought into a new realm. It is as far from everyday life as anybody had imagined. But what it recognizes is how the notion of 'life'—like our understanding of the human, or of nature—would never be the same given our knowledge of evolution and genetics, and the beginnings of a bioscience devoted to transforming both.

One young intellectual who would play a crucial role in the development of cultural studies and the observation of everyday life was certainly paying attention. By the time Charles Madge went up to Cambridge in 1931, where he had won a scholarship to study at Magdalene—Ogden's and Richards' College—he had already drafted a book intended for inclusion in the series entitled 'Arethusa or the Future of Enthusiasm' which dealt with 'applied psychology in the context of industrial society'.[27] In the typed up version of the autograph manuscript, the title-word 'Arethusa' (the nymph transformed into a fountain, associated by Virgil with poetic inspiration) has been replaced with the name of the pioneering orator Isocrates. When he recalled writing it in his autobiography sixty years later he

---

[25] J. D. Bernal, *The World, the Flesh and the Devil* (1929) does not mention George Bernard Shaw's *Back to Methuselah* (1921) by title (nor does it mention Joad), but it does refer to 'Shaw's Immortals' (68).

[26] E. A. Mowrer's *Sinon; or, The Future of Politics* (1930), 61, writes of 'the still dubious thesis of Lamarck'. For an example of neo-Lamarckian thought in the series, see W. Russell Brain's *Galatea; or, The Future of Darwinism* (1927); discussed in Chapter 1.

[27] The quotation is from Charles Madge's unpublished autobiography (1987), 23, in the University of Sussex archives with the manuscript and typescript of 'Arethusa'. I am grateful to Rose Lock, the Senior Archive Assistant at the University, for information about the manuscript. Kegan Paul did not have a series called 'Books of the Future' (though the Science Fiction Club of London did in the 1950s). Neither the archive of Madge's correspondence at Sussex, nor the various collections of Ogden's papers, include any evidence of whether the manuscript was submitted for publication.

mis-remembered the series title as 'Books of the Future'. But it is clear from his choices of classical title, the futurological subtitle, and length of the text—and indeed from his citing of *Daedalus* and *Lars Porsena* as representative volumes—that Madge meant To-Day and To-Morrow. Nick Hubble in his excellent study of Mass Observation, says of this, and Madge's voracious reading at the time: 'it can be seen that even before he reached Cambridge, Madge's education had already fitted him for the uniquely varied career he was to follow':[28] surrealist poet, journalist, communist, founder (with Tom Harrisson) of the Mass Observation project in 1937, and later, professor of Sociology. What can also be seen is that his reading of, and writing for, To-Day and To-Morrow was part of his preparation for this transformational career exploring the analysis of everyday life.

Fig. 6. J. B. S. Haldane (left), Aldous Huxley (centre), and Lewis Gielgud at Oxford, 1914

---

[28] Nick Hubble, *Mass Observation and Everyday Life: Culture, history, theory* (Basingstoke: Palgrave Macmillan, 2005), 46.

LARS PORSENA
OR
THE FUTURE OF SWEARING AND IMPROPER LANGUAGE
By
ROBERT GRAVES

The author discusses modern swearing with a poet's frankness; as a breach of religious and social taboo—here he points out that the decline of blasphemy can only mean the decline of religious faith; as an act—here he declares the modern standard-isation of the oath; as a psychological weapon—here he quotes Sterne, Coleridge, and the Aldershot Gymnastic Staff. He also examines with ethnological comment the efforts at the secret dialect of porno-graphy on legitimate... and adds a note defending... charge of dis... present direct... one to put to...

TIMOTHEUS
THE FUTURE OF THE THEATRE
By
BONAMY DOBRÉE

"A witty anacharynous little book, to be read with delight."—*Times Literary Supplement*

"This is a delightfully witty book."—*Spectator*

"In a subtly satirical vein he visualizes various kinds of theatres in two hundred years' time. His gay little book makes delightful reading."—*Nation*

"It hardly pretends... yet when... at all... of the..."—*Guardian*

THE FUTURE OF FUTURISM
JOHN RODKER

IT ISN'T DONE
THE FUTURE OF TABOO AMONG THE BRITISH ISLANDERS
By
ARCHIBALD LYALL

Not since Robert Graves's *Lars Porsena*, or the Future of Swearing from... in the Today and... this... intellectual... this... Today... To-Day... this... Series... an admirable... a provocation to... Assuming that nobody of the island... Mr Lyall... a close... like... in a... example... to... reviewer... position... like... Among us as a Melanesian Islands looking his report draws... in... disillusion... above an outcome in a more... night. This brilliant and... of our... institutions... and its... by taboos... examines taboo... governed by... disappointing, for labour... at... and...

MORPHEUS
OR
THE FUTURE OF SLEEP
By
D. F. FRASER-HARRIS
M.D. D.Sc., F.R.S.E.

This is not a text-book of the physiology of Sleep although in the nature of things some physiology comes into it. It is, in the first place, a popularly written account of what sleep consists in as regards the body, the brain, and the mind.
In the second place, it gives a somewhat detailed description of dreaming and certain states allied to it, walking in sleep, talking in sleep, and trance.
Lastly, the chapter on the Future of Sleep contains a plea for the suppression of all noises which are not absolutely inevitable in our highly mechanized civilization.

"An interesting volume about sleep and the part it plays in maintaining health. It contains valuable suggestions for sufferers from insomnia, discusses dreams and their causes, and suggests the probable line of investigation of sleep problems."
—*Daily Mirror.*

SCHEHERAZADE
OR THE FUTURE OF THE ENGLISH NOVEL
JOHN CARRUTHERS

6

To-Day and To-Morrow, Literature, and Modernism

To-Day and to-Morrow had many superb writers contributing to it, with a number of excellent literary writers among them—Vernon Lee, Graves, Maurois, Holtby, Brittain, MacDiarmid, etc.—though the visionary imaginations and rhetorical ingenuities of many of the scientists, philosophers, psychologists, and others render the distinction between literary and non-literary irrelevant. The series' conjunction of the arts and sciences is one of its significant achievements. To borrow Vernon Lee's phrase, but not her irony, 'Creative Intellects' abound in it (*Proteus*, p. 57). This chapter investigates the two-way traffic between To-Day and To-Morrow and modern literature and the arts. The preliminary section considers the series' response to modernism, arguing that despite all the good modern writers enlisted by Ogden, the judgements in the series of major figures such as Joyce, Eliot, Proust, or Woolf now appear to undervalue them; and that the books barely attend to the visual arts or to modern music. Nevertheless, four outstanding volumes, on the novel, contemporary criticism, the modern arts, and modern dress Shakespeare, are discussed in detail; and the volumes dealing with music, poetry, the English language, and censorship are also considered.

The major section is devoted to other ways in which the series is relevant to modern and modernist literature, looking at how other writers responded to it, and were perhaps influenced by it. The key case studies here are Robert Graves, and Aldous Huxley, whose *Brave New World* is arguably informed by several of the volumes; also Joyce, Eliot, Lewis, and Waugh. It turns out the series was followed by a surprising number of important modern and modernist figures.

Literature and the Arts in To-Day and To-Morrow

Scheherazade; or, The Future of the English Novel (1927) is an illuminating case, since it is the author's interest in the scientific developments animating the series which militates against his appreciation of modernism. It was written by John Young Thomson Greig, who also wrote *Breaking Priscian's Head* for the series, four novels during the 1920s, and biographies of Hume and Thackeray; but it was published under his novelist pseudonym of 'John Carruthers'. He shares the analysis of many of the contributors, that the prevailing factors shaping culture

Imagined Futures: Writing, Science and Modernity in the To-Day and To-Morrow. Max Saunders, Oxford University Press (2019). © Max Saunders. DOI: 10.1093/oso/9780198829454.001.0001

were the after-effects of the war, and the advances of science. He sees literature as in a 'transitional' state (15) of a form of agnosticism (21). Post-war disillusion has destroyed traditional belief systems, replacing them with a cynical view of money as the only intelligible motive (25). But 'the oddly confusing literary and scientific influences that have been brought to bear on post-war novelists' (16) offer no clear sense of direction.

He praises the 'remarkable powers' of Proust, Joyce, and Richardson (62). But he sees them as writers formed by the pre-war world, who aim at 'the entirely frank revelation in detail of their own inner consciousness' (62). This 'subjectivist' position seems to Carruthers a dead end: 'there has been in European fiction during the last fifty or more years a persistent tendency away from objectivity and towards the ever more minute and analytic exposition of mental life; and Mr Joyce has carried this tendency as far as it apparently can go' (63-4). While he recognizes that tighter forms may offer some compensation for spiritual confusion, he argues that the novel cannot turn from representation to abstraction as other arts have been doing (28). He also disapproves of psycho-analysis as a method in fiction (56-8).

He is thus a critic aware of modernist aims and achievements, writing as modernists had just published works now considered the defining masterpieces of the period in English—*Ulysses, The Waste Land, Mrs Dalloway*, the first three volumes of *Parade's End*—yet too lacking in sympathy with their methods to recognize them as constituting the movement, and therefore the guidance, which he feels is required.

His prescription makes it clear why. He quotes a passage from *To the Lighthouse* (just out that year) as an example of the 'belief, the product of incomplete and abstract scientific theory, that life does not progress according to plan, but just happens':

> What was it then? What did it mean? Could things thrust their hands up and grip one; could the blade cut; the fist grasp? Was there no safety? No learning by heart of the ways of the world? No guide, no shelter, but all was miracle, and leaping from the pinnacle of a tower into the air? Could it be, even for elderly people, this was life?—startling, unexpected, unknown.   (84)

For Carruthers, such an intuition of perplexity is a delusion:

> People in real life may be permitted to suffer from it, and so may characters in books; but novelists may not. Plan, shape, form, organic pattern [...] that is the ultimate fact about life, and not until novelists apprehend it, not until their apprehension of it possesses them like a mystical revelation of truth, will their work attain to classic rank.   (85)

The shape he has in mind is that of story. He is clearly aware of Woolf's landmark essay 'Modern Fiction' (also very recently revised for inclusion in *The Common*

Reader, 1925), and comments on the influence of Chekhov on certain post-war novels: 'so that, instead of a continuous narrative of interconnected events, or a series of careful and detailed psychological analyses of mental processes, they give us a succession of vivid and revealing but seemingly disconnected episodes' (66).

It would be easy to characterize Carruthers' argument thus far as middlebrow. But it would be unjust. The rejection of 'story', advocated by Woolf and Pound, had not yet hardened into critical dogma. Eliot's formulation of the 'mythic method' in his response to *Ulysses* was after all an argument for imposing a narrative pattern on 'the immense panorama of futility and anarchy which is contemporary history'.[1] Others had good reasons for querying modernism's divagation from story, such as William Empson, arguing in 1931 that Woolf's 'impressionist method' 'tries to substitute for telling a story, as the main centre of interest, what is in fact one of the by-products of telling a story; it tries to correlate sensations rather than the impulses that make the sensations interesting'.[2] Modernism's subjective turn struck some leftward-leaning writers and critics as a disturbing retreat from the social. Jesse Matz posits a 'world-wide trend away from psychological aesthetics toward explicit politics from the 1930s onward'.[3] Where today's critics of modernism find radical potential in the extreme subjectivism of Proust or Woolf, *Scheherazade* shows how to some contemporaries such writing appeared troublingly solipsistic; and to that extent, rather than lagging behind modernist experimentation, he was ahead of the coming political turn. Better, then, to align Carruthers not only with Empson, but also Walter Benjamin. When he turns to predictions (which are clearly also his desiderata) he says novels will be shorter; have more plot; and return to the story-teller (92). Hence his title. In some ways *Scheherazade* can lay claim to providing an English precursor of Benjamin's famous essay of a decade later, 'The Storyteller' (1936); its analysis of the aftermath of war as precipitating a narrative crisis having points of contact with Benjamin's argument. Yet where Benjamin locates the source of the crisis in the lack of communicable experience, Carruthers's emphasis on the lack of story tells another story; and one which allows of another way of historicizing modernism's antipathy to plot: less as traumatic disillusion, and more as the result of a crisis of narrative logic in the war-theatre of the absurd.

The second strand of Carruthers' prescription for the fiction of the future chimes with the scientific volumes of To-Day and To-Morrow, and particularly with their advocacy of a new sense of the interpenetration of mind and matter. He thinks post-relativistic science has precipitated a 'new philosophical synthesis'

---

[1] T. S. Eliot 'Ulysses, Order, and Myth' (1923), in *Selected Prose of T. S. Eliot*, Frank Kermode (New York: Harcourt, 1975), 175–8 (178).
[2] William Empson, 'Virginia Woolf' (1931), in *Argufying* (London: Chatto and Windus, 1987), 443–9 (448).
[3] Jesse Matz, *Lasting Impressions* (New York: Columbia University Press, 2016), 137.

(75, 73), which he too sees re-instating the metaphysical (76). He concludes his argument against modernist aims by invoking totality:

> Contemporary novelists do not believe with all their heart in the *whole*, the comprehensive pattern which is made up of lesser patterns interlocking and interfusing, *no one of which is sacrificed to any other* but each one of which finds its reality and fulfilment *in* the others[.]   (81)

That is the ground of his objection to the Jamesian point of view, Proust's inward quest, or Woolf's stream of consciousness. You might expect to find it justified with reference to Hegel, or Darwin, or Marx. But Carruthers quotes a passage from Whitehead's *Science and the Modern World* about 'prehension', which *Scheherazade* glosses as 'unconscious patterning' (80).

Like *Scheherazade*, Geoffrey West's *Deucalion; or, The Future of Literary Criticism* (1930) is illuminating about how its subject appeared during the disorientating flux of the postwar period. West was the pseudonym of G. H. Wells, who wisely adopted it when writing a biography of H. G. Wells, and who also wrote on Bennett, Shaw, and others.[4] Deucalion is Greek mythology's equivalent of a Noah figure, who survives Zeus's deluge by building an ark. West calls criticism 'that DEUCALION of the spirit' because in a time of chaos it is what's looked towards to find literary and human values (94). West juxtaposes Eliot's *Criterion*, as the citadel of Catholic classicism, with John Middleton Murry's *Adelphi*, as a champion of humanism. West, who is well-informed about critical developments, invokes T. E. Hulme's distinction between romanticism and classicism.[5] But he rejects Hulme's argument for classicism, countering that the Renaissance represented a wholesale rejection of Catholic authority, dogma, and traditionalism, along with the notion of original sin. 'Post-Renaissance man is Romantic', he says: 'for him Romanticism alone serves'; 'so to a truly Romantic criticism must he look for his salvation' (64). Romanticism, he argues, is based on 'an autonomous individualism' (65). The 'immediate task' of a Romantic criticism is 'the creation of an individualist tradition by the discovery and exposition of a series of truly Romantic individuals' (65). What he means by this is essentially a tradition of biographical criticism. He cites Lawrence's *Studies in Classical American Literature* (1923) as an example, along with studies of Beethoven by two To-Day and To-Morrow authors, W. J. Turner, and J. W. N. Sullivan. But it is in Murry's work (such as his 1916 book *Fyodor Dostoevsky*) 'that this type of criticism is seen at its best' (66).

Deucalion's final chapter, 'Towards the Future', then juxtaposes Murry with I. A. Richards as signalling the two significant directions of contemporary criticism: Richards as epitome of the scientific and intellectual approach; Murry of the intuitive. The book is dedicated to the two men, 'linked in a common admiration'.

---

[4] Geoffrey West, *H. G. Wells: Sketch for a portrait* (1930).
[5] T. E. Hulme, 'Romanticism and Classicism', in *Speculations*, ed. Herbert Read (London: Kegan Paul, 1924), 111–40.

West predicts that criticism will follow either of these examples, or attempt to combine the two. It is an impressively accurate prediction, given that Richards (together with Ogden, and later with Richards' student Empson) was a pioneer of the combination of close verbal analysis with scientific theory that prepared the way for structuralism and post-structuralist theory; and that Murry's approach has much in common with that of Leavis and the *Scrutiny* group, especially in his valuing of Lawrence, and the passionate commitment to close engagement with literature as a source of moral value. The accuracy was perhaps facilitated by the fact that the directions were already becoming manifest in the Cambridge of the late 1920s. But *Deucalion* stands out for its astute accounts of the most contemporary and transformative criticism of the period in English; and stands apart from *Scheherazade* in being more appreciative of the developments it discusses.

John Rodker's *The Future of Futurism* (1926) mentions one contemporary modernist movement, though oddly barely discusses the Italian Futurism of Marinetti, Balla, Russolo, etc., focusing instead on the English literature Rodker worked with. Rodker had been one of the 'Whitechapel Boys', with Isaac Rosenberg, David Bomberg, and Mark Gertler. His Ovid Press published Ezra Pound, T. S. Eliot, and Wyndham Lewis. He told Ford Madox Ford that his novel *The Good Soldier* was 'the finest French novel in the English language'.[6] If he seems slightly behind the times in intimating that 'the complexities of Dostoievsky's characters, not to mention Tchekhov, are about to descend upon these shores' (28)—Lawrence, Woolf, and Mansfield had surely already been exploring just those complexities and techniques—*The Future of Futurism* is the one To-Day and To-Morrow book on the arts that gets their future right. Rodker argues that what he calls 'futurism only exists as a state of flux, immediately it is accepted becoming the classical of its own generation and of posterity' (21), and identifying Picasso, Stravinsky, and Joyce as the exemplary figures (21-2). Though like Carruthers, Rodker too mentions *The Arabian Nights*, and hopes that 'the story is about to come into its own again [...]' (82). He cites Stein, e. e. cummings, Pound, and Epstein, and also refers to Ogden and Richards' *The Meaning of Meaning* (73).

Rodker's book is also striking for the way it invokes exactly those arguments discussed in Chapter 4 about the effects on the human of technological change. 'Mr Wells gives us a number of comprehensive but disturbing visions of posterity' (15), he says, such as libraries which 'turn on the speaking romances of that day, while other switches will fill the empty picture frame with any abstract arrangement of the units supplied, not omitting stage-noises, rustle of leaves, murmur of water, and battery of pastoral sounds' (15)—our audio books in the first case, and in the second, something between digital picture frames, virtual reality and screensavers. But it is possible, he says, that 'before even so much happens, men may acquire a

---

[6] Ford Madox Ford, *The Good Soldier*, ed. Max Saunders, Oxford World's Classics (Oxford: Oxford University Press, 2012), 5.

new sense or two, and with them new standards' (16). He thinks it impossible to predict their effect on the arts; and anyway, he thinks such developments unlikely. Yet the words in which he envisages them gives a new twist to the term then in vogue, 'air-minded':[7]

> And, though the airman is said to be growing a new kind of mind, as if like a bird, his spiritual skeleton grew hollow and could soar, and though life in submarines may cause profound organic changes, yet the expression of these activities has so far meant nothing more than a slight alteration in the hæmoglobin index and additional bric-a-brac to the what-not of the arts.
>
> However, there has not been time enough for these vocations to modify deeply the minds of those engaged in them, but perhaps the mind itself is incapable of a transition commensurate with our taking to the air and the depths of the sea. (16-17)

Insofar as the idea of the airman 'growing a new kind of mind' sounds dubiously Lamarckian, Rodker is right to be sceptical. His scepticism that man's mentality has yet adjusted to the advances in his science and technology is close to Carruthers' view that literature has so far failed to engage with the new science; but goes further, approaching Günther Anders' notion of a 'Promethean gap' (according to which we fail to imagine or conceptualize the effects of our new technologies).[8] It is a view that does not recognize Wells's science fiction or futurology as an adequate response to modernity (nor, one might add, the expository prose of To-Day and To-Morrow), presumably on the grounds that though its *subject* is technological change, it does not reflect that change in its own techniques and forms and language, remaining locked in nineteenth-century modes of realist representation and rational debate. What is striking now is that it does not occur to Rodker that his modern classics might represent just such a transformation of mentality. True, artists like Joyce, Picasso, or Stravinsky were not celebrating the machine as the Italian Futurists were—were not painting triptychs of trimotors or symphonies of the submarine. But their vision of the mind, and their language for presenting it, were something new; as Ford recognized, writing just after he had read *Ulysses* that it 'contains the undiscovered mind of man; it is human consciousness analyzed as it has never before been analyzed. Certain books change the world. This, success or failure, *Ulysses* does'.[9]

The series' response to Joyce is telling. He is unignorable, and mentioned by a number of contributors: not just *Scheherazade*, *Deucalion*, and *The Future of*

---

[7] The earliest historical example of the term given by the *OED* is 1927: '*Times* 28 Feb. 9/4 Flying clubs...offer one of the most economical and direct ways of making the nation, in the words of Sir Samuel Hoare, "air-minded"'.

[8] See Chapter 4, and the Conclusions for further discussion of Anders' 'Promethean gap'.

[9] Ford Madox Ford, ed., 'A Haughty and Proud Generation', *Yale Review*, 11 (July 1922), 703–17; in Ford Madox Ford, *Critical Essays*, ed. Max Saunders and Richard Stang (Manchester: Carcanet, 2002), 208–17 (217).

Futurism. We saw Robert Graves, in *Lars Porsena*, invoke him as a test case for obscenity; and George Godwin, in *Columbia; or, The Future of Canada*, quote him (though anonymously) as providing an example of the language of the future. In the other book Carruthers wrote for the series (under his own name, J. Y. T. Greig)— *Breaking Priscian's Head; or, English as She Will Be Spoke and Wrote* (1928), it is for Joyce's contribution to 'the enrichment of Standard English' (92) that he is introduced at the end. But though Greig admires the dexterity of Joyce's neologisms, giving over several pages to a discussion of his compound words, he does not think they will last (94-6). In other words, for him they are not the language of the future. (That, he suggests, will be forged instead out of new words 'to name new material objects (*photograph, magneto, aeroplane*), new processes (motoring, broadcasting), and new scientific or philosophical concepts (*bacterium, electron, exogamy, prehension*)'; 68-9). Greig's examples are all from *Ulysses*, though given his argument about literature's influence on everyday language, one doubts whether the portmanteau compounds of *Finnegans Wake* would have changed his mind. Passages from the latter had been appearing since 1924 under the provisional title 'Work in Progress'. The first extract came out in Ford's *transatlantic review*, which published other modernist writers who were indeed producing what must have seemed to many like the literature of the future: Pound, Gertrude Stein, Hemingway, Jean Rhys, Djuna Barnes, Dorothy Richardson, e. e. cummings, H. D., and Tristan Tzara. Robert Graves, in his second book for the series, *Mrs Fisher; or, The Future of Humour* (1928) does quote from 'Work in Progress'— the version of 'the Ant and Grasshopper fable' (93-4)—as a prophetic antecedent of that future of humour he sees his Mrs Fisher as ushering in.

Yet for all Joyce's appearances through the series, and regardless of whether the writers are admiring or mocking him, the nearest we get to sustained critical engagement with his achievement is Carruthers' verdict of the *cul de sac* of subjectivism. Oddly, Joyce is not even mentioned in the otherwise important section of Bolton C. Waller's *Hibernia; or, The Future of Ireland* (1928) covering Gaelic literature, culture, and language (54-65): though the denigration of a 'cult of unintelligibility, or a display of mental acrobatics' (63) may have had him in mind; and may offer a suggestion as to why these authors were struggling to place him.

Does this suggest a parochialism of outlook in the series? Perhaps; if only to the extent that it reflects the postwar literary scene in Britain. Joyce, Ford, Lawrence, and Pound were all living abroad. Joyce and Lawrence had even had to publish abroad to avoid censorship. That doesn't mean advanced critics (like Greig, West, and Rodker) were not aware of their work. Leavis caused a scandal by expecting his students to have read *Ulysses* in 1926 when it was still illegal to possess a copy.[10] But it does mean that the figures that we now tend to think of as central to

---

[10] See Paul Vanderham, *James Joyce and Censorship: The trials of Ulysses* (Basingstoke: Palgrave Macmillan, 1998), 4.

the modernist movement were much more contested. Not all readers and critics who did know their work admired it; and for many, their names would have been familiar only as the objects of the scorn of reviewers in the popular press.

The series was certainly not parochial in the sense of isolationist. Just as its treatment of postwar geopolitics is profoundly internationalist, so its discussions of the arts display modernism's internationalism rather than any fetishizing of Britishness (though De Sélincourt's celebration of the English language in *Pomona* is complacently insular). Rodker is the most internationalist of its critics, also bringing into the series discussion of James, Marinetti, Stein, cummings, Lawrence, and Mallarmé. Ogden himself was anything but parochial, devoting most of his efforts to the cause of international understanding and intellectual debate. Anyone who finds that claim belied by BASIC English's aim of facilitating trans-language communication under the sign of English,[11] would do well to remember Dora Russell's praise of his courage in publishing material from the German press during the war; and his determination in encouraging English minds to engage with European ideas in the International Library.

What is at stake, however, is a troubling sense that the series touches hardly at all on some of the most dynamic and disruptive artists, writers, thinkers, and movements of the early twentieth century: notably the proponents of Expressionism, Fauvism, Post-Impressionism, the Bauhaus, *Die Brücke*, *Der Blaue Reiter*, Cubism, Vorticism, Dada, Constructivism, Suprematism, *Neue Sachlichkeit*, *Pittura metafisica*, *De Stijl*, atonality and serialism, Russian Formalism, Socialist Realism, or Surrealism. Some of these omissions are the result of a different kind of omission: the lack of any volumes dealing with painting, drawing, sculpture, or photography. Yet some of these movements cut across media; and the writers on film or architecture or literature, who must have been aware of them, seemed not to think them worth discussing, or perhaps did not think they pointed the way to the future.

It was possible in 1935 for Kenneth Clark to write on 'The Future of Painting'.[12] Did it not seem an important topic for Ogden in the late 1920s? Surrealist manifestos were issued in 1924 and 1929, at the start and towards the end of To-Day and To-Morrow. Did they not seem worth addressing? There were extraordinarily visionary figures in the period. Fortunato Depero, for example, described by Hal Foster as 'a talented jack-of-all-the-arts who designed ads for Campari', who predicted in 1931 (the last year of the series) that '[t]he art of the future will...be the art of advertising'.[13] Perhaps few others had seen so clearly the trajectory that

---

[11]   See for example Michael Silverstein, 'From The Meaning of Meaning to the Empires of the Mind: Ogden's orthological English', *Pragmatics* 5:2 (1995) 185–95, for a critique of BASIC as inflected by Anglo-American imperialism.

[12]   Kenneth Clark, 'The Future of Painting', *Listener*, Issue 351 (2 October 1935), 543–4, 578.

[13]   Hal Foster, 'At the Guggenheim', *LRB* (20 March 2014), 38.

would lead to Pop Art. Yet given the series' interest in media and advertising, one might have expected more from it on the visual imagination of the future.

One possible explanation for this blind spot is Ogden's focus on language and communication. He may simply have been too committed to a notion of verbal communication to have been much concerned with the visual as a language. Similarly, his commitment to communication theory perhaps rendered Surrealism unpalatable. As a rationalist, he doubtless saw the irrational as something to be subdued rather than exalted. It is a tendency evident in the work of I. A. Richards too, who may have been advising Ogden about literature and criticism. Richards' *Practical Criticism*, with its innovative human sciences approach to literary responses, was a radical and modern book in 1929. But its view of the process of literary communication as prone to classifiable errors implies a model of a correctly communicable meaning problematic to later theorists. The emergence of 'Practical Criticism' as the literary pedagogy of the future coincided with the last few years of the series. So again, it is disappointing—given Ogden's close friend-ship with Richards—that it does not receive more attention. True, the publication of Leavis' first major book *New Bearings in English Poetry*, and founding of the magazine *Scrutiny*, did not happen till 1932, the year after the series concluded. But he had begun publishing earlier. And William Empson, Richards' loyal and brilliant student, whose work nonetheless both sophisticated and undermined Richards' communication model of poetic language, had published his landmark first book *Seven Types of Ambiguity* in 1930. That too goes unmentioned in To-Day and To-Morrow, along with the work by Robert Graves which Empson was later prompted to acknowledge as influential on him, *Poetic Unreason and Other Studies* (London: Cecil Palmer, 1925).

To-Day and To-Morrow was never intended to provide exhaustive surveys of the existing cultural domain. The small scale of its volumes enforced a selective approach. Its scope appears to have evolved as the series progressed; there is no evidence of its having been blocked out in advance. We don't have a prospectus or plan other than the blurb that appeared in all but the earliest volumes and the Classified Index that appeared in many of the later ones. So we do not know which other subjects, trends, movements, disciplines Ogden may have wanted eventually to include. That makes it impossible to rule out the possibility that, had the publishers wanted to continue the series beyond 1931, missing fields and developments would have been covered in later volumes. Even given the impro-visatory nature of the commissioning, it should be apparent from the discussion thus far that a creditable range of international modernism is covered; and not just in Anglo-American literature. The coverage of some fields is inevitably better than that of others. Film, for example, was relatively well-served by *Heraclitus*, in which Ernest Betts comments: 'In Russia, Eisenstein and Pudolfkin have devel-oped an expressionist technique which aims at making the mass and the machine say what the individual once said—the voice of Russia, of the workers, of those labouring for speech' (20).[14] Yet the lack of a volume (or even part of one) dealing with photography is puzzling. There had been experiments in colour for both cinema and still images since the start of the century; but effective and affordable colour film only began to appear in the 1930s. Perhaps the introduction of sound in cinema, and the development of television, called the future of still photography into question. Overall, whatever the reasons, it is unfortunate that the significance of figures like Kafka, Thomas Mann, Pirandello, Apollinaire, Brecht, and Weill, or Man Ray is left unregistered.

It is the volumes devoted to opera, music and poetry especially which fail to deliver convincing accounts of the modernist developments in these fields, let alone any prognostications of their futures. *Eurydice; or, The Nature of Opera* (1929), for example, by Dyneley Hussey, has disappointingly little to say about music after Wagner—which is perhaps why his subtitle speaks of the 'Nature' rather than the 'Future' of opera. Franz Hueffer (the father of Ford Madox Ford) had written a book called *Richard Wagner and the Music of the Future*; but that was in 1874, when the composer was still living and finishing the *Ring*. Nearly half a century after Wagner's death, he scarcely still seemed avant-garde. Hussey, who was an art and music critic, writes well enough about *Tristan*. Subsequent composers he mentions are Richard Strauss, Vaughan Williams (for *Hugh the Drover*), Charles Villiers Stanford, and Charpentier. His only reference to Debussy is as '[a]nother Frenchman with real genius' (64); but his *Pélleas et Mélisande* is said to have carried out Wagner's theories so literally as to have 'proved conclusively their unsoundness' (64), judging that 'it fails to be interesting as music, beautiful though it is as sound from one moment to the next' (64-5). He seems unwilling to address the more challenging modern works that he must have been aware of. There is nothing on Bartok, Berg, or Stravinsky, let alone on Brecht and Weill's *Threepenny Opera*.

The same is true of the two volumes ostensibly dealing with the future of music. E. J. Dent's *Terpander; or, Music and the Future* (1926) is more of a dull history of harmony and tonality than an assessment of contemporary directions.[15] He does not mention composers after Wagner, Scriabin, Elgar, and Strauss. But Scriabin had died in 1915; and though the last two were still working, their genres and idioms were distinctly pre-war; their late Romanticism even harking back to the nineteenth century. Dent make digs at people writing fragmentary, sketch-like work, but doesn't name any names, as if he didn't want to offend anyone.

W. J. Turner's *Orpheus; or, The Music of the Future* (1926)—discussed at end of Chapter 5—is even more classical in taste and historical in method, for example

[14] 'Pudolfkin' is a variant transliteration for Vsevolod Pudovkin, whose *Mat* (Mother) was reviewed by 'V. P', 'The Movies in Moscow', *Manchester Guardian* (5 January 1927), 16.

[15] Dent was the music critic of the *Athenaeum*, and Professor of Music at Cambridge University from 1926 to 1941.

explaining the notion of 'Progress in Music' by contrasting Bach with Froberger (37–42).[16] He mentions Debussy's *Prélude à L'après-midi d'un Faune* (1894), but then goes on to argue for Beethoven's pre-eminence above Debussy or Strauss, let alone 'the fatiguing excitements of Stravinsky and Jazz' (80). Nonetheless, he does at least offers the following attempt at theorizing aesthetic innovation:

> every new wave of artistic expression is preluded by a breakdown of the abstract combinations of symbols in which the symbols had become most completely devitalized, and a return to a sense of a meaning, a colour, a life in the symbol itself. This results in simplification, which ultimately gives place to a new complication. What is called progress in art consists mainly of this process.   (25)

R. C. Trevelyan's thesis, in *Thamyris; or, Is There a Future for Poetry?* (1925), is that historically poetry has declined rather than progressed. Hence the questioning in his subtitle of whether it has a future at all. Thamyris was a Thracian singer who boasted his superiority to the Muses. They challenged him to a contest, and when Apollo judged him the loser, he was blinded and robbed of his poetic gifts in punishment. Trevelyan—the brother of historian George Macaulay Trevelyan, a Cambridge Apostle, classicist, and minor poet—tells a variant of the myth (81–3) in which Thamyris retains his gifts and keeps producing masterpieces. Trevelyan characterizes modern poets as 'Children of Thamyris': rebellious innovators, whose art lost its rationale when it separated from song. He quotes Pound, though without naming him, as an example of un-poetic *vers libre*:

> Come, my songs, let us express our baser passions.
> Let us express our envy for the man with a steady job and no
> worry about the future.[17]

commenting that 'it would almost seem that at times free verse is no more than an excuse for uttering futilities and ineptitudes that we should not have dared to express in honest prose' (25). That is the only look-in modernism gets. There is nothing on Yeats; nothing on Imagism; nothing on Eliot (this in 1925, three years after the appearance of *The Waste Land*). He mentions Waley appreciatively, but as insubstantial. Otherwise the references are to Bridges, Lascelles Abercrombie, or Sturge Moore. He appears not to have noticed that most of the poets he discusses not only shared his view that poetry's relation to song had become problematic, but had made the problem part of their subject and technique—as in those lines of Pound's, from a poem which pits its flat, white-collar title, 'Further Instructions', against the lyric invocation to lyric itself: 'Come, my *songs*'. Nor does Trevelyan

---

[16] Dent gives Johann Jakob Froberger's name in the form 'Frohberger'.
[17] Ezra Pound, 'Further Instructions', in *The New Poetry: An anthology*, ed. Harriet Monroe (New York: Macmillan, 1917), 265–6.

appear to have caught Pound's futurological anxiety: he too was concerned what future poetry might have in an era when the language of corporate man is everywhere rampant. The pre-eminent prose writers striving for a language of intelligence to resist the instant gratification and commercialization of language and media, Proust and James, are invoked, but only as bad models for poets:

> Narrative, when it ceases to narrate, very easily becomes a bore. Such writers as Proust and Henry James may have been able successfully to dispense with many of the functions of story-telling, by laboriously evolving a peculiar prose instrument of their own for the expression of psychological subtleties. But it is doubtful whether anything of the kind would be possible in verse, or, if possible, whether it would be readable.   (58)

It is not hard to imagine what such champions of James as Pound, Eliot, or Ford would have made of that. Fortunately we do not even have to try to imagine what Robert Graves thought of *Thamyris*, since he felt strongly enough that someone else should have written a volume on the future of poetry that really engaged with modernism and modernity, as to do it himself, in a pamphlet directly replying to it, *Another Future of Poetry*, published by the Woolfs' Hogarth Press in 1926.[18] Denouncing Trevelyan as parochial, Graves insists that '[t]he fact is, poetry read silently and poetry spoken aloud are divergent arts' (7); and that therefore 'the importance of the first visual impact must not be sentimentally discounted' (6). He rejects Trevelyan's argument basing the difference between poetry and prose on verbal patterning, countering that 'in reading prose or in reading verse quite a different attitude is adopted by the reader, and it is this attitude more than the intrinsic quality of the writing that logically decides whether it is prose or poetry that is being read' (15-16). He also disagrees with Trevelyan's narrative of degeneration, expressing skepticism about how far the best poets have ever been in touch with the common man. Graves suspects that the future of poetry depends on the class antagonism he describes as then in full swing. He is more in tune with the mentality of contemporary listeners, in a way that makes him in tune with many of To-Day and To-Morrow's more alert observers: 'The public that is acquiring a short-story sense and a film sense and a fast-traffic sense and a radio sense is not a dull public' (23).

While he is at it he takes issue with Haldane's plea in *Daedalus* that poets ought to be educated in science (16); this apparently because he reserves for poetry the right 'to use both the method of logic and the method of fantastic thought'; defining the latter, in a phrase which anticipates Pound's formulation of the 'ideogrammic method',[19] as '*sensorial hieroglyphic*' (26). Poetic Unreason was clearly still on his

---

[18] A revised version was later published as 'The Future of Poetry' in *The Common Asphodel: Collected essays on poetry, 1922-1949* (London: Hamish Hamilton, 1949), 51-9.

[19] Pound's first use of the phrase is in his *ABC of Reading* (London: G. Routledge, 1934), 11; though the method, or this way of conceiving it, was perhaps suggested by his reading before the war of Ernest Fenollosa's manuscript 'The Chinese Written Character as a Medium for Poetry'.

mind; and contributed to another visionary anticipation, this time of the New Critical dogma that poems should not mean, but be; and that it was therefore heretical to attempt to paraphrase them: 'Modern poetry and modern painting do not set out to translate or interpret in the traditional sense', says Graves: 'but to provide an independent experience' (30).[20] This challenge to the traditional notion of representation enables Graves to pose poetry as taking on science on its own terms. He writes of 'this new poetic Relativity' (30-1); which is also a comment on technique, since he argues that the modernist method does not claim to be better than its predecessors; merely different.

The year after *Another Future of Poetry* appeared, Graves and Laura Riding published *A Survey of Modernist Poetry*—another version of the charting of the contemporary and likely future that the series had still failed to provide for poetry. The following year Graves produced his own two volumes for To-Day and To-Morrow, on swearing and humour. He and Ogden must have both wanted to have his futurological projections contributing to the series from within.

The fact that Graves's pamphlet was published by the Hogarth Press means that Virginia Woolf would have been aware of it. She probably would already have been aware of *Thamyris*. Trevelyan was published by the Hogarth Press too, and was associated with the Bloomsbury Group. Woolf's lover Vita Sackville-West reviewed *Thamyris*—also unfavourably—for the *Nation and Athenaeum*, of which Leonard Woolf was then the literary editor.[21] Although Virginia Woolf did not comment on the series, her husband was certainly well aware of it. He had reviewed *Daedalus* and *Icarus* himself, foretelling that '[i]f the series maintains the standards set by these two books, it will be a notable achievement'. He concentrated on Haldane's volume, which he thought gave 'an extraordinarily interesting and imaginative sketch of the new discoveries which may be expected [...]'. 'But what to me is even more interesting', adds Woolf, 'is his theory that Einstein's discovery will have important effects upon practical life, since for a few centuries "many practical activities will probably be conducted on a basis, not of materialism, but of Kantian idealism" '.[22] It was an idea which chimed with the criticism of Edwardian fiction Virginia Woolf had been writing since the war—especially in the essay 'Modern Novels' (1919), revised into 'Modern Fiction' (1925), with its critique of Wells, Galsworthy, and Bennett as 'materialist'.[23] Leonard Woolf also reviewed *Lysistrata* for the *Nation and Athenaeum*, unsurprisingly finding Ludovici's 'conclusions [...] as strained and false as his premises'—especially his

---

[20] See for example Archibald MacLeish's poem 'Ars Poetica'; and the chapter 'The Heresy of Paraphrase' in Cleanth Brooks, *The Well-Wrought Urn* (New York: Harcourt, Brace, 1947).
[21] V. Sackville-West, 'The Future of Poetry', *Nation and Athenaeum*, 37:19 (Aug. 8, 1925), 572.
[22] Leonard Woolf, 'Daedalus and Icarus', 'The World of Books' column, *Nation and Athenaeum*, 34 (22 March 1924), 890.
[23] Virginia Woolf, 'Modern Novels' (1919; subsequently revised as 'Modern Fiction'), and 'Character in Fiction' (1924; subsequently revised as 'Mr Bennett and Mrs Brown'), in *The Essays of Virginia Woolf*, vol. 3, ed. Andrew McNeillie (London: The Hogarth Press, 1988), 30-7, 420-38.

eugenicist assumptions about contemporary degeneracy. 'The book is not up to the standards set by others in this excellent little series', he judged.[24] *Icarus* remained in the Woolfs' library, along with only one other To-Day and To-Morrow volume: H. F. Scott Stokes's *Perseus; or, Of Dragons* (1924).[25] It is unlikely he would have been remembering that as a volume contributing to the high standard. As *Lysistrata* and *Perseus* were probably the eighth and ninth volumes to appear, Woolf is perhaps referring back to Haldane and Russell. He also reviewed Russell's *What I Believe* three months later, calling it '[o]ne of the most brilliant and thought-stimulating little books that I have read'.[26] Over the next few years he went on to review at least six others in the *Nation and Athenaeum*, and may well have read more besides: his reviews show that he read volumes that did not stay in their library.[27] The magazine carried reviews of at least twenty other volumes. For example, in 1925 the anonymous review of *Hypatia* said 'no intelligent woman would disagree with Mrs. Russell's essential position or fail to admire her courage' but criticized its 'polemical' vein, worrying that 'its defiant tone may alienate or amuse others whom it is more necessary to convince'.[28] In late 1926 or early 1927 Woolf delegated reviews of two volumes to T. S. Eliot (discussed below).

It was in 1927 that Virginia Woolf briefly turned futurologist. In an essay titled 'Poetry, Fiction and the Future', she notes that most critics ignore the present and 'gaze steadily into the past':

> But one has sometimes asked one's self, must the duty of a critic always be to the past, must his gaze always be fixed backward? Could he not sometimes turn round and, shading his eyes in the manner of Robinson Crusoe on the desert island, look into the future and trace on its mist the faint lines of the land which some day perhaps we may reach? The truth of such speculations can never be proved, of course, but in an age like ours there is a great temptation to indulge in them. For it is an age clearly when we are not fast anchored where we are; things

[24] Leonard Woolf, 'The Future of Woman', *Nation and Athenaeum*, 36:15 (10 January 1925), 526.

[25] See *The Library of Leonard and Virginia Woolf: A short-title catalog* compiled and edited by Julia King and Laila Miletic-Vejzovic; foreword by Laila Miletic-Vejzovic; introduction by Diane F. Gillespie: http://ntserver1.wsulibs.wsu.edu/masc/onlinebooks/woolflibrary/woolflibraryonline.htm

[26] Leonard Woolf, 'The Religion of A ----', 'World of Books', *Nation and Athenaeum* 37 (25 April 1925), 106.

[27] The *Nation and Athenaeum*'s 'The World of Books' section included Leonard Woolf's reviews of *Scheherazade*, 'The Novel of To-Day', 42 (3 December 1927), 356; *Archon*, 'Fools Contest', 42 (14 January 1928), 569; *Alma Mater*, 'Youth among the Ruins', 44 (22 December 1928), 446; *Cato*, 'A Censorship at Work', 46 (8 February 1930), 642; *Deucalion*, 'The Ideals of Journalism', 46 (15 February 1930), 674; and *Chronos*, 'Marriage and the Family', 47 (28 June 1930), 412. Vera Brittain's *Halcyon; or, The Future of Monogamy* (1929) was reviewed by Ray Strachey (sister-in-law to Lytton Strachey, and whose sister married Virginia Woolf's brother Adrian Stephen): 'Monogamy', *Nation and Athenaeum*, 46:1 (5 October 1929), 18, 20.

[28] Anon., 'Hypatia', *Nation and Anthenaeum*, 37 (23 May 1925), 244.

are moving round us; we are moving ourselves. Is it not the critic's duty to tell us, or to guess at least, where we are going?[29]

So she makes the attempt; and, as she does so, imagines a rather different future for poetry. She starts by wondering about what she sees as the demise of verse drama ('the one form which seems dead beyond all possibility of resurrection today'; 430). She attributes this to the ambivalences and inter-connectedness of 'the modern mind' (433); to 'the strange way in which things that have no apparent connection are associated' in it. Her analysis of why human character has changed in these ways invokes the same changes in technology, media, and society which were exercising To-Day and To-Morrow's writers; especially the way the mediations of communications technologies increasingly stand in for social contact. She conjures a vision of people living in long brick avenues of locked houses for privacy, yet with each 'linked to his fellows by wires which pass overhead, by waves of sound which pour through the roof and speak aloud to him of battles and murders and strikes and revolutions all over the world' (433).

Poetry, Woolf suggests, may no longer be suitable to express such mentality: 'It may be', she writes,

> that the emotions here sketched in such rude outline and imputed to the modern mind submit more readily to prose than to poetry. It may be possible that prose is going to take over—has, indeed, already taken over—some of the duties which were once discharged by poetry.   (434)

Prose had indeed already taken over many poetic functions in *To the Lighthouse*, published just two weeks before Woolf presented these ideas to Oxford students; and it would do again, differently, in *Orlando*, the novel she would write next. Doubtless the development of her own work lay behind her argument that: 'If, then, we are daring and risk ridicule and try to see in what direction we who seem to be moving so fast are going, we may guess that we are going in the direction of prose [...]' (434-5). But given the number of the volumes reviewed in the *Nation and Athenaeum*, and given Leonard Woolf's review of *Scheherazade*, with its analysis of her fiction, she was surely also aware of the series. It is thus also probable, with so much involvement in To-Day and To-Morrow among the people around her—writing for and against the series, and reviewing it—that whether she read any of the volumes or not, the series not only contributed to her sense of the rapidity of change, and its effect on the modern mind, but prompted her to imagine the future of literature for herself.

---

[29] Virginia Woolf, 'Poetry, Fiction and the Future', *The Essays of Virginia Woolf*, pp. 428–41 (428–9). The essay was derived from a paper read to the Oxford University English Club on 18 May 1927, and was first published in the *New York Herald Tribune* on 14 and 21 August 1927.

The relationships between To-Day and To-Morrow and modern literature are thus complex, and any strictures about the adequacy of the series' dealings with contemporary literature and art only touch one aspect. It contributed many excellent volumes to that literature, specifically through the inclusion of books by modern writers who were already significant figures—Russell, Jeans, Paget, Pankhurst, etc.—and by others who would soon prove to be: such as Haldane, Graves, Brittain, MacDiarmid, Maurois, or Radhakrishnan. The engagements of figures like Graves and Leonard Woolf testify to the impact volumes were having on contemporary writers; and that impact is the subject of the second half of this chapter.

First, though, it is time to consider other contributions the series made to contemporary debates about literature and culture; since some especially interesting volumes think about the future of the literature of the past; and about the future of censorship.

Iconoclastes; or, The Future of Shakespeare (1927), by the playwright and commentator on Soviet Russia, Hubert Griffith, approaches his topic via a discussion of the questions, central to Eliot's modernism, of the tradition and the classic. Griffith takes a diametrically opposed view, however: 'the word classic is detested' he tells us, 'because it is generally taken to mean "dead" ' (7). Whereas for him, '*A Classic is simply a work of such intense vitality that it is always modern*' (14). He had been convinced by H. K. Ayliff's modern dress production of *Hamlet* in 1925 that 'the future of Shakespeare lies in doing Shakespeare as a modern playwright' (48).[30] Shakespearean productions, he argues, have evolved a 'tradition' of absurd conventions that kill the works. This explains what he describes as two 'perverse paradoxes' (24): that Shakespeare is unpopular (by which he means that it takes a star actor, or an extraneous design gimmick, to make productions commercially viable); this despite the good taste of the public. Griffith—an enthusiast for music hall too (30)—is committed to a view of classic art as popular (6) but also as superlative: '[t]he Classic of art owes its position to one thing and to one thing only: that in the absolute quality of its achievement it is supreme and has never been surpassed' (15). 'To my disappointment I found myself in complete agreement with nearly all its author's arguments', confessed Nigel Playfair, the actor-manager of the Lyric, Hammersmith in the *Evening Standard*.[31]

Griffith's argument sets him at odds with those contributors claiming that modernity was changing humanity. 'Drama is the art of arousing emotion by staging a conflict of will, character, intelligence, aspiration—whatever you like to call it', he says: 'Men do not change, or change only infinitesimally slowly' (21).

---

[30] Though there had been experiments with modern dress Shakespeare before the war, H. K. Ayliff's 1923 *Cymbeline* and 1925 *Hamlet* gave the concept a new urgency.

[31] Quoted from the end-matter of C. P. Harvey's *Solon; or, The Price of Justice* (1931).

Though he is dismissive of the idea of 'a dramatization of the Einstein theory' (26), it is nonetheless typical of the series that the possibility occurs to him. (May he be watching Michael Frayn's *Copenhagen* somewhere in a parallel universe!) Yet while this commits him to a universalist position that 'a first-rate work of art [...] rises utterly clear of its period' (15), it simultaneously makes him radical—iconoclastic indeed!—in his desire to transform the modes of theatre production. The virtue of a classic is not that it embodies a past glory from which we have declined, but that it was modern ahead of its time—a work of implicit futurology. Also, though he sees the human situations that make for drama as being trans-historical, that does not make him a naïve realist about how they should be represented. His advocacy of modern dress does not make a fetish of fashion, but simply wants to discard conventions of theatrical costume that have come to seem threadbare. When he says: 'I would have the great truth—the truth to minute and immediate personal experience—insisted on rather than the lesser, fantastically unimportant, truth, to the detail of period costume' (78), he recognizes that Shakespeare's way of achieving that truth to experience is through a transformation of the mundane; through the convention that characters in plays 'are always allowed to speak *better* than they would ever do in ordinary life' (70). Ayliff's *Hamlet* stayed with him as 'incomparably his greatest experience in the theatre' (52). One of the things it brought home to him was a Stanislavskian—though also socialist—appreciation of the importance of the ensemble. The production showed that 'Hamlet is not the principal figure in his own play' (61).

For all its ahistoricism about classic works, Griffith's celebration of their vitality for keeping them 'always modern' does at least recognize that modernity is always changing. It was doubtless a sense that change had been so rapid and seismic because of the war that made modernized modes of Shakespeare production seem necessary after it. That sense of disruption in language and behaviour is evident across many of the To-Day and To-Morrow volumes; and especially so in those dealing with conventions of the sayable or writeable. We have seen Graves's fantasia on obscenity and swearing in *Lars Porsena* (in Chapter 2). The series is of particular interest to modernist studies is in its discussions of taboo and censorship; not least because of the censoring of works by figures such as Radcliffe Hall, Lawrence, and Joyce.

In *It Isn't Done; or, The Future of Taboo among the British Islanders* (1930), Archibald Lyall satirizes a range of mostly class-specific prohibitions: 'It is at least possible that our children will be free from the body taboo altogether', he writes: 'but it is almost the only taboo from which there seems any prospect of their emancipation' (95); this by contrast with '[t]he snob taboos, the clothes taboos, the sporting taboos, the religious taboos', and the taboo on money (95). It is his attention to the shifts in conventions of permissibility in the literary representation of the body, and of sexuality, that is of especial interest to students of modern literature. He discusses the shock effect of Shaw's use of the word 'bloody' in *Pygmalion*, and says of the rapidity of the change of 'taboos with regard to "bad" language' (51):

> The Islanders were deeply shocked when, after decades of '—'s and 'b—'s, Mr Masefield, or whoever it was, first printed the word 'bloody' in full. And yet in 1927 Mr Robert Graves referred to two of the most strictly tabooed words as 'x–ing' and 'y–ing'. By 1929 he had progressed to 'b–ing' and 'f–ing', and I am not aware that anyone so much as commented on it.   (51)[32]

He goes on to note that *The Middle Parts of Fortune* (by Frederic Manning, though it had to be published anonymously at first as by 'Private 19022') printed the words in full; though the first edition (of 1929) was sold only to private subscribers (52).[33] Lyall argues that as taboos lose their force, they are replaced with 'antitaboos'; as for example when the young appear more ashamed at being spotted in a church than a pub (83–4). He identifies himself clearly as one of the series' progressive authors: 'For myself I think it is no bad thing for adolescents to discover that a thing is not necessarily a fact because their parents and pedagogues have said that it is' (33).

The taboos Lyall discusses are a form of censorship diffused through society, and policed by other citizens, families and institutions such as schools and churches—and even, when fully internalized, by the self. The elisions in print are also self-imposed (whether by authors or publishers); but adopted to escape prosecution from laws prohibiting obscenity or blasphemy or sedition. Print censorship is thus only one aspect of Lyall's taboos; a special case of where taboo meets law. It is the sole subject of William Seagle's trenchant book of the same year, *Cato; or, The Future of Censorship*.[34]

Seagle contrasts the 'great martyrs' of the past—Socrates, Jesus, Galileo—with the present's 'intimate conversations of Mr. George Moore, the prefaces at large of Mr. Bernard Shaw, and the anti-puritanical homilies of Mr. H. L. Mencken' (8–9). 'As in the past the great battles against censorship have been fought in the name of the freedom of thought', he says: 'they are now fought in the name of the freedom of art' (9). Nonetheless, he still believes that '[i]n the last analysis all censorship is

---

[32] The first reference is to Robert Graves, *Lars Porsena; or, The Future of Swearing and Improper Language* (1927), 43; the second probably to his *Good-Bye to All That*, which includes several usages of 'f—ing'.

[33] See the discussion of Archibald Lyall's remarks in the Introduction to Ford Madox Ford's *No More Parades*, ed. Joseph Wiesenfarth (Manchester: Carcanet, 2011), lv; and also John Attridge's discussion of Lyall in '"A Taboo on the Mention of Taboo": Taciturnity and Englishness in *Parade's End* and André Maurois' *Les Silences du Colonel Bramble*', in *Ford Madox Ford's* Parade's End: *The First World War, culture and modernity*, ed. Ashley Chantler and Rob Hawkes (Rodopi: Amsterdam and New York, 2014), 23–35.

[34] Both *Cato* and *To the Pure…: A Study of Obscenity and the Censor* by Morris L. Ernst and William Seagle (New York: Viking, 1928), are discussed in *Prudes on the Prowl: Fiction and obscenity in England, 1850 to the present day*, ed. David Bradshaw and Rachel Potter (Oxford: Oxford University Press, 2013).

political censorship' (10); though this has been organized in terms of 'three great formulæ: those of political, theological, and sexual absolutism' (11); the third characterizing the present: 'Our age is the asterisk age' (22). He distinguishes between two types of obscenity. First, 'an excessive sexualism or eroticism in any work which contravenes the sense of shame resulting from the mores of the community'—he terms this 'the obscenity of established sin'. Second, 'bringing accepted morality into contumely or contempt'; which he terms 'critical obscenity'. The first is tolerated, whereas the second 'is always regarded with suspicion, and is suppressed as soon as its implications are understood'. 'Radicalism in sexual morals is the worst kind of obscenity', he observes, revealing his progressive streak: 'All discussions of birth control are considered, *ipso facto*, obscene' (26-7). 'Cato would never have understood Comstock' (33), he says, referring to Anthony Comstock, the US Postal Inspector who founded the New York Society for the Suppression of Vice, and campaigned to censor birth control information.

Seagle's comment that '[t]he democratization of life had still to be completed by the secularization of life' (33) might sound like an augury of freedom from such censorship. But his penultimate chapter takes a curious turn—though one characteristic of the series—when it turns to 'Mechanism and Censorship'. Though much of the 'progress of democratic institutions' is ascribed to 'the mechanisation of the means of human expression', he argues, in fact 'with increasing mechanization freedom has suffered more and more' (69). This is in part a straightforward argument about capitalist complexity. 'As long as the machine remains comparatively simple the effect is to expand the possibilities of human personality and human expression' (70). Thus far it is also an argument about prosthetic emancipation. The revolutionist with a hand-press hidden in a cellar is a more potent threat than a man with a pen. But a complex printing process such as is required for books or newspapers needs substantial investment of capital; and capitalists exert control over what is printed (70-1). For similar reasons, he says that cinema has proven 'even easier to control' (73); though he attributes this ease not only to 'even greater concentrations of capital' (as we saw), but to what he calls 'Psychological perversions which have resulted from the high degree of mechanization in film art [...]' (73-4). What he means by this is that the effect of cinema on the viewer is at the opposite pole of the machine-man conjunction from prosthetic creativity. He sees film as inducing a form of passivity described in terms of anthropological primitivism; something which other contributors compared anxiously (as we shall see) to hypnosis:

> The psychological process involved really amounts to a complicated animism which has both points of resemblance and dissimilarity from more primitive forms. The printing press still seems simply another 'mechanical arm' of man which he uses to write as he does with a pen. But the cinema projects a life that seems to have a force and vitality of its own. Man, the creator, is in the background, and it is the 'magic shadow-shapes that come and go' that occupy the whole

foreground. It is they who are endowed with thought and emotion and the ability
to move and act.   (74-5)

The quotation is from Fitzgerald's *Rubaiyat of Omar Khayyám* (stanza 68); but the
analysis is of the process of fetishism, whether out of anthropology, or Marx's
concept of commodity fetishism. Implicit here too is the notion that cinema
infantilizes its audience, and is thus capable of exerting a powerful influence.
Seagle's discussion thus also brings out how the question of censorship relates to
the ideas of propaganda and public opinion discussed in the previous chapter in
relation to *Stentor* and *The Next Chapter*, and their visions of the power of the
press. Seagle thinks the talkies only heighten the animistic effect, while their
added technological complexity makes them yet more susceptible to censorship.
Where Archibald Low thought radio brought a man into your room, Seagle worries that it breaks the connection between speaker and listener, so that '[a] speaker
can be censored without himself or the audience being aware of the fact' (78). He
argues that 'radio television', when perfected, will bring the talkie into the home,
and '[a] great part of the distinction between public and private performances
will have been destroyed' (79-80). 'Homo sapiens will sit in his cave like an insect
with antennæ' (79). If web 2.0 and its prosumers seem the logical extension of this
vision of hive mentality, so do the new forms in which the internet has posed the
questions of private and public, susceptibility, surveillance, and censorship.
Indeed, Seagle's final chapter—'The Certainty of Censorship'—argues that the
technologization of media will ensure that censorship continues. 'The last censorship will be a psychological censorship which will last for countless thousands of
years', he prophesies; 'The perfection of the mind of man will be the ruling
passion of the governors of society' (94). This anticipates a eugenicist future in
which crime is redescribed as disease; and with an Orwellian Thought Police of
'Psychological Comptrollers' (94), as suggested in Chapter 2, with the term
'censorship' itself becoming airbrushed out of history. But that image of the already-
censored being brought into the insect's private cave also suggests how that
'psychological censorship' is also a matter of the increasing internalization of
censorship by the individual psyche; and thus a further example of alteration
of mind by machine.

*   *   *

In some respects, then, the series' account of literature and the arts is more variable
in quality than its coverage of other fields. In particular, its representation of
modernism, interesting though it is, is less impressive than might have been
expected, and on two counts. Hardly any of the contributors are major *modernist*
writers: MacDiarmid, certainly; but the others, though accomplished, popular,
and writing on modern subjects, are unlikely to be described as modernists. The
high modernists are given little sustained or serious discussion. Joyce is invoked

chiefly in relation to obscenity or unintelligibility. Woolf, Stein, Ford, Eliot, Pound, and Lewis receive some attention but only slight analysis and ambivalent evaluation. They were the producers of the literature of the future: not because they were producing futurology, but because, as Lewis said about himself, Joyce, Pound, and Eliot, they seemed too far ahead of their time: '*We are the first men of a future which has not materialized*'.[35] The contrast with the criticism by those writers of their contemporaries, or with the criticism beginning to appear from Ogden's associates Richards and Empson, is telling.

It could be countered that Ogden was publishing major cutting-edge work in several disciplines in his other series, including landmark criticism and theory by Richards and T. E. Hulme. Or it might be objected that the aim of the series was to speculate *about* the art, criticism, philosophy, etc. of the future, rather than try to provide it. But even that is what the works on art and literature only intermittently do. Which may be why literary studies have rarely attended to the series in general to the extent it deserves. However, as the next section will demonstrate, important writers of the period were attending closely.

Modernist Responses: Case Studies

Aldous Huxley

To-Day and To-Morrow is a major element of Huxley's intellectual context, and his relation to his contemporaries. Roy Lewis wrote of the series that 'It is easy to see whence came many of the ideas for Huxley's *Brave New World*, and similar books'.[36] The main aim of the rest of this chapter will be to try to convey why readers and scholars might find the series relevant to modern writers like Huxley, Joyce, Eliot, Lewis, Waugh, and others. Huxley was writing *Brave New World* when To-Day and To-Morrow wound up in 1931. He was one of many writers who had been watching the series closely, if not actually contributing to it. Several volumes were written by people who feature in his biography: especially Russell, Maurois, Graves, E. S. P. Haynes, Gerald Heard, C. E. M. Joad, and J. W. N. Sullivan. Doubtless he knew other contributors. What is more, those he knew were among those most involved with the series, in that Russell, Graves, and Joad each wrote two volumes for it.[37] That is one reason for thinking Huxley was following the series. Another is that the volume that is of most relevance to his work, and

---

[35] Wyndham Lewis, *Blasting & Bombardiering* (London: John Calder, 1982), 256.

[36] Roy Lewis, 'C. K. Ogden's To-Day & To-Morrow Series', *The Private Library*, 3rd Series 10:4 (1987), [140]–52 (147). This is the fullest account of the series, with the most complete listing, though it omits the three USA-only volumes, and also *Achates* and *Chronos*.

[37] Only nine of the authors wrote two volumes for the series. The others were E. E. Fournier d'Albe, J. F. C. Fuller, George Godwin, J. Y. T. Greig (pseud. 'John Carruthers'), and F. C. S. Schiller.

especially to *Brave New World*, was the first and most important one, written by his close friend J. B. S. Haldane (who also provided two volumes).

Huxley had got to know the Haldanes before entering Oxford as an undergraduate. The summer before he had been staying with them, acting in a play by Naomi Haldane, later Naomi Mitchison, the sister of J. B. S.[38] The connections between *Daedalus* and *Brave New World* are striking. Though, as Aline Ferreira has argued, it isn't simply a case of Huxley getting the idea from *Daedalus*, since he had already written about ectogenesis, albeit more fleetingly, in *Crome Yellow* two years earlier, in 1921:[39]

> '[…] An impersonal generation will take the place of Nature's hideous system. In vast state incubators, rows upon rows of gravid bottles will supply the world with the population it requires. The family system will disappear; society, sapped at its very base, will have to find new foundations; and Eros, beautifully and irresponsibly free, will flit like a gay butterfly from flower to flower through a sunlit world.'
>
> 'It sounds lovely,' said Anne.
>
> 'The distant future always does.'

We cannot quite say, then, that Huxley got his ideas of ectogenesis from Haldane's *Daedalus*. The character Scogan who offers this utopian vision is said to be based on Bertrand Russell; though it seems likely that in this earlier sketch of the idea, Huxley was drawing on *conversations* with Haldane.[40] Certainly, in 'A Note on Eugenics', Huxley attributed the idea to Haldane, writing: 'It is quite possible, as Mr. J. B. S. Haldane has suggested, that biological technique will soon have advanced to such a pitch that scientists will succeed in doing what Dr. Erasmus Darwin and Miss Anna Seward, the Swan of Lichfield, tried, it is said, and failed to do: they will learn to breed babies in bottles.'[41]

There was, doubtless, influence running the other way too, with Haldane, writing his paper in 1923, recalling Huxley's novel of 1921, and developing its suggestion of ectogenesis into a fuller elaboration of a possible 'distant future' world in which it was the norm—a utopian vision that Huxley could then draw upon in his turn, and turn to dystopia when fully realized in *Brave New World*. Surely he would have been interested in how his friend had developed the concept in *Daedalus*. But even if not, he would have been reminded of it by his

---

[38] Sybille Bedford, *Aldous Huxley: A biography*, 2 vols, vol. 1 (London: Quartet, 1979), 40, 43.

[39] Aline Ferreira, 'The Sexual Politics of Ectogenesis in the To-Day and To-Morrow Series', *Interdisciplinary Science Reviews*, 34:1 (March 2009), 32–55. But, as Peter Firchow argues, it's impossible to determine influence either way: 'Science and Conscience in Huxley's *Brave New World*', *Contemporary Literature*, 16:3 (Summer 1975), 301–16. Also see Angus McLaren, *Reproduction by Design: Sex, robots, trees, and test-tube babies in interwar Britain* (Chicago: University of Chicago Press, 2012).

[40] Huxley also satirized him as the character of Shearwater in his 1923 novel *Antic Hay*. See Ronald Clark, *JBS: The life and work of J. B. S. Haldane* (London: Hodder and Stoughton, 1968), 57.

[41] Aldous Huxley, *Proper Studies* (London: Chatto & Windus, 1927), 272–82 (278). See Susan M. Squier, *Babies in Bottles: Twentieth-century visions of reproductive technology* (New Brunswick, NJ: Rutgers University Press, 1994).

brother Julian's book *What Dare I Think?* of 1931—the year Aldous was writing *Brave New World*:

> Many of my readers will remember how Mr Haldane in his *Daedalus* envisaged the possibility of ectogenesis or the bringing up of babies in incubators instead of in their mothers' bodies. We are a long way from realizing that possibility, and yet, in the short space of time since he wrote, the first step has been successfully taken. Professor Warren Lewis, of Baltimore, has succeeded in cultivating rabbits' eggs outside the body, from a moment immediately after fertilization to about a week later, when they have enlarged considerably and the embryo is showing the beginnings of organization. He has even recorded their development on the cinematograph; and it is one of the most astonishing spectacles to see, on the speeded up film, the processes of cell-division, of organization, of growth, which have never before in any mammal taken place in the light of day, going on in the unfamiliar environment of a drop of nutrient fluid in a glass dish just as happily as in the dark recesses of the Fallopian tube, just as regularly as if the eggs were the eggs of sea-urchin or starfish in which development customarily takes place outside the body.[42]

Remember that cinematograph.

We saw how Haldane used the trope of future history, writing an imaginary student's essay of the future, summarizing the history of biological science. So where Julian Huxley in 1931 could look back to Haldane's 1923 predictions and say 'the first step has been successfully taken', Haldane describes lots of future steps as having already been taken—indeed including how he himself had grown embryonic rats in serum for ten days' as early as 1925 (*Daedalus*, 63). Not unlike the effect of a speeded up film...

> France was the first country to adopt ectogenesis officially, and by 1968 was producing 60,000 children annually by this method. In most countries the opposition was far stronger, and was intensified by the Papal Bull 'Nunquam prius audito', and by the similar fetwa of the Khalif, both of which appeared in 1960.
>
> As we know ectogenesis is now universal, and in this country less than 30 per cent of children are now born of woman. The effect on human psychology and social life of the separation of sexual love and reproduction which was begun in the 19th century and completed in the 20th is by no means wholly satisfactory. The old family life had certainly a good deal to commend it, and although nowadays we bring on lactation in women by injection of placentin as a routine, and thus conserve much of what was best in the former instinctive cycle, we must admit that in certain respects our great grandparents had the advantage of us. On the other hand it is generally admitted that the effects of selection have more than counterbalanced these evils. The small proportion of men and women who are selected as ancestors for the next generation are so undoubtedly

---

[42] Julian Huxley, *What Dare I Think?* (London: Chatto and Windus, 1931), pp. 53–4.

superior to the average that the advance in each generation in any single respect, from the increased output of first-class music to the decreased convictions for theft, is very startling. (65-6)

Underneath the parody of the undergraduate trying to sound authoritative seems to be a claim that any ways we might find of talking about such issues are less interesting than the possibilities themselves. If only we could get over our religious, instinctive, or habitual ways of thinking about such ideas, we'd be able to realize the benefits, and realize we have nothing to fear. But then Haldane (who was sceptical of Eugenics) plants that eugenicist idea about selection, and the improbable closing flourish about both art and crime, which can only ironize the undergraduate's whiggish tone, and introduce a doubt as to whether the vision really is of a better new world.

The antitheses of this passage anticipate *Brave New World*. The novel, too, sets the eugenic and cultural changes against the instinctive ways of bearing children and the traditional ways of educating them. But whereas the World State considers the innovations to be improvements, as Haldane's imaginary undergraduate does, Huxley reverses the values: the story of John Savage shows how the losses outweigh any gains. Where the undergraduate damns the past with faint praise—'The old family life had certainly a good deal to commend it'—Huxley sees such visions of the future as too cavalier in their abandonment of the human.

Or, to put it another way, Huxley can see the power of the future history trope—how it might make radical transformation seem achievable, nothing to worry about; and that might have been part of what disturbed him about *Daedalus*. In *Brave New World* he turns that attitude against itself; creating Haldane's world in which things like ectogenesis are taken for granted, and the past and its traditions and cultures condescended towards, and shows us why he thinks we should worry about it.

As Patrick Parrinder too argues, there is a clear line from *Daedalus* to *Brave New World*.[43] But in two major respects Huxley takes the exploration a stage further. He adds a prophetic invention of his own: 'Malthusian belts' containing chemical contraception, which ensure that sex remains casual and recreational. We have seen how Birth control was an important cause running through a number of To-Day and To-Morrow volumes. The contraceptive pill did not become a reality until two decades later. But it completed the separation *Daedalus* had predicted between sexual love and reproduction (65).

Huxley also extrapolates the familiar figure of 'machine man', imagining a version of him not just altered by machines, but manufactured like them—the 'machined man' of the 'Bokanovsky groups' of cloned workers.[44]

[43] Patrick Parrinder, *Utopian Literature and Science* (Basingstoke: Palgrave Macmillan, 2015), 54.
[44] Though Cecil Chisholm in *Vulcan* does imagine a future factory in which: 'Only one room never knows monotony; the sunny room where the sub-normals ply their routine tasks' (85). If the discourse

Russell's *Icarus* might well have attracted Huxley's attention too. He certainly got to know Russell through Ottoline Morrell's circle at Garsington. There is evidence that Huxley's circle was aware of Russell's book (and thus also of Haldane's). In early March 1924, J. W. N. Sullivan told J. M. Murry that he was writing a novel (at Huxley's house outside Florence). 'I get very little conversation. Even the Huxleys have been away the last week or so, and I'm alone here with the nurse and baby... Have you seen the review of B. Russell's "Icarus" in the New Statesman? An extraordinarily downright condemnation. It sounds as if Russell had declined into a sniggering vicious futility.'[45] Russell's sense that science was likely to be used in the wrong way to become repressive and totalitarian could be seen as another influence (among many) on *Brave New World*.

But there are two further ways in which the series may be more interestingly relevant to Huxley; and specifically to two of the most famous technological predictions of *Brave New World*; hypnopaedia and the feelies. As with ectogenesis, neither of these can be attributed as originating with Huxley, nor with To-Day and To-Morrow. Huxley has a good eye for the eye-catching developments that scientists and journalists were talking about as just beyond the horizon of the future. And, at the very least, To-Day and To-Morrow represents a set of good examples of this kind of science talk; examples of which he would surely have been aware.

Hypnopaedia—literally, 'sleep education', could be found in literature before the war. Hugo Gernsback's 1911 novel *Ralph 124C 41+* features a 'Hypnobioscope': a sleep learning device.[46] But the term 'hypnopaedia' also connotes the phenomenon of hypnosis—of course newly fascinating and fashionable after Freud and Breuer's *Studies in Hysteria* of 1895 as offering a way into the mind, in order to modify behaviour and cure mental illness. Perhaps you didn't have to be J. B. S. Haldane to think that hypnosis had plenty of potential that remained to be explored scientifically and applied to different areas of life. But what Haldane says about it, again in *Daedalus*, offers a further reason for thinking the book had its effect on Huxley:

> Psychology is hardly a science yet. Like biology it has arrived at certain generalizations of a rather abstract and philosophic character, but these are still to some extent matters of controversy. And though a vast number of most important empirical facts are known, only a few great generalizations from them—such as the existence of the subconscious mind—have yet been made.

of 'sub-normals' sounds eugenicist, Chisholm is advocating fulfilment rather than elimination. It is not impossible that the image might have contributed to Huxley's Epsilons.

---

[45] Sullivan to Murry, 9 March 1924; Harry Ransom Center; I'm grateful to David Bradshaw for drawing my attention to this letter. The *New Statesman* review, 22:640 (8 March 1924), 515, complained of 'thin and spiteful politico-economic anticipations'.

[46] Hugo Gernsback, *Ralph 124C 41+*, first published as a serial in *Modern Electrics* from April 1911.

But anyone who has seen even a single example of the power of hypnotism and suggestion must realise that the face of the world and the possibilities of existence will be totally altered when we can control their effects and standardize their application, as has been possible, for example, with drugs which were once regarded as equally magical.   (74-5)

Julian Huxley was interested in hypnosis too, so again, the precise lines of influence are hard to trace in such a group actively discussing each other's ideas.[47] But it seems to me that Aldous Huxley appears more stimulated by Haldane's more extreme prophecies. In *Brave New World* he extrapolates Haldane's suggestion: showing us that altered face of the world in which the effects of hypnosis can be controlled and its application standardized.

In *Brave New World* the technique is discovered by accident when a Polish boy hears an English radio broadcast in his sleep, and is able to reproduce it even though he doesn't understand it. Why the radio? Well, from one point of view, the broadcasting technology gets the alien language into the domestic space. But there is also a sense that the technology enables a more direct connection to the mind than with normal speech. Would it have been as effective an image if the boy had unconsciously overheard a conversation, through his open bedroom window, of some English travellers outside? Huxley's radio does not just bring a man (or woman) into the room; it brings a voice into the head—rather as with Bernal's radio-receptive brains.

The media offer both a means of mass dissemination, and also of repetition through recording. So the effects can be controlled and standardized, as Haldane's scientific imagination required. In Gernsbach's story, the 'Hypnobioscope' would have reminded readers of the 'Bioscope show', a travelling cinema that was a popular fairground attraction before the war. But what this example, and Huxley's Polish boy also reveal, is that the conjunction of hypnosis and media is addressing a specific anxiety of the period, which is that the media themselves appear to have hypnotic properties.

This is where the topic of hypnopedia intersects with that of the 'feelies'. The 'feelies' are famously an extrapolation of the 'talkies'; which had just arrived four years before, with *The Jazz Singer* in 1927; and which, before then, had been the utopian future that the industry had been eagerly predicting. Not so all its film critics though. The Introductions discussed the consummate bad timing of Ernest Betts's prophecy, made just as the first talkie was released, that: 'The film of a hundred years hence, if it is true to itself, will still be silent, but it will be saying more than ever' (*Heraclitus* 88). Yet *Heraclitus* has other qualities to

---

[47] See Julian Huxley, *Essays of a Biologist* (London: Chatto, 1923), Preface, p. ix on hypnosis: 'all the main claims of its founders have been verified, and many new facts unearthed'. 'The mind can be raised to an abnormal sensitiveness [...]'.

recommend it, including its suggestive remarks about precisely this concern about film and hypnosis:

> But it is not, unfortunately, the arts which sway the world—not truth by itself, revealed by the imagination, but half-truth, or opinion, and in the forming of opinion insufficient note seems to have been taken of the strange, hypnotic, unanalysed power of the film to sink its message into the minds and memories of people in a way that has no parallel among the recognised arts.
>
> It is very unlikely that this new and fatal gun-powder will be left alone when the merest touch from mankind can make it dangerous; for as one armed nation forces arms upon another, so one country has only to utilize 'the pictures' for propaganda and its neighbour must do likewise. For this reason, leaving out of account the film's separate responsibilities, it is of immense importance that it should be in the right hands, in the control of people who realize that they are under some obligation to civilization to serve it decently and intelligently—always, of course, putting the interests of the shareholders first.   (82-3)

This not just about the *emotional* manipulativeness of a cinema which ministers to multiple senses. It is also about the medium's potential for *political and economic* manipulativeness too; whether in advertising or public information broadcasts—the kind of power satirized by Orwell in *Nineteen Eighty-Four* with the two minute hate.

So readers might turn to David Fraser-Harris's volume in the series, *Morpheus; or, The Future of Sleep*, also from 1928, expecting that he too would have something to say about future uses of sleep such as hypnopaedia. From that point of view, *Morpheus* is rather disappointing. True, Fraser-Harris (who was a professor of physiology and histology and, like several other contributors, was interested in psychical research) presents an exciting picture of sleep as a subject only beginning to be treated scientifically, and thus having everything to play for. He thinks the science of sleep will be able to tell us more about dreaming—hence the title, since Morpheus in mythology can assume any form and appear in dreams. But Fraser-Harris, who one can only assume was drawn to the topic because he was a light sleeper, if not an insomniac, is, like his great precursor writing about dreams, De Quincey, obsessed by noise: the noisiness of society that disturbs the sleeper. He advocates what he calls 'The Hygiene of Sleep'.

His book ends with a chapter on 'The Future of Sleep', which introduces Freudian dream theory, but predicts its being challenged by future research. Fraser-Harris is more concerned with future legislation trying to prevent neighbours being noisy nuisances, however, rather than any Huxleyan predictions. Nevertheless, the phrase 'the future of sleep' (both in the title of the book and of the last chapter) may have been enough to set the novelist's imagination dreaming about the ways in which society might attempt to control and standardize sleep, as it uses it for processes of indoctrination or advertisement.

But it is not just the phrase 'the future of sleep' that readers might wish to connect with Huxley's novel. Take this sentence, near the beginning: "The savage in the remotest ages considered, as does the savage of our own day, that the state of sleep was full of significance' (10). That combination of thinking about the future of sleep, and thinking about the category of 'the savage' as both prehistoric and contemporary, is striking. But also, the structure of ideas here is comparable to that of *Brave New World*. In the novel, John Savage is brought up on the 'Savage Reservation', remote in space from the technocratic civilized world. But this 'savage of our own day' turns out to be more in tune with traditional civiliza-tion—more cultured—than those who adhere to modern principles rather than ancient ones. In Fraser-Harris' text, that phrase 'the savage of our own day' is ambiguous. It could mean those 'primitive' tribes who were the subject of the modern anthropological observation beginning to be defined in this period (by writers such as Bronisław Malinowski, who was also very much part of Ogden's circle, publishing in his other series, though not To-Day and To-Morrow. *Crime and Custom in Savage Society*, 1926, and *Sex and Repression in Savage Society*, 1927, for example, were published in the International Library).

But it could also mean 'we savages'; and thus be ironic about our flattering ourselves that modern civilization distances us from the savage. Fraser-Harris was no Freudian, and part of his irony is to suggest that Freudian dream-interpretation is not so distant from ancient theories of dream interpretation. But it is a genuine irony rather than a sarcasm, since it was his attraction to ideas of psychical research that made him sceptical of psycho-analysis. So he is acknowledging his kinship with what anthropologists used to call 'the savage mind'.

I dwell on this example not just because of its relevance to *Brave New World*, but because the trope of reverse anthropology—of viewing the civilized as the savage—comes up elsewhere in To-Day and To-Morrow, in Archibald Lyall's fine book (discussed briefly above in relation to censorship), *It Isn't Done; or, The Future of Taboo Among the British Islanders*, published in 1930—the year before Huxley wrote *Brave New World*. Referring to his own society as 'the British island-ers' does more than just make them sound insular—little Englanders, provincial in their moral and social codes. It puts them on a par with, say, the Trobriand islanders near New Guinea, famously visited by Malinowski during the First World War, his studies of their sexual and social customs becoming foundational texts of modern anthropology. When you look at British society objectively, the trope implies, it is as 'other' as any you might want to call 'primitive' or 'savage', its prescriptions and taboos as mysterious as any fetishistic or animistic practices. That is Huxley's trope in the novel too. The citizens in the World State visit the Reservation as tourists, in search of the exotic. But the Savage they find there is simply early twentieth-century man. His commitment to natural processes, family bonds, literature, seem bizarre to his visitors. But as readers identify with Savage, they see that it is the World State that is bizarre. And if its citizens are taking an anthropological field trip to the reservation, the novel anthropologizes them in return, making explicit the rules by which their society works.[48] The novel's anthropologically-minded visitors, that is, are not just from a zone distant in space, but in time. Their modernity is more modern than the twentieth century whose anthropologists were visiting the South Seas. They are anthropologists from the future. That innovative double displacement is in Lyall's book too: in order to get the distance on British culture of the twentieth century, he has to imagine how the taboos of the future will differ from those of the present.

We saw Lyall imagining the next generation casting off 'the body taboo', but remaining in thrall to those in other areas, such as class, everyday life, and religion. Huxley imagines not only sexual de-repression, but the casting off of the religious taboos of Christianity or snake worship outside the Reservation. Yet in two paradoxical ways religious taboo appears harder to escape. The substitution of Ford for Christ suggests a persistence of magical thinking. Whereas, conversely, the rejection of traditional religions and *mores* might be argued to have turned into what Lyall calls 'antitaboos' (83-4).[49] Lyall's 'snob taboos' (95), by contrast, remains firmly in place in *Brave New World*, newly underwritten by the pseudo-scientific Eugenic classifications of aptitude from alpha to epsilon.

Some of the individual connections proposed here may seem mere coincidence; too tenuous a basis for a claim of influence. Huxley could arguably have come up with his reversals of contemporary moral positions without needing Lyall's or Seagle's elegant and ironized statements of those positions. But To-Day and To-Morrow imagines the future across a number of fields, most of which in fact provide the main co-ordinates for *Brave New World*: the Wellsian ideal of a post-national politics; reproduction, birth control and eugenics; anthropology; sleep; mass production; leisure and so on. It is that combination of futurology across a range of concerns which strengthens the case for influence.

There is one volume which, alongside *Daedalus*, provides the best evidence for thinking the series relevant to *Brave New World*. This is *Timotheus; The Future of the Theatre*, by the well-known literary critic Bonamy Dobrée: one of the earlier volumes, dating from 1925. Dobrée was a specialist in the Augustan period, and *Timotheus* is an accomplished Swiftean satire of theatre developments, ostensibly just charting the future, but actually criticizing the present. The impressionable narrator manages to borrow H. G. Wells's *Time Machine* and actually visit the future that other authors in the series can only guess about. When there, he takes

---

[48] As Hisashi Ozawa has shown, Huxley was also probably drawing on a striking real-life case of bi-directional anthropology: 'John and Ishi, "Savage" Visitors to "Civilization": A reconsideration of Aldous Huxley's *Brave New World*, imperialism and anthropology', *Aldous Huxley Annual*, 12/13 (Münster: LIT Verlag, 2014), 123-47.

[49] See above, pp. 303-04. William Seagle's related concept of 'critical obscenity' in *Cato*, discussed above, p. 305, may also have contributed to Huxley's imagining of future mores in which what is deemed shocking is any departure from 'the separation of sexual love and reproduction'.

an air-taxi to the National Theatre (which didn't exist until 1963, though it had been under discussion since the First World War). He is taken to a kind of play there called a 'clutch'—

> the name given to a drama of the kind about to take place, where everything was under the control of one man, the 'fairfusser' as he is called,[50] who designs the movement, the emotional sequences, the voices, and whatever else is needed.   (11-12)

There is a parody of the emerging kind of meticulously controlling director, whether in Stanislavsky's realist mode or Harley Granville Barker's more symbolist one. The individual control of the fairfusser might make us think of subsequent *auteur* in theory in cinema. But we can also note that, as in *Morpheus*, there is a combination of hypnosis and control. For the theatre in *Timotheus* is an immersive, multi-sensory experience, involving throbbing, rhythms, aromas, psychotropic gases, and spectacle and movement designed for maximum intensity of effect (25-6). For example:

> The naming of nitrous oxide, or laughing gas as it used to be called, brings me to the perfumes, which, I learnt, were led along each row of seats by what I had taken for hot-water pipes. This again, Fabian said, was a legacy of the third (1914-1918) Great War of European Settlement, and he gave me to read an account I have since recovered of a gas which caused 'the most appalling mental distress and misery'.[51] Of course the means had been much refined, and the fairfusser could at will set free gases which brought about sorrow, fear, joy, shame, the love of glory or of animals, and indeed any emotion, all without the least risk of harm; though it is true that some serious mishaps, especially in the early stages, had unluckily happened. The combined result was that almost any feeling, and any required degree of that feeling, could be produced by the fairfusser, and this the government found of the greatest use at times of political or European crisis, when wars were to be declared or averted, or any controversial measure passed.   (26-8)

Dobrée explicitly invokes Freud and hypnosis, quoting Freud's *Group Psychology and the Analysis of the Ego*, where it says:

> Thus the indirect methods of hypnotising, like many of the technical procedures used in making jokes, have the effect of checking certain distributions of mental energy which would interfere with the course of events in the unconscious, and

---

[50] Perhaps with a suggestion of the German *Vierfüssler*, or quadruped.

[51] Dobrée here footnotes 'J. B. S. Haldane, *Callinicus*'. The quotation is on p. 10, describing arsenic compounds with powerful but largely temporary effects. Note how, as in Graves's *Lars Porsena*, the future historian has redescribed our history. The Great War becomes the 'third (1914-1918) Great War of European Settlement'—not unlike the way it would actually get redesignated as the 'First World War' after the occurrence of its sequel.

they lead eventually to the same result as the direct methods of influence by means of staring or stroking.[52]

The narrator adds: 'From there the high road is plain to see; the phrases of the clutch check or loosen "certain distributions of mental energy," for art is only a kind of hypnotism'. Like Ernest Betts in *Heraclitus* writing of 'the strange, hypnotic, unanalysed power of the film', Dobrée worries that the power of this new form of immersive, hypnotic theatre, will be used to manipulate public opinion and behaviour; as an instrument of propaganda (28).

Indeed, it is used as a kind of subliminal advertising for government funds. It soon becomes clear that Dobrée isn't only talking about theatre, but about cinema, and in much the same way as Betts's *Heraclitus*. But Dobrée's futurology is more inventive. His narrator observes another kind of theatre, with signs above them saying '"Two Minutes," or "Thirty Seconds," or some like period of time' (63). Had Orwell read this, we might wonder? The narrator learns that these are called 'Hurry Theatres', where busy commuters can drop in for a dose of 'organised emotion' (64). I. A. Richards had been lecturing in Cambridge while Dobrée was a student there, and this phrase—very redolent of the neurological basis of Richards' work of the 1920s—suggests that the satire is also directed at the literary criticism of the future. Indeed, describing the physical sensations of the 'clutch' theatre, he quotes Richards to comment on the way the air was made to throb— another detail anticipating Huxley's 'feelies'. This throbbing, Dobrée writes, was:

> merely to create a rhythm, the effects of which had been keenly studied. Again to copy a passage I have traced:
>
> 'Among the results of rhythm susceptibility and vivacity of emotion, limitations of the field of attention, marked differences in the incidence of belief feelings closely analogous to those which alcohol and nitrous oxide can induce...may be noted.' (25-6)[53]

The 'Hurry Theatres' are also anticipations of the talkies: 'I had seen the backs of men standing in lines, with pads clamped over their ears and their faces pushed forward into a sort of camera' (64), says the narrator. But it turns out that what looks like a camera is really: 'a stereoscopic glass directed on a double film screen, and the pads were the telephone receivers through which one heard the voices of the actors, which seemed to come from their mouths' (66). But as in the clutches, the words aren't there for their own sake, or for the communication of ideas, but for a hypnotic production of sensation and affect. Such ideas were in the air even

---

[52] Dobrée *Timotheus*, pp. 22–3. Quoting Sigmund Freud, *Group Psychology and the Analysis of the Ego* page 97. The text appears to be that of the International Psycho-Analytical Press, London and Vienna, 1922.

[53] Quoting I. A. Richards, *The Principles of Literary Criticism*—published in Ogden's International Library (London: Kegan Paul, 1924), 143.

before the First World War. Indeed, in some ways they hark back to the Wagnerian ideal of the *Gesamtkunstwerk*, or total work of art combining drama, music, and the visual arts. In *The New Spirit in Drama* (1912), Huntly Carter had written:

> My own idea of the finest form of national drama which this country will see adopted comprises a rhythmic conception of play, player, decoration, and music. This drama will be represented in a rhythmic form of theatre. Everything henceforth is to be orchestrated to produce a single but infinitely varied total effect. We need a stage which lends itself to the simple and single vision, that brings even the most unintelligent spectator into the action of the drama and holds him there, that promotes a direction of effort on the part of all concerned which will unify the results.[54]

The year after *Timotheus* appeared, Terence Gray, who ran the Festival Theatre Cambridge, wrote in *Dance-Drama: Experiments in the art of the theatre* that words in a dramatic medium were 'a strikingly inadequate medium for the expression of the emotion that they attempt to convey'.[55]

For today's readers, however, what Dobrée seems prescient about is not only what has happened in theatre, but even more so, what has happened in cinema; as dialogue has increasingly given way to music, visual images, and more recently, to 3D and other special effects. He even seems to anticipate developments in video, holograms, and virtual reality, postulating a 3D video recorder (46). To readers of Huxley, though, the parallel is evident with the 'feelies'. Dobrée is more focused on emotional rather than haptic 'feeling'. But it is nonetheless possible that his vision of theatre entirely at the service of manipulating 'feeling' contributed to Huxley's playful coinage of 'feelies' as the next goal of the industry after the 'talkies' (which had emerged between *Timotheus* and *Brave New World*).

The First World War had ushered in a new kind of sustained, intense propaganda operation; and the postwar period earnestly debated public opinion and the media's role in forming it, as discussed in Chapter 5.[56] The concerns about media power suggested by *Brave New World* were widespread, and Huxley could have been drawing on many other sources for them. Or none other than his own analysis. But such concerns are certainly elsewhere in To-Day and To-Morrow. In *Plato's American Republic* (1929) by Douglas Woodruff, Socrates says Americans 'are the least free of all the peoples of the earth' because of the tyrant 'Public Opinion', who is worse than Procrustes, because 'he seems to fashion and control not the

---

[54] Huntly Carter, *The New Spirit in Drama* (London: Frank Palmer, 1912), preface, p. vi.

[55] Terence Gray, *Dance-Drama* (Cambridge: W. Heffer & Sons, 1926), 25. See Andrzej Gasiorek, *A History of Modernist Literature* (Chichester: Wiley-Blackwell, 2015), 493.

[56] See Peter Buitenhuis. *The Great War of Words: British, American, and Canadian propaganda and fiction, 1914–1933* (Vancouver: University of British Columbia Press, 1987); Mark Wollaeger, *Modernism, Media, and Propaganda: British narrative from 1900 to 1945* (Princeton: Princeton University Press, 2006); Patrick Deer, *Culture in Camouflage: War, empire, and modern British literature*, (Oxford: Oxford University Press, 2009).

body, as is the way of ordinary tyrants, but the soul itself. He standardizes their souls wherever he is strong'; he is 'the offspring of Propaganda' (42). We saw in Chapter 2 how in André Maurois' *The Next Chapter; The War against the Moon* (1927) the press barons manufacture public opinion for political control. If the wireless movie, telephotophones, and especially the Hertzian police in Maurois' book sound like Huxleyan and Orwellian themes, they are explored in a comic vein.

Timotheus, like the other volumes discussed in this chapter, was concerned with future art. Yet we saw how the other volume on drama—*Iconoclastes; or, The Future of Shakespeare* (1927)—attended to the future of *past* literature—again with putative parallels to *Brave New World*. Shakespeare too was being made new, and Huxley could conceivably have drawn his own projection of the Bard's future from the postwar modern-dress productions themselves, or other commentaries on them. But what he does in the novel is not just wonder about whether a modernist future might lose the ability to appreciate the classics altogether. He also reimagines *The Tempest*—not in modern dress exactly, in the normal sense of contemporary dress; but in 'future-dress' instead. Is it not possible that it was *Iconoclastes*' conjunction of modern dress and future Shakespeare that prompted such a move?

To conclude this section: in the absence of any definitive evidence confirming Huxley's familiarity with the series, one can only establish a cumulative probability. The presence across the To-Day and To-Morrow series of so many of the preoccupations of *Brave New World* adds up to a reasonable probability that he knew more of the volumes than *Daedalus* (among them perhaps *Scheherazade*, which mentions him as 'disillusionment embodied'; 45). If it is not possible to prove that he read any other specific volumes, it is scarcely conceivable he would not have known of the ones by his friends; and he would probably have been aware of others from reviews (often highly favourable), and of how the series was contributing to the public debates about issues such as birth control, sexual relationships, a world state, mass production, and mass media.

Indeed, given the close affiliations between To-Day and To-Morrow and Ogden's other publishing ventures, the net should perhaps be drawn more widely. Not just Malinowski's volumes on 'Savage Society' for the International Library, but perhaps also some of the Psyche Miniatures, such as H. Stafford Hatfield's *The Conquest of Thought by Invention in the Mechanical State of the Future* (London: Kegan Paul, Trench, Trübner & Co., 1929), whose vision of a mechanized society predicts an applied psychology which will grade individuals to allocate their jobs:

> Before very long each individual will pass through a machine which will state, with an air of complete finality, what that individual is fitted to do. The mental effect of this will be to replace all doubts, fears, [o]ver-weening ambitions and despairing self-searching by a kind of hypnotic state, in which the subject will be aware of no other course than the one for which he is told that he is suited.   (111-12)

'And that', put in the Director sententiously, 'that is the secret of happiness and virtue—liking what you've *got* to do. All conditioning aims at that: making people like their unescapable social destiny.'[57]

Hatfield also envisions technologies of leisure designed to sustain such hypnotic docility:

> Life in the Mechanical State will be so full of harmless distractions that none will have any excuse for communing with his soul. What is left of the more dangerous instincts will be painlessly reacted off in the Cinema, in athletics, in perusal of the daily newspaper. A mild if somewhat perverted eroticism will provide gentle sport for all ages and both sexes. Originality of thought and character will be gently but firmly canalized off into institutions provided for this purpose.   (110)

—such as, perhaps, the Directorate of Hatcheries and Conditioning in which Bernard Marx works on hypnopaedia.

The To-Day and To-Morrow volumes mentioned here include those which Huxley is most likely to have known, and those which seem to offer the closest parallels to *Brave New World*. But they form a small proportion of the whole series. If Huxley had read any of the volumes discussed in this chapter, he would have been aware of many of the others, since by 1927 they all carried a substantial gathering of end-matter including a list of available titles with a description or reviews of each one. It would have been hard for writers not to be aware of the series, given its often admiring reception in the press and the responses to it in other creative works. If, like Huxley, you were writing a fictional dystopian future, it would be strange if you did not look at what contemporary futurology was saying, if only so that your account of everyday life in the future would have some scientific credibility. What the rest of this chapter will make clear is that writers interested in time and modernity were indeed following To-Day and To-Morrow.

James Joyce

Whether or not Haldane had read *Ulysses*, Joyce certainly read *Daedalus*. One of the notebooks he kept while working on *Finnegans Wake* contain numerous fragments jotted down from Haldane's book. As Geert Lernout (one of the editors of the scholarly transcription of the notebook) explains, Joyce appeared to have started his reading, or at least his annotating, *in medias res*, perhaps drawn by Haldane's discussion of the mythological figure of Daedalus. He then worked through to the end of the pastiche student essay, returned to the middle, and worked back through the volume towards the beginning.[58] Lernout observes that

---

[57] Aldous Huxley, *Brave New World* (Harmondsworth: Penguin, 1972), 24.
[58] Geert Lernout, 'Introduction', in *The* Finnegans Wake *Notebooks at Buffalo. Notebook VI.B.1*, ed. Vincent Deane, Daniel Ferrer, and Geert Lernout (Turnhout: Brepols Publishers, 2003), 4–14 (4–6). The notes from *Daedalus* are reproduced, transcribed, and contextualized on pp. 33–41.

'It is not possible to deduce from Joyce's choice of notes what his main interest in this book was'.[59] Another way of putting that would be to say that he was interested in many of the ideas in *Daedalus*, from Haldane's claim that Einstein's physics was returning science from materialism to Kantian idealism, to his argument that vaccination had made the traditional English system of land ownership collapse (because increasing longevity meant that elder sons had to go off and learn another career before inheriting, by which time it was too late 'to learn the art of managing an estate'; 55-6). However, that theme of the cycle of generations, the relation of parents to children, and age to youth, is arguably the central strand running through the passages Joyce annotated; that, and how science might alter the cycle through eugenics and biomedical interventions.

Though Joyce's notebook proves he read *Daedalus* closely, and indicates what caught his eye when reading, they demonstrate little about what use he would make of them in his published work. Very few of his notes on Haldane's book are recognizable in *Finnegans Wake* as allusions or echoes. However, five passages are identified as drawing (however obliquely) on the notes from *Daedalus*.[60] These don't convey Haldane's arguments (though arguably those provide a penumbra of context and suggestion). Rather, Joyce fastens on a word or a phrase. Sometimes, even as he transcribes it into the notebook, he starts playing on it. In one note that doesn't register in the *Wake*, Haldane's student's word 'ectogenic' gestates inexplicably (unless by error) into 'octogenic'.[61] In another example which does get used, Joyce's note that 'plants turn sugar into starch / & cellulose' becomes more specific in the book: 'changing cane sugar into sethulose starch'; as he compounds 'cellulose' with the name 'Seth', the younger brother of Cain (whose name likewise particularizes the sugar).[62] If the phrase appears to function as a hook for one of the *Wake*'s main themes of fraternal conflict, Haldane's description of photosynthesis and plant growth may also have suggested the process of transformations in gestating a book (both starch and cellulose are used in paper manufacture).

Haldane (who later became an Indian citizen) includes a footnote in *Daedalus* arguing that Hinduism has recognized 'the special and physiological relation of man to the cow' by making the latter holy, leading to 'extensive use of cow dung in Indian religious ceremonies' which he says is 'disgusting to the average European'. By contrast, Europeans are 'insensitive to the equally loathsome injunctions of the Catholic Church with regard to human marriage', he argues, concluding that 'It would perhaps be better if both marriage and milking could be secularized' (45n).

---

[59] Ibid., p. 6.
[60] Lernout and his fellow editors helpfully tabulate which passages of the *Wake* bear traces of the notebook entries, on pp. 218–24. They also indicate in their notes on the transcribed notebook entries which passages in the *Wake* relate to these entries. Yet several of these do not figure in their 'Table of usage in *Finnegans Wake*'.
[61] Ibid., p. 34.
[62] Ibid., p. 39; James Joyce, *Finnegans Wake*, third edition (London: Faber, 1964)—henceforth referred to as '*FW*': 29.28.

Joyce wrote 'secularise marriage & / milking' in his notebook.[63] The conjunction of milk and marriage crops up in the *Wake* with 'music' added, parodying the phrase 'wine, women, and song'. Such secularization as that may evoke, though, is produced by yoking together the angelic and the diabolic (or a diabolic Englishman): '(an engles to the teeth who, nomened Nash of Girahash, would go anyold where in the weeping world on his mottled belly (the rab, the kreepon-skneed!) for milk, music or married missusses)'.[64] It is characteristic of Joyce's recycling of material that though it is intelligible how he got from *Daedalus* to such verbal hedonism, we'd never have guessed without the notebook, and the corresponding passage in the *Wake* doesn't depend on its source text for its intelligibility (or suggestivity).

In the other instances, the connection is more tenuous. Or rather, while the concept referred to in Joyce's note is detectable in his text, the language is less recognizable. For example, Haldane argues that as advances in medicine and hygiene have extended longevity, 'religion has come to lay less and less stress on a good death, and more and more on a good life, and its whole outlook has gradually changed in consequence' (54-5). Joyce's note—'death has receded'—quotes from Haldane's 'Death has receded so far into the background of our normal thoughts [...]' (54). But the *Finnegans Wake* passage corresponding to this note transposes the idea to the context of Irish history and legend: 'famine with Englisch sweat and oppedemics, the twotoothed dragon worms a with allsort serpents has compolitely seceded from this landleague of many nations [....]'[65] 'English Sweat' was an epidemic that hit Dublin in 1528. (*Oppidum* is the Latin for town.) The *Dublin Annals* record 'Ireland visited by a plague of strange worms, having two teeth, which devoured everything green in the land; supposed to have been locusts' in 897.[66] While the subject still includes the death and plagues of Haldane's argument, there is no allusion or quotation; just an echo of 'receded' in the very different verb 'seceded'.

Nonetheless, *Daedalus* appears to have incited Joyce to read more widely in To-Day and To-Morrow. After reading at least half of another of the earliest volumes, Crookshank's *The Mongol in Our Midst*, Joyce took out a further eight volumes in 1925 from the lending library of Sylvia Beach's Paris bookshop Shakespeare and Company at 12, Rue de l'Odéon:

1. A.M. Low, *Wireless Possibilities*

2. E.E. Fournier d'Albe, *Quo Vadimus? Glimpses of the Future*[67]

---

[63] Lernout, *The* Finnegans Wake *Notebooks at Buffalo. Notebook VI.B.1*, 37.   [64] *FW*, 75.22.

[65] *FW*, 539-40.

[66] See Roland McHugh, *Annotations to Finnegans Wake*, revised edition (Baltimore: Johns Hopkins University Press, 1991), 540.

[67] Joyce knew of Fournier d'Albe as the compiler of *An English-Irish Dictionary and Phrase Book with Synonyms, Idioms, and the Genders and Declensions of Nouns* (Dublin: M. H. Gill & Son, Ltd, n.d.), since he had a copy of it in his library in Paris. See Thomas Connolly, *The Personal Library of James Joyce: A descriptive bibliography* (Buffalo: University of Buffalo, 1955).

3. F. C. S. Schiller, *Tantalus; or, The Future of Man*

4. J. B. S. Haldane, *Callinicus; A Defence of Chemical Warfare*

5. C. J. Patten, *The Passing of the Phantoms; A Study of Evolutionary Psychology and Morals*

6. Dora Russell, *Hypatia; or, Woman and Knowledge*

7. Gerald Heard, *Narcissus; an, Anatomy of Clothes*

8. H. F. Scott-Stokes, *Perseus; or, Of Dragons*[68]

Joyce's use of these books is the subject of the only extended consideration I have seen of how a modern writer might have made use of the series: an article on Joyce's 'Lost Notebook', 'D1', by Robbert-Jan Henkes and Mikio Fuse. Besides being an impressive piece of detective work about Joyce's processes of note-taking and composition, it is a cogent demonstration of one of the most important modernist writer's extensive knowledge of To-Day and To-Morrow. In it, they explore Joyce's reading across the series, and the traces of that reading detectable in the composition of *Finnegans Wake*.[69] Henkes comments:

> Nor would he bid goodbye to this unique opportunity to supply his word hoard with scientific terms of the future. In 1930 he would read Richard Paget's *Babel; or, The Past, Present, and Future of Human Speech* (VI.B.32.14-146), and most probably he also read Robert Graves' *Lars Porsena; or, The Future of Swearing*, with its long chapter [*sic*] on *Ulysses*, held up by Graves as 'perhaps the least obscene book ever published.' At any rate, Joyce mentions this 'amusing book' in a letter to Harriet Weaver of 22 July 1932[.]

While it is not surprising that the creator of Stephen Dedalus would want to read Haldane's *Daedalus*, nor that the quality of that volume would make him want to try others, it is striking that he read at least twelve of the volumes in the series. He would have seen the lists of published and announced volumes in the end-matter to later volumes. Given his choice of two of the books on language, he might have been interested in others advertised in the series under the subheading 'Language and Literature', such as:

[68] H. F. Scott-Stokes, *Perseus; or, Of* Dragons (1924) is an oddity in the series, with little to say about the future. An early, short volume, perhaps a debating society paper, its 'dragons' are the 'incredible things men believed almost down to our own day, and still believe' (19–20); the modern equivalents being 'respectability, bigotry, and cant' (13).

[69] Robbert-Jan Henkes and Mikio Fuse, 'Inside D1', *Genetic Joyce Studies*, 12 (Spring 2012): http://www.geneticjoycestudies.org/GJS12/GJS12_Henkes_Fuse.html accessed 31 October 2013. They explain: D1 is 'a Notebook that we only know through Mme Raphael's partial transcription, in the C-series, of the items Joyce didn't cross out in his original Notebook and had left unused up till that moment'; which means *Finnegans Wake* may draw on more material from the series than is shown here. His eyesight failing, Joyce worried that he would become unable to read his own notes, so enlisted Mme Raphael to copy them out more legibly. I haven't included their extensive references to Joyce's notes and manuscripts, as Joycean geneticists will need to consult their article directly.

Thamyris; or, Is There a Future for Poetry? R. C. Trevelyan (1925)

The Future of Futurism. John Rodker (1926)

Pomona; or, The Future of English. Basil de Selincourt (1926)

Delphos; The Future of International Language. E. Sylvia Pankhurst (1927)

Scheherazade; or, The Future of the English Novel. 'John Carruthers' (i.e. J. Y. T. Greig) (1927)

Breaking Priscian's Head; or, English as She Will Be Spoke and Wrote. Greig again. (1928)

Mrs Fisher; or, the Future of Humour. Robert Graves (1928)

Pons Asinorum; or, The Future of Nonsense. George Edinger and E. J. C. Neep (1929)

Democritus; or, The Future of Laughter. Gerald Gould (1929)

We have seen how he is discussed in three of these too, as well as in *Columbia*.

What happens to Joyce's other To-Day and To-Morrow reading is again characteristically Joycean. Though he made notes of particular passages, he doesn't quote them, paraphrase their arguments, discuss them or dispute them. They function as suggesting additions to the 'word hoard'; often, again, not because he lifts a word verbatim, but because it suggested another (often portmanteau-) word; or because a sentence suggests a variation on both its language and its story or idea. Henkes and Fuse provide a marvellous appendix tracing how Joyce expanded the 'Night Lessons' chapter of *Finnegans Wake* (II. 2) using notes that had been transcribed from the lost notebook into a surviving one by his amanuensis Mme Raphael.

For example, a text which provides a source for ten different moments in the *Wake* (the most traces of any of the To-Day and To-Morrow volumes) is Gerald Heard's *Narcissus: An anatomy of clothes* (1924). The central idea of this bizarre book appears to be a metaphorical (or perhaps mystical) application of the idea of evolution (not exactly Darwinian, but vitalist) to clothes and architecture. The connection seems to be that they both offer outer shells, like a hermit crab's. Evolution, he says, 'is going on no longer in but around the man, and the faster because working in a less resistant medium' (11). The style is Carlylean, and the whole exercise is very much a reworking of *Sartor Resartus* (which Heard mentions on p. 3) using evolution instead of Carlyle's transcendental idealism. This might mean that the attitude to evolution is ironic, except that it appears not to be. Instead, Heard documents with drawings the ways in which clothing styles parallel architectural ones. It is easy to see how Joyce might have found this exponent of the idea of evolving human consciousness provoking thoughts, even if they were not the thoughts Heard was expounding.

Henkes and Fuse cite a representative passage from *Narcissus*, which they connect with two of Joyce's notes that were worked into *Finnegans Wake*:

Nature had already given man such legs that the Psalmist had definitely, as a true Semite, to declare that their Maker did not delight in them. The tailor could only unveil as on him worked the imitative passion to translate in terms of his own art the invention of the architect. Tights sweep clean up to the apex, round the athletic arch of the thighs, to the trunk borne like a tower above the crossing. The tunic, to display this, the final organic architecture, shrinks into the jupon, a body-glove, and the build of man, though his flesh be covered to his palms and chin, is more visible to every eye than ever since the closing of the Gymnasium.   (86-7)

Both notes refer to the last sentence. In one, it is the portmanteau-word 'body-glove' which catches Joyce's eye. At least, it's not clear if he saw the 'g' or not, since the note says 'body-love'; though again it's unclear whether, if a scribal error, it was on Joyce's part or Mme Raphael's, or whether Joyce was already holding it up to his Narcissean distorting mirrors. The published version becomes: 'So long as beautylife is bodylove'.[70]

The second note reads just 'gym (naked)'. This takes up Heard's idea that close-fitting Early Modern clothing makes the form of the flesh visible. The 'Gymnasium' refers to the Athenian institutions of athletics and education, such as Plato's Academy. The name derives from the Greek adjective γυμνός (*gymnos*) meaning 'naked'. In the *Wake* Joyce transforms 'gym (naked)' into 'gymnufleshed' *FW* 271; footnote 4; translating 'naked' into the French 'nu', and getting in Heard's 'flesh'. It also arguably gets in Heard's semitic legs, through a puns on 'understandings' and 'genuflect'. And possibly a hint of his argument too, which traces the evolution of attitudes towards the body from Old Testament and medieval bowed mortification to Renaissance neo-classical celebration.

Another such note reads simply 'the parent / offers sweetmeat'. Henkes and Fuse connect this to the behaviourist/mechanistic passage from Patten's *The Passing of the Phantoms*:

Let us now examine the same faculties, viz. *sorrow* and *joy* under different con-ditions, and see how the Brain machinery is called forth into action. The child trips over the door-mat and falls in its eagerness to reach the sweetmeat held up in the parent's hand at the other end of the room.   (24-5)

The phrase 'parent who offers sweetmeats' was a manuscript insertion to the pas-sage eventually published in the *Wake* as: 'where as and when Heavysciugardaddy, parent who offers sweetmeats, will gift uns his Noblett's surprize' (*FW* 306.03-04).

As Helmut Bonheim has shown, the German 'uns' alerts us to the translingual pun in 'gift' ('poison' in German).[71] The sugar-daddy turns into an ambivalent patriarch or god, offering pleasures which lead to pain or mortality. What looks like the ultimate reward—the Nobel Prize—blows up in your face: not just because

---

[70] *FW*, 271.09.
[71] Helmut Bonheim, *Joyce's Benefictions* (University of California Press, 1964), 54.

Alfred Nobel invented dynamite, but because the windows of Noblett's sweet shop[72] were among those smashed by an explosion in the 1916 Easter Rising, looting children dodging bullets for their first taste of chocolate, some of them possibly among the forty children killed during the Rising.

The manuscript already had the Father tempting the child with sweets, leading to danger. It is not hard to see why Joyce latched onto Patten's image. It provides the child, and the fall. The word 'sweetmeats' brings out the 'sugar' in 'sciugardaddy', connects the sugar to the prize in 'surprize'; and it also introduces fleshly pleasures. The passage was already playing with ideas of theology, temptation, and punishment. The kind of scene Patten describes is already implied—the parent, the sweet, the child, the unpleasant surprise—but presumably Joyce enjoyed the correspondence, introducing a new phrase echoing Patten's version. But the actual words taken from Patten are too minimal to constitute an allusion: just 'parent' and 'sweetmeat' (which he makes plural). It isn't credible that Joyce would have expected anyone to recognize it as a reference and look it up.

So it might be rash to speculate about Joyce's engagement with Patten's argument on the basis of such slender trace. Yet Patten's thesis—that animal behaviour 'places in our hands the master-key which unlocks the secrets regarding the Evolution of Human Morality' (5) is also something Joyce could have enjoyed. Like many of the To-Day and To-Morrow books, *The Passing of the Phantoms*, with its Nietzschean title suggesting a sweeping away of religion, is resolutely secularizing in its scientific bearings. Patten uses observations of animal behavior to argue that 'morality is not an exclusively human characteristic' (65), and that the moral sense, where based upon superstition, is 'bound to be permeated with falsities and absurdities' (93). Ultimately, in religious terms he is an agnostic, quoting T. H. Huxley saying 'a man shall not say he knows or believes that which he has no scientific grounds for professing to know or believe' (69).[73] But he is an empiricist about morality, since he thinks that—luckily for us—natural selection has implanted a moral sense in us which works for the good of the community (93). (It is a position given an explanatory basis in Richard Dawkins' theory of *The Selfish Gene*.)

Knowing Patten's book might thus make the parent/child image more benign, or at least less malign. Parents, not having divine foreknowledge, do not want their children to experience pain when anticipating pleasure. But accidents happen; and we learn that excitement, like pride, or even prize, can come before a fall. So our evolution, both as a species and as individuals, forms the ground of our moral sense. Joyce, like psychoanalysis, would also have shared this sense that religious morality is a projection of, or translates back to, familial desires and prohibitions, pleasures and pains.

If what Joyce was annotating from the series were suggestions for lexical inventions, that is because lexical invention was the revolution he was engaged in.

---

[72] See McHugh, *Annotations to Finnegans Wake*, p. 306.
[73] The quotation is from T. H. Huxley, *Life and Letters of Thomas Henry Huxley*, vol. 3 (London: Macmillan, 1913), 97.

But the words being played with in these examples invoke the everyday life that his writing revelled in: parents, children, the body, food, education, religion. To-Day and To-Morrow as a series has a form of encyclopedic compendiousness, as it gradually covered more and more of human life and knowledge. Absorbing elements from the series, Joyce was attempting to cover all these subjects in one book. Ultimately, though, it is perhaps To-Day and To-Morrow's temporal aspect that may have appealed most strongly to someone with Joyce's Viconian sense of historical cycles, as well as its interest in language and reinvention of myth.[74] Ogden's conception of the series wasn't Viconian at all. The aim was to consolidate a new way of thinking about time, as we have seen, by imagining the future as theoretically more predictable in a scientific age. Yet the ways in which the authors go about their brief, moving back and forth between different epochs; and the way in which the frame of the series connects the Classical past, the present, and the projected future, puts different historical periods in dialogue with each other. If the effect is rarely the Viconian one of recognizing historical repetitions, it does what Joyce did by calling his novel about a twenty-four-hour journey around 1904 Dublin *Ulysses*; and what he was doing in his all-time-consuming *Finnegans Wake*: in T. S. Eliot's terms, making all time eternally present, whether past, present or future.

T. S. Eliot

The promotional material introduced as end-matter after the early volumes included a quotation from T. S. Eliot:

> *Nation:*   'We are able to peer into the future by means of that brilliant series [which] will constitute a precious document upon the present time.'—T. S. ELIOT.

It was somewhat disingenuous to have cherry-picked these clauses out of context. Eliot certainly approved of one of the volumes he was reviewing, John Rodker's *The Future of Futurism*. But what he wrote expresses a more hostile view of the entire futurological project:

> To be interested in 'the future' is a symptom of demoralization and debility. Messrs. Kegan Paul are to be commended for instituting a series of little books which fully exposes this contemporary weakness. We are, at least officially, prohibited from consulting the oracles, and from having our horoscopes cast in the Tottenham Court Road; but we are able to peer into the future by means of that brilliant series of little books called 'To-day and To-morrow'. The volumes are, inevitably, of varying interest; but the series will constitute a precious document upon the present time. There are, of course, two futures: there is the future

---

[74] See D. P. Verene, 'Vico's Scienza Nuova and Joyce's *Finnegans Wake*', *Philosophy and Literature*, 21:2 (1997), 392–404; and his edited collection *Vico and Joyce* (New York: SUNY Press, 1987).

of the present, the future which we are actually working upon, and there is the future of the future, the future beyond our power, the future of the housemaid's dream of marriage; the latter is the future with which the series is concerned.[75]

The word 'brilliant' sparkles less in that setting. Yes, some of the writing is clever; but its glitter is crystal balls, the series representing to his mind an acceptable 'modern' substitute for superstitious and wishful fantasy. This is wilfully to miss the point of a scientific futurology, which, as Wells had clearly explained, was not concerned with the future of individuals: 'Scientific prophecy will not be fortune-telling, whatever else it may be'; 'The knowledge of the future we may hope to gain will be general, and not individual'.[76] Ogden's progressive contributors certainly felt the future they were writing about was the one they were working on, and which it was in their power to influence. Yet the interest of the series for Eliot is its symptomatic quality, which 'exposes' 'contemporary weakness'. That was certainly not the aim, either of Ogden or his contributors. Eliot refuses their offer of a vision of the future, turning the instrument upon itself; saying it reveals more about 'to-day' than 'to-morrow'.

The notes of moral and social superiority ('debility'; 'the housemaid's dream of marriage') indicate that his objection is grounded in religion and politics, and is of a piece with his announcement the following year, in the Preface to the essays *For Lancelot Andrewes* (1928), of a conversion to Anglo-Catholicisim, Toryism, and royalism. What he calls 'the future of the future' is 'beyond our power' for Eliot because he sees it as at god's disposition. What is being implicitly rejected is any radical or socialist utopianism in the series, together with its implicit claim that science should be the basis for thinking about the future, rather than religion or divination. He praises Rodker for his debts to the reactionaries Wyndham Lewis and T. E. Hulme. But any praise for *The Future of Futurism* is tempered by his contempt for the other To-Day and To-Morrow volume he is reviewing in the same article (which also takes in Gertrude Stein and Rose Macaulay), Basil de Sélincourt's *Pomona; or, The Future of English* (1926):

> While Miss Macaulay, fixing her eye upon a few of the more conventional con-ventionalities of present speech, such as 'not cricket', provides us with a pleasant half-hour of amusing triviality, Mr. de Sélincourt contrives in his half-hour to be equally trivial, but not half so amusing. One wishes, indeed, that Mr. de Sélincourt, before knitting his brows over the future of English, had taken a little more thought for the present.

---

[75] 'Charleston, Hey! Hey!', *Nation and Athenaeum*, 40 (29 Jan 1927), 595. In *The Complete Prose of T. S. Eliot. The critical edition: Literature, politics, belief, 1927–1929*, edited by Frances Dickey, Jennifer Formichelli, and Ronald Schuchard (Baltimore: Johns Hopkins University Press, 2015), 25–9 (http://muse.jhu.edu/chapter/1634627). In addition to John Rodker, *The Future of Futurism* (1926) and Basil de Sélincourt's *Pomona; or, The Future of English* (1926), Eliot was reviewing *Composition as Explanation* (1926), by Gertrude Stein, and *Catchwords and Claptrap* (1926), by Rose Macaulay.

[76] H. G. Wells, *The Discovery of the Future* (London: T. Fisher Unwin, 1902), 71, 72.

Eliot's comment about the 'varying interest' of the series suggests he had read more than just these two. We do not know how many more, but his friendship with Bertrand Russell makes it likely he would have known *Icarus* and *What I Believe*. Bonamy Dobrée's *Timotheus; The Future of the Theatre* (1925) and Trevelyan's *Thamyris; or, Is There a Future for Poetry?* might also have caught his eye. The two volumes he was reviewing were both from 1926, still relatively early on in the series. *Scheherazade; or, The Future of the English Novel* (1927) and *Deucalion; or, The Future of Literary Criticism* (1930) were still to appear. Also Sylvia Pankhurst's *Delphos; The Future of International Language* (1927), *Gallio; or, The Tyranny of Science* (1927), *Iconoclastes; or, The Future of Shakespeare* (1927), and *Breaking Priscian's Head; or, English as She Will Be Spoke and Wrote* (1928), J. Y. T Greig's scathing riposte to *Pomona*. Eliot was certainly concerned with all these subjects. Neither *Pomona* nor *The Future of Futurism* included the Classified Index yet, but they did append a list of volumes ready or in preparation, including favourable notices. So Eliot would certainly have been aware of the scale and shape of the series by 1927.

He would also have known of Haldane's inaugurating volume, since de Sélincourt cites the 'brilliant little essay *Daedalus*' on his first page:

> Before discussing the future of English, one is forced, in the bustle of these scientific days, to inquire whether language itself has a future. 'We are working,' wrote Mr. J. B. S. Haldane [...] 'towards a condition when any two persons on earth will be able to be completely present to one another in not more than a twenty-fourth of a second'. Is speech quick-moving enough to keep a place in such a picture?   (5-6)

It is unlikely such a question would have struck Eliot as intelligent, and it is as likely to have deterred him from *Daedalus* as recommended it to him. But *Daedalus* was the volume that had attracted most attention, and again given his intimacy with Russell he is likely to have heard about it; and of course if he read *Icarus* he would have had a clearer sense of what was impressive about Haldane's book. The point of such speculation is first to suggest that Eliot is likely to have known more of the series than just the two volumes under review; and second, to suggest that if he had read *Daedalus*, the review might be seen as adopting the tactic of 'future history' Haldane uses there (see Chapter 2). It is not just that Eliot's distinction between 'the future of the present' and 'the future of the future' may have been suggested by that concept of looking back at one future from the vantage point of a more distant one. It is also that Eliot's ironic reversal of the poles of futurology, so that the present's attempts to predict the future will be read back by later ages as symptoms of that age making the attempt, might itself be provoked by Haldane's trope, but turning it against itself so as to undermine its claim to any predictive power. (You thought you were telling us about the future, but you're only exposing the degeneration of yourself.)

That suggestion is highly speculative. Eliot's discrimination of futures may owe nothing to Haldane's 'future history' trope, and may simply be his rebuke to what he saw as the presumption of people dressing up speculation and fantasy as science. Even Rodker does not quite get off that hook, as Eliot slyly insinuates: 'Mr. Rodker is up-to-the-minute, if anyone is; we feel sure that he knows all about hormones, W. H. R. Rivers and the Mongol in our midst'—demonstrating, at the same time, that he knew of at least one other early To-Day and To-Morrow title.[77]

Eliot's attitude presents a further reason why the series, for all its contemporary prestige, lost traction in literary studies. Disdainfully aware of it, he barely mentions it again. The only volume to receive more than a mention in his journal, the *Criterion*, was *Deucalion*: the one devoted to literary criticism.[78]

However, Eliot's review also suggests why the very act of formulating his sceptical rejection of the pleasures of futurology was important to him for a different reason. In inciting him think about 'the future of the present' and 'the future of the future', it had elicited a new and paradoxical discourse about temporality. In one sense, he might have felt he had seen it all before. The application of prophecy to everyday life was the torment of his Tiresias in *The Waste Land*, who had already 'foresuffered all' of the typist's encounter with the young man carbuncular in 'A Game of Chess'. But the language of 'the future of the present' is different from anything in *The Waste Land*, anticipating instead *Four Quartets*. It is the language of metaphysics, and Christopher Ricks and Jim McCue cite a number of theological and philosophical sources for the first lines of the sequence, from *Ecclesiastes* and Augustine to F. H. Bradley, William James, and Eliot's own annotations to Hegel. They are probably right not to speculate about any debt to Ogden's series; though an echo of Eliot's discussion of it in the *Nation* seems at least possible. In which case, it might be the opening of *Burnt Norton* that represents Eliot's last words or last judgment on To-Day and To-Morrow, or at least on its variety of futurology's 'world of speculation':

> Time present and time past
> Are both perhaps present in time future,
> And time future contained in time past.
> If all time is eternally present
> All time is unredeemable.
> What might have been is an abstraction
> Remaining a perpetual possibility
> Only in a world of speculation.[79]

---

[77] For a discussion of F. G. Crookshank's *The Mongol in Our Midst* (1924), see Chapter 1. C. K. Ogden published four of W. H. R. Rivers' books in the International Library: *Conflict and Dream* (1923); *Psychology and Politics, and Other Essays* (1923); *Medicine, Magic, and Religion* (1924); and *Psychology and Ethnology* (1926).

[78] Reviewed favourably by 'J. G. F.' (John Gould Fletcher), *Criterion*, 9:36 (April 1930), 575–7: 'This little book is a model of the sort of writing and thinking we should expect, but do not always get, from this famous series'.

[79] *The Poems of T. S. Eliot*, vol. 1, ed. Christopher Ricks and Jim McCue (London: Faber, 2015), 907–9, 179.

That word 'speculation', and the pun in the phrase 'world of speculation', suggesting both the culture of the speculator, and the world being imagined, do not clinch the proposition that Eliot was recalling the past time when To-Day and To-Morrow had been present, but they strengthen the case. Though Eliot may have been recalling another book, T. E. Hulme's *Speculations*, published posthumously in 1924, at the same time as the early To-Day and To-Morrow volumes, and in Ogden's International Library. Hulme's speculations are philosophical; but his evocation of a world of 'Cinders', is reminiscent of *The Waste Land* it preceded; its dystopian vision a stark contrast with the progressive hope of much of To-Day and To-Morrow.

Wyndham Lewis

Wyndham Lewis was another who was attending to the series. In *The Art of Being Ruled* (1926) he took issue with the prediction in Russell's *Icarus* of a (Wellsian) 'world-government', arguing that it was already taking shape, not in the form Russell anticipated, but through what he terms '(in one form or other) castration', due to 'the feminization of the white European and American [...]'.[80] However, his criticism of the idea of scientific 'impersonality'—that 'it is an ideal cloak for the personal will' (47) to manipulate other people with—is very close to Russell's cynicism about how scientific knowledge will be monopolized by the powerful to further their own ends.

Lewis's low opinion of Anthony Ludovici may have disinclined him to read *Lysistrata*; but his views on feminism and masculinity were close.[81] The other To-Day and To-Morrow volume he does mention in *The Art of Being Ruled* is *Daedalus*, mainly to accuse Haldane of mocking the reaction he anticipates from the public to ectogenesis as indecent because he himself finds natural processes indecent—an attitude Lewis claims is representative of the scientific outlook: 'the "substitution of the doctor for the priest" is not really, as it would seem to be, in the interest of carnal joys' (187; quoting *Daedalus*, 54). We know Lewis read the book to the end, because he didn't like the ending (the atheism too sentimental). But his summing up makes one wonder if his determined rejection of Haldane's confident intelligence hasn't made him read it the wrong way round. He says 'the man of science' such as Haldane is 'romantically destructive' (228), and that

> The large lay audience of such a book as *Daedalus* is left with nothing more useful than the conviction that it will shortly be finished off in a most ingenious manner, and so all its trouble brought to a timely conclusion.   (230)

---

[80] In *The Art of Being Ruled*, ed. Reed Way Dasenbrock (Santa Rosa: Black Sparrow Press, 1989), 53–5.

[81] Dan Stone, *Breeding Superman: Nietzsche, race and eugenics in Edwardian and interwar Britain* (Liverpool University Press, 2002), 38.

Jealous, *ego*? True, Haldane begins with a speculation about an exploding star perhaps signifying extra-terrestrial scientific hubris. But he also begins with the First World War, in which he, like Lewis, had fought. He does not shy away from the fact of mass slaughter. But his future history narrative implies precisely that mankind is not on the verge of self-destruction, but can learn—from science, and a scientifically-informed politics—how to preserve, and enhance, life.

In *Time and Western Man* (1927), it becomes clear that Lewis's view of Haldane probably owes more to *Callinicus; A Defence of Chemical Warfare* (1925). He professes to find it strange that *The Art of Being Ruled*, with its anti-liberal argument than humankind really does not desire the freedom it thinks it does, was greeted as a 'Bill of Hate' 117), whereas *Callinicus* was 'everywhere received with gratitude' (117). (Again, the spectre of review and sales-figure envy is summoned up.) An ex-artilleryman like Lewis could hardly be expected to find Haldane's justification of poison gas anything but obscene. Yet, as suggested (in Chapter 2), Haldane's point is that that smart weapons reduce obscenity. The debate is still with us, though about drones as well as chemical weapons. But drones are being deployed because there is so little enthusiasm for the anticipated casualties of mass ground wars.

Richard Aldington's review of Lewis' *The Art of Being Ruled* refers to the book as 'a whole "To-Day and To-Morrow" series crushed into one volume'. The review is titled 'Mr. Lewis on Everything'.[82] There were perhaps some thirty volumes out by then. Not a third of the total extent; but even so, Aldington's gist is clear. His suggestive description indicates one aspect of the series that might have attracted Lewis: its encyclopedic scope. Its sceptical, radical questioning of all conventions is another. But the futurological premise of the whole project would surely have stimulated the author of *Time and Western Man*—if only into contempt, as yet another demonstration of the tyranny of what he called the 'time-mind'.

Evelyn Waugh and Others

There are two very different kinds of evidence of Evelyn Waugh's engagement with To-Day and To-Morrow. He appears to have thought highly enough of the series to have wanted to contribute to it, writing to Kegan Paul in October 1926 proposing a volume to be called *Noah; or, The Future of Intoxication*.[83] 'To my surprise and pleasure they welcome the idea enthusiastically', he wrote.[84] The

---

[82] Richard Aldington, *Saturday Review* (31 July 1926), 4. I am grateful to Nathan Waddell for drawing my attention to this review. The 'Books of the Quarter' section of Eliot's *New Criterion*, 4:2 (April 1926) carried Aldington's review (381–4) of five books by Bonamy Dobrée (who was also a reviewer for the magazine). This includes *Timotheus*, only to call it 'a brisk little satire under the innocent disguise of prophecy' (382).

[83] Martin Stannard, *Evelyn Waugh: The early years 1903–1939* (London: Dent, 1986), 129–30.

[84] *The Diaries of Evelyn Waugh*, ed. Michael Davie (London: Weidenfeld and Nicolson, 1976). Entry for 30 October 1926 (not 1925), as implied by Jeffrey M. Heath, *The Picturesque Prison: Evelyn Waugh and his writing* (Kingston and Montreal: McGill-Queen's University Press, 1982), 64.

previous year he had been toying with writing a book about Silenus—in Greek mythology the Satyr who was tutor to Dionysus, the god of wine.[85] Now he switched to the Old Testament patriarch who had got drunk and been seen in his nakedness by his youngest son.[86] He started writing it at once, and noted in his diary that its style was 'mannered and "literary"'.[87] But by December he had run out of steam, writing: 'I have had an idea or two for the finishing of *Noah* but lack the energy to put them into form'.[88] At the end of the year he left for a trip to Greece, noting on Christmas Day: 'Before I left London I finished off *Noah*, though badly, and sent it to Kegan Paul'.[89] Whoever read it—either Ogden or a publisher's reader—appears to have agreed. In January it was rejected. The refusal was 'rather a blow', said Waugh, 'as I was counting on the money for it but perhaps it is a good thing. I was not pleased with it'.[90] By this date Waugh was an unknown quantity: he had only published a handful of pieces in Oxford magazines. His first novel, *Decline and Fall*, did not appear until 1928. Unfortunately the manuscript of *Noah* has not survived.[91]

The other kind of evidence is a number of allusions to the series in Waugh's subsequent novels. These mainly function to mock it, and the modernity it represents. *Vile Bodies* (1930) mentions a 'Huxdane-Halley bomb', interestingly conflating Haldane with Huxley, and suggesting Waugh may have read Haldane's *Callinicus*.[92] In *Black Mischief* (1932), the Oxford-educated Seth returns to the African state of Azania to become its Emperor. He is determined to modernize the country, appointing his devious university friend Basil Seal as Minister for Modernization. 'I am the Future', Seth proclaims: 'I have read modern books', and he cites evolution, woman's suffrage, vaccination, and vivisection: 'I am the New Age.' (17). A devotee of the wireless and the tank, he is convinced he will win the war against his usurper because: 'We are Light and Speed and Strength, Steel and Steam, youth, Today and Tomorrow'.[93] Later in the novel there are glimpses of specific volumes. 'Do you realize the magnitude of the fixed stars? They are immense. I have read a book which says that the mind boggles at their distances' (150). 'Even while discussing the topic that immediately interested him', writes Waugh: 'he would often break off in the middle of a sentence with an irrelevant question. "How much are autogyros?"' (151). In the most direct allusion he appears to be reading *Daedalus*:

> But next day he was absorbed in ectogenesis. 'I have read here', he said, tapping a volume of speculative biology, 'that there is to be no more birth. The ovum is

[85] See Robert Reginald Garnett, *From Grimes to Brideshead: The early novels of Evelyn Waugh* (Lewisburg, PA: Bucknell University Press, 1990), 49.

[86] *Genesis*, 9:20–23.   [87] *Diaries*, 10 November 1926, p. 270.

[88] *Diaries*, 6 December 1926, p. 272.   [89] *Diaries*, 25 December 1926, p. 273.

[90] *Diaries*, 24 January 1927, p. 280.

[91] His grandson Alexander Waugh thinks it must have been destroyed.

[92] Evelyn Waugh, *Vile Bodies* (Harmondsworth: Penguin, 1976), 248.

[93] Evelyn Waugh, *Black Mischief* (London: Penguin, 2000), 17, 40.

fertilized in the laboratory and then the foetus is matured in bottles. It is a splendid idea. Get me some of those bottles [....]'   (150-1)

Waugh's double-edged satire targets both the purveyors of the modern and its gullible enthusiastic readers (perhaps with a troubling suggestion that only someone lacking the traditional European and Catholic civilized mentality would be persuaded by such prophecies). Of course To-Day and To-Morrow is not the only instance of futuristic thought in his sights. Seth has also proudly read 'Shaw, Arlen, Priestley' (17), and presumably the magazine *The New Age*. While there may be a sour note of fermented grapes over the rejection of *Noah*, it is also possible that the satire preceded the rejection, and indeed may have been the reason for it, if Ogden felt the manuscript was making fun of the modernity of the series, without thinking seriously about the future.

You didn't have to be a modernist to contribute to the series or be interested in it. Douglas Woodruff became editor of the Roman Catholic magazine the *Tablet*. Hilaire Belloc was listed as preparing a volume, though it did not appear. The novelist Compton Mackenzie wrote a short essay about it, 'The Triple Tyranny', which appeared in his book *Unconsidered Trifles* (1932).[94] The terms of his response are similar to Waugh's. He offers a comic meditation wonder about contributing a volume, which he then sketches out: giving what is effectively a prediction of a prediction.

As illustrated in the previous chapters, there is a high degree of internal cross-reference in the series; arising in part from the aim of stimulating debate, and indicating that the volumes were also studied by other contributors. Winifred Holtby's *Eutychus* cites Dora Russell's *Hypatia* and mentions Ludovici and Norman Haire, for example. Paget's *Babel* refers to both *Icarus* and *Tantalus*. Eden Paul's *Chronos* refers to both to *The World, the Flesh and the Devil* and *Daedalus*. C. E. M. Joad made extensive notes in his copy of Russell's *What I Believe* to review it.[95] *Daedalus* is certainly the volume other contributors refer to most. While that could simply reflect the attention it received (it was one of the series' two runaway bestsellers), in the absence of any evidence of a brief for contributors, it may be that Ogden just recommended *Daedalus* to them as a model.

We have also seen one contributor (Graves) debating with another (Trevelyan) outside the series. The psychologist William McDougall, who wrote *Janus* for the series, referred to *Daedalus* (as an example of pioneering new scientific mentality seeing materialism as superseded by new sense of interpenetration of mind and

[94] I'm very grateful to Nathan Waddell for alerting me to this essay.
[95] Joad's copy was described by the London bookshop Any Amount of Books on ABE Books; accessed 5 August 2016. His review appeared in the *New Leader* (24 April 1925), 12–13, contrasting Chesterton's *The Superstitions of the Sceptic* with *What I Believe*. It describes Russell as 'one of the greatest and the most disturbing thinkers of our day; he is our most severe and weighty critic of the present, and he has profoundly influenced the minds of those who seek to mould the future'. (12).

matter) in the Psyche Miniature *The Battle of Behaviorism*.[96] But the kinds of external reference detailed in this chapter are more significant.

The modernist writers considered here each respond to To-Day and To-Morrow in distinct and characteristic ways. Graves was prompted to write a counterblast expressing his vision of poetry's future. Huxley elaborates an imagined world which resembles the futures projected by some of the scientific volumes—as if the predictions of the series, or something like them, had actually come to pass. Joyce mines the volumes for lexical inspiration, and is perhaps diverted by the temporal layerings of futurology and future history. Eliot criticizes the scientific faith of the contributors, and is prompted to muse about time and attitudes to the future which would continue to resonate through his later work. Lewis too criticizes the way Haldane's book exemplifies a belief that science will sweep away religion. If he shares Bertrand Russell's objection that scientific developments are likely to worsen the human lot, he doesn't hold the politicians to blame as Russell does, but the scientists themselves. Waugh fastens on to the comic potential of the project: first, as an opportunity to contribute to its attention to everyday human activities; then as evidence of what he sees as a fatuous belief in the superiority of the modern (at least in its readers). When their responses are taken together, two things stand out. A number of the most important modernist writers are known to have read some of the books (or in Huxley's case are almost certain to have known some); and they were engaged enough by them to comment, criticize, or respond in their own imaginative work. Even the heterodox group of writers who drafted a contribution that was not published (Charles Madge and Ashley Montagu as well as Waugh), or who were advertised as working on a volume which never appeared (Hilaire Belloc, Rebecca West, the American poet Alan Porter, and several others) provides a telling cross-section of the literati and intelligentsia of the period. It would have been hard for writers not to be aware of the series, given its reception in the press and the responses to it in other creative works. To-Day and To-Morrow was followed closely by modernists. The Portuguese poet Fernando Pessoa's library includes copies of *Icarus*, *Lars Porsena*, and *Stentor*.[97] In some ways a modernist project itself, the series is also a project that alters the received picture of modernism. Classic modernism, at least, often expresses its modernity through a vision of the past, often the classical or mythological past; or by projecting yesterday onto today. To-Day and To-Morrow, by contrast, represents a strain in modernism imagining the future.

[96] John B. Watson and William MacDougall, *The Battle of Behaviorism: An exposition and an exposure* (London: Kegan Paul, Trench and Trubner, 1928), 43. refers to *Daedalus*, pp. 87–8 n.
[97] See: http://casafernandopessoa.cm-lisboa.pt/index.php?id=6433 accessed 22 July 2017.

AEOLUS
OR THE FUTURE OF
THE FLYING MACHINE

OLIVER STEWART

ICARUS
OR
THE FUTURE OF SCIENCE

By
BERTRAND RUSSELL, F.R.S.

"Startling possibilities of the future."—
Daily Express.

"Utter pessimism."—Observer.

"Mr Russell refuses to believe that the
progress of Science must be a boon to
mankind."—Morning Post.

"The whole essay deserves to be read."—
Daily Chronicle.

"A stimulating ... that brevity nor
... sold luridly, leaves
... "—Daily Herald.

PROTEUS
OR
THE FUTURE OF INTELLIGENCE

By
VERNON LEE

"Profoundly stimulating. Should be
read by everyone who is perturbed by the
true conditions of modern thought. It is
a delight to follow Vernon Lee's supple
intelligence on its exciting course."

"A concise, outspoken piece of work."
—Saturday Review.

"The function of this genius is to stimulate
intelligence. That genius is the stimulus
here in Vernon Lee's book, we find an
unanswerable, comprehensive. We are intelligent as
critical comparison... Quick, intelligence as
many other things... amount of the given
in a very interesting Vernon Lee."
—Times Literary Supplement.

"A very stimulating essay."—Discovery.

"She has attacked a great subject, and a
subject peculiarly suited to her genius and
has produced a brilliant but remote
extemporization."—Manchester Guardian.

PROMETHEUS
OR
BIOLOGY AND THE
ADVANCEMENT OF MAN

By
H. S. JENNINGS
Henry Walters Professor of Zoology and Director of the Zoological
Laboratory, The Johns Hopkins University

An exceedingly brilliant little book
which seems to me to knock the bottom
completely out of Weismann's theory, as
it also appears to settle once and for all
this old controversy about the respective
influences of heredity and environment."
C. E. M. Joad in New Leader

KALKI
OR
THE FUTURE OF CIVILIZATION

By
S. RADHAKRISHNAN

A book of unusual interest for English
readers as being a considered statement of
the prospects of world civilization by an
Indian and a philosopher. An analysis of
Western science leads to the conclusion
that East and West are being drawn closer
together in a physical sense. But a
psychological rapprochement is not at hand;
unhappiness and increasing friction prevail.
Spengler's thesis of the decline of the West
is analysed, and the conclusion reached
that co-operation of East and West is
possible without an amalgamation of their
contrasted cultures.

Conclusion

The Ending of the Series

There were eight To-Day and To-Morrow volumes published in the UK in 1930; but only four, the last in the series, in 1931. Why did it stop then? It continued to receive enthusiastic reviews to the end, words like 'brilliant' and 'thought-provoking' still echoing through them, as shown by the examples excerpted in the appendix added to most of the volumes advertising the series. Some reviewers marvelled that the excitement was being sustained. The *Observer*, reviewing *Democritus; or, The Future of Laughter* by Gerald Gould in 1929, commented: that 'With nearly 100 volumes to its credit, the series frisks on as briskly as in its first youth', adding that: '*Democritus* is bound to be among the favourites', and praising Gould's 'Wise and witty writing'.

Unsurprisingly, given the variety of the series, views varied. *Time* magazine, for instance, had felt in 1926 that though 'The "Today and Tomorrow Series" continues to increase and multiply. It cannot be said that it is maintaining the standard of excellence set by its first few volumes'; and judging that many of the subsequent ones 'have enjoyed prestige that was largely borrowed'.[1] True, few were able to match the authority and panache of Haldane and Russell. But the rumours of the decline of the series, just two years into its eight-year run, were premature. Many of the best volumes were still to come. The reviewer acknowledged, oddly, that:

> Bertrand Russell wrote a second book (What I Believe), as did Dr. Crookshank (Aesculapius) that stood on independent merits. The feminist controversy between Mrs. Russell and Captain Ludovici (Hypatia v. Lysistrata) was very readable, though biased on both sides. Gerald Heard's Narcissus—An Anatomy of Clothes qualified in its own right.

Oddly, because though *Aesculapius* was advertised, it was not published (or if it was, has disappeared without trace).[2] Otherwise, the review accuses the publisher of having 'gone unwisely far afield for writers and subjects', and of 'thinning out a

---

[1] 'Non-Fiction, Fiction: Gladstone v. Disraeli', *Time*, 7:12 (22 March 1926). See http://content.time.com/time/magazine/article/0,9171,721804-3,00.html Similar views were expressed by Carroll Mason Sparrow, 'Phoebus, or the Future of Prophecy', *Virginia Quarterly Review*, 2:2 (Spring 1926), 275–84; and by 'E. M. K.' in the *Sewanee Review*, 34:3 (July–September 1926), 359–61.
[2] See the note on this mystery volume in Appendix B.

Imagined Futures: Writing, Science and Modernity in the To-Day and To-Morrow. Max Saunders, Oxford University Press (2019). © Max Saunders. DOI: 10.1093/oso/9780198829454.001.0001

superb vintage with hasty and insipid dilutions'. When he, or she, gets to the four latest volumes under review, some of the grounds for the adverse judgement become clearer.

> In *Lycurgus*, Mr. Haynes endeavors to write for the laity but waxes excessively technical and seldom escapes his insular British point of view. His style is unrelieved by the figures and crispness that have become part of the 'Today and Tomorrow' tradition.

But it is C. E. M. Joad who caused offence, for being 'scornful' of morality, and because he: 'vitiates his discussion by the employment of flippant paradox, unrepresentative facts and overstrained, somewhat splenetic deductions'. But from the example given—the claim that 'American civilization' actually seeks 'to substitute cleanliness for beauty, mechanism for men and hypocrisy for morals' (*Thrasymachus*, p. 33)—one suspects that it was his cultural condescension that was really being objected to. Tellingly, it is only the American author the reviewer warms to:

> Only one of the four [...] is of compelling interest and originality [....] Mr. Garrett's *Ouroboros* has the merits of a central idea, an impersonal viewpoint, a cool wit. He traces the growth of machinery from Adam's pastoral day to our pasteurized one, when it has become an essential of our existence, an 'extension' of human nature with which humanity will have to harmonize itself or starve.

The reviewer criticizes the US publisher, Dutton, for commissioning British writers who patronize or insult America, not seeming to realize the series was a British import. What comes across nonetheless is that the allegation of decline sits oddly with the characterization of the series in general as 'a superb vintage', with its signature 'figures and crispness'; these somehow survive the occasional dip in quality. Which is perhaps a reflection of the broader reception, the reviews often recognizing the import of the series as a whole—as when the *Spectator* wrote that: 'Few wittier or wiser books have appeared in this stimulating series than *Eutychus*'. For some reviewers of the later volumes such as *Halcyon* the momentum and excitement were still being sustained. *The World, the Flesh and the Devil* was greeted as 'one of the most startlingly original in that clever To-day and To-morrow series of books'.[3] The last volumes included some of the best, such as these, from 1929; or *Babel*, *It Isn't Done*, and *Sinon* from 1930; and *Chiron* and *Aphrodite* from 1931.

Any doubts about the continuing quality or reception of the series can thus scarcely be why it was discontinued. What about the forces of the market? Here there are three kinds of relevant evidence. First, that provided by Ogden's other two major book series, which were relatively unaffected by the Depression.

---

[3] 'Book of the Week', *Aberdeen Journal* (23 September 1929), 6.

The International Library carried on until Ogden's death in 1957, and indeed beyond. Psyche Miniatures—the more comparable to To-Day and To-Morrow in terms of scale, price, and audacious pitch to the general reader, and indeed often interchangeable in terms of topic, continued to appear throughout the 1930s and into the Second World War. Possibly the proximity of these two series of short volumes was a reason to consolidate, and channel any future To-Day and To-Morrow plans into the Psyche Miniatures. But even if so, the buoyancy of the other series shows that such projects remained viable. And To-Day and To-Morrow had a distinctive rationale, which still had mileage.

The second kind of evidence is to be found in the Routledge and Kegan Paul archive at University College London.[4] This is fairly minimal, consisting mainly of the publisher's 'journals', ledgers recording publications, print runs and reprints, and some correspondence from readers. But it sheds interesting light on the course of the series. A more granular analysis is given in Appendix A, so only a summary is outlined here. The initial print runs were relatively modest for most volumes—2,000 in most cases, apart from nine volumes which had initial print runs of 3,000 or more. Almost a quarter of the books were reprinted, some many times, with a few key volumes edging into 'best-seller' territory. By 1931, six titles had at least 6,000 copies printed. Five sold more than 10,000, with *Daedalus* and *What I Believe* topping the list at 17,000 and 18,000 respectively.[5]

Though most of the best-sellers were the earlier volumes (doubtless helped by continual references to them from later additions), it is thus not the case that sales fizzled out. Several volumes from the last three years were among those reprinted: two from 1928 and two from 1929. Even after the Wall Street Crash, *It Isn't Done* (1930) went into three impressions, and *Aphrodite* (1931) into two. The sales figures thus indicate that, in Britain at least, the series remained commercially a modest success, with many volumes exceeding initial expectations. It was not reaching a wide, popular audience. Instead, the figures support the idea that it was reaching the elite, educated audience it was directed towards.

However, the third kind of evidence concerns what was happening in the US market. The relationship between the series and its US publisher, E. P. Dutton, shifted several times (as detailed in Appendix A). After about two-thirds of the eventual volumes had been published, Dutton stopped publishing its own editions of them. This must have reduced the profitability of the series for Kegan Paul, which is likely to have been a factor in the decision to discontinue it.

To-Day and To-Morrow could have continued. There were many important topics still to be covered. Besides those mentioned in the introduction: among the

---

[4] The UCL archive contains ledgers, authors' agreements, printed catalogues and other papers 1853–1973.

[5] Fredric Warburg, *An Occupation for Gentlemen* (London: Hutchinson, 1959), 110, says that *Daedalus* sold over 20,000 copies altogether. The UCL archives include Haldane's royalty statements up to 1946 showing that it was still selling steadily after the war.

scientific or technological ones, readers might have expected volumes on subjects like electricity, television, cars, trains, ships, as well as ones on specific disciplines like sociology, psycho-analysis, geology, metallurgy, meteorology, etc. Some of these are touched on in other volumes. Or a very partial account is given, rather than a sense of the intellectual foundations of the discipline. It is possible to imagine more niche ideas for volumes that might have appealed to the time—cryptography, perhaps, or camouflage; or topics that might have been expected to appeal to Ogden—language-teaching through recordings, say (which Linguaphone had been offering since 1901), or the future of knowledge, or neurology, or of time (Ogden was a passionate collector of clocks as well as books and manuscripts).

Such a list just scratches the surface. But it shows how it couldn't have been thought that the most promising subjects had already been covered. Indeed, some of the volumes that were advertised but did not appear sound as if they could well have provoked the most interest: *The Future of Sex*; *Mercurius; or, The World on Wings*; *Pandarus; or, The Future of Traffic in Women*; or *Caliban; or, The Future of Industrial Capitalism*.[6] The commissioning of such volumes shows that the series could have been, and nearly was, more extensive. Ogden may have had other topics on a putative list, but may have been slowed down by the publisher, or may not have been able to find the appropriate authors.

So, yes, the series could have been longer—much longer. In a sense it is, in that some work that could have gone into it was diverted into the adjacent Psyche Miniatures.[7] That points to what is another, and perhaps the most salient, reason for winding the series down. Ogden had decided that the future, at least as far as he was concerned, consisted mainly of psychology, and BASIC English, and he devoted most of his time and considerable energy to them (though even the journal *Psyche* was scaled down from 1932, switching from quarterly to annual publication).

Perhaps the future of these missing subjects did not seem interesting or urgent enough; nor the futures that seem most pressing to us now—of the environment, of water, of terror, of population, or of oil—though the last of these was also urgent between the wars. Nevertheless, at 110 volumes (including the three US-only volumes), the range is still vast and the content rich. Many of the volumes merit a chapter-length discussion each, which would have made this book ten or twenty times longer. An exploratory study like this cannot hope to do much more than blaze a trail, and hope that others will think it worth following.

The archive allows alternative speculations about the fate of the series. The printing figures, that is, could be made to tell a different story; one about the publisher's prudence. They show that the books were doing well until 1928; but

---

[6] See the end of Appendix B for full details of these phantom volumes.
[7] For examples, see Appendix A, p. 386.

from 1929 onwards only four of the new volumes went into reprints. *Kalki; or, The Future of Civilization*, and *Shiva; or, The Future of India* (both from 1929)—which presumably sold well thanks to India's larger readership. Otherwise only two volumes, both touching on sexuality—*It Isn't Done* (1930) and *Aphrodite* (1931)—warranted a second impression. Some of the earlier volumes were still being reprinted in 1930 or 1931; but it was harder for new volumes to make a mark. There were no new titles in the series after 1931, and only two volumes were reprinted after that: *Aphrodite* in 1932, and *What I Believe* in 1932 and 1933.[8] This may be because the series was no longer news; but the more likely reason is the background of the Depression. Book sales generally had slumped; and two shillings and sixpence must have seemed harder to find for a small book. But also, such economic convulsions, as they highlight the future-orientation of the economy, change attitudes towards the future. Marc Augé contrasts insurance and credit as embodying opposing conceptions of the future. You insure yourself against the risks of life, whereas to live on credit is 'to show confidence in life, to take risks'.[9] Such attitudes are themselves overdetermined by economic conditions. When the economy melts down, the blow to economic confidence is a blow to confidence in the future more generally.

The changing political context may also have had an effect. Political debate became increasingly polarized with the rise of communism and fascism. The series pitted reactionaries against progressives. Some volumes, like *Sinon*, attempted a balanced view of left and right. Such even-handedness became less tenable, though, first during the Spanish Civil War, then after the Nazi-Soviet Non-Aggression Pact of 1939. The concerns of the 1920s weren't the same as those of the 1930s. A book like Arthur Keith's *Ethnos* on race is humane about the relation between race and nation. The biological and social volumes debate Eugenics. By the end of the 1930s writers were taking their stand on fascism, and were beginning to envisage the murderous consequences to which such discourses could be turned.[10]

The volume by F. G. Crookshank with the troubling title *The Mongol in our Midst* was greatly expanded in 1931 to 540 pages, when it was published outside the series. (He had a way with titles. His *Flatulence and Shock* was a blast.) Some other volumes had undergone smaller-scale revision by that date. Otherwise, the

[8] Routledge and Kegan Paul archive at the UCL Library; see Appendix A for a more detailed discussion.

[9] Marc Augé, *The Future*, trans. John Howe (London: Verso, 2014), 96.

[10] One later commentator on Money-Kyrle's book *Aspasia* complains of exactly that. Riccardo Steiner describes *Aspasia* as 'a sort of science-fictional novel', arguing that in it Money-Kyrle 'sketched out a utopian "sane society" of the future. His statements regarding eugenics, a pseudo-science fashionable amongst upper-class English intellectuals of the time, are, however, rather disturbing'. 'The (Ir)resistible Lightness of Our Past', paper published on the British Psychoanalytical Society website, http://www.psychoanalysis.org.uk/articles/the-irresistible-lightness-of-our-past-riccardo-steiner accessed on 1 February 2019.

only new publications relating to the series was an attempt to relaunch it in 1936, when seven of the better-selling volumes were expanded and published under the revised version of the series title, 'To-day, Tomorrow and After'. None of these were on scientific or technological topics, but mostly on the relations between the sexes, and associated topics like taboo and swearing. The classical titles were dropped, and these volumes were all called 'The Future of' their subject. After the New Deal in the US, and rearmament worldwide, the more buoyant economic situation perhaps seemed propitious for futurology again. But the publisher's archive doesn't indicate any reprints after the first 2,000 copies for any of these relaunched volumes. If they'd hoped that dropping the classical titles would broaden their readership, they were disappointed. By 1936 it appeared that the Future didn't have much of a future; or at least, as far as people thought about the future, they could see that it was going to be grim; the rhetoric was more of the coming struggle for Europe, as the utopian hopes for the League of Nations and increasing integration now rang hollow. As Joad wrote in *The Future of Morals*, 'To-day the post-War era has definitely ended and the pre-War era begun' (93).

That was in 1936. Yet the archive indicates that the critical reception may have grown out of kilter with the sales, and that the series was losing its commercial momentum as early as 1928—before the Wall Street Crash and the Depression—with only three of the volumes from that year going into second impressions: *Diogenes*, *Eos*, and *Mrs Fisher*. Whereas another book from 1928 shows that the public appetite for futurology was certainly not yet sated. *The Day after To-Morrow: What is going to happen to the world*, by the well-known journalist, war-correspondent, and novelist Philip Gibbs, went through at least ten impressions by 1929.[11] Its success suggests several further reasons why the series might have been losing traction. Gibbs, who had made his name in tabloid journalism, presents himself as one of the 'men in the street' (10) who should be paying attention to the scientific developments that are going to change their lives. 'We really ought to watch those scientists!' he cautions (11). He has been watching them himself; and indeed has clearly been reading To-Day and To-Morrow. He doesn't name the series, saying only that the scientists have lately 'been writing little books to tell the man-in-the-street something of what he may expect in the near or distant future' (10). But he quotes from several of its volumes, though again he doesn't identify most of them.[12] Pretending to 'ignorance', he implies that the scientist's attempts at popularization (characterized by their use of 'words of three syllables' when talking to him (10); and implicitly, their polysyllabic classical titles and terms such as ectogenesis) are themselves in need of popularization.

[11] Philip Gibbs, *The Day After To-Morrow: What is going to happen to the world* (London: Hutchinson 1928).

[12] For example, Gibbs quotes from *Daedalus* (12, 23, 44, 49–50), Low's *Wireless Possibilities* (39), Russell's *Icarus* (44), Schiller's *Tantalus* (44–6), and Jennings' *Prometheus* (83); in each case mentioning the author but not the source. He does mention the title of Garrett's *Ouroboros* (111).

In another, and two-syllable, word of the period, the series is high-brow, for an elite and mainly university-educated audience. What he is offering is to interpret it for a more popular readership: to repopularize the popularizations.

That act of mediation itself suggests another potential difficulty To-Day and To-Morrow was facing. It was the earlier volumes that had generated the most excitement. True, they included some of the best. But also, the extent of the series was more manageable. Two volumes, or ten, or fifteen, seemed intriguing; an opening out of possibilities. By the end of 1928 more than eighty had appeared; and that number, or a hundred, presented a more daunting challenge. Gibbs's book is an example of what other writers were also offering in the period: a one-volume survey of the entire range of technological, social, and cultural developments. Archibald Low, for example, had followed *Wireless Possibilities* with a single book simply promising *The Future*.[13] We have even seen examples within To-Day and To-Morrow: *Daedalus* ranged widely across fields such as reproduction, energy, agriculture, and pollution. F. C. S. Schiller's *Tantalus* looked at man's future in general terms. Fournier D'Albe's *Quo Vadimus?* considered numerous changes across different time-scales. A one-volume stop that promised to encapsulate the future would have been a more attractive proposition to publishers and busy readers alike.

Gibbs's strategy of not mentioning the series or its volumes explicitly for the most part, even while using their predictions, was probably a combination of attempting to cover his tracks, plus a canny publishing tactic of not diverting readers away from his own work to that of some of his sources. (He mentions a number of other scientists and commentators too, especially his friend Julian Huxley, the radiochemist Frederick Soddy, and inevitably, Henry Ford and H. G. Wells.) Yet to those who knew the series, the book's title is a clear allusion to it: a claim of going beyond it; going one better. The claim is absurd in intellectual terms. The To-Day and To-Morrow volumes go well beyond Gibbs's pedestrian book in their ideas, their ingenuity, and their timescales. Gibbs's novelistic title promises to turn a multiplicity of visions into a coherent narrative, perhaps. But it also suggests a third reason why the series may have been perceived as losing its

---

[13] A. M. Low, *The Future* (London: G. Routledge & Sons, 1925); discussed further in Appendix A. Low was a prolific writer on technology and futurology, also publishing *Tendencies of Modern Science; or, Science and Modern Life* (London: E. Mathews & Marrot, 1930), *Our Wonderful World of Tomorrow: A scientific forecast of the men, women, and the world of the future* (London: Ward, Lock & Co., Limited, 1934)—incidentally showing that the market for futurology continued into the 30s; and the wonderfully-titled *Science in Wonderland* (London: L. Dickson & Thomson, 1935). Lord Birkenhead's ghost-written volume *The World in 2030 A.D.* (London: Hodder and Stoughton, [1930]) was another indication of a vogue for the single-volume futurological compendium; one that caused a scandal when Haldane noticed that he had been plagiarized in it: see Ronald Clark, *JBS: The life and work of J. B. S. Haldane* (London: Hodder and Stoughton, 1968), 86–8. Also see Peter Bowler's *A History of the Future: Prophets of progress from H. G. Wells to Isaac Asimov* (Cambridge: Cambridge University Press, 2017) for later examples such as Ritchie Calder's *The Birth of the Future* (London: Arthur Barker, 1934); or John Langdon-Davies' *A Short History of the Future* (London: Routledge, 1936).

cutting edge. Tomorrow, it implies, no longer felt like the future. We are already too familiar with what has been predicted for it. If this is in part a comment on the fact that the series had already been running for five years—so the tomorrows being predicted at its start might already seem yesterday's news—it is also perhaps reflects the ever-accelerating pace of change with which Gibbs starts.

Another way of putting this is to say that a further possible reason for winding the series up is the speed with which (as anticipated in the Introductions) the future goes out of date. In 1927 To-Day and To-Morrow had only been running for three years when T. S. Eliot could imagine how 'the series will constitute a precious document upon the present time'.[14] My argument is that it does indeed constitute such a document, not in the sense Eliot intended, of exposing the symptoms of the age's demoralization and debility, but because it reveals the creative energy with which its writers were trying to reimagine man's place in the world, in history, in time, and in relation to technology—nothing less than a crucial document in the intellectual history of modernity. But history has a way of overtaking such attempts. Some of the contributors comment on the problem of foreseen obsolescence. E. E. Fournier d'Albe wrote in Hephaestus that 'What we write to-day is obsolete to-morrow' (42). This is a predicament that falls between Jameson's two poles of utopian speculation (if it stays too close to contemporary reality it reads like reformist political critique; if it strays too far, it reads like science fiction). In between, and history merely overtakes it, whether proving it true or false. In some unfortunate cases, as we saw in the Introductions, the predictions proved false soon after publication.

By 1931 To-Day and To-Morrow had been running for eight years, and its very longevity may have come to seem a liability, the earlier volumes by then hailing from the early years of a previous decade. As another world war loomed, then broke out, the future changed. Gertrude Stein's comment about youth at the end of the Second World War was beginning to be true even in the years before it began:

> One of the things that is most striking about the young generation is that they never talk about their own futures, there are no futures for this generation, not any of them and so naturally they never think of them. It is very striking, they do not live in the present they just live, as well as they can, and they do not plan. It is extraordinary that whole populations have no projects for a future, none at all. It certainly is extraordinary, but it is certainly true.[15]

It is all the more extraordinary because the language of conceiving of the future in terms of 'projects' was also that of Existentialism, at least in its Sartrean version; a product of the furnace of the same war. It is in Existentialism's Absurdist strain

---

[14] T. S. Eliot, 'Charleston, Hey! Hey!', Nation and Athenaeum, 40 (29 January 1927) 595.
[15] Gertrude Stein, Wars I Have Seen (New York: Random House, 1945), 190.

that one hears a more anguished attitude towards the future, as in Camus' account of the absurdity of human relations to time:

> We live on the future: 'tomorrow', 'later on', 'when you have made your way' [….] Yet a time comes when a man notices […] that he stands on a certain point on a curve that he acknowledges having to travel to its end. He belongs to time and, by the horror that seizes him, he recognizes his worst enemy. Tomorrow, he was longing for tomorrow, whereas everything in him ought to reject it. The revolt of the flesh is the absurd.[16]

That time comes in an individual life, as the individual future foreshortens. But in 1942 that time, that recognition of the proximity of death, had come for a generation, as Stein recognized. When the economic and political crises led to war, the future must have seemed a distant luxury. After the Depression, the rise of fascism, the Nazi-Soviet pact, the war, and then the Cold War, and the prospect of nuclear annihilation, little wonder that any faith in the future offered by dialectical materialism offered scant consolation. The shift outlined in the Introduction from Bloch's view of Marxism as providing a scientific blueprint of the future, to Popper's rejection of its predictive claims, was…inevitable.

People didn't stop thinking about tomorrow, of course. But the future seemed more likely to offer disaster than hope; one symptom of which was a sense of belatedness; of defining ourselves as coming after the event, rather than looking forward to realization. Elaborating on her term 'postmemory', Marianne Hirsch locates it in relation to a cluster of late twentieth-century terms bearing the 'post-' prefix:

> Postmemory is the term I came to on the basis of my autobiographical readings of works by second generation writers and visual artists. The 'post' in 'postmemory' signals more than a temporal delay and more than a location in an aftermath. Postmodern, for example, inscribes both a critical distance and a profound interrelation with the modern; postcolonial does not mean the end of the colonial but its troubling continuity, though, in contrast, postfeminist has been used to mark a sequel to feminism. We certainly are, still, in the era of 'posts', which continue to proliferate: 'post-secular', 'post-human', 'postcolony', 'post-white'. Postmemory shares the layering of these other 'posts' and their belatedness, aligning itself with the practice of citation and mediation that characterize them, marking a particular end-of-century/turn-of-century moment of looking backward rather than ahead and of defining the present in relation to a troubled past rather than initiating new paradigms. Like them, it reflects an uneasy oscillation between continuity and rupture.[17]

---

[16] Albert Camus, *The Myth of Sisyphus*, trans. Justin O'Brien (London: Penguin, 2000), 19–20.
[17] Marianne Hirsch, 'The Generation of Postmemory' *Poetics Today*, 29:1 (Spring 2008), 103–28 (106).

The writers in question are 'second generation' in relation to the Shoah. But in principle the syndrome she describes applies to the aftermath of other traumatic events: 'Postmemory describes the relationship of the second generation to powerful, often traumatic, experiences that preceded their births but that were nevertheless transmitted to them so deeply as to seem to constitute memories in their own right'.[18] For children of traumatized combatants from the First World War doubtless predicaments from that war were transmitted with comparable depth. The generation born after the end of the war did not start to come of age until the start of the Second World War. But arguably even for those born between the wars, the cultural memory of the war was transmitted as to constitute, if not 'memories in their own right', a sense of the war as the defining experience of modernity that they had just missed. That is to say, Hirsch's 'moment of looking backward rather than ahead and of defining the present in relation to a troubled past rather than initiating new paradigms' also describes those coming of age in the late 1920s and throughout the 30s. Which may account for why a series written largely by forward-looking survivors in the 20s may have resonated less with readers of the following decade.

Read retrospectively, however, from a distance of about a century, To-Day and To-Morrow's refusal of monolithic pessimism (despite the pessimism of some volumes) is historically significant, and for both periods. Its ludic speculativeness contrasts not only with the 1930s' sense of what William Empson (before Winston Churchill) called *The Gathering Storm* (1940), but also with the post-1989 sense of futurelessness, whether from a selection of environmental or geopolitical catastrophes; or from a sense of 'The End of History' (as Francis Fukuyama was famously to term it),[19] thanks to rampant globalized neo-liberal capitalism; or from the related imaginary of a technophiliac consumer utopia which, in Augé's analysis, fosters a rhetoric of Future-Now-ism which tends to short-circuit any creative exhilaration:

> The real problems with democratic life today stem from the fact that technological innovations exploited by financial capitalism have replaced yesterday's myths in the definition of happiness for all, and are promoting an ideology of the present, an ideology of the future *now*, which in turn paralyses all thought about the future. (3)

After all, if the future is already here, we have nothing to look forward to. Except ever more 'innovation', of course, which has become an institutional cant term, and really means 'competition', but in a specifically product-based form. Or ever more 'disruption', which equally cantingly, is confined in meaning to making

---

[18] Ibid., Abstract.
[19] See Francis Fukuyama, 'The End of History?', *The National Interest* (Summer 1989); expanded into *The End of History and the Last Man* (New York: Free Press, 1992).

employees less secure, not their employers; changing the 'business model', not the model of business. Given that the models for these things are often the 'tech' giants of Apple, Google, Amazon, Facebook, and their ilk, it is worth pointing out two things. First that, though we certainly use such tech for shopping for products, we use it more for people, information, and ideas: for friendship, aesthetics, social life, knowledge. Second, that these corporations invoke the future when they present themselves (it is good for their businesses if they can persuade people they *are* the future). But from another point of view, what they represent is that we are now arguably inhabiting *a post-future era*. As George Myerson has said, there are times when there are more (possible) futures than others; and the 1920s was such a time of future cornucopia.[20] The period of To-Day and To-Morrow acquires poignancy now when seen as a moment when you could imagine futures other than that of militant fascism and imminent world war. In 1968—significantly another moment of surging utopianism—it was possible for Arthur C. Clarke to choose 2001 as the point when the future seemed to begin. Why 2001? Presumably because it would be the first unequivocal year of the twenty-first century, which had become shorthand for the future itself throughout the twentieth. The reality of the dawn of the new century? Of the new millennium? First, the anxiety about the havoc that might be caused by the 'millennium bug' (causing older computers to malfunction because their date functions couldn't cope with more than two digits) but which then failed to fail. Then 9/11, and the 'War on Terror', which has thrown us back into the barbarity of religious warfare reminiscent of the medieval crusades. It is because our age is one in which it scarcely seems possible to imagine a future we want to live in that it seems more important than ever to reflect on imaginative futurologists such as To-Day and To-Morrow's writers.

Concluding Evaluation

The preceding chapters have included a number of suggestions about the possible or demonstrable influences To-Day and To-Morrow had on other writers and thinkers. These connections and speculations are revealing, not only demonstrating that prominent cultural figures were reading the series as well as writing for it; but also suggesting how their reading of its volumes might have fed into their own work. But 'influence' is not the only way, and not necessarily the best way, to think about the significance of the series. A more useful concept may be *confluence*: the flow or movement of ideas and images in particular directions at particular times. What comes across again and again in the volumes is what a good barometer the series was of the intellectual pressures of the era. If it is sometimes tempting to

---

[20] In conversation, 28 January 2014.

draw a line from To-Day and To-Morrow and a particular literary or critical work, it may be that both are responding to what Stephen Greenblatt calls the 'social energy' of the period, rather than that one directly influenced the other. After all, the main fields outlined here—science, war, the human, the machine, the everyday, the arts—are so enormous as to have thousands of writers and intellectuals contributing to their development. Yet if one is tempted to think that volumes in the series had influences, it is because they often precede important related developments elsewhere. What that indicates is not that To-Day and To-Morrow was simply a sign of the times, reflecting the intellectual fashions of the 1920s and early 30s; but that it was in the avant-garde, actually leading the way into the future, or the future of the future.

In Chapter 1, I argued that Haldane's vignette of the birth of a new star showed how the new astronomy and physics ushered in the possibility of new plots, with human agency supplanting the natural or the divine. Yet he also considers the plot as being one of a last judgement on an alien civilization; a possibility that appears to drag plot back towards a traditional, religious world view. But Susan Sontag's claim that 'Science fiction films are not about science. They are about disaster, which is one of the oldest subjects of art', suggests how Haldane's film-like vignette can be made to reveal a further aspect of To-Day and To-Morrow's generic versatility.[21] When the books switch into science fiction mode, disaster looms, bearing out Sontag's analysis. The oceans turn purple. The Moon strikes back. The whole of north-west London is blown up. But elsewhere, it is the series' resistance to science fiction—its ways of doing the future differently, as speculative exposition, as future history, as satire—that enables it to postulate non-disastrous futures.

One of the many virtues of Paul Saint-Amour's book *Tense Future* is the way it focuses attention on the affect of futurology between the wars. That is implicit in the argument he explores that it is possible to conceive as trauma as produced not only by the past, but by the anticipation of future.[22] If that proposition runs against the grain of received trauma theory, it should not, since the prospect of death is surely the future which traumatizes most of us, producing tell-tale distortions and denials and repetition-compulsions.

Traumatic anxiety about the future is consonant with Günther Anders' concept of the 'Promethean gap' (discussed in Chapter 4) in two reciprocal respects. A sense that we struggle to conceive the significance of what our technology is capable of, issues in an anxiety about what it *will* be capable of. Conversely, that cognitive gap could be construed as the sign of a repression of a full realization of

---

[21] Susan Sontag, 'The Imagination of Disaster' (1965), reprinted in *Against Interpretation* (New York: Farrar, Straus, and Giroux, 1966), 213.

[22] Paul Saint-Amour, 'Introduction', *Tense Future* (Oxford: Oxford University Press, 2015), 1–43.

what our technologies mean—the repression itself being the sign of trauma in the face of the realization of such horrifying potentialities.

In some ways To-Day and To-Morrow bears out such a trauma-theory shaped analysis of thinking about the future. Volumes such as Joad's *Diogenes* and Bernal's *The World, the Flesh and the Devil* are evidently invested in imagining futures in which personal death can be avoided. One reason why we desire futurology in general is arguably to counter the traumatic anticipation of mortality; to imagine life after (our own) death—even if we are not planning, like Ray Kurzweil, to have ourselves frozen until the future has learnt how to reanimate us. But even in Saint-Amour's terms, the imagining of future trauma of mass destruction is powerfully active, especially in the volumes about, or representing, war. The First World War had barely been over for five years when the series started appearing. So soon afterwards, it was inevitable that to look forwards was to look back to the catastrophe of the Western Front; and that to look back was to fear a return of the horror to come. No wonder William McDougall called his book about war *Janus*. As Saint-Amour shows (20-1), the idea of an 'inter-war period' is not just a retrospective construction; it was the growing anticipation of a sequel to the world war that made people at the time feel that was what they were inhabiting. That was certainly Ogden's concern. As he wrote in 1931, as the series drew to a close, the 'Great' War might prove to have been:

> only a little one—a sort of one act play before the curtain is lifted on a more serious military outburst.... Something has to be done for the development of international feeling, or another War will take our breath away in more sensed than one. Where there is no breath, there is no language—only a system of signs or marks on paper; but where there is no international language, the breath even of nations may be turned into some new chemical substance by gases of such power that there will be no signs of the British Museum, or the Committee for the Study of International Relations, having ever been in existence.[23]

Ogden's life's work was largely devoted to trying to make such catastrophes less likely. Accordingly, most of the volumes in the series tell a different story from trauma. This is most startlingly the case with those writers who would become most closely associated for British readers with narratives of the traumatic horrors of the war—Robert Graves and Vera Brittain. A future trauma theorist might be able to construct an argument for how *Lars Porsena*'s future historian, struggling to reconstruct a lexicon of obscene language completely censored from the historical record, represents the mind struggling to come to terms with repressed traumatic memories; or that Brittain's use of the future history trope proves that

---

[23] C. K. Ogden, *Brighter Basic*, Psyche Miniatures (London: Kegan Paul, 1931), 25–7. See Kristin Bluemel, *George Orwell and the Radical Eccentrics: Intermodernism in literary London* (New York: Palgrave Macmillan, 2004), 112–15.

she is only able to imagine her utopia coming to pass from the perspective of the far future, well after the death of her entire generation. But *Lars Porsena* and *Halcyon* are both amusing, light-hearted books. And trauma doesn't do comedy (even if comedy sometimes does trauma, as in Roberto Benigni's controversial 1997 film about the Concentration Camps, *La Vita e Bella*). These, and many other volumes in the series, demonstrate a range of affects associated with their imagined futures. In addition to anxiety and comedy, there are utopian wish, desire, creative exhilaration, even denial (though treated comically rather than psycho-analytically, in *Cassandra* by Schiller).

On the day Britain declared war on Germany in 1914, Kipling wrote in his wife's diary: 'Incidentally, Armageddon begins'.[24] It became a common trope during and after the war to describe it as Armageddon—in Christian eschatology the battle presaging the end of the world and the last judgement.[25] To use such a trope during or after the war is in a sense the antithesis of projecting the war into the anticipatory trauma of future destruction shadowing utopian hope. It is to anticipate the end of war. Trauma studies understandably focuses on the guilt of the survivor. But what that guilt is for is not just for having survived when others have not; but for the feeling of exhilaration at having survived. And that exhilaration contributes to the futurological imagination. Augé's comment that people believe in the future in a post-war period is borne out by the launching of a series of four *Future Books* just after the Second World War.[26] Certainly, thinking of the future, having survived the disaster, enables you both to look back on the conflict, at the same time as worrying about any future recurrence. But it constructs a different relation between war and the future. Instead of seeing the future as being brought to an end by war, it sees the possibility of the future *after* war. For the progressive contributors to the series, the technological power unleashed in the war, did not so much signal the destruction of humanity, as announce humanity's ability to rethink its place in the world.

Saint-Amour's turning of trauma to face forwards as well as back is a fascinating move, which can clearly capture important aspects of interwar writing— including much in To-Day and To-Morrow—and indeed help define its interwar condition. But in doing so it extends trauma's dominion, in a culture which is already prone to devaluing the concept by applying it loosely, to less disturbing and distorting affects. Traumatized by the past? Don't worry, the future will be just as bad. This is not to make light of trauma, nor to suggest that the prospect of

---

[24] See Cecil D. Eby, *The Road to Armageddon: The martial spirit in English popular literature, 1870–1914* (Durham, NC: Duke University Press, 1987), p. 171.

[25] See for example Ford Madox Ford, *War Prose*, ed. Max Saunders (Manchester: Carcanet, 1999), 42, 59–60, 190, 195, and 264.

[26] *Future Books: Industry Government science arts. Volume 1: Overture* (London: Leathley Publications Ltd, [1946]), ed. Marjorie Bruce Milne, is a compilation of essays includes contributions by Stephen Spender, Cecil Day Lewis, Osbert Lancaster, and W. J. Turner. It announces three further volumes: 'The Stage is Set', 'The Crowded Scene', and 'Transformation'.

nuclear annihilation did not have traumatic effects on some imaginations. What is at stake though is the attempt to keep open the possibility of a non-traumatic future. That is what the energy and humour with which the series imagines a multiplicity of possible futures stands for, and is the ground of its achievement. As a response it is analogous to Nietzsche's account of tragedy's articulation and confrontation of traumatic experience as a form of joyful affirmation.[27] Which is unsurprising. As we have seen, the recurrent quest in the series to liberate humanity from the prison house of outworn religion and morality is frequently accompanied by Nietzschean ideas and echoes; though the quest itself is framed in terms of scientific rigour rather than philosophic inspiration.

Saint-Amour argues that we need 'a loose rubric for work that applies sceptical pressure to reflexive invocations of the future', and proposes that we 'Call it *critical futurities*: scholarship that takes as its object past and present conscriptions of "the future", the rhetoric, poetics, and ideology of such conscriptions, and their ethical, political, and historiographic import' (24). Under this rubric he focuses on three 'currents of thought' contributing to critical futurities: 'nuclear criticism, queer temporalities scholarship, and work that strives to reemplot or reactivate futures past' (24). The present book is clearly first and foremost a contribution to the third current, taking a particular archive of works elaborating what Reinhart Koselleck calls past or superseded futures.[28] Saint-Amour describes such past imaginings of futurity as among the 'strangest, most important' documents, 'the traces of a past moment's orientation "to the not-yet, to the nonexperienced, to that which is to be revealed"'.[29] Critical futurities research on such material needs to strive 'to reemplot or reactivate futures past' because (as Saint-Amour paraphrases David Scott) 'The living [...] need to be able to renarrate futures-past so as not to be constrained by now-obsolete emplotments of those futures by earlier generations'.[30]

This is an admirable and necessary position; and indeed one which sheds light on the value of an archive such as To-Day and To-Morrow. In neo-liberal times it seems especially important to keep open a sense that the future might be otherwise. What Fukuyama's thesis of 'The End of History' really means is the end of the *future*: the idea that the triumph of liberal democracy and global capitalism

---

[27] See for example *Ecce Homo*, trans. R. J. Hollingdale (London: Penguin, 1992), on his apprehension of 'a formula of supreme affirmation born out of fullness, of superfluity, an affirmation without reservation even of suffering, even of guilt, even of all that is strange and questionable in existence... This ultimate, joyfullest, boundlessly exuberant Yes to life is not only the highest insight, it is also the profoundest, the insight most strictly confirmed and maintained by truth and knowledge' (79–80).

[28] Reinhart Koselleck, *Futures Past: On the semantics of historical time*, trans. Keith Tribe (Cambridge, MA: MIT Press, 1985).

[29] Saint-Amour, *Tense Future*, p. 31, quoting Koselleck, *Futures Past*, p. 259.

[30] Saint-Amour, *Tense Future*, p. 31, citing David Scott, *Conscripts of Modernity: The tragedy of colonial enlightenment* (Durham, NC: Duke University Press, 2004).

means that no other systems of social organization or political aspiration are possible or necessary, or ever will be. Another reason why the future seems harder to imagine in the twenty-first century; or harder to imagine as anything other than either neo-liberal stasis or environmental disaster. To-Day and To-Morrow's speculative excitement reminds us of another, more liberating way of relating to time.

However, it also shows up problems with Saint-Amour's other two currents of critical futurities. Admittedly his book, *Tense Future*, does not discuss To-Day and To-Morrow, but concentrates instead on modern literary works by authors such as Woolf, Ford, and Joyce. His approach illuminates their concern with futurity; and to that extent is not vitiated by texts out of its field of vision. Yet from another point of view, it is extraordinary that a book taking as its subject 'the relationship between warfare and futurity' in the interwar period (7), and which does take in texts of military strategy and policy, should be unaware of the most extensive grouping of texts explicitly discussing futurity, including writing by some of the twentieth century's major writers about war such as Robert Graves, Vera Brittain, J. B. S. Haldane, and Bertrand Russell.[31] He does discuss Basil Liddell Hart's *Paris*; but omits any mention the series, even though the Dutton edition of *Paris* included a list of twenty other To-Day and To-Morrow volumes, Haldane's *Daedalus* and *Callinicus* and Russell's *Icarus* among them. These, together with other volumes such as Maurois' *The Next Chapter*, and McDougall's *Janus*, offer important evidence both for and against the thesis of *Tense Future*. If the series bears out Saint-Amour's argument to some extent that 'the memory of one world war was already joined to the specter of a second, future one, framing the period in real time as an *interwar* era whose terminus in global conflict seemed to many, foreordained', it also demonstrates that even among those primarily focused on projecting the future, not everyone had a sense of an 'apparent foreclosure of the future' (8). *Janus* in particular—the volume making the series' most significant contribution to the air war theory of the period which is central to Saint-Amour's argument—is the volume most challenging to it. Yes, *Janus* articulates a psychological approach to future war anxiety; yet McDougall also has a solution to propose. The sheer speculative exuberance of the series challenges the reading of the period framed in terms of trauma theory. It also demonstrates how the imperative of replotting the future as an exercise in liberation from the restrictive fix of ideological orthodoxies was not something the interwar writers needed to wait for later critical futurists to show them how to achieve.

The critical futurities Saint-Amour applies to interwar writing are all—as he freely acknowledges—anachronisms in the literal sense: products of later, post

---

[31] Tyrus Miller's *Time Images: Alternative temporalities in 20th-century theory, history, and art* (Cambridge: Cambridge Scholars Publishing, 2009) is another example of a book about temporality by a leading modernist scholar compromised by its omission of modernism's prime site of futurology.

Second World War times—the anti-nuclear movement, queer theory and post-colonial theory—back-projected onto the modernism of the 1920s and 30s. Futurology is itself a species of anachrony, and to that extent it is deeply appropriate that a critic should have the freedom to approach it with a correspondingly innovative temporal licence. Anachronism is in that sense constitutive of his project, as it is of this book. The analysis of texts in relation to subsequent theory applied retrospectively is virtually definitional of contemporary humanities criticism, and has great potential for illumination, as in Saint-Amour's discussions of modernist fiction. However, the To-Day and To-Morrow books show up the limitations of nuclear criticism and queer temporalities as heuristics for a wide cross-section of interwar writing.

First, apropos of nuclear criticism: as we have seen, the scale of mass destruction of the First World War overshadows much of the writing in the series, and several writers contemplate humanity's future self-destruction through war or war-technology. Several also contemplate the advent of nuclear power, and were well aware of its weapons potential. Thus, as in Haldane's vision of an exploding star at the start of *Daedalus*, the concept of nuclear holocaust is already present in To-Day and To-Morrow as a potential catastrophe scenario. Admittedly, it is part of Saint-Amour's argument that pre-1945 futures 'looked nuclear' in a 'broader' sense of the term; but this broader sense is explained via Jacques Derrida's belief that 'the nuclear epoch is dealt with more "seriously" in texts by Mallarmé, of Kafka, of Joyce, for example, than in present-day novels that would offer direct and realistic descriptions of a "real" nuclear catastrophe'.[32] Derrida is characteristically imagining the concept of a nuclear war not in terms of bombs and lives but writing; imagining the destruction of the archive and thereby (allegedly) the annulling of the symbolic order. But such dubious manoeuvres are scarcely necessary when the texts themselves, in To-Day and To-Morrow and elsewhere, are already explicitly 'nuclear' in the narrower, literal sense of imagining a human-produced nuclear disaster.

Haldane's work in particular (though James Jeans's *Eos* could be enlisted for further evidence) reveals a further limitation of a post-1945 nuclear approach. Nuclear criticism is mainly about destroying humanity, not the planet. Nuclear holocaust scenarios imagined making the planet uninhabitable to humans and most other species, due to the environmental catastrophes of radioactive fallout and a dust-induced nuclear ice age. The planet itself remains; a sterile graveyard or monument to human folly.

However, the new physics and astronomy reveal humanity does not have a monopoly on nuclear energy. Haldane, as we saw, also contemplated the possibility

---

[32] Saint-Amour, *Tense Future*, p. 27. Jacques Derrida, 'No Apocalypse, Not Now (full speed ahead, seven missiles, seven missives)', trans. Catherine Porter and Philip Lewis, *diacritics* 14:2 (Summer 1984), 20–31 (27–8).

that the stellar explosion might have been a 'last judgement' on an alien world. Three years later, he elaborated what he meant by that phrase in the essay 'The Last Judgement: A Scientist Turns to Prophecy'.[33] This is another characteristically bravura piece of writing. Sixty per cent of the text is in the form of an account written by the descendants of humans on Venus forty million years in the future, long after life on earth has become extinct—and is thus yet another, spectacular, example of the trope of future history. The cause was not nuclear annihilation, but a combination of lack of foresight and astronomical chaos. Having exhausted fossil fuel, man turns to tidal power, but develops it so recklessly as to slow the Earth's rotation, and draw the Moon nearer. Subject to increased gravitational pull from the Earth, the Moon breaks up and its fragments rain down on Earth with devastating consequences.[34] Such an ending qualifies as apocalyptic, but perhaps not as 'nuclear' even in the Derridean sense, since human descendants have not only survived but written the history of the destruction. The archive and symbolic order have not perished. Yet they are not the same. Haldane has commented that he can imagine a future forty million years ahead because that long ago our ancestors were already mammals and probably monkeys; whereas he finds it impossible to project his imagination forwards by ten times as much, since four hundred million years ago our ancestors were fish-like, and 'a corresponding change in our descendants' is too alien to imagine. Yet the Venusian narrative ends with a much more farsighted prophecy:

> Our galaxy has a probable life of at least eighty million million years. Before that time has elapsed it is our ideal that all the matter in it available for life should be within the power of the heirs of the species whose original home has just been destroyed. If that ideal is even approximately fulfilled, the end of the world which we have just witnessed was an episode of entirely negligible importance. And there are other galaxies.   (309)

His point is that the post-humans would need to be as distant as this in time before such indifference to the end of the world is conceivable. It would probably also require a corresponding alteration in mentality. Haldane's Venusians have evolved into what they call a 'super-organism' (303), through a development that imagines via long-timescale biology what Bernal (who was probably influenced by this essay) was to envisage through more immediate cyborg engineering:

> The evolution of the individual has been brought under complete social control, and besides enormously enhanced intellectual powers we possess two new senses. The one enables us to apprehend radiation of wave-lengths between 100 and 1200 metres, and thus places every individual at all moments of life, both

---

[33] Haldane, 'The Last Judgement: A scientist turns to prophecy', *Harper's* (March 1927); reprinted in *Possible Worlds and Other Essays* (London: Chatto & Windus, 1927), 287–312.

[34] Compare Sir Harold Jeffreys, *The Future of the Earth* (London: Kegan Paul, Trench, Trübner and Co., 1929); discussed in Chapter 1, n. 100.

asleep and awake, under the influence of the voice of the community. It is difficult to see how else we could have achieved as complete a solidarity as has been possible. We can never close our consciousness to those wave-lengths on which we are told of our nature as components of a super-organism or deity, possibly the only one in space time, and of its past, present, and future.   (304)

(They are also sensitive to magnetism, useful for flying and navigating through Venus' opaque atmosphere.) This is an early figuring of what has become known as the 'hive mind', and its transhumanism testifies to how far ahead of the intellectual curve some of To-Day and To-Morrow's authors were.[35] In Haldane's light-speed imagination, the machine man of 1925 had become *homo deus* by 1927. Its congruence with the Marxist idea comes across in that word 'solidarity', more explicitly than in Bernal's scenario of networked cyber-spacemen. But the subordination of the individual to the state is presented as another matter 'of entirely negligible importance', given the immense gain of intellectual development. Haldane's conclusion, back in *propria persona*, says that he has contrasted humanity's 'pursuit of individual happiness' with the 'monstrous ant-heap' of Venus, and that his 'own ideal is naturally somewhere in between' (310). So presumably he would not be able to view the world's destruction with Venusian detachment. But the important point is that he is able to imagine it being imagined thus; and in doing so is able to present us with a vision of the annihilation of human life on Earth without traumatic anticipation. As he says in the conclusion—and it is here that the kind of 'judgment' he has in mind becomes clear:

> Man's little world will end. The human mind can already envisage that end. If humanity can enlarge the scope of his will as it has enlarged the reach of its intellect, it will escape that end. If not, the judgment will have gone against it, and man and all his works will perish eternally.   (312).

That last clause summons the nuclear apocalypse, at least in the Derridean sense: 'man and all his works', the archive, the symbolic order, all finished. No human future. The 'judgment' in question here is not that of a personified god, but either of the social organization developing into a 'super-organism' equivalent to a deity; or even of impersonal science: forces like gravity and processes of geology. Call it destiny or evolution or history—or even judgement by the future. Yet, just as in

---

[35] See Aline Ferreira, 'Mechanized Humanity', in *Discourses and Narrations in the Biosciences*, ed. Brian Hurwitz and Paola Spinozzi (Goettingen: V&R unipress GmbH, 2011), 145–58 (149). Contrast Julian Huxley, who as late as the 1960s still saw the human control of evolution as merely a way of finessing humanism: 'Today, in twentieth-century man, the evolutionary process is at last becoming conscious of itself and is beginning to study itself with a view to directing its future course. Human knowledge worked over by human imagination is seen as the basis of human understanding and belief, and the ultimate guide to human progress. The distillation of raw knowledge according to Humanist recipes can produce ideas and principles which illuminate the human condition in general and have the widest range of particular application.' *The Humanist Frame*, ed. Julian Huxley (London: George Allen & Unwin, 1961), Preface, p. 7.

Daedalus he recounts watching a star-birth from Earth, and speculating about its signifying the end of a world elsewhere, so here, but in reverse, he imagines the ending of our world witnessed from elsewhere. The colonization of Venus thus offsets the apocalypse with another set of possibilities; indeed of 'Possible Worlds'. This casts science then as the source of potential salvation, imagining ways to spread humanity around the universe as an insurance policy against both human negligence but also obliterating acts of astronomy indifferent or even inimical to human life (as Jeans portrayed them). It would take actual nuclear war, and the confrontation with the Shoah, to effect a radical turn away from the instrumental scientific reason that had delivered the atomic bomb and now threatened the entire world with thermo-nuclear Apocalypse.

The second current of Saint-Amour's triad of critical futurities, queer temporalities, is similarly challenged by the heterodoxy of To-Day and To-Morrow's presentations both of temporality and sexuality. His argument is that 'one of the chief temporalities from which queer subjects are variously excluded and dissenting' is

> the 'reproductive futurism' that conscripts the child as mascot for a heteronormative politics of hope—that is, for a future that can only be imagined in terms of biological reproduction and the modes of kinship, inheritance, and political succession it undergirds. (29)

This is an important concept, and the repressive ideology of 'reproductive futurism' is undeniable in advertising and politics, say. But what traction does it have when brought to bear on To-Day and To-Morrow?

The series does not explicitly discuss homosexuality—arguably one of its major omissions, given the prominence of sexological and criminological debate about it from—say—the trial of Oscar Wilde in 1895 to that of Radclyffe Hall's *The Well of Loneliness* for obscenity in 1928. The omission is perhaps accounted for precisely by concern about comparable prosecution; but it sets the To-Day and to-Morrow circle apart from the Decadents of the 1890s, say, or the Bloomsbury Group. The eugenic discourse of 'degeneracy' pervading some of the volumes might have been taken to include homosexuality by their authors and readers. Similarly, the series could be described as adopting a sexual ideology of tacit hetero-normativity by not addressing the issue more explicitly.

Where it might seem especially germane is in the fact that the question of reproductive futurism could be said to be at the core of the series—ectogenesis, eugenics, the relations between the sexes, sex education, marriage, birth control, the family, the home, education, etc. Yes, these all concern heterosexual reproduction conceived futuristically. But where the claim breaks down is in the fact that these topics are hardly ever treated hetero-normatively in the series. From *Daedalus* onward, the emphasis is precisely on the future's postulated *difference* from the status quo. Arguably all the envisaged reforms are aimed at freeing people from what are perceived as the oppressive burdens of recurrent child-bearing. Where the volumes advocate birth control they are advancing what *Daedalus*'s future undergraduate saw as the gradual 'separation of sexual love and reproduction' (65), as was Vera Brittain through her projection of long-distance monogamy. Bernal too downplays reproduction in *The World, the Flesh and the Devil*. Of evolution, he says: 'if we can find a more direct way by the use of intelligence, that way is bound to supersede the unconscious mechanism of growth and reproduction' (39). He adopts Haldane's ectogenesis, and imagines that his humans, before they leave their bodies, will 'perhaps incidentally take part in the reproductive activity' (45); so presumably also perhaps not. He refers to this phase as a 'larval' one. His vision required reproduction, but he is more interested in brains than babies. Once the brains are hard-wired into their vats during their chrysalis phase, and then during their final metamorphosis, reproduction is irrelevant, at least in the biological sense; though the speculation about transferring thought processes to other hosts to achieve immortality might be seen as an alternative form of reproduction—if a form which has completely transformed it into a reproduction of the mind rather than (and without the intervention of) the body. If medals were being handed out for future reproductivistics, queer temporalities would now be looking a bit staid and old-fashioned...

The work in the series which most clearly does address homosexuality, if with necessary implicitness, is Bertrand Russell's *What I Believe*:

> It should be recognized that, in the absence of children, sexual relations are a purely private matter, which does not concern either the State or the neighbours. Certain forms of sex which do not lead to children are at present punished by the criminal law: this is purely superstitious, since the matter is one which affects no one except the parties directly concerned.   (57)

While this might gesture towards bestiality too (also summoned up by Haldane's use of the Daedalus myth), it seems primarily to refer to homosexuality (though it might also refer to heterosexual buggery). Either way, clear evidence that not all futurologists in the period were locked into a hetero-normative model of reproduction.

It is apparent, then, that on three counts To-Day and To-Morrow's past futures both anticipate and problematize a queer temporalities approach. As with nuclear criticism, they already incorporate a vision of queer dissidence. They dissent too from hetero-normative reproduction; not because they dissent from heterosexuality, but by imagining a range of non-normative possibilities for it, including a marginalizing or suspending or cerebralizing of its reproductive aspect. And finally, because their *temporalities* are already fundamentally non-normative too. Predicting the future may be a common enough practice in flashes—calling a match or an election or the future of a friend's relationship. But to remain in future-vision mode for several thousand words is something else. However, even that could be claimed as standard in fields such as political or economic journalism. But To-Day and To-Morrow is non-standard in other ways. Its titles make it jump between the modern and the classical ages. Its future history offers further dislocations and multiplicities of temporality. While these might be described as queered temporalities, it is important to recognize that they were arrived at independently of queer theory.

Such arguments represent To-Day and To-Morrow as an original and significant achievement; and as a representative product of the modernist period. Both claims have been central to the present study. But they are joined by a third: that the series also illuminates the nature and practice of futurology. That claim has been argued primarily in relation to interwar projections. Yet to complete the assessment, let us consider To-Day and To-Morrow's futurology in relation to that of our age.

In his Introduction to Oxford University Press's 1999 collection, *Predictions*, Jonathan Weiner argues that to achieve a futurology 'schooled and chastened by the scientific process', instead of thinking about the future 'in terms of the magic sudden knowledge of the diviner', we should consider 'a few of the future's greatest experiments'; and he identifies five of these processes, which he describes as 'experiments already in progress and that are too big for anyone to stop'.[36] Of the five he selects, the first two were not yet concerns for the To-Day and To-Morrow generation. Global warming had not been identified as a problem, even if some of the contributors could foresee fuel resources being used up, and disturbances to the ecosystem. Similarly, the term 'population explosion' might have sounded like its opposite to the generation that had witnessed over seventeen million deaths in the war. Those, followed by the deaths of 3-5 per cent of the world's population from the 1918-20 influenza pandemic meant that any idea of a dangerous rise in populations was far from people's minds; even more so as a second world war loomed. In these areas, the unexpected happened, as Haldane predicted it would.

The other three of Weiner's 'experiments', by contrast, are all extremely important in To-Day and To-Morrow, and to our exploration of the series. The 'progress of technology' is a central concern, affecting every branch of life, whether extreme or everyday. The technologies themselves have changed, the mechanical giving way to the electronic on many fronts. The 'progress of evolution', similarly, detains a number of the volumes. Here too the scientific paradigm has shifted, as eugenics gave way to molecular biology, genomics, and now genetic modification and epigenetics. But that has left us with a new version of the same problem: should we alter our species, and how? For Weiner's final 'experiment' he takes the biologist E. O. Wilson's term 'consilience': 'This is the dream, hope, or prayer that everything we are learning about ourselves and our universe will fit together

---

[36] Jonathan Weiner, 'Introduction', *Predictions*, ed. Sian Griffiths (Oxford: Oxford University Press, 1999), xi–xxi (xii).

someday soon [...]' (xii–xiii). That, as we have seen in a number of the volumes, was the belief in the 1920s: that a unified field of human science would be able to redefine the nature of existence, as traditional divisions between physics, chemistry and biology were eroded by new developments in each, and new hybrid fields such as biochemistry and neurology—the resulting developments in scientific method then being extensible to the human sciences.

Weiner's thought experiment about experiments suggests a form of meta-futurology, which attends less to actual predictions, or predictions of specific developments, and more to the fields in which things are likely to arise that might require us to predict them. To say that the To-Day and To-Morrow team were concentrating on three out of five of the areas which late twentieth-century (and today's) futurologists are exercised over is not to say that 60 per cent of their specific predictions were correct, though they may have been. Accuracy is usually impossible to quantify in such textual rather than numerical predictions. Even when the predictions do involve figures, judgements need to be made about a margin of error. More often than not, predictions posit sets of likely facts, which may deviate from historical outcomes to different extents. For example, J. Leslie Mitchell predicted in *Hanno* (1928) that man would reach the Moon 'Within the next half century' (84). It seems impressive that he is correct (Apollo 11 took men there in 1969, well within the limit he had anticipated of 1978), especially since his confidence might have seemed extravagant given that the first solo flight across the Atlantic had only been managed (by Charles Lindbergh) the previous year. Yet Mitchell thought that the propulsion would be ballistic (the jet not yet having been invented); the first crew to land would consist of five people, not two; that they would be accompanied by a Reuters reporter; and that the Moon would have an atmosphere. Does it vitiate the accuracy of the main prophecy about the date of a landing if the details differ? When does the *how* become so different that the prediction of *when* scarcely seems to refer to the same event? Given such interpretative difficulties in evaluation, Weiner's set of experiments is helpful, in that it enables us to see a bigger picture.

The fact that To-Day and To-Morrow was exercised by three out of five core themes of futurologists three-quarters of a century later might simply mean that those themes are so broad—so crucial to any sense of modernity and knowledge— as to signify very little. That seems to me probably the case with the 'progress of technology' experiment. It is in the nature of technology usually to progress, and it is hard to see it not being a key issue, even for a post-Apocalyptic society of Luddites. What *is* significant in the way the series approaches technological process, as Chapter 4 here on Machine Man in particular argued, is its focus on prosthetics and bionics. In the case of the other two themes, there too the writers had a glimmering of just how important the issues of evolution and consilience were to become. That is to say, To-Day and To-Morrow was far-sighted not only in its specific projections, but in its understanding of which areas would be key to the shape of the future: especially these three of the cyborg, genetics, and of consilience.

In the case of genetics, eugenics might simply have revealed itself as a dead end (on scientific grounds, as not being able to deliver significant improvements, as Jennings argued) even without being shown up as a pseudoscience through its inhumane use in Nazi hands. Haldane explains the difficulties of scale of working on genes in a precise, targeted way.[37] So one can imagine a world in which eugenics had become unfashionable; the double helix hadn't been discovered; and there still seemed no prospect of genetic modification. People might still have been predicting exciting things to come when such breakthroughs would eventually occur. But it is as likely that genetics might have simply have stopped arousing interest, and stopped figuring as a key to the future. Yet even those like Jennings and Haldane who cast doubt on eugenics' claim to scientific validity nonetheless felt that genetics would be a central scientific quest of the future.

The objection to Weiner's notion of 'the future's greatest experiments' is that his selection of them may be seen as distorting. All five of his proposals seem important, not least because they are all still clearly relevant today. That is less surprising over a span of fewer than twenty years than of around seventy. Yet even so, most futurologists would draw up a different list today, at least to the extent that it would almost certainly have artificial intelligence (AI) and neuroscience on it. (Of course there are many other candidates too—pharmacology and resistance to antibiotics; gerontology; nuclear fusion; alternative power sources; and so on.) It is possible Weiner was including computers under technology. Though the example he gives of probable developments is of what he calls 'Organomics'—the implanting of electronic devices into the body enabling us to interact directly with technologies. That, of course, is an area absolutely continuous with the prosthetic and cyborg imagination we have been charting in Bernal and many of the series contributors. For a futurologist on the threshold of the third millennium not to make more of developments in computing and AI seems like an omission. It is an omission all the more evident to the present, because of the enormous current investments in neuroscience projects. The two areas are closely interdependent; using the computer as a conceptual model of the human brain (very much as Havelock Ellis observed, saying we find our machines inside our own bodies); then using computers to map the brain's neural networks, in the hope that the map might lead to a computer simulation of an actual brain.

Yet this very interdependence throws up a question about the notion of consilience. Research such as the Human Brain Project may increase consilience between neuroscience and informatics if the workings of anatomically-structured processors are shown to behave in comparable ways to human brains, and to be better at activities such as learning, remembering, or conversing, than current

[37] See J. B. S. Haldane, 'The Future of Biology', *Possible Worlds* (London: Chatto and Windus, 1927), 139–53 (143–4).

digital programs. But alternatively, it may not; either if the results are negative; or if they are positive, but observers still feel the computer is only simulating experiences rather than having them. Consilience here is not simply between two scientific disciplines, neurology and computer science; but between two different world views about the reducibility of experience to matter or function—again, very much a To-Day and To-Morrow debate. Similarly, the jury is out on consilience elsewhere in the sciences, especially in physics, where the quest for a unified field theory or a theory of everything still proves elusive.

It would be unreasonable to expect thinkers and scientists of the 1920s to see what those in later decades could not, and to criticize them for not having said more explicitly: 'the great challenges of the next century will be to develop technologies that can substitute for some of the work done by the human brain; and also to understand how the brain itself actually works'. Nonetheless, we have seen the stirrings of such anticipations, as in Hatfield's thoughts about the mechanical or chemical brain; Bernal's about transferring the brain's thoughts to communications networks; and in Whyte's wonderings about the relationship between the structures and functions of the brain on the one hand, and the qualia of experience and consciousness on the other. If the criteria are relaxed to admit implicit predictions of this kind, then the work of To-Day and To-Morrow seems even more spectacularly prophetic.

However, such moments have as much to do with what Weiner calls 'the magic, sudden knowledge of the diviner' as with 'the slow hard-won knowledge of the experiment' (xii). That is to say that, even though those three men were scientists, they were also among the most visionary; that what is most impressive in their projections is when they go beyond hard-won empirical proof and are able to trust their imaginative speculations. But then good scientists know that new scientific insights depend on just such moments of inspiration and vision—provided you have done the hard experimental work to base the visions on.

Such moments are also revealing in that they take these professional scientific experts outside their disciplines. They provide some of the best evidence of the importance of interdisciplinarity to much truly transformative thought. They also indicate ways in which consilience operates within To-Day and To-Morrow. It does so within individual volumes, as this study has sought to show, when writers move between fields, using the metaphors and tropes of one to discuss another. N. Katherine Hayles has argued that studies in literature and science which merely postulate parallels between a scientific theory and a literary passage need to be challenged with a series of questions, such as: 'What do the parallels signify? How do you explain their existence?' and 'What keeps the selection of some theoretical features and some literary texts from being capricious?'[38] Part of the answer to these questions in the case of To-Day and To-Morrow is that rather

[38] N. Katherine Hayles, 'Introduction', in *Chaos and Order: Complex dynamics in literature and science* (Chicago: University of Chicago Press, 1991), p. 19.

than the critic bringing together a scientific theorem and an extract from a novel, in a conjunction that may reflect his caprice, what we are dealing with in the series are books in which the connections are made explicitly by the authors themselves. That still leaves them open to the charge that it may be the author who is being capricious, rather than the critic. The answer to that is that the writers are not making casual references to other fields, but there is frequently a genuine interest in what those working in them are doing. We see this specifically in the numerous cross-references within the series, indicating that many of the authors had a keen interest in what their fellow-contributors were saying, and how the discoveries and anticipations they were describing in distant disciplines might relate to their own work.[39] What such parallels signify then is also a more general sense of a shared perspective—often configured around ideas of science, scientific method, and a scientific outlook and impartiality, as discussed throughout this book. The radicalism of most of the contributors, that is, was already bound up with a sense that the discoveries of a scientific age were stimulating them to challenge their own beliefs and reimagine their own disciplines. This represents a form of consilience across the series: an aspiration that taken together, the books will amount to a new, all-inclusive philosophy. That inclusiveness is not merely a matter of reconciling quantum mechanics with relativity, say, or those with genetics and neurology and informatics.[40] It is also an aspiration that the knowledge of the future, and its epistemology, will reconcile arts and sciences; men and women; languages and nations and races; and East and West. The form of the series itself, that is, represents a version of consilience. That is why it is important that it is not a monograph, or the purportedly monologic report of a think-tank; but instead builds up, collectively, into something resembling an encyclopedia of the future.

But why, it might be asked, have *different* versions of the future in contrasting volumes? Does that not detract from the authority of any single projection? Does it not render the combined prophecies self-defeating (in a different way from that posed by Schiller in *Cassandra*), because contradictory? No, because the point is not to offer the vision as endorsed by any mystical or magical or theological guarantee. These are not the actual future, pulled back into the present through some kink in time. They are speculations; imaginative exercises; thought experiments. The idea is that by conducting these experiments you get a better sense of likely directions, of what matters, of which decisions are likely to have which

---

[39] It is interesting to note that the notion of consilience itself is anticipated in some of the Vienna School philosophy Ogden was publishing. Carnap's *The Unity of Science* was published as a Psyche Miniature in 1934. The subtitle of Wilson's *Consilience* (1998) is 'The Unity of Knowledge'.

[40] The infamous hoax of 1996, when the physicist Alan Sokal submitted a pastiche paper, 'Transgressing the Boundaries: Towards a transformative hermeneutics of quantum gravity', which was duly published by the journal *Social Text*, 46/47 (spring/summer 1996), 217–52, is perhaps indicative of contemporary cynicism about comparable consilience-hope. On the other hand, the plausibility of the hoax demonstrates the persistence and pervasiveness of the hope.

consequences etc. They inculcate a new attitude to the future, as something we can work experimentally towards, collectively anticipate, ameliorate. They also constitute a dialogic view of epistemology. The actual future will emerge from processes of dispute and contestation. It is likely to be multiple; unfolding differently and at different speeds in different areas. A futurology grounded in debate and multiplicity may provide a better preparation for it. Its authority derives from its very multivocality, not despite it.

The most common question when people discover the series, and doubtless with any historical predictions, is to ask how accurate the prophecies were.[41] We are curious about past futurology, not only as historians, but also for what it tells us about the chances of our own predictions proving reliable. Yet one of the major insights of To-Day and To-Morrow's multivocal futurology is that treating futurology as a form of gambling may be to miss the point.

From one point of view today's professionalized foresight expert groups have made us better at predicting our own behaviour. We are now more future-oriented than ever; constantly trying to anticipate trends through foresight, scenario planning, horizon scanning, forecasting, assessing risk and threat, genome analysis, mining big data etc. Yet from another point of view, what has been lost is precisely the *imagination* of the future. The attempt is often to replace 'psyche' with the predictability of algorithm. That it shows up the limits of such a tendency is, ultimately, a crucial aspect of the value of the To-Day and To-Morrow series. We should also consider such works of projection as works of art. The novelist creates situations that do not exist in a world that for the most part does. The details of names, places, buildings, geographies, might alter or recombine, but the world is still recognizably ours. The futurologist creates a world that does not exist, or not yet; then populates it with people like us. But virtually everything else can be reimagined—including, eventually, the nature of people. Such imagined worlds normally follow the laws of the natural sciences, but not necessarily any other. Many of these books are themselves imaginative works of a high order; not just because of what they predict accurately, but also because their imaginations set the agenda for other writers—and other scientists and engineers as well as creative writers. To-Day and To-Morrow reminds us of the human (as opposed to the economic) value of speculation; of the need to exercise our minds to free ourselves from the bonds of what Ogden called 'word magic', as from the spells of fates and figures; and to realize our freedom to make the world different; to 'make it new'. That is to say, in a world in which we are fixated on the accuracy of forecasts and opinion polls, we risk becoming supine in relation to a future we conceive as deterministic. There will only be one outcome, which is inevitable, and we have to struggle to predict it. Whereas multivocal futurology, by encouraging

---

[41] See for example Roy Lewis, 'Looking Back 50 Years to the Predictions that were Made for the Times we Live in: How accurate were the visions of the twenties prophets?', *Times* (26 August 1974), 6.

us to imagine different possible futures, makes other worlds conceiveable. As Badiou says: 'It is a matter of showing how the space of the possible is larger than the one we are assigned—that something else is possible'.[42] It is by imagining the future that we can begin to change it, and the value of futurology needs to be gauged less in terms of commercial innovation and more in terms of human freedom, including the freedom to imagine better everyday lives.

Dmitri Levitin argues that 'the case can be made that the humanities, not the natural sciences, were the prime mover in the emergence of "modernity"' in the Renaissance, and suggests that perhaps that fact, 'and not the more usual moralising, is the proper basis for a defence of the humanities today'.[43] It is too one-sided a case to advance apropos of To-Day and To-Morrow, because it was the conjunction of the scientific and the imaginative across the series, but also often in the same mind, that made it such a landmark in the era of modernism. As the question of the public understanding of science, and clashes between religion and science, have presented themselves as urgent once more, To-Day and To-Morrow offers a model for how such debates might be advanced creatively and compellingly. It also offers a model of how the arts and humanities can not only contribute to discussion of the relations between culture and technological and social change, but also have the potential to enhance contemporary futurological thought. One effect of To-Day and To-Morrow, itself often visionary, is to stimulate readers' own visions of the future.

Julian Huxley had made the converse case in 1922 of how science was necessarily transforming philosophy:

> The time has gone by when the intelligent public needs to be reminded of the practical utility of science, or of the fact that investigation of any problem, however apparently remote from every-day life, may be fraught with the most valuable consequences. But it should not be forgotten that there is another utility besides that of creature comforts and improved machinery. Science is not only a useful drudge, inventing telephones and electric light or teaching us how best to breed cattle. Man demands a philosophy of life, a point of view under whose wings he may exist, and science gives him the knowledge from which he may build this philosophy and this point of view. [...]

> Man primitively tends to draw both his philosophy and his religion almost exclusively from within himself; but as the generations pass, he finds gradually that his wishes, his imaginations, his symbols, his ideals, do not correspond properly with the realities of the universe in which he lives or even with the realities of his own nature. To attempt to understand this universe, including the nature of man, is the task of science; and as she makes progress with this task,

---

[42] Alain Badiou, Ethics: An essay on the understanding of evil, trans. Peter Hallward (London: Verso, 2002), 115.
[43] Dmitri Levitin, 'Such Matters as the Soul', LRB (22 September 2016), 29–30, 32 (32).

so will she become more and more an indispensable part of philosophy and religion— imagination's touchstone, thought's background, action's base.[44]

But the last word—the last judgement—should go to Haldane, or come from him, since it was his intelligence which launched the series. He was, according to Isiah Berlin, 'one of our major intellectual emancipators'.[45] And what he says of the 'more speculative' essays in his collection *Possible Worlds* could stand as the rationale for To-Day and To-Morrow too:

In scientific work the imagination must work in harness. But there is no reason why it should not play with the fruits of such work, and it is perhaps only by so doing that one can realize the possibilities which research is opening up. In the past these results have always taken the public and the politicians completely by surprise. The present disturbed condition of humanity is largely the result of this unpreparedness.[46]

[44] Julian Huxley, 'Searching for the Elixir of Life', *Century* (February 1922), 621–9 (629).

[45] Isiah Berlin in Julian Huxley, ed. *Aldous Huxley, 1894–1963: A memorial volume* (London, 1965), 144.

[46] Haldane, 'Preface', *Possible Worlds*, pp. v–vi (vi).

DAEDALUS
OR
SCIENCE & THE FUTURE
By
J. B. S. HALDANE
Sir William Dunn Reader in Biochemistry,
University of Cambridge

"The principal merit of this little book lies in the recognition ..."

HEPHÆSTUS
OR
The Soul of the Machine
✳ ✳ ✳
E. E. FOURNIER D'ALBE

Morpheus
or
THE FUTURE OF
SLEEP
By
PROFESSOR D. F. FRASER-HARRIS
M.D., D.Sc., F.R.S.E.
Author of "Nerves, Life and Science,"
"Coloured Thinking," "The Sixth Sense"

Procrustes
or
THE FUTURE OF ENGLISH
EDUCATION
By
M. ALDERTON PINK, M.A.

Socrates
or the
EMANCIPATION OF
MANKIND
By
H. F. CARLILL

The Book History of the Series

Kegan Paul specialized in book series. So did Ogden. He joined the firm as consulting editor in 1922, and stayed till his death in 1957. He created five series for them, several of over a hundred volumes. The most substantial was International Library of Psychology, Philosophy and Scientific Method (from 1922). It is also extremely significant in terms of intellectual history, and deserves a study to itself. It specialized in importing and translating leading contemporary European thinkers (with Plato, Parmenides, and Bentham granted honorary contemporaneity), but combined them with British and some American writers. By the end of the 1930s the series had published at least 120 volumes, including works by many of the major living European thinkers apart from Freud (whose works were all published in English translation by the Hogarth Press). By the time of Ogden's death in 1957 there were over 150 volumes. The series continued, its title modified to The International Library of Philosophy, under the editorship of Bernard Williams, Ted Honderich, and others, into the twenty-first century, eventually including over 200 titles. By 1923-4, when To-Day and To-Morrow began, it had already published Jung, Adler, G. E. Moore, C. S. Peirce, I. A. Richards, W. H. R. Rivers, and T. E. Hulme.

Ogden's other book series were The History of Civilization (from 1924), To-Day and To-Morrow (also from 1924), Science for You (from 1928—fewer volumes), and Psyche Miniatures (from 1926). The last was an offshoot from the journal *Psyche* which he also edited. There was a 'General Series' of 'Psyche Miniatures' of at least ninety-six titles, plus a smaller 'Medical Series' of at least fourteen volumes, followed by a series of 'Psyche Monographs' of at least thirteen titles.

To-Day & To-Morrow was by no means his most ambitious project; but it was the most original. The main interest of the series, and the main concern of this book, is the thought, the writing, the intriguing generic and rhetorical manoeuvres the contributors engage in, rather than the publishing history. But the structure and course of the series is also fascinating, and this Appendix reconstructs its development as far as possible. The development can only be described conjecturally in places, as the archival evidence is slight, and the bibliographical evidence sometimes ambiguous (because some of the book impressions exist in different states, with different paratextual material; and because some of the evidence comes from the dust-jackets, which are rare, but which also sometimes exist in different states for a single impression).

The conception appears to have developed gradually as the first few volumes were published. One striking feature is how little description is given of the overall rationale. When *Daedalus* was first published (in November 1923), it contained no mention of To-Day and To-Morrow. Neither editor nor publishers appear to have foreseen the series the book would spawn. It was produced as a stand-alone book, with matt brown boards, and orange labels on the front cover and spine, with a leaf-pattern border round the front-cover label.[1]

---

[1] Thus Krishna Dronamraju's comment in the introduction to his Haldane's Daedalus Revisited (Oxford: Oxford University Press, 1995), 1, that 'Ogden encouraged Haldane to write up his lecture in a publishable form to be included in the new series *Today and Tomorrow*, which his firm was about to launch' is wrong to suggest the idea of the series had already been conceived.

The physical appearance of the Kegan Paul volumes evolved as the first few books were published. As others were added, the design was eventually changed to an attractive deep glossy aubergine colour for the boards, with cream labels decorated simply with two rectangles, the thinner enclosed within the thicker; these and the title and author's name printed in black. However, some of the first impressions of the volumes immediately following *Daedalus—Icarus* and *The Mongol in Our Midst*—have lighter-coloured boards: a rich maroon colour, closely related to the aubergine, but distinguishable; though the labels are the same.[2] After nearly a century of possible exposure to direct sunlight or water-damage it is impossible to be sure that these haven't faded. But the effect of sun-bleaching on the spines of the later volumes is normally to turn them bluish rather than red. It appears that while the design of dark colour and simple cream labels was in place from the second volume, *Icarus*, onwards, the final colour wasn't settled until the fourth, *Wireless Possibilities* (after which, later impressions of the earlier volumes were produced uniform with the darker colour boards).

No dust-jackets for the first state of the first UK edition of *Daedalus* have been traced.[3] The earliest jacket for it which I have seen illustrated (and which covers an aubergine binding, so a later impression or state) doesn't advertise To-Day and To-Morrow either, but Ogden's other most important book series: The International Library.

Daedalus had created a stir. That encouraged Ogden to get Russell to reply.[4] *Icarus* appeared in February 1924. That too was a success. A single book had become a pair. The blurb on the earliest traced dust-jacket for *Icarus* advises: 'The essay should be read as a companion to Mr Haldane's *Daedalus*'.[5] There was thus—somewhat ironically—an improvisatory quality to To-Day and To-Morrow in its early stages. The idea of its being a series at all makes its first appearance on the back of the same *Icarus* dust-jacket. The fact that no reviews of *Icarus*—nor of the two subsequent titles—are quoted on it suggests it is the first jacket state issued, and may thus date from as early as February 1924. On the other hand, Fredric Warburg, who handled the series for Kegan Paul, wrote that after *Daedalus* and *Icarus*:

> it had become clear that there was a considerable market for books about the future, and we discussed the possibility of a whole series of little books and a title for it. After a good deal of deliberation, the clumsy but not inappropriate title was found, the Today and Tomorrow Series.[6]

---

[2] Second impressions of *Daedalus* and *Icarus* exist in this form too.

[3] Roy Lewis, 'C. K. Ogden's To-Day & To-Morrow Series', *The Private Library*, third series, 10:4 (1987), [140]-52 (p. 142) says that 'a white printed jacket was added at a later stage'. He perhaps follows Fredric Warburg, *An Occupation for Gentlemen* (London: Hutchinson, 1959), 110, who thought the first edition of *Daedalus* was issued without one. However, the Kegan Paul archive records jackets having been printed for the first run. Jackets of course are printed after books, or at least after books have been typeset. They were printed in smaller batches and more frequently than the impressions, so they could be revised to incorporate good reviews.

[4] See Dora Russell's reminiscence, discussed in Chapter 2.

[5] The Kegan Paul jackets initially featured a blurb on the front cover. This was frequently replaced with quotations from favourable reviews in later printings. A revised second impression of *Icarus* was published in May 1924. The text of the book inside still announced its relation to its companion in its opening sentence: 'Mr Haldane's *Daedalus* has set forth an attractive picture of the future as it may become through the use of scientific discoveries to promote human happiness'. The front of the jacket however no longer associates Russell's book with Haldane's, replacing the original precis with some of the excited praise *Icarus* had already garnered in its reviews, such as: 'Startling possibilities of the future' (*Daily Express*).

[6] Warburg, *An Occupation for Gentlemen*, p. 113.

That the series is first mentioned on *Icarus'* jacket rather than inside the book may support this recollection that it was conceived after the book was printed; but equally, it may simply mean that it did not seem necessary to name or list the series internally, so long as it was small enough for the details to fit on the jacket. At this stage the list only included the first four titles: *Daedalus, Icarus, The Mongol in Our Midst*, and *Wireless Possibilities*.

The changing early descriptions of the series indicate how the conception of it, and of what its title signified, was also evolving rapidly. The blurb before the list on this early jacket of *Icarus* emphasizes 'new discoveries' and 'novel theories'. That is understandable given the focus on science and technology in these first four books: two on science in general; one on biology and evolution; one on communication technology. Yet surprisingly, though the series has been named with a clearly futurological element, no mention is made here either of this aspect. True, some of the reviews discuss it: 'Extraordinary predictions', the *Daily Mail* commented on *Daedalus*; the *New York Times* said Haldane 'exposes the inadequacy of all purely technical and political forecasts of the future'; and the back of the jacket says that Low's book is 'A remarkable prognostication of the future of wireless'—as if its title needed a nudge to make its futurology more explicit. Low had also been working on a more extended book for Routledge called *The Future* (1925), which is advertised at the back of the first British edition of *Wireless Possibilities* (1924). In a way, that book reads like an attempt to cover the entire field of To-Day and To-Morrow on his own, with twenty-four chapters on topics including: artificial light; planet communication; motoring; cities and traffic; men, women, and trousers; doctors; warfare; invention; telepathy; and religion. It was presumably because Ogden was aware that Low was making a name for himself as a futurologist that he was invited to contribute to the series.

The most striking thing about this early jacket description of the series is what little resemblance it bears to what To-Day and To-Morrow eventually became. Rather than making scientific or technical journal papers more accessible,[7] it commissioned authors—who may or may not have been the kind of authors who wrote for professional journals—to write popularizing accounts which might include discussion of the 'new discoveries'; and not just the new discoveries that had been made, but those that hadn't yet. Also, the phrase 'this little series' may denote a series of short texts; but it may equally indicate that at this stage no-one anticipated the eventual extent of To-Day and To-Morrow.

The discrepancy between this early description and the eventual series relates to the disparity between two forms of title that appears in these early volumes. *Daedalus*, and Russell's riposte, *Icarus*, set the form that most titles in the series would eventually follow: a classical name as the title, followed by a subtitle identifying the field, and invoking its future: 'Daedalus; or, science and the future'; 'Icarus; or, the future of science'.[8] There were

---

[7] In fact none of the first four volumes fit the description (though *The Mongol in Our Midst* looks more like a medical or biological journal article, with numerous footnotes and a bibliography). The only one previously published in a periodical was Haldane's, but that had appeared not in a learned journal but in the popular *Century* magazine.

[8] Two of the titles included classical references but in a different form from the general run:
Plato's American Republic (1926); *Breaking Priscian's Head; or, English as She Will Be Spoke and Wrote* (1928). Though *Autolycus; or, The Future for Miscreant Youth* (1928) has a classical ring the allusion is to Shakespeare's *The Winter's Tale*. Some of the volumes drew on traditions outside Greece and Rome for their titles, such as: *The Dance of Çiva* (1927); *Scheherazade; or, The Future of the English Novel* (1927); *Cain; or, The Future of Crime* (1928); *Kalki; or, The Future of Civilization* (1929); *Shiva; or, The Future of India* (1929); *Babel; or, The Past, Present and Future of Human Speech* (1930). Of those that didn't use the classical/mythological form, *Mrs. Fisher; or, The Future of Humour* (1928) at least retained the syntactic pattern; as did *It Isn't Done; or The Future of Taboo among the British Islanders* (1930). Only ten volumes ignored both: *The Mongol in Our Midst* (1924); *Wireless Possibilities* (1924);

F'cap 8vo.   Each 2s. 6d. net

TO-DAY & TO-MORROW

In every department of knowledge new discoveries are constantly being made, and novel theories of the utmost
importance put forward. Too often these contributions are
lost in the files of learned journals and in other inaccessible
places. Yet many of them cannot fail to be of the greatest
interest to the public. It will be the object of this little
series to make such papers available in a handy format.

DAEDALUS, or Science and the Future
By J. B. S. HALDANE

States the case for Science in the most startling manner. " The essay
is brilliant, sparkling with wit, and bristling with challenges. No scientific
man will find himself looking at the facts of life and possibilities of the
future in quite the same way as he did when he took it up." *British
Medical Journal.*   "Extraordinary predictions."—*Daily Mail.*

ICARUS, or The Future of Science
By BERTRAND RUSSELL, F.R.S.

Traces the sinister influence of Science on the world, and the dangers of
its exploitation. Deals in particular with the Power of the Press ; of
the Influence of Propaganda, official and otherwise ; and foresees the
unification of the world under a nation or group of nations probably
despotic and militaristic.

THE MONGOL IN OUR MIDST,
or Man and His Three Faces
By F. G. CROOKSHANK, M.D., F.R.C.P.

The author, a well-known London physician, brings forward a mass of
new evidence in favour of a three–fold origin of the human race. Whether
we think of them as White, Black, and Yellow, or, symbolically, as the three
sons of Noah, there are three irreducible stocks corresponding to the three
types of Great Ape. Other contents include The ' Scientific Basis ' of
Palmistry, The Posture of Buddha, and The Causes of ' Mongolian
Imbecility.'

WIRELESS POSSIBILITIES
By Prof. A. M. LOW

A remarkable prognostication of the future of wireless.

KEGAN   PAUL,   TRENCH,   TRUBNER   &   CO.,   LTD.

Verso of early (and possibly the first state) dust-jacket for *Icarus*, early 1924.

variations on this form, certainly: *Gallio; or, The Tyranny of Science*—here the issue is less the future, than the present: the need, as J. W. N. Sullivan sees it, to wrest the future from a science he wants to restrict to the physical world, and prevent from pronouncing on the metaphysical, where he thinks it has no jurisdiction. Others played with the format: such as J. Y. T. Greig's *Breaking Priscian's Head; or, English as She Will Be Spoke and Wrote* (Priscian being the Latin grammarian whose *Institutiones grammaticae* became the standard textbook for the study of Latin during the Middle Ages). The point here is precisely the breaking away from a classical formalism. A small number of the later volumes departed from the classical formula altogether. André Maurois' *The Next Chapter: The war against the moon* is probably the book that was announced before publication as *Clio; or, The Future of History*. It is written in the form of an imaginary history in the future; but was perhaps felt not to be sufficiently *about* history for that title to work.[9] *The Dance of Çiva; or, Life's Unity and Rhythm* needed a non-Western title figure to make its Eastern point. *The Future of Futurism* was too good an opportunity for a play on words (as well, perhaps, as a nod to Ogden's and Richards' *The Meaning of Meaning*); and you couldn't expect futurists to tolerate being subordinated to anything classical. J. D. Bernal's *The World, the Flesh and the Devil* needed its Biblical title to play its secular eschatology against. Nevertheless, such volumes conformed exactly to what became the vision of the series: to draw upon cutting-edge developments in order to predict where they might lead in the century or so ahead.

Thus the series title was decided upon in early 1924, and as a marketing device to associate a second tranche of titles with the success of *Daedalus*. The books themselves bear out this account. There is no indication inside the first impressions of the first four, nor on their covers, that they are included a series.

By contrast, when Dutton launched the books in the US it was *as* a series from the start. What is probably the first US impression of *Daedalus* did carry the series title and first four volumes inside, as well as on the jacket, which quoted from the British reviews of *Daedalus*, but also from the one in the *New York Times*—thus enabling us to date the US launch as around 11 May 1924 or after; some six months after the initial volume had appeared in the UK.

This jacket for Dutton's *Daedalus* carried the same headnote as Kegan Paul's about the 'new discoveries' and 'novel theories' needing to be rescued from the oblivion of 'learned journals and […] other inaccessible places'. The blurb is a better description of *The Mongol in Our Midst* and *Narcissus*, both of which offered 'novel theories'; or *Wireless Possibilities*, which discusses 'new discoveries', than it is of the first two volumes. *Daedalus* predicts discoveries and inventions not yet made; *Icarus* does not really advance a theory of science, though it has a strong thesis about (in the words of the jacket again) its 'sinister influence' on the world.

In short, once the decision had been taken to launch a series, the first conception of it was as a platform for popularizing new and interesting ideas. The format was adjusted as

What I Believe (1925); *The Conquest of Cancer* (1925); *The Passing of the phantoms* (1925); *Birth Control and the State* (1926); *The Future of Israel* (1926); *The Future of Futurism* (1926); *The Next Chapter: The war against the moon* (1927); *The World, the Flesh and the Devil* (1929). Clearly exceptions were permitted from the first year of the series. Vernon Lee's comment in *Proteus* that she has used that title 'partly because I am attracted by the classical titles, *Daedalus, Icarus, Tantalus*, of my predecessors' (5) suggests that classical titles were not being prescribed by Ogden.

[9] The announcement in some printings of *Balbus* (1926), for example, described *Clio* under the heading 'NEARLY READY' as 'A whimsical and fantastic picture of the world in the not-so-far distant future, showing the power of a world press organization'.

Ogden and his contacts started generating ideas for more and yet more volumes. By the second UK impression of *Icarus*, the jacket listed the first five volumes under the series title, but dropped the explanatory gloss. There were by now reviews of *Icarus* quoted, but none yet for *The Mongol in Our Midst*, *Wireless Possibilities*, or *Narcissus*. *Daedalus* was announced as in its third impression (which was dated as April 1924 in later impressions), and *Icarus* in its second (so this jacket dates from May 1924 or later). Other titles were thus being added slowly. The jacket for *Wireless Possibilities* still only lists five volumes. The conjunction in the title was perhaps thought of at this point as offering a set of alternatives: some of these ideas will be about 'To-Morrow', like *Daedalus*; other volumes will offer new ideas about 'To-Day'. Futurology was a major component from the start, and the basis for three of the first four books. But it only became the standard model for the series after the first ten volumes.

A series page, giving the title and listing the volumes, started being included inside the UK volumes from the fifth (*Narcissus*) onwards. Initially it faced the title page. That in *Narcissus* gives eight titles; adding *Tantalus; or, The Future of Man*; and two more that don't follow the classical formula: *The Passing of the Phantoms*, and *Of Dragons*. Or don't yet. For though *The Passing of the Phantoms* duly appeared as announced, *Of Dragons* acquired the classical title *Perseus* when it was published, also in 1924, with its jacket including a ninth title, *Lysistrata*, absent from the list inside, still of eight, though with *Perseus'* own title updated, facing the title page.[10]

The series format was still inchoate. When *Tantalus* appeared, it lacked the series list and gave a list of F. C. S. Schiller's previous books facing the title page instead. The series list was resumed in *Lysistrata*, in *Perseus* (another short volume, at eighty pages), in *Callinicus*, Haldane's second contribution, and in *Quo Vadimus?* (classical title but not a person). *Quo* indeed! At around this point the series list was moved to the end of the books.[11] That's where it is in the first impression of Bertrand Russell's second contribution, *What I Believe*, dated 1925 by the publisher, and with Russell's preface dated 1st January 1925. Another non-classical title, please note. There the list only just fits on a single page, and was perhaps moved once it was clear more space would soon be needed.

Several volumes repeat this formula: *The Conquest of Cancer*, *Proteus*, and *Hypatia*, all have a simple listing of volumes at the end, with no reviews. These are thirteenth, fourteenth, and sixteenth respectively in the Kegan Paul ledger. The fifteenth is *Prometheus*, but that has the later format of series page followed by a listing including reviews. Actually the

---

[10] Interestingly, *The Passing of the Phantoms* was omitted from the one-page 'Classified Index' included in later volumes, for example *Gallio* (1927) or *Aphrodite* (1931). This may have been inadvertence, or because of the increasing difficulty of fitting all the titles onto one page. But it may have indicated a feeling that Ogden felt less convinced that it fitted the brief—especially given its scant attention to the future.

[11] 'Around', because according the sequence in which the books are entered in the publisher's ledger, *What I Believe* is tenth, and *Callinicus* eleventh; but the evidence of the series lists suggests the reverse: not just the placing of the lists, but the fact that the one in *Callinicus* lists only ten books, that on *What I Believe*, fifteen. My descriptions in this chapter are of the Kegan Paul UK editions. The US Dutton editions followed a similar course, the early volumes including a series list facing the title page. But instead of the end-matter in the Kegan Paul volumes, some of the later Dutton ones included two-page spreads listing volumes ready and in preparation, the same series list inserted as the front and rear end-papers. In some volumes these replace the list facing the title page, though some include both. The end-paper lists give only very brief synopses, no reviews. Dutton used the jacket flaps (which Kegan Paul left blank) for reviews of the whole series. In some of the Dutton volumes these jacket flaps bear the only indication of membership of a series, and no details are given of any of the other volumes.

length of the lists at the back of the other three suggest that the order in the ledger might not give the true publication sequence: *Hypatia* lists sixteen titles including itself; *Conquest* seventeen including itself; and *Proteus* eighteen (also including itself). The listings on the back of the jackets tell yet a different story: *Conquest*, fifteen; *Hypatia*, sixteen; *Proteus*, eighteen. These lists are themselves unreliable, especially the internal ones, in that they include volumes which were never published (as discussed below). The disparities most likely indicate that the books were published in batches, with the various elements of text, end-matter, and jackets, being worked on separately.

Thus in this early phase, as the conception of the series emerged it also altered. It might seem that *Daedalus*, and then *Icarus*, provided a template which Ogden realized he could use for a whole series. So they did, and so did he, eventually. But his first move appears to have been to group around Haldane's and then Russell's successful books others which didn't especially conform to the four most distinctive features of the eventual series: its futurological rationale; its classical titles; its standard length and standard paratextual format.

The Mongol in Our Midst is focused on our evolutionary past. *Perseus: Of Dragons* spends most of its pages tracing past superstitions. It barely addresses the future at all, except in a half-hearted last sentence about whether a future Perseus will be able to rescue us from the dragon. *The Passing of the Phantoms: A study of evolutionary psychology and morals* is more concerned with the light animal behaviour can shed on the history of human morality. These volumes all have implications for future thought about questions of religion, morality, and race. But they have little to say about that future, concentrating instead on how modern thought has reinterpreted the past. Similarly, *Narcissus: An anatomy of clothes*—as its subtitle suggests—is more concerned with the relation between bodies and clothes, and with the histories of evolution and of fashion, than with the future. What they have in common is not, then, a focus on futurology.

Two of the first four volumes stand out as not adopting the classical formula: *The Mongol in Our Midst: A study of man and his three faces*; and the short wave at *Wireless Possibilities*—no classics, no subtitle.[12] Low's book too was short: seventy-seven pages, in a series where the norm would become ninety-six, with the font adjusted for a largely uniform extent. Again, there were exceptions later. But there was much greater variety of scale during the early stages. *Icarus* was a crisp sixty-four pages. Whereas *The Mongol in Our Midst* ran to 118, and 128 including the scholarly references at the end—which none of the subsequent volumes had.[13] The longest in the entire series is the volume published fifth:[14] *Narcissus: An anatomy of clothes*, by Gerald Heard. This ran to 156 pages of noticeably smaller type than most of the volumes, and ran to over 30,000 words of text, as opposed to the norm of around 12,000 to 15,000.[15]

[12] Crookshank, in the Preface to the enlarged 1931 edition of *The Mongol in Our Midst* says (p. xiii) that it was 'originally the second volume' of To-Day and To-Morrow. But the ledger at UCL has *Icarus* preceding it. Warburg, *An Occupation for Gentlemen*, p. 113, recalled *Icarus* as following *Daedalus* immediately.

[13] A small number, including *Archimedes*, and *Sinon; or, The Future of Politics*, had endnotes.

[14] According to Kegan Paul's ledger—the best guide we have to the sequence in which the books were published, though approximate in places. Some dustjackets bear volume numbers at the foot of the spine. But this appears to have been an afterthought. Jackets for volumes appearing in the last two years of the series exist without the numbers. The jacket numbering corresponds approximately to the order in the ledger, but appears to have been introduced for later printings of the jackets (which were also revised to include favourable reviews as they appeared).

[15] Some were shorter. Russell's *Icarus* is under 7,000 words.

After the first fifteen volumes or so, in mid-1925, a page was added at the end, devoted to a fuller and strikingly different description of the series, which finally draws attention to the futurological aspect:

> This series of books, by some of the most distinguished English thinkers, scientists, philosophers, doctors, critics and artists, was recognized on publication as a note-worthy event. Written from various points of view, one book frequently opposing the argument of another, they provide the reader with a stimulating survey of the most modern thought in many departments of life. Several volumes are devoted to the future trend of Civilization, conceived as a whole; while others deal with particular provinces, and cover the future of Woman, War, Population, Clothes, Wireless, Morals, Drama, Poetry, Art, Sex, Law, etc.
>
> It is interesting to see in these neat little volumes, issued at a low price, the revival of a form of literature, the Pamphlet, which has been in disuse for 200 years.[16]

That last sentence is an odd pitch for futurology; that it has resurrected and dusted off a worn out mode. This text too evolved with the series. By 1927, in *Albyn*, for example, by which time some sixty volumes had appeared, the one-sentence list of hot topics no longer sufficed. The comment harking back to pamphlet wars was dropped, and the text broadened but shortened to end on a more up-to-date note, with 'a survey of numerous aspects of most modern thought'. What should we make of the shift from 'the most modern thought' (cutting edge) to 'most modern thought' (we cover almost everything)? Was the article dropped inadvertently? Apart from the series title, the phrase 'the future trend' had been the only description of the whole future-orientation of the series. Now even that had disappeared. The space gained was given to endorsements from reviews. In these too, not only was there no reference to the books' predictive assays, but the review highlighted by being the only one above the series title—T. S. Eliot's from the *Nation*, though attributed only to the magazine—describes the series as 'A precious document on the *present* time' (my emphasis). This chronological ineptness, and the fact the page underwent numerous revisions between volumes, perhaps indicates that the paratexts were the responsibility of an inexperienced member of Kegan Paul's staff rather than Ogden himself. But either way, they indicate a gradual and uncertain process of definition.

This raises the question of whether the authors were given any more detailed brief about how to frame their contributions: any guidelines about titles, style, polemical stance, how far ahead to project, cross-reference, balance between present and future, etc. If there were a template it has not been discovered.[17] If any such a document did exist, the authors certainly do not appear to feel bound by it. The variety of styles, approaches, lengths, kinds of attention to the future, and even forms of title, indicate that Ogden as editor was no Procrustes. His input was probably more at the conceptual than the copy-editing stage; and probably conducted more through conversations in Oxbridge Colleges or London clubs than by letter.[18] We have seen how he wanted Russell to answer *Daedalus*. The series page perhaps stood in for a brief from 1925, signalling the essential points about future trends, modern thought, and 'one book frequently opposing the argument of another'.

---

[16] Taken from *Prometheus* (1925).

[17] There isn't any material in the Kegan Paul archive at UCL that illuminates these questions, such as any information given to prospective authors. The main collections of Ogden's correspondence are at the Cambridge University Library and McMaster University Library, but neither contains much significant material relating to To-Day and To-Morrow.

[18] According to Lewis, 'C. K. Ogden's To-Day & To-Morrow Series', pp. [140]-52, Ogden 'held court in a corner of the Athenaeum drawing room' (p. 146).

Perhaps all Ogden felt it necessary to say otherwise, was that contributors should have a look at *Daedalus* and some of the others, and try to keep the extent between 10,000 and 20,000 words (which most, but not all, managed).

The first conception of the series, then, was less focused on futurology, and more on provocative examples of 'the most modern thought'. That was, after all, Ogden's speciality. And it may have seemed the most salient aspect of *Daedalus* initially; though perhaps one effect of positioning it at the head of a series was to refocus it eventually onto the futurological.

Unlike Ogden's International Library, To-Day and To-Morrow didn't publish work in translation, and only published new work, most of it (with the possible exception of some of the earliest volumes) commissioned or written specifically for the series. That, together with its increasing attention to the future; its address to the general, non-specialist reader; its comparative lightness of tone; its frequent humour, satire, and irony; and the fact that many of the authors refer to other volumes in the series; gives it a thematic focus and a coherence that sets it apart from the International Library. From another point of view, its scope is much broader. It doesn't popularize and futurologize about just psychology, philosophy, and scientific method—though it certainly has much to say about all three—but takes potentially any human domain as being within its remit: including politics, society, art, language, technology, and everyday life. Nevertheless, the International Library represents very much the kind of modern thought To-Day and To-Morrow seeks to popularize.

Thus *Daedalus* and *Icarus* could have been seen as examples of modern thinking about the future; that is, as one aspect of what the series might have turned into: a more popularizing equivalent of the International Library. That would explain why several of the earlier volumes seem disengaged from either the trope of the classical titles, or futurology, or both: either because they had already been written, and arrived on Ogden's desk shortly after the publication of *Daedalus*; or because they were already near enough to completion for it to be too late to recast them in terms of future projections. According to this hypothesis, the series was still publishing titles exemplifying an earlier conception of it as popularizing contemporary thought, for about a year after the decision had been taken to use the To-Day and To-Morrow name, and make futurology integral to the project. Other volumes, and titles—besides *The Mongol in Our Midst*, *Wireless Possibilities*, *Narcissus*, *Perseus*, and *The Passing of the Phantoms*—that could be seen as the legacy of an earlier, pre-To-Day and To-Morrow conception, are Russell's *What I Believe*; and *The Conquest of Cancer*, by H. W. S. Wright—the tenth and thirteenth in the ledger. This latter too was short—just eighty-six pages; and would have been too short for the series without the thirty-two-page introduction—by F. G. Crookshank. As Crookshank explains (p. 6), Wright's book is based on a lecture he had given two or three years earlier in the Christian University, Tsinan, China, where he worked in the School of Medicine. In this case, Ogden was bringing in work that had already been written, prior to the To-Day and To-Morrow brief, under the umbrella of the series once he had unfurled it. In doing so, he was fulfilling the mission of the original blurb: to disseminate 'new discoveries' and 'novel theories'. That was after all how the series had started, by publishing the paper read to the Heretics, which became *Daedalus*. Haldane's other volume for the series—*Callinicus: A defence of chemical warfare* (1925)—had also begun as a lecture, in Mürren, Switzerland, in 1924 (thus in this case after the series was well-defined; so it may have been written expressly for it). Doubtless some of the other miscellaneous early volumes also originated as talks. H. F. Scott Stokes refers to his *Perseus* as a 'paper' (it reads more like a talk given to a folklore society than a paper for a psychology journal). Among the later ones, at least Bernal's *The World, the Flesh, and the Devil*, began as a Cambridge paper.

The somewhat haphazard evolution of the series was matched by unpredictability in the production process. Some titles that were offered or commissioned didn't materialize or were rejected. The bibliographic evidence suggests that several volumes were in production at the same time, and that different parts of the process had got out of sync. For example, at least one binding of *The Passing of the Phantoms* has both the list at the front and not even the simple list at the end, but ten pages of end-matter including the series page and reviews. This was the end-matter that all the volumes carried after these pioneering ones: the page describing the series, followed by a catalogue of its volumes, whether published or imminent.[19] In this case the list facing the title page was presumably set with the main text, but the end-matter, which has separate page numbering, could be added later as a separate gathering. Here the list facing the title page includes just six other volumes; whereas the end-matter includes twenty-four 'Volumes Ready', five 'Volumes Just Published', and nine announced as 'Ready Shortly'. As one of these—'Mercurius; or, The World on Wings' was another that was never published, and two others don't have here the classical titles they were later to acquire (*Pomona* and *Balbus*), 'Ready Shortly' was presumably a wishful way of referring to books at various stages of production, from in press to still being written or even not being written. This copy is thus probably a later state of the first impression, using sheets for the main text that might have been printed originally, or reprinted without revision, but to which the later end-matter of series page and reviews was appended to bring it more up to date. The existence of such hybrids complicates the establishment of a linear publication sequence. But what is clear is that after around a dozen volumes, the material pertaining to the series was moved to the end of the volumes; and that after around fifteen, the basic format had been arrived at that would remain in place (with slight revisions) for all subsequent volumes, which included an additional gathering after the text, with its own page number sequence. This began with a series page with the heading 'TO-DAY AND TO-MORROW', and some descriptive text and later extracts from reviews of the series as a whole. The series page was followed by an annotated listing of volumes, usually four per page, giving a synopsis, and/or where available, commendatory reviews. This section ran from seven pages (*Hephaestus* and *Thamyris*) up to twenty in the later volumes (and occasionally even twenty-four).[20]

The end-matter had thus metamorphosed into a catalogue and advertisement for the series. At the risk of deterring all but the most perverse bibliophiliacs, this substantial section (eventually a quarter the length of the texts themselves) also deserves comment. It was excised from all volumes for the 2008 Routledge re-issuing of (most of) the series—understandably so, since inevitably most of the material—the description of the series, the synopses, the reviews—is repeated, with variations, from volume to volume. But it

[19] The publisher's journal covering most of the volumes has pages recording 'Miscellaneous Lists, Catalogues, etc.', which include repeated orders from 1929 of 'Today & Tomorrow Lists' of twenty or twenty-four pages. The first of these specifies '500 Bd.' and 7,000 'flat'. If that means some copies were bound separately, they may have been used as catalogues for promotional purposes, but I have not found any.

[20] There are nonetheless anomalies. There are copies of the ninth impression of *Daedalus* (1930) with no end-matter at all, though printed while the series was in full flight (and in the case of my copy, with a jacket that carries the series list on the back cover). As these copies are bound in pale grey-blue-green or bright red boards instead of the usual aubergine, they may have been bound later from the 1930 sheets—possibly after rest of the series had gone out of print. There are certainly also copies of the 1930 ninth impression in the standard binding. The sixth impression of *Eos* (1931) exists in maroon binding, in the same colour as the earliest few volumes after the original *Daedalus*; but in this case with leather-textured boards. These disparate late bindings suggest that after the series was terminated in 1931 the uniform presentation was abandoned and old sheets were bound up with material at hand.

represents an important element of the project, giving a sense of how the editor and publishers wanted it to be received as a whole. And there are also variations and evolutions from one volume to the next. It isn't just a matter of more books being added, and synopses being replaced by reviews. This end-matter gives the best insight into the conception and development of the series: into how Ogden conceived of its purpose, organization, and its effect; and also into how the plans kept changing, as titles changed, and volumes were announced which were never published. It doesn't just record what the series contains, but attempts to track what it achieved (through excerpting the reviews). It records its progress, and gestures—appropriately!—towards its future, dividing up the descriptions of the books into subsections (varied from volume to volume) of 'Volumes Ready', 'Recently Published', 'Just Published', 'Nearly Ready', or 'Volumes in Preparation'. These anticipatory subsections also sketch out Ogden's aspirations for what he wanted the series to include, even when they were not realized.

The end-matter thus grew with the series. There were also two later additional elements, inserted between the series page and the details of the individual volumes. At around forty volumes, and by 1927, a page was added immediately after the series page headed 'From the Reviews', excerpting comments about the series in general.[21] In Sylvia Pankhurst's *Delphos* of 1927, for example, the selection begins with the *Times Literary Supplement*'s comment: 'An entertaining series', placed first presumably to dispel any anxiety prospective customers and readers might have had that prognostication by any other means than crystal balls might be a chore. This is followed by the *Observer*, praising the series as 'brilliant' (a word many of the reviews were to echo) and congratulating it for the seemingly impossible task of keeping up 'the sport' for more than forty volumes. Then T. S. Eliot's comment (here attributed) from the *Nation*: 'We are able to peer into the future by means of that brilliant series [which] will constitute a precious document upon the present time'.[22] His playful turn of do-it-yourself futurology predicts the future of the series itself, with a double edge as he tarnishes the brilliance of its futurology by predicting its value as chiefly historical. It's easy to see why the remaining excerpts were included. *The Manchester Dispatch* provided the marketing department's dream of addiction: 'The more one reads of these pamphlets, the more avid becomes the appetite'. The *Irish Statesman* admired the 'lively controversy'— an aspect the series page was eager to promote ('Written from various points of view, one book frequently opposing the argument of another...'). The *Daily Herald* admired the 'many monographs of brilliance and discernment', praising 'The stylistic excellencies of this provocative series'. The *Field* magazine, whose rural traditionalist huntin' shootin' fishin' ethos makes it the last place one would expect To-Day and To-Morrow's radical modernism to find fertile soil, and which clearly had more manly things to attend to than stylistic excellencies, nonetheless got out at last that 'We have long desired to express the deep admiration felt by every thinking scholar and worker at the present day for this series'. If it is surprising that Kegan Paul left in the sentence that takes the intellectual gleam off the compliment—'As small gift-books, austerely yet prettily produced, they remain

[21] Here too the evidence is inconclusive. The 'From the Reviews' page appears sporadically in the volumes from 1926 and 1927, from the 38th to the 45th book listed in the Kegan Paul ledger; again indicating that this record was out of sync with this part of the production process. The earliest first impression I have found this 'From the Reviews' page in is *Procrustes* (1926); all the others are from 1927.

[22] 'Charleston, Hey! Hey!', *Nation and Athenaeum*, 40 (29 January 1927) 595. In *The Complete Prose of T. S. Eliot: The critical edition. Literature, politics, belief, 1927–1929*, ed. Frances Dickey, Jennifer Formichelli, and Ronald Schuchard (Baltimore: Johns Hopkins University Press, 2015), pp. 25–9; http://muse.jhu.edu/chapter/1634627 Discussed further in Chapter 6.

unequalled of their kind'—it was probably that commercial hope overcame critical doubt, in a surreal vision of To-Day and To-Morrow books saving the day for present-hunters desperate to find something to give county ladies and gentlemen who had everything. The remaining reviews were from further afield: the *Japan Chronicle* admiring the wisdom of the series; and the *New York World* saying it 'Holds the palm in the speculative and interpretative thought of the age'. Ogden was a committed internationalist, driven by an Enlightenment 'republic of letters' ideal rather than that of a Socialist International. One aim of To-Day and To-morrow, as with his International Library, was to perform the very kind of international communication volumes in the series described and advocated, as making future national and imperialist wars less likely. Ogden wanted not only to reach readers in other continents, but to demonstrate the international impact To-Day and To-Morrow was already beginning to have. Besides the US issues, there were translations by 1930 of at least three volumes into German (*Daedalus, Icarus,* and *The Mongol in Our Midst*), and six into Spanish (*Icarus, Callinicus, Tantalus, Lysistrata, Hypatia,* and *Prometheus*).[23] *Daedalus* and *Icarus* were published together in a single volume in Swedish. *Icarus* was also translated into Russian and Chinese.[24] *Typhoeus; or The Future of Socialism* also got a Chinese translation. *Eos* was translated into Polish. *Lysistrata* appeared in Dutch. By about 1935 there were three Hungarian translations—*Daedalus, Icarus,* and *Tantalus*—published separately, but also together as the *Daedalus* trilogy.

Towards the end of the run of 1927 volumes—*Archon, Caledonia, Iconoclastes, Bacchus*—the announcement began to appear above the series title: 'Sixty Volumes are Now Published'. In these four books the end-matter ran to nineteen pages. The list and the encomia were impressive. But they were becoming unwieldy; and in danger of taking longer to read, in order to understand what the series covered, and how, than potential book-buyers and even book-sellers might be prepared to spend. So soon after the series turned sixty, the volumes began to include a two-page 'Classified Index' tabulating all the volumes into groups, so that the scope and structure of the series could be more readily grasped, and giving page references next to each volume to the descriptions in the following pages. These indices started appearing in some volumes towards the end of 1927 (*Gallio, Albyn*), and in almost all volumes in 1928 (but not in at least some copies of *Atalanta, Lares et Penates,* and *Breaking Priscian's Head*), and all thereafter.[25] The categories into which the now over eighty volumes were divided were to remain unchanged:

[23] There was also a later single volume including *Hephaestus, Quo Vadimus,* and *Hermes* in Spanish translation published in Spain and Argentina: *Efestos. Quo vadimus. Hermes* (Buenos Aires and Madrid: Espasa-Calpe, 1947).
[24] *A Bibliography of Bertrand Russell,* ed. Kenneth Blackwell, Harry Ruja, Sheila Turcon (London: Routledge, 2003), vol. 1, 97–101.
[25] One exception to this pattern I have seen is a copy of *Birth Control and the State,* the title page dated 1926 and the text a first impression, but with the ' Classified Index' and twenty-four pages of end-matter. This twenty-four-page extent makes it clear that the end-matter dates from much later than 1926, which suggests that Kegan Paul was again producing hybrid bindings, combining unbound sheets of the original edition of the book with the new end-matter after 1927. (If they had had to reprint the text, surely they would have advertised the fact.) My copy of *Proteus* is a comparable bibliographic hybrid of old sheets and revised end-matter. There is no evidence (in the book or on the jacket) of it being a later impression than the first, from 1925 and only the fourteenth in the series. It includes the early series list of two pages (including three volumes never published, but implying they already had been). But it follows that with a much later version of the end-matter, including the later series page, and listings and reviews of volumes not published till 1928. After the 'Classified Index' was introduced, the page 'From the Reviews' was eventually discontinued, the series page text—which had not given a very helpful or attractive account of the series—being condensed to allow space to quote from some of the series reviews (as described above). Yet some transitional volumes included both, such as *Cain, Hanno, Metanthropos, Heraclitus, Fortuna, Autolycus,* and some copies of *Eos*.

CLASSIFIED INDEX

GENERAL   PAGE
Daedalus, or Science and the Future. J. B. S. Haldane . . . 5
Icarus, or the Future of Science. Bertrand Russell . . . 5
Tantalus, or the Future of Man. F. C. S. Schiller . . . 5
The World, the Flesh and the Devil. J. D. Bernal . . . 18
Quo Vadimus? Glimpses of the Future. E. E. Fournier D'Albe . 6
Socrates, or the Emancipation of Mankind. H. F. Carlill . . 12
What I Believe. Bertrand Russell 5
Sibylla, or the Revival of Prophecy. C. A. Mace . . . 10
The Next Chapter. André Maurois 13
Kalki, or the Future of Civilization. S. Radhakrishnan . . 17
Ethnos, or the Problem of Race. Sir Arthur Keith . . . 20
Diogenes, or the Future of Leisure. C. E. M. Joad . . 16
The Dance of Civa, Life's Unity and Rhythm. Collum . . 8

MARRIAGE AND MORALS
Hypatia, or Woman and Knowledge. Dora Russell . . . 6
Lysistrata, or Woman's Future and Future Woman. A. M. Ludovici . 6
Hymen, or the Future of Marriage. Norman Haire . . . 13
Aphrodite, or the Future of Love. R. de Pomerai . . . 20
Thrasymachus, or the Future of Morals. C. E. M. Joad . . 6
Halcyon, or the Future of Monogamy. Vera Brittain . . 18
Chronos, or the Future of the Family. Eden Paul . . . 19
Birth Control and the State. C. P. Blacker . . . 9
Romulus, or the Future of the Child. R. T. Lewis . . . 17
Lares et Penates, or the Home of the Future. H. J. Birnstingl . 15

SCIENCE AND MEDICINE
Gallio, or the Tyranny of Science. J. W. N. Sullivan . . 12
Archimedes, or the Future of Physics. L. L. Whyte . . 14
Eos, or the Wider Aspects of Cosmogony. Sir J. H. Jeans . 16
Hermes, or the Future of Chemistry. T. W. Jones . . . 14
Prometheus, or Biology and the Advancement of Man. H. S. Jennings . 7
Galatea, or the Future of Darwinism. W. Russell Brain . . 7
Apollonius, or the Future of Psychical Research. E. N. Bennett . 12
Sisyphus, or the Limits of Psychology. M. Jaeger . . . 19
Metanthropos, or the Future of the Body. R. C. Macfie . . 16
Morpheus, or the Future of Sleep. D. F. Fraser-Harris . . 15
The Conquest of Cancer. H. W. S. Wright . . . 7
Automaton, or the Future of Mechanical Man. H. S. Hatfield . 7

INDUSTRY AND THE MACHINE
Ouroboros, or the Mechanical Extension of Mankind. G. Garrett . 9
Vulcan, or the Future of Labour. Cecil Chisholm . . . 13
Typhoeus, or the Future of Socialism. Arthur Shadwell . . 17
Hephaestus, or the Soul of the Machine. E. E. Fournier D'Albe . 6
Artifex, or the Future of Craftsmanship. John Gloag . . 9
Pegasus, or Problems of Transport. J. F. C. Fuller . . 9
Aeolus, or the Future of the Flying Machine. Oliver Stewart . 12
Wireless Possibilities. A. M. Low 8

WAR
Janus, or the Conquest of War. William McDougall . . 13
Callinicus, a Defence of Chemical Warfare. J. B. S. Haldane . 5

FOOD AND DRINK
Lucullus, or the Food of the Future. Olga Hartley and C. F. Leyel . 10
Bacchus, or the Future of Wine. P. Morton Shand . . . 14

MISCELLANEOUS
Narcissus, an Anatomy of Clothes. Gerald Heard . . . 7
Perseus, of Dragons. H. F. Scott Stokes 8

[2]

CLASSIFIED INDEX

SOCIETY AND THE STATE   PAGE
Archon, or the Future of Government. Hamilton Fyfe . . 13
Sinon, or the Future of Politics. E. A. Mowrer . . . 20
Cain, or the Future of Crime. George Godwin . . . 15
Autolycus, or the Future of Miscreant Youth. R. G. Gordon . 17
Cato, or the Future of Censorship. William Seagle . . 19
Lycurgus, or the Future of Law. E. S. P. Haynes . . . 8
Stentor, or the Press of To-Day and To-Morrow. D. Ockham . 12
Nuntius, or Advertising and its Future. Gilbert Russell . . 9
Rusticus, or the Future of the Countryside. Martin S. Briggs . 13
Procrustes, or the Future of Education. M. Alderton Pink . 10
Eleutheros, or the Future of the Public Schools. J. F. Roxburgh . 20
Chiron, or the Education of a Citizen of the World. M. C. Pearce . 20
Alma Mater, or the Future of the Universities. Julian Hall . 17
Isis, or the Future of Oxford. W. J. K. Diplock . . . 19
Apella, or the Future of the Jews. A Quarterly Reviewer. . 11
Eutychus, or the Future of the Pulpit. Winifred Holtby . . 17
Vicisti Galilaee? or The Church of England. E. B. Powley . 18

GREAT BRITAIN, THE EMPIRE, AND AMERICA
Cassandra, or the Future of the British Empire. F. C. S. Schiller . 6
Caledonia, or the Future of the Scots. G. Malcolm Thomson . 14
Hibernia, or the Future of Ireland. Bolton C. Waller . . 15
Columbia, or the Future of Canada. George Godwin . . 18
Achates, or Canada in the Empire. W. Eric Harris . . . 18
Shiva, or the Future of India. R. J. Minney . . . 17
Plato's American Republic. J. Douglas Woodruff . . . 10
Midas, or the United States and the Future. C. H. Bretherton . 9
Atlantis, or America and the Future. J. F. C. Fuller . . 9

LANGUAGE AND LITERATURE
Pomona, or the Future of English. Basil de Selincourt . . 11
Breaking Priscian's Head. J. Y. T. Greig . . . 15
Saxo Grammaticus. Ernest Weekley 19
Babel, or the Future of Human Speech. Sir Richard Paget . 20
Lars Porsena, or the Future of Swearing. Robert Graves . . 11
It Isn't Done. Archibald Lyall 20
Delphos, or the Future of International Language. E. Sylvia Pankhurst . 12
Scheherazade, or the Future of the Novel. John Carruthers . 14
Deucalion, or the Future of Criticism. Geoffrey West . . 19
Thamyris, or Is There a Future for Poetry? R. C. Trevelyan . 7
The Future of Futurism. John Rodker . . . 11
Mrs. Fisher, or the Future of Humour. Robert Graves . . 11
Pons Asinorum, or the Future of Nonsense. George Edinger . 18
Democritus, or the Future of Laughter. Gerald Gould . . 19

ART, ARCHITECTURE, MUSIC, DRAMA, ETC
Euterpe, or the Future of Art. Lionel R. McColvin . . 8
Proteus, or the Future of Intelligence. Vernon Lee. . . 8
Balbus, or the Future of Architecture. Christian Barman . 11
Orpheus, or the Music of the Future. W. J. Turner . . 10
Terpander, or Music and the Future. E. J. Dent . . . 10
Eurydice, or the Nature of Opera. Dyneley Hussey . . 18
Iconoclastes, or the Future of Shakespeare. Hubert Griffith . 14
Timotheus, or the Future of the Theatre. Bonamy Dobrée . 8
Heraclitus, or the Future of Films. Ernest Betts . . . 16

SPORT AND EXPLORATION
Atalanta, or the Future of Sport. G. S. Sandilands . . 15
Fortuna, or Chance and Design. Norwood Young . . . 16
Hanno, or the Future of Exploration. J. L. Mitchell . . 16

[3]

The 'Classified Index' from *Aphrodite*.

The version of the 'Classified Index' in *Aphrodite* (1931), the penultimate volume, lists 102 volumes, including itself, but omitting *The Future of Israel*, *Hygieia*, and *Thinking about Thinking*, presumably because they were published only in the US (all in 1926); and *Solon*—the final volume, perhaps not yet out. But it also omits four earlier books. *The Passing of the Phantoms* as suggested, may have been passed over as inadequately futurological. Perhaps *The Mongol in Our Midst* was dropped for the same reason; though it was more probably because Crookshank brought out a revised and greatly expanded edition that was now outside the series in the same year, 1931. The exclusions of *Pygmalion* and *Paris* are harder to account for.

Of the groupings in the Classified Indices, the 'General' category is the only puzzle, as it starts with *Daedalus* and *Icarus*. These clearly could have been put into the 'Science and Medicine' group, as science is their main concern; but Ogden perhaps wanted to indicate how much more far-reaching they were, and that they sat better with the volumes contemplating the future of humanity and civilisation in general. Otherwise the categories are unexceptional. For today's readers, they might be rearranged under three broader headings (given here in square brackets):

[Science and Technology]
SCIENCE AND MEDICINE
INDUSTRY AND THE MACHINE

[Socio-Political]
MARRIAGE AND MORALS
SOCIETY AND THE STATE

GREAT BRITAIN, THE EMPIRE, AND AMERICA
WAR
[Culture and Everyday Life]
LANGUAGE AND LITERATURE
ART, ARCHITECTURE, MUSIC, DRAMA, ETC.
FOOD AND DRINK
SPORT AND EXPLORATION

The only other category excluded from this putative regrouping is 'Miscellaneous': which only ever included two titles: *Narcissus: An anatomy of clothes*, and *Perseus; or, Of Dragons*: those two early and not particularly futurological volumes, which still, the index seems to concede, couldn't be made to fit into the series' map of contemporary and future life. It is perhaps, further evidence, if more were needed, that the overall futurological project hadn't crystallized until after the first few books had appeared, and that these two early volumes were really a survival of the prior conception of disseminating research of general interest.

The early blurb casting the series as popularizing obscure new ideas describes an essentially journalistic conception. It was a brilliant publishing ploy to follow where Haldane's vision had led him, and recast the series as considering the future of everything. That produced something genuinely innovative, and which allowed a space for forms of imagination not easily accommodated elsewhere. One reason for tracing the series' development this minutely is thus to track the gestation of a publishing invention—one that is itself a futurological exercise, projecting not only what shape the series would take, but how well it would be received.

Sales Figures

The Kegan Paul archives for this period are in the Special Collections department of the UCL library.[26] The archives include what are described as publisher's 'journals', which detail expenditure on each impression or edition of each volume—printing costs, jackets, the labels which they all had on the covers and so on. Though the books themselves tend to list reprintings, you need to see the publishers' records to find out the number of copies. The figures here are only for the editions printed in the UK (presumably including copies sent to dominions and colonies; and possibly also, in some cases discussed below, to the US);[27] And they only cover the years the series was being published, 1923-31. They are not *sales* figures exactly. But they give the maximum figure and probable minimum, since the publishers would not have reprinted the next batch until the previous batch had (nearly) sold out.

Most titles had an initial print run of 2,000, except the following eight, which started with 3,000: *Narcissus, Tantalus, Lysistrata, Callinicus, Proteus, Birth Control, Achates; or, The Future of Canada* (1929) by W. Eric Harris, and *Halcyon*. Only one title, *What I Believe*, had 4,000 for its first impression. Several of these came early in the series. This suggests that Kegan Paul thought it would make a splash, and it did initially, but that after the first twenty volumes or so it became clear that only the occasional volume would sell more than

---

[26] Held temporarily at the National Archives, Kew, at the time of writing.
[27] E. P. Dutton archives: http://library.syr.edu/digital/guides/e/ep_dutton.htm Try Foreign Correspondence/ Box 74 Ka-Le.

2,000 copies. The number of volumes having more than 2,000 printed (either because reprinted after the first 2,000 or because the first run was 3,000 or more) was twenty-eight; or a quarter of the total. The number of titles which had more than the initial run printed was twenty-five; in that case, just under a quarter of the series. Seven of those that were reprinted had a second impression of fewer than 2,000): *The Mongol in Our Midst*, *Thrasymachus*, *Cassandra*, *Diogenes*, *Aphrodite*. Also, curiously, *Lysistrata*, which went into a third impression, and *Daedalus*, which turned out to sell far more.

The other eighteen had second or later impressions of at least 2,000:

Icarus
Callinicus
What I Believe
Tantalus
Quo Vadimus
Prometheus
Hypatia
Plato's American Republic
Orpheus
Lars Porsena
Gallio
Hymen
Caledonia
Eos
Kalki
Mrs Fisher
Shiva
It Isn't Done

Because some of the reprint runs were of fewer than 2,000 copies, the number of volumes achieving aggregated print runs of 4,000 is the slightly lower figure of twenty-two.

Eleven of those—10 per cent of the total—sold much better. Five titles had 6,000 copies printed, or just over:

Tantalus 6,500 (two impressions, one revised edition)
Hymen 6,350 (three impressions)
Lysistrata 6,000 (three impressions)
Hypatia 6,000 (three impressions)
It Isn't Done 6,000 (three impressions)

But there were another six volumes that did much better still:

Icarus 10,000 (five impressions)[28]
Plato's American Republic 10,000 (five impressions)
Eos 12,000 (six impressions)
Lars Porsena 12,000 (six impressions)

---

[28] *A Bibliography of Bertrand Russell*, pp. 97–8, says the second impression of *Icarus* was of 4,000 copies, based on royalty statements. However, the publisher's journal gives it as 2,000, and the numbers of labels and jackets recorded there are also for 2,000 copies. There may be confusion with the first impression of *What I Believe*, for which the run was the unusually high number for the series of 4,000.

Daedalus 17,000 (nine impressions)[29]
What I Believe 18,000 (eight 'impressions')[30]

Several of the science volumes were thus among the strongest sellers; and three of the top six were on science. One reason *Daedalus* may have sold so many copies was because so many subsequent volumes referred to it. Nevertheless, the printing figures suggest that the series fulfilled the ambitions implicit in its scientific start, of stimulating debate about pressing contemporary issues, of which the uses of science was a predominant one.

The US sales told much the same story for the better sellers. There was a ninth printing there of *Daedalus* in June 1925; and eighth printings of *Icarus* in 1926 and of *What I Believe* in 1933. However, the association of the series with Dutton was variable. The first four Kegan Paul volumes did not mention Dutton on their title pages. After that, they mostly do for the next six years. The decision to co-publish with the American firm was evidently an afterthought. Fredric Warburg describes how John Macrae, the head of Dutton, would visit London every year to decide which British books to take for the US market.[31] Dutton published their own distinct editions, in differently coloured cloth bindings, with their own labels and jackets; and without the Kegan Paul end-matter.

However, by no means did all the volumes appear in separate Dutton editions. The series list that appeared in Dutton's catalogue for 1930 includes nearly all the Kegan Paul titles out by the end of 1929.[32] This gives the impression that the New York firm was handling the entire series. However, there are three indications to the contrary. Dutton's catalogue for 1932 (the year after Kegan Paul's last volume in the series) lists fewer titles, adding no more from 1929, and none for 1930 or 1931.[33] Dutton evidently stopped taking on new titles in the series in 1929, even though Kegan Paul continued to issue them for two more years. As a result, some of the most important volumes—such as *The World, the Flesh and the Devil, Halcyon, It Isn't Done, Babel, Cato, Deucalion,* or *Aphrodite*—were not marketed in the US. Nonetheless, Kegan Paul continued to put both publishers' names on its title pages through 1929 and into 1930.[34] Perhaps it hoped the continued success of the series

<hr/>

[29] Warburg, *An Occupation for Gentlemen,* p. 110, claims that 'over 20,000 copies were sold'. The Kegan Paul journal lists no impressions after the ninth (1930), though it lists later impressions of other books into the 1940s. Kegan Paul royalty statements in UCL's archive show that *Daedalus* was still selling after the Second World War.
[30] The 'eighth impression' was in fact a second UK edition: see *A Bibliography of Bertrand Russell,* p. 102.
[31] Warburg, *An Occupation for Gentlemen,* pp. 103–6.
[32] Its ninety-six titles include the three Dutton-only ones, and four that never materialized; so eighty-nine of the ninety-five Kegan Paul titles published before 1930. The omitted titles are all from 1929: *Pons Asinorum, The World, the Flesh and the Devil, Halcyon, Isis, Democritus,* and *Sisyphus.* Dutton's catalogues are among the publisher's archive at the Special Collections Research Center, Syracuse University Libraries. I'm very grateful to Abby Houston and Jacklyn Hoyt there, for their help in tracing them.
[33] Dutton's 1932 catalogue listed ninety-two Kegan Paul volumes. Those from 1929 are *Achates, Romulus, Shiva, Vicisti, Galilaee?, Kalki,* and *Typhoeus,* the last listed by its subtitle only: 'The Future of Socialism'. *Eurydice* had been on the 1930 list (as 'The Future of Opera'). Its omission in 1932 may mean it had sold out; or may be another indication of the lists' unreliability. Fyfe's *Archon* (1927) is missing from the 1932 list but appears on earlier and later lists. Whereas Low's early *Wireless Possibilities,* issued separately by Dutton, was listed in 1930 but stays off after 1932. They also included (as did the Kegan Paul lists) several titles that failed to appear; and even continued to include these phantom volumes long after the UK series had wound up.
[34] With the single exception of *Achates,* about Canada, which has the name of the Toronto publisher Musson instead.

in the UK would persuade Dutton to fill the gaps in its list. But, second, the last nine volumes, from 1930 and 1931, no longer carry Dutton's name on the UK title pages, indicating that the arrangement to co-publish the series had been terminated. Dutton continued to advertise it throughout the 1930s, but was reprinting best-sellers and clearing old stock rather than issuing new titles.

The third indication of Dutton's uncoupling from the series is that far fewer than the ninety-odd volumes on Dutton's lists appear actually to have materialized in separate US editions. In this case the process began earlier. There are separate cloth-bound Dutton editions of most of the first forty-one titles (with possibly four exceptions),[35] up to (probably late) 1926. After that, the take-up becomes intermittent, with Dutton-only editions of only around eighteen out of the next forty-one volumes being recorded, to late 1928. This correlates with Warburg's account of how, in 1926, Dutton flooded the US market with what was probably 'the largest remainder sale ever in the history of the American book-trade and it ruined the market for months to come' (106). That suggests that Kegan Paul's business with Dutton was affected—a sizeable proportion of which consisted of To-Day and to-Morrow volumes. Macrae, whom Warburg describes as a gambler, may have hoped that tempting readers with bargain volumes would increase their appetite for the series. If so, it did not work, since Dutton only published selected titles from then to late 1928; and appears to have produced US editions of none of the To-Day and To-Morrow titles coming out (in the UK) after that, from 1929-31.[36]

I have only been able to trace Dutton copies of seventy-one volumes: 65 per cent of the total of 110.

Some of the others will doubtless surface eventually. It would be surprising if *Hermes* on chemistry, or *Columbia*, on the future of Canada, were not thought to be of interest to American readers. Further research will be necessary to establish the final figure. While it is possible a few more will be found, it seems improbable that as many as the twenty volumes listed by Dutton but still missing could have indeed disappeared, leaving no other trace than the entries in the publisher's lists—particularly given the legal requirement that all the US imprints should have been deposited for Library of Congress use.

It is not hard to see why some volumes may have been deemed unsuitable for the US market. Americans may have been thought unlikely to want to be lectured by Brits on sky-scrapers, automation, or advertising. Joad on leisure may have seemed too Anglocentric; *Pons Asinorum* on nonsense, too nonsensical. Fuller's scathing portrayal of the American character in *Atlantis*, or Holtby's scepticism about religious authority, might have just seemed to be offering the wrong messages for a US readership. Furthermore Macrae may simply not have liked some of these, or other volumes.

The smallest estimate for the number Dutton did not publish—based on the assumption that absence from their lists means they didn't publish the volumes—is twenty-two, or 20 per cent of the total. The largest estimate would be thirty-nine titles, or 35 per cent. So between a quarter and a third of the titles do not exist in Dutton's own editions. The actual figure must be between these two, and is probably nearer the high end of the range. Dutton almost certainly didn't issue the last twenty-four volumes; and probably didn't publish most of the other nineteen.

---

[35] I have not seen evidence of *Atlantis*, *Balbus*, *Lucullus*, or *Nuntius* in Dutton bindings, though they are all claimed on its 1930 series list.

[36] With the single exception of Ernest Weekley's *Saxo-Grammaticus*; though Dutton published that under the new title of *Cruelty to Words*, and in 1931, when the series ended. See below, p. 385.

The absence of nearly forty Dutton-style editions from the Library of Congress, which holds Kegan Paul copies of most of the corresponding volumes, suggests that, for some titles, inclusion on the Dutton series list meant that the firm may have simply been importing the UK editions rather than producing its own copies (though it may have lodged the UK copies with the Library to secure US copyright before issuing their own).

The story is complicated by the existence of several different kinds of Dutton edition. The early Dutton volumes were printed in the US. But from late 1927 or more probably early 1928, volumes were produced made from sheets printed in the UK, identical to those in Kegan Paul's aubergine volumes, but bound in cloth, in similar colours to the earlier Dutton volumes. These mostly had a new style of US label, without any lined border, and printed in larger fonts matching those used for the later style of jacket Dutton had adopted for the series in early 1926.

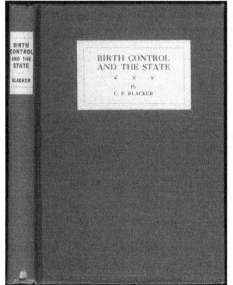 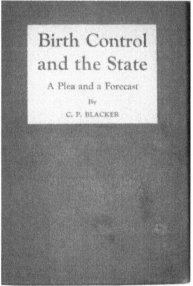

The first printing (June 1926) and second printing (July 1929) of one of Dutton's editions. In this case the one bearing the later label was also printed in the US—presumably because it was a reprint rather than a new title.

The earlier US jackets echo the plain cream of the Kegan Paul ones, and usually bore a blurb on the front. The later ones include a striking framed Art Deco image of a classical charioteer, in black and white plus a single colour, the colour varying from volume to volume. (They either drop the blurb or put it on the back cover.)

As the later-style labels are also affixed to some of the volumes printed in the US, they were probably provided by Dutton. The arrangement of importing sheets or copies indicates less confidence in the US sales; and a corresponding lack of anxiety about piracy (since, under the International Copyright Act of 1891, all books were required to be manufactured in the United States in order to obtain American copyright).

The history of Dutton's involvement sheds light on the rarity of many of the volumes in two ways. For those not published in the US, the Kegan Paul print run is the global total

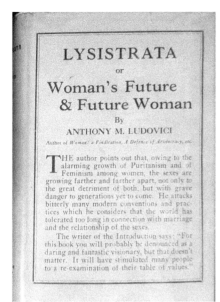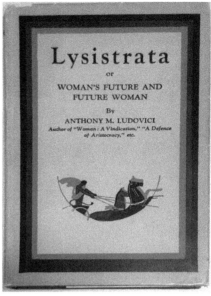

The earlier and later style of Dutton's dust-jackets for the series; here for the first and third impressions of *Lysistrata* (June 1925 and March 1926)

(some copies being exported for the colonial markets). Where Dutton printed their own editions, the worldwide totals would be much larger, especially with the better selling volumes—a fact that helps account for the reach and impact of those by Haldane, Russell, Graves, and Jeans. But what of the volumes printed in the UK for the US market? The Kegan Paul journals don't record extra sheets being printed for these. If that means that the print runs indicated in the journals *included* copies for the US, then both the Kegan Paul and Dutton editions of those volumes would have numbered far fewer than the standard initial run of 2,000 copies. That would explain why so many of the volumes are so scarce in either form.

The Depression was doubtless a factor in Dutton's eventual decision to discontinue publishing new volumes in the series altogether, especially for relatively expensively-priced books. Yet two pieces of evidence militate against taking the economic situation as the sole cause. Dutton did publish one of the volumes from the 1930s, Weekley's *Saxo-Grammaticus* (1930 from Kegan Paul); but as a stand-alone volume under a catchier title—*Cruelty to Words* (1931)—in a different design, and with no mention of To-Day and To-Morrow. It also re-issued another book—one it had published in the series: Jeans' *Eos*—under the new title of *Man and the Stars*, also in 1931, and again separated from To-Day and To-Morrow. Dutton could still sell books, but had lost confidence it could sell the series with its predominantly classical titles. This story of the gradual winding down and loss of the US market for it during the Depression must have been a decisive reason for Kegan Paul's shelving of it. The timing was unfortunate. The election of Roosevelt in 1932 and his ensuing New Deal programme offered the sole moment of utopian hope in the 1930s, which could have made the series timely once more.

To grasp the significance of the UK sales figures some comparators may be useful. The Kegan Paul journals also record the production figures for better-known works by

I. A. Richards, Ogden, and Russell. Ogden's and Richards' *The Meaning of Meaning* went through three editions, selling 4,000 copies from 1922–30. Russell's *ABC of Relativity* went through four impressions between 1925 and 1931, totalling 7,500 copies. Equally, 7,500 copies were produced of Richards' *Principles of Literary Criticism* from 1923–33. His *Practical Criticism* went through three editions, from 1929 to 1934, totalling 5,370 copies.

All these continued to sell for years, generating further impressions and editions; the Richards books especially, as foundational texts of the Cambridge criticism that was revolutionizing the teaching of English in schools as well as universities in the mid-twentieth century. But over the same period as the To-Day and To-Morrow series, the comparison is illuminating. A major popular science book like the *ABC of Relativity* and a landmark book on literary criticism like *Practical Criticism* were selling considerably less than *Icarus* and less than half of the sales of *What I Believe*; with the other two books on criticism and semantics doing less well, but selling a comparable number of copies to a To-Day and To-Morrow book that had gone to only one reprint. Nearly a quarter of the To-Day and To-Morrow books had 4,000 copies printed. The top eleven titles had 6,000 or more printed; the top five were selling more than two, three, or four times as many as these other influential books. By the standards of serious academic books, the sales figures were very strong for a large proportion of the series. They may sound small compared to today's mass-market 'blockbuster' sales; but when you look at the figures for a broader range of even today's UK 'best-sellers', the top five from To-Day and To-Morrow are comparable.

The volumes cost 2/6 (two shillings and sixpence; one-eighth of a pound); or $1 in the US. That was less than, for example, literary novels, for which a standard price around 1925–30 was around 7/6, then reduced to 3/6 for a cheaper reprint. But these were longer, larger books. Kegan Paul also published a sixpenny series and a sevenpenny series. Ogden had originally suggested publishing *Daedalus* as a 'sixpenny pamphlet' but the publisher thought it deserved a less ephemeral presentation.[37] For such short volumes, the To-Day and To-Morrow books were clearly not cheap. They were produced to a high standard; labels as well as jackets, a deep colour, and attractive design. This all suggests that the books were aimed at an upper and middle class audience; to stimulate debate and inform opinion among the educated powerful elite, rather than as a project of mass popularization.

Besides the impact on literary writers explored in Chapter 6, the series had another form of influence. Several books appeared from 1928 with titles that appeared to imitate the successful formula for To-Day and To-Morrow. Two of these appeared in Ogden's series of Psyche Miniatures:

Montgomery Evans, *Prodigal Sons; or, The Future of Caste* (1928)
Sir Harold Jeffreys, *The Future of the Earth* (1929)

The classical title of a third Psyche Miniature, *Selene; or, Sex and the Moon* (1928), by Harold Munro Fox, suggests it may originally have been intended for To-Day and To-Morrow—the Psyche Miniatures did not go in for classical titles, unless you count Greek medical terms (*Aphasia*, *Hypochondria*) or the translation into BASIC English of the *Meno* of Plato. Perhaps Selene was not futurological enough for To-Day and To-Morrow? Or perhaps Ogden wanted to suggest interconnections between the two series—perhaps to draw readers of the longer-established series towards the newer one? (The first Psyche Miniature, I. A. Richards' *Science and Poetry*—the juxtaposition very much in the spirit of To-Day and To-Morrow as well—appeared in 1926).

---

[37] Warburg, *An Occupation for Gentlemen*, p. 109.

Roger Money-Kyrle's *Aspasia: The future of amorality* (1932) was published by Kegan Paul. It was not part of a series, but carried a list of volumes on the back of the dust jacket of the series its title seemed designed to join.[38]

Another work whose title follows the formula but which had no connection to any of Ogden's series nor even to Kegan Paul was *Cedric Dover's Cimmerii? Or Eurasians and Their Future*, published in Calcutta (The Modern Art Press, 1929). This does not refer to To-Day and To-Morrow, but its case for a more respectful attitude to mixed race colonial progeny could well have been intended as a contribution to the debates in the series about the British Empire and race. (Though the echo could be a co-incidental result of the stance that Eurasians have as much right to the classical past—and to neo-classical Dryden's line 'Near the Cimmerians in his dark abode'.)

There are other books that might have been intended to coast in the slipstream of the series. *Prometheus, USA*, by Ernest Greenwood (New York: Harper and Brothers, 1929) was a larger-scale work at 213 pages. But its story of fire, from legend, myth, and religion, through wood, to the age of coal, and into that of oil, includes a chapter entitled: 'Petroleum Today and Tomorrow'. As suggested, the phrase was too ready a publishing cliché for any contemplation of the future for its use to count as evidence of a specific debt; but coupled with the classical figure in the title to figure a story of modern technology the probability of an intentional alignment cannot be discounted. Many works continued to appear from other publishers bearing the title 'Today and Tomorrow' or its variants.

Afterlives of the Series

In 1936 there was an attempt to regain the earlier momentum of To-Day and To-Morrow. At least seven of the volumes were relaunched in rewritten, expanded, and retitled versions, under the new heading 'To-Day, Tomorrow and After'.[39] These were volumes that had all sold well in their first versions:

Ralph de Pomerai, *The Future of Sex Relationships*. (A revised edition of *Aphrodite*)

Anthony M. Ludovici, *The Future of Woman*. (A rewritten edition of *Lysistrata*)

F. C. S. Schiller, *The Future of the British Empire after Ten Years*. (An enlarged edition of *Cassandra*, doubling its length with a new second half including chapters on 'The Decline of "Democracy"', 'The Disintegration of the British Empire', 'Universal Misgovernment', and ending on the chillingly prophetic note: 'Armageddon II?')

C. E. M. Joad, *The Future of Morals*. (A revised edition of *Thrasymachus*)[40]

Archibald Lyall, *The Future of Taboo in these Islands*. (A revised edition of *It Isn't Done*)

---

[38] *Aspasia* is discussed in Chapter 3.

[39] This reprise appears to have been started in as improvisatory way as the original series. I have seen one unjacketed copy of *The Future of Morals* with no indication of the series; and a second, also dated 1936, which has pages at the end advertising the series and the volumes by Joad, Graves, and Lyall; this copy also has a jacket advertising those, plus a fourth volume, Norman Haire's. *The Future of Swearing* and *The Future of Taboo* both have a list at the front of the volumes (facing the title page), giving five titles; all of the above, plus George Thomson's *The Future of Scotland* (a revised edition of *Caledonia*), which appears not to have been published. While *The Future of Swearing* lacks the end-matter, *The Future of Taboo* includes it.

[40] On p. 92 Joad explains that the preceding ninety-one pages were reprinted from *Thrasymachus* (the corresponding portion of that book is up to p. 86); but that he has deleted most of the rest, and replaced it with a mostly new chapter, 'Nineteen Thirty-Six and What Next?'.

Robert Graves, *The Future of Swearing and Improper Language*. (A revised edition of *Lars Porsena*)

Norman Haire, *The Future of Marriage* (a revised edition of *Hymen*)

None of these volumes was on science. As with the original series, the initial print runs were set to 2,000.[41] None of the volumes was reprinted.

Joad's *The Future of Morals* was revised again in 1946 and published under the same title by another London publisher, John Westhouse. This edition has a dust-jacket saying 'JOAD / on the future of / MORALS / herd morality & the / new liberty of action; / marriage, birth control and / divorce; parents and children; patriotism; pacifism, religion, drink'. The title page explains that the 1936 re-issue had 'a new chapter covering developments during the period between 1924 and 1936. A further chapter, *Nineteen Forty-Five and What Now?* has been written for the present edition, bringing the discussion down to contemporary events'.

The volume that may well have been the most widely sold eventually was Radhakrishnan's *Kalki*. It was one of just three volumes reprinted by Kegan Paul after 1931 (with *What I Believe* and *Aphrodite*.) From 1943 it was issued in at least twelve translations into different languages of India, as well as being republished in English by the Bombay publisher Hind Kitabs in 1948 (the year after the Indian Independence he had predicted).

Volume II of The Collected Works of Cassius Jackson Keyser, *The Rational and the Superrational: Studies in thinking* (New York: Scripta Mathematica, Yeshiva University, 1952), 127-67, reprints *Thinking About Thinking*. The same publisher also re-issued *Thinking About Thinking* as a separate pamphlet in 1953.

Russell's *Icarus* was re-issued by the Philosophical Library in New York in 1959 under the title *The Future of Science*; and re-issued in the UK as *Icarus* in 1973. Though his *What I Believe* had no further separate re-issues after 1933, Russell's bibliography lists nine reprints (entire or partial) between 1957 and 1967.[42] Dent's *Terpander* was republished as *The Future of Music* in 1965.[43]

At least ten other titles were reanimated in the last third of the century. Jeans's *Eos* was re-issued by Books for Libraries Press in 1969. Bernal's *The World, the Flesh and the Devil* was re-issued by Indiana University Press in 1969 and by Jonathan Cape in 1970. Graves's *Lars Porsena* reverted to its classical title for a 1972 edition (London: Martin Brian & O'Keefe, 1972), with a new preface by the author. His *Mrs Fisher* was re-issued by four different US publishers in the 1970s.[44] Two volumes were published as part of the 360-title Garland Library of War and Peace in 1972: *Paris* with a new Introduction by S. J. Stearns; and *Janus*, with a new introduction by John Wing. Bretherton's *Midas* was reprinted by the Arno Press, New York, 1974, in the series Foreign Travelers in America, 1810-1935. A number of the titles were re-issued by Folcroft Library Editions in the 1970s: at least *Deucalion, Hypatia, Lars Porsena, Mrs Fisher, Saxo-Grammaticus, Thamyris,* and *Timotheus*. Of these, *Deucalion* and *Timotheus* also had Norwood editions. Hugh MacDiarmid's *Albyn* was republished in *Albyn: shorter books and monographs*, ed. Alan Riach (Manchester: Carcanet, 1996). Fittingly, the first volume, *Daedalus*, was reprinted in Krishna Dronamraju's collection *Haldane's Daedalus Revisited* (Oxford: Oxford University Press, 1995).

[41] Recorded in the Kegan Paul archive in UCL Special Collections.
[42] *A Bibliography of Bertrand Russell*, p. 101.
[43] In The Commonwealth and International Library (Oxford/London: Pergamon/Curwen).
[44] *Timotheus* (Folcroft, PA: Folcroft Library Editions, 1974. New York: Haskell House Publishers, 1974. Norwood, PA: Norwood Editions, 1974 and 1975. Philadelphia: R. West, 1977).

Most of the volumes were not re-issued, and the series sank further into oblivion.[45] Ogden's obituary in the *Times* didn't even mention it, focusing instead on BASIC and the International Library.[46]

Routledge Library Edition

Routledge's re-issuing of the To-Day and To-Morrow series in 2008 was extremely welcome on many counts, and offered the possibility of reclaiming the project for literary and cultural studies.[47] The original Kegan Paul books are scarce (three-quarters having had only 2,000 copies printed). The majority have aged badly, the labels soiling, the boards scuffing, and the spines detaching. The cream jackets have rarely worn well. Well-preserved examples are now highly collectible. These reprints are facsimiles of the original texts, but with the page blocks enlarged by about 25 per cent, to make them easier on the eye. Three, four, or five of the books have been combined to fit 104 titles into twenty-five heftier volumes.[48]

As a publishing exercise, though, it is extremely odd. Effectively, it resembles a print-on-demand re-issue of classic but out-of-print texts. What's lacking is any indication of Routledge's rationale for reviving them. There is no introduction to the whole series, let alone to individual volumes; no annotation; no biographical notes on contributors now scarcely known. How many readers outside India know today that the author of *Kalki; or, The Future of Civilization*, S. Radhakrishnan, later became President of India? How many outside Scotland will identify C. M. Grieve or J. Leslie Mitchell with their respectively better-known pseudonyms of Hugh MacDiarmid and Lewis Grassic Gibbon? And who, beyond certain readers of literary biographies, will recognize Ernest Weekley, the author of *Saxo Grammaticus*—essentially a humorous catalogue of grammatical errors and how to avoid them—as the first husband of Frieda von Richthofen, who left him to elope with D. H. Lawrence?

Nor are there any indications of editorial decisions taken, including alterations to the presentation and the exclusion of six volumes. So it seems necessary to note them here. Some of the Routledge volumes retain the original categories given in the 'Classified Index' which made its appearance midway through the series, and which gives the intellectual flavour of the project: 'Science and Medicine', 'Language and Literature', 'Industry and the Machine', 'Society and the State', or 'Great Britain, The Empire, And America'. But they don't always contain the same individual titles. The series eventually outgrew several of the headings, some of which, like the loose 'General' category, were anyway candidly provisional. Some were intelligently recombined by Routledge, in ways that better describe the shape the series eventually assumed, or which sound less dated. Thus some of the 'General' titles lead off in two volumes on 'Mankind and Civilization'. 'Marriage and Morals' became 'Women, Marriage and the Family'. *Lares et Penates; or, The Home of the Future*, originally listed in the former, was put in a new grouping, 'Home, Clothes and Food', which gathers up not only the titles on food and wine, but also one Kegan Paul could only describe as 'Miscellaneous': Gerald Heard's wacky volume *Narcissus: An anatomy of clothes* (1924).

---

[45] Some titles were posted online; others made available through the Internet Archive. Many have been made available through print-on-demand this century.

[46] 'Mr. C. K. Ogden', *Times* (23 March 1957), 11.

[47] *To-Day and To-Morrow*, 25 vols (London and New York: Routledge; Tokyo: Edition Synapse, 2008). ISBN: 10: 0-415-43596-X (Set) / 13:978-0-415-43596-3 (Set).

[48] The Routledge publicity counts 103 volumes, but their spreadsheet listing which titles appear in which library volumes shows two titles both counted as eighty-nine.

There was certainly a case for dressing the series up in newer and better-fitting exteriors. But it is irresponsible not to tell readers that this is what has been done.

Some of the new Routledge configurations are less welcome. John Rodker's book on *The Future of Futurism* is now in the volume on 'Art and Architecture'. But it's really about whether there's any future for Futurist literature. It was originally grouped under 'Language and Literature', but was perhaps excluded from the two Routledge volumes using that heading because they already contained four titles each. Norwood Young's *Fortuna; or, Chance and Design* was originally under 'Sport and Leisure', which suited its emphasis on probability and gambling much better than its new home in 'Society and the State'.

There are, unfortunately, some more serious defects which compromise the set of reprints as a resource for cultural as well as book history. Most damagingly, there are three major omissions which are nowhere acknowledged: the two volumes by Bertrand Russell; and *Hypatia; or, Woman and Knowledge* by his wife, Dora Russell.[49] This is trebly unfortunate: not only are they among the best, and best-written, of the series, but *Icarus* is one of the volumes most referred to by the others; and *Hypatia* is the strongest statement of feminism, making a powerful case against Ludovici's *Lysistrata; or, Woman's Future and Future Woman*, which in the Routledge set thus goes relatively unchallenged.

The three volumes which only appeared in the US publisher's version of the series are also omitted: *Hygieia; or, Disease and Evolution* by Burton Peter Thom; *The Future of Israel* by James Wise Waterman; and *Thinking about Thinking* by Cassius Keyser. These omissions are perplexing too, since all three books contribute to debates within the series. Thom's supplements several volumes engaging with medicine or evolution; Waterman's adds another perspective on what Laurie Magnus' otherwise solitary volume *Apella* (published under the pseudonym 'A Quarterly Reviewer', which the reprint does not decrypt) subtitles *The Future of the Jews*. Keyser's is a scintillating philosophical exposition.

The decision to exclude the volumes published only by Dutton would be intelligible if only the Kegan Paul texts had been used. But they are not. Several have been copied from the Dutton texts, including some of the most interesting volumes, such as *Hephaestus*, by E. E. Fournier d'Albe, or André Maurois' *The Next Chapter: The war against the moon*. The case of *The World, the Flesh and the Devil* is odder still. Bernal's text here is taken not from its appearance in To-Day and To-Morrow, but from the 1970 Jonathan Cape reprint, complete with a table of contents promising a bibliography and 'A Note on the Author', neither of which have been reproduced.

Where the texts do stick to the Kegan Paul originals, book-history purists will also be disconcerted by the inconsistency about the impression used. If there is a good reason why F. C. S. Schiller's *Tantalus; or, The Future of Man* is copied from the second impression of three, or *Daedalus* from the fourth impression of nine, we are not told it.[50] The publisher's archives at University College London include several letters, mainly from contributors but also occasionally irate readers, noting errors to be corrected in any re-issues. Some of these were corrected in subsequent Kegan Paul impressions, but most have been left uncorrected in the Routledge reprints. Nor is there any indication of which volumes were revised when reprinted.

The original Kegan Paul books also included the lists of volumes in various states of readiness, or unreadiness. Part of the fascination of the series is seeing how it was received;

---

[49] It is all the more surprising since Routledge had re-issued *What I Believe* (as a 'Routledge Classic') four years earlier (London: Routledge, 2004), with a preface by Alan Ryan.
[50] In fact the fifth impression (of January 1925) would have been a better choice, since it included a new two-page preface.

how the titles changed; and especially how some were promised but never appeared. Books which turned out not to have a future included *The Future of our Magnates* and *Methuselah; or, The Future of Old Age*. *The Evocation of Genius* by Alan Porter was revoked. We can guess at the nature of *Pandarus; or, The Future of Traffic in Women* from its author H. Wilson Harris's book on *Human Merchandise: A study of the international traffic in women*. But it would have been good to have *Mercurius; or, The World on Wings* (by C. Thompson Walker) to set alongside *Aeolus*; or *Caliban; or, The Future of Industrial Capitalism* by Hilaire Belloc, just for the hell of it;[51] not to mention the title that represents the greatest loss to literary modernism—Rebecca West's *The Future of Sex*. Even she appeared shy of that version of the title. In later advertisements it became *The Future of the Sexes*.[52] Among West's manuscript notebooks at the University of Tulsa is one entitled 'Europa or the Future of the Sex'. But the catalogue comments tantalizingly: 'Contents appear to have been removed'. Ouch!

Including nearly a hundred slightly different versions of the end-matter would have been redundant, making the edition 20-25 per cent longer, more expensive, and unfriendlier to rainforests. Nor would it have satisfied book historians, who would still need to consult the originals and compare impressions. There was perhaps a case for re-issuing the texts in electronic form, so that samples of this material could have been incorporated, along with other contextual information essential to understand the evolution of the series. Routledge's website quoted some of the reviews, but combined them into a palimpsest with 2008 marketing descriptions which tie themselves in knots trying to present the books as still 'relevant', whereas, in extreme cases at least, it would have been better to acknowledge their fantastical or even perverse qualities. Readers turning to *Lysistrata*, for example, expecting to find 'an attack on many modern conventions and practices which, according to the author, the world has tolerated too long in connection with marriage and the relationship between the sexes', will be surprised by Ludovici's paranoid fantasy of women unsexing themselves and slaughtering men.

Electronic publication would have also added the massive advantage of making the whole collection easily searchable as well as more easily navigable. Having decided to stick to the non-futuristic format of the book, Routledge surely should have provided an index. Given the way certain names and themes thread their way through the series, a single cumulative index would make it a much more valuable collection for teachers and researchers. It is to be hoped that the publishers will still consider adding this online, perhaps combined with an introduction to the whole series. Otherwise, it will remain extraordinary that Ogden is nowhere credited as the inspired editor of the whole series.

Such cavils apart, however, those interested in the literature and intellectual history of the 1920s and 1930s have reason to be grateful to Routledge for putting these important and engaging books back into circulation.

[51] It was perhaps the success of Belloc's *The Servile State* (1912) and *Economics for Helen* (1924) that prompted Ogden to include him.
[52] West's missing title is announced as *The Future of Sex* at the end of *Thamyris*; but it is given at the end of *Chronos, Deucalion, Columbia*, and *Eleutheros* as 'The Future of the Sexes'.

APPENDIX B

Complete Chronological Listing of the To-Day and To-Morrow Series

Order (in Kegan Paul journal)	Title	Author	Year of First UK Edition
1	Daedalus; or, Science and the Future	Haldane, J. B. S.	1923
2	Icarus; or, The Future of Science	Russell, Bertrand	1924
3	Wireless Possibilities	Low, A. M.	1924
4	The Mongol in Our Midst; A Study of Man and His Three Faces	Crookshank, F. G.	1924
5	Narcissus; An Anatomy of Clothes	Heard, Gerald	1924
6	Tantalus; or, The Future of Man	Schiller, F. C. S.	1924
7	The Passing of the Phantoms; A Study of Evolutionary Psychology and Morals	Patten, Charles Joseph	1924
8	Lysistrata; or, Woman's Future and Future Woman	Ludovici, Anthony M.	1924
9	Perseus; or, Of Dragons	Scott-Stokes, H. F.	1924
10	What I Believe	Russell, Bertrand	1925
11	Callinicus; A Defence of Chemical Warfare	Haldane, J. B. S.	1925
12	Quo Vadimus? Glimpses of the Future	Fournier d'Albe, E. E.	1925
13	The Conquest of Cancer	Wright, H. W. S.	1925
14	Proteus; or, The Future of Intelligence	Lee, Vernon	1925
15	Prometheus; or, Biology and the Advancement of Man	Jennings, H. S.	1925
16	Hypatia; or, Woman and Knowledge	Russell, Dora	1925
17	Hephaestus; or, The Soul of the Machine	Fournier d'Albe, E. E.	1925
18	Thamyris; or, Is There a Future for Poetry?	Trevelyan, R. C.	1925
19	Paris; or, The Future of War	Liddell Hart, Basil Henry	1925

Continued

Continued

Order (in Kegan Paul journal)	Title	Author	Year of First UK Edition
20	*Thrasymachus; The Future of Morals*	Joad, C. E. M.	1925
21	*Timotheus; The Future of the Theatre*	Dobrée, Bonamy	1925
22	*Pygmalion; or, The Doctor of the Future*	Wilson, R. McNair	1925
23	*Lycurgus; or, The Future of Law*	Haynes, E. S. P.	1925
24	*Euterpe; or, The Future of Art*	McColvin, Lionel R.	1926
25	*Cassandra; or, The Future of the British Empire*	Schiller, F. C. S.	1926
26	*Atlantis; or, America and the Future*	Fuller, J. F. C.	1925
27	*Pegasus; or, Problems of Transport*	Fuller, J. F. C.	1925
28	*Nuntius; Advertising and its Future*	Russell, Gilbert	1926
29	*Midas; or, The United States and the Future*	Bretherton, C. H.	1926
30	*Birth Control and the State*	Blacker, C. P.	1926
31	*Plato's American Republic*	Woodruff, J. Douglas	1926
32	*Ouroboros; or, The Mechanical Extension of Mankind*	Garrett, Garet	1926
33	*Orpheus; or, The Music of the Future*	Turner, W. J.	1926
34	*Sibylla; or, The Revival of Prophecy*	Mace, C. A.	1926
35	*Artifex; or, The Future of Craftsmanship*	Gloag, John	1926
36	*Terpander; or, Music and the Future*	Dent, E. J.	1926
37	*The Future of Futurism*	Rodker, John	1926
38	*Procrustes; or, The Future of English Education*	Pink, Alderton M.	1926
39	*Balbus; or, The Future of Architecture*	Barman, Christian	1926
40	*The Dance of Çiva; or, Life's Unity and Rhythm*	Collum	1927
41	*Lucullus; or, The Food of the Future*	Hartley, Olga and Leyel, Mrs C. F.	1926
42	*Janus; The Conquest of War: A Psychological Inquiry*	McDougall, William	1927
43	*Pomona; or, The Future of English*	de Sélincourt, Basil	1926
44	*Apella; or, The Future of the Jews*	A Quarterly Reviewer [Laurie Magnus]	1925
45	*Lars Porsena; or, The Future of Swearing and Improper Language*	Graves, Robert	1927
46	*Socrates; or, The Emancipation of Mankind*	Carlill, H. F.	1927
47	*Gallio; or, The Tyranny of Science*	Sullivan, J. W. N.	1927
48	*Apollonius; or, The Present and Future of Psychical Research*	Bennett, E. N.	1927
49	*Delphos; The Future of International Language*	Pankhurst, E. Sylvia	1927
50	*Stentor; or, The Press of To-Day and To-Morrow*	Ockham, David	1927

51	*Aeolus; or, The Future of the Flying Machine*	Stewart, Oliver	1927
52	*Rusticus; or, The Future of the Countryside.*	Briggs, Martin S.	1927
53	*Vulcan; or, The Future of Labour*	Chisholm, Cecil	1927
54	*Hymen; or, The Future of Marriage*	Haire, Norman	1927
55	*The Next Chapter; The War Against the Moon*	Maurois, André	1927
56	*Caledonia; or, The Future of the Scots*	Thomson, G. M.	1927
57	*Scheherazade; or, The Future of the English Novel*	Carruthers, John [= pseud. for J. Y. T. Greig]	1927
58	*Galatea; or, The Future of Darwinism*	Brain, W. Russell	1927
59	*Lares et penates; or, The Home of the Future*	Birnstingl, H. J.	1928
60	*Archon; or, The Future of Government*	Fyfe, Hamilton	1927
61	*Albyn; or, Scotland and the Future*	Grieve, C. M. [= Hugh MacDiarmid (pseud.)]	1927
62	*Hermes; or, The Future of Chemistry*	Jones, T. W.	1927
63	*Iconoclastes; or, The Future of Shakespeare*	Griffith, Hubert	1927
64	*Bacchus; or, Wine To-Day and To-Morrow*	Shand, P. Morton	1927
65	*Breaking Priscian's Head; or, English as She Will Be Spoke and Wrote*	Greig, J. Y. T.	1928
66	*Archimedes; or, The Future of Physics*	Whyte, L. L.	1927
67	*Atalanta; or, The Future of Sport*	Sandilands, G. S.	1928
68	*Hibernia; or, The Future of Ireland*	Waller, Bolton C.	1928
69	*Cain; or, The Future of Crime*	Godwin, George	1928
70	*Morpheus; or, The Future of Sleep*	Fraser-Harris, David	1928
71	*Hanno; or, The Future of Exploration*	Mitchell, J. Leslie [= Lewis Grassic Gibbon (pseud.)]	1928
72	*Metanthropos; or, The Body of the Future*	Macfie, R. Campbell	1928
73	*Heraclitus; or, The Future of Films*	Betts, Ernest	1928
74	*Autolycus; or, The Future for Miscreant Youth*	Gordon, R. G.	1928
75	*Fortuna; or, Chance and Design*	Young, Norwood	1928
76	*Diogenes; or, The Future of Leisure*	Joad, C. E. M.	1928
77	*Eos; or, The Wider Aspects of Cosmogony*	Jeans, J. H.	1928
78	*Eutychus; or, The Future of the Pulpit*	Holtby, Winifred	1928
79	*Kalki; or, The Future of Civilization*	Radhakrishnan, S.	1929
80	*Columbia; or, The Future of Canada*	Godwin, George	1928
81	*Mrs Fisher; or, The Future of Humour*	Graves, Robert	1928
82	*Alma Mater; or, The Future of Oxford and Cambridge*	Hall, Julian	1928
83	*Automaton; or, The Future of the Mechanical Man*	Hatfield, H. Stafford	1928

Continued

Continued

Order (in Kegan Paul journal)	Title	Author	Year of First UK Edition
84	*Achates; or, The Future of Canada*	Harris, W. Eric	1929
85	*Pons Asinorum; or, The Future of Nonsense*	Edinger, George and Neep, E. J. C.	1929
86	*Romulus; or, The Future of the Child*	Lewis, Robert T.	1929
87	*Typhoeus; or, The Future of Socialism*	Shadwell, Arthur	1929
88	*Vicisti, Galilaee? or, Religion in England: A Survey and Forecast*	Powley, Edward B.	1929
89	*Shiva; or, The Future of India*	Minney, R. J.	1929
90	*Eurydice; or, The Nature of Opera*	Hussey, Dyneley	1929
91	*Saxo Grammaticus; or, First Aid for the Best-seller*	Weekley, Ernest	1930
92	*The World, the Flesh and the Devil; An Enquiry into the Future of the Three Enemies of the Rational Soul*	Bernal, J. D.	1929
93	*Halcyon; or, The Future of Monogamy*	Brittain, Vera	1929
94	*Isis; or, The Future of Oxford*	Diplock, W. J. K.	1929
95	*Deucalion; or, The Future of Criticism*	West, Geoffrey	1930
96	*Democritus; or, The Future of Laughter*	Gould, Gerald	1929
97	*Sisyphus; or, The Limits of Psychology*	Jaeger, M.	1929
98	*Cato; or, The Future of Censorship*	Seagle, William	1930
99	*Chronos; or, The Future of the Family*	Paul, Eden	1930
100	*Eleutheros; or, The Future of the Public Schools*	Roxburgh, J. F.	1930
101	*Babel; or, The Past, Present and Future of Human Speech*	Paget, Richard	1930
102	*Ethnos; or, The Problem of Race*	Keith, Arthur	1931
103	*Chiron; or, The Education of a Citizen of the World*	Pearce, M. Chaning	1931
104	*It Isn't Done; or, The Future of Taboo Among the British Islanders*	Lyall, Archibald	1930
105	*Sinon; or, The Future of Politics*	Mowrer, Edgar Ansel	1930
106	*Aphrodite; or, The Future of Sexual Relationships*	de Pomerai, R.	1931
107	*Solon; or, The Price of Justice*	Harvey, C. P.	1931

Continued

VOLUMES PUBLISHED ONLY IN THE US

Hygieia; or, Disease and Evolution	Thom, Burton Peter	1926
The Future of Israel	Wise, James Waterman	1926
Thinking about Thinking	Keyser, Cassius Jackson	1926

RELATED VOLUME NOT PUBLISHED IN THE SERIES

Aspasia; The Future of Amorality	Money-Kyrle, R. E.	1932

TITLES ADVERTISED IN THE END-MATTER OF OTHER VOLUMES BUT NOT PUBLISHED

'Clio; or, The Future of History'	Maurois, André	Advertised, but presumably a working title of the book published as *The Next Chapter*
'The Future of Sex' [thus at the end of *Thamyris*; but also advertised in *Chronos, Deuacalion, Columbia,* and *Eleutheros* as "The Future of the Sexes']	West, Rebecca	
'Mercurius; or, The World on Wings'	Walker, C. Thompson	
'The Evocation of Genius'	Porter, Alan	
'The Future of India'	Welby, T. Earle	
'Aesculapius; or, Disease and the Man' [also advertised on jacket of *The Conquest of Cancer* as 'Aesculapius; or, Man and Disease']^[1]	Crookshank, F. G.	
'Pandarus; or, The Future of Traffic in Women' [advertised as 'in preparation' at end of *Diogenes*]	Harris, H. Wilson, author of 'Human Merchandise'	
'Methuselah; or, The Future of Old Age'	Haire, Norman	
'The Future of Our Magnates'	Thomas, Sir W. Beach	
'Hestia; or, The Future of Home Life'	Spielman, Winifred	
also advertised with the title 'Davus'; as in the end-matter of *Pomona* and *Pygmalion*]	Belloc, Hilaire	

Continued

Order (in Kegan Paul journal)	Title	Author	Year of First UK Edition
	VOLUMES WRITTEN BUT NOT ADVERTISED OR PUBLISHED		
	'Androgyne; or, The Future of the Sexes'	Montagu, Ashley	1924–5
	'Noah; or, The Future of Intoxication' [MS lost or destroyed]	Waugh, Evelyn	1927
	'Arethusa; or, The Future of Enthusiasm' [MS at the University of Sussex in Mass Observation archive. See p. 284 in Chapter 5]	Madge, Charles	1930–1

Note: The order of the volumes is taken from the Kegan Paul 'journals' in the UCL Archives. The numbering does not always correspond to the numbers given on the dust-jackets (which anyway were not included on all jackets).

[1] *Aesculapius* is something of a mystery. The volume is advertised in the end-matter of a number of 1925 volumes as 'In Preparation.' Then it disappears; not only from the promotional material for the series, but from the public record altogether, with the exception of one review (in *Time*, 22 March 1926; discussed in the Conclusions, pp. 337–38). Perhaps the reviewer read something in proof or manuscript; but the comment is generic enough to make one suspect the announcement was being reviewed rather than the book; or that the reviewer was looking at a list such as the one included in the front matter of the 1925 Dutton edition of *Paris*, which listed *Aesculapius* as if it were published. The title is usually given as *Aesculapius; or, Disease and the Man*; but it is advertised on back of the jacket of *The Conquest of Cancer* (1925) as *Aesculapius; or, Man and Disease*, in a series listing, as if already out. It is described (in the end-matter announcements) as 'A consideration of the most modern methods of controlling disease'; in which case perhaps some of the material ended up in the pieces collected in Crookshank's later *Epidemiological Essays* (1930). But the contrast between the disease and the man suggests that it may relate to the work published in the Psyche Miniature *Diagnosis; and Spiritual Healing* (1930). The first part of this book was based on Crookshank's November 1926 Bradshaw lecture on the theory of diagnosis, contrasting the methods associated with Hippocrates and Galen. The review of *Diagnosis; and Spiritual Healing* in the *Journal of Neurology, Neurosurgery & Psychiatry*, 8:31 (1928), 280–3 (279–80), by 'R. G. G.' (probably R. G. Gordon, who also wrote for To-Day and To-Morrow and the International Library), explains how, whereas the Galenic method seeks to classify diseases:

Dr. Crookshank gives a scholarly exposition of the contrasting views of Hippocrates and Galen. The latter, which sought for a classification of diseases, has dominated medicine for the last thousand years and culminated in the absurdity of an official nomenclature. The author welcomes the signs of a return to the naturalistic method of Hippocrates, which aimed at a diagnosis of the patient as a whole with special relation to his particular disability and the method of a relief from this.

In other words, classify the disease or understand the man and his needs. So it may be that Ogden diverted the book into another series because it was a better fit for the brief of Psyche Miniatures; or because he didn't feel it was futurological enough for what To-Day and To-Morrow had become.

Bibliography

Note: the individual volumes of To-Day and To-Morrow are not included here. A full listing is provided in Appendix B. 104 of the original 110 volumes were reissued in a 25 volume library edition: *To-Day and To-Morrow*, (London and New York: Routledge; Tokyo: Edition Synapse, 2008).

Abir-Am, Pnina, 'The Biotheoretical Gathering, Transdisciplinary Authority, and the Incipient Legitimation of Molecular Biology in the 1930s: New Historical Perspectives on the Historical Sociology of Science', *History of Science*, 25 (1987), 1–71

Adrian, Edgar, *The Basis of Sensation* (London: Christophers, 1928)

Adrian, Edgar, 'Animal Electricity', *Realist*, 2:1 (October 1929), 1–12

Agassi, Joseph, *Science in Flux* (Dordrecht: D. Reidel, 1975)

Albright, Daniel, *Quantum Poetics* (Cambridge: Cambridge University Press, 1997)

Aldington, Richard, 'The Poetry of the Future', *Poetry*, 14: 5 (August 1919), 266–9

Aldington, Richard, *Death of a Hero* (London: Chatto & Windus, 1929)

Anderson, Perry, 'The River of Time', *New Left Review*, 26 (March–April 2004), 67–77

Annan, Noel, 'The Intellectual Aristocracy' (1955), in *The Dons: Mentors, Eccentrics and Geniuses* (Chicago: University of Chicago Press, 1999)

Annan, Noel, *Roxburgh of Stowe* (London: Longmans, 1965)

Anon, 'Survey of Current Literature' section, *Psyche*, 3:4 (April 1923), 375–8

Anon, 'News of the Future', *Daily Mail* Ideal Home Exhibition Special (28 February 1928)

Anon, 'Francis Graham Crookshank, M.D.', *Journal of Nervous & Mental Disease*, 79:1 (January 1934), 122–3

Anon 'The Second International Congress for the Unity of Science', *Science*, 83 (17 April 1936), 363

Anon, 'L. L. Whyte 1896–1972', obituary, *British Journal for the Philosophy of Science*, 24:1 (1973), 91–2. doi: 10.1093/bjps/24.1.91

Appadurai, Arjun, *The Future as Cultural Fact: Essays on the Global Condition* (London: Verso, 2013)

Armstrong, Tim, *Modernism, Technology, and the Body: A Cultural Study* (Cambridge: Cambridge University Press, 1998)

Ascari, Maurizio, 'From Spiritualism to Syncretism: Twentieth-Century Pseudo-Science and the Quest for Wholeness', *Interdisciplinary Science Reviews*, 34:1 (March 2009), 9–21

Asimov, Isaac, and Jean Marc Côté, *Futuredays: A Nineteenth-Century Vision of the Year 2000* (New York: Henry Holt and Company, 1986)

Attridge, John, '"A Taboo on the Mention of Taboo": Taciturnity and Englishness in *Parade's End* and André Maurois' *Les Silences du Colonel Bramble*', in *Ford Madox Ford's Parade's End: The First World War, Culture and Modernity*, ed. Ashley Chantler and Rob Hawkes (Rodopi: Amsterdam and New York, 2014), 23–35

Augé, Marc, *The Future*, trans. John Howe (London: Verso, 2014)

Badiou, Alain, *Ethics: An Essay on the Understanding of Evil*, trans. Peter Hallward (London: Verso, 2002)

Badiou, Alain, *The Century* (Cambridge: Polity Press 2007)

Barthes, Roland, *Sade, Fourier, Loyola* (Paris: Editions de Seuil, 1971)

Bedford, Sybille, *Aldous Huxley: A Biography*, 2 vols, vol. 1 (London: Quartet, 1979)

Beer, Gillian, *Darwin's Plots: Evolutionary Narrative in Darwin, George Eliot, and Nineteenth-Century Fiction* (London, Routledge & Kegan Paul, 1983)

Beer, Gillian, *Open Fields: Science in Cultural Encounter* (Oxford: Oxford University Press, 1996)

Benson, A. C., *The Upton Letters* (London: Smith, Elder, 1905)

Berman, Marhall, *All that Solid Melts into Air* (New York and London: Penguin, 1988)

Bernal, J. D. 'The World, the Flesh and the Devil', *Psyche*, 9:4 (April 1929), 3–26

Bernal, J. D., 'Foreword to the Second Edition' of *The World, the Flesh, and the Devil* (London: Jonathan Cape, 1970), 9–10

Bernal, J. D., *The Extension of Man: A History of Physics Before 1900* (London: Weidenfeld & Nicolson, 1972)

Birkenhead, Lord, *The World in 2030 A.D.* (London: Hodder and Stoughton, [1930])

Black, Jeremy, 'Why the Industrial Revolution Happened Here', BBC 2, 14 January 2013: http://www.bbc.co.uk/programmes/b01pz9d6

Black, Nick, David Boswell, Alastair Gray, Sean Murphy, and Jennie Popay, *Health and Disease: A Reader* (Milton Keynes, Open University, 1993)

Blackwell, Kenneth, Harry Ruja, Sheila Turcon, eds, *A Bibliography of Bertrand Russell* (London: Routledge, 2003)

Bleiler, Richard J., and Everett F. Bleiler, *Science-Fiction: The Gernsback Years* (Kent, OH: Kent State University Press, 1998)

Bluemel, Kristin, *George Orwell and the Radical Eccentrics: Intermodernism in Literary London* (New York: Palgrave Macmillan, 2004)

Bod, Rens, Julia Kursell, Jaap Maat, and Thijs Weststeijn, 'A New Field: *History of Humanities*', *History of Humanities*, 1:1 (2016), 1–8

Boehmer, Elleke, 'Global and Textual Webs in an Age of Transnational Capitalism; or, what isn't new about Empire', *Postcolonial Studies*, 7:1 (2004), 11–26

Bonheim, Helmut, *Joyce's Benefictions*, Issue 16 of Perspectives in Criticism (Berkeley: University of California Press, 1964)

Bostrom, Nick, 'A History of Transhumanist Thought', *Journal of Evolution and Technology*, 14:1 (April 2005), 1–25

Bowler, Peter J., *Science for All: The Popularization of Science in Early Twentieth-Century Britain* (Chicago: University of Chicago Press, 2009)

Bowler, Peter J., *A History of the Future: Prophets of Progress from H. G. Wells to Isaac Asimov* (Cambridge: Cambridge University Press, 2017)

Bradshaw, David, ed. *The Hidden Huxley* (London: Faber, 1995)

Bradshaw, David, 'The Best of Companions', *Review of English Studies*, 47 (1996), 188–206, 352–68

Bradshaw, David, and Rachel Potter, eds, *Prudes on the Prowl: Fiction and Obscenity in England, 1850 to the Present Day* (Oxford: Oxford University Press, 2013)

Brain, Robert, 'Representation on the Line: The Graphic Method and the Instruments of Scientific Modernism', in *From Energy to Information: Representation in Science, Art, and Literature*, ed. B. Clark and L. D. Henderson (Stanford: Stanford University Press, 2002), pp. 155–78

Brant, Clare, 'Aeolus: Futurism's Flights of Fancy', *Interdisciplinary Science Reviews*, 34:1 (March 2007), 79–90

Brockington, Grace, 'Translating Peace: Pacifist Publishing and the Transmission of Foreign Texts', in *Publishing in the First World War: Essays in Book History*, ed. Mary Hammond and Shafquat Towheed (Basingstoke: Palgrave, 2007), 46–58

Brooke, Stephen, 'The Body and Socialism: Dora Russell in the 1920s', *Past & Present*, 189:1 (2005), 147–77. doi: 10.1093/pastj/gti024

[Brooke-Rose, C.], 'A Conversation with Christine Brooke-Rose by Ellen G. Friedman and Miriam Fuchs', from the *Review of Contemporary Fiction*, 9:3 (Fall 1989), 81–90.

Brooks, Cleanth, *The Well-Wrought Urn* (New York: Harcourt, Brace, 1947)

Brown, Andrew, *J. D. Bernal: the Sage of Science* (Oxford: Oxford University Press, 2005)

Buchanan, Scott, *Possibility* (London: Kegan Paul, 1927)

Bud, Robert, 'Life, DNA and the Model', *British Journal for the History of Science*, 46 (June 2013), 311–34

Buitenhuis, Peter, *The Great War of Words: British, American, and Canadian Propaganda and Fiction, 1914–1933* (Vancouver: University of British Columbia Press, 1987)

Burke, Kenneth, *The Philosophy of Literary Form* (Louisiana State University Press, 1941)

Bush, Vannevar, 'As We May Think', *Atlantic*, 176 (July 1945), 101–8

Calder, Ritchie, *The Birth of the Future* (London: Arthur Barker, 1934)

Camus, Albert, *The Myth of Sisyphus*, trans. Justin O'Brien (London: Penguin, 2000)

Carnap, Rudolf, *The Unity of Science* (London: Kegan Paul, Trench and Trübner, 1934)

Carter, Huntly, *The New Spirit in Drama* (London: Frank Palmer, 1912)

Cassata, Francesco, *Building the New Man: Eugenics, Racial Science and Genetics in Twentieth-Century Italy* (Budapest: Central European University Press, 2011)

Castells, Manuel, *The Information Age: Economy, Society and Culture. Volumes I, II, and III: The Rise of The Network Society/The Power of Identity/End of The Millennium* (Oxford: Blackwell, 1999)

Chekhov, Anton, *Ivanov, The Seagull and Three Sisters*, trans. Ronald Hingley (London: Oxford University Press, 1968)

Churchill, Winston, 'Shall We All Commit Suicide?', *Nash's Pall Mall Magazine* (September 1924), 12–13, 80–1

Cianci, Giovanni, and Jason Harding, ed., *T. S. Eliot and the Concept of Tradition* (Cambridge: Cambridge University Press, 2007)

Clark, Kenneth, 'The Future of Painting', *Listener*, Issue 351 (2 October 1935), 543–4, 578.

Clark, Ronald, *JBS: The Life and Work of J. B. S. Haldane* (London: Hodder and Stoughton, 1968)

Clarke, Arthur C., 'Haldane and Space', in *Haldane and Modern Biology*, ed. K. R. Dronamraju (Baltimore: Johns Hopkins Press, 1968), 243–8

Clarke, Arthur C., *Greetings, Carbon-Based Bipeds* (New York: St Martin's Griffin, 2000)

Clarke, I. F., *The Tale of the Future: From the Beginning to the Present Day* (London: Library Association, 1961)

Clarke, I. F., *The Pattern of Expectation: 1644–2001* (London: Cape, 1979)

Clayton, Jay, 'The Modern Synthesis: Genetics and Dystopia in the Huxley Circle', *Modernism/modernity*, 23:4 (November 2016), 875–96

Crangle, Sara, *Prosaic Desires: Modernist Knowledge, Boredom, Laughter, and Anticipation* (Edinburgh: Edinburgh University Press, 2010)

Dawkins, Richard, *The God Delusion* (London: Bantam Press, 2006)

Deer, Patrick, *Culture in Camouflage: War, Empire, and Modern British Literature* (Oxford: Oxford University Press, 2009)

Derrida, Jacques, 'No Apocalypse, Not Now (full speed ahead, seven missiles, seven missives)', trans. Catherine Porter and Philip Lewis, *diacritics* 14:2 (Summer 1984), 20–31

Dilthey, W., *W. Dilthey: Selected Writings*, ed. H. P. Rickman (Cambridge: Cambridge University Press, 1979)

Doyle, Charles, *Richard Aldington: A Biography* (Carbondale and Edwardsville, IL: Southern Illinois University Press, 1989)

Dronamraju, K. R., ed., *Haldane and Modern Biology* (Baltimore: Johns Hopkins Press, 1968)

Dronamraju, K. R., ed., *Haldane's Daedalus Revisited* (Oxford: Oxford University Press, 1995)

Dronamraju, Krishna, *Popularizing Science: The Life and Work of JBS Haldane* (Oxford: Oxford University Press, 2017)

Dunbar, Robin, 'The Social Brain Hypothesis', *Evolutionary Anthropology: Issues, News, and Reviews*, 6:5 (1998) 178–90

Duncan, Isadora, *The Dance of the Future* (Leipzig: Eugen Diedrichs, 1903)

Dyson, Freeman, 'Daedalus after Seventy Years' in K. R. Dronamraju, ed. (1995) *Haldane's Daedalus Revisited* (Oxford: Oxford University Press, 1995), 55–63

Eby, Cecil D., *The Road to Armageddon: The Martial Spirit in English Popular Literature, 1870–1914* (Durham, NC: Duke University Press, 1987)

Eliot, T. S. 'The Man of Letters and the Future of Europe', *Sewanee Review*, 53:3 (Summer 1945), 333–42

Eliot, T. S., 'Tradition and the Individual Talent', *Selected Essays*, third enlarged edition (London: Faber and Faber Limited, 1951), 13–22

Eliot, T. S., 'Ulysses, Order, and Myth' [1923], in *Selected Prose of T. S. Eliot*, ed. Frank Kermode (New York: Harcourt, 1975), 175–8

Eliot, T. S., 'Charleston, Hey! Hey!', *Nation and Athenaeum*, 40 (29 January 1927), 595, in *The Complete Prose of T. S. Eliot: The Critical Edition. Literature, Politics, Belief, 1927–1929*, ed. Frances Dickey, Jennifer Formichelli, and Ronald Schuchard (Baltimore: Johns Hopkins University Press, 2015), 25–9. http://muse.jhu.edu/chapter/1634627

Eliot, T. S., *The Poems of T. S. Eliot*, vol. 1, ed. Christopher Ricks and Jim McCue (London: Faber, 2015)

Ellis, Havelock, 'The Machine and the Future', *Today and Tomorrow*, 3:3 (Spring 1933), 261–6

Empson, William, 'Virginia Woolf' [1931], in *Argufying* (London: Chatto and Windus, 1987), 443–9

Esty, Jed, *A Shrinking Island: Modernism and National Culture in England* (Princeton University Press, 2004)

Farmelo, Graham, *Churchill's Bomb* (London: Faber, 2013)

Felski, Rita, 'The Invention of Everyday Life', in *Doing Time: Feminist Theory and Postmodern Culture* (New York: New York University Press, 2000)

Felski, Rita, 'Introduction' to *Special Issue: Everyday Life*, *New Literary History*, 33:4 (Autumn 2002), 607–22

Ferreira, Aline, 'Mechanized Humanity', in *Discourses and Narrations in the Biosciences*, ed. Brian Hurwitz and Paola Spinozzi (Göttingen: V&R unipress GmbH, 2011), 145–58

Fink, Howard, 'Newspeak: The Epitome of Parody Techniques in *Nineteen Eighty-Four*', *Critical Survey*, 5:2 (Summer 1971), 155–63

Firchow, Peter, 'Science and Conscience in Huxley's *Brave New World*', *Contemporary Literature*, 16:3 (Summer, 1975), 301–16

Firestone, Shulamith, *The Dialectic of Sex: The Case for Feminist Revolution* (New York: William Morrow, 1970)

Flagg, Francis, 'The Machine Man of Ardathia', *Amazing Stories* (November 1927), 798–804

Florence, P. Sargent and J. R. L. Anderson, eds, *C. K. Ogden: A Collective Memoir* (London: Elek Pemberton, 1977)

Fodor, Jerry, 'You Can't Argue with a Novel', *London Review of Books* (4 March 2004), 30–1

Ford, Ford Madox (as Ford Madox Hueffer), *England and the English* (New York: McClure, 1907)

Ford, Ford Madox (as Hueffer), *When Blood is Their Argument: An Analysis of Prussian Culture* (London: Hodder and Stoughton, 1915)

Ford, Ford Madox (as Hueffer), *Thus to Revisit* (London: Chapman and Hall, 1921)

Ford, Ford Madox (as Hueffer), 'A Haughty and Proud Generation', *Yale Review*, 11 (July 1922), 703–17; in Ford, *Critical Essays*, ed. Max Saunders and Richard Stang (Manchester: Carcanet, 2002), 208–17

Ford, Ford Madox, *War Prose*, ed. Max Saunders (Manchester: Carcanet, 1999)

Ford, Ford Madox, *A Man Could Stand Up—* [1926], ed. Sara Haslam (Manchester: Carcanet, 2011)

Ford, Ford Madox, *No More Parades*, ed. Joseph Wiesenfarth (Manchester: Carcanet, 2011)

Ford, Ford Madox, *The Good Soldier*, ed. Max Saunders, Oxford World's Classics (Oxford: Oxford University Press, 2012)

Ford, Henry, *To-day and To-morrow* (Garden City, NY: Doubleday Page, 1926).

Forrester, John, 'The Psychoanalytic Passion of J. D. Bernal in 1920s Cambridge', *British Journal of Psychotherapy*, 26 (2010), 397–404

Forrester, John, and Laura Cameron, *Freud in Cambridge* (Cambridge: Cambridge University Press, 2017)

Forster, E. M., 'The Machine Stops', *Oxford and Cambridge Review* (November 1909); collected in *The Eternal Moment and Other Stories* (London: Sidgwick and Jackson, 1928), 1–61

Foster, Hal, 'Postmodernism in Parallax', *October*, 63 (Winter 1993), 3–20

Foster, Hal, 'Prosthetic Gods', *Modernism/modernity*, 4:2 (April 1997), 5–38

Foster, Hal, 'At the Guggenheim', *LRB* (20 March 2014), 38

Foucault, Michel, *Discipline and Punish: The Birth of the Prison* (New York: Random House 1975)

Franke, Damon, *Modernist Heresies: British Literary History, 1883–1924* (Columbus, OH: Ohio State University Press, 2008)

Frayn, Andrew, *Writing Disenchantment* (Manchester: Manchester University Press, 2014)

Freud, Sigmund, *Civilization and its Discontents*, in the *Standard Edition of the Complete Psychological Works of Sigmund Freud, Volume XXI (1927–1931)* (London: Hogarth Press, 1930), 59–145

Fukuyama, Francis. 'The End of History?', *The National Interest* (Summer 1989); expanded into *The End of History and the Last Man* (New York: Free Press, 1992)

Fukuyama, Francis, *Our Posthuman Future: Consequences of the Biotechnology Revolution* (New York: Farrar Straus & Giroux, 2002)

Fuller, Steve, *Preparing for Life in Humanity 2.0* (Basingstoke: Palgrave Macmillan, 2012)

Gardiner, Michael, *Critiques of Everyday Life* (London and New York: Routledge, 2000)

Garnett, Robert Reginald, *From Grimes to Brideshead: The Early Novels of Evelyn Waugh* (Lewisburg, PA: Bucknell University Press, 1990)

Gasiorek, Andrzej, *A History of Modernist Literature* (Chichester: Wiley-Blackwell, 2015)

Gelfand, Scott, and John, R. Shook, eds, *Ectogenesis: Artificial Womb Technology and the Future of Human Reproduction* (Amsterdam: Rodopi, 2006)

Gere, C., introducing a special issue on 'The Brain in a Vat', *Studies in History and Philosophy of Science*, 35:2 (June 2004), 219–25

Gibbs, Philip, *The Day After To-Morrow* (London: Hutchinson 1928)

Giddens, Anthony, *The Consequences of Modernity* (London: Polity, 1990)

Giddens, Anthony, *Conversations with Anthony Giddens: Making Sense of Modernity* (Stanford, CA: Stanford University Press, 1998)

Giddens, Anthony, 'Risk and Responsibility', *Modern Law Review*, 62:1 (1999), 1–10

Giedion, Siegfried, *Mechanization Takes Command: A Contribution to Anonymous History* (New York: Oxford University Press 1948)

Gloag, John, *Tomorrow's Yesterday* (London: Allen & Unwin, 1932)

Glover, Jon, and Jon Silkin, eds, *The Penguin Book of First World War Prose* (London: Penguin, 1990)

Gordon, W. Terrence, *C. K. Ogden: A Bio-Bibliographic Study* (Metuchen, NJ, and London: The Scarecrow Press, 1990)

Gould, Stephen Jay, 'Unpredictable Patterns', in *Predictions*, ed. Sian Griffiths (Oxford: Oxford University Press, 1999), 145–6

Gould, Stephen Jay, *The Lying Stones of Marrakech* (Cambridge, MA: Harvard University Press, 2011)

Graves, Robert, *Another Future of Poetry* (London: The Hogarth Press, 1926)

Gray, John, *The Immortalization Commission: The Strange Quest to Cheat Death* (London: Allen Lane, 2011)

Gray, Terence, *Dance-Drama* (Cambridge: W. Heffer & Sons, 1926)

Greer, Tom, *A Modern Daedalus* (London: Griffith, Farran, Okeden & Welsh, 1885)

Griffiths, Sian, ed., *Predictions* (Oxford University Press, 1999)

Habermas, Jürgen, *The Future of Human Nature: Towards a Liberal Eugenics?* trans. Hella Beister, Max Pensky, and William Rehg (Cambridge: Polity, 2003)

Haldane, J. B. S., 'If You Were Alive in 2123 A. D.', *Century*, 106 (August 1923), 549–66

Haldane, J. B. S., 'Chemistry and Peace', in the *Atlantic Monthly*, 135:1 (January 1925), 1–18

Haldane, J. B. S., 'The Last Judgement: A Scientist Turns to Prophecy', *Harper's* (March 1927); reprinted in *Possible Worlds and Other Essays* (London: Chatto & Windus, 1927), 287–312

Haldane, J. B. S., 'The Future of Biology', *Possible Worlds* (London: Chatto and Windus, 1927)

Haldane, J. B. S., *Science and Well-Being* (London: Kegan Paul, 1935)

Haldane, J. B. S., *Science and Everyday Life* (London: Lawrence and Wishart, 1939)

Haldane, J. B. S., 'Machines that Think', *Daily Worker* (29 August 1940) 4–5. Collected in *A Banned Broadcast and Other Essays* (London: Chatto and Windus, 1946), 85–7

Haldane, J. B. S., 'Biological Possibilities for the Human Species in the Next Ten Thousand Years', in *Man and his Future*, ed. Gordon Wolstenholme (London: J. & A. Churchill, 1963), 337–61

Haldane, J. B. S., 'A Scientific Revolution? Yes. Will We Be Happier? Maybe', *New York Times Magazine* (19 April 1964), 90, 113, 114

Haldane, J. B. S., 'On Being Finite', *Rationalist Review*, 1965; collected in *Science and Life* (The Humanist Library, Pemberton Publishing Co. Ltd, in association with Barrie & Rockliff, 1968), 192–203

Hansen, Mark, *Feed Forward: On the Future of Twenty-First-Century Media* (University of Chicago Press, 2015)

Haraway, Donna, 'A Cyborg Manifesto: Science, Technology, and Socialist-Feminism in the Late Twentieth Century', in *Simians, Cyborgs and Women: The Reinvention of Nature* (New York: Routledge, 1991), 149–81

Harman, Claire, 'Futurity Man', *TLS* (6 August 2010), 7–8

Harman, Gilbert, *Thought* (Princeton, NJ: Princeton University Press, 1973)

Hatfield, H. Stafford, *The Conquest of Thought by Invention* (London: Kegan Paul, Trench, Trübner & Co., 1929)

Hatfield, H. Stafford, *The Inventor and his World* (London: Kegan Paul, Trench, Trübner & Co., 1933)

Hawhee, Debra, 'Language as Sensuous Action: Sir Richard Paget, Kenneth Burke, and Gesture-Speech Theory', *Quarterly Journal of Speech*, 92:4 (November 2006), 331–54

Hayles, N. Katherine Introduction, *Chaos and Order: Complex Dynamics in Literature and Science* (Chicago: University of Chicago Press, 1991)

Heath, Jeffrey M., *The Picturesque Prison: Evelyn Waugh and His Writing* (Kingston and Montreal: McGill-Queen's University Press, 1982)

Henkes, Robbert-Jan, and Mikio Fuse, 'Inside D1', *Genetic Joyce Studies*, 12 (Spring 2012): http://www.geneticjoycestudies.org/GJS12/GJS12_Henkes_Fuse.html accessed 31 October 2013

Herf, Jeffrey, *Reactionary Modernism: Technology, Culture and Politics in Weimar and the Third Reich* (Cambridge: Cambridge University Press, 1984)

Highmore, Ben, *Everyday Life and Cultural Theory* (London and New York: Routledge, 2002)

Highmore, Ben, ed., *The Everyday Life Reader* (London and New York: Routledge, 2002)

Highmore, Ben, *Ordinary Lives: Studies in the Everyday* (London: Routledge, 2010)

Hirsch, Marianne, 'The Generation of Postmemory', *Poetics Today*, 29:1 (Spring 2008), 103–28

Hirschkop, Ken, 'Why Rhetoric is Magic to Modernism', *Affirmations of the Modern*, 3:1 (2015). https://am.ubiquitypress.com/articles/52/

Hodgkin, D. M., 'John Desmond Bernal', 'Biographical memoirs of the Fellows of the Royal Society', *Proceedings of the Royal Society*, 26 (1980), 17–84

Holman, Brett, 'Airminded'. https://airminded.org/bibliography/to-day-and-to-morrow/

Horkheimer, Max, *Eclipse of Reason* (New York: Oxford University Press, 1947)

Horkheimer, Max, and Theodor Adorno, *Dialektik der Aufklärung* [*Dialectic of Enlightenment*] (Amsterdam: Querido Verlag, 1947)

Hounshell, David A., *From the American System to Mass Production* (Baltimore: Johns Hopkins University Press, 1984)

Howsam, Leslie, *Kegan Paul—A Victorian Imprint: Publishers, Books and Cultural History* (Toronto: University of Toronto Press, 1999)

Howsam, Leslie, 'An Experiment with Science for the Nineteenth-Century Book Trade: The International Scientific Series', *British Journal for the History of Science*, 33:2 (June 2000), 187–207

Hubble, Nick, *Mass Observation and Everyday Life: Culture, History, Theory* (Basingstoke: Palgrave Macmillan, 2005)

Huber, Bettina J., 'Studies of the Future: A Selected and Annotated Bibliography', in *Sociology of the Future: Theory, Cases and Annotated Bibliography*, ed. Wendell Bell and James Wau (New York: Russell Sage Foundation, 1971), 339–437; item no. 236.

Hughes, J. J., 'Back to the future: Contemporary Biopolitics in 1920s' British Futurism', EMBO Reports. 2008 July; 9 (Suppl 1): S59–S63. doi: 10.1038/embor.2008.68

Hurwitz, Brian, and Max Saunders, eds, special issue of *Interdisciplinary Science Reviews*, 34:1 (March 2009)

Hutcheon, Linda, *A Poetics of Postmodernism* (New York and London: Routledge, 1988)

Huxley, Aldous, *Proper Studies* (London: Chatto & Windus, 1927)

Huxley, Aldous, *Brave New World* (Harmondsworth: Penguin, 1972)

Huxley, Julian, 'Searching for the Elixir of Life', *Century* (February 1922), 621–9

Huxley, Julian, *Essays of a Biologist* (London: Chatto and Windus, 1923)

Huxley, Julian, 'The Tissue-Culture King', *Yale Review*, 15 (April 1926), 479–504. Reprinted in *Amazing Stories*, 2:5 (August 1927), 451–9

Huxley, Julian, *What Dare I Think?* (London: Chatto and Windus, 1931)

Huxley, Julian, *Evolution: The Modern Synthesis* (London: George Allen and Unwin, 1942)

Huxley, Julian, ed., *The Humanist Frame* (London: George Allen and Unwin, 1961)

Huxley, Julian, ed., *Aldous Huxley, 1894–1963: A Memorial Volume* (London: Chatto and Windus, 1965)

James, Simon J. *Maps of Utopia: H. G. Wells, Modernity and the End of Culture* (Oxford: Oxford University Press, 2012)

Jameson, Fredric, 'Politics of Utopia', *New Left Review*, 25 (January–February 2004), 35–54

Jameson, Fredric, *Archaeologies of the Future: The Desire Called Utopia and Other Science Fictions* (London: Verso, 2007)

Jeffreys, Harold, *The Future of the Earth* (London: Kegan Paul, Trench, Trübner and Co., 1929)

Jencks, Charles, *The Language of Post-Modern Architecture* (New York: Rizzoli, 1977)

Joad, C. E. M. *The Horrors of the Countryside* (London: The Hogarth Press, 1931)

Joad, C. E. M. *The Untutored Townsman's Invasion of the Country* (London: Faber, 1946)

Johnson, Richard, 'What Is Cultural Studies Anyway?', *Social Text*, 16 (Winter 1986–7), 38–80

Joyce, James, 'Opening Pages of a Work in Progress', *transition*, 1 (April 1927), 9–30

Joyce, James, *Finnegans Wake*, third edition (London: Faber, 1964)

Joyce, James, *A Portrait of the Artist as a Young Man*, ed. Jeri Johnson (Oxford: Oxford University Press, 2000)

Jünger, Ernst, 'Photography and the "Second Consciousness"', in *Photography in the Modern Era*, ed. Christopher Phillips (New York: Metropolitan Museum, 1989), 207–10

Kahn, Herman, and Anthony Wiener, *The Year 2000: A Framework for Speculation on the Next Thirty-Three Years* (New York: Macmillan, 1967)

Kaku, Michio, 'The Universe in a Nutshell': https://www.youtube.com/watch?v=0NbBjNiw4tk accessed 1 February 2019

Kaku, Michio, BBC4's 2007 series 'Visions of the Future'. http://docunow.blogspot.co.uk/2013/05/dr-michio-kaku-revolution-series.html

Kermode, Frank, 'Educating the planet', *LRB*, 2:5 (20 March 1980), 1–4

Kern, Stephen, *The Culture of Time and Space, 1880–1918*, new edition (Cambridge, MA: Harvard University Press, 2003)

Kevles, Daniel, *In the Name of Eugenics: Genetics and the Uses of Human Heredity* (Cambridge, MA: Harvard University Press, 1985)

Keynes, John Maynard, *The General Theory of Employment Interest and Money* (London: Macmillan, 1936)

Kittler, Friedrich, *Gramophone, Film, Typewriter* (Stanford, CA: Stanford University Press, 1999)

Kołakowski, Lesjek, *Main Currents of Marxism*, revised omnibus edition (New York: W. W. Norton, 2005)

Koselleck, Reinhart, *Futures Past: On the Semantics of Historical Time*, trans. Keith Tribe (Cambridge, MA: MIT Press, 1985)

Kurzweil, Ray, *The Singularity Is Near: When Humans Transcend Biology* (New York: Viking, 2005)

Lamberti, Elena, *Marshall McLuhan's Mosaic: Probing the Literary Origins of Media Studies* (Toronto: University of Toronto Press, 2012)

Langdon-Davies, John, *A Short History of the Future* (London: Routledge, 1936)

Lawrence, D. H., *Psychoanalysis and the Unconscious*, in *Fantasia of the Unconscious* and *Psychoanalysis and the Unconscious* (Harmondsworth, Penguin, 1983)

Le Corbusier, *Towards a New Architecture*, trans. Frederick Etchells (London: The Architectural Press, 1927)

Le Corbusier, *Urbanisme* [*The City of Tomorrow*], trans. Frederick Etchells (London: John Rodker, 1929)

Leavis, F. R., *Mass Civilization and Minority Culture* (Cambridge: Gordon Fraser, The Minority Press, 1930)

Leavis, F. R., *For Continuity* (Cambridge: Minority Press, 1933)

Lee, Vernon, *The Beautiful: An Introduction to Psychological Aesthetics* (Cambridge: Cambridge University Press, 1913)

Lernout, Geert, 'Introduction', *The* Finnegans Wake *Notebooks at Buffalo. Notebook VI.B.1*, ed. Vincent Deane, Daniel Ferrer, and Geert Lernout (Turnhout: Brepols Publishers, 2003), 4–14

Leung, Colette, in the 'Encyclopedia' section of the 'Eugenics Archive'. http://eugenicsarchive.ca/discover/encyclopedia/535eed7a7095aa000000024a

Levitin, Dmitri, 'Such Matters as the Soul', *LRB* (22 September 2016), 29–30, 32

Lewis, C. S., *That Hideous Strength* (London: The Bodley Head, 1945)

Lewis, P. Wyndham, *Time and Western Man* (London: Chatto & Windus, 1927)

Lewis, P. Wyndham, *Blasting & Bombardiering* (London: John Calder, 1982)

Lewis, P. Wyndham, *The Art of Being Ruled*, ed. Reed Way Dasenbrock (Santa Rosa: Black Sparrow Press, 1989)

Lewis, Roy, 'Looking Back 50 Years to the Predictions that were Made for the Times we Live in', *Times* (26 August 1974), 6

Lewis, Roy, 'C. K. Ogden's To-Day & To-Morrow Series', *The Private Library*, third series, 10:4 (1987), [140]–52

Low, A. M., *The Future* (London: G. Routledge & Sons, 1925)

Ludovici, Anthony, 'Art: A Question of Finish', *New Age*, 12:21 (1913), 508

Ludovici, Anthony, 'Art: An Open Letter to my Friends', *New Age*, 14: 9 (1914), 278–81

Lukács, György, *History and Class Consciousness: Studies in Marxist Dialectics* [1923], trans. Rodney Livingstone (London: Merlin Press, 1971)

Lukács, György, *The Historical Novel*, trans. Hannah and Stanley Mitchell (Harmondsworth: Penguin, 1976)

Macaulay, Thomas Babington, review of Leopold von Ranke's *Die römische Papste* [*The Ecclesiastical and Political History of the Popes During the Sixteenth and Seventeenth Centuries*], trans. S. Austin (London, 1840); *Edinburgh Review* 72, October 1840, 227–58

Marett, Paul, 'Making Science Public: The Today and Tomorrow Series and the Place of Science in Early 20th Century Britain' (Senior thesis, University of Pennsylvania, 2015). https://cpb-us-w2.wpmucdn.com/web.sas.upenn.edu/dist/c/253/files/2016/10/making_science_public-2dijcxg.pdf

Marsh, Charles, 'The War against the Moon: *Andre Maurois' 1927 "Fantasy on the Coming Power of the Press"'*, *Journalism & Mass Communication Quarterly*, 86:2 (June 2009), 419–38

Matz, Jesse, *Lasting Impressions: The Legacies of Impressionism in Contemporary Culture* (New York: Columbia University Press, 2016)

McElvenny, James, 'Meaning in the Age of Modernism: C. K. Ogden and his Contemporaries' (Thesis submitted in fulfilment of the requirements for the degree of Doctor of Philosophy Department of English University of Sydney, 2013)

McElvenny, James, *Language and Meaning in the Age of Modernism: C.K. Ogden and His Contemporaries* (Edinburgh: Edinburgh University Press, 2017)

McHugh, Roland, *Annotations to* Finnegans Wake, revised edition (Baltimore: Johns Hopkins University Press, 1991)

McLaren, Angus, *Reproduction by Design: Sex, Robots, Trees, and Test-Tube Babies in Interwar Britain* (Chicago: University of Chicago Press, 2012)

McLuhan, Marshall, *Understanding Media: The Extensions of Man* (New York: McGraw-Hill, 1964)

Miller, Tyrus, *Time Images: Alternative Temporalities in 20th-Century Theory, History, and Art* (Newcastle: Cambridge Scholars Publishing, 2009)

Milne, Marjorie Bruce, ed., *Future Books: Industry Government Science Arts. Volume 1: Overture* (London: Leathley Publications Ltd, [1946])

Monk, Ray, *Bertrand Russell: The Ghost of Madness. 1921–1970* (London: Vintage, 2001)

Monk, Ray, entry on Bertrand Russell in the *Oxford Dictionary of National Biography* (Oxford: Oxford University Press, n.d.)

Moore, G. E., *Principia Ethica* (Cambridge: Cambridge University Press, 1903)

Morrisson, Mark S., *Modernism, Science, and Technology* (London: Bloomsbury, 2017)

Muir, Edwin, *The Structure of the Novel* (London: Hogarth Press, 1928)

Myerson, George, 'Utopia@second_millennium. Daedalus_meets_Job', *History of the Human Sciences*, 16:1 (2003), 79–92

Myerson, George, and Yvonne Rydin, 'No Limits to Imagining London's future', *Imagining the Future City: London 2062*, ed. S. Bell and J. Paskins (London: Ubiquity Press, 2013), 155–8

Nagel, Thomas, 'What Is It Like to Be a Bat?', *Philosophical Review*, 83:4 (October 1974), 435–50

Nietzsche, Friedrich, *Ecce Homo*, trans. R. J. Hollingdale (London: Penguin, 1992)

Nordmann, Charles, *The Tyranny of Time: Einstein or Bergson?*, trans. E. E. Fournier d'Albe (London: T. Fisher Unwin, 1925)

Ogden, C. K., 'Editorial', *Psyche*, 8:1 (July 1927), 1–7

Ogden, C. K., 'Editorial', *Psyche*, 8:3 (January 1928), 1–2

Ogden, C. K., 'Editorial', *Psyche*, 9:3 (January 1929), 1–9

Ogden, C. K., *ABC of Psychology* (London: Kegan Paul, 1929; third edition 1934). The *ABC* was a revised version of his *The Meaning of Psychology* (New York: Harper & Brothers, 1926)

Ogden, C. K., *Brighter Basic*, Psyche Miniatures (London: Kegan Paul, 1931)

Ogden, C. K., *Debabelization: With a Survey of Contemporary Opinion on the Problem of a Universal Language* (London: Kegan Paul, Trench, Trubner and Co., 1931)

Ogden, C. K., 'The Orthological Institute', *Psyche*, 12:2 (October 1931), 92–6; reprinted in *transition*, 21 (March 1932)

[Ogden, C. K., and Mary Sargant Florence], *Militarism versus Feminism: Writings on Women and War*, ed. Margaret Kamester and Jo Vellacott (London: Virago Press, 1987)

Olson, Liesl, *Modernism and the Ordinary* (Oxford: Oxford University Press, 2009)

Olson, Liesl, 'Everyday Life Studies: A Review', *Modernism/modernity*, 18:1 (January 2011), 175–80

Orwell, George, 'Wells, Hitler and the World State', *Horizon* (August 1941), 133–8

Orwell, George, *Nineteen Eighty-Four* (London: Penguin, 2000)

Osler, Mirabel, *The Rain Tree* (London: Bloomsbury, 2011)

Ozawa, Hisashi, 'John and Ishi, "Savage" Visitors to "Civilization": A Reconsideration of Aldous Huxley's *Brave New World*, Imperialism and Anthropology'. *Aldous Huxley Annual*, 12/13 (Münster: LIT Verlag, 2014), 123–47

Paget, Richard, 'The Origin of Language', *Psyche*, 8 (July 1927), 35–9

Parrinder, Patrick, *Shadows of the Future: H. G. Wells, Science Fiction, and Prophecy* (Syracuse, NY: Syracuse University Press, 1995)

Parrinder, Patrick, *Utopian Literature and Science: From the Scientific Revolution to Brave New World and Beyond* (Basingstoke: Palgrave Macmillan, 2015)

Parry, Bronwyn, 'Technologies of Immortality: The Brain on Ice', *Studies in History and Philosophy of Science*, 35:2 (June 2004), 391–413

Partington, John S., 'H. G. Wells and the World State: A Liberal Cosmopolitan in a Totalitarian Age', *International Relations*, 17:2 (2003), 233–46

Pick, Daniel, *Faces of Degeneration: A European Disorder, c.1848–1918* (Cambridge: Cambridge University Press, 1993)

Pick, Daniel, *War Machine: The Rationalisation of Slaughter in the Modern Age* (New Haven, Conn.: Yale University Press, 1993)

Popper, Karl, *The Poverty of Historicism* (London: Routledge, 2002)

Pound, Ezra, 'Further Instructions', in *The New Poetry: An Anthology*, ed. Harriet Monroe (New York: Macmillan, 1917), 265–6

Pound, Ezra, *ABC of Reading* (London: G. Routledge, 1934)

Priest, Susanna Hornig, ed., *Encyclopedia of Science and Technology Communication* (Los Angeles: Sage, 2010)

Rabaté, Jean-Michel, 'Joyce and Jolas: Late Modernism and Early Babelism', *Journal of Modern Literature*, 22:2, Joyce and the Joyceans (Winter 1998–9), 245–52

Randall, Bryony, *Modernism, Daily Time, and Everyday Life* (Cambridge: Cambridge University Press, 2007)

Reuter, E. B., '*Prometheus or Biology and the Advancement of Man*. H. S. Jennings', *American Journal of Sociology*, 31:5 (March 1926), 692

Richards, I. A., *Principles of Literary Criticism* (London: Kegan Paul, 1924)

Richards, I. A., *Science and Poetry* (London: Kegan Paul, 1926)

Richards, I. A., *Practical Criticism* (London: Kegan Paul, 1929)

Richards, I. A., 'Some Recollections of *C. K. Ogden*', in *Encounter*, 9:3 (September 1957), 10–12

Richardson, Dorothy, 'Women and the Future', reprinted in Scott, Bonnie Kime, ed., *The Gender of Modernism* (Bloomington, IN: Indiana University Press, 1990), 411–14

Roberts, John, *Philosophizing the Everyday* (London and New York: Pluto Press, 2006)

Rose, Steven, 'How to Get Another Thorax', *London Review of Books*, 38:17 (8 September 2016), 15–17

Rowse, A. L., *On History: A Study of Present Tendencies*, Psyche Miniatures (London: Kegan Paul, Trench, Trübner & Co., 1927)

Rubin, Charles T., 'Daedalus and Icarus Revisited', *New Atlantis* (Spring 2005), 73–91

Russell, Bertrand, 'Science and Civilization', *Daily Herald* (16, 19, 20, and 21 November 1923), p. 4 each issue

Russell, Bertrand, 'The Effect of Science on Social Institutions', *The Survey: Graphic Number* (New York), 52:1 (1 April 1924), 5–11

Russell, Bertrand, 'What I Believe', *Forum*, 82 (September 1929), 129–34

Russell, Bertrand, 'What I Believe', *Nation* (New York), 132 (29 April 1931), 469–70

Russell, Bertrand, 'Some Prospects: Cheerful and Otherwise', in *Sceptical Essays* (London: Routledge, 2004), 202–17

Russell, Dora, 'Portrait of C. K. Ogden', letter to the editor, *Listener* (21 March 1963), 505

Sackville-West, V., 'The Future of Poetry', *Nation and Athenaeum*, 37:19 (8 August 1925), 572

Saint-Amour, Paul, *Tense Future: Modernism, Total War, Encyclopedic Form* (Oxford: Oxford University Press, 2015)

Santayana, George, *Soliloquies in England and Later Soliloquies* (New York: C. Scribner's Sons, 1922)

Sargent, Lyman, *Utopian Literature in English: An Annotated Bibliography From 1516 to the Present*. http://openpublishing.psu.edu/utopia/ accessed 29 October 2016

Saunders, Max, 'Lawrence, Freud and Civilisation's Discontents', *D. H. Lawrence Review*, 27:2–3 (1997–8), 269–88

Saunders, Max, 'Ford and European Modernism: War, Time, and *Parade's End*', *Ford Madox Ford and 'The Republic of Letters'*, ed. Vita Fortunati and Elena Lamberti (Bologna: CLUEB [Cooperativa Libraria Universitaria Editrice Bologna], 2002), 3–21

Saunders, Max, 'Future Sublime', 'Commentary', *TLS* (26 June 2009), 14–15

Saunders, Max, 'Science and Futurology in the To-Day and To-Morrow Series: Matter, Consciousness, Time and Language', *Interdisciplinary Science Reviews*, 34:1 (March 2009), 69–79; in a special issue devoted to To-Day and To-Morrow, ed. Max Saunders and Brian Hurwitz. DOI: 10.1179/174327909X421461

Saunders, Max, *Self Impression* (Oxford: Oxford University Press, 2010)

Saunders, Max, 'All These Fellows are Ourselves': Ford Madox Ford, Race, and Europe', in *Modernism and Race*, ed. Len Platt (Cambridge: Cambridge University Press, 2011), 39–57

Saunders, Max, 'Empire of the Future: *The Inheritors*, Ford, Liberalism and Imperialism', *The Edwardian Ford Madox Ford*, ed. Laura Colombino and Max Saunders (Amsterdam and New York: Rodopi, 2013), pp. 125–40

Scheffler, Samuel H., *Death and the Afterlife* (Oxford: Oxford University Press, 2014)

Scholes, Robert, and Eric S. Rabkin, *Science Backgrounds*, *Science Fiction: History, Science, Vision* (London: Oxford University Press, 1977)

Scott, David, *Conscripts of Modernity: The Tragedy of Colonial Enlightenment* (Durham, NC: Duke University Press, 2004)

Scott, J. W., 'Ogden, Charles Kay (1889–1957)', revised by W. Terrence Gordon, *Oxford Dictionary of National Biography* (Oxford: Oxford University Press, n.d.)

Seltzer, Mark, *Bodies and Machines* (New York: Routledge, 1992)

Shapin, Steven, 'The Superhuman Upgrade', *LRB*, 39:14 (13 July 2017), 29–31

Shaw, George Bernard *Back to Methuselah (A Metabiological Pentateuch)* (London: Constable, 1921)

Shaw, Rosalind, 'Provocation: Futurizing Memory'. http://www.culanth.org/fieldsights/ 376-provocation-futurizing-memory

Sheringham, Michael, *Everyday Life: Theories and Practices from Surrealism to the Present* (Oxford and New York: Oxford University Press, 2006)

Shiach, Morag, '"To Purify the Dialect of the Tribe": Modernism and Language Reform', *Modernism/modernity*, 14:1 (January 2007), 21–34

Shklovskij, Viktor, 'Art as Technique', *Literary Theory: An Anthology*, ed. Julie Rivkin and Michael Ryan (Malden: Blackwell Publishing Ltd, 1998), 15–21

Silverstein, Michael, 'From the Meaning of Meaning to the Empires of the Mind: Ogden's Orthological English', *Pragmatics* 5:2 (1995), 185–95

Simmel, Georg, 'Die Grosstadt und das Geistesleben', in *Die Grosstadt. Jahrbuch der Gehe-Stiftung*, 9, (1903). Available in English translation in Kurt H. Wolff, *The Sociology of Georg Simmel* (Glencoe, IL: The Free Press, 1950)

Snow, C. P., 'The Two Cultures and the Scientific Revolution', *Encounter*, 12 (June 1959), 17–24; 13 (July 1959), 22–7

Sokal, Alan, 'Transgressing the Boundaries: Towards a Transformative Hermeneutics of Quantum Gravity', *Social Text*, 46/47 (Spring/Summer 1996), 217–52

Sontag, Susan, 'The Imagination of Disaster' [1965], reprinted in *Against Interpretation* (New York: Farrar, Straus, and Giroux, 1966)

Soyfer, Valery N., 'The Consequences of Political Dictatorship for Russian Science', *Nature Reviews Genetics*, 2 (2001), 723–9

Spengler, Oswald, *The Decline of the West* (New York: Knopf, 1927)

Squier, Susan Merrill, *Babies in Bottles: Twentieth-Century Visions of Reproductive Technology* (New Brunswick, NJ: Rutgers University Press, 1994)

Stableford, Brian, 'Science Fiction Between the Wars', in *Anatomy Of Wonder: A Critical Guide to Science Fiction*, ed. Neil Barron, fourth edition (New Providence, NJ: Bowker, 1995), 62–114

Stableford, Brian, *Biotechnology and Speculative Fiction*. http://www.lysator.liu.se/lsff/mb-nr41/Biotechnology_and_Speculative_Fiction.html accessed 8 August 2014

Stannard, Martin, *Evelyn Waugh: The Early Years 1903–1939* (London: Dent, 1986)

Stein, Gertrude, *Wars I Have Seen* (New York: Random House, 1945)

Steiner, Riccardo, 'The (Ir)resistible Lightness of Our Past'. http://www.psychoanalysis.org.uk/articles/the-irresistible-lightness-of-our-past-riccardo-steiner accessed on 1 February 2019

Sterling, Bruce, *Schismatrix Plus* (New York: Ace Books, 1996)

Stevenson, Randall, *Modernist Fiction* (Lexington: University Press of Kentucky, 1992)

Stock, Adam, 'The Future-as-Past in Dystopian Fiction', *Poetics Today*, 37:3 (2016), 416–42

Stodart-Walker, Archibald, *Robert Buchanan: The Poet of Modern Revolt* (London: Grant Richards, 1901)

Stone, Dan *Breeding Superman: Nietzsche, Race and Eugenics in Edwardian and Interwar Britain* (Liverpool University Press, 2002)

Strauss. E. B., 'L'Homme Machine: A Brief Account of Pavlov's Conditioned Reflexes', *Realist*, 1:4 (July 1929), 89–98

Sullivan, J. W. N., *Aspects of Science* (London: R. Cobden-Sanderson, 1923)

Tagore, Rabindranath, *The Religion of Man* (New York: Macmillan, 1931)

Thompson, Mark, *Enough Said: What's Gone Wrong with the Language of Politics?* (London: Bodley Head, 2016)

Toscano, Alberto, 'The Promethean Gap: Modernism, Machines, and the Obsolescence of Man', *Modernism/modernity*, 23:3 (September 2016), 593–609

Tresch, John, 'In a Solitary Place: Raymond Roussel's Brain and the French Cult of Unreason', *Studies in History and Philosophy of Science*, 35:2 (June 2004), 307–32

Trotter, David, *Literature in the First Media Age: Britain between the Wars* (Cambridge, MA: Harvard University Press, 2013)

Trotter, David, 'In the Soup', *LRB*, 36:19 (9 October 2014), 27–8

Valéry, Paul, 'The Future of Literature', *New York Herald Tribune, Books* (April 1928): *Collected Works. Volume 11: Occasions*, trans. Malcolm Cowley, ed. Roger Shattuck and Frederick Brown (Princeton, NJ: Princeton University Press, 2015), 151–7

Vanderham, Paul, *James Joyce and Censorship: The Trials of Ulysses* (Basingstoke: Palgrave Macmillan, 1998)

Verene, D. P., 'Vico's Scienza Nuova and Joyce's *Finnegans Wake*', *Philosophy and Literature*, 21:2 (1997), 392–404

Vickers, Neil, 'Roger Money-Kyrle's *Aspasia: The Future of Amorality* (1932)', *Interdisciplinary Science Reviews*, 34:1 (March 2009), 91–106

Warburg, Fredric, *An Occupation for Gentlemen* (London: Hutchinson, 1959)

Watson, John B., 'Psychology as the behaviorist views it', *Psychological Review*, 20 (1913) 158–77. Later incorporated into the first chapter of *Behavior: A Textbook of Comparative Psychology* (New York: Henry Holt & Co. 1914)

Watson, John B., and William MacDougall, *The Battle of Behaviorism: An Exposition and an Exposure* (London: Kegan Paul, Trench and Trubner, 1928)

Waugh, *Vile Bodies* (Harmondsworth: Penguin, 1976)

Waugh, *Black Mischief* (London: Penguin, 2000)

Waugh, Evelyn, *Decline and Fall* (Harmondsworth: Penguin, 1980)

Waugh, Evelyn, *A Little Learning* (Harmondsworth: Penguin, 1983)

Waugh, Evelyn, *The Diaries of Evelyn Waugh*, ed. Michael Davie (London: Weidenfeld and Nicolson, 1976)

Weiner, Jonathan, 'Introduction', *Predictions*, ed. Sian Griffiths (Oxford: Oxford University Press, 1999), xi–xxi

Wells, *The Open Conspiracy* (London: Waterlow and Sons [printers], [1933])

Wells, H. G., *Anticipations of the Reactions of Mechanical and Scientific Progress upon Human Life and Thought*, fourth edition (London: Chapman and Hall, 1902)

Wells, H. G., *The Discovery of the Future* (London: T. Fisher Unwin, 1902)

Wells, H. G., *The Dream* (London: Cape, 1924)

Wells, H. G., 'Preface' to *Seven Famous Novels* (New York: Alfred A. Knopf, 1934), vii–x

Wells, H. G., *World Brain* (London: Methuen, 1938)

Wells, H. G., *The Correspondence of H.G. Wells*, ed. David C. Smith, 4 vols (London: Pickering & Chatto, 1998)

Werskey, Gary, *The Visible College: A Collective Biography of British Scientists and Socialists of the 1930s* (London: Allen & Unwin, 1978)

Werskey, Gary, 'The Visible College Revisited: Second Opinions on the Red Scientists of the 1930s', *Minerva*, 45 (2007), 305–19

White, Paul, 'Ministers of Culture: Arnold, Huxley and Liberal Anglican Reform of Learning', *History of Science*, 43 (2005), 115–38

Whitehead, A. N., *Science and the Modern World* (New York: Macmillan, 1925)

Whitrow, O. J., 'L. L. Whyte 1896—1972', *British Journal for the Philosophy of Science*, 24 (1973), 91–2

Whitworth, Michael, *Einstein's Wake* (Oxford: Oxford University Press, 2001)

Wiener, Martin J., *An Empire on Trial: Race, Murder, and Justice under British Rule, 1870–1935* (Cambridge: Cambridge University Press, 2008)

Wilson, Edward O., *Consilience: The Unity of Knowledge* (New York: Knopf, 1998)

Wilson, Leigh, *Modernism and Magic: Experiments with Spiritualism, Theosophy and the Occult* (Edinburgh: Edinburgh University Press, 2012)

Wollaeger, Mark, *Modernism, Media, and Propaganda: British Narrative from 1900 to 1945* (Princeton: Princeton University Press, 2006)

Woolf, Leonard, 'Daedalus and Icarus', 'The World of Books' column, *Nation and Athenaeum*, 34 (22 March 1924), 890

Woolf, Leonard, 'The Future of Woman', *Nation and Athenaeum*, 36:15 (10 January 1925), 526

Woolf, Leonard, 'The Religion of A ----', 'World of Books', *Nation and Athenaeum*, 37 (25 April 1925), 106

Woolf, Leonard, 'The Novel of To-Day', *Nation and Athenaeum*, 42 (3 December 1927), 356

Woolf, Leonard, 'Fools Contest', *Nation and Athenaeum*, 42 (14 January 1928), 569

Woolf, Leonard, 'A Censorship at Work', *Nation and Athenaeum*, 46 (8 February 1930), 642

Woolf, Leonard, 'The Ideals of Journalism', *Nation and Athenaeum*, 46 (15 February 1930), 674

Woolf, Leonard, 'Marriage and the Family', *Nation and Athenaeum*, 47 (28 June 1930), 412

Woolf, Virginia, 'Modern Fiction', in *The Essays of Virginia Woolf*, vol. 4, ed. Andrew McNeillie (London: The Hogarth Press, 1984), 157–65

Woolf, Virginia, 'Character in Fiction' [1924; subsequently revised as 'Mr Bennett and Mrs Brown'], in *The Essays of Virginia Woolf*, vol. 3, ed. Andrew McNeillie (London: The Hogarth Press, 1988), 420–38

Woolf, Virginia, 'Poetry, Fiction and the Future', *The Essays of Virginia Woolf*, vol. 4, ed. Andrew McNeilie (London: Hogarth Press, 1994), 428–41

Wright, Patrick, *Tank* (London: Faber, 2000)

Wright, Patrick, *Iron Curtain: From Stage to Cold War* (Oxford: Oxford University Press, 2007)

Zuckerman, Solly, 'Apes, Idiots, and Men', *Spectator* (13 June 1931), 939–40. Review of expanded edition of F. G. Crookshank's *The Mongol in Our Midst*

Index

ABC of Psychology 85–6, 213–15, 236–7
Achates; or, The Future of Canada 160n.62
advertising 193, 252–3, 258–64, 275, 313
Aeolus; or, The Future of the Flying Machine 5–6, 23–4, 55, 133, 146, 222n.4, 390–1
Aesculapius; or, Disease and the Man 98, 337–8
Africa 12–13, 174–5
Albyn; or, Scotland and the Future 136, 159–60, 239–40, 374, 388
Aldington, Richard 122, 133–4, 282, 332
Alma Mater; or, The Future of Oxford and Cambridge 200–1
anthropology 31, 85–6, 89, 109–10, 156–7, 169–71, 180, 189, 211–13, 305–6, 314–15
Anders, Günther 249–52, 292, 348–9
Anticipations 44–7, 137–8, 161
Apella; or, The Future of the Jews 178–9, 390
Aphrodite; or, The Future of Sexual Relationships 15–16, 96–7, 209–11, 237, 338–41, 382–3, 387–8
Apollonius; or, The Present and Future of Psychical Research 75, 185–6
Appadurai, Arjun 37–8, 134–5
Archimedes; or, The Future of Physics 4, 55, 92, 101–6, 185–6
architecture 11, 82, 232, 258–9, 261–2, 274, 294, 324–5, 380
Archon; or, The Future of Government 82, 191–2, 239–40
arts 12–13, 81–2, 88, 100, 108–9, 111, 175, 182–3, 191–2, 210, 212, 214–16, 221, 228, 230–3, 248, 253, 280–1, 294–5, 298–9, 306–7, 361–2, 374–5, 380
artificial intelligence (AI) 26–7, 40, 53, 56–7, 76–7, 79, 111–12, 245, 247, 278–9, 360
Artifex; or, The Future of Craftsmanship 222n.4, 266
Asimov, Isaac 54
Aspasia; The Future of Amorality 12–13, 211, 341n.10, 387
astronomy 40, 64, 85–6, 109–10, 112–16, 131, 150, 173–4, 212, 254, 348, 353–6
Atalanta; or, The Future of Sport 280–1
Atlantis; or, America and the Future 236
atom 53–4, 63, 66, 69, 78–9, 94–5, 112–13, 117–18, 121–2, 131, 143–4, 150–1, 173–4, 191, 249–50, 350–6, 360

Augé, Marc 42–3, 50, 79–80, 122, 340–1, 346, 350
Autolycus; or, The Future for Miscreant Youth 177–8, 189–90
Automaton; or, The Future of the Mechanical Man 12–13, 82–3, 222, 239–40, 244–7, 252n.67
automobiles 12–13, 15, 46–7, 57, 73–4, 112, 138, 228, 233–5, 262–3, 269, 274–6, 292–3, 298, 339–40, 369
aviation 11, 23–4, 43, 57, 65–7, 80, 112, 125–8, 133, 144–5, 222, 237, 241, 262–3, 281, 292–3, 340, 376

Babel; or, The Past, Present and Future of Human Speech 84–5, 259–60, 323, 334, 338, 382–3
Bacchus; or, Wine To-Day and To-Morrow 33–4, 238
Badiou, Alain 50–2, 363–4
Balbus; or, The Future of Architecture 269–74, 376
Barman, Christian 269–74
BASIC English 4, 82–3, 85–6, 162, 171, 253, 259–60, 294, 340, 386, 389
BBC 142, 231, 263
Behaviourism 80, 105, 164, 174, 214–15, 217, 236–7, 334–5
Bellamy, Edward 44, 141
Belloc, Hilaire 334–5, 390–1
Benjamin, Walter 230, 289
Bennett, E. N. 75, 185–6, 252n.67
Bentham, Jeremy 84–5, 169–70, 367
Berman, Marshall 42, 91, 121–2
Bernal, J. D. 7–8, 17–18, 22–3, 27–8, 32–3, 40–2, 47, 55–7, 64, 70–82, 86, 88–9, 106–12, 116–17, 128, 137, 152–5, 164, 212–13, 221, 224, 239–41, 243–7, 250, 254, 279, 283–4, 312, 349, 354–7, 360–1, 369–71, 375, 388, 390
Betts, Ernest 24–5, 114, 154–5, 185, 295–6, 312–13, 317
biology 29, 40, 56–7, 64–70, 78–82, 92–3, 99–101, 151, 154, 164, 182–3, 186–7, 189, 192, 212, 221, 225–6, 279, 309, 311–12, 333–4, 356–9, 369
bionic 108, 221, 359–60
biospheres 39–42, 71, 111–12
Birnstingl, H. J. 14, 265–8

Birth Control and the State 15–16, 17n.41, 19n.46, 154, 206–7, 384*f*

Blacker, C. P. 15–16, 17n.41, 19n.46, 32–3, 154, 206–7

Bloch, Ernst 51, 345

body 12–13, 36, 89, 229, 278–9, 283–4, 303–4, 326–7

brain (also see 'compound mind') 71, 75–6, 91–3, 101, 104–5, 111–12, 221, 226, 229, 238, 242–4, 247, 312, 325, 356–7, 360–1

Brain, W. Russell 28–9, 99–101

Brave New World 3–4, 25, 27, 111–12, 115, 161, 196, 307–20

Breaking Priscian's Head; or, English as She Will Be Spoke and Wrote 83–4, 287–8, 292–3, 324, 329, 369–71

Bretherton, C. H. 228–30, 250

Briggs, Martin S. 14, 274–5

Brittain, Vera 8, 10, 13n.33, 21–2, 28–30, 32–5, 55, 88, 139–40, 144–6, 153, 211, 237, 287, 302, 349–50, 352, 356–7

Butler, Samuel 65, 116, 177–8, 224, 226–7, 251

Cain; or, The Future of Crime 15–16, 17n.41, 18n.45, 176–7, 189–90

Caledonia; or, The Future of the Scots 146–7, 232n.25, 387n.39

Callinicus; A Defence of Chemical Warfare 7–8, 117–18, 132–3, 133n.25, 316n.51, 323, 332–3, 352, 372, 375, 377–8

Cambridge 32–4, 81–2, 92, 103, 109–10, 117–18, 138–40, 195–6, 200–4, 212–13, 232, 253, 259–60, 284–5, 290–1, 297, 374–5, 386

Cambridge Magazine 4, 203–4

Canada 10, 29–30, 82–4, 146–7, 159–60

Čapek, Karel 91–2, 239–40

Carlill, H. F. 164, 217

Carnap, Rudolf 3–4, 171–2

Carruthers, John 287–93, 324

Cassandra; or, The Future of the British Empire 156–7, 159–62, 349–50, 362–3, 387

Cato; or, The Future of Censorship 140–1, 237, 239–40, 304–6

censorship 140–1, 149, 151, 237, 287, 303–6

Chekhov, Anton 43, 135–6, 288–9, 291

chemistry 29, 64–7, 77–8, 80, 92–3, 110, 112, 138, 147–8, 201, 212, 221, 246–7, 254, 279, 358–9

Chiron; or, The Education of a Citizen of the World 82, 198–200, 338

Chisholm, Cecil 153, 237–8, 247, 280, 310n.44

Chronos; or, The Future of the Family 15–16, 17n.41, 34, 268, 334

Churchill, Winston 27, 125–7, 346

cinema 11, 24, 40–1, 80, 83–4, 111–12, 114–16, 130–1, 169–70, 185, 193, 222, 228, 232, 234–5, 240, 252–3, 259–61, 263–4, 294–6, 298, 305–6, 309, 312–13, 320

city 133, 153, 226–7, 258, 269, 271–3, 275–6, 369

Clarke, Arthur C. 23–4, 65, 76–7, 245–6, 346–7

Clarke, I. F. 44–5, 55, 88

class 85–6, 88, 162, 237–8, 267, 275, 298, 303–4, 315

Classics 9, 65, 70–1, 105, 109, 111, 172–3, 195–7, 201, 216, 297, 302–3, 341–3, 357–8, 369n.8, 372–3

Classified index 11, 12n.27

climate change 26–7, 87–8, 358

Cloning 3n.8, 7, 21, 112

Collum 186–8

Columbia; or, The Future of Canada 15–16, 83–4, 139–40, 159–60, 292–3, 324

compound mind 76–7, 111–12, 124–5, 155, 163–5, 226–7, 250, 354–5

computers 25, 39–40, 53–4, 56–7, 72, 76–9, 87, 93, 223, 226, 242–7, 266, 360–2

Conquest of Cancer, The 98, 372–3, 375

consilience 100–1, 358–62

contraception 33, 67, 147–8, 154, 163, 174, 205–8, 304–5, 310, 315, 356–7

countryside 267, 274–8

craft 266

crime 172, 174, 176–8

criticism 170–1, 196, 212, 262–3, 287–96, 306–7, 386

Crookshank, F. G. 15–16, 32–3, 98, 123–4, 322, 337, 341–2, 375

cultural studies 29, 88, 119, 134–5, 169–70, 199, 232, 257–85

cyborg 7, 22–3, 72–80, 89, 111–12, 224, 239–40, 247, 354, 359–60

Daedalus; or, Science and the Future 1–3, 5–8, 22–3, 26–9, 47–9, 55, 63–70, 73, 77, 82–4, 86, 92–3, 107, 111–12, 123–4, 131, 133, 136, 149–52, 201–2, 208, 213, 221, 245–6, 252n.67, 284–5, 298–300, 308–11, 315–16, 319, 323, 329, 331, 333–5, 339, 343, 352–3, 355–7, 367–75, 377–9, 382, 386, 388, 390

Dance of Çiva; or, Life's Unity and Rhythm, The 186–8, 369–71

Darwin 32–3, 46, 88, 99–101, 103, 112, 138, 144–5, 156–7, 213, 290, 324

Dawkins, Richard 8–9, 77, 101, 174–5, 326

de Pomerai, Ralph 15–16, 96–7, 209–11, 237, 387

de Sélincourt, Basil 16n.36, 83–4, 238, 294, 324, 328, 328n.75

Debabelization 83–5

Debussy, Claude 296–7

Delphos; The Future of International Language 7–8, 29–30, 83–4, 154–5, 162, 239–40, 324, 329, 377–8

Democritus; or, The Future of Laughter 159, 183, 324, 337

Dent, E. J. 32–3, 231n.23, 296, 388

Derrida, Jacques 104, 106, 353, 355–6

Deucalion; or, The Future of Criticism 290–3, 329–30, 382–3, 388

Diogenes; or, The Future of Leisure 14, 82, 143–4, 158, 275–80, 342–3, 349

Diplock, W. J. K. 201

Discovery of the Future 44–6

DNA 53, 78–9

Dobrée, Bonamy 25, 32–4, 83–4, 136, 315–19, 329

Dronamraju, Krishna 67, 81–2, 388

Dutton, E. P. 10, 123–4, 338–9, 352, 371–90

Dyson, Freeman 27, 67, 81–2

economics 12–13, 40, 66, 87, 89, 154, 160–1, 169, 182–3, 189, 203, 211–13, 252–3, 303–4, 306, 313, 340

ectogenesis 2–3, 27, 41–2, 49, 68, 73–4, 81–2, 107, 116, 172, 174, 243, 308–11, 331, 333–4, 342–3, 356–7

Edinger, George 83–4, 184–5, 324

Eddington, Arthur 13–14, 63, 96

education 34, 82, 85, 89, 124, 134–5, 146–8, 174, 191–2, 195–203, 206–7, 212–13, 230–1, 261, 264, 268, 310, 326–7, 356–7

Einstein, Albert 29, 63–4, 66–7, 88, 90–2, 94–6, 100–2, 104, 111–13, 117–18, 174, 184, 186–7, 191, 213, 299–300, 302

Eleutheros; or, The Future of the Public Schools 15–16, 34, 82, 196–8

Eliot, T. S. 1–4, 9, 12–13, 29–30, 51, 110, 135, 235, 259–60, 266, 282, 287–91, 297–300, 302, 306–8, 326–31, 335, 344, 377–8

Ellis, Havelock 223–7, 360

Empire, the British 10–12, 44, 158–63, 172, 174–5, 189, 197, 212–13, 263, 266, 380, 389–90

Empson, William 85–6, 109–11, 253, 259–60, 289–91, 295, 306–7

engineering 188, 346

Environmentalism 40

Eos; or, The Wider Aspects of Cosmogony 112–16, 342–3, 353, 377–8, 381, 385

Ethnos; or, The Problem of Race 19, 151–2, 341

Eugenics 14–16, 21–2, 36, 56, 67–8, 82, 89–90, 98–9, 112, 124, 154–7, 160–1, 174–8, 197, 207–8, 211, 216, 268, 273–4, 308, 310, 315, 320–1, 341, 356–7, 360

Eurydice; or, The Nature of Opera 296

Euterpe; or, The Future of Art 230–3, 238–40

Eutychus; or, The Future of the Pulpit 82, 94, 179–82, 189, 334, 338

everyday life 29–30, 40–1, 106, 119, 136, 169–70, 208–9, 212–13, 221, 237–8, 257–85, 315, 326–7, 375

evolution 15–22, 74–5, 89, 92, 98–101, 103–4, 138, 156–7, 160–1, 173–4, 211–12, 225, 228, 247, 251, 279, 283–4, 324, 326, 354–60, 369, 373

Fascism 10, 121–2, 149, 158, 175–6, 179, 191–4, 207–8, 216, 227, 241, 251–2, 261, 341, 345–7, 360

Feminism 82, 88, 139–40, 147–8, 151, 201–3, 243, 270

Finnegans Wake 320–7

'Flagg, Francis' [pseud. of Henry George Weiss] 72–3

Ford, Ford Madox 44, 49–50, 57–8, 134, 142nn.40, 42, 157n.60, 198, 207, 281, 288, 291–4, 296, 298, 306–7

Ford, Henry 222, 235, 280, 315, 343–4

form 99–100, 232–3, 270–1

Forster, E.M. 1–2, 41n.87

Fortuna; or, Chance and Design 390

Foster, Hal 239, 241–3, 294–5

Fournier d'Albe, E. E. 12–16, 55, 103–4, 136, 142–3, 153–5, 161, 226–7, 240, 247–8, 250–1, 264–5, 307n.37, 322, 343–4

Fraser-Harris, David 313

Freud, Sigmund 77, 94–5, 106, 111, 147–8, 164, 174, 181, 185, 192, 209, 214–15, 217, 241–2, 248, 251–2, 276, 311, 313–14, 316, 367

Fukuyama, Francis 346, 351–2

Fuller, J. F. C. 126–7, 129–30, 236, 307n.37

function 100

future history 21–2, 67–8, 83–4, 124, 134–52, 212–13, 309–10, 329–30, 349–50, 353–4

Future of Futurism, The 48, 291–3, 324, 327, 369–71, 390

Future of Israel, The 179, 379, 390

'Future of Sex, The' (Rebecca West) 340, 390–1

Futurism (Italian art movement) 39–40, 44, 226, 249–50, 266, 291–2

Fyfe, Hamilton 82, 191–2

Galatea; or, The Future of Darwinism 99–100, 279

Gallio; or, The Tyranny of Science 93–4, 100–1, 185–6, 329, 369–71

Garrett, Garet 12–13, 22, 137, 234n.28, 240, 251–4, 261, 338

Gasiorek, Andrzej 49–51, 235

gender 30, 144–6, 162, 172, 175, 197, 201, 210, 224, 235, 262, 270–1, 273, 281, 331, 340, 361–2, 369, 374, 389–90 genetics 11, 17–18, 21, 39–40, 67–8, 78, 81–2, 89, 92–3, 99–100, 112, 174–5, 221, 283–4, 310, 358–62

General Strike 150, 163, 237–8, 263

Germany 163, 191, 193

Gibbon, Lewis Grassic 10, 24, 389

Gibbs, Philip 342–4

Giddens, Anthony 13–15, 42, 51, 87, 146, 215–16

Gloag, John 222n.4, 266

Godwin, George 15–16, 17n.41, 18n.45, 29–30, 83–4, 139–40, 159–60, 176–8, 292–3, 307n.37

Gordon, R. G. 177–8

Gould, Gerald 28–9, 32–3, 159, 183–4, 324, 337

Gould, Stephen Jay 8–9, 52, 132n.24

Graves, Robert 8–9, 28, 31–3, 83–4, 133, 147–50, 183–4, 287, 292–3, 295, 298–300, 302–4, 307–8, 316n.51, 323–4, 334–5, 349–50, 352, 384–5, 388

Greig, J. Y. T. 83–4, 287–94, 307n.37, 324, 329, 369–71

Grieve, C. M.[i.e. Hugh MacDiarmid] 10, 136, 159–60, 287, 389

Griffith, Hubert 232n.26, 302–3

Haire, Norman 15–16, 34–5, 181, 206–9, 334, 388

Halcyon; or, The Future of Monogamy 21–2, 88, 144–6, 207, 338

Haldane, J. B. S. 1–8, 14–15, 17–18, 22–3, 25–8, 32–5, 40–2, 47–9, 55–7, 64–70, 73–4, 77–82, 85–6, 88–9, 92–3, 99–100, 102, 106–12, 115–19, 123–4, 126–8, 131–3, 138–40, 145, 157, 169, 172, 181, 199–201, 206, 215–16, 221, 226–7, 239–40, 243, 246–7, 250–2, 252n.67, 279, 283–4, 298–300, 302, 307–8, 310–12, 316n.51, 320–3, 329–33, 335, 337, 348–50, 352–3, 356–8, 360, 365, 369, 375, 380, 384–5

Hall, Julian 200–1

Hanno; or, The Future of Exploration 24, 359

Harris, W. Eric 160n.62

Hartley, Olga 139–40, 150–1, 238

Harvey, C. P. 269

Hatfield, H. Stafford 12–13, 82–3, 240, 244–7, 247n.59, 252n.67, 319–20, 361

Haynes, E. S. P. 177n.15, 268–9, 307–8, 338

Heard, Gerald 8–9, 17n.41, 22, 28–9, 123–4, 225, 240, 307–8, 323–4, 337, 373, 389–90

helicopter 23–4

Hephaestus; or, The Soul of the Machine 12–13, 103–4, 240, 247–8, 250–1, 344, 376

Heraclitus; or, The Future of Films 24, 114, 295–6, 312–13, 317

Heretics, The 1–2, 32–3, 109, 139, 204

Hermes; or, The Future of Chemistry 92–3, 138, 140

Hibernia; or, The Future of Ireland 157–8, 293

history (*see also* 'future history') 89–90, 144, 163, 212–13

Hitler, Adolf 175–6

Holocaust, The 249–50

Holtby, Winifred 34–5, 82, 94, 179–82, 189, 208–9, 287, 334

home 212–13, 253, 258–9, 264–8

Hulme, T. E. 171, 290, 306–7, 328, 331, 367

humour 82, 148, 159, 183–5, 212–13, 324, 349–50

Hussey, Dyneley 28–9, 296

Huxley, Aldous 3–4, 12–13, 25, 27, 29–30, 32–3, 68, 111–12, 121–2, 132, 147, 161, 196, 287, 307–20, 333, 335

Huxley, Julian 12–13, 32–3, 47–8, 68, 73–4, 308–9, 312, 343–4, 364

Hygieia; or, Disease and Evolution 23, 98–9, 379, 390

Hymen; or, The Future of Marriage 15–16, 206–9, 381, 388

Hypatia; or, Woman and Knowledge 15–16, 82, 175, 201–4, 209, 299–300, 323, 334, 337, 372–3, 377–8, 381, 388, 390

hypnosis 311–13, 316–17

Icarus; or, The Future of Science 2–3, 5–6, 15–16, 19, 26, 28–9, 55, 64, 88, 107, 112, 123–4, 172–4, 202, 213, 254n.71, 259–60, 299–300, 311, 329, 331, 334–5, 352, 368–73, 370f, 375, 377–9, 381–2, 386, 388, 390

Iconoclastes; or, The Future of Shakespeare 232n.26, 302, 319, 329

'If You Were Alive in 2123 A.D.' 1–2, 73–4

India 10, 28, 159–60, 187–90, 195, 340–1

interconnection 39–40, 76–7, 85, 96–7, 108, 111–12, 124, 129–31, 152–65, 170–1, 188–9, 226–7, 233, 243, 250, 265, 267, 283–4, 288–9, 301, 355

International Library of Psychology, Philosophy, and Scientific Method 3–4, 10, 32–3, 86, 103, 170–1, 176–8, 212–13, 236–7, 253, 294, 314, 319, 331, 338–9, 367–8, 375, 377–8, 389

internet 76–7, 89, 155, 164, 265, 306

Ireland 10, 146–7, 156–8, 293

Isis; or, The Future of Oxford 201

It Isn't Done; or, The Future of Taboo Among the British Islanders 83–4, 156–7, 303–4, 314, 338–41, 381–3, 387

Italy 193–4, 216

Jaeger, Muriel 214–15

Jameson, Fredric 37, 55–8, 142, 344

Janus; The Conquest of War: A Psychological Inquiry 8, 124–7, 133, 236–7, 334–5, 349, 352, 388

jazz 230, 240, 296–7
Jeans, James 10, 13–14, 30–1, 63, 96, 112–15, 302, 353, 355–6, 384–5
Jennings, H. S. 20–1, 92–3, 360
Joad, C. E. M. 8–9, 14, 28–35, 82, 143–4, 146–7, 158, 204–7, 211, 227–8, 259–60, 275–84, 307–8, 334, 338, 341–2, 349, 387–8
Jones, T. W. 92–3, 138, 140
Joyce, James 2–4, 9, 29–30, 51, 57–8, 83–4, 105, 109–10, 149, 259–60, 287–9, 291–4, 303, 306–8, 320–7, 335, 353

Kalki; or, The Future of Civilization 28, 127n.20, 159–60, 187–90, 195–6, 340–1, 388–9
Kahn, Herman 53–4
Kaku, Michio 78, 249
Kegan Paul, Trench, Trübner & Co. 1–2, 10–11, 28, 38, 83–4, 103, 123–4, 268, 332–3, 339, 367–91
Keith, Arthur 19, 155–7, 160–2, 341
Keyser, Cassius Jackson 213–16, 388, 390
Kuhn, Thomas S. 53

Lamarckianism 99–100, 194, 279, 283–4, 292
language 9, 31, 33, 64, 82–6, 91, 104, 106, 121, 147–50, 154–5, 160–2, 169–70, 180, 185, 212, 238, 253, 295, 297–8, 303, 323, 339–40, 349, 361–2, 369, 375, 380, 389–90
Lares et penates; or, The Home of the Future 14, 265–8, 389–90
Lars Porsena; or, The Future of Swearing and Improper Language 83–4, 147–50, 183–4, 284–5, 292–3, 303, 316n.51, 323, 335, 349–50, 381, 388
'Last Judgement, The' (Haldane) 353–4
law 174, 177n.15, 211–12, 225, 268–9, 374
Lawrence, D. H. 94–6, 179, 197, 236–7, 276, 282–3, 290–1, 293–4, 303, 389
League of Nations 10, 127–8, 140–1, 147–9, 151–2, 154, 156–8, 162, 179, 195, 199–200, 261–2, 341–2
Leavis, F. R. 12–13, 222–3, 232, 235, 258–61, 290–1, 293–5
Le Corbusier 40, 224–7, 272
Lee, Vernon 10, 32–3, 215–16, 287
leisure 106, 143–4, 258–9, 277, 283–4, 315
Lewis, C. S. 27, 77
Lewis, Percy Wyndham 13–14, 29–30, 49–50, 115, 235–6, 239, 241–2, 264, 287, 291, 306–8, 328, 331–2, 335
Lewis, Robert T. 196
Leyel, Hilda (Mrs C. F.) 139–40, 150–1, 238
Liddell Hart, Basil Henry 28, 57–8, 126–7, 129–33, 146, 206, 227, 352

literature 69, 110, 116, 169–70, 182–3, 196–7, 230, 287–335, 389–90
Low, Archibald M. 123–4, 153–5, 240–1, 244–5, 306, 322, 343, 369
Lucullus; or, The Food of the Future 139–40, 150–1, 238
Lukács, Georg 122, 190–1
Ludovici, Anthony M. 17n.41, 123–4, 175–6, 181, 202, 299–300, 331, 334, 337, 387, 390–1
Lyall, Archibald 83–4, 156–7, 303–4, 314–15, 387
Lycurgus; or, The Future of Law 177n.15, 268, 338
Lysistrata; or, Woman's Future and Future Woman 17n.41, 123–4, 175–6, 202, 216, 299–300, 331, 337, 372, 377–8, 381, 387, 390–1

MacDiarmid, Hugh 8–10, 136, 159–60, 239–40, 287, 302, 306–7, 389
Mace, C. A. 7–8, 26, 90–2, 252n.67
Macfie, R. Campbell 12–13, 17–20, 103–4, 240
'Machine Man of Ardathia, The' 72–4, 224
machines 9, 11–13, 22, 36, 66, 71–4, 87–9, 94–6, 100–1, 103–4, 187–8, 194, 198, 212–13, 221–54, 266–7, 271, 276, 279, 292, 295–6, 305–6, 310, 319, 338, 355, 359–60, 375, 379, 389–90
Madge, Charles 284–5, 335
Magnus, Laurie 178–9, 390
Malinowski, Bronislaw 3–4, 31, 171, 314, 319
Mannheim, Karl 171, 176, 180
Marinetti, Filippo Tommaso 239, 241–2, 270, 291, 294
Marxism 42, 51–2, 70–1, 75–7, 81–2, 88, 90, 97, 104, 107–8, 121–2, 136, 147–8, 161, 163, 182–3, 185, 190–4, 212–13, 227, 237–8, 243, 268, 277–8, 290, 302–3, 306, 341, 345, 355
Mass Observation 5, 284–5
mass production 185, 222–3, 233–8, 280, 315
Maurois, André 8, 28, 82, 136, 139–40, 142–4, 153, 262, 287, 302, 307–8, 318–19, 352, 369–71
McColvin, Lionel R. 230–3, 238–40, 253
McDougall, William 124–5, 127–9, 236–7, 334–5, 349, 352
McLuhan, Marshall 239, 252–4, 257, 259–60
Meaning of Meaning, The 4, 8, 85–6, 253, 291, 369–71, 385–6
media 9, 15, 29–30, 34, 130–1, 136, 212–13, 221–2, 230–2, 241, 252–4, 257–66, 297–8, 301, 312, 369
medicine 12, 15–16, 67, 77, 97–9, 134–5, 154–5, 169, 206–7, 217, 225, 322, 369, 379, 389–90
Metanthropos; or, The Body of the Future 12–13, 17–21, 103–4, 240, 279
Midas; or, The United States and the Future 228–30, 235–6, 250, 252, 388
Minney, R. J. 159–60
Mitchell, J. Leslie 10, 24, 359, 389

modernism 287–335
Money-Kyrle, R E 12–13, 211, 341n.10, 387
Mongol in Our Midst; A Study of Man and His Three Faces, The 98, 123–4, 322, 329–30, 341–2, 368–9, 371–3, 375, 377–9
Moon 24, 54, 110, 117n.98, 136, 142–3, 353–4, 359
Moore, G. E. 171, 367
morality 67, 107, 144–5, 172, 174, 182–3, 189–90, 204–6, 211, 225, 227–8, 326, 373–4, 379, 389–90
Morpheus; or, The Future of Sleep 313–14, 316
Mowrer, Edgar Ansel 82, 192–5, 226, 259–60
Mrs Fisher; or, The Future of Humour 183–4, 292–3, 324, 342–3, 388
music 11, 82, 113, 212, 230–1, 283, 287, 296–7, 380
Mussolini, Benito 193
Myerson, George 38–9
myth 85, 134, 191, 198, 247–8, 251–2, 283, 289, 357

Narcissus; An Anatomy of Clothes 17n.41, 22, 123–4, 225, 240, 323–5, 337, 371–3, 375, 380, 389–90
Needham, Joseph 99–100
Neep, E. J. C. 83–4, 184–5, 324
neurology 92–4, 103, 108–10, 169, 358–62
newspapers 146–7, 193, 237, 252–3, 260–4, 306
Next Chapter; The War Against the Moon, The 55, 82, 142–4, 262, 306, 318–19, 352, 369–71
Nietzsche, Friedrich 50–1, 69, 91, 102–4, 174–6, 189–92, 204, 326, 350
Nineteen Eighty-Four 27, 111–12, 195, 313
'Noah; or, The Future of Intoxication' (Evelyn Waugh) 332–3
Nuntius; Advertising and its Future 7–8, 259–62

Ockham, David 262–4
Ogden, C. K. 1–5, 8, 10, 12, 28–33, 35, 38, 48, 60, 77, 80, 82–6, 92, 98–9, 103, 109–10, 121, 123–4, 136, 144, 164, 169–71, 176, 185, 202–4, 212–15, 217–18, 236–8, 240, 253, 259–60, 284–5, 287, 290–1, 294–6, 299, 306–7, 314, 319, 326–8, 330–4, 338–40, 349–50, 363–4, 367–71, 373–8, 385–7, 389, 391
Open Conspiracy, The 46–8, 200
Orwell, George 23–4, 27–8, 82–3, 111–12, 141–2, 161, 195, 306, 313, 317
Orpheus; or, The Music of the Future 112–13, 283, 296–7
Ouroboros; or, The Mechanical Extension of Mankind 12–13, 22, 55, 137, 212–13, 234n.28, 240, 251–4, 261, 338
Oxford 32–4, 65, 109, 144–5, 148, 187–9, 195–6, 200–2, 212–13, 374–5

Paget, Richard 84–5, 259–60, 302, 323, 334
Pankhurst, E. Sylvia 7–8, 10, 29–30, 83–4, 154–5, 162, 185, 302, 324, 329, 377–8
Paris; or, The Future of War 57–8, 129–33, 146, 227, 352, 379, 388
Parrinder, Patrick 37, 70n.15, 91–2, 239–40, 310
Passing of the Phantoms; A Study of Evolutionary Psychology and Morals, The 211–12, 323, 325–7, 372–3, 375–6, 379
Patten, Charles Joseph 211–12, 323, 325–7
Paul, Eden 15–16, 17n.41, 34, 268, 334
Pearce, M. Chaning 82, 198–200
Pegasus; or, Problems of Transport 129–30, 265
Perseus; or, Of Dragons 299–300, 323, 372–3, 375, 380
philosophy 69, 81–2, 94, 103, 170–2, 180, 182–3, 201, 211–18, 287, 306–7, 330, 361–2, 364–5, 375
photography 228, 231, 262–3, 269–70, 292–6
physics 29, 36, 63–6, 80, 91–7, 101–6, 109–13, 115, 164, 173–4, 186–7, 212, 348
Pink, Alderton M. 82, 196, 232
Plato's American Republic 82, 187, 233–6, 318–19, 381
poetry 172, 287, 296–301, 374
politics 69, 81–2, 87, 107–8, 113, 124, 136, 145, 160–1, 169–70, 174–5, 178–9, 182–3, 190–5, 200, 212, 216, 226, 263–4, 313, 315–16, 318–19, 328, 369, 375
Pomona; or, The Future of English 16n.36, 83–4, 137, 238, 294, 324, 328, 328n.75, 376
Pons Asinorum; or, The Future of Nonsense 83–4, 184–5, 324
Popper, Karl 52–3, 90, 345
popularization 28–9, 41–2, 58–9, 63–119, 124–5, 206–7, 209, 342–3
Possible Worlds 85–6, 131–2, 215, 365
post-human 17–18, 22, 56, 70, 72, 101, 103–4, 221–2, 239–40, 254, 354–5
post-modern 87, 104, 112
Pound, Ezra 9, 12–13, 30, 48–50, 289, 291–4, 297–9, 306–7
Powley, Edward B. 181–3
Predictions 31–2, 52, 358–62
print runs 380–5
Procrustes; or, The Future of English Education 82, 196, 232
Prometheus; or, Biology and the Advancement of Man 20–1, 55, 92–3, 372–3
propaganda 122, 130–1, 142–3, 149, 243, 260–3, 306, 313, 317–19
prosthesis 18, 22–3, 25, 27, 39–40, 74–5, 89, 108, 111–12, 174, 221–54, 257, 277, 283–4, 305, 359–60

Proteus; or, The Future of Intelligence 215–16, 372–3

Proust, Marcel 287–90, 297–8

Psyche (journal) 1–2, 77, 85–6, 340, 367

Psyche Miniatures 3–4, 85–6, 103, 164, 171, 212, 236–7, 253, 259–60, 319, 334–5, 338–9, 362n.39, 367, 386

psychical research 12, 18, 40, 47, 74–5, 124–5, 145, 185–6, 313–14, 369

psycho-analysis 12–13, 57–8, 75, 77, 89, 97–8, 107–10, 140–1, 164, 170–1, 174, 176–8, 183–4, 200, 206–7, 209, 211–15, 242, 248, 288, 314, 326, 339–40, 349–50

psychology 9, 41, 56–7, 68–9, 82–3, 85–6, 89, 91–3, 97, 99–101, 103, 106–11, 113, 169–71, 174, 177–8, 182–3, 189, 192–3, 196–7, 211–18, 236–7, 242, 287, 298, 305–6, 309–12, 340, 375

Pygmalion; or, The Doctor of the Future 97–8, 217, 379

quantum mechanics 40, 66, 106, 361–2

'Quarterly Reviewer, A' (*see* Magnus, Laurie) 178, 390

Quo vadimus? Glimpses of the Future 14–16, 55, 136–7, 153–5, 158, 250, 264–5, 322, 343, 372

race 12–13, 17, 19–20, 34, 113, 121, 151–2, 154–8, 160–2, 197–9, 212–13, 216, 273–4, 361–2, 373

Radhakrishnan, Sarvepalli 28, 127n.20, 159–60, 187–90, 302, 388

radio 9, 11, 43–4, 65–6, 72, 75, 80, 112, 125, 144–5, 152–4, 169–70, 183, 186–7, 190, 193, 222, 231, 237, 240–1, 243, 247, 252–3, 257–9, 261, 264, 292–3, 298, 312, 333, 374, 389

Realist, The 34–5, 169n.1, 173n.7, 237n.34

recording 169–70, 222, 230–1, 238–9, 242–3, 253, 257, 264–5, 318, 339–40

relativity, theory of 40, 63, 102, 106, 118, 184, 289–90, 298–9, 361–2

religion 34, 39–40, 42–3, 67, 69–71, 75–8, 82, 87–8, 90, 94, 97, 100, 108, 112, 117–18, 134–6, 147–8, 157–8, 169–70, 172–83, 185, 189–90, 192–3, 198, 200, 202, 204–6, 209, 211–13, 215–16, 248, 277–8, 303–5, 310, 315, 321–2, 326–8, 330, 335, 350–1, 364–5, 369, 373

Richards, I. A. 4, 8, 12–13, 82–3, 85–6, 93–4, 103, 109–10, 124, 171, 253, 259–60, 284–5, 290–1, 295, 306–7, 367, 369–71, 385–6

robots 7, 14–15, 23, 36, 39–40, 54, 57, 191–2, 226, 228–9, 237–40, 244–7, 252

Rodker, John 48, 291–4, 324, 327–30, 390

Romulus; or, The Future of the Child 196

Routledge 5–6, 9–12, 28–9, 376–7, 389–91

Roxburgh, J. F. 15–16, 34, 82, 196–8

Russell, Bertrand 1–3, 5–10, 15–16, 19, 26, 28, 30–5, 47–8, 56–7, 63–4, 80–2, 88, 106–7, 111–12, 123–4, 136, 172–5, 181, 185, 190–1, 206–8, 212, 216, 236–7, 254n.71, 299–300, 302, 307–8, 311, 329, 331, 334–5, 337, 352, 357, 368, 372, 374–5, 384–6, 388, 390

Russell, Dora Winifred 15–16, 31–3, 82, 88, 123–4, 175, 181, 201–7, 209–10, 294, 299–300, 323, 334, 337, 390

Russell, Gilbert 7–8, 259–64

Russia 10, 50–1, 163, 191, 193–4, 261, 295–6, 302

Rusticus; or, The Future of the Countryside 14, 274–6

Saint-Amour, Paul 57–9, 281–2, 348–58

Sandilands, G. S. 280–4

Sargent, Lyman 37, 55

Saxo Grammaticus; or, First Aid for the Best-seller 385, 388–9

Scheherazade; or, The Future of the English Novel 287–93, 301

Schiller, F. C. S. 19n.46, 22, 28–33, 103–4, 156–7, 159–62, 213, 216, 239, 307n.37, 319, 323–4, 329, 343, 349–50, 362–3, 372, 387

science fiction 9, 14–15, 23–4, 27, 37–9, 41–2, 44, 49–50, 55–7, 74, 79, 81–2, 110–12, 116, 136, 144, 186–7, 245–6, 279, 292

Scotland 10, 82, 136, 146–7, 151, 156–60

Scott-Stokes, H. F. 299–300, 323, 375

Seagle, William 140–1, 237, 304–6

'Searching for the Elixir of Life' 73

sexuality 9, 11–12, 15–17, 30, 34, 36, 68, 89, 96–7, 113, 124, 144–6, 169, 174, 180, 188, 202–11, 216, 237, 273–4, 303–4, 341–2, 356–8, 374, 390–1

Shadwell, Arthur 191

Shakespeare, William 176–7, 302–3, 319

Shand, P. Morton 33–4, 238

Shaw, George Bernard 1–2, 204–5, 278, 283–4, 290, 303–5, 334

Shiva; or, The Future of India 159–60, 340–1

Sibylla; or, The Revival of Prophecy 7–8, 26, 90–2, 252n.67

Sinon; or, The Future of Politics 82, 192–5, 226, 338, 341

Sisyphus; or, The Limits of Psychology 214–15

Snow, C. P. 7–8, 110–11, 199, 201

Social media 76–7, 155, 243

social sciences 89, 103, 157–8, 164, 169–71, 176–8, 183, 189, 196, 199–200, 211–13, 224, 230–1, 258, 268, 284–5, 339–40, 375, 389–90

Socrates; or, The Emancipation of Mankind 55, 164, 217, 239–40

Solon; or, The Price of Justice 269

space travel 14–15, 23, 27, 66, 71, 77, 79, 108, 111–12, 283–4

Spanish Civil War 81–2, 341

speculative non-fiction 9, 44–5, 56–7, 79, 116, 131–2, 137

Squier, Susan 68, 73

Stapledon, Olaf 141, 245–6

state 56, 121–2, 151–2, 156–64, 169, 178–9, 190–5, 199, 361–2, 379, 389–90

Stein, Gertrude 291–3, 306–7, 328, 344

Stentor; or, The Press of To-Day and To-Morrow 262, 306, 335

Stewart, Oliver 5–6, 23–4, 146, 222n.4

Strauss, Richard 296–7

Stravinsky, Igor 292, 296–7

Sullivan, J. W. N. 28–9, 93–4, 100–1, 185–6, 290, 307–8, 311, 369–71

Surrealism 12–13, 294–5

tank 115–16, 222, 333

Tantalus; or, The Future of Man 5, 17n.41, 19n.46, 22, 103–4, 213, 239, 259–60, 323, 334, 343, 372, 377–8, 381

Taylorism 12–13, 91–2, 217, 237–8, 280

telephone 23, 39–40, 57, 72, 75, 152–3, 169–70, 190, 240, 257, 264–5, 271, 364

television 112, 141, 144–5, 153, 222, 237, 240, 242–3, 247, 253, 257, 261–4, 295–6, 306, 318–19, 339–40

Terpander; or, Music and the Future 231n.23, 296, 388

Thamyris; or, Is There a Future for Poetry? 137, 297–300, 324, 329, 376, 388

theatre 212, 287, 374, 380

Thinking about Thinking 51, 213–14, 379, 388, 390

Thom, Burton Peter 23, 98–9, 390

Thomson, G. M. 146–7, 387n.39

Thrasymachus; The Future of Morals 204–7, 209, 227–8, 338, 387

Time Machine, The 16–17, 25, 46–7, 72–5, 136, 141, 315–16

Timotheus; The Future of the Theatre 25, 34, 82–4, 136, 315–19, 329, 332n.82, 388

translations of To-Day and To-Morrow volumes 377–8

transport 129–30, 264–6, 272–3

Trevelyan, R. C. 297–300, 324, 329, 334–5

Turner, W. J. 32–3, 112–13, 283, 290, 296–7

Two Cultures, The 7–9, 110–11, 199, 201

Typhoeus; or, The Future of Socialism 191, 377–8

USA 10, 27, 82–4, 98–9, 123–4, 146–7, 158–9, 171, 185, 187, 227–30, 233–6, 272–5, 277–8, 295–6, 338–9, 341–2, 371, 380, 389–90

utopia 9, 18, 37, 44, 46, 49, 55–7, 70, 85, 88, 106, 112, 117, 121–2, 127, 133–4, 137, 139–40, 146, 154–8, 164, 173–4, 176, 180, 183, 194–5, 204, 207, 214–15, 237–8, 257, 272–4, 277–8, 308, 312–13, 328, 331, 341–2, 349–50, 385

Versailles Treaty, the 10, 123, 156–9

video phone 40–1, 54, 142, 318–19

Vicisti, Galilee? or, Religion in England: A Survey and Forecast 181–2

Vorticism 223, 226, 235–6

Vulcan; or, The Future of Labour 153, 237–40, 247, 280, 310n.44

Wagner, Richard 296, 317–18

Waller, Bolton C. 157–8, 293

war 9–12, 23–4, 30, 33, 35–6, 48–50, 53–4, 57–8, 65, 86–7, 89, 92, 98–9, 107–8, 112, 115–18, 121–64, 174, 178–9, 182, 189, 192–5, 200, 202–6, 209–13, 221, 227, 240–51, 253, 258, 263, 269, 274–5, 279–83, 287–9, 315–18, 338–42, 345–7, 349–50, 352–3, 355–6, 369, 374, 380

Warburg, Fredric 1–2, 9, 28, 368, 382–3

Watson, J. B. 214–15, 236–7

Waugh, Evelyn 29–30, 139, 196n.34, 200, 268, 287, 307–8, 332–5

Weekley, Ernest 389

Weiner, Jonathan 358–62

Wells, H. G. 5, 8–9, 12–13, 16–17, 19, 23–5, 34–5, 40–8, 63, 65–6, 69, 72–5, 83–4, 91–2, 110, 117–18, 127, 136–9, 141, 161, 163–5, 194, 200, 242, 247, 290–2, 299–300, 315–16, 328, 331, 343–4

West, Geoffrey 34–5, 290–1, 293–4

West, Rebecca 34–5, 335, 390–1

What I Believe 7–8, 172–5, 181, 207–8, 299–300, 329, 334, 337, 339–41, 357, 372, 375, 382, 386, 388

Whitehead, Alfred North 63, 239, 244, 290

Whyte, L. L. 4, 32–3, 80, 92–7, 101–7, 112–13, 185–6, 361

Williams, Raymond 258

Wilson, E. O. 100–1, 358–9

Wilson, R. McNair 97–8, 217

Wireless Possibilities 123–4, 153, 240, 244–5, 322, 343, 368–9, 371–3, 375

Wise, James Waterman 179, 390

Wittgenstein, Ludwig 1–4, 31, 171–2, 212

Woodruff, J. Douglas 82, 187, 233–5, 318–19, 334

Woolf, Leonard 34–5, 299–302

Woolf, Virginia 1–4, 282, 287–301, 306–7

World, the Flesh and the Devil; An Enquiry into the Future of the Three Enemies of the Rational Soul, The 7–8, 22–3, 47, 55, 64, 70–82, 86, 164, 221, 245–6, 283–4, 334, 338, 349, 356–7, 369–71, 375, 382–3, 388

world state 69, 127, 142, 153–4, 161–2, 164, 194, 310, 314–15, 331

Wright, H. W. S. 98, 375

Year 2000, The 53–4

Young, Norwood 390

Zuckerman, Solly 98n.78, 171, 253

.